Official Guide to
Camping & Cara
in Britain

CW00521145

BRITAIN

Where to Stay 2001
England • Scotland • Wales

Where to Stay in Britain 2001
Contents

WELCOME TO WHERE TO STAY

PLACES TO STAY AND THINGS TO DO
Camping and caravan parks, places to visit, regional
tourist board contact details and travel to the area

EVENTS FOR 2001

FURTHER INFORMATION

- Competition
  Win a week's family holiday park break.   See page 16
- Concours
  Gagnez un séjour d'une semaine pour toute la famille
  dans un parc de vacances.   Voir en page 16
- Preisausschreiben
  Gewinnen Sie einen einwöchigen Familienurlaub in einem Feirenpark.   Siehe Seite 16
- Prijsvraag
  Win een vakantie van een week voor het hele gezin op een vakantiepark.   Zie pagina 16
- Concorso
  Vincete una vacanza di una settimana per tutta
  la famiglia in un parco vacanze.   Vedere pagina 16

Front Cover:
Luss Camping and Caravanning Club Site, Scotland

Touring Britain

Britain is a country of beautiful landscapes and historic interest where the traveller can enjoy a great variety of scenery within short distances. Camping or caravanning is a good way to see Britain. You can go as you please without sticking to a set programme, enjoy the country air and have a lot of fun. Wherever you stay, you can use your park as a base for sightseeing and touring the surrounding area.

 As the birthplace of camping, Britain has a large number of places to stay of every kind - from small, quiet spots to big lively parks offering a wide range of facilities and entertainment. Many have a restaurant, bar, nightclub, regular barbecues and evening entertainment (eg dinner dance, cabaret).

An increasing number of parks now make ideal centres for an activity holiday. Fishing, sailing and golfing are just three of the more popular activities offered by more and more parks. Many also have indoor swimming pools, tennis courts, games room and provide a wide range of facilities and activities to keep the children amused.

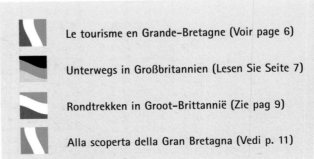

Le tourisme en Grande-Bretagne (Voir page 6)

Unterwegs in Großbritannien (Lesen Sie Seite 7)

Rondtrekken in Groot-Brittannië (Zie pag 9)

Alla scoperta della Gran Bretagna (Vedi p. 11)

Most parks admit tents, touring and motor caravans and provide a wide range of central facilities for the tourer. Many have caravan holiday homes for hire. These are often very spacious, luxurious and well equipped with two to three good sized bedrooms, a lounge with comfortable furnishings and a separate dining area. Many have modern conveniences such as colour televisions, fridges, hot showers, en-suite bathrooms and microwaves. In addition to caravan holiday homes, many parks also have chalets and lodges for hire, designed and equipped to the same standard as the caravans. All are truly a home from home, giving you the facilities and freedom you need to enjoy your holiday.

To help you select the type of park to suit you, with the facilities and standards you require, the British Graded Holiday Parks Rating Scheme will be of great assistance. Each park involved in this scheme has been visited by an independent assessor and given a rating based on cleanliness, environment and the quality of facilities and services provided. An explanation of the scheme can be found on page 17.

Many parks are open all year and can be an excellent way to have a short break in the spring, autumn and even in the winter months. Prices will be cheaper than during the main season and many facilities will still be available (although it might be wise to check).

If you intend to stay in a popular holiday area during the main season (June to September), you are advised to book in advance. It is essential either to send written confirmation of any reservations made or to arrive very early at your chosen park.

Le tourisme en
Grande-Bretagne

La Grande-Bretagne est un pays qui abonde en panoramas superbes et en sites d'intérêt historique, où les touristes n'ont pas besoin de parcourir des kilomètres pour pouvoir admirer des paysages très variés. Le camping et le caravaning sont d'excellents moyens d'explorer la Grande-Bretagne. On peut aller où on le désire sans adhérer à un plan fixe, profiter du bon air de la campagne et se divertir. Quelle que soit la région où se trouve le terrain dans lequel on séjourne, on peut s'en servir comme point de chute pour faire du tourisme et rayonner dans la région.

C'est en Grande-Bretagne qu'est né le camping, on y trouve donc un grand nombre de terrains de toutes sortes, allant de petits terrains tranquilles à de grands parcs pleins d'animation proposant une vaste gamme d'équipements et de distractions. Un grand nombre de terrains possèdent des restaurants, bars, night-clubs, et organisent régulièrement des barbecues et des distractions nocturnes (par ex. dîners dansants, spectacles de cabaret).

Les terrains de camping sont des endroits merveilleux pour passer des vacances à thème, et un nombre de plus en plus important de terrains proposent cette formule. La pêche, la navigation de plaisance et le golf, entre autres, font partie des activités les plus populaires qu'on peut pratiquer dans des terrains de plus en plus nombreux. Un grand nombre de terrains mettent également à la disposition des vacanciers des piscines couvertes chauffées, des courts de tennis, des salles de jeux, et proposent une large gamme d'installations et d'activités destinées aux enfants.

La plupart de terrains acceptent les tentes, les caravanes de tourisme et les camping-cars, et mettent un vaste éventail d'équipements à la disposition des vacanciers. Un grand nombre de terrains louent des caravanes fixes, qui sont souvent très spacieuses, luxueuses et bien aménagées, comportant deux ou trois belles chambres à coucher, un salon confortable et un coin salle à manger séparé.

Un grand nombre de ces logements de vacances ont tout le confort moderne: télévision couleur, réfrigérateur, douche avec eau chaude, salle de bains et four à

micro-ondes. En plus des caravanes de vacances, de nombreux terrains louent également des chalets et des pavillons, conçus et équipés avec le même soin et dotés du même confort. Vous vous sentirez comme chez vous dans tous ces terrains et vous y trouverez les aménagements et la liberté dont vous avez besoin pour profiter au mieux de vos vacances.

Pour sélectionner le meilleur terrain/centre offrant les services et normes dont vous avez besoin, le nouveau British Graded Holiday Parks Rating Scheme (système d'évaluation des centres de vacances/terrains de camping britanniques) vous sera très utile. Des inspecteurs indépendants ont visité chaque terrain participant à ce projet et les ont classés selon la propreté, l'environnement et la qualité de leurs services. Vous trouverez une explication de ce projet page 20.

De nombreux terrains sont ouverts toute l'année, et permettent ainsi de prendre quelques jours de vacances agréables au printemps, en automne et même en hiver. Les tarifs sont moins élevés que pendant la haute saison, et de nombreux équipements sont encore à la disposition des vacanciers (il est toutefois prudent de vérifier).

Si vous avez l'intention de séjourner, en haute saison (de juin à septembre), dans une région de villégiature très fréquentée, nous vous conseillons de réserver à l'avance. Il est indispensable soit de confirmer toute réservation par écrit, soit d'arriver très tôt au terrain de votre choix.

Unterwegs in
Großbritannien

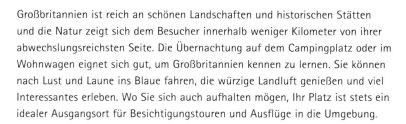

Großbritannien ist reich an schönen Landschaften und historischen Stätten und die Natur zeigt sich dem Besucher innerhalb weniger Kilometer von ihrer abwechslungsreichsten Seite. Die Übernachtung auf dem Campingplatz oder im Wohnwagen eignet sich gut, um Großbritannien kennen zu lernen. Sie können nach Lust und Laune ins Blaue fahren, die würzige Landluft genießen und viel Interessantes erleben. Wo Sie sich auch aufhalten mögen, Ihr Platz ist stets ein idealer Ausgangsort für Besichtigungstouren und Ausflüge in die Umgebung.

Großbritannien ist der Geburtsort des Zeltens und bietet eine große Anzahl an Plätzen jeder Art - von kleinen, ruhigen bis zu großen, lebhaften Plätzen mit einer großen Auswahl an Einrichtungen und einem reichen Unterhaltungsprogramm. Zahlreiche Plätze verfügen über ein Restaurant, eine Bar, einen Nachtklub und veranstalten regelmäßige Grillpartys und Abendunterhaltung (z.B. Abendessen mit Tanz, Kabarett).

Immer mehr Plätze sind ideale Ferienorte für Aktivferien. Angeln, Segeln und Golf, nur drei der beliebtesten Aktivitäten, werden von einer wachsenden Zahl von Plätzen angeboten. Viele verfügen auch über ein Hallenbad, Tennisplätze, Spielzimmer und bieten eine große Auswahl an Einrichtungen und Aktivitäten für Kinder.

Die meisten Plätze sind für Zelte, Wohnwagen und Wohnmobile eingerichtet und bieten dem Besucher eine Reihe von Einrichtungen. Zahlreiche Plätze vermieten Wohnwagen. Diese sind oft äußerst geräumig, luxuriös und gut ausgestattet und verfügen über zwei oder drei Schlafzimmer, ein Wohnzimmer mit komfortablen Möbeln und einen getrennten Essbereich. Viele bieten auch Farbfernseher, Kühlschrank, Dusche mit warmem Wasser, Bad und Mikrowellenherd. Zusätzlich zu den Wohnwagen gibt es auf zahlreichen Plätzen auch Chalets und Hütten mit demselben Komfort. Alle sind in der Tat ein zweites Zuhause und bieten die Einrichtungen und die Unabhängigkeit, die für erfolgreiche Ferien unerlässlich sind.

Um Ihnen bei der Auswahl des Parktyps zu helfen, dessen Standards und Leistungsumfang Ihren Anforderungen und Wünschen am besten entspricht, wird Ihnen das British Graded Holiday Parks Rating Scheme (Beurteilungs-system für britische Ferienparks) von großem Nutzen sein. Alle an diesem System beteiligten Parks sind von unabhängigen Gutachtern besucht und im Hinblick auf Sauberkeit, Umwelt und Qualität von Angebot und Service beurteilt worden. Eine Erklärung des Systems finden Sie auf Seite 24.

Zahlreiche Plätze sind ganzjährig geöffnet und ideal für Kurzurlaube im Frühling, Herbst oder auch Winter. Die Preise sind während der Nebensaison billiger als während der Hochsaison und zahlreiche Einrichtungen sind immer in Betrieb (es ist jedoch ratsam, sich zuerst zu erkundigen).

Falls Sie während der Hochsaison(Juni bis September) eine beliebte Feriendestination wählen, ist es ratsam, im Voraus zu buchen. Sie müssen die Buchung entweder schriftlich bestätigen oder sehr früh auf dem Platz Ihrer Wahl eintreffen.

Rondtrekken in
Groot-Brittannië

In Groot-Brittannië vindt u prachtige landschappen en een interessante geschiedenis. De reiziger treft op korte afstand van elkaar allerlei verschillende gebieden aan, en kamperen met de tent of de caravan is de ideale manier om echt van Groot-Brittannië te genieten. Ga en sta waar u wilt, zonder aan een programma vast te zitten, geniet van de frisse lucht en maak plezier! Waar u ook bent, u kunt uw kampeerplaats uw basis maken en in het omliggende gebied rondtrekken.

Groot-Brittannië is het geboorteland van het kamperen, en wij hebben dan ook een groot aantal terreinen in allerlei soorten en maten: vanaf kleine rustige terreintjes tot en met grote gezellige parken met allerlei faciliteiten en amusement. Vele hebben een restaurant, bar, nachtclub, en organiseren regelmatig barbecues en amusement 's avonds (zoals diner dansant, cabaret).

Steeds meer parken vormen tegenwoordig een ideaal centrum voor een actieve vakantie. Vissen, zeilen en golfen zijn slechts drie mogelijkheden die steeds meer terreinen organiseren. Vaak vindt u ook overdekte zwembaden, tennisbanen, spellenkamers en allerlei faciliteiten en activiteiten om de kinderen bezig te houden.

Op de meeste terreinen worden tenten, trekcaravans en kampeerauto's toegelaten en vindt u een groot aantal centrale faciliteiten voor de trekker. Ook zijn er vaak stacaravans te huur: deze zijn vaak zeer ruim, luxueus en goed uitgerust, met twee of drie ruime slaapkamers, een zitkamer met gerieflijk meubilair en een aparte eetkamer. Vaak vindt u er ook moderne gemakken zoals kleuren t.v., ijskast, warme douches, en-suite badkamers en magnetronovens.

Vele parken bieden niet alleen stacaravans maar ook huisjes te huur, die al net zo goed zijn ingericht en uitgerust. Geniet van de faciliteiten en de vrijheid om echt vakantie te vieren.

Om u te helpen met het selecteren van een bepaald type park metvoorzieningen en op het niveau dat u zoekt, zal het British Graded Holiday Parks Rating Scheme u zeker van pas komen. Elk park dat aan ditsysteem meedoet is bezocht door een onafhankelijke controleur en heeft een classificatie gekregen op basis van hygiëne, omgeving en de kwaliteit van de voorzieningen en diensten die er aanwezig zijn. Een verklaring van dit systeem kan op pagina 28 gevonden worden.

Vele parken zijn het hele jaar open en bieden de ideale manier om er even tussenuit te gaan in de lente, herfst of zelfs in de winter. De prijzen zijn dan lager dan in het hoogseizoen, terwijl toch vele faciliteiten beschikbaar zijn (het is wel raadzaam dit van te voren na te gaan).

Als u in een populair vakantiegebied denkt te verblijven in het hoogseizoen (juni tot september), raden wij u aan van te voren te reserveren. Bevestig de reservering schriftelijk of kom zeer vroeg aan op het terrein.

Alla scoperta della
Gran Bretagna

La Gran Bretagna è uno stupendo paese di grande interesse storico che offre un'ampia varietà di paesaggi. Il campeggio in tenda o roulotte è uno dei modi più efficaci di visitare la Gran Bretagna, dato che consente di viaggiare quando e dove si vuole, senza dover rispettare un itinerario prestabilito, divertendosi e respirando l'aria fresca della campagna. Ovunque si decida di andare, il campeggio può servire da base dalla quale il turista può visitare la zona circostante.

Il campeggio è un'invenzione britannica, ne consegue che in Gran Bretagna vi sono numerosissimi campeggi di tutti i tipi: da quelli piccoli e tranquilli a quelli grandi e animatissimi che offrono un'ampia gamma di strutture e intrattenimenti. Molti campeggi offrono anche ristoranti, bar, locali notturni, banchetti all'aperto con barbecue e spettacoli serali (p.es. serate di ballo, cabaret).

Molti campeggi sono ideali per trascorrere periodi di vacanza di tipo più dinamico, dato che un numero sempre maggiore di essi offre la possibilità, ad esempio, di pescare, praticare la vela o giocare al golf.

Molti dispongono di piscine, campi da tennis e palestre al coperto e di numerose strutture e attività per il divertimento dei bambini.

La maggior parte dei campeggi accetta tende, campers e roulottes e offre un'ampia gamma di strutture centralizzate per il campeggiatore. Molti offrono anche roulottes a noleggio

Queste roulottes sono spesso spaziosissime, lussuose e ben attrezzate con due o tre camere doppie, un salotto comodamente ammobiliato e una sala da pranzo separata. Molte offrono anche altre moderne comodità come televisioni a colori, frigoriferi, docce calde, camere con bagno e forni a microonde. Oltre alle roulottes a noleggio, molti campeggi offrono anche chalet e casette a noleggio progettate e attrezzate con gli stessi criteri. Sono tutte abitazioni dove ci si sente come a casa propria, e che offrono libertà e tutte le attrezzature necessarie a godersi la propria vacanza.

Per aiutare a scegliere il tipo di parco più adatto, che offra i requisiti e gli standard richiesti, sarà molto utile il British Graded Holiday Parks Rating Scheme (progetto di assegnazione di punteggio ai parchi vacanze del Regno Unito). Ogni parco iscritto viene ispezionato da ispettori indipendenti, con assegnazione di punteggio sulla base dei criteri di pulizia, qualità dell'ambiente e delle risorse e dei servizi offerti. Una spiegazione di come la valutazione funziona è reperibile a pagina 32.

Molti dei campeggi sono aperti tutto l'anno e sono dunque ideali per trascorrere una breve vacanza anche in primavera, in autunno o in inverno, stagioni in cui i prezzi sono più bassi che durante i mesi di alta stagione, anche se restano disponibili molte delle strutture (consigliamo comunque di controllare prima dell'arrivo).

Si consiglia a chi intenda trascorrere una vacanza in una delle località turistiche più frequentate durante i mesi di alta stagione (da giugno a settembre) di prenotare in anticipo. È essenziale confermare la prenotazione per iscritto o arrivare molto presto al campeggio prescelto.

South Coast
& New Forest

With two high quality destinations to choose from, Shorefield Country Parks offers you the best of both worlds in touring locations

LYTTON LAWN

Set in beautiful natural parkland close to Milford beach and the historic New Forest with views to the Isle of Wight. Peaceful, unspoilt and relaxing. Electricity hook-up, showers, laundrette, shop, 'Premier Pitches' and a children's area. Free Leisure Club facilities 2½ miles away, at Shorefield

OAKDENE
FOREST PARK

Over 55 acres of beautiful parkland giving direct access to the Avon Forest, and only 9 miles from Bournemouth's sandy beaches. New indoor and outdoor pools, sauna, steam room, spa bath, flume, gym, riding stables, adventure playground, club with entertainment, cafeteria, takeaway, general store and launderette.

SHOREFIELD
HOLIDAYS LIMITED

RALLIES WELCOME AT BOTH SITES

1999
DAVID BELLAMY
CONSERVATION AWARD
GOLD

For further details telephone
01590 648331 Ref. WTST

ENGLAND FOR EXCELLENCE
THE ENGLISH TOURIST BOARD
AWARDS FOR TOURISM

Oakdene Forest Park, St. Leonards, Ringwood, Hants BH24 2RZ
Lytton Lawn, Lymore Lane, Milford on Sea, Hants SO41 0TX
e-mail: holidays@shorefield.co.uk **www.shorefield.co.uk**

14

Want To Win A Holiday?

Just answer the question below!

British Holidays and **Where to Stay**: Camping and Caravan Parks are delighted to offer you the chance to win a wonderful seven night self-catering family holiday, with three runners-up prizes of family breaks at a British Holidays Park.

With a choice of 19 coastal locations throughout England, Scotland and Wales, all parks offer an extensive range of facilities such as Indoor and Outdoor Heated Swimming Pools, meet Bradley Bear at the Kids Club, Teen Activities, Excellent Sports, Family Entertainment, Great Bars and Restaurants and much more.

The lucky 1st Prize Winner will stay in a top of the range Gold Olympic Holiday Home, sleeping two to six people and superbly equipped with luxury utilities and furnishings.

Q What is the name of our British Holidays bear?

Fill in your answer and details on the coupon below and send to: Teresa O'Connor, Bta Competition, British Holidays, Normandy Court, 1 Wolsey Road, Hemel Hempstead, Herts HP2 4TU.

Closing date 30th November 2001
Please see p246 for competition rules

Answer:

Name:

Address:

Postcode:

Telephone Number:

For reservations or enquiries outside the U.K. please call 00 44 1442 248 66
Visit our website www.british-holidays.co.uk or ca

BRITISH HOLIDAYS

0845 607 8099

How to use
this guide

Most parks listed here have accommodation for touring caravans or tents or both and most welcome motor caravans. Many parks also have caravan holiday homes to let.

The Quality Assurance Scheme

When you're looking for a place to stay, you need a rating system you can trust. The British Graded Holiday Parks Scheme, relaunched in 2000 gives you a clear guide of what you can expect, in an easy-to-understand form. The scheme has quality at its heart and reflects consumer expectation.

The English Tourism Council uses Stars to show the quality rating of parks participating in the scheme. Parks are visited annually by trained, impartial assessors who award a rating from One to Five Stars. These are based on cleanliness, environment and the quality of facilities and services provided.

Parks are also given a 'designator' so you can identify the type of site at-a-glance - a Holiday Park, a Touring Park or a Camping Park, for example. (If no rating or designator is shown, the park was awaiting assessment at the time of going to press.)

The British Graded Holiday Parks Scheme was devised jointly by the national tourist boards for England, Northern Ireland, Scotland and Wales in association with the British Holiday & Home Parks Association (see page 31) and the National Caravan Council (see page 35).

Facilities

Facilities are indicated by means of the at-a-glance symbols explained on the fold-out back cover flap.

Prices

Prices given for touring pitches are based on the minimum and maximum charges for one night for two persons, car and either caravan or tent. It is more usual in Britain to charge simply for the use of the pitch, but a number of parks charge separately for car, caravan or tent, and for each person. Some parks may charge extra for caravan awnings. Minimum and maximum prices for caravan holiday homes are given per week. Prices quoted are those supplied to us by the park operators concerned, and are intended to give an indication of the prices which will be charged during the currency of this publication. Prices are shown in pounds (£) and pence (p). VAT (Value Added Tax) at 17.50% is included in the prices shown. **In order to avoid misunderstandings, it is particularly advisable to check prices with the park concerned when making reservations.**

Making a Booking

When enquiring about accommodation, as well as checking prices and other details, you will need to state your requirements clearly and precisely - for example:

- arrival and departure dates with acceptable alternatives if appropriate.
- the accommodation you need.
- tell the management about any particular requirements.

Misunderstandings can occur very easily over the telephone so we recommend that all bookings be confirmed in writing if time permits. Remember to include your name and address and please enclose a stamped addressed envelope or an international reply coupon (if writing from outside Britain) for each reply.

Deposits and Advance Payments

In the case of caravan, camping and chalet parks and holiday centres the full charge often has to be paid in advance. This may be in two instalments - a deposit at the time of booking and the balance by, say, two weeks before the start of the booked period.

Cancellations

When you accept offered accommodation, in writing or on the telephone, you are entering into a legally binding contract with the proprietor of the establishment. This means that if you cancel a reservation, fail to take up the accommodation or leave prematurely (regardless of the reasons) the proprietor may be entitled to compensation if it cannot be relet for all or a good part of the booked period. If a deposit has been paid it is likely to be forfeited and an additional payment may be demanded.

It is therefore in your interest to advise the management immediately if you have to change your travel plans, cancel a booking or leave prematurely.

Electric hook-up points

Most parks now have electric hook-up points for caravans and tents. Voltage is generally 240v AC, 50 cycles, although variations between 200v and 250v may still be found. An adaptor for use with hook-ups may be necessary. Parks will usually charge extra for this facility, and it is advisable to check rates when making a booking.

Finding your Park

Parks in this guide are listed in England by region followed by Scotland and Wales. They are listed alphabetically under the name of the town in or near which they are situated. The Town Index on page 255 and colour location maps at the back of the guide show all cities, towns and villages with park listings in this guide. Use these as a quick and easy way to find suitable accommodation. If you know which park you wish to stay at, check under the Index to Parks on page 251.

If the place you wish to stay is included in the Town Index, turn to the page number given to find the parks available there. The town names appear in black on the maps at the back of the guide as indicated by the map reference in the entry. Also check on the colour maps to find other places nearby which also have parks listed in this guide.

If the place you want is not in the town index – or you only have a general idea of the area in which you wish to stay – use the colour location maps.

The maps show all place names under which a park is listed in this guide. For a precise location read the directions in each entry. If you have any difficulties

 finding a particular park, we suggest that you ask for final directions within the neighbourhood.

The International Direction Signs shown above are in use in Britain and are designed to help visitors find their park. They have not yet been erected for all parks and do not display the name of any particular one. They do show, however, whether the park is for tents or caravans or both.

The International Camping Carnet is rarely recognised in Britain except at parks organised by the major clubs.

London sites
London is a great attraction to many visitors, so the camping and caravan parks in the Greater London area tend to become full very quickly, and early booking is required. Parks are also available at most ports of entry to the country and many of these are listed in this guide and marked on the maps at the back.

Park finding services
Tourist Information Centres throughout Britain (see end pages) are able to give campers and caravanners information about parks in their areas.

Some Tourist Information Centres have camping and caravanning advisory services which provide details of park availability and often assist with park booking. At present, in England, these advisory Tourist Information Centres cover areas in the **New Forest**, (0131) 314 6505; and **Cornwall**, (01872) 274057. In Wales, many Tourist Information Centres can supply information on pitch availability in their area from the end of May to the end of August.

Avoiding Peak Season Problems

In the summer months of June to September, parks in popular areas such as North Wales, Cumbria, the West Country or the New Forest in Hampshire may become full. Campers should aim to arrive at parks early in the day or, where possible, should book in advance. Some

parks have overnight holding areas for visitors who arrive late. This helps to prevent disturbing other campers and caravanners late at night and means that fewer visitors are turned away. Caravans or tents are directed to a pitch the following morning.

Other Caravan and Camping Places

If you enjoy making your own route through Britain's countryside, it may interest you to know that the Forestry Commission operates forest camp parks in Britain's seven Forest Parks as well as in the New Forest. Some offer reduced charges for youth organisations on organised camping trips, and all enquiries about them should be made, well in advance of your intended stay, to the Forestry Commission.

Camping Barns

These are usually redundant farm buildings which have been converted to provide simple accommodation, for up to 15 visitors, at a reasonable cost. Facilities are basic with somewhere to sleep, eat and prepare food, a supply of cold running water and flush toilet.

The Youth Hostels Association has a network of camping barns stretching from the Forest of Bowland in Lancashire, through Durham and into North Yorkshire. Further information and bookings details can be obtained from the YHA, Trevelyan House, 8 St Stephen's Hill, St Albans, Hertfordshire ALI 2DY. Tel: (01727) 855215.

Camping barns are also available in the Peak National Park. Further information and details can be obtained from Peak District National Park Authority, Aldern House, Baslow Road, Bakewell, Derbyshire DE45 1AE.

Pets

Many places accept guests with dogs, but we do advise that you check this when you book, and ask if there are any extra charges or rules about exactly where your pet is allowed. The acceptance of dogs is not always extended to cats and it is strongly advised that cat owners contact the establishment well in advance. Some establishments do not accept pets at all. These places are indicated with the symbol ✖.

Bringing Pets to Britain
The quarantine laws have recently changed in England and a pilot Pet Travel Scheme (PETS) is currently in operation. Under this new scheme pet dogs are able to come into Britain from over 35 countries via certain sea, air and rail routes into England.

Dogs that have been resident in these countries for more than 6 months may enter the UK under the Pilot Scheme providing they are accompanied by the appropriate documentation.

For dogs to be able to enter the UK without quarantine under the PETS Pilot Scheme they will have to meet certain conditions and travel with the following documents: the Official PETS Certificate, a certificate of treatment against tapeworm and ticks and a declaration of residence.

For details of participating countries, routes, operators and further information about the PETS Pilot Scheme please contact the Ministry of Agriculture, Fisheries and Food, 1a Page Street, London SW1P 4PQ

Tel: +44 (0) 870 241 1710 Fax: +44 (0) 20 7904 6834 Email: pets@ahvg.maff.gsi.gov.uk, or visit their web site at www.maff.gov.uk/animalh/quarantine

Drugs Warnings for Incoming Tourists

The United Kingdom has severe penalties against drug smuggling. Drug traffickers may try to trick travellers. If you are travelling to the United Kingdom avoid any involvement with drugs. Never carry luggage or parcels through customs for someone else.

Legal Points

The best source of legal advice for motorists in Britain will be your motoring organisation. What the caravanner or camper needs to know in addition is relatively simple.

If you are towing a caravan or camping trailer you must not exceed 96 kph (60 mph) on dual carriageways and motorways, 80 kph (50 mph) on single carriageways, and on a motorway with three lanes each side you must not enter the third (fastest) lane. Do not light cooking stoves in motorway service areas.

In most towns parking is restricted both by regulations and practical difficulties. Cars with trailers may not use meter-controlled parking spaces, and many town car parks are designed with spaces for single vehicles only. However, a number can accommodate long vehicles as well as cars.

At night a trailer or a car attached to a trailer, if parked on the roadway, must show two front and two rear lights even where a car by itself would be exempt.

The brakes, lights, weight etc. of foreign vehicles do not have to comply with British technical requirements. However, a trailer must not exceed the British size limits - 7 metres (23 feet) long and 2.3 metres (7 feet 6 inches) wide. They must carry your national identification plates. Do not stop overnight on roadside grass verges or lay-bys, because these are considered by law to be part of the road.

Finally, it is important to find out the time you are expected to vacate your pitch on your departure day. You should then leave in good time in the morning, or you may be asked to pay an extra day's charge.

Advice for Visitors

The British Tourist Authority welcomes your comments on any aspects of your stay in Britain, whether favourable or otherwise. We hope that you will have no cause to complain, but if you do, the best advice is to take up the complaint immediately with the management of the enterprise concerned: for example the park, shop or transport company. If you cannot obtain satisfaction in this way, please let us know and we ourselves may investigate the matter or suggest what action you might take.

You may bring currency in any denomination and up to any amount into Britain and there is no restriction on the number of travellers' cheques you can change. If you need to change money when the banks are closed you can do so at some large hotels, travel agents and stores or at independent bureaux de change. Be sure to check in advance the rate of exchange and the commission charges. All large shops, department stores and most hotels and restaurants will accept the usual internationally recognised credit cards. If you go shopping in local street markets, patronise only the large, recognised ones, and examine goods carefully.

Always ask the price of goods and services before committing yourself. Beware of pick-pockets in crowded places.

If your possessions are stolen or if you are involved in an accident or fire, telephone 999 (no charge will be made) and ask for the police, the ambulance service or the fire brigade.

Every effort has been made by the British Tourist Authority to ensure accuracy in this publication at the time of going to press. The information is given in good faith on the basis of information submitted to the British Tourist Authority by the promotors of the caravan parks listed. However, BTA cannot guarantee the accuracy of this information and accepts no responsibility for any error or misrepresentation. All liability for loss, disappointment, negligence or other damage caused by the reliance on the information contained in this guide or in the event of the bankruptcy or liquidation of any company, individual or firm mentioned, or in the event of any company, individual or firm ceasing to trade, is hereby excluded. It is advisable to confirm the information given with the establishments concerned at the time of booking.

All parks in this guide conform to Tourism Council Standards. A list of these Standards for Camping and Caravan Parks may be found on page 225.

All the establishments listed have paid for inclusion in this guide.

Mode d'emploi
du guide

La plupart des terrains répertoriés ici possèdent des emplacements pour les caravanes de tourisme ou les tentes, ou les deux, et la plupart accueillent volontiers les camping-cars De nombreux terrains ont aussi des caravanes fixes à louer.

Le Systeme d'Assurance-Qualite

Lorsque vous cherchez un endroit où faire étape, vous voulez un système d'évaluation de confiance. Le British Holiday Parks Scheme, relancé en l'an 2000, vous indique clairement et en toute simplicité à quoi vous attendre. La qualité reste la préoccupation principale de ce système, en réponse aux exigences des consommateurs.

L'English Tourism Council (office de tourisme anglais) utilise des Etoiles pour indiquer la qualité des terrains et centres de vacances participant à ce système. Des inspecteurs agréés et impartiaux visitent ces terrains chaque année et les récompensent de une à cinq Etoiles. Celles-ci indiquent la propreté, l'environnement et la qualité des services fournis.

Les terrains reçoivent également un symbole pour vous permettre d'identifier le type de terrain en un clin d'œil - centre de vacances familial, terrain de camping ou de caravanes, par exemple (si aucun symbole/aucune étoile n'est indiqué pour un terrain/centre particulier, celui-ci n'a pas encore reçu son évaluation à l'heure de mise sous presse).

Le British Graded Holiday Parks Scheme (système d'évaluation des centres de vacances/terrains de camping britanniques) a été conçu par les agences de tourisme d'Angleterre, d'Irlande du Nord, d'Ecosse et du Pays de Galles en collaboration avec The British Holiday & Home Parks Association (l'Association britannique des centres familiaux de vacances et de terrains de camping) (voir page 31) et le National Caravan Council (le bureau national des caravaniers) (voir page 35).

Equipements

Les installations sont indiquées au moyen de symboles illustratifs, dont la légende est donnée ici.

SIGNES CONVENTIONNELS

M Membre d'un Office de tourisme régional
BH& British Holiday
HPA & Home Parks Association (voir page 31)
NCC National Caravan Council (voir page 33)
🚐 Caravanes admises (suivi du nombre d'emplacements et des tarifs)
🚍 Camping-cars admis (suivi du nombre d'emplacements et des tarifs). Dans certains cas, les emplacements pour camping-cars sont compris dans le total des emplacements pour caravanes
Å Tentes admises (suivi du nombre d'emplacements et des tarifs)
🏠 Nombre de caravanes disponibles pour la location (voir la rubrique "emplacements" ci-dessous)
🛏 Location de bungalows et logements similaires
🚗 Place de parking à côté de l'unité
P Parking dans le terrain
Aire de séjour d'une nuit
Branchements électriques pour caravanes (voir la rubrique "alimentation électrique pour caravanes" ci-dessous)
Douches
Eau chaude à tous les lavabos
Eclairage dans les compartiments WC, etc.
Décharge pour WC chimiques
Service de remplacement des bouteilles de gaz butane ou propane
Magasin d'alimentation fixe/itinérant
✕ Café/restaurant

🍷 Club/bar/magasin avec vente de boissons alcoolisées
📺 Salle de télévision couleur
📞 Cabine(s) téléphonique(s)
🔲 Laverie
Dispositifs de séchage du linge
Matériel de repassage
☉ Prises électriques pour rasoirs
Salle de jeux
Aire de jeux pour les enfants
🚲 Location de vélos
Piscine couverte chauffée sur le terrain
Piscine de plein air sur le terrain
Installations de plongée sous-marine (avec compresseur)
Ski nautique depuis le terrain
Canotage/canoë sur le terrain
Voile depuis le terrain
Equitation/randonnée à dos de poney depuis le terrain
Tennis sur le terrain
Pêche sur le terrain
Golf sur le terrain ou à proximité
Chasse privée
✕ Les chiens ne sont PAS acceptés
Distractions nocturnes
Réservations recommandées l'été
T Les réservations peuvent s'effectuer par l'intermédiaire d'une agence de voyages
WH Agréé "Welcome Host"

Tarifs

Les tarifs indiqués pour les emplacements sont établis sur la base du tarif minimum et du tarif maximum pour une nuitée et pour 2 personnes accompagnées d'une voiture et d'une tente ou d'une caravane La pratique générale veut qu'en Grande-Bretagne on ne fasse payer que l'emplacement, mais certains terrains de camping pratiquent des tarifs séparés pour la voiture, la tente ou la caravane ainsi que pour chaque personne. Certains terrains appliquent parfois des suppléments pour les auvents des caravanes. Les tarifs minimum et maximum de location des caravanes sont donnés par semaine. Les prix indiqués nous ont été fournis par les responsables des terrains concernés, et ont pour but de donner une idée des prix en vigueur au moment de la publication de ce guide. Les prix sont libellés en livres (£) et pence (p). La T.V.A. (Taxe à la Valeur Ajoutée) de 17,5% est comprise dans les tarifs indiqués Afin d'éviter tout malentendu, il est fortement conseillé de vérifier les prix auprès du terrain de camping concerné au moment d'effectuer les réservations.

Modalités de réservation

Lorsque vous vous renseignerez sur l'hebergement offert ainsi que sur les tarifs et autres détails, vous devrez énoncer avec clarté et précision quels sont vos besoins, notamment ;

- dates d'arrivée et de départ, avec dates de remplacement acceptables le cas échéant.
- type d'hebergement requis.
- autres besoins particuliers à signaler à la direction.

Les malentendus sont très courants par téléphone, aussi vous est-il recommandé de confirmer par écrit toutes vos réservations si les délais vous le permettent. N'oubliez pas de mentionner votre nom et votre adresse et prenez soin de joindre une enveloppe timbrée à votre adresse ou un coupon-réponse international (si vous écrivez depuis l'étranger) pour la réponse.

Arrhes et paiements anticipés

Les terrains de camping, de caravaning, ou avec bungalows, ainsi que les centres de vacances exigent souvent le versement intégral du paiement à l'avance. Celui-ci peut s'effectuer en deux fois: vous devez payer des arrhes lors de la réservation et vous acquitter du solde deux semaines avant le début de la période de location, par exemple.

Annulations

Lorsque vous acceptez l'hébergement qui vous est offert par écrit ou par téléphone, bous êtes lié par contrat avec le propriétaire de l'établissement. Cela signifie que si vous annulez une réservation, si vous ne venez pas prendre possession du logement ou si vous partez plus tôt que prévu (quelle qu'en soit la raison), le propriétaire est en droit d'exiger un dédommagement s'il ne peut pas relouer pour la durée totale ou une grande partie de la location. Si vous avez versé des arrhes, vous ne serez probablement pas remboursé, et l'on peut vous demander de payer une somme supplémentaire.

Vous avez donc intérêt à aviser immédiatement la direction si vous devez changer vos projets de voyage, annuler une réservation ou partir plus tôt que prévu.

Point de branchement électrique:

La plupart des terrains ont à présent des points de branchement électrique pour les caravanes et les tentes. Le voltage est en général de 240v 50Hz en courant alternatif, bien qu'on puisse encore trouver des courants variant entre 200v et 250v. Il se peut qu'un adaptateur soit nécessaire pour le branchement. En général, les terrains font payer un supplément pour ce service, et il est conseillé de se renseigner sur les tarifs en vigueur au moment de la réservation.

Comment choisir un terrain

Les terrains sont répertoriés dans ce guide en plusieurs sections : Angleterre (par région), Écosse et Pays de Galles. Dans chaque section, ils sont répertoriés par ordre alphabétique selon le nom de la ville la plus proche. L'Index des Villes en page 255 ainsi que les cartes en couleur au dos du guide vous indiquent toutes les villes et villages pour lesquels un terrain apparaît dans ce guide. Utilisez-les pour trouver un terrain rapidement et très facilement. Si vous savez quel est le terrain où vous voulez séjourner, vous le trouverez immédiatement en consultant l'index des terrains en page 251. Si le lieu où vous désirez séjourner figure dans l'index des villes, reportez-vous au numéro de page indiqué pour voir quels terrains y sont disponibles.

Le nom de la ville est indiqué en noir sur les cartes au dos du guide à l'endroit indiqué par la référence carte donnée dans chaque entrée. Consultez également les cartes encouleur pour trouver des lieux proches pour lesquels des terrains sont également répertoriés dans ce guide.

Si le lieu où vous désirez séjourner ne figure pas dans l'index des villes (ou bien si vous avez seulement une idée générale du lieu dans lequel vous désirez séjourner), utilisez les cartes en couleur. Certaines régions apparaissent sur plus d'une carte mais les noms de villes (imprimés en noir sur les cartes) sont indiqués une fois seulement.

Toutes les localités dans lesquelles un terrain est répertorié dans le guide figurent sur la carte. Pour avoir la position précise du terrain, veuillez consultez la rubrique qui lui est consacrée. Si vous avez des difficultés pour trouver un terrain donné, nous vous suggérons de demander votre chemin une fois que vous serez vous trouvez dans le voisinage.

Pour aider les visiteurs à trouver leur terrain de camping, La Grande-Bretagne emploie les panneaux de signalisation internationaux ci-dessus. Tous les terrains ne sont pas encore signalés de cette manière et les panneaux n'affichent pas le nom de terrains particuliers. Ces panneaux indiquent en revanche si le terrain peut accueillir des tentes, des caravanes ou les deux.

21

L'International Camping Carnet est rarement reconnu en Grande-Bretagne sauf dans les terrains gérés par les grands clubs.

Sites Londres

Londres attire de nombreux visiteurs, aussi les terrains de Camping-caravaning du Grand Londres ont-ils tendance à se remplir tres rapidement. Des terrains sont également disponibles dans la plupart des ports d'entrée du pays: bon nombre d'entre eux sont répertoriés dans ce guide et indiqués sur les cartes en fin de guide.

Services–conseils disponibles

Les Centres d'Information Touristique de toute la Grande-Bretagne (voir dernières pages) sont en mesure de donner aux campeurs et au caravaniers des renseignements sur les terrains de leur région.

Certains Centres d'Information Touristique possèdent des services-conseils pour le camping-caravaning qui vous donneront des détails sur les terrains disponibles et pourront souvent vous aider à effectuer votre réservation. A l'heure actuelle, en Angleterre, ces Centres d'Information Touristique couvrent les régions suivantes: **New Forest**, (0131) 314 6505; et **Cornouailles**, (01872) 274057. Au Pays de Galles, de nombreux Centres d'Information touristique peuvent fournir des renseignements sur les emplacements disponibles dans leur région depuis la fin du mois de mai jusqu'à la fin du mois d'août.

Précautions à prendre en haute saison

Lors des mois d'été, de juin à septembre, les terrains situés dans des régions très fréquentées comme le Nord Gallois, le Cumbria, le Sud-Ouest de l'Angleterre ou la New Forest, dans le Hampshire, risquent d'être complets. Les campeurs doivent s'efforcer d'arriver sur les terrains de bonne heure dans la journée ou, si c'est possible, de réserver à l'avance. Certains terrains ont des aires de séjour temporaire ou les visiteurs arrivant tard le soir peuvent passer la nuit. Cela permet de ne pas déranger les autres campeurs et caravaniers pendant la nuit et d'accepter un plus grand nombre de vacanciers. Les caravanes et les tentes se voient attribuer un emplacement le lendemain matin.

Autres terrains de camping–caravaning

Si vous souhaitez suivre votre propre itinéraire dans la campagne britannique, il peut vous être utile de savoir que la Forestry Commission gère des terrains de camping en forêt dans les sept Parcs forestiers de Grande-Bretagne ainsi que dans la New Forest. Certains terrains offrent des tarifs réduits pour les organisations de jeunesse effectuant des séjours de groupes: il vous est conseillé de vous renseigner à ce sujet auprès de la Forestry Commission très à l'avance.

Granges aménagées pour le camping (Camping Barns)

Ce sont en général des bâtiments de ferme aujourd'hui superflus qui ont été aménagés pour permettre d'héberger - en toute simplicité - jusqu'à 15 personnes,

à un prix raisonnable. Les installations sont ce qu'il y a de plus simple: un endroit pour dormir, manger et préparer les repas, l'eau froide et les WC avec chasse d'eau.

La Youth Hostels Association exploite un réseau de granges aménagées pour le camping qui va de la région de Forest Bowland dans le Lancashire au North Yorkshire, en passant par Durham. Pour obtenir de plus amples renseignements et des détails sur la façon de réserver, veuillez vous adresser à: YHA, Trevelyan House, 8 St Stephen's Hill, St Albans, Hertfordshire ALI 2DY. Tel: (01727) 855215.

On peut également séjourner dans des granges aménagées pour le camping dans le Peak National Park. Pour obtenir de plus amples renseignements et des détails, veuillez vous adresser auprès du Peak District National Park Authority, Aldern House, Baslow Road, Bakewell, Derbyshire DE45 1AE.

Les animaux

De nombreux terrains acceptent les chiens, mais nous vous conseillons de vérifier si c'est bien le cas lorsque vous réservez. Demandez également s'il y a des frais supplémentaires et si votre chien sera exclu de certaines zones. Lorsque les chiens sont acceptés, les chats ne le sont pas automatiquement et nous conseillons vivement aux propriétaires de chats de contacter l'établissement longtemps à l'avance. Certains terrains n'acceptent aucun animal familier. Ceci est indiqué par le symbole 🐕.

Amener votre animal en Grande-Bretagne

Les lois sur la quarantaine ont récemment changé en Angleterre. Un nouveau système, appelé Pet Travel Scheme (PETS) est actuellement à l'essai. Ce système autorise les chiens venus de 35 autres pays d'entrer en Angleterre à certains points (par avion, bateau et train).

Les chiens qui résident dans ces pays depuis plus de 6 mois peuvent entrer au Royaume-Uni grâce au système PETS, pourvu qu'ils possèdent la documentation nécessaire.

Pour que les chiens puissent entrer au Royaume-Uni sans quarantaine grâce au système PETS, ils doivent répondre à certaines conditions et avoir les documents suivants: certificat officiel PETS, certificat de traitement contre le ténia et les tiques et déclaration de résidence.

Pour avoir la liste des pays participant à ce programme, ainsi que la liste des points d'entrée et des opérateurs, ou pour tout complément d'information sur le projet pilote PETS, veuillez contacter le Ministère de l'Agriculture, de la Pêche et de l'Alimentation, 1a Page Street, London SW1P 4PQ.

Tél: +44 (0) 870 241 1710 Fax: +44 (0) 20 7904 6834

Email: pets@ahvg.maff.gsi.gov.uk, ou visitez le site web www.maff.gov.uk/animalh/quarantine

Réglementation contre la drogue

Le Royaume-Uni applique des sanctions sévères contre la contrebande de la drogue. Les trafiquants de drogue peuvent essayer de duper les voyageurs. Si vous voyagez à destination du Royaume-Uni, ne soyez pas mêlé au trafic de drogue. Ne passez jamais de bagages ou de colis pour autrui par les douanes.

Aspects juridiques

La meilleure source de renseignements juridiques pour les automobilistes voyageant en Grande-Bretagne reste l'association des automobilistes de leur pays d'origine. Les détails supplémentaires que doivent connaître le campeur ou le caravanier sont relativement simples.

Si vous tractez une caravane ou une remorque de camping, vous ne devez pas dépasser 96 km/h sur les voies express ou sur les autoroutes, 80 km/h sur les routes à deux voies; en outre, sur les autoroutes ayant trois voies dans chaque direction, vous ne devez pas rouler sur la troisième voie (la plus rapide). N'allumez pas de réchauds à gaz sur les aires de service des autoroutes.

Dans la plupart des villes, le stationnement est limité à la fois par la réglementation et par le manque de place. Les voitures dotées de remorques ne peuvent pas occuper les espaces de stationnement limité à parcmètres et de nombreux parcs de stationnement de ville ne sont conçus que pour accueillir des véhicules indépendants. Toutefois, certains parcs peuvent accueillir des véhicules plus longs en plus des voitures.

La nuit, les remorques ou les voitures dotées de remorques, lorsqu'elles sont en stationnement au bord de la route, doivent avoir les deux feux avant et les deux feux arrière allumés même dans le cas où cela n'est pas jugé nécessaire pour une voiture seule.

Les freins, l'éclairage, le poids, etc. des véhicules étrangers n'ont pas à respecter les prescriptions techniques britanniques. Toutefois, une remorque ne doit pas dépasser les limites dimensionnelles britanniques: 7m de long et 2,3m de large. Elle doit être munie de votre plaque d'immatriculation nationale. Vous ne devez pas vous arrêter pour la nuit sur les accotements ou sur les petites aires de stationnement des bas-côtés car la loi stipule que ces emplacements font partie de la route.

Enfin, il est important de vous renseigner sur l'heure à laquelle il vous est demandé de libérer votre emplacement le jour du départ. Vous devrez prévoir de partir assez tôt, sans quoi vous risquez d'avoir à payer une journée de location supplémentaire.

Conseils aux visiteurs

L'Office de Tourisme de Grande-Bretagne vous invite à formuler vos observations sur tout aspect de votre séjour en Grande-Bretagne, qu'elles soient favorables ou non. Nous espérons que vous n'aurez pas lieu de vous plaindre, mais dans l'affirmative, il vous est conseillé de faire part de votre mécontentement immédiatement auprès de la direction de l'établissement concerné comme par exemple: camping, magasin ou société de transport. Si vous ne pouvez pas obtenir satisfaction de cette manière, veuillez nous le faire savoir et nous examinerons la question nous-mêmes ou nous vous suggèrerons une procédure éventuelle à suivre.

Vous pouvez emporter en Grande-Bretagne les devises de votre choix en quantité illimitée et aucune restriction ne s'applique a la quantité de chèques de voyage changés. Si vous avez besoin de devises britanniques pendant les heures de fermeture des banques, vous pouvez vous les procurer dans certains grands hôtels, agences de voyages, grands magasins ou dans les bureaux de change indépendants. **Ne manquez pas de vérifier à l'avance le taux de change et la commission appliqués.**

Tous les grands magasins et boutiques et la plupart des hôtels et restaurants accepteront les cartes de crédit usuelles reconnues dans le monde entier. Si vous aimez faire vos achats au marché, limitez-vous aux grands marchés de rue officiels et examinez toujours les articles soigneusement.

Demandez toujours le prix des marchandises avant de vous engager. Prenez garde aux pickpockets en cas d'affluence. Si l'on vous vole des objets personnels ou si vous vous trouvez sur le lieu d'un incendie ou d'un accident, composez le 999 (numéro gratuit) et demandez la police, les services d'ambulance ou les pompiers.

L'Office de Tourisme de Grande-Bretagne (BTA) a pris toutes les dispositions nécessaires pour assurer l'exactitude des Informations contenues dans la présente publication au moment de mettre sous presse. Ces Informations sont fournies en toute bonne foi sur la base des renseignements donnés à la BTA par les exploitants des terrains de camping répertoriés. Toutefois, la BTA ne peut pas garantir l'exactitude de ces renseignements et décline toute responsabilité en cas d'erreur ou de déformation des faits. Toute responsabilité est également déclinée pour toutes pertes, déceptions, négligences ou autres dommages que pourrait subir quiconque se fie aux renseignements contenus dans le présent guide, pour les cas de faillite ou de liquidation de toute personne morale ou physique mentionnée, et pour les cas de cessation d'activités de toute personne morale ou physique. Il est conseillé de se faire confirmer les renseignements fournis par les établissements concernés lors de la réservation.

Tous les terrains inclus dans ce guide respectent les normes du Tourism Council (bureau national de tourisme). On trouvera à la page 225 une liste de ces normes relatives aux terrains de camping-caravaning.

Tous les établissements répertoriés figurent dans le présent guide à titre payant.

Hinweise zur Benutzung
dieses Reiseführers

Die meisten der hier aufgeführten Parks verfügen über Stellplätze für Wohnwagen bzw. Zelte oder beides und die meisten nehmen auch Wohnmobile auf. Des Weiteren vermieten viele Parks auch Ferienwohnwagen.

Das Programm zur Gewährleistung der Qualität

Bei der Suche nach einer geeigneten Unterkunft braucht man ein verlässliches Einstufungssystem. Das 'British Graded Holiday Parks Scheme' (britisches Beurteilungssystem für Ferienparks), das im Jahr 2000 neu lanciert wurde, vermittelt Ihnen in leicht verständlicher Form einen klaren Eindruck von dem, was Sie erwarten können. Das System spiegelt die Kundenerwartungen und beurteilt in erster Linie die Qualität.

Das English Tourism Council (englischer Fremdenverkehrsrat) kennzeichnet die Qualitätsstufe der an diesem Programm teilnehmenden Parks durch die Vergabe von Sternen. Die betreffenden Parks werden jährlich von sachlich geschulten, unparteiischen Prüfern inspiziert und dann mittels einer Skala von einem bis fünf Sterne eingestuft. Die Anzahl der vergebenen Sterne hängt von der

Sauberkeit, dem Ambiente sowie der Qualität der vorhandenen Einrichtungen und gebotenen Dienstleistungen ab.

Außerdem werden die einzelnen Parks nach Typ gekennzeichnet, so dass man auf einen Blick erkennt, um was für eine Art von Gelände es sich handelt – z.B. Ferienpark, Touringpark oder Campingpark. (Weist der Park keine Einstufung oder Kennzeichnung auf, so bedeutet das, dass die Beurteilung zum Zeitpunkt der Drucklegung noch nicht stattgefunden hat.)

Das 'British Graded Holiday Parks Scheme' entstand in partnerschaftlicher Zusammenarbeit der nationalen Fremdenverkehrsstellen für England, Nordirland, Schottland und Wales, in Verbindung mit der British Holiday & Home Parks Association (siehe Seite 31) und dem National Caravan Council (siehe Seite 35).

Einrichtungen

Die jeweiligen Einrichtungen sind durch Symbole bezeichnet, deren Bedeutung Sie der Zeichenerklärung auf einen Blick entnehmen können.

ZEICHENERKLÄRUNG

⚎ Mitglied eines regionalen Tourist Board
BH& British Holiday
HPA & Home Parks Association (siehe Seite 31)
NCC National Caravan Council (siehe Seite 35)
⚎ Wohnwagen zugelassen (mit Anzahl der Stellplätze und Preisen)
⚎ Wohnmobile zugelassen (mit Anzahl der Stellplätze und Preisen)
Å Zelte zugelassen (mit Anzahl der Stellplätze und Preisen)
⊡ Anzahl der vermietbaren Ferienwohnwagen (mit Anzahl und Preisen)
⚎ Bungalows, Chalets, Wohnkabinen zum Vermieten
⚎ Parkmöglichkeit neben der Wohneinheit
P Parkplatz auf dem Gelände
⚎ Auffangstelle für spät im Park eintreffende Gäste
⚎ Stromanschluß für Wohnwagen und Zelte
⚎ Duschen
⚎ Heißes Wasser für alle Waschbecken
⚎ Beleuchtung im Toilettenbau
⚎ Chemische Toiletten
⚎ Umtauschstelle für Butan- oder Propangaszylinder
⚎ Lebensmittelgeschäft/Wagen für Lebensmittelverkauf

✕ Restaurant
⚎ Klub mit Alkoholausschank Bar
TV Aufenthaltsraum mit Farbfernseher
⚎ Öffentliche Fernsprechzellen
⚎ Wäscherei
⚎ Wäschetrockner
⚎ Bügelmöglichkeiten
☉ Anschlüsse für Elektrorasierer
⚎ Hallenspiele
⚎ Kinderspielplatz
⚎ Fahrradverleih
⚎ Hallenbad
⚎ Freibad
⚎ Tauchen
⚎ Wasserski vom Park aus
⚎ Bootsfahrten/Kanufahrten
△ Segeln
U Reiten/Ponyreiten in der Nähe
⚎ Tennis
⚎ Angeln
⚎ Golf im Park oder in der Nähe
✓ Private Jagdrechte
⚎ Hunde NICHT erlaubt
♫ Abendunterhaltung
⚎ Im Sommer Reservierung empfohlen
T Buchung durch Reisebüros möglich
WH Welcome Host

Preise

Die angegebenen Preise für Stellplätze beruhen auf den Mindest- bzw. Höchstgebühren pro Nacht für zwei Personen, ein Auto und einen Wohnwagen bzw. ein Zelt. In Großbritannien ist es im Allgemeinen üblich, einfach eine Gebühr für die Nutzung des Stellplatzes zu berechnen, allerdings erheben einige Parks separate Gebühren für das Auto, den Wohnwagen bzw. das Zelt und pro Person. Manche Parks verlangen unter Umständen eine Zusatzgebühr für am Wohnwagen angebrachte Sonnenzelte. Die Mindest- und Höchstpreise für Ferienwohnwagen sind pro Woche angegeben. Die Preise wurden jeweils von der betreffenden Parkleitung zur Verfügung gestellt und bilden lediglich eine Richtschnur für die tatsächlich berechneten Preise während der Gültigkeit der vorliegenden Veröffentlichung. Die Preise sind in Pfund Sterling (£) und Pence (p) angegeben. Die Mehrwertsteuer (VAT) zum Satz von 17,5% ist im Preis enthalten. Um etwaigen Missverständnissen vorzubeugen, ist es ratsam, sich bei der Reservierung nach den genauen Preisen zu erkundigen.

Reservierungen

Bei Anfragen über mögliche Unterkünfte, Preise und weitere Angaben sollten Sie Ihre Wünsche klar und genau angeben - zum Beispiel:

- Ankunfts- und Abreisetermin, falls möglich mit akzeptablen Ausweichterminen
- gewünschte Unterkunft
- Teilen Sie der Parkleitung mit, falls Sie besondere Anforderungen haben.

Bei Telefongesprächen kommt es leicht zu Missverständnissen. Deshalb empfehlen wir Ihnen, Ihre Reservierung schriftlich zu bestätigen, falls dies zeitlich möglich ist. Denken Sie bitte daran, Ihren Namen und Ihre Anschrift anzugeben und einen adressierten Freiumschlag, bei Anfragen aus dem Ausland einen internationalen Antwortschein, beizulegen.

Anzahlung aen und Vorauszahlungen

Bei Wohnwagen-, Camping-, Chaletparks und Ferienzentren ist der gesamte Betrag häufig im Voraus zu entrichten. Die Zahlung kann in zwei Raten erfolgen: bei der Reservierung wird eine Anzahlung fällig und der Restbetrag ist zwei Wochen vor Beginn des Aufenthalts zu leisten.

Stornierungen

Wenn Sie ein Unterkunftsangebot schriftlich oder telefonisch akzeptieren, gehen Sie mit dem Besitzer der betreffenden Unterkunft einen rechtlich bindenden Vertrag ein. Das hat zur Folge, dass der Besitzer, wenn Sie eine Reservierung stornieren, nicht wahrnehmen oder die Unterkunft (gleichgültig aus welchen Gründen) vorzeitig räumen, unter Umständen berechtigt ist, Schadensersatz zu verlangen, sofern er nicht in der Lage ist, die Unterkunft für den ganzen bzw. einen Teil des gebuchten Zeitraums weiterzuvermieten. Falls eine

Anzahlung geleistet wurde, wird sie wahrscheinlich hierfür angerechnet und unter Umständen erfolgt eine weitere Zahlungsforderung.

Es ist daher in Ihrem Interesse, die Geschäftsleitung umgehend zu benachrichtigen, wenn Sie Ihre Reisepläne ändern, eine Reservierung stornieren oder die Unterkunft vorzeitig verlassen möchten.

Anschluss ans Stromnetz

Die meisten Parks verfügen inzwischen über Stromanschlussstellen für Wohnwagen und Zelte. Es handelt sich dabei im Allgemeinen um Wechselstrom mit einer Spannung von 240 Volt, 50 Schwingungen, allerdings können Spannungsschwankungen zwischen 200 V und 250 V auftreten. Unter Umständen benötigen Sie einen Adapter. Die Parks erheben normalerweise eine Zusatzgebühr für diesen Service und es ist ratsam, sich bei der Reservierung nach deren Höhe zu erkundigen.

So finden Sie Ihren Park

In der vorliegenden Broschüre sind die Parks in England nach Region, danach die Parks in Schottland und Wales aufgeführt. Sie sind in alphabetischer Reihenfolge unter dem Namen der Ortschaft, in der oder in deren Nähe sie liegen, verzeichnet. Im Ortsverzeichnis auf Seite 255 und auf den farbigen Lagekarten am Ende dieser Veröffentlichung sind alle Städte, Ortschaften und Dörfer aufgeführt, die in dieser Broschüre mit einem Park vertreten sind. Anhand des Verzeichnisses und der Karten finden Sie schnell und mühelos eine geeignete Unterkunft. Wenn Sie bereits wissen, in welchem Park Sie übernachten möchten, schlagen Sie im Verzeichnis der Parks auf Seite 251 nach.

Wenn die Ortschaft, in der Sie übernachten möchten, im Ortsverzeichnis aufgeführt ist, schlagen Sie auf der angegebenen Seite nach, wo die dort vorhandenen Parks verzeichnet sind. Die Namen der Ortschaften sind gemäß des beim betreffenden Eintrag genannten Planquadrats auf den Karten am Ende dieses Reiseführers schwarz gedruckt. Sehen Sie auch auf den farbigen Karten nach, um Ortschaften in der Nähe zu finden, wo sich ebenfalls Parks befinden, die in dieser Veröffentlichung aufgeführt sind.

Falls die Ortschaft, in der Sie übernachten möchten, nicht im Ortsverzeichnis aufgeführt ist oder Sie nur eine ungefähre Vorstellung von der Gegend haben, in der Sie übernachten möchten, so benutzen Sie die farbigen Lagekarten.

Auf den Karten sind alle Orte verzeichnet, die in der vorliegenden Veröffentlichung mit einem Park vertreten sind. Die genaue Lage ist jeweils in den betreffenden Einträgen beschrieben. Sollten Sie Schwierigkeiten haben,

 einen bestimmten Park zu finden, so schlagen wir vor, dass Sie sich vor Ort eine genaue Wegbeschreibung geben lassen.

Die oben abgebildeten internationalen Hinweisschilder, die in Großbritannien vielfach zu finden sind, erleichtern Ihnen das Auffinden eines Parks. Allerdings

sind sie noch nicht für alle Camping-, Wohnwagen- bzw. Ferienparks vorhanden und geben nicht den Namen des Parks an, doch zeigen sie, ob es sich um einen Park für Wohnwagen, Zelte oder beides handelt.

Der internationale Campingausweis ist in Großbritannien nur in Parks gültig, die von größeren Klubs verwaltet werden.

Plätze in London

Da London ein großer Anziehungspunkt für Besucher ist, sind die Camping- und Wohnwagenparks im Umkreis der britischen Hauptstadt schnell ausgebucht, daher ist eine frühzeitige Reservierung ratsam. Auch in den meisten Einreisehäfen gibt es entsprechende Parks, von denen viele in dieser Veröffentlichung aufgeführt und auf den Karten verzeichnet sind.

Informationsdienste

Die Touristeninformationszentren in allen Teilen Großbritanniens (auf den letzten Seiten aufgeführt) geben Ihnen gerne Auskunft über die Camping- und Wohnwagenparks in ihrem Gebiet.

Einige Touristeninformationszentren haben einen Wohnwagen- und Camping-Beratungsdienst, der über freie Plätze Auskunft geben und häufig auch Reservierungen vornehmen kann. Zur Zeit sind in England folgende Beratungsdienste vorhanden: **New Forest**, (0131) 314 6505 und **Cornwall** (01872) 274057. Viele Touristeninformationszentren in Wales können Ihnen Auskunft über von Ende Mai bis Ende August verfügbare Stellplätze in ihrem Gebiet geben.

Vermeiden von Problemen in der Hochsaison

In den Sommermonaten Juni bis September sind die Camping- und Wohnwagenparks in den beliebten Urlaubsgebieten wie etwa Nordwales, Cumbria, im West Country oder im New Forest in Hampshire schnell ausgebucht. Treffen Sie daher frühzeitig am Tag am Park ein oder buchen Sie nach Möglichkeit im Voraus. Manche Parks verfügen über Auffangstellen für spät eintreffende Gäste. Auf diese Weise werden die anderen Gäste zu fortgeschrittener Stunde nicht gestört und es werden weniger Besucher abgewiesen. Es wird dann am nächsten Morgen ein Stellplatz zugewiesen.

Sonstige Wohnwagen- und Campingplätze

Wenn Sie Ihre Reiseroute durch die britische Landschaft lieber auf eigene Faust planen, dürften Sie an den Campingplätzen in Waldgebieten interessiert sein, die von der Forestry Commission verwaltet werden. Hierzu gehören sieben Forest Parks und der New Forest. In einigen erhalten Jugendorganisationen beim Campingurlaub Preisermäßigungen. Alle diesbezüglichen Anfragen sind frühzeitig im Voraus an die Forest Commission zu richten.

Camping in der Scheune

Bei dieser Campingalternative handelt es sich um ehemalige Scheunen, die zu einfachen, günstigen Unterkünften für bis zu 15 Personen umgebaut wurden.

Die Einrichtungen sind anspruchslos. Es gibt eine Schlaf-, Koch- und Essstelle, kaltes Wasser und ein WC.

Die Youth Hostels Association (der Jugendherbergsverband) verfügt über ein Netz von Camping-Scheunen, das sich vom Forest of Bowland in Lancashire über Durham bis nach North Yorkshire erstreckt. Für weitere Informationen und Reservierungen wenden Sie sich bitte an die YHA, Trevelyan House, 8 St Stephen's Hill, St Albans, Hertfordshire AL1 2DY. Tel: (01727) 855215.

Camping-Scheunen sind auch im Peak Nationalpark zu finden. Für weitere Auskünfte wenden Sie sich bitte an die Peak District National Park Authority, Aldern House, Baslow Road, Bakewell, Derbyshire DE45 1AE.

Haustiere

In vielen Unterkünften werden Gäste mit Hunden aufgenommen, allerdings raten wir Ihnen, sich bei der Reservierung danach zu erkundigen. Außerdem sollten Sie fragen, ob für den Hund eine zusätzliche Gebühr berechnet wird, und ob es Regeln gibt, wo genau Ihr Haustier sich aufhalten darf. Der Umstand, dass Hunde aufgenommen werden, bedeutet nicht unbedingt, dass das Gleiche auch für Katzen gilt und wir raten Katzenbesitzern dringend, sich diesbezüglich frühzeitig mit der betreffenden Unterkunft zu verständigen. Manche Unterkünfte lassen überhaupt keine Haustiere zu und sind mit folgendem Symbol gekennzeichnet ✖

Das Mitbringen von Haustieren nach Großbritannien

In England wurden kürzlich die Quarantänevorschriften novelliert und momentan läuft das Pilotprogramm 'Pet Travel Scheme (PETS)'. Im Rahmen dieser neuen Aktion können als Haustier gehaltene Hunde auf bestimmten Schiffs-, Flug- und Bahnstrecken aus über 35 Ländern nach England mitgebracht werden.

Hunde, die länger als 6 Monate in den betreffenden Ländern gehalten wurden, können im Rahmen des Pilotprogramms nach Großbritannien eingeführt werden, vorausgesetzt, dass die entsprechenden Dokumente vorhanden sind.

Um im Rahmen des Pilotprogramms PETS ohne Quarantäne nach Großbritannien einreisen zu können, müssen Hunde bestimmten Kriterien erfüllen und es müssen folgende Unterlagen vorgelegt werden: das offizielle PETS-Zertifikat, eine Behandlungsbescheinigung gegen Bandwurm und Zecken sowie eine Erklärung des Haltungsorts.

Für weitere Auskünfte über die an diesem Programm teilnehmenden Länder, die Strecken, Reiseunternehmer sowie ausführlichere Informationen über das Pilotprogramm PETS wenden Sie sich bitte an: Ministry of Agriculture, Fisheries and Food, 1a Page Street, London SW1P 4PQ,

Tel: +44 (0) 870 241 1710 Fax: +44 (0) 20 7904 6834

E-Mail: pets@ahvg.maff.gsi.gov.uk oder schauen Sie auf der Website vorbei: www.maff.gov.uk/animalh/quarantine

Drogenwarnung für einreisende Touristen

Großbritannien geht gegen Rauschgiftschmuggel seht scharf vor. Drogenhändler versuchen häufig, unschuldige Reisende in ihre Geschäfte zu verwickeln. Seien Sie daher bei der Reise nach Großbritannien sehr auf der Hut und tragen Sie niemals Gepäckstücke für andere Personen durch die Zollkontrolle.

Rechtliches

Wenden Sie sich vor dem Antritt Ihrer Reise am besten an Ihren Automobilverband, der Ihnen gerne Auskunft über alle rechtlichen Fragen in Bezug auf Reisen in Großbritannien gibt. Wenn Sie mit dem Wohnwagen oder Zelt unterwegs sind, sollten Sie zusätzlich ein paar einfache Regeln beachten.

Wenn Sie mit einem Wohnwagen oder einem Camping-Anhänger unterwegs sind, dürfen Sie auf vierspurigen Fernstraßen und Autobahnen höchstens 96 km/h fahren. Auf zweispurigen Fernstraßen gilt das Tempolimit 80 km/h. Auf sechsspurigen Autobahnen dürfen Sie niemals - auch nicht zum Überholen - in der dritten (schnellsten) Spur fahren. Auf den Raststätten an der Autobahn dürfen keine Kochöfen angezündet werden.

In den meisten Städten ist das Parken durch gesetzliche Bestimmungen oder praktische Probleme stark eingeschränkt. Autos mit Anhängern dürfen nicht an Parkuhren parken. Ferner nehmen die meisten Parkplätze nur Wagen ohne Anhänger auf. Allerdings sind einige Parkplätze vorhanden, die überlange Fahrzeuge und Fahrzeuge mit Anhängern zulassen.

Nachts müssen auf der Straße geparkte Anhänger bzw. Autos mit Anhänger vorn und hinten jeweils zwei Lampen aufweisen. Dies gilt auch an Stellen, wo ein Auto ohne Anhänger davon ausgenommen wäre.

Die britischen Vorschriften über Bremsen, Beleuchtung, zulässiges Gewicht und sonstige technische Punkte gelten nicht für ausländische Fahrzeuge. Ein Anhänger muss jedoch die britischen Vorschriften erfüllen und darf nicht länger als 7 m und nicht breiter als 2,30 m sein. Anhänger müssen mit den amtlichen Zulassungsschildern Ihres Heimatlandes versehen sein. Übernachten Sie nicht auf dem Grasrand einer Straße oder in einer Ausweichbucht, weil diese Stellen als zur Straße gehörig angesehen werden.

Abschließend sei betont, wie wichtig es ist, dass Sie sich erkundigen, wann Sie den Stellplatz in einem Camping- oder Wohnwagenpark am Abreisetag räumen müssen. Reisen Sie morgens rechtzeitig ab, sonst müssen Sie vielleicht die Gebühr für einen weiteren Tag bezahlen.

Ratschläge für Besucher

Die British Tourist Authority würde sich über Ihren Kommentar hinsichtlich aller Gesichtspunkte Ihres Aufenthalts in Großbritannien freuen, ganz gleich, ob er positiv oder negativ ausfällt. Wir hoffen, dass Sie keinen Grund zur Beanstandung haben, falls Sie aber doch Anlass zu Beschwerden haben sollten, ist es am besten, sich sofort an die Leitung des entsprechenden Unternehmens zu wenden, z. B. des Parks, des Geschäfts oder der Verkehrsgesellschaft. Wenn Sie mit der Behandlung, die Sie dort erfahren, nicht zufrieden sind, so geben Sie uns bitte Bescheid. Wir werden dann der Angelegenheit entweder selbst nachgehen oder Sie darüber beraten, welche Maßnahmen Sie ergreifen können.

Sie können Währungen jeder Art in beliebiger Höhe nach Großbritannien mitbringen. Reiseschecks werden in beliebiger Anzahl eingelöst. Wenn Ihnen das Bargeld ausgeht, wenn die Banken geschlossen sind, so können Sie Geld in einigen großen Hotels, Reisebüros, Kaufhäusern und in unabhängigen Wechselstuben umtauschen. Prüfen Sie vor dem Geldumtausch, welcher Wechselkurs Anwendung findet und wie hoch die Bearbeitungsgebühr ist. Alle größeren Geschäfte, Kaufhäuser und die meisten Hotels und Restaurants akzeptieren international gängige Kreditkarten als Zahlungsmittel. Wenn Sie auf örtlichen Straßenmärkten einkaufen, so halten Sie sich an die großen, bekannten Märkte und prüfen Sie die Waren sorgfältig.

Erkundigen Sie sich vor dem Kauf stets nach dem Preis der Waren oder Dienstleistungen. Nehmen Sie sich in Menschenmengen vor Taschendieben in Acht.

Wenn Sie Opfer eines Diebstahls oder Zeuge eines Unfalls oder Brands werden, wählen Sie den Notruf unter der Nummer 999 (der Anruf ist kostenlos) und verlangen Sie die Polizei (police), einen Krankenwagen (ambulance) oder die Feuerwehr (fire brigade).

Die British Tourist Authority hat sich alle erdenkliche Mühe gegeben, die Richtigkeit der in der vorliegenden Veröffentlichung gemachten Angaben zum Zeitpunkt der Drucklegung zu gewährleisten. Die Informationen werden in gutem Glauben erteilt und beruhen auf den Angaben, die der British Tourist Authority von den aufgeführten Wohnwagenparks erteilt wurden. Die BTA gibt jedoch keine Garantie für die Genauigkeit der Angaben und übernimmt keinerlei Verantwortung für Fehler oder fälschliche Darstellungen. Hiermit ausgeschlossen wird die Haftung für Verluste, nicht erfüllte Erwartungen, Fahrlässigkeit oder andere Schäden, die sich daraus ergeben, dass sich Leser auf die Informationen in der vorliegenden Veröffentlichung verlassen, oder die sich daraus ergeben, dass in der Veröffentlichung genannte Unternehmen, Firmen oder Einzelpersonen Konkurs anmelden, in Liquidation gehen oder ihre Geschäftstätigkeit einstellen. Es wird empfohlen, sich die in der vorliegenden Veröffentlichung gemachten Angaben bei der Reservierung von den betreffenden Stellen bestätigen zu lassen.

Alle in diesem Reiseführer genannten Parks entsprechen den Standards des Tourism Council (Fremdenverkehrsrat). Eine Liste der Standardbedingungen für Camping- und Wohnwagenparks befindet sich auf Seite 225.

Sämtliche genannten Stellen haben für die Aufnahme in dieser Veröffentlichung eine Gebühr entrichtet.

Hoe u deze gids moet
Gebruiken

Op de meeste vermelde terreinen zijn trekcaravans, tenten of kampeerauto's of alledrie welkom. Bij de meeste zijn vakantiecaravans te huur.

Het Kwaliteits Garantie Systeem

Als u een verblijfsplaats zoekt, dan heeft u een classificatiesysteem nodig dat u kunt vertrouwen. De British Graded Holiday Parks Scheme, in 2000 opnieuw gepubliceerd, geeft u een duidelijk overzicht van wat u kunt verwachten in een gemakkelijk te begrijpen formaat. Het systeem houdt kwaliteit hoog in het vaandel en weerspiegelt de verwachtingen van de consument.

De English Tourism Council gebruikt sterren om de kwaliteitsclassificatie van de deelnemende parken weer te geven. De parken worden jaarlijks door getrainde, onafhankelijke controleurs bezocht, die 1 tot 5 sterren toekennen. Deze zijn gebaseerd op hygiëne,omgeving en kwaliteit van de voorzieningen en diensten, die er aanwezig zijn.

De parken hebben ook een 'aanwijzer' zodat u het type standplaats in één oogopslag kunt herkennen b.v. een

vakantie park, een tourcaravan park en een camping. (als er geen gradatie of aanwijzer is gegeven dan is men in afwachting van een classifcatie ten tijde van het drukken van deze brochure.)

The British Graded Holiday Parks Scheme is gezamelijk ontworpen door de nationale touristen centra van Engeland, Noord-Ierland, Schotland en Wales en de British Holiday & Home Parks Association (zie pagina 31) en de National Caravan Council (zie pagina 35).

Faciliteiten

De faciliteiten worden aangeduid d.m.v. de hieronder in het kort verklaarde tekens.

Prijzen

De vermelde tarievan zijn de minimale en maximale prijzen voor een overnachting voor 2 personen, auto plus caravan of tent. Over het algemeen berekent men in Groot-Brittannië voor de staanplaats, maar een aantal terreinen belast u apart voor de auto, caravan of tent, en elke persoon. Bij sommige parken moet u

VERKLARING VAN DE TEKENS

❁ lid van een regionale toeristenraad
BH& British Holiday
HPA & Home Parks Association (zie blz 31)
NCC National Caravan Council (zie blz 35)
🚐 caravans toegestaan (met aantal staanplaatsen en tarieven)
🚐 kampeerauto's toegestaan (met aantal staanplaatsen en tarieven) In sommige gevallen is het aantal plekjes voor kampeerauto's opgenomen in het totaal voor toercaravans
Å tenten toegestaan (met aantal plekjes en tarieven)
aantal vakantiecaravans te huur (Zie 'Vakantiecaravans')
🔩 bungalows/chalets/huisjes te huur
🚗 parkeerplaats naast staanplaats
P parkeerruimte op terrein
terrein voor late aankomers op het park
🔌 elektrische aansluiting voor caravans (zie 'Elektriciteit. Elektrische aansluiting voor caravans)
douches
alle wastafels hebben warm water
verlichting in toiletten, etc.
lozing van chemische toiletten mogelijk
omwisseling van butaan- en propaangasflessen
levensmiddelenwinkel/rijdende winkel
✕ café/restaurant

klub/barwinkel met vergunning
📺 Zitkamer met kleuren televisie
openbare telefoons
wasserette op terrein aanwezig
drogen van wasgoed mogelijk
strijken van wasgoed mogelijk
⊙ stopcontacten voor scheerapparaten
recreatiekamer
speeltuin
🚲 fietsen verhuur
verwarmd binnenbad op park
openluchtbad op park
onderwaterzwemmen op terrein (zuurstofflessen verkrijgbaar)
waterskiën op terrein
boten/kano's op terrein aanwezig
zeilen op terrein
U manège (paard/pony) op terrein
tennis op terrein
vissen op terrein
golf op of bij park
particuliere jachtvergunning
✕ honden NIET toegestaan
♫ amusement's avonds
raadzaam voor de zomermaanden te boeken
🆃 kan geboekt worden bij reisbureaus
WH Welcome Host

eventueel extra betalen voor een tent of voortent die aan een caravan vastgebouwd is. Minimale en maximale tarieven voor vakantiecaravans zijn per week. Vermelde prijzen werden verstrekt door de terreinbeheerders en dienen als richtlijn voor de prijzen die tijdens de geldendheid van dit boekje gerekend zullen worden. Vermelde prijzen zijn in ponden (£) en pence (p). VAT (BTW) à 17.5% is bij de prijzen inbegrepen. Om misverstanden te vermijden, raden wij u dringend aan de prijzen te controleren als u een reservering maakt.

Reserveren

Bij het maken van een reservering, of het inwinnen van inlichtingen, moet u vooral duidelijk en precies aangeven wat u wilt - bij voorbeeld:

- aankomst- en vertrekdata met mogelike alternatieven.

- gewenste accommodatie.

- vertel de beheerder vooral wat voor speciale wensen of eisen u heeft.

Misverstanden kunnen heel gemakkelijk voorkomen over de telefoon en wij raden u daarom aan alle reserveringen, als de tijd dat toelaat, schriftelijk te bevestigen. Vergeet vooral niet uw naam en adres te vermelden en een uzelf geadresseerde envelop met postzegel of internationale antwoordcoupon (als u uit het buitenland schrijft) in te sluiten voor elk antwoord.

Aan- en vooruitbetalingen

Campings, caravanterreinen, bungalow- en vakantieparken moeten meestal van tevoren geheel betaald worden. Dit kan gedaan worden in tweeën - een aanbetaling bij de reservering en betaling van het saldo bijvoorbeeld twee weken voor de aanvang van de geboekte periode.

Annuleren

De aanvaarding van geboden accommodatie, hetzij schriftelijk of telefonisch, wordt over het algemeen beschouwd als een wettelijk bindend contract. Dit betekent dat als u annuleert, niet verschijnt op het park, of vroegtijdig het park verlaat (het geeft niet om welke reden), de eigenaar compensatie van u kan verlangen als de staanplaats voor het overgrote deel van de geboekte periode niet opnieuw verhuurd kan worden. Als u een aanbetaling gedaan heeft, kan deze vervallen worden verklaard en een aanvullend bedrag van u verlangd worden.

Het is daarom in uw eigen belang de bedrijfsleiding onmiddelijk in kennis te stellen, als u uw reisplannen moet wijzigen, een boeking moet annulemren, of voortijdig moet vertrekken.

Elektrische aansluiting:

De meeste parken hebben elektrische aansluitpunten voor caravans en tenten. De voltage is meestal 240v AC, 50Hz, hoewel nog steeds voltages tussen 200v en 250v kunnen worden aangetroffen. Het kan zijn dat u een adaptor nodig heeft voor de aansluiting. Meestal moet u extra betalen voor deze faciliteit. Het is raadzaam de tarieven na te vragen voor u reserveert.

Het vinden van een park of terrein

De parken in dit gidsje zijn ingedeeld in Engeland per regio, gevolgd door Schotland en Wales. Zij staan in alfabetische volgorde onder de naam van de meest nabijgelegen plaats. De index van plaatsen op blz 255 en de gekleurde lokatiekaarten achterin de gids vertonen alle steden, plaatsen en dorpen met parken die in deze gids voorkomen. Zo kunt u snel en gemakkelijk ergens een park vinden. Als u al weet op welk park u wilt staan, kunt u de index van parken raadplegen op blz 251.

Als uw bestemming in de index van plaatsen voorkomt, raadpleeg dan de gegeven bladzij, waar de aldaar gevestigde parken worden vermeld. De plaatsnamen staan in zwart op de kaarten achterin het gidsje, aangeduid met coördinaten bij de vermelding. Ook kunt u de kleurenkaarten raadplegen om nabijgelegen plaatsen te vinden die ook in de gids voorkomende parken hebben.

Als uw bestemming niet in de index van plaatsen voorkomt, of als u alleen een vaag idee heeft van het gebied dat u wilt bezoeken, kunt u eveneens de kleurenkaarten raadplegen. De kaarten bevatten alle plaatsnamen waaronder een park in het gidsje wordt vermeld. Voor de precieze locatie dient u de routebeschrijvingen bij iedere vermelding te raadplegen. Heeft u moeite met het vinden van een bepaald park, dan raden wij u aan in de buurt om verdere aanwijzingen te vragen.

  De hierboven vermelde internationale verkeersborden worden in Groot-Brittannië gebruikt en zijn speciaal ontworpen voor het gebruik van de parkbezoekers en kampeerders. Ze zijn nog niet bij alle parken opgesteld en vermelden niet de naam van een park of camping. Ze duiden echter wel aan of het park geschikt is voor caravans, tenten of beide.

Het Internationale Kampeerkarnet wordt maar weinig in Groot-Brittannië erkend, behalve op terreinen die beheerd worden door de grote clubs.

Campings bij Londen

Londen is een grote trekpleister voor toeristen en daarom raken de campings en caravanterreinen in de streek van Greater London erg snel vol en boeking ver van tevoren is daarom noodzakelijk. Bij de meeste aankomsthavens zijn ook campings te vinden en de meeste worden vermeld in deze gids en aangeduid op de kaarten achterin.

Hulp bij het vinden van een park

De Toeristische Informatiecentra over heel Groot-Brittannië (zie aan het einde van deze gids) kunnen kampeerders en caravaneigenaars informatie verschaffen over lokale parken en terreinen. Een aantal Toeristische Informatiecentra biedt ook een adviesdienst, die inlichtingen kan geven over mogelijke plaats op campings en vaak kan helpen met het maken van een reservering. Momenteel beslaan de volgende TIC's in Engeland de streken: **New Forest,**

0131-314-6505; en **Cornwall**, 01872-274057. In Wales kan tussen mei en eind augustus een groot aantal Tourist Information Centres inlichtingen verstrekken over beschikbare staanplaatsen in hun streek.

Vermijding van problemen in het hoogseizoen

In de zomermaanden juni t/m september kunnen parken in populaire gebieden, zoals Noord-Wales, Cumbria, de West Country en het New Forest in Hampshire bijzonder vol raken. Bezoekers moeten proberen zo vroeg mogelijk op de dag bij het park aan te komen, of nog beter, van tevoren boeken. Een aantal parken heeft een speciaal terrein voor bezoekers die laat in de avond arriveren. Dit is om te voorkomen dat andere bezoekers in hun slaap gestoord worden en minder kampeerders weggestuurd worden. De volgende morgen worden de caravans en tenten dan een juiste plek gegeven.

Andere mogelijkheden voor caravans en tenten

Als u ervan houdt om door landelijke streken in Groot-Brittanië te trekken, vindt u het misschien interessant te weten, dat de Forestry Commission (staatsbosbeheer) bos-kampeerterreinen in zeven van Groot-Brittanië's Forest Parks en het New Forest beheert. Sommige bieden gereduceerde tarieven voor jeugdorganisaties op georganiseerde kampeertochten, en alle inlichtingen hierover moeten ver van tevoren ingewonnen worden bij de Forestry Commission.

Kampeerschuren

Dit zijn meestal niet meer in gebruik zijnde boerengebouwen die zijn verbouwd tot simpele logies voor een groep tot 15 personen, tegen redelijke prijs. De faciliteiten zijn eenvoudig: u kunt er slapen, eten, en eten bereiden, er is koud stromend water en een doortrek w.c. De Jeugherberg Vereniging heeft een heel netwerk van kampeerschuren, van de Forest of Bowland in Lancashire tot en met Durham en Noord-Yorkshire. Meer informatie bij de YHA, Trevelyan House, 8 St Stephen's Hill, St Albans, Hertfordshire ALI 2DY. Tel: 01727-855215.

Kampeerschuren zijn ook in het Peak National Park beschikbaar. Meer informatie verkrijgbaar bij Peak District National Park Authority, Aldern House, Baslow Road, Bakewell, Derbyshire DE45 1AE.

Huisdieren

Op veel parken zijn honden toegestaan, maar we raden u aan voor het reserveren na te vragen of dit het geval is, of er een extra tarief wordt geheven, en waar uw hond precies is toegestaan. Als er honden worden toegelaten, wil dit niet altijd zeggen dat ook katten toegestaan zijn, en we raden u ten sterkste aan van te voren contact op te nemen met het etablissement als u uw kat mee wilt nemen. Op sommige parken zijn huisdieren in het geheel niet toegestaan. Deze worden aangegeven met het volgende symbool 🐕.

Uw huisdier meenemen op vakantie in Groot-Brittannië

De quarantainewetten zijn onlangs gewijzigd in Engeland, en er wordt op dit moment een proefsysteem, het Pet Travel Scheme (PETS) uitgeprobeerd. Onder dit systeem kunnen honden uit meer dan 35 landen Engeland binnen via bepaalde zee-, lucht- en treinroutes.

Honden die langer dan zes maanden in die landen hebben vertoefd mogen Groot-Brittannië binnen mits de eigenaar de juiste documentatie bij zich heeft voor de dieren.

Als u een hond mee wilt nemen naar Groot-Brittannië onder het PETS-systeem dan moet het dier aan bepaalde voorwaarden voldoen en u over de volgende documentatie beschikken: het officiële PETS-certificaat, een certificaat van behandeling tegen lintworm en teken, en een verklaring van verblijf.

Neem voor meer informatie over deelnemende landen, toegestane routes, reisoperators en andere details over het PETS-systeem contact op met het Ministry of Agriculture, Fisheries and Food, 1a Page Street, Londen SW1P 4PQ, Engeland.

Tel: +44 (0) 870 241 1710, Fax: +44 (0) 20 7904 6834.

E-mail: pets@ahvg.maff.gsi.gov.uk, of bezoek hun website op www.maff.gov.uk/animalh/quarantine

Drugswaarschuwing voor inkomende toeristen

In het Vereningd Koninkrijk staan er zware straffen op het illegaal invoeren van drugs. Drugshandelaars proberen onschuldige reizigers te misleiden en wij raden u daarom aan alle betrokkenheid met drugs te vermijden. Draag nooit pakjes of bagage door de douane die niet van uzelf zijn.

Wettelijke bepalingen

De allerbeste bron van wettelijk advies voor automobilisten is een Club voor Automobilisten (b.v. ANWB). Wat de kampeerder of caravaneigenaar nog meer moet weten is betrekkelijk eenvoudig. Als u een caravan of kampeerwagentje achter de auto heeft, mag u niet meer dan 96 km (60 mijl) per uur rijden op tweebaanswegen of snelwegen, 80 km (50 mijl) per uur op eenbaanswegen, en op snelwegen met drie banen aan elke kant mag u niet in de derde (snelste) baan. Kooktoestellen mogen niet bij een wegrestaurant met benzinestation aangestoken worden.

In de meeste steden is parkeren beperkt, zowel door wettelijke bepalingen als uit praktische overwegingen. Auto's met aanhangende caravans mogen niet parkeren bij een parkeermeter en vele stadsparkeerterreinen zijn alleen geschikt voor auto's zonder aanhangende caravans of kampeerwagentjes.

's Nachts moet een kampeerwagen, of een auto verbonden met een aanhangwagen, die aan de weg geparkeerd staat, zowel z'n twee voorlichten als z'n achterlichten aanhebben, terwijl een auto alleen dit niet hoeft.

De remmen, lampen, het gewicht, etc. van buitenlandse voertuigen hoeven niet te voldoen aan de Britse technische voorschriten. Hoe dan ook, een aanhangwagen mag de Britse wettelijke afmetingsbepalingen - 23 feet (7m) lang en 7 feet 6 inches (2,3m) breed - niet overschrijden. Ze moeten het internationale kenteken (NL of B) voeren en niet overnachten in de berm of op de parkeerhavens, daar deze wettelijk onderdeel uitmaken van de weg.

Tenslotte is het ook heel belangrijk van tevoren uit te vinden hoe laat u op de dag van vertrek moet opbreken. U moet zich daar aan houden, anders kan men u een extra dag in rekening brengen.

Advies aan bezoekers

De BTA stelt er prijs op uw op- of aanmerkingen op uw verblijf in Groot-Brittannië te vernemen. wij hopen dat u geen reden tot klagen heeft, maar mocht dit toch het geval zijn, raden wij u dringend aan om uw klacht onmiddelijk kenbaar te maken aan de leiding van het desbetreffende park, de winkel of vervoersmaatschappij. Indien u hieruit geen genoegdoening verkrijgt, laat u ons dit dan weten, zodat wij zelf een onderzoek kunnen instellen, of u kunnen adviseren over eventuele verder te nemen stappen.

U mag het geeft niet hoeveel geld, en in welke munteenheid dan ook, meenemen en er bestaan geen beperkingen op het aantal inwisselbare reischeques. Als u geld wilt wisselen als de banken gesloten zijn, kunt u dit doen bij de grotere hotels, reisbureaus en warenhuizen of bij onafhankelijke wisselkantoren. **Controleer vooral van tevoren de berekende wisselkoers en commissietarieven.**

Alle grote winkels, warenhuizen, en de meeste hotels en restaurants accepteren de gebruikelijke, internationaal erkende credit cards. Als u ook graag op markten winkelt, koop dan alleen op grote, erkende markten, en bekijk de artikelen eerst zorgvuldig.

Vraag altijd wat de prijs is voor u tot de aankoop overgaat. Pas op voor zakkenrollers in drukke menigten.

Indien u bestolen bent, of betrokken bent bij een ongeval of brand, ben dan 999 (waarvoor geen geld nodig is) en vraag om de 'police' (politie), 'ambulance service' (ambulance) of de 'fire brigade' (brandweer).

De British Tourist Authority heeft alle pogingen in het werk gesteld om deze publicatie bij het ter perse gaan van nauwkeurigheid te verzekeren. De informatie werd in goed vertrouwen verstrekt, gebaseerd op inlichtingen gegeven aan de British Tourist Authority door de organisatoren van de vermelde caravanparken en campings. De BTA kan echter niet garanderen dat deze informatie correct is en kan geen verantwoording aanvaarden voor foute of onjuiste voorstellingen. De BTA kan beslist niet verantwoordelijk worden gesteld voor verlies, teleurstelling, nalatigheid of enige andere schade die voortvloeit uit het vertrouwen in de informatie in deze gids, of problemen voortkomend uit

het faillisement of liquidatie van enige vermelde maatschappij, individu of bedrijf, of indien een maatschappij, individu of bedrijf ophoudt handel te drijven. Het is daarom raadzaam de gegeven informatie bij het maken van een reservering goed te controleren.

Alle parken in deze gids houden zich aan de richtlijnen van de Tourism Council. Een lijst van de aan de campings en caravanparken gestelde eisen kunt u vinden op pagina 225.

All genoemde instellingen hebben betaald voor hun vermelding in deze gids.

BRITISH HOLIDAY AND HOME PARKS ASSOCIATION

The Association represents commercial operators of all kinds throughout Britain. Its aim is to ensure a high standard of excellence in members' parks for the satisfaction of the visitor.

Parks listed in this Guide all conform to the standards set by the British Tourist Authority but BH&HPA Members' Parks, which are identified in the Guide by (BH&HPA), must also abide by the BH&HPA Code of Conduct. This gives the visitor an assurance of a high standard of facilities and reliability.

The BH&HPA works with the British Tourist Authority, English Tourism Council, and the national and regional tourist boards to safeguard tourist interests. It also works with Government and local government authorities to ensure that all aspects of legislation and control are applied and that proper safety measures are carried out for the comfort and protection of the visitor.

The BH&HPA will investigate problems encountered by visitors and can provide details of self-catering holidays and residential parks. Contact:

British Holiday and Home Parks Association Ltd, Chichester House, 6 Pullman Court, Great Western Road, Gloucester GL1 3ND.
Telephone: (01452) 526911
Fax: (01452) 508508.

Come usare questa
Guida

I campeggi elencati in questa guida sono per la maggior parte aperti sia alle roulottes che alle tende e molti di essi accolgono anche i camper e le motorhome. Molti campeggi dispongono anche di roulottes a noleggio.

Programma di garanzia di qualità

Per chi va in cerca di un posto dove soggiornare, è necessario un sistema di classificazione affidabile. Il programma britannico di classificazione dei parchi vacanze (British Graded Holiday Parks Scheme) del 2000 offre una guida chiara e comprensibile su ciò che ci si può aspettare. Il programma è sempre imperniato sulla qualità e rispecchia le aspettative del cliente.

L'organo per il turismo inglese (English Tourism Council) utilizza ora delle stelle per illustrare le categorie dei parchi partecipanti al programma. I parchi vengono ispezionati annualmente da funzionari competenti e imparziali, che assegnano una classificazione da una a cinque stelle, basandosi sulla pulizia, sull'ambiente e sulla qualità delle strutture e dei servizi offerti.

Inoltre, i parchi vengono ora contrassegnati da un simbolo, in modo che se ne possa identificare immediatamente il tipo - ad esempio Parco Vacanze, Parco Turistico o Campeggio. (L'assenza di classifica o contrassegno significa che il parco in oggetto non è stato ancora valutato al momento di andare in stampa).

Il programma di classificazione è stato ideato congiuntamente dagli enti nazionali per il turismo dell'Inghilterra, dell'Irlanda del Nord, della Scozia e del Galles in collaborazione con l'associazione britannica dei parchi per roulotte e vacanze (British Holiday & Home Parks Association) (vedere a pagina 31) e con l'organo nazionale per le roulotte (National Caravan Council) (vedere a pagina 35).

Strutture

Le strutture vengono indicate per mezzo di simboli, comprensibili a prima vista, spiegati qui di seguito.

Prezzi

I prezzi indicati per i posteggio sono il prezzo minimo e il prezzo massimo di un pernottamento per 2 persone, un'automobile e una tenda o una roulotte. I campeggi

SPIEGAZIONE DEI SIMBOLI

M Socio del Regional Tourist Board
BH& British Holiday
HPA & Home Parks Association (v. pagina 31)
NCC National Caravan Council (v. pagina 35)
⊕ Roulottes ammesse (con numero di posteggi e prezzi)
☎ Camper/motorhome ammessi (con numero di posteggi e prezzi) In alcuni casi il numero di posteggi per camper/motorhome è compreso nel numero di posteggi per roulottes
⋀ Tende ammesse
⊞ Numero di roulottes a noleggio (v. posteggi per roulottes a noleggio a seguito)
◫ Bungalow/chalet/casette a noleggio
◚ Parcheggio vicino all'alloggio
P Parcheggio sul post
◨ Zona di pernottamento temporaneo
◙ Allacciamento elettrico per roulottes (v. Alimentazione elettrica: prese di allacciamento per roulottes)
⌂ Docce
⚒ Aqua calda per tutti i lavandini
◌ Illuminazione dei WC ecc.
♟ WC a trattamento chimico
⊖ Cambio di bombole di gas butano o propano
⚖ Negozio/negozio ambulante di alimentari
✕ Bar/ristorante

⚲ Club/bar/negozio autorizzato alla vendita di bevande alcoliche
TV Salone con televisione a colori
☏ Telefono pubblico
⊟ Lavanderia sul posto
⟋ Attrezzature per asciugare la biancheria
◢ Attrezzature per stirare i vestiti
⊙ Prese per rasoi elettrici
◕ Sala giochi
⚠ Zona giochi per i bambini
⚶ Locazione biciclette
⤳ Piscina riscaldata al coperto sul posto
⤳ Piscina all'aperto sul posto
⚓ Strutture per gli sport subacquei sul posto (comprese le bombole di ossigeno)
⚘ Sci d'acqua sul posto
⚓ Imbarcazioni/canottaggio sul posto
⚐ Vela sul posto
U Equitazione/escursioni a dorso di pony partendo dal campeggio
Q⚌ Tennis sul posto
⤙ Pesca sul posto o nelle vicinanze
⇂₁₈ Golf sul posto o nelle vicinanze
⟋ Galleria per armi da fuoco privata
✖ NON si ammettono cani
♫ Spettacoli/intrattenimenti serali
♤ Si consiglia di prenotare in estate
T Prenotazione possibile tramite agenzie di viaggio
WH Welcome Host

britannici preferiscono in genere includere tutto in un solo prezzo, benché in alcuni vi siano prezzi separati per automobili, roulottes o tende e per ogni persona. In alcuni campeggi possono essere richiesti supplementi per i tendoni delle roulottes. I prezzi minimi e massimi delle roulottes a noleggio sono i prezzi per settimana. I prezzi indicati sono quelli forniti dagli esercenti dei campeggi in questione, e sono un'indicazione dei prezzi che verranno praticati per il periodo di validità di questa pubblicazione. I prezzi indicati sono in sterline (£) e pence (p). L'IVA (Imposta sul Valore Aggiunto) al 17,5% è compresa nei prezzi indicati. Per evitare qualsiasi equivoco, si consiglia vivamente di controllare i prezzi al momento di effettuare la prenotazione.

Prenotazione

Nel richiedere informazioni sulle possibilità di sistemazione, è necessario, oltre a controllare il prezzo, dire chiaramente quali siano le proprie esigenze, per esempio:

- date di arrivo e partenza, e se possibile date alternative;
- il tipo di sistemazione richiesto;
- qualsiasi particolare esigenza.

Quando si prenota per telefono c'è sempre il rischio di errori. Tempo permettendo, si consiglia dunque di confermare sempre le prenotazioni per iscritto. Ricordarsi di indicare il proprio nome e indirizzo e di accludere, per ogni risposta, una busta preindirizzata e preaafrancata o un buono internazionale per riposta pagata.

Anticipi

Per la prenotazione di posti nei campeggi per tende, roulottes e chalets, il prezzo intero va normalmente versato in anticipo. Il versamento può normalmente essere effettuato in due rate: un anticipo al momento della prenotazione e il saldo circa due settimane prima dell'inizio del periodo prenotato.

Annullamenti

Nel Regno Unito, l'accettazione di un alloggio offerto, sia per iscritto che per telefono, equivale per legge alla firma di un contratto vincolante tra l'inquilino e il proprietario dell'alloggio. Ciò significa che se l'inquilino annulla la propria prenotazione, non prende domicilio o parte prima del previsto (per qualsiasi ragione), il proprietario potrebbe avere diritto a un risarcimento qualora non riesca a riaffittare l'alloggio per tutto o parte del periodo prenotato. Se è stato versato un anticipo, è probabile che venga ritenuto dal proprietario, il quale potrebbe anche esigere un ulteriore addebito.

È consigliabile dunque avvisare immediatamente il proprietario sia di qualsiasi cambiamento di itinerario, sia dell'intenzione di annullare una prenotazione o di partire prima del previsto.

Prese di allacciamento elettrico:

I campeggi dispongono, per la maggior parte di prese di allacciamento alla rete di distribuzione dell'energia elettrica adoperabili sia per la roulottes che per le tende. La tensione è di 240V circa e 50Hz, benchè in alcuni casi possa ancora variare tra 200V e 250V. In alcuni campeggi potrebbe essere necessario un adattatore per l'allacciamento. La fornitura di energia elettrica è normalmente soggetta ad un addebito supplementare e si consiglia di controllare le tariffe al momento della prenotazione.

Come trovare il campeggio prescelto

I campeggi in questa guida sono raggruppati per regione in Inghilterra, seguiti dalle liste relative a Scozia e Galles, e sono stati elencati in ordine alfabetico sotto il nome della città in cui si trovano, o vicino a cui si trovano. L'Indice delle Città a pagina 255 e le Mappe a colori nell'ultima parte della guida riportano tutte le città, i centri e i villaggi che hanno un campeggio elencato in questa guida. Usate questi riferimenti per trovare in un modo facile e veloce un alloggio adatto. Se sapete in quale campeggio volete stare, controllate l'Indice dei Campeggi a pagina 251.

Se il luogo dove volete stare è compreso nell'indice delle città, andate alla pagina indicata per trovarvi i campeggi disponibili. I nomi delle città appaiono in nero sulla mappa nell'ultima pagina della guida nel modo in cui sono stati indicati dal riferimento alla mappa nella voce relativa. Controllate anche le mappe a colori per trovarvi altri luoghi vicini che hanno anche dei campeggi elencati in questa guida.

Se il luogo dove volete stare non si trova nell'indice delle città – o avete solo un'idea generale della zona in cui volete stare – usate le cartine a colori.

Le cartine illustrano tutti i nomi delle località in cui viene elencato un campeggio nella guida. Per trovare la località precisa leggete le indicazioni di ogni voce. In

 caso di difficoltà è consigliabile chiedere indicazioni a qualcuno nelle vicinanze del campeggio.

I segnali internazionali indicati qui sopra vengono usati in Gran Bretagna per aiutare i visitatori a trovare i campeggi. Non sono ancora stati installati per tutti i campeggi e non indicano il nome di nessun campeggio. Indicano però se il campeggio è per tende, roulottes o ambedue.

Il carnet internazionale del campeggiatore è raramente riconosciuto in Gran Bretagna, salvo nei campeggi organizzati dai principali club.

Campeggi di Londra

Londra rappresenta una grande attrazione per molti visitatori, per cui i campeggi per tende e roulotte nell'area della Grande Londra tendono a riempirsi molto rapidamente, e bisogna prenotare molto in anticipo.

Sono anche disponibili campeggi presso la maggior parte dei porti d'entrata nel paese, e molti di questi sono elencati in questa guida e indicati sulla mappa sul retro.

Servizi di ricerca campeggi

I Tourist Information Centres di tutta la Gran Bretagna (v. pagine finali) possono fornire ai campeggiatori informazioni sui campeggi nelle loro zone di responsabilità.

Alcuni Tourist Information Centres offrono servizi di ricerca campeggi che forniscono informazioni sulla disponibilità di posteggi e spesso aiutano a effettuare le prenotazioni. I Tourist Information Centres che attualmente offrono questo servizio coprono le seguenti zone del paese: **New Forest**, (0131) 314 6505; **Cornovaglia**, (01872) 274057. Nel Galles, molti Tourist Information Centres possono fornire informazioni sulla disponibilità di posti dalla fine di maggio alla fine di agosto.

Come evitare i problemi dell'alta stagione

Nei mesi estivi, da giugno a settembre, i campeggi nelle zone più frequentate del paese: Galles settentrionale, Cumbria, Inghilterra sud-occidentale e la New Forest nel Hampshire, registrano molto presto il tutto esaurito. Si consiglia ai campeggiatori di arrivare presto o, se possibile, di prenotare in anticipo. Alcuni campeggi dispongono di zone di pernottamento temporaneo per i campeggiatori che arrivano tardi. Queste zone di pernottamento consentono di non disturbare gli altri campeggiatori durante la notte e di accogliere un maggior numero di nuovi arrivati, i quali vengono condotti a uno dei posti liberi la mattina seguente.

Altri luoghi di campeggio

A chi preferisce seguire il proprio itinerario attraverso la campagna britannica potrebbe interessare sapere che la Forestry Commission gestisce dei campeggi forestali nei sette parchi forestali del paese e nella New Forest. Alcuni offrono tariffe ridotte a gruppi organizzati di giovani in campeggio. Tutte le richieste d'informazioni vanno indirizzate direttamente alla Forestry Commission con qualche mese di anticipo sulla data di arrivo.

Granai da campeggio

Sono spesso degli edifici agricoli inutilizzati e trasformati in semplici alloggi per un massimo di 15 visitatori a prezzi ragionevoli. Le strutture sono le minime indispensabili: un posto per dormire, mangiare e cucinare, acqua corrente fredda e WC.

La Youth Hostel Association dispone di una rete di granai da campeggio che copre la zona tra Forest Bowland nel Lancashire, Durham e lo Yorkshire settentrionale. Per ulteriori informazioni, anche sulle modalità di prenotazione, rivolgersi a: YHA, Trevelyan House, 8 St. Stephen's Hill, St. Albans, Hertfordshire ALI 2DY. Tel: (01727) 855215.

I granai da campeggio esistono anche nel Peak National Park. Per ulteriori informazioni, scrivere al seguente indirizzo: Peak District National Park Authority, Aldern House, Baslow Road, Bakewell, Derbyshire DE45 1AE.

Animali domestici

Molti campeggi accettano ospiti con cani, ma si consiglia di controllare al momento della prenotazione e di chiedere se è necessario versare un supplemento o se esistono delle regole particolari per l'ammissione degli animali domestici. Spesso anche se sono ammessi i cani, non è consentito portare gatti; è consigliabile per i proprietari di gatti contattare l'esercizio in anticipo. Alcuni esercizi non accettano animali domestici. Questi luoghi sono indicati dal seguente simbolo 🐾.

Ingresso degli animali domestici in Gran Bretagna

Ultimamente in Inghilterra la normativa sulla quarantena è stata modificata; attualmente è in vigore PETS, un programma pilota per l'ingresso degli animali domestici, che consente l'ingresso in Gran Bretagna dei cani provenienti da oltre 35 paesi diversi attraverso determinati itinerari in nave, aereo e treno.

L'ingresso nel Regno Unito dei cani residenti da oltre 6 mesi in questi paesi è consentito ai sensi del Programma pilota, a condizione che gli animali siano accompagnati dalla relativa documentazione.

Per entrare nel Regno Unito senza quarantena ai sensi del programma PETS, i cani devono rispondere a determinate condizioni e viaggiare con i seguenti documenti: Certificato ufficiale PETS, un certificato di cura contro tenia e zecche e dichiarazione di residenza.

Per particolari sui paesi partecipanti, gli itinerari, gli operatori e altre informazioni sul programma PETS, rivolgersi a: Ministry of Agriculture, Fisheries and Food, 1a Page Street, London SW1P 4PQ.

Tel: +44 (0) 870 241 1710 Fax: +44 (0) 20 7904 6834

Email: pets@ahvg.maff.gsi.gov.uk o visitare il sito web www.maff.gov.uk/animalh/quarantine

Avvertimento sugli stupefacenti per i turisti in arrivo

Le leggi britanniche sul contrabbando di stupefacenti prevedono delle sanzioni estremamente severe per i trasgressori. I trafficanti di droga tentano a volte di ingannare i viaggiatori. Si consiglia a chiunque abbia deciso di visitare il Regno Unito di evitare qualsiasi coinvolgimento con lo spaccio di stupefacenti e di non attraversare mai la dogana portando le valige o i pacchi di altri viaggiatori.

Aspetti giuridici

La migliore fonte d'informazioni per gli automobilisti che intendono visitare la Gran Bretagna è l'organizzazione automobilistica del paese di origine. Le regole che deve conoscere l'automobilista campeggiatore sono relativamente semplici.

Le automobili con roulotte o rimorchi al traino non devono superare i 96 chilometri orari (60 miglia all'ora) sulle strade a doppia carreggiata e sulle autostrade, e gli 80 chilometri orari (50 miglia all'ora) sulle strade normali. Sulle autostrade a tre carreggiate in ogni direzione, le roulotte ed i rimorchi non sono ammessi nella terza carreggiata (la più veloce). È vietato accendere fornellini nelle aree di servizio autostradali.

Nella maggior parte delle città, parcheggiare è reso difficile sia dai regolamenti che da difficoltà pratiche. Alle automobili con rimorchio è vietato l'uso di spazi con parchimetri e i posteggi di molti parcheggi cittadini sono intesi per automobili senza rimorchio, sebbene in alcuni di essi vi siano spazi anche per veicoli più lunghi.

Se parcheggiati sulla strada di notte, i rimorchi, o le automobili attaccate ai rimorchi, devono avere due luci anteriori e due luci posteriori accese, anche dove l'automobile senza il rimorchio sarebbe esonerata da quest'obbligo.

I freni, le luci, il peso ecc. dei veicoli provenienti dall'estero non devono soddisfare i criteri tecnici delle norme britanniche. I rimorchi tuttavia non devono superare i limiti britannici, che sono: 7 metri di lunghezza e 2,3 metri di larghezza. I rimorchi devono recare il numero di targa del paese di provenienza. È vietato sostare di notte sui lati erbosi o nelle piazzole di sosta delle strade, dato che queste zone sono per legge considerate parti della strada.

Per concludere, è importante sapere l'ora entro la quale si è obbligati a liberare il posteggio nel giorno previsto per la partenza. Si consiglia di partire presto la mattina per evitare di dover pagare il prezzo di una giornata in più.

Consigli per i visitatori

La British Tourist Authority è sempre lieta di ricevere i commenti e le osservazioni dei turisti su qualsiasi aspetto del loro soggiorno in Gran Bretagna, che siano o meno favorevoli. Ci auguriamo che chiunque visiti il nostro paese non abbia mai occasione di lamentarsi. Se vi fosse ragione di lamentarsi, il consiglio è di rivolgersi in primo luogo alla gestione del campeggio, negozio o società di trasporti. Qualora la risposta non sia soddisfacente, consigliamo ai turisti di rivolgersi alla BTA che prenderà in esame la questione o suggerirà le misure da prendere.

Si possono portare in Gran Bretagna valute di qualsiasi denominazione senza limiti di quantità. Si può cambiare anche qualsiasi numero di traveller's cheque. Per cambiare le valute straniere durante le ore di chiusura delle banche ci si può rivolgere alle ricezioni di alcuni grandi alberghi, alle agenzie di viaggio, alle agenzie di cambiavalute indipendenti. **Raccomandiamo di controllare il tasso e la commissione di cambio prima di cambiare i soldi.**

Tutti i grandi negozi, i grandi magazzini la maggior parte degli alberghi e dei ristoranti accettano le carte di credito normalmente riconosciute nel mondo. A chi decida di fare spese nei mercati consigliamo di comprare solo in quelli grandi e riconosciuti e di esaminare accuratamente gli articoli prima di acquistarli.

Consigliamo di chiedere sempre il prezzo dei beni e dei servizi prima di impegnarsi all'acquisto e di fare attenzione ai borsaioli nei luoghi affollati.

Chiunque sia vittima di un furto, o coinvolto in un incidente o un incendio può telefonare al 999 (chiamata gratuita) e chiedere la polizia, il servizio ambulanze o i vigili del fuoco.

La British Tourist Authority si è adoperata per garantire l'esattezza delle informazioni contenute in questa pubblicazione al momento di andare in stampa. Le informazioni vengono date in buona fede in base ai dati forniti alla British Tourist Authority dai promotori del campeggi elencati. La BTA non può tuttavia né garantire l'esattezza delle informazioni né assumersi la responsabilità di qualsiasi errore o falsità. È esclusa tutta la responsabilità di perdite, delusioni, negligenza o di altri danni che risultino dall'aver fatto affidamento sulle informazioni contenute in questa guida o dal fallimento o dalla liquidazione di qualsiasi società, individuo o ditta, o dalla cessazione delle attività di qualsiasi società, individuo o ditta. Si consiglia di verificare l'esattezza delle informazioni al momento di effettuare la prenotazione.

Tutti i parchi elencati in questa guida sono conformi agli Standard del Tourism Council. A pagina 225 riportiamo un elenco di queste norme applicabili ai campeggi per tende e roulottes.

Tutti i campeggi elencati hanno pagato per la loro inserzione nella guida.

THE NATIONAL CARAVAN COUNCIL

The National Caravan Council is the representative body of the British caravan industry.

The Council operates an approval system for caravans, certifying that they are manufactured in accordance with the British Standard. All Dealer members and Park Operator members, which are identified in the Guide by **(NCC)**, agree to comply with Conditions of Membership which require them to provide their customers with a high standard of service.

The Council works closely with the British Tourist Authority, English Tourism Council, and the national and regional tourist boards to promote tourism and particularly to promote the important role which all kinds of caravans play in providing tourists with the facilities they require.

Full information on its members and its activities together with assistance on any difficulties encountered can be obtained from:

The National Caravan Council,
Catherine House, Victoria Road, Aldershot,
Hampshire GU11 1SS.
Telephone: (01252) 318251
Fax: (01252) 322596.

Caravan Holiday Home
Award Scheme

Rose Award, English Tourism Council, Thames Tower, Black's Road, Hammersmith, London W6 9EL.	Thistle Award, Scottish Tourist Board, Thistle House, Beechwood Park North, Inverness IV2 3ED.	Dragon Award, Wales Tourist Board, Brunel House, 2 Fitzalan Road, Cardiff CF24 0UY.

The English Tourism Council and the national tourist boards for Scotland and Wales run similar Award schemes for holiday caravan homes on highly graded caravan parks. They recognise high standards of caravan accommodation and enable you to step into a comfortable, fully furnished holiday home set amongst landscaped surroundings with all amenities you could wish for.

All the caravan parks included in the Award scheme have been inspected and meet the criteria demanded by the scheme. In addition to complying to joint tourist board standards for 'Holiday Caravan Parks and in Caravan Holiday Homes' all Award caravans must have a shower or bath, toilet, mains electricity and water heating (at no extra charge) and a refrigerator (many also have a colour television).

A complete list of the parks in each country, plus further information about them, can be obtained free from the national tourist boards (see page 238). Look out for these plaques displayed by all Award winning parks, and by each caravan which meets the required standards. Many parks listed in this guide are participating in these schemes and are indicated accordingly.

CAMPING AND CARAVAN PARKS IN BRITAIN

Published by: British Tourist Authority, Thames Tower, Black's Road, Hammersmith, London W6 9EL.
ISBN 0 7095 7260 3
Managing Editor: Michael Dewing
Technical Manager: Marita Sen
Compilation & Production: Guide Associates, London
Design & Cartography: Jackson Lowe Marketing, Lewes, East Sussex. Tel: (01273) 487487
Typesetting: Tradespools Ltd, Somerset and Jackson Lowe Marketing, Lewes, East Sussex
Printing and Binding: Acorn Web Offset Ltd, Normanton, West Yorkshire
Advertisement Sales: Jackson Lowe Marketing, Lewes, East Sussex. Tel: (01273) 487487
© British Tourist Authority (except where stated)

Photo Credits:
Cumbria – Cumbria Tourist Board; **Northumbria** – Northumbria Tourist Board, Graeme Peacock, Mike Kipling, Colin Cuthbert and Michael Busselle; **North West** – North West Tourist Board, Cheshire County Council, Lancashire County Council, Marketing Manchester; **Yorkshire** – Yorkshire Tourist Board; **Heart of England** – Heart of England Tourist Board; **East of England** – East of England Tourist Board Collection; **South West** – South West Tourism; **South of England** – Southern Tourist Board, Peter Titmuss, Chris Cove-Smith and Iris Buckley; **South East England** – South East England Tourist Board, Chris Parker and Iris Buckley; **Scotland** – Scottish Tourist Board; **Wales** – Wales Tourist Board

London LONDON

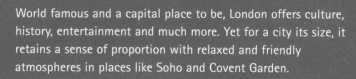

World famous and a capital place to be, London offers culture, history, entertainment and much more. Yet for a city its size, it retains a sense of proportion with relaxed and friendly atmospheres in places like Soho and Covent Garden.

Shoppers can spend, spend, spend in swanky Knightsbridge, or save, save, save at the Petticoat Lane, Brick Lane and Portobello markets. And for eating out, London is an explosion of tastes – traditional, international, and exotic. The outskirts of the city have their attractions, too, such as the Royal Observatory in Greenwich, and the botanical gardens at Kew.

For the perfect overview, book a flight on the world's highest observation wheel, 'The London Eye', open daily.

Greater London, comprising the 32 London Boroughs

FOR MORE INFORMATION CONTACT:
London Tourist Board
6th floor, Glen House, Stag Place,
London SW1E 5LT
Telephone enquiries – see Visitorcall on page 42
Internet: www.LondonTown.com

Where to Go in London – see pages 38–42
Where to Stay in London – see pages 43–45

The Pictures:
1 Piccadilly Circus;
2 Tower Bridge;
3 The maze at Hampton Court;
4 Canary Wharf.

Whilst in

LONDON ...

You will find hundreds of interesting places to visit during your stay, just some of which are listed in these pages.

Contact any Tourist Information Centre in and around London for more ideas on days out.

Chessington World of Adventures

Leatherhead Road, Chessington KT9 2NE
Tel: (01372) 729560
Dr Chessington, creator of the World of Adventures, has invented thrilling rides and attractions for all the family, with crazy entertainers and rare animals in themed lands.

Design Museum

Shad Thames, London SE1 2YD
Tel: (020) 7403 6933
One of London's most inspiring attractions, concerned solely with the products, technologies and buildings of the 20th and 21st centuries.

Hampton Court Palace

Hampton Court, East Molesey KT8 9AU
Tel: (020) 8781 9500
The oldest Tudor palace in England with many attractions including the Tudor kitchens, tennis courts, maze, State Apartments and King's Apartments.

HMS Belfast

Morgan's Lane, Tooley Street, London SE1 2JH
Tel: (020) 7940 6300
World War II cruiser weighing 11,500 tonnes, now a floating naval museum with nine decks to explore. Many naval exhibitions also on show.

Kensington Palace State Apartments

Kensington Gardens, London W8 4PX
Tel: (020) 7937 7079
Furniture and ceiling paintings from the Stuart-Hanoverian periods, rooms from the Victorian era and works of art from the Royal Collection. Also Royal Ceremonial Dress Collection.

Kew Gardens (Royal Botanic Gardens)

Kew, Richmond TW9 3AB
Tel: (020) 8940 1171
Three hundred acres containing living collections of over 40,000 varieties of plants. Seven spectacular glasshouses, two art galleries, Japanese and rock garden.

London Aquarium

Riverside Building, London SE1 7PB
Tel: (020) 7967 8000
Dive down deep beneath the Thames and submerge yourself in one of Europe's largest displays of aquatic life.

London Dungeon

Tooley Street, London SE1 2SZ
Tel: 0891 600 0666
The world's first medieval horror museum. Now featuring two major shows, 'The Jack the Ripper Experience' and 'The Judgement Day Ride'.

London Eye

Jubilee Gardens, South Bank, London SE1
Tel: 0870 5000 600
At 135 metres (443ft) high, this is the world's highest observation wheel. It provides a 30-minute slow-moving flight over London.

London Planetarium

Marylebone Road, London NW1 5LR
Tel: (020) 7935 6861
Visitors can experience a virtual reality trip through space and wander through the interactive Space Zones before the show.

London Transport Museum

Covent Garden Piazza, London WC2E 7BB
Tel: (020) 7379 6344
The history of transport for everyone, from spectacular vehicles, special exhibitions, actors and guided tours to film shows, gallery talks and children's craft workshops.

London Zoo

Regent's Park, London NW1 4RY
Tel: (020) 7722 3333
One of the world's most famous zoos and home to over 600 species. Including the new 'Web of Life' exhibition, and a full daily events programme.

Madame Tussaud's

Marylebone Road, London NW1 5LR
Tel: (020) 7935 6861
World-famous collection of wax figures in themed settings which include The Garden Party, 200 Years, Superstars, The Grand Hall, The Chamber of Horrors and The Spirit of London.

Museum of London

London Wall, London EC2Y 5HN
Tel: (020) 7600 3699
Discover over 2,000 years of the capital's history, from prehistoric to modern times. Regular temporary exhibitions and lunchtime lecture programmes.

National Gallery

Trafalgar Square, London WC2N 5DN
Tel: (020) 7747 2885
Gallery displaying Western European paintings from about 1260-1900. Includes work by Botticelli, Leonardo da Vinci, Rembrandt, Gainsborough, Turner, Renoir, Cezanne.

National Maritime Museum

Romney Road, London SE10 9NF
Tel: (020) 8858 4422
This national museum explains Britain's worldwide influence through its explorers, traders, migrants and naval power. Features on ship models, costume and ecology of the sea.

National Portrait Gallery

St Martin's Place, London WC2H 0HE
Tel: (020) 7306 0055
Permanent collection of portraits of famous men and women from the Middle Ages to the present day. Usually free, but a charge may be made for some exhibitions.

Natural History Museum

Cromwell Road, London SW7 5BD
Tel: (020) 7942 5000
One of the most popular museums in the world and one of London's finest landmarks, it houses the natural wonders of the world.

Rock Circus

Piccadilly Circus, London W1V 9LA
Tel: (020) 7734 7203
Madame Tussaud's new Rock Circus features special audio, visual and animatronic effects, plus wax figures of the pop world's biggest names of past and present.

Royal Air Force Museum

Grahame Park Way, Hendon, London NW9 5LL
Tel: (020) 8205 2266
Britain's National Museum of Aviation features over 70 full-sized aircraft, Flight Simulator, 'Touch and Try' Jet Provost Trainer and Eurofighter 2000 Theatre.

The Pictures:
1 Harrods;
2 Big Ben;
3 The Whitechapel at the Tower of London;
4 Trafalgar Square;
5 Battersea Park Pagoda;
6 Hays Galleria;
7 China Town;
8 Richmond Lock.

Royal Observatory Greenwich

Greenwich Park, London SE10 9NF
Tel: (020) 8858 4422
Museum of time and space, and site of the Greenwich Meridian. Working telescopes and planetarium, timeball, Wren's Octagon Room and intricate clocks and computer simulations.

St Paul's Cathedral

St Paul's Churchyard, London EC4M 8AD
Tel: (020) 7236 4128
Wren's famous cathedral church of the diocese of London incorporating the Crypt, Ambulatory and Whispering Gallery.

Science Museum

Exhibition Road, London SW7 2DD
Tel: (020) 7942 4454
See, touch and experience the major scientific advances of the past 300 years. The world's finest collections in the history of science, technology and medicine.

Shakespeare's Globe Theatre Tours and Exhibition

New Globe Walk, Bankside, London SE1 9DT
Tel: (020) 7902 1500
Against the historical background of Elizabethan Bankside — the City of London's playground in Shakespeare's time — the exhibition focuses on actors, architecture and audiences.

Tate Modern

Bankside Power Station, Sumner Street, London SE1
Tel: (020) 7401 5081
Home of the Tate Gallery of Modern Art with displays of 20thC art ranging from Andy Warhol to Rachel Whiteread and Henri Matisse to Henry Moore.

Tower Bridge Experience

Tower Bridge, London SE1 2UP
Tel: (020) 7403 3761
Exhibition explaining the history of the bridge and how it operates. Original steam-powered engines on view. Panoramic views from fully-glazed walkways. Gift shop.

Tower of London

Tower Hill, London EC3N 4AB
Tel: (020) 7709 0765
Home of the 'Beefeaters' and ravens, the building spans 900 years of British history. On display are the nation's Crown Jewels, regalia and armoury robes.

Victoria and Albert Museum

Cromwell Road, London SW7 2RL
Tel: (020) 7942 2000
The V&A holds one of the world's largest and most diverse collections of the decorative arts, dating from 3000BC to the present day.

Vinopolis, City of Wine

Bank End, London SE1 9BU
Tel: (020) 7645 3700
Vinopolis offers all the pleasures of wine under one roof. The Wine Odyssey tour includes free tastings from over 200 wines. Four restaurants on site.

Westminster Abbey

Parliament Square, London SW1P 3PA
Tel: (020) 7222 5152
One of Britain's finest Gothic buildings. Scene of the coronation, marriage and burial of British monarchs. Includes nave and cloisters, Royal Chapels and Undercroft Museum.

The Pictures:
1 Guards at Buckingham Palace;
2 St Paul's Cathedral;
3 Tower Bridge at night;
4 Eros in Piccadilly Circus;
5 Big Ben and the Houses of Parliament.

Find out more about
LONDON ...

A free information pack about holidays and attractions in London is available on written request from:

LONDON TOURIST BOARD AND CONVENTION BUREAU
6th Floor, Glen House, Stag Place, London SW1E 5LT.

TOURIST INFORMATION CENTRES

POINT OF ARRIVAL
- Heathrow Terminals 1, 2, 3 Underground Station Concourse, Heathrow Airport, TW6 2JA.
Open: Daily 0800-1800; 1 Jun-30 Sep, Mon-Sat 0800-1900, Sun 0800-1800.
- Liverpool Street Underground Station, EC2M 7PN.
Open: Daily 0800-1800; 1 Jun-30 Sep, Mon-Sat 0800-1900, Sun 0800-1800.
- Victoria Station Forecourt, SW1V 1JU.
Open: 1 Jun-30 Sep, Mon-Sat 0800-2100, Sun 0800-1800; 1 Oct-Easter, daily 0800-1800; Easter-31 May, Mon-Sat 0800-2000, Sun 0800-1800.
- Waterloo International Terminal
Arrivals Hall, London SE1 7LT. *Open: Daily 0830-2230.*

INNER LONDON
- Britain Visitor Centre
1 Regent Street, Piccadilly Circus, SW1Y 4XT.
Open: Mon 0930-1830, Tue-Fri 0900-1830, Sat & Sun 1000-1600; Jun-Oct, Sat 0900-1700.
- Greenwich Tourist Information Centre
Pepys House, 2 Cutty Sark Gardens SE10 9LW.
Tel: 0870 608 2000; Fax: (020) 8853 4607.
Open: Daily 1000-1700; 1 Jul-31 Aug, daily 1000-2000.
- Lewisham Tourist Information Centre
Lewisham Library,
199-201 Lewisham High Street, SE13 6LG.
Tel: (020) 8297 8317.
Open: Mon 1000-1700, Tue-Fri 0900-1700, Sat 1000-1600.
- Southwark Information Centre
London Bridge, 6 Tooley Street, SE1 2SY.
Tel: (020) 7403 8299.
Open: Easter-31 Oct, Mon-Sat 1000-1800, Sun 1030-1730; 1 Nov-Easter, Mon-Sat 1000-1600, Sun 1100-1600.

- Tower Hamlets Tourist Information Centre
18 Lamb Street, E1 6EA.
Fax: (020) 7375 2539.
Open: Mon, Tues, Thur & Fri 0930-1330,1430-1630, 0930-1300; Sun 1130-1430.

OUTER LONDON
- Bexley Hall Place Visitor Centre
Bourne Road, Bexley, Kent DA5 1PQ.
Tel: (01322) 558676; Fax: (01322) 522921.
Open: Mon-Sat 1000-1630, Sun 1400-1730.
- Croydon Tourist Information Centre
Katharine Street, Croydon CR9 1ET.
Tel: (020) 8253 1009; Fax: (020) 8253 1008.
Open: Mon-Wed 0900-1800, Thu 0930-1800, Fri 0900-1800, Sat 0900-1700, Sun 1400-1700.
- Harrow Tourist Information Centre
Civic Centre, Station Road, Harrow HA1 2XF.
Tel: (020) 8424 1103; Fax: (020) 8424 1134.
Open: Mon-Fri 0900-1700.
- Hillingdon Tourist Information Centre
Central Library, 14 High Street, Uxbridge UB8 1HD.
Tel: (01895) 250706; Fax: (01895) 239794.
Open: Mon, Tue & Thu 0930-2000, Wed 0930-1730, Fri 1000-1730, Sat 0930-1600.

● **Hounslow Tourist Information Centre**
24 The Treaty Centre,
Hounslow High Street, Hounslow TW3 1ES.
Tel: (020) 8583 2929; Fax: (020) 8583 4714.
Open: Mon, Wed, Fri & Sat 0930-1730, Tue & Thu 0930-2000.

● **Kingston Tourist Information Centre**
Market House, Market Place,
Kingston upon Thames KT1 1JS.
Tel: (020) 8547 5592; Fax: (020) 8547 5594.
Open: Mon-Fri 1000-1700, Sat 0900-1600.

● **Richmond Tourist Information Centre**
Old Town Hall, Whittaker Avenue, Richmond TW9 1TP.
Tel: (020) 8940 9125; Fax: (020) 8940 6899.
Open: Mon-Sat 1000-1700; Easter Sunday-end Sep,
Sun 1030-1330.

● **Swanley Tourist Information Centre**
London Road, BR8 7AE.
Tel: (01322) 614660.
Open: Mon-Thu 0930-1730, Fri 0930-1800, Sat 0900-1600.

● **Twickenham Tourist Information Centre**
The Atrium, Civic Centre, York Street, Twickenham,
Middlesex TW1 3BZ.
Tel: (020) 8891 7272.
Open: Mon-Thu 0900-1715; Fri 0900-1700.

VISITORCALL

The London Tourist Board and Convention Bureau's
'Phone Guide to London' operates 24 hours a day.
To access a full range of information call 09064 123456.
To access specific lines dial 09064 123 followed by:

What's on this week	- 400
What's on next 3 months	- 401
Rock and pop concerts	- 422
Visitor attractions	- 480
Where to take children	- 424
Museums and galleries	- 429
Palaces (including Buckingham Palace)	- 481
Current exhibitions	- 403
Changing the Guard	- 411
West End shows	- 416
Eating out	- 485
London line 2000:	**09064 663344**

Calls cost 60p per minute at all times (as at
June 2000). To order a Visitorcall card please
call (020) 7971 0026.

ARTSLINE

London's information and advice service for disabled
people on arts and entertainment. Call (020) 7388 2227.

The Pictures:
1 River Thames at night
2 Buckingham Palace;
3 Westminster Abbey.

Getting to
LONDON ...

BY ROAD: Major trunk roads into London include: A1, M1, A5, A10, A11, M11, A13, A2,
M2, A23, A3, M3, A4, M4, A40, M40, A41, M25 (London orbital).
London Transport is responsible for running London's bus services and the underground
rail network. (020) 7222 1234 (24 hour telephone service; calls answered in rotation).

BY RAIL: Main rail termini:
Victoria/Waterloo/Charing Cross - serving the South/South East;
King's Cross - serving the North East; Euston - serving the North West/Midlands;
Liverpool Street - serving the East; Paddington - serving the Thames Valley/West.

WHERE TO STAY (LONDON)

Parks in London are listed in alphabetical order of place name,
and then in alphabetical order of park.

Map references refer to the colour location maps at the back of this guide.
The first number indicates the map to use; the letter and number which follow refer to the
grid reference on the map.

At-a-glance symbols can be found inside the back cover flap.
Keep this open for easy reference.

CHINGFORD

Map ref 3D2

Lee Valley Campsite ⚠
★★★★
Touring and Camping Park
Sewardstone Road, Chingford,
London E4 7RA
T: (020) 8529 5689
F: (020) 8559 4070
E: scs@leevalleypark.org.uk
I: www.leevalleypark.org.uk
*Take junction 26 off the M25, then
follow signs to Chingford. Turn left at
the roundabout and the campsite is 2
miles on the right. Signposted.*
5.2 hectares (13 acres). Level,
sloping, grassy, hard.
200 touring pitches.

200	🚐	£11.00
	🚏	£11.00
	⛺	£11.00

Open April–October
Cards accepted: Barclaycard, Delta,
JCB, Maestro, Mastercard, Solo,
Switch, Visa, Visa Electron

🚗 P 🖥 ⭐ 🎣 ⛱ 🛁 🔥 🛎 💷 🗑
☘ 🎱 ☉ ⚠ 🛝 Wh

Ad See display advertisement on
page 45

EDMONTON

Map ref 3D2

Lee Valley Leisure Centre ⚠
★★★★
Touring and Camping Park
Meridian Way, London N9 0AS
T: (020) 8345 6666 & 8803 6900
F: (020) 8884 4975
E: leisurecentre@
leevalleypark.org.uk
I: www.leevalleypark.org.uk
*Turn from the A406 on to Montagu
Road, which leads into Meridian Way.
From the M25 take the A10 towards
London and then turn left onto the
A1055. The site is about 5 miles along
the A1055. Signposted.*
2.4 hectares (6 acres). Level, grassy,
hard.
160 touring pitches.

160	🚐	£11.00—£11.00
	🚏	£11.00—£11.00
	⛺	£11.00—£11.00

Open all year round
Cards accepted: Barclaycard, Delta,
Maestro, Mastercard, Solo, Switch,
Visa, Visa Electron

🚗 P 🖥 ⭐ 🎣 ⛱ 🛁 🔥 🛎 × 💷
🗑 ☘ 🚌 ☉ 🔍 ⚠ 🍴 ∪ ⚲ ▶ 🛝 Wh

Ad See display advertisement on
page 45

LOUGHTON

Map ref 3D1

The Elms Caravan and Camping Park
★★★
Touring and Camping Park
Member BH&HPA
Lippitts Hill, High Beech, Loughton,
IG10 4AW
T: (020) 8508 3749 & 8508 1000
F: (020) 8502 0016
E: elmscar@aol.com
I: members.aol.com/elmscar
*Jct 26 off M25. Follow signs to
Waltham Abbey (A121), turn left at
traffic lights (A112) for 1.3 miles, 3rd
left turn by Plough pub, half a mile to
Lippitts Hill. Signposted.*
1.2 hectares (3 acres). Level, grassy,
hard, sheltered.
50 touring pitches.

50	🚐	£9.50—£9.50
50	🚏	£9.50—£9.50
50	⛺	£9.50—£9.50
2	🚚	£200.00

Open March–October

🚗 ⭐ 🎣 ⛱ 🛁 🔥 🛎 💷 ☘ 🚌
☉ ⚠

Ad See display advertisement on this
page

The ⚠ symbol after a
park name indicates that
it is a Regional Tourist
Board member.

You are advised to confirm
your booking in writing.

Please check prices and other
details at the time of booking.

LONDON – THE ELMS CARAVAN AND CAMPING PARK
LIPPITTS HILL, HIGH BEECH, LOUGHTON, ESSEX

Ideal base for visiting London. The Elms is situated in Epping Forest Conservation Area. A small, quiet family run park just 3 miles from the underground,
30 minutes journey time to London. Shopping basics on site. Pub with children's room within 200 yards. Our individual shower and toilet cubicles second to none.
Riding, fishing, golf, boating, swimming, restaurants and shops all nearby. Booking advisable. Tel: 020 8508 3749/1000; Fax: 020 8502 0016.
Junction 26 off M25. Follow signs to Waltham Abbey (A121), turn left at traffic lights (A112) for 1.3 miles, third turning left beside Plough Pub, half a mile to
Lippitts Hill. Or from Loughton Station, 'phone for pick-up. **Free bus to/from underground station for backpackers and motorhome owners.**

STANSTED

Map ref 4B3

Thriftwood Caravan & Camping Park

★ ★ ★ ★ ★

Holiday, Touring and Camping Park
Rose Award
Member BH&HPA
Plaxdale Green Road, Stansted,
Wrotham, Sevenoaks, Kent
TN15 7PB
T: (01732) 822261
F: (01732) 822261
I: www.ukparks.co.uk/thriftwood
*Situated 3.75 miles south of Brands
Hatch motor racing circuit on A20.
Signposted.*
8 hectares (20 acres). Level, grassy,
hard, sheltered.
150 touring pitches.

150	🚐	£8.00—£11.00
150	🚍	£8.00—£11.00
150	⛺	£6.00—£8.00
5	🏠	£138.00—£340.00

Open January, March–December
Cards accepted: Barclaycard, Delta,
Eurocard, JCB, Mastercard, Solo,
Switch, Visa, Visa Electron

🅿 P 📶 🎱 ⛳ 🎣 🔔 🛒 ♿ 🍴
📺 🏪 📞 🚿 🛢 ☺ ⛰ 🐾 ⚓

USE YOUR *i*s

There are more than 550
Tourist Information Centres
throughout England offering friendly
help with accommodation and
holiday ideas as well as
suggestions of places to visit
and things to do. There may well be
a centre in your home town which
can help you before you set out.
You'll find addresses in the
local Phone Book.

Perfectly Placed for the
City of London,
and the countryside of Hertfordshire and Essex

There are plenty of camping and caravan sites to choose from in Lee Valley Regional Park. All sites have modern facilities, offer value for money and are located in pleasant surroundings with their own local leisure attractions.

**Lee Valley Leisure Centre Campsite,
Picketts Lock, Edmonton,
North London**
Only 34 mins from the West End. The site also boasts a large leisure centre, 18 hole golf course and 12 screen UCI cinema.
Tel: 020 8803 6900
Fax: 020 8884 4975

**Lee Valley Caravan Park,
Dobbs Weir, Hoddesdon, Herts**
Enjoy the peace and tranquillity of this riverside site with good fishing, walking and boating nearby. Get to the West End by train and tube in under an hour.
Tel/Fax: 01992 462090

**Lee Valley Campsite,
Chingford, London**
Situated on the edge of Epping Forest and close to the historic town of Waltham Abbey, this site is easily accessible from the M25 and just 42 minutes from the West End by public transport.
Tel: 020 8529 5689
Fax: 020 8559 4070

For more information, call our Information Centre on 01992 702200 or find us on the web at:
www.leevalleypark.org.uk

Lee Valley Park

USE YOUR *i*s

There are more than 550 Tourist Information Centres throughout England offering friendly help with accommodation and holiday ideas as well as suggestions of places to visit and things to do. There may well be a centre in your home town which can help you before you set out. You'll find addresses in the local Phone Book.

On-line Information

In-depth information about travelling in Britain is now available on BTA's VisitBritain website.

Covering everything from castles to leisure parks and from festivals to road and rail links, the site complements Where to Stay perfectly, giving you up-to-the-minute details to help you with your travel plans.

BRITAIN on the internet
www.visitbritain.com

Cumbria

Cumbria can be admired from many angles - from the heights of Scafell Pike, England's tallest mountain, from the glassy waters of the magnificent Lakes or even from the windows of one of the many scenic railway trains.

The Lake District is also Beatrix Potter country and you can visit her charming house at Hilltop near Sawrey. Or take a leisurely cruise across Lakes Windermere or Coniston. Cumbria's coastline boasts superb sands. And if you yearn for the bustle of city life, head for historic Carlisle.

Fell racing attracts competitors from all over the world. It's a sprint to the top of a fell (or peak) and is nearly as exhausting to watch as to run!

The county of Cumbria

FOR MORE INFORMATION CONTACT:
Cumbria Tourist Board
Ashleigh, Holly Road, Windermere,
Cumbria LA23 2AQ
Tel: (015394) 44444
Fax: (015394) 44041
Email: mail@cumbria-tourist-board.co.uk
Internet: www.gocumbria.co.uk

The Pictures:
1 Great Langdale;
2 Walking at Wasdale;
3 Ullswater;
4 Derwentwater.

Where to Go in Cumbria - see pages 48-51
Where to Stay in Cumbria - see pages 52-56

Whilst in
CUMBRIA ...

You will find hundreds of interesting places to visit during your stay, just some of which are listed in these pages.

Contact any Tourist Information Centre in the region for more ideas on days out in Cumbria.

Appleby Castle
Appleby-in-Westmorland, Cumbria CA16 6XH
Tel: (017683) 51402
A beautiful castle with breathtaking views, steeped in history. The Great Hall is a must for anyone to see.

Aquarium of the Lakes
Newby Bridge, Ulverston, Cumbria LA12 8AS
Tel: (015395) 30153
Discover the UK's largest collection of freshwater fish in Britain's award-winning freshwater aquarium. Meet mischievous otters, diving ducks, sharks and rays.

Brantwood, Home of John Ruskin
Coniston, Cumbria LA21 8AD
Tel: (015394) 41396
Superb lake and mountain views. Works by Ruskin and contemporaries, memorabilia. Ruskin watercolours. Craft and picture gallery, gardens.

Brockhole Visitor Centre
National Park Authority, Windermere,
Cumbria LA23 1LJ
Tel: (015394) 46601
Interactive exhibitions, audio-visual show, shop, gardens, grounds, adventure playground, dry-stone walling area, trails, events and croquet. Cafe with home cooked food.

Cars of the Stars Motor Museum
Keswick, Cumbria CA12 5LS
Tel: (017687) 73757
Features TV and film vehicles including the Batmobile, Chitty Chitty Bang Bang, the James Bond collection, Herbie, FAB 1 plus many other famous cars and motorcycles.

The Dock Museum
Barrow-in-Furness, Cumbria LA14 2PW
Tel: (01229) 894444
The museum, which straddles a Victorian graving dock, presents the story of steel shipbuilding for which Barrow is famous. Interactive displays and nautical adventure playground.

Dove Cottage and Wordsworth Museum
Town End, Grasmere, Cumbria LA22 9SH
Tel: (015394) 35544
Wordsworth's home from 1799-1808. Poet's possessions, museum with manuscripts, farmhouse reconstruction, paintings and drawings. Special events throughout the year.

Eden Ostrich World
Langwathby, Penrith, Cumbria CA10 1LW
Tel: (01768) 881771
Working farm with lots of farm animals, some of them rare breeds. Covered and outdoor play areas, picnic areas, tearoom and craft shop.

Furness Abbey

Barrow-in-Furness, Cumbria LA13 0TJ
Tel: (01229) 823420
Ruins of a 12thC Cistercian abbey, the second wealthiest in England. Extensive remains include transepts, choir and west tower of church, canopied seats and arches.

Graythwaite Hall Gardens

Newby Bridge, Ulverston, Cumbria LA12 8BA
Tel: (015395) 31248
Rhododendrons, azaleas and flowering shrubs. Laid out by T Mawson, 1888-1890.

Heron Corn Mill and Museum of Papermaking

Waterhouse Mills, Beetha, Milnthorpe,
Cumbria LA7 7AR
Tel: (015395) 65027
Restored working corn mill featuring 4.9-metre (14ft) high breastshot waterwheel. The museum shows paper making both historic and modern with artefacts, displays and diagrams.

Hill Top

Near Sawrey, Ambleside, Cumbria LA22 0LF
Tel: (015394) 36269
Beatrix Potter wrote many of her popular Peter Rabbit stories and other books in this charming little house. It still contains her own china and furniture.

K Village Heritage Centre

Netherfield, Kendal, Cumbria LA9 7DA
Tel: (01539) 732363
Heritage centre within the 'K' Village where visitors can follow numbered exhibits detailing the history of K Shoes in Kendal and the Lake District since 1842.

Lakeland Motor Museum

Holker Hall, Cark in Cartmel,
Grange-over-Sands, Cumbria LA11 7PL
Tel: (015395) 58509
Over 10,000 exhibits including rare motoring automobilia. A 1930s garage recreation and the Campbell Legend Bluebird Exhibition.

Lakeland Sheep and Wool Centre

Cockermouth, Cumbria CA13 0QX
Tel: (01900) 822673
An all-weather attraction with live sheep shows including working dog demonstrations. Also large screen and other exhibitions on the area. Gift shop and cafe.

Lakeside and Haverthwaite Railway

Haverthwaite Station, Ulverston, Cumbria LA12 8AL
Tel: (015395) 31594
Standard gauge steam railway operating a daily seasonal service through the beautiful Leven Valley. Steam and diesel locomotives on display.

Levens Hall

Levens, Kendal, Cumbria LA8 0PD
Tel: (015395) 60321
Elizabethan mansion incorporating a pele tower. Famous topiary garden laid out in 1694, steam collection and plant centre. Shop, play area, picnic area.

Linton Tweeds

Shaddon Mills, Shaddon Gate, Carlisle, Cumbria CA2 5TZ
Tel: (01228) 527569
Centre shows history of weaving in Carlisle up to Linton's today. Visitors can try weaving and other hands-on activities.

Lowther Leisure and Wildlife Park

Hackthorpe, Penrith, Cumbria CA10 2HG
Tel: (01931) 712523
Attractions include exotic birds and animals, rides, miniature railway, boating lake, play areas, adventure fort, Tarzan trail, international circus and a puppet theatre.

Muncaster Castle, Gardens and Owl Centre

Ravenglass, Cumbria CA18 1RQ
Tel: (01229) 717614
The most beautifully situated Owl Centre in the world. See the birds fly, picnic in the gardens and visit the Pennington family home.

The Pictures:
1 Buttermere;
2 Kirkstile Inn;
3 Watendlath Bridge;
4 Derwentwater;
5 Green Gable;
6 Carlisle Castle.

Ravenglass and Eskdale Railway

Ravenglass, Cumbria CA18 1SW
Tel: (01229) 717171
England's oldest narrow-gauge railway runs for 11km (7 miles) through glorious scenery to the foot of England's highest hills. Most trains are steam hauled.

Senhouse Roman Museum

The Battery Sea, Brows, Maryport, Cumbria CA15 6JD
Tel: (01900) 816168
Once the headquarters of Hadrian's Coastal Defence system. The UK's largest group of Roman altar stones and inscriptions from one site. Roman military equipment, stunning sculpture.

Sizergh Castle

Kendal, Cumbria LA8 8AE
Tel: (015395) 60070
Strickland family home for 750 years, now National Trust owned. With 14thC pele tower, 15thC great hall, 16thC wings. Stuart connections. Rock garden, rose garden, daffodils.

South Lakes Wild Animal Park

Dalton-in-Furness, Cumbria LA15 8JR
Tel: (01229) 466086
Wild zoo park in over 17 acres of grounds. Over 120 species of animals from all around the world. Large waterfowl ponds, miniature railway, cafe.

Townend

Troutbeck, Windermere, Cumbria LA23 1LB
Tel: (015394) 32628
Typical Lakeland statesman farmer's house c1626. All original interiors, carved woodwork and domestic implements from the family who lived there for over three centuries.

Trotters World of Animals

Coalbeck Farm, Bassenthwaite, Cumbria CA12 4RE
Tel: (017687) 76239
Farm park with collection of rare and interesting farm animals, poultry and baby animals, reptile house and bird of prey centre.

Tullie House Museum and Art Gallery

Carlisle, Cumbria CA3 8TP
Tel: (01228) 534781
Major tourist complex housing museum, art gallery, education facility, lecture theatre, shops, herb garden restaurant and terrace bars.

Ullswater Steamers

Kendal, Cumbria LA9 4QD
Tel: (017684) 82229
Relax and enjoy beautiful Ullswater combining a cruise with a visit to other local attractions. All boats have bar and toilet facilities.

Windermere Steamboat Museum

Bowness-on-Windermere, Cumbria LA23 1BN
Tel: (015394) 45565
A wealth of interest and information about life on bygone Windermere. Regular steam launch trips, vintage vessels and classic motorboats. Model boat pond and lakeside picnic area.

The World of Beatrix Potter

Bowness-on-Windermere, Cumbria LA23 3BX
Tel: (015394) 88444
The life and works of Beatrix Potter presented on a 9-screen video-wall. Beautiful three dimensional scenes bring her stories to life.

The Pictures:
1 Shoreline, Derwantwater;
2 Windermere Steamer;
3 Maryport;
4 Brundholme Wood;
5 Lake Windermere;
6 Cycling at Coniston;
7 Holker Hall, Grange-over-Sands;
8 Muncaster Castle;
9 Loughrigg.

Find out more about
CUMBRIA ...

Further information about holidays and attractions in Cumbria is available from:

CUMBRIA TOURIST BOARD

Ashleigh, Holly Road, Windermere, Cumbria LA23 2AQ.

Tel: (015394) 44444

Fax: (015394) 44041

Email: mail@cumbria-tourist-board.co.uk

Internet: www.gocumbria.co.uk

The following publications are available from Cumbria Tourist Board:

Cumbria Tourist Board Holiday Guide (free)
Tel: 08705 133059

Events Listings (free)

Cumbria The Lake District Touring Map
including tourist information and touring caravan and camping parks £3.95
Laminated Poster - £4.50

Getting to
CUMBRIA ...

BY ROAD: The M1/M6/M25/M40 provide a link with London and the South East and the M5/M6 provide access from the South West. The M62/M6 link Hull and Manchester with the region. Approximate journey time from London is 5 hours, from Manchester 2 hours.

BY RAIL: From London (Euston) to Oxenholme (Kendal) takes approximately 3 hours 30 minutes. From Oxenholme (connecting station for all main line trains) to Windermere takes approximately 20 minutes. From Carlisle to Barrow-in-Furness via the coastal route, with stops at many of the towns in between, takes approximately 2 hours. Trains from Edinburgh to Carlisle take 1 hour 45 minutes. The historic Settle-Carlisle line also runs through the county bringing passengers from Yorkshire via the Eden Valley.

www.travelcumbria.co.uk

WHERE TO STAY (CUMBRIA)

Parks in this region are listed in alphabetical order of place name, and then in alphabetical order of park.

Map references refer to the colour location maps at the back of this guide.
The first number indicates the map to use; the letter and number which follow refer to the grid reference on the map.

At-a-glance symbols can be found inside the back cover flap.
Keep this open for easy reference.

AMBLESIDE

Cumbria
Map ref 6A3

Market town situated at the head of Lake Windermere and surrounded by fells. The historic town centre is now a conservation area and the country around Ambleside is rich in historic and literary associations. Good centre for touring, walking and climbing.
Tourist Information Centre
T: (015394) 32582

Greenhowe Caravan Park ⚠
★★★
Holiday Park
Member BH&HPA
Great Langdale, Ambleside
LA22 9JU
T: (015394) 37231 (24 hours.)
F: (015394) 37464
From Ambleside take the A593 then the B5343. The site is on the right-hand side. Signposted.
1.6 hectares (4 acres). Sloping, stony, sheltered.

| 46 | 🚐 | £150.00—£395.00 |

Open March—November
⚓P🏕🏪⛽🛁🕮📺✂�'🚗☺🔫🏔☾⛄Ⓣ

WELCOME HOST

This is a nationally recognised customer care programme which aims to promote the highest standards of service and a warm welcome. Parks taking part in this initiative are indicated by the [WH] symbol.

APPLEBY-IN-WESTMORLAND

Cumbria
Map ref 6B3

Former county town of Westmorland, at the foot of the Pennines in the Eden Valley. The castle was rebuilt in the 17th C, except for its Norman keep, ditches and ramparts. It now houses a Rare Breeds Survival Trust Centre. Good centre for exploring the Eden Valley.
Tourist Information Centre
T: (017683) 51177

Wild Rose Park ⚠
★★★★★
Holiday, Touring and Camping Park
Member BH&HPA
Ormside, Appleby-in-Westmorland
CA16 6EJ
T: (017683) 51077
F: (017683) 52551
E: hs@wildrose.co.uk
I: www.wildrose.co.uk
Turn off the B6260 (Appleby to Tebay) at Burrells. Follow the signposts to Ormside. After approximately 2 miles the park is on right-hand side. Signposted.
16 hectares (40 acres). Level, sloping, grassy, hard.
240 touring pitches.

240	🚐	£7.80—£13.30
80	🚏	£7.80—£13.30
80	⛺	£7.80—£13.30

240 units privately owned
Open all year round
Cards accepted: Barclaycard, Delta, Eurocard, JCB, Mastercard, Solo, Switch, Visa, Visa Electron
🎮🚗📸🏪⛽🛁🕮👕🚻✗📺📻🚂🚗☺🔫🏔🚲🍴🛁[WH]

You are advised to confirm your booking in writing.

CARLISLE

Cumbria
Map ref 6A2

Cumbria's only city is rich in history. Attractions include the small red sandstone cathedral and 900-year-old castle with magnificent view from the keep. Award-winning Tullie House Museum and Art Gallery brings 2,000 years of Border history dramatically to life. Excellent centre for shopping.
Tourist Information Centre
T: (01228) 625600

Dandy Dinmont Caravan and Camping Site ⚠
★★★★
Touring and Camping Park
Blackford, Carlisle CA6 4EA
T: (01228) 674611
Exit the M6 at jct 44. Take A7 north, 1.5 miles. After Blackford sign follow the road directional signs to site. Site is on the right-hand side of the A7. Signposted.
1.6 hectares (4 acres). Level, grassy, hard.
47 touring pitches.

27	🚐	£7.75—£8.00
27	🚏	£7.75—£8.00
20	⛺	£6.50—£7.00

15 units privately owned
Open March—October
🚗P🍴📸🏪🛁👕🕮📺✂☺Ⓣ

Star ratings were correct at the time of going to press but are subject to change. Please check at the time of booking.

Orton Grange Caravan Park ⚠

★★★★
Holiday, Touring and Camping Park
Member BH&HPA
Wigton Road, Carlisle CA5 6LA
T: (01228) 710252
F: (01228) 710252
E: chris@ortongrange.flyer.co.uk
*Four miles west of Carlisle on the A595
(south side of the road). Signposted.*
2 hectares (5 acres). Level, grassy,
sheltered.
50 touring pitches.

30	🚐	£8.00—£9.50
30	🚏	£8.00—£9.50
20	⛺	£8.00—£9.50
4	🏠	£112.00—£202.00

18 units privately owned
Open all year round
Cards accepted: Amex, Barclaycard,
Delta, Mastercard, Solo, Switch, Visa

🚗🎏🅰️👜🏕️🛁👕👂♨️✕🖺 TV
🍴🗄️🚿🚪☉🔍🛆🔺🎣♨️

CONISTON

Cumbria
Map ref 6A3

The 803m fell Coniston Old Man
dominates the skyline to the east of
this village at the northern end of
Coniston Water. Arthur Ransome
set his "Swallows and Amazons"
stories here. Coniston's most
famous resident was John Ruskin,
whose home, Brantwood, is open to
the public. Good centre for walking.

Crake Valley Holiday Park ⚠

★★★★★
Holiday Park
Rose Award
Member BH&HPA
Water Yeat, Blawith, Ulverston
LA12 8DL
T: (01229) 885203
F: (01229) 885203
*Turn right off the A590 Barrow road at
Greenodd. Go onto the A5902, within 2
miles fork right onto the A5084 for
Coniston. The park is 3 miles along on
your left-hand side.*
Level, sloping, grassy, stony.

10	🏠	£165.00—£440.00

Open January, March–December
🎏🚗P🌲🏕️🛁🍴🗄️♨️🚪☉♨️

**Please check prices and other
details at the time of booking.**

ESKDALE

Cumbria
Map ref 6A3

Several minor roads lead to the west
end of this beautiful valley, or it can
be approached via the east over the
Hardknott Pass, the Lake District's
steepest pass. Scafell Pike and Bow
Fell lie to the north and a miniature
railway links the Eskdale Valley with
Ravenglass on the coast.

Fisherground Farm Campsite ⚠

★★
Camping Park
Fisherground, Eskdale, Holmrook
CA19 1TF
T: (019467) 23319
E: holidays@fisherground.co.uk
I: www.fisherground.campsite.co.uk
*At King George IV inn in middle of
Eskdale turn towards Boot (east).
Fisherground is 400m on the left.
Signposted.*
64 hectares (160 acres). Level,
grassy, sheltered.
30 touring pitches.

30	🚐	£8.00—£8.00
30	⛺	£8.00—£8.00
	🏠	£190.00—£490.00

Open March–November
🎏🚗P🌲🏕️🛁👕🍴🗄️♨️🚪
☉🔺

FLOOKBURGH

Cumbria
Map ref 6A3

Village, once a market town,
renowned for winkle and fluke
fishing.

Lakeland Leisure Park ⚠

★★★★
Holiday, Touring and Camping Park
Member BH&HPA/NCC
Moor Lane, Flookburgh, Grange-
over-Sands LA11 7LT
T: 0870 2425678
F: (01442) 254956
I: www.british-holidays.co.uk
*Leave the M6 at jct 36 and go onto the
A590. Turn left onto the A6/A590 for
Barrow-in-Furness. Take the B5277
through Grange-over-Sands to
Flookburgh. The park is 1 mile down
this road.*
42 hectares (105 acres). Level,
grassy.
125 touring pitches.

100	🚐	£8.30—£22.00
100	🚏	£8.30—£22.00
25	⛺	£8.30—£17.50
250	🏠	£149.00—£624.00

400 units privately owned
Open April–October

Cards accepted: Amex, Barclaycard,
Delta, JCB, Mastercard, Solo, Switch,
Visa

🚗P🎏🌲🏕️🛁👜👕🖺✕🍴
TV🍴🗄️🅰️☉🔺🎣♨️🔍U
🔍🎵🅰️ T WH
Ad See display advertisement on
page 10

GRANGE-OVER-SANDS

Cumbria
Map ref 6A3

Set on the beautiful Cartmel
Peninsula, this tranquil resort,
known as Lakeland's Riviera,
overlooks Morecambe Bay. Pleasant
seafront walks and beautiful gardens.
The bay attracts many species of
wading birds.
*Tourist Information Centre
T: (015395) 34026*

Greaves Farm Caravan Park ⚠

★★★★
Holiday and Touring Park
Member BH&HPA
Field Broughton, Grange-over-Sands
LA11 6HR
T: (015395) 36329 & 36587
*Leave the A590 1 mile south of Newby
Bridge, signed Cartmel 4. Proceed 2
miles to 3 bungalows on the left.
Approximately 200 yards before Field
Broughton church. Signposted.*
1.2 hectares (3 acres). Level, grassy,
hard.
8 touring pitches.

3	🚐	£8.50—£9.50
3	🚏	£8.50—£9.50
5	⛺	£7.50—£8.50
2	🏠	£180.00—£240.00

18 units privately owned
Open March–October
🚗P🌲🏕️🛁👕🚪🍴🗄️☉♨️ WH

HAWKSHEAD

Cumbria
Map ref 6A3

Lying near Esthwaite Water, this
village has great charm and
character. Its small squares are
linked by flagged or cobbled alleys
and the main square is dominated by
the market house, or Shambles,
where the butchers had their stalls
in days gone by.

The Croft Caravan and Camp Site ⚠

★★★
Touring and Camping Park
North Lonsdale Road, Hawkshead,
Ambleside LA22 0NX
T: (015394) 36374
F: (015394) 36544
E: enquiries@hawkshead-croft.com
I: www.hawkshead-croft.com

Continued ▶

HAWKSHEAD
Continued

From Ambleside follow B5286, 8 miles to Hawkshead. Signposted.
2 hectares (5 acres). Level, grassy, sheltered.
100 touring pitches.

15	🚐	£11.00
		£10.50
85	⛺	£10.50
18	🚃	£180.00—£295.00

Open March—October
Cards accepted: Barclaycard, Delta, Eurocard, Mastercard, Solo, Switch, Visa, Visa Electron

KENDAL
Cumbria
Map ref 6B3

The "Auld Grey Town" lies in the valley of the River Kent with a backcloth of limestone fells. Situated just outside the Lake District National Park, it is a good centre for touring the Lakes and surrounding country. Ruined castle, reputed birthplace of Catherine Parr.
Tourist Information Centre
T: (01539) 725758

Waters Edge Caravan Park ⚠
★★★★
Touring and Camping Park
Member BH&HPA
Crooklands, Kendal LA7 7NN
T: (015395) 67708 & 67527
F: (015395) 67610
E: cromoco@aol.com
Leave M6 at jct 36. Take A65 to Crooklands. Site about 4 miles on the right. Signposted.
1.2 hectares (3 acres). Level, grassy, hard, sheltered.
35 touring pitches.

30	🚐	£10.00—£15.00
30	🚃	£10.00—£15.00
5	⛺	£5.00—£13.00

Open March—October

Cards accepted: Barclaycard, Mastercard, Visa

[icons]

KESWICK
Cumbria
Map ref 6A3

Beautifully positioned town beside Derwentwater and below the mountains of Skiddaw and Blencathra. Excellent base for walking, climbing, watersports and touring. Motor-launches operate on Derwentwater and motor boats, rowing boats and canoes can be hired.
Tourist Information Centre
T: (017687) 72645

Castlerigg Hall Caravan and Camping Park ⚠
★★★★
Holiday, Touring and Camping Park
Member BH&HPA
Castlerigg Hall, Keswick CA12 4TE
T: (017687) 72437
F: (017687) 72437
I: www.castlerigg.co.uk
About 1.5 miles south east of Keswick off A591, turn right 100 yards on the right. Signposted.
6 hectares (15 acres). Level, sloping, grassy, stony, hard, sheltered.
165 touring pitches.

45	🚐	£9.50—£11.75
45	🚃	£8.75—£9.95
120	⛺	£7.50—£9.50
7	🚃	£170.00—£340.00

23 units privately owned
Open March—October
Cards accepted: JCB, Mastercard, Solo, Switch, Visa

[icons]

Ad See display advertisement on this page

Lakeside Holiday Park ⚠
★★★★
Holiday and Touring Park
Member BH&HPA
Norman Garner Ltd, Crow Park Road, Keswick CA12 5EW
T: (017687) 72878 (0900-1700)
F: (017687) 72017
E: welcome@lakesideholidaypark.co.uk
I: www.lakesideholidaypark.co.uk
Leave the M6 at jct 40. Exit A66 at roundabout near Keswick (16 miles). Follow signs for town centre. Follow camping and carvan signs. Signposted.
2.2 hectares (5.5 acres). Level, grassy, hard, sheltered.
14 touring pitches.

	🚐	£8.00—£17.50
14	🚃	£8.00—£17.50
12	🚃	£190.00—£460.00

20 units privately owned
Open March—November
Cards accepted: Barclaycard, Delta, JCB, Mastercard, Solo, Switch, Visa, Visa Electron

[icons]

Scotgate Holiday Park ⚠
★★★★
Holiday, Touring and Camping Park
Member BH&HPA
Braithwaite, Keswick CA12 5TF
T: (017687) 78343
F: (017687) 78099
Two miles west of Keswick just off the A66 on the B5292. Signposted.
3.6 hectares (9 acres). Level, grassy.
165 touring pitches.

15	🚐	£11.50—£15.00
165	🚃	£6.50—£9.00
165	⛺	£8.00—£9.00
27	🚃	£140.00—£300.00

Open March—November
Cards accepted: Barclaycard, Delta, Eurocard, Mastercard, Solo, Switch, Visa

[icons]

Ad See display advertisement on this page

NEWBY BRIDGE

Cumbria
Map ref 6A3

At the southern end of Windermere on the River Leven, this village has an unusual stone bridge with arches of unequal size. The Lakeside and Haverthwaite Railway has a stop here, and steamer cruises on Lake Windermere leave from nearby Lakeside.

Newby Bridge Caravan Park ♠
★★★★★
Holiday Park
Rose Award
Member BH&HPA
Canny Hill, Newby Bridge,
Ulverston LA12 8NF
T: (015395) 31030
F: (015395) 30105
E: newbybridge@
hopps.freeserve.co.uk
Just before entering Newby Bridge about 2.25 miles beyond High Newton turn left off the A590 signposted Canny Hill. Park entrance 200yds on the right-hand side. Signposted.
10.4 hectares (26 acres). Sloping, hard, sheltered.
9 touring pitches.

9	🚐	£15.00—£17.00
9	🚎	£15.00—£17.00
7	🏠	£110.00—£390.00

69 units privately owned
Open March—October

PENRITH

Cumbria
Map ref 6B2

Ancient and historic market town, the northern gateway to the Lake District. Penrith Castle was built as a defence against the Scots. Its ruins, open to the public, stand in the public park. High above the town is the Penrith Beacon, made famous by William Wordsworth.
Tourist Information Centre
T: (01768) 867466

Melmerby Caravan Park
★★★★
Holiday and Touring Park
Member BH&HPA
Melmerby, Penrith CA10 1HE
T: (01768) 881311
F: (01768) 881311
Take A686 Penrith to Alston road. Signposted.
.9 hectare (2.2 acres). Level, grassy, hard, sheltered.
5 touring pitches.

5	🚐	£8.00—£8.00
5	🚎	£8.00—£8.00

40 units privately owned
Open March—November

POOLEY BRIDGE

Cumbria
Map ref 6A3

The bridge is on the northern tip of Lake Ullswater and spans the River Eamont where it emerges from the lake. Good centre for exploring, walking and sailing.

Waterside House Campsite ♠
★★★
Touring and Camping Park
Waterside House, Howtown Road, Pooley Bridge, Penrith CA10 2NA
T: (017684) 86332
F: (017684) 86332
Leave the M6 at jct 40, take the A66 for 1 mile. Turn left onto the A592 for Ullswater and Pooley Bridge. Turn right at church, 1 mile along, Howtown Road on the right. Signposted.
111.6 hectares (279 acres). Grassy.
90 touring pitches.

90	🚎	£8.00—£10.00
90	⛺	£8.00—£10.00

Open March—October

SILLOTH

Cumbria
Map ref 6A2

Small port and coastal resort on the Solway Firth with wide cobbled roads and an attractive green leading to the promenade and seashore known for its magnificent sunsets.
Tourist Information Centre
T: (016973) 31944

Stanwix Park Holiday Centre ♠
★★★★★
Holiday, Touring and Camping Park
Rose Award
Member BH&HPA/NCC
Greenrow, West Silloth, Silloth, Carlisle CA7 4HH
T: (016973) 32666
F: (016973) 32555
E: stanwix.park@btinternet.com
I: www.stanwix.com
Leave M6 at jct 44, follow signs to Carlisle, Wigton and Silloth. From south leave M6 at jct 40, follow signs to Wigton and Silloth. Signposted.
7 hectares (17.5 acres). Level, grassy, sheltered.
121 touring pitches.

121	🚐	£13.00—£16.00
121	🚎	£13.00—£16.00
121	🚎	£13.00—£16.00
77	🏠	£130.00—£330.00

135 units privately owned
Open all year round
Cards accepted: Barclaycard, Delta, Eurocard, Mastercard, Solo, Switch, Visa

ULLSWATER

Cumbria
Map ref 6A3

This beautiful lake, which is over 7 miles long, runs from Glenridding to Pooley Bridge. Lofty peaks ranging around the lake make an impressive background. A steamer service operates along the lake between Pooley Bridge, Howtown and Glenridding in the summer.

Waterfoot Caravan Park ♠
★★★★★
Holiday and Touring Park
Member BH&HPA
Pooley Bridge, Penrith CA11 0JF
T: (017684) 86302 (Answerphone 24 hours.)
F: (01784) 86728
Leave the M6 at jct 40, take the A66 west for 1 mile. Follow the A592 for 3.5 miles, site on the right. Signposted.
8.8 hectares (22 acres). Level, sloping, grassy, hard, sheltered.
57 touring pitches.

57	🚐	£12.00—£14.00
57	🚎	£12.00—£14.00

126 units privately owned
Open March—October

WELCOME HOST
This is a nationally recognised customer care programme which aims to promote the highest standards of service and a warm welcome. Parks taking part in this initiative are indicated by the WH symbol.

All accommodation in this guide has been rated, or is awaiting a rating, by a trained Tourist Board assessor.

WINDERMERE

Cumbria
Map ref 6A3

Once a tiny hamlet before the introduction of the railway in 1847, now adjoins Bowness which is on the lakeside. Centre for sailing and boating. A good way to see the lake is a trip on a passenger steamer. Steamboat Museum has a fine collection of old boats.
Tourist Information Centre
T: (015394) 46499

Fallbarrow Park
★★★★★
Holiday and Touring Park
Rose Award
Member BH&HPA
Rayrigg Road, Windermere
LA23 3DL
T: (015394) 44427 (Caravan enquiries.) & 44428 (Touring pitch enquiries.)
F: (015394) 88736
I: www.fallbarrow.co.uk
From Windermere take the B5284. At Bowness turn right, park on the left. Signposted.
12.8 hectares (32 acres). Level, grassy, hard.
79 touring pitches.

79	🚐	£14.50—£20.50
79	🚚	£14.50—£20.50
71	🛖	£126.00—£530.00

180 units privately owned
Open March–October
Cards accepted: Amex, Barclaycard, Delta, Mastercard, Switch, Visa

Limefitt Park
★★★★★
Holiday, Touring and Camping Park
Rose Award
Member BH&HPA
Windermere LA23 1PA
T: (015394) 32300
I: www.limefitt.co.uk
Four miles north of Windermere on the A592 to Ullswater. Signposted.
45.2 hectares (113 acres). Level, grassy, hard, sheltered.
165 touring pitches.

110	🚐	£9.50—£13.00
110	🚚	£9.50—£13.00
55	⛺	£9.50—£13.00
9	🛖	£175.00—£430.00

45 units privately owned
Open April–October
Cards accepted: Amex, Barclaycard, Delta, Mastercard, Switch, Visa

Park Cliffe Caravan and Camping Estate
★★★★★
Holiday, Touring and Camping Park
Member BH&HPA
Birks Road, Windermere LA23 3PG
T: (015395) 31344
F: (015395) 31971
E: info@parkcliffe.co.uk
I: www.parkcliffe.co.uk
Exit the M6 at jct 36, A590 towards Barrow. At Newby Bridge turn right onto the A592 towards Windermere. After 4 miles turn right into Birks Road, 0.3 miles on the right. Signposted.
10 hectares (25 acres). Level, sloping, grassy, hard, sheltered.
250 touring pitches.

70	🚐	£13.00—£19.00
70	🚚	£13.00—£19.00
180	⛺	£10.00—£12.80

50 units privately owned
Open March–November
Cards accepted: Barclaycard, Delta, Eurocard, Mastercard, Solo, Switch, Visa, Visa Electron

COUNTRY CODE

Always follow the Country Code 🌿 Enjoy the countryside and respect its life and work 🌿 Guard against all risk of fire 🌿 Fasten all gates 🌿 Keep your dogs under close control 🌿 Keep to public paths across farmland 🌿 Use gates and stiles to cross fences, hedges and walls 🌿 Leave livestock, crops and machinery alone 🌿 Take your litter home 🌿 Help to keep all water clean 🌿 Protect wildlife, plants and trees 🌿 Take special care on country roads 🌿 Make no unnecessary noise

NORTHUMBRIA
Northumbria

From the sublime to the magnificent, Northumbria is rich in variety with an enormous expanse of coastline, countryside and culture. Stately homes and castles, designer gardens and open air museums all wait to share their secrets.

Discover Durham with its imposing Cathedral where the Venerable Bede, England's first historian, is buried. And from the beautiful fishing village of Seahouses, nature lovers will enjoy the boat trip around the Farne Islands to see eider duck, puffins and grey seals.

On the last Saturday in June the week long medieval Alnwick Fair begins. Be sure to catch unique events such as dwyle flonking - hitting your opponent with a beer-soaked rag on a stick!

The counties of
County Durham, Northumberland,
Tees Valley and Tyne & Wear

FOR MORE INFORMATION CONTACT:
Northumbria Tourist Board
Aykley Heads, Durham DH1 5UX
Tel: (0191) 375 3000
Fax: (0191) 386 0899
Internet: www.ntb.org.uk

Where to Go in Northumbria - see pages 58-61
Where to Stay in Northumbria - see pages 62-64

The Pictures:
1 Hadrian's Wall, Northumberland;
2 Kielder Water, Northumberland;
3 Washington Old Hall,
   Tyne & Wear;
4 Durham Cathedral.

Whilst in
NORTHUMBRIA ...

You will find hundreds of interesting places to visit during your stay, just some of which are listed in these pages.

Contact any Tourist Information Centre in the region for more ideas on days out in Northumbria.

Auckland Castle

Bishop Auckland, County Durham DL14 7NR
Tel: (01388) 601627
Principal country residence of the Bishops of Durham since Norman times. The chapel and staterooms are open to the public.

Bamburgh Castle

Bamburgh, Northumberland NE69 7DF
Tel: (01668) 214515
Magnificent coastal castle completely restored in 1900. Collections of china, porcelain, furniture, paintings, arms and armour.

Bede's World

Jarrow, Tyne & Wear NE32 3DY
Tel: (0191) 489 2106
Discover the exciting world of the Venerable Bede, early medieval Europe's greatest scholar. Church, monastic site, museum with exhibitions and recreated Anglo-Saxon farm.

Belsay Hall, Castle and Gardens

Belsay, Newcastle upon Tyne NE20 0DX
Tel: (01661) 881636
House of the Middleton family for 600 years in 30 acres of landscaped gardens and winter garden. 14thC castle, ruined 17thC manor house and neo-classical hall.

Captain Cook Birthplace Museum

Marton, Middlesbrough, Cleveland TS7 6AS
Tel: (01642) 311211
Early life and voyages of Captain Cook and the countries he visited. Temporary exhibitions.

Cragside House, Gardens and Grounds

Rothbury, Morpeth, Northumberland NE65 7PX
Tel: (01669) 620333
House built 1864-1884 for the first Lord Armstrong, a Tyneside industrialist. Cragside was the first house to be lit by electricity generated by water power.

Discovery Museum

Blandford Square, Newcastle upon Tyne NE1 4JA
Tel: (0191) 232 6789
Discovery Museum offers a wide variety of experiences for all the family to enjoy. Visit the Science Factory, Great City, Fashion Works and maritime history.

Dunstanburgh Castle

Craster, Alnwick, Northumberland NE66 3TT
Tel: (01665) 576231
Romantic ruins of extensive 14thC castle in dramatic coastal situation on 30-metre (100ft) cliffs. Built by Thomas, Earl of Lancaster. Remains include gatehouse and curtain wall.

Durham Castle

Palace Green, Durham DH1 3RW
Tel: (0191) 374 3863
Castle founded in 1072, Norman chapel dating from 1080. Kitchens and great hall dated 1499 and 1284 respectively. Fine example of motte-and-bailey castle.

Gisborough Priory

Guisborough, Cleveland TS14 6HG
Tel: (01287) 633801
*Remains of a priory founded by Robert de Brus in
AD1119 for Augustinian canons in the grounds of
Gisborough Hall. Main arch and window of east wall
virtually intact.*

Hall Hill Farm

Lanchester, Durham DH7 0TA
Tel: (01388) 730300
*Family fun set in attractive countryside. See and touch
the animals at close quarters. Farm trailer ride, riverside
walk, teashop and play area.*

Hartlepool Historic Quay

Hartlepool, Cleveland TS24 0XZ
Tel: (01429) 860006
*An exciting reconstruction of a seaport of the 1800s
with buildings and a lively quayside.*

Housesteads Roman Fort

Haydon Bridge, Hadrian's Wall, Hexham,
Northumberland NE47 6NN
Tel: (01434) 344363
*Best preserved and most impressive of the Roman forts.
Vercovicium was a 5-acre fort for an extensive 800 civil
settlement. Only example of a Roman hospital.*

Josephine and John Bowes Museum

Barnard Castle, Durham DL12 8NP
Tel: (01833) 690606
*French-style chateau housing art collections of national
importance plus archaeology of south west Durham.*

Killhope, the North of England Lead Mining Museum

Cowshill, St John's Chapel, County Durham DL13 1AR
Tel: (01388) 537505
*Most complete lead mining site in Great Britain. Mine
tours available, 10-metre (34ft) diameter waterwheel,
reconstruction of Victorian machinery, miners lodging
and woodland walks.*

Life Interactive World

Times Square, Newcastle upon Tyne NE1 4EP
Tel: (0191) 261 6006
*This remarkable visitor experience is at the heart of the
International Centre for Life, a £58 million landmark
Millennium project.*

Lindisfarne Castle

Holy Island, Berwick-upon-Tweed,
Northumberland TD15 2SH
Tel: (01289) 389244
*Fort converted into a private home for Edward Hudson
by the architect Sir Edwin Lutyens in 1903.*

National Glass Centre

Sunderland, Tyne & Wear SR6 0GL
Tel: (0191) 515 5555
*A large gallery presenting the best in contemporary
and historical glass. Master craftspeople demonstrate
glass-making techniques. Classes and workshops
available.*

Natures World at the Botanic Centre

Acklam, Middlesbrough, Tees Valley TS5 7YN
Tel: (01642) 594895
*Demonstration gardens, wildlife pond, gold medal-
winning white garden, environmental exhibition hall,
shop, tearoom and river Tees model.*

Newcastle Cathedral

Church of St Nicholas, Newcastle upon Tyne NE1 1PF
Tel: (0191) 232 1939
*13thC and 14thC church, added to in 18thC-20thC.
Famous lantern tower, pre-reformation font and font
cover, 15thC stained-glass roundel in the side chapel.*

The Pictures:
1   The Angel of the North,
    Gateshead;
2   Boulby Cliff, Cleveland;
3   Tynemouth Priory and Castle,
    Tyne & Wear;
4   Dustanburgh, Northumberland;
5   Alnwick, Northumberland;
6   Beamish, County Durham;
7   Bridges over the Tyne, Newcastle;
8   Bamburgh, Northumberland.

The North of England Open Air Museum

Beamish, County Durham DH9 0RG
Tel: (01207) 231811
Visit the town, colliery village, farm, railway station, Pockerley Manor and 1825 railway, recreating life in the North East in the early 1800s and 1900s.

Otter Trust's North Pennines Reserve

Vale House Farm, Bowes, County Durham DL12 9RH
Tel: (01833) 628339
A branch of the famous Otter Trust. Visitors can see Asian and British otters, red and fallow deer and several rare breeds of farm animals in this 230-acre wildlife reserve.

Raby Castle

Staindrop, County Durham DL2 3AY
Tel: (01833) 660202
Medieval castle in 200-acre park. Includes a 600-year-old kitchen, carriage collection, walled gardens and deer park. Home of Lord Barnard's family for over 370 years.

Sea Life Aquarium

Long Sands, Tynemouth, Tyne & Wear NE30 4JF
Tel: (0191) 257 6100
More than 30 hi-tech displays provide encounters with dozens of sea creatures. Journey beneath the North Sea and discover thousands of amazing creatures.

South Shields Museum and Art Gallery

Ocean Road, South Shields, Tyne & Wear NE33 2JA
Tel: (0191) 456 8740
Galleries of Catherine Cookson memorabilia and local history. Also an exciting programme of exhibitions and events.

Thomas Bewick Birthplace Museum

Cherryburn, Mickley, Northumberland NE43 7DB
Tel: (01661) 843276
Birthplace cottage (1700) and farmyard. Printing house using original printing blocks. Introductory exhibition of the life, work and countryside.

Wallington House, Walled Garden and Grounds

Wallington Cambo, Morpeth,
Northumberland NE61 4AR
Tel: (01670) 774283
Built in 1688 on the site of an earlier medieval castle and altered in the 1740s. Interior has plasterwork, porcelain, furniture, pictures, needlework and a dolls house. Walled garden.

Washington Old Hall

Washington, Tyne & Wear NE38 7LE
Tel: (0191) 416 6879
The home of George Washington's ancestors, from 1183-1288, remaining in the family until 1613. The manor, from which the family took its name, was restored in 1936.

Wet 'N Wild

Royal Quays, North Shields NE29 6DA
Tel: (0191) 296 1333
Tropical indoor water park. A fun water playground providing the wildest and wettest indoor rapid experience. Whirlpools, slides and meandering lazy river.

Wildfowl and Wetlands Trust

Washington, Tyne & Wear NE38 8LE
Tel: (0191) 416 5454
Collection of 1,250 wildfowl of 108 varieties. Viewing gallery, picnic areas, hides and winter wild bird feeding station, flamingos and wild grey heron. Food available.

The Pictures:
1 Freeborough Hill, Cleveland;
2 Roseberry Topping, Northumberland;
3 Cragside Estate, nr. Rothbury, Northumberland;
4 Alnwick Castle, Northumberland;
5 Bamburgh, Northumberland.

Find out more about
NORTHUMBRIA ...

Further information about holidays and
attractions in Northumbria is available from:

NORTHUMBRIA TOURIST BOARD
Aykley Heads, Durham DH1 5UX.
Tel: (0191) 375 3000
Fax: (0191) 386 0899
Internet: www.ntb.org.uk

*The following publications are available free from the
Northumbria Tourist Board, unless otherwise stated:*

Northumbria 2000

*information on the region, including hotels, bed and
breakfast and self-catering accommodation, caravan
and camping parks, attractions, shopping, eating and
drinking*

North of England Bed & Breakfast Map

*value for money bed and breakfast accommodation in
Northumbria and Yorkshire*

Going Places

*information on where to go, what to see and what to
do. Combined with the award-winning Powerpass
promotion which offers 2-for-1 entry into many of the
region's top attractions*

Group Travel Directory

*guide designed specifically for group organisers,
detailing group accommodation providers, places to
visit, suggested itineraries, coaching information and
events*

Educational Visits

*information to help plan educational visits within the
region. Uncover a wide variety of places to visit with
unique learning opportunities*

Discover Northumbria on two wheels

*information on cycling in the region including an order
form allowing the reader to order maps/leaflets from a
central ordering point*

Freedom

*caravan and camping guide to the North of England.
Available from Freedom Holidays, tel: 01202 252179*

Getting to
NORTHUMBRIA ...

BY ROAD: The north/south routes on the A1 and A19 thread the region as does the
A68. East/west routes like the A66 and A69 easily link with the western side of the
country. Within Northumbria you will find fast, modern interconnecting roads between
all the main centres, a vast network of scenic, traffic-free country roads to make
motoring a pleasure and frequent local bus services operating to all towns and villages.

BY RAIL: London to Edinburgh InterCity service stops at Darlington, Durham,
Newcastle and Berwick upon Tweed. 26 trains daily make the journey between
London and Newcastle in just under 3 hours. The London to Middlesbrough journey
takes 3 hours. Birmingham to Darlington 3 hours 15 minutes. Bristol to Durham
5 hours and Sheffield to Newcastle just over 2 hours. Direct services operate to
Newcastle from Liverpool, Manchester, Glasgow, Stranraer and Carlisle. Regional
services to areas of scenic beauty operate frequently, allowing the traveller easy
access. The Tyne & Wear Metro makes it possible to travel to many destinations
within the Tyneside area, such as Gateshead, South Shields, Whitley Bay and
Newcastle International Airport, in minutes.

WHERE TO STAY (NORTHUMBRIA)

Parks in this region are listed in alphabetical order of place name, and then in alphabetical order of park.

Map references refer to the colour location maps at the back of this guide. The first number indicates the map to use; the letter and number which follow refer to the grid reference on the map.

At-a-glance symbols can be found inside the back cover flap.
Keep this open for easy reference.

BAMBURGH

Northumberland
Map ref 6C1

Village with a spectacular red sandstone castle standing 150 ft above the sea. On the village green the magnificent Norman church stands opposite a museum containing mementoes of the heroine Grace Darling.

Bradford Kaims Caravan Park ⚠

★★

Holiday, Touring and Camping Park
Bamburgh NE70 7JT
T: (01668) 213432 & 213595
F: (01668) 213891
Take the A1(M) north, turn right to Lucker and take the B1341 for 1 mile. Follow the signs. Signposted.
16 hectares (40 acres). Sheltered.
80 touring pitches.

80	🚐	£8.00—£10.00
80	🚙	£8.00—£10.00
80	⛺	£8.00—£10.00

270 units privately owned
Open March–November
Cards accepted: Amex, Barclaycard, Delta, Diners, Eurocard, Mastercard, Switch, Visa

IMPORTANT NOTE

Information on accommodation listed in this guide has been supplied by the proprietors. As changes may occur you are advised to check details at the time of booking.

Glororum Caravan Park ⚠

★★★

Holiday and Touring Park
Glororum, Bamburgh NE69 7AW
T: (01668) 214457 & 214205
F: (01668) 214622
From the A1 take the B1431 at Adderstone garage, signposted.
8 hectares (20 acres). Level, grassy, sheltered.
100 touring pitches.

100	🚐	£8.00—£9.00
100	🚙	£8.00—£9.00
	⛺	£8.00—£9.00

150 units privately owned
Open April–October

Waren Caravan Park ⚠

★★★★

Holiday, Touring and Camping Park
Rose Award
Member BH&HPA
Waren Mill, Belford NE70 7EE
T: (01668) 214366
F: (01668) 214224
E: enquiries@warencp.demon.co.uk
I: www.meadowhead.co.uk/waren
Follow A1 to Waren Mill towards Bamburgh. By Budle Bay turn right, follow Waren Caravan Park signs. Signposted.
40 hectares (100 acres). Level, sloping, grassy, sheltered.
180 touring pitches.

180	🚐	£8.00—£13.50
180	🚙	£8.00—£13.50
180	⛺	£8.00—£13.50
27	🏕	£160.00—£425.00

250 units privately owned
Open March–October
Cards accepted: Barclaycard, Delta, Maestro, Mastercard, Switch, Visa

BEADNELL

Northumberland
Map ref 6C1

Charming fishing village on Beadnell Bay. Seashore lime kilns (National Trust), dating from the 18th C, recall busier days as a coal and lime port and a pub is built on to a medieval pele tower which survives from days of the border wars.

Beadnell Links Caravan Park

★★★★

Holiday and Touring Park
Member BH&HPA
Beadnell Harbour, Beadnell, Chathill NE67 5BN
T: (01665) 720993 (Admin office)
E: jameshall@
beadnell.freeserve78.co.uk
I: www.ukparks.co.uk/beadnell
Follow roads B6347 or B1342 from A1. Signed thereafter.
4 hectares (10 acres). Level, grassy.
17 touring pitches.

17	🚐	£9.00—£15.00
17	🚙	£9.00—£15.00

150 units privately owned
Open April–October
Cards accepted: Barclaycard, Delta, Eurocard, JCB, Mastercard, Solo, Switch, Visa, Visa Electron

Star ratings were correct at the time of going to press but are subject to change.
Please check at the time of booking.

BEAL

Northumberland
Map ref 6B1

Tiny hamlet with an inn at the junction of the A1 which leads on to the causeway to Holy Island. Some farmhouses and buildings are dated 1674.

Haggerston Castle **
★★★★
Holiday and Touring Park
Rose Award
Member BH&HPA/NCC
Beal, Berwick-upon-Tweed
TD15 2PA
T: 0870 2425678
F: (01442) 254956
I: www.british-holidays.co.uk
The park is signposted from the A1, 7 miles south of Berwick-upon-Tweed. Situated just off the A1 between Edinburgh and Newcastle. Signposted.
80 hectares (200 acres). Level, grassy.
156 touring pitches.

156	🚐	£9.30—£26.00
156	🚛	£9.30—£26.00
574	🏠	£149.00—£639.00

415 units privately owned
Open April–October
Cards accepted: Amex, Barclaycard, Delta, Mastercard, Solo, Switch, Visa, Visa Electron
🚗 P ⌂ 🔧 🍴 🛁 🚿 🛒 🕙 🖃 ✕ 🍷
📺 🛋 🖥 ✉ 🍺 🌳 ⊙ 🔍 /ⅢΛ ♿ 🎿 🎣
🏹 ∪ 🔦 ▶ 🎵 🛎 ᴛ ᵂᴴ
Ad See display advertisement on page 10

BERWICK-UPON-TWEED

Northumberland
Map ref 6B1

Guarding the mouth of the Tweed, England's northernmost town with the best 16th C city walls in Europe. The handsome Guildhall and barracks date from the 18th C. Three bridges cross to Tweedmouth, the oldest built in 1634.
Tourist Information Centre
T: (01289) 330733

Berwick Holiday Centre **
★★★
Holiday Park
Member BH&HPA/NCC
Magdalene Fields, Berwick-upon-Tweed TD15 1NE
T: 0870 2425678
F: (01442) 254956
I: www.british-holidays.co.uk
From A1 north, exit off the 1st roundabout for Safeway and town centre. Straight forward to town for 0.5 miles. Over railway bridge, turn left, holiday centre at end of road. Same

directions from south once at Safeway. Signposted.
20 hectares (50 acres). Level, grassy, hard.

| 322 | 🏠 | £135.00—£552.00 |

451 units privately owned
Open April–October
Cards accepted: Barclaycard, Delta, Mastercard, Solo, Switch, Visa, Visa Electron
🚗 P ⌂ 🔧 🍴 🛁 🚿 🛒 🕙 🖃 ✕ 🍷
📺 🛋 🖥 ✉ 🍺 ⊙ 🔍 /ⅢΛ ᶠ 🎣
🎵 🛎 ᴛ ᵂᴴ
Ad See display advertisement on page 10

CASTLESIDE

Durham
Map ref 6B2

Village on the edge of the North Pennines on the A68, one of the main routes from England to Scotland.

Manor Park Caravan Park **
★★★★
Holiday, Touring and Camping Park
Member BH&HPA
Broadmeadows, Rippon Burn, Castleside, Consett, County Durham DH8 9HD
T: (01207) 501000
F: (01207) 509271
Just off A68, 2.5 miles south of Castleside and 5 miles north of Tow Law, signposted Broadmeadows. Signposted.
2.8 hectares (7 acres). Sloping, grassy, sheltered.
30 touring pitches.

30	🚐	£5.50—£7.00
7	🚛	£5.50—£7.00
5	🏕	£5.50—£7.00

Open April–October
🚗 P 🖃 🔧 🍴 🛁 🛒 🕙 🍺 ᶠ
🛁 ⊙ ᵂᴴ

GREENHEAD

Northumberland
Map ref 6B2

Small hamlet, overlooked by the ruins of Thirlwall Castle, at the junction of the A69 and the B6318 which runs alongside Hadrian's Wall. Some of the finest sections of the wall and the Carvoran Roman Military Museum are nearby.

Roam-n-Rest Caravan Park **
★★★
Touring and Camping Park
Raylton House, Greenhead
CA8 7HA
T: (016977) 47213
Leave the A69 at Greenhead jct and follow the short link road, turn direct

left up the hill. After 250m the park is on the right-hand side. Signposted.
.4 hectare (1 acre). Level, grassy, sheltered.
15 touring pitches.

15	🚐	£8.50—£9.00
15	🚛	£8.50—£9.00
15	🏕	£8.50—£9.00

Open March–October
🚗 P 🖃 🔧 🍴 🛁 🛒 🕙 ⊙ /ⅢΛ
▶ 🛁

HARTLEPOOL

Tees Valley
Map ref 6C2

Major industrial port north of Tees Bay. Occupying an ancient site, the town's buildings are predominantly modern. Local history can be followed in the Museum of Hartlepool and adjacent historic quay and there is a marina with restored ships.
Tourist Information Centre
T: (01429) 869706

Ash Vale Homes & Holiday Park **
★★
Holiday and Touring Park
Member BH&HPA
Easington Road, Hartlepool, Cleveland TS24 9RF
T: (01429) 862111
E: ashvale@compuserve.com
I: www.ashvalepark.demon.co.uk
From A19 take A179 at 3rd roundabout. Turn left onto A1086 towards Blackhall. Continue through next roundabout and the park is 300yds on left.
8 hectares (20 acres). Level, sloping, grassy.
20 touring pitches.

20	🚐	£6.00—£8.00
20	🚛	£6.00—£8.00
20	🏕	£3.00—£8.00
26	🏠	£80.00—£250.00

27 units privately owned
Open March–October
🚗 🖃 🔧 🍴 🛁 🛒 🕙 🍺 🛋 🖥 ᶠ
🛁 ⊙ /ⅢΛ 🛎 ᴛ

NEWTON-BY-THE-SEA

Northumberland
Map ref 6C1

Attractive hamlet at the south end of Beadnell Bay with a sandy beach and splendid view of Dunstanburgh Castle. In a designated Area of Outstanding Natural Beauty, Low Newton, part of the village, is now owned by the National Trust.

Newton Hall Caravan Park
★★★★
Holiday and Touring Park
Member BH&HPA
Newton Hall, Newton-by-the-Sea, Alnwick NE66 3DZ
T: (01665) 576239
F: (01665) 576239
E: patterson@
newtonhall.prestel.co.uk
I: www.commercepark.co.uk/
newtonhall
Turn off A1 trunk road, take the B1430 then the unclassified road to Newton-by-the-Sea. Signposted.
1.6 hectares (4 acres). Level, grassy, hard, sheltered.
15 touring pitches.

15	🚐	£9.00—£12.50
15	🚎	£9.00—£12.50

51 units privately owned
Open all year round
Cards accepted: Barclaycard, Delta, Eurocard, JCB, Mastercard, Switch, Visa, Visa Electron

OVINGHAM

Northumberland
Map ref 6B2

This quiet village on the north bank of the River Tyne and with a 17th C packhorse bridge was the birthplace of Thomas Bewick, the famous artist and engraver. Each June the villagers celebrate the traditional Goose Fair.

The High Hermitage Caravan Park
★★★
Holiday and Touring Park
Member BH&HPA
The Hermitage, Ovingham, Prudhoe NE42 6HH
T: (01661) 832250
F: (01661) 834848
Take Wylam exit on A69 west from Newcastle upon Tyne and take Ovingham Riverside Road from Wylam. Caravan park is 0.5 miles along on right. Signposted.
.6 hectare (1.5 acres). Sloping, grassy, hard, sheltered.
5 touring pitches.

5	🚐	£10.00—£10.00
5	🚎	£10.00—£10.00

28 units privately owned
Open April–October

SEAHOUSES

Northumberland
Map ref 6C1

Small modern resort developed around a 19th C herring port. Just offshore, and reached by boat from here, are the rocky Farne Islands (National Trust) where there is an important bird reserve. The bird observatory occupies a medieval pele tower.

Seafield Caravan Park
★★★★
Holiday and Touring Park
Rose Award
Member BH&HPA
Seafield Road, Seahouses NE68 7SP
T: (01665) 720628
F: (01665) 720088
E: info@
seafield-caravan.demon.co.uk
I: www.seafieldpark.co.uk
Take the B1340 from Alnwick for 14 miles. East to coast. Signposted.
8 hectares (20 acres). Level, grassy.
22 touring pitches.

22	🚐	£9.00—£18.00
22	🚎	£9.00—£18.00
9	🛏	£150.00—£450.00

202 units privately owned
Open March–December
Cards accepted: Barclaycard, Delta, Eurocard, JCB, Mastercard, Solo, Switch, Visa, Visa Electron

---

COUNTRY CODE

Always follow the Country Code 🌳 Enjoy the countryside and respect its life and work 🌳 Guard against all risk of fire 🌳 Fasten all gates 🌳 Keep your dogs under close control 🌳 Keep to public paths across farmland 🌳 Use gates and stiles to cross fences, hedges and walls 🌳 Leave livestock, crops and machinery alone 🌳 Take your litter home 🌳 Help to keep all water clean 🌳 Protect wildlife, plants and trees 🌳 Take special care on country roads 🌳 Make no unnecessary noise

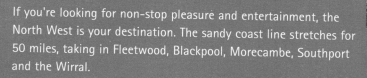

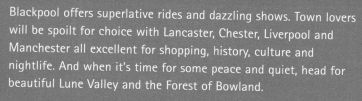

If you're looking for non-stop pleasure and entertainment, the North West is your destination. The sandy coast line stretches for 50 miles, taking in Fleetwood, Blackpool, Morecambe, Southport and the Wirral.

Blackpool offers superlative rides and dazzling shows. Town lovers will be spoilt for choice with Lancaster, Chester, Liverpool and Manchester all excellent for shopping, history, culture and nightlife. And when it's time for some peace and quiet, head for beautiful Lune Valley and the Forest of Bowland.

The annual Lancashire food festival in early March is an excellent opportunity to taste local delicacies, including Lancashire Hotpot and Black Pudding.

The counties of Cheshire, Greater Manchester, Lancashire, Merseyside and the High Peak District of Derbyshire

FOR MORE INFORMATION CONTACT:
North West Tourist Board
Swan House, Swan Meadow Road,
Wigan Pier, Wigan WN3 5BB
Tel: (01942) 821222
Fax: (01942) 820002
Internet: www.visitnorthwest.com

Where to Go in the North West - see pages 66-69
Where to Stay in the North West - see pages 70-71

The Pictures:
1 Blackpool Pleasure Beach;
2 Knowsley Safari Park, Merseyside;
3 Japanese Garden, Tatton Park.

Whilst in the
NORTH WEST ...

You will find hundreds of interesting places to visit during your stay, just some of which are listed in these pages.

Contact any Tourist Information Centre in the region for more ideas on days out in the North West.

Arley Hall and Gardens

Arley, Northwich, Cheshire CW9 6NA
Tel: (01565) 777353
Early Victorian building set in 12 acres of magnificent gardens. 15thC tithe barn and a unique collection of watercolours of the area.

Astley Hall Museum and Art Gallery

Astley Park, Chorley, Lancashire PR7 1NP
Tel: (01257) 515555
Dates from 1580 with subsequent additions. Unique collections of furniture including a fine Elizabethan bed and the famous Shovel Board Table.

The Beatles Story

Albert Dock, Liverpool, Merseyside L3 4AA
Tel: (0151) 709 1963
Liverpool's award-winning visitor attraction with a replica of the original Cavern Club. Available for private parties.

Beeston Castle

Beeston, Tarporley, Cheshire CW6 9TX
Tel: (01829) 260464
A ruined 13thC castle situated on top of the Peckforton Hills, with views of the surrounding countryside. Exhibitions are held featuring the castle's history.

Blackpool Sea Life Centre

The Promenade, Blackpool, Lancashire FY1 5AA
Tel: (01253) 622445
Tropical sharks up to 2.5m (8ft) in length housed in a 100,000-gallon water display, with an underwater walkway. The new 'Lost City of Atlantis' is back.

Blackpool Tower

The Promenade, Blackpool, Lancashire FY1 4BJ
Tel: (01253) 622242
Inside the Tower you will find the Tower Ballroom, a circus, entertainment for the children, the Tower Top Ride and Undersea World.

Boat Museum

Ellesmere Port, Cheshire CH5 4FW
Tel: (0151) 355 5017
Over 50 historic craft, the largest floating collection in the world. Restored buildings, traditional cottages, workshops, steam engines, boat trips, shop and cafe.

CATALYST: The Museum of the Chemical Industry

Widnes, Cheshire WA8 0DF
Tel: (0151) 420 1121
Catalyst is the award-winning family day out where science and technology come alive.

Chester Zoo

Upton-by-Chester, Cheshire CH2 1LH
Tel: (01244) 380280
One of Europe's leading conservation zoos with over 5,000 animals in spacious and natural enclosures. Now featuring the new 'Twilight Zone'.

Croxteth Hall and Country Park

Liverpool, Merseyside L12 0HB
Tel: (0151) 228 5311
An Edwardian stately home set in 500 acres of countryside (woodlands and pasture), featuring a Victorian walled garden and animal collection.

Dunham Massey Hall Park and Garden

Altrincham, Cheshire WA14 4SJ
Tel: (0161) 941 1025
An 18thC mansion in a 250-acre wooded deer park. Over 30 rooms open to the public. Collections of furniture, paintings and silver. Restaurant and shop.

East Lancashire Railway

Bury, Greater Manchester BL9 0EY
Tel: (0161) 764 7790
Thirteen kilometres (8 miles) of preserved railway operated principally by steam. Traction Transport Museum close by.

Frontierland Western Theme Park

Promenade, Morecambe, Lancashire LA4 4DG
Tel: (01524) 410024
Over 40 thrilling rides and attractions including the Texas Tornado, Polo Tower, Perculator and Stampede rollercoaster. The indoor Fun House complex features live shows in summer.

Gawsworth Hall

Gawsworth, Macclesfield, Cheshire SK11 9RN
Tel: (01260) 223456
Beautiful Tudor half-timbered manor-house with tilting ground. Pictures, sculpture and furniture on display. Open-air theatre.

Granada Studios

Water Street, Manchester M60 9EA
Tel: (0161) 832 9090
Europe's only major television theme park, providing a unique insight into the fascinating world behind the television screen.

Jodrell Bank Science Centre, Planetarium and Arboretum

Lower Withington, Macclesfield, Cheshire SK11 9DL
Tel: (01477) 571339
Exhibition and interactive exhibits on astronomy, space, energy and the environment. Planetarium and the world-famous Lovell telescope, plus a 35-acre arboretum.

Knowsley Safari Park

Prescot, Merseyside L34 4AN
Tel: (0151) 430 9009
An 8km (5 mile) safari through 500 acres of rolling countryside. See the world's wildest animals roaming free. Picnic area, shops, cafeteria.

Lady Lever Art Gallery

Port Sunlight Village, Higher Bebington, Wirral CH62 5EQ
Tel: (0151) 478 4136
The first Lord Leverhulme's magnificent collection of British paintings dated 1750-1900. British furniture, Wedgwood pottery and oriental porcelain.

Lancaster Castle

Shire Hall, Castle Parade, Lancaster, Lancashire LA1 1YJ
Tel: (01524) 64998
Shire Hall has a collection of coats of arms, a crown court, a grand jury room, a 'drop room' and dungeons. External tour of the castle.

Lyme Park

Disley, Stockport, Greater Manchester SK12 2NX
Tel: (01663) 762023
A National Trust country estate set in 1,377 acres of moorland, woodland and park. This magnificent house has 17 acres of historic gardens.

The Pictures:
1 Little Moreton, Congleton, Cheshire;
2 Bridgewater Hall, Manchester;
3 Peckforton, Cheshire;
4 Blackpool Beach;
5 Rural Cheshire, Marbury;
6 Liverpool Football Club Stadium.

Macclesfield Silk Museum

The Heritage Centre, Macclesfield, Cheshire SK11 6UT
Tel: (01625) 613210
Tells the story of the silk industry in Macclesfield. Features textiles, garments, models and room settings.

Merseyside Maritime Museum

Albert Dock, Liverpool, Merseyside L3 4AQ
Tel: (0151) 478 4499
Set in the heart of Liverpool's historic waterfront. The museum holds craft demonstrations, working displays and permanent galleries.

The Museum of Science & Industry in Manchester

Castlefield, Manchester M3 4FP
Tel: (0161) 832 2244
Based in the world's oldest passenger railway station with working exhibits which bring the past to life. The galleries will amaze, amuse and entertain.

Norton Priory Museum and Gardens

Runcorn, Cheshire WA7 1SX
Tel: (01928) 569895
Medieval priory remains, purpose-built museum, St Christopher's statue, sculpture trail and award-winning walled garden, all set in 39 acres of beautiful gardens.

Rufford Old Hall

Rufford, Ormskirk, Lancashire L40 1SG
Tel: (01704) 821254
One of the finest 16thC buildings in Lancashire with a magnificent hall, particularly noted for its immense moveable screen.

Southport Zoo and Conservation Park

Princes Park, Southport, Merseyside PR8 1RX
Tel: (01704) 538102
Lion, snow leopards, chimpanzees, monkeys, penguins, giant tortoise, reptile house, aquarium and much more. Snack bar, gift shop, picnic area.

Tate Gallery, Liverpool

Albert Dock, Liverpool, Merseyside L3 4BB
Tel: (0151) 702 7400
The National Collection of Modern Art is housed here in a converted warehouse.

Tatton Park

Knutsford, Cheshire WA16 6QN
Tel: (01625) 534400
Historic mansion with a 50-acre garden, traditional working farm, medieval manor-house and a 2,000 acre deer park. Sailing and outdoor centre, and an adventure playground.

Wigan Pier

Wallgate, Wigan, Lancashire WN3 4EF
Tel: (01942) 323666
Wigan Pier combines interaction with displays and reconstructions plus the Wigan Pier Theatre Company. Facilities include shops and a cafe.

Wildfowl and Wetland Trust

Martin Mere, Burscough, Lancashire L40 0TA
Tel: (01704) 895181
A 376-acre wild area, 20-acre lake and 45 acres of gardens. Rare and exotic ducks, geese, swans and flamingoes. Pantry, gift shop, art/craft gallery.

Find out more about the
NORTH WEST ...

Further information about holidays and attractions
in the North West is available from:

NORTH WEST TOURIST BOARD

Swan House, Swan Meadow Road, Wigan Pier, Wigan WN3 5BB.

Tel: (01942) 821222

Fax: (01942) 820002

Internet: www.visitnorthwest.com

The following publications are available free from the North West Tourist Board:

Best of the North West

*a guide to information on the region including hotels,
self-catering establishments, caravan and camping
parks. Also includes attractions, major events, shops
and restaurants*

Discovery Map

*a non-accommodation guide, A1 folded to A4 map
including list of visitor attractions, what to see and
where to go*

Bed and Breakfast Map

*forming part of a family of maps for England, this guide
provides information on bed and breakfast
establishments in the North West region*

Freedom

*forming part of a family of publications about caravan
and camping parks in the north of England*

Stay on a Farm

a guide to farm accommodation in the north of England

Group Travel Planner

*a guide to choosing the right accommodation,
attraction or venue for group organisers*

Venues

*a 6-monthly newsletter about conference venues in the
North West region*

Schools Out

*a 6-monthly newsletter aimed at schools providing
information about where to go and what to see*

The Pictures:
1 Healey Dell, Rochdale;
2 Pavilion Gardens,
   Buxton;
3 Bridgewater Canal,
   Manchester;
4 Lytham, Lancashire;
5 The Rows, Chester;
6 Barca Cafe Bar,
   Manchester;
7 Albert Dock, Liverpool.

Getting to the
NORTH WEST ...

BY ROAD:
Motorways intersect within the region which has the best road network in the
country. Travelling north or south use the M6 and east or west the M62.

BY RAIL:
Most North West coastal resorts are connected to InterCity routes with trains from
many parts of the country and there are through trains to major cities and towns.

WHERE TO STAY (NORTH WEST)

Parks in this region are listed in alphabetical order of place name,
and then in alphabetical order of park.

Map references refer to the colour location maps at the back of this guide.
The first number indicates the map to use; the letter and number which follow refer to the
grid reference on the map.

At-a-glance symbols can be found inside the back cover flap.
Keep this open for easy reference.

BLACKPOOL

Lancashire
Map ref 5A1

Britain's largest fun resort, with Blackpool Pleasure Beach, 3 piers and the famous Tower. Host to the spectacular autumn illuminations - "the greatest free show on earth".
Tourist Information Centre
T: (01253) 478222

Gillett Farm Caravan Park
★★★
Touring and Camping Park
Member BH&HPA
Peel Road, Peel, Blackpool,
Lancashire FY4 5JU
T: (01253) 761676
Exit the M55 at jct 4, turn left onto the A583, proceed for 0.25 miles. Turn right and immediate left onto Peel Road. Signposted.
4.4 hectares (11 acres). Sloping, grassy, hard.
76 touring pitches.

46	🚐	£8.25—£11.25
6	🚚	£8.25—£11.25
30	▲	£6.00—£8.25

100 units privately owned
Open March–October
Cards accepted: Barclaycard, Eurocard, Mastercard, Visa

Marton Mere Holiday Village ⚠
★★★★
Holiday and Touring Park
Member BH&HPA/NCC
Mythop Road, Blackpool FY4 4XN
T: 0870 2425678
F: (01442) 254956
Leave the M55 at jct 4, take the A583 to Blackpool. Turn right at the 2nd set of traffic lights into Mythop Road. The Park is 150 yards down on the left-hand side. Signposted.

37.2 hectares (93 acres). Level, grassy, stony, hard.
323 touring pitches.

323	🚐	£14.50—£27.00
323	🚚	£14.50—£27.00
110	🛖	£167.00—£673.00

852 units privately owned
Open March–October
Cards accepted: Barclaycard, Delta, Eurocard, Mastercard, Solo, Switch, Visa, Visa Electron

Ad See display advertisement on page 10

Newton Hall Caravan Park ⚠
★★★
Holiday and Touring Park
Staining Road, Staining, Blackpool
FY3 0AX
T: (01253) 882512 & 885465
F: (01253) 893101
E: parthols@netcomuk.co.uk
Leave the M55 at junction 4 onto the A583. Take the second set of lights, turn right onto Mythop Road. Take the first left onto Chain Lane. This leads to Staining Road. Newton Hall is on the left-hand side. Signposted.
11.2 hectares (28 acres). Level, sloping, grassy.
33 touring pitches.

33	🚐	£10.50—£15.50
33	🚚	£10.50—£15.50
45	🛖	£120.00—£410.00

380 units privately owned
Open March–October

For ideas on places to visit refer to the introduction at the beginning of this section.

CLEVELEYS

Lancashire
Map ref 5A1

Popular holiday resort on the Fylde coast close to Blackpool, with pleasant promenade, sandy beaches and shopping area. Close by, at Thornton, is a historic Marsh Windmill.
Tourist Information Centre
T: (01253) 853378

Kneps Farm Holiday Park ⚠
★★★★
Holiday, Touring and Camping Park
Member BH&HPA
River Road, Stanah, Cleveleys,
Blackpool FY5 5LR
T: (01253) 823632 (Answerphone)
F: (01253) 863967
I: www.kneps-farm.co.uk
Leave the A585 at the roundabout, turn right onto the B5412 signposted to Little Thornton. Turn right after the school onto Stanah Road leading to River Road. Signposted.
4 hectares (10 acres). Level, grassy, stony, hard, sheltered.
70 touring pitches.

45	🚐	£10.00—£12.50
10	🚚	£10.00—£12.50
15	▲	£10.00—£12.50
2	🛖	£175.00—£350.00

78 units privately owned
Open March–November
Cards accepted: Amex, Barclaycard, Delta, Diners, Eurocard, JCB, Mastercard, Solo, Switch, Visa, Visa Electron

Please check prices and other details at the time of booking.

FLEETWOOD

Lancashire
Map ref 5A1

Major fishing port and resort bounded by the sea on 3 sides. Fine sands, bathing and large model-yacht pond. Good views across Morecambe Bay and peaks of Lake District.
Tourist Information Centre
T: (01253) 773953

Cala Gran ⚑
★★★
Holiday Park
Member BH&HPA/NCC
Fleetwood Road, Fleetwood
FY7 8JX
T: (0870) 2425678
F: (01442) 254956
Exit the M55 at junction 3. Follow the A585 to Fleetwood. At the fourth roundabout take the third turning. The park is 500 yards down on the left-hand side. Signposted.
17.6 hectares (44 acres). Level, grassy.

300	🚐	£142.00—£607.00

540 units privately owned
Open March–November
Cards accepted: Barclaycard, Delta, Mastercard, Switch, Visa, Visa Electron

See display advertisement on page 10

LANCASTER

Lancashire
Map ref 6A3

Interesting old county town on the River Lune with history dating back to Roman times. Norman castle, St Mary's Church, Customs House, City and Maritime Museums, Ashton Memorial and Butterfly House are among places of note. Good centre for touring the Lake District.
Tourist Information Centre
T: (01524) 32878 or 792181 (M6 Bay Horse)

New Parkside Farm Caravan Park
★★★
Touring Park
Member BH&HPA
Denny Beck, Caton Road, Lancaster
LA2 9HH
T: (01524) 770723 & 770337
I: www.ukparks.co.uk/newparkside
Leave the M6 at jct 34 and go onto the A683 towards Caton and Kirkby Lonsdale, 1 mile from jct. Signposted.

1.6 hectares (4 acres). Level, sloping, grassy.
40 touring pitches.

40	🚐	£5.00—£8.00
10	🚖	£5.00—£8.00
15	⛺	£5.00—£8.00

Open March–October

LITTLEBOROUGH

Greater Manchester
Map ref 5B1

Attractive small town on the edge of the South Pennine Moors, with many historic buildings and industrial heritage features. Attractions include Hollingworth Lake, the Rochdale Canal and access to the Pennine Way.

Hollingworth Lake Caravan Park ⚑
★★★
Touring and Camping Park
Member BH&HPA
Rakewood, Littleborough, Lancashire OL15 0AT
T: (01706) 378661
Exit the M62 at jct 21. Follow Hollingworth Lake Country Park signs. Take Rakewood Road. Country Park signs. Signposted.
52 hectares (130 acres). Level, sloping, grassy, hard, sheltered.
45 touring pitches.

25	🚐	£8.00—£10.00
10	🚖	£6.00—£10.00
10	⛺	£5.00—£10.00
	🚐	£150.00—£350.00

40 units privately owned
Open all year round

LYTHAM ST ANNES

Lancashire
Map ref 5A1

Pleasant resort famous for its championship golf-courses, notably the Royal Lytham and St Annes. Fine sands and attractive gardens. Some half-timbered buildings and an old restored windmill.
Tourist Information Centre
T: (01253) 725610

Eastham Hall Caravan Park ⚑
★★
Holiday and Touring Park
Member BH&HPA
Saltcotes Road, Lytham St Annes
FY8 4LS
T: (01253) 737907

On the B5259, 1 mile north of A584 at Lytham. Signposted.
10 hectares (25 acres). Level, grassy, hard.
140 touring pitches.

140	🚐	£10.00—£11.50
20	🚖	£10.00—£11.50

290 units privately owned
Open March–October

WARRINGTON

Cheshire
Map ref 5A2

Has prehistoric and Roman origins. Once the "beer capital of Britain" because so much beer was brewed here. Developed in the 18th and 19th C as a commercial and industrial town. The cast-iron gates in front of the town hall were originally destined for Sandringham.
Tourist Information Centre
T: (01925) 442180 or 442146

Holly Bank Caravan Park ⚑
★★★★
Touring and Camping Park
Member BH&HPA
Warburton Bridge Road, Rixton, Warrington WA3 6HU
T: (0161) 775 2842
Two miles east of jct 21 off the M6 onto the A57 Irlam. Turn right at the lights onto Warburton Bridge Road. Entry to the site is on the left. Signposted.
3.2 hectares (8 acres). Level, grassy, hard, sheltered.
75 touring pitches.

50	🚐	£11.00—£13.00
10	🚖	£11.00—£13.00
15	⛺	£10.00—£12.00

Open all year round

For an explanation of the Quality Assurance Scheme, represented by Stars, please refer to the front of the guide.

DAVID BELLAMY CONSERVATION AWARDS

If you are looking for a site that's environmentally friendly look for those that have achieved the David Bellamy Conservation Award. Recently launched in conjunction with the British Holiday & Home Parks Association, this award is given to sites which are committed to protecting and enhancing the environment – from care of the hedgerows and wildlife to recycling waste – and are members of the Association. More information about this award scheme can be found at the front of the guide.

USE YOUR *i*s

There are more than 550 Tourist Information Centres throughout England offering friendly help with accommodation and holiday ideas as well as suggestions of places to visit and things to do. There may well be a centre in your home town which can help you before you set out. You'll find addresses in the local Phone Book.

Yorkshire

Yorkshire is the land of the white rose of England and traditional English fare - hearty roast beef and Yorkshire pudding. Boasting 1,000 square miles of National Parks, including the Dales, the Pennines and the northern Peak District, it's dotted with beauty spots.

Abbeys and castles, quiet country lanes and inns, coastline, museums, designer shopping, and café society, Yorkshire's got it all. Cruise the network of historic canals, and discover the industrial past at the National Coal Mining Museum in Wakefield, or Grimsby's National Fishing Heritage Centre.

The Egton Bridge Old Gooseberry Show on the first Tuesday in August is something different. It includes a competition to find the heaviest gooseberry.

The counties of
North, South, East and West Yorkshire and
Northern Lincolnshire

FOR MORE INFORMATION CONTACT:
Yorkshire Tourist Board
312 Tadcaster Road, York YO24 1GS
Tel: (01904) 707070 (24-hour brochure line)
Fax: (01904) 701414
Email: info@ytb.org.uk
Internet: www.yorkshirevisitor.com

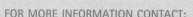

Where to Go in Yorkshire - see pages 74-77
Where to Stay in Yorkshire - see pages 78-82

The Pictures:
1 Hull Fair;
2 Castle Howard, North Yorkshire;
3 Spurn Lighthouse, Holderness.

Whilst in
YORKSHIRE ...

You will find hundreds of interesting places to visit during your stay, just some of which are listed in these pages.

Contact any Tourist Information Centre in the region for more ideas on days out in Yorkshire.

Bolton Abbey Estate

Bolton Abbey, Skipton, North Yorkshire BD23 6EX
Tel: (01756) 710533
Ruins of a 12thC priory in a park setting by the river Wharfe. Tearooms, nature trails, fishing, fell-walking and picturesque countryside.

Cusworth Hall Museum of South Yorkshire Life

Cusworth Hall, Doncaster, South Yorkshire DN5 7TU
Tel: (01302) 782342
Georgian mansion in landscaped park containing Museum of South Yorkshire Life. Special educational facilities.

Deep Sea Experience Centre

Cleethorpes, North East Lincolnshire DN35 8SE
Tel: (01472) 290220
Touch the rays, watch the sharks being fed and see fish from coastal waters. Dine in the famous Shark Bite Restaurant or stroll around Davy Jones' gift shop.

Elsham Hall Country & Wildlife Park

Elsham, Brigg, North Lincolnshire DN20 0QZ
Tel: (01652) 688698
Trout and carp lakes, wild butterfly garden walkway, animal farm, pets' corner, adventure playground, new falconry centre, craft centre, art gallery and shop.

Eureka! The Museum for Children

Discovery Road, Halifax, West Yorkshire HX1 2NE
Tel: (01422) 330069
Eureka! is the first museum of its kind designed especially for children up to the age of 12 with over 400 hands-on exhibits.

Flamingo Land Theme Park, Zoo and Holiday Village

Kirby, Malton, North Yorkshire YO17 6UX
Tel: (01653) 668287
One-price family funpark with over 100 attractions and 8 shows. Europe's largest privately-owned zoo and its only triple looping coaster!

Fountains Abbey and Studley Royal

Studley Park, Ripon, North Yorkshire HG4 3DY
Tel: (01765) 608888
Largest monastic ruin in Britain, founded by Cistercian monks in 1132. Landscaped garden laid between 1720-1740 with lake, formal water garden, temples and deer park.

Helmsley Castle

Helmsley, York YO62 5AB
Tel: (01439) 770442
The great ruined keep dominates the town. Other remains include a 16thC domestic range with original panelling and plasterwork. Spectacular earthwork defences.

Jorvik Viking Centre

Coppergate, York YO1 9WT
Tel: (01904) 643211
Travel back in time in a 'time car' to a recreation of Viking York. See excavated remains of Viking houses and a display of objects found.

Last of the Summer Wine Exhibition (Compo's House)

30 Huddersfield Road, Holmfirth, Huddersfield HD6 1JS
Tel: (01484) 681408
Collection of photographs and memorabilia connected with the television series 'Last of the Summer Wine'.

Leeds City Art Gallery

The Headrow, Leeds LS1 3AA
Tel: (0113) 247 8248
British paintings, sculptures, prints and drawings of the 19thC and 20thC. Henry Moore gallery with permanent collection of 20thC sculpture.

Life Force – The National Millennium Faith Experience

St Peter's House, 8 Petergate, Bradford BD1 1DN
Tel: (01274) 224540
A unique interactive experience exploring the faiths and beliefs of different cultures, and how they have influenced some of Bradford's famous people, including the Bronte sisters. Exciting restaurant serving international cuisine.

Lightwater Valley Theme Park

North Stainley, Ripon, North Yorkshire HG4 3HT
Tel: (01765) 635321
Set in 175 acres of parkland, Lightwater Valley features a number of white-knuckle rides and children's rides along with shopping malls, a restaurant and picnic areas.

Mother Shipton's Cave & the Petrifying Well

High Bridge, Knaresborough, North Yorkshire HG5 8DD
Tel: (01423) 864600
The oldest tourist attractions in Britain, opened in 1630. Cave, well, museum, playground and 12 acres of riverside grounds.

The Pictures:
1 North Yorkshire Moors, Westerdale;
2 Countryside near Grimsby;
3 Keighley and Worth Valley Railway;
4 Felixkirk, North Yorkshire Moors;
5 The Humber Bridge;
6 Victoria Quarter, Leeds;
7 Nora Batty's Cottage, Holmfirth;
8 Skidby Windmill.

National Fishing Heritage Centre

Alexandra Dock, Grimsby,
North East Lincolnshire DN31 1UZ
Tel: (01472) 323345
A journey of discovery, experience the reality of life on a deep-sea trawler. Interactive games and displays. Children's area.

National Museum of Photography, Film & Television

Bradford, West Yorkshire BD1 1NQ
Tel: (01274) 202030
This fascinating and innovative museum houses the three types of media that have transformed the 20thC. Includes galleries dedicated to digital imaging, news, light and magic.

National Railway Museum

Leeman Road, York YO26 4XJ
Tel: (01904) 621261
From rocket to Eurostar, from giants of the steam age to a miniature railway ride – discover it all in a fun-packed family day.

Newby Hall & Gardens

Ripon, Yorkshire HG4 5AE
Tel: (01423) 322583
Late 17thC house with additions. Exceptional interior by Robert Adam. Classical sculpture, Gobelins tapestries, 25 acres of gardens, miniature railway and children's adventure garden.

North Yorkshire Moors Railway

Pickering, North Yorkshire YO18 7AJ
Tel: (01751) 472508
Evening and Sunday lunchtime dining service trains offer a unique and nostalgic experience with a wonderful selection of menus to suit all tastes.

Nunnington Hall

Nunnington, York YO62 5UY
Tel: (01439) 748283
Large 17thC manor house situated on the banks of the river Rye. Hall, bedrooms, nursery, maid's room (haunted) and Carlisle collection of miniature rooms. National Trust shop.

Piece Hall

Halifax, West Yorkshire HX1 1RE
Tel: (01422) 358087
Built in 1779 and restored in 1976, this Grade I Listed building forms a unique and striking monument to the wealth and importance of the wool trade.

Pleasure Island Family Theme Park

Kings Road, Cleethorpes,
North East Lincolnshire DN35 0PL
Tel: (01472) 211511
The east coast's biggest fun day out, with over 50 rides and attractions. Whatever the weather, fun is guaranteed. Interactive play area, undercover attractions and shows from around the world.

Ripley Castle

Ripley, Harrogate, North Yorkshire HG3 3AY
Te: (01423) 770152
Home to the Ingilby family for over 26 generations. Set in the heart of a delightful estate with Victorian walled gardens, deer park and pleasure grounds.

Ryedale Folk Museum

Hutton-le-Hole, York YO62 6UA
Tel: (01751) 417367
Reconstructed local buildings including cruck-framed long houses, Elizabethan manor house, furnished cottages, craftsmen's tools, household and agricultural implements.

Sea Life Centre

Scalby Mills, Scarborough, North Yorkshire YO12 6RP
Tel: (01723) 376125
Meet creatures that live in and around the oceans of the British Isles, ranging from starfish and crabs to rays and seals.

Sheffield Botanical Gardens

Clarkehouse Road, Sheffield S10 2LN
Tel: (0114) 250 0500
Extensive gardens with over 5,500 species of plants. Landscape by Robert Marnock, famous 19thC landscape designer.

Skipton Castle

Skipton, North Yorkshire BD23 1AQ
Tel: (01756) 792442
One of the most complete and well-preserved medieval castles in England. Civil War royalist stronghold.

Wensleydale Cheese Visitor Centre

Gayle Lane, Hawes, North Yorkshire DL8 3RN
Tel: (01969) 667664
Museum, video and interpretation area, plus viewing gallery. Handmade Wensleydale cheese, licensed restaurant, specialist cheese shop, farm animals in a natural environment.

Wigfield Farm

Worsbrough Bridge, Barnsley, South Yorkshire S70 5NQ
Tel: (01226) 733702
Open working farm with rare and commercial breeds of farm animals including pigs, cattle, sheep, goats, donkeys, ponies, small animals, snakes and other reptiles.

York Minster

Deangate, York YO1 7HH
Tel: (01904) 557200
The largest medieval Gothic cathedral in England. Museum of Saxon and Norman remains. Chapter house. Unrivalled views from the tower.

Find out more about
YORKSHIRE ...

Further information about holidays and attractions in the Yorkshire region is available from:

YORKSHIRE TOURIST BOARD

312 Tadcaster Road, York YO24 1GS.
Tel: (01904) 707070 (24-hour brochure line)
Fax: (01904) 701414
Email: info@ytb.org.uk
Internet: www.yorkshirevisitor.com

The following publications are available free from the Yorkshire Tourist Board:

Yorkshire Visitor Guide 2001
information on the region, including hotels, self-catering, caravan and camping parks. Also attractions, shops, restaurants and major events

Yorkshire – A Great Day Out
non-accommodation A5 guide listing where to go, what to see and where to eat, the list goes on! Including map

Bed & Breakfast Touring Map
forming part of a 'family' of maps covering England, this guide provides information on bed and breakfast establishments in the Yorkshire and Northumbria regions

What's On
listing of events. Published three times a year

Stay on a Farm in the North of England
farm holiday accommodation in the North of England

Freedom
caravan and camping guide to the North of England

Group Operators' Guide 2001
a guide to choosing the right venue for travel trade and group organisers including hotels, attractions and unusual venues

Conference and Venue Guide 2001
a full-colour, comprehensive guide to conference facilities in the region

The Pictures:
1 North Yorkshire Moors, Railway Steam Train;
2 Worsbrough Mill Museum, South Yorkshire;
3 York Minster;
4 Thixendale in the Wolds, East Yorkshire;
5 The beach at Bridlington, East Riding of Yorkshire;
6 Low Petergate and Minster Towers, York;
7 The Mills at Luddenden;
8 Flamborough, East Riding of Yorkshire.

Getting to
YORKSHIRE ...

BY ROAD: Motorways: M1, M62, M606, M621, M18, M180, M181, A1(M). Trunk roads: A1, A19, A57, A58, A59, A61, A62, A63, A64, A65, A66.

BY RAIL: InterCity services to Bradford, Doncaster, Harrogate, Kingston upon Hull, Leeds, Sheffield, Wakefield and York. Frequent regional railway services city centre to city centre including Manchester Airport service to Scarborough, York and Leeds.

WHERE TO STAY (YORKSHIRE)

Parks in this region are listed in alphabetical order of place name, and then in alphabetical order of park.

Map references refer to the colour location maps at the back of this guide. The first number indicates the map to use; the letter and number which follow refer to the grid reference on the map.

At-a-glance symbols can be found inside the back cover flap. Keep this open for easy reference.

BEDALE

North Yorkshire
Map ref 6C3

Ancient church of St Gregory and Georgian Bedale Hall occupy commanding positions over this market town situated in good hunting country. The hall, which contains interesting architectural features including great ballroom and flying-type staircase, now houses a library and museum.

Pembroke Caravan Park ▲▲
★★★★
Touring and Camping Park
19 Low Street, Leeming Bar, Northallerton DL7 9BW
T: (01677) 422608 & 422652
One mile from the A1 and 0.5 miles from the A684. Signposted.
.6 hectare (1.5 acres). Grassy, sheltered.
25 touring pitches.

25	🚐	£6.00—£7.00
25	🚍	£6.00—£7.00
25	▲	£5.00—£6.00
	🏕	£80.00—£120.00

Open March—October

🛒 P 🏪 🌳 🛡 🍴 🎱 🛍 🕓
⛰ 🛟

WELCOME HOST
This is a nationally recognised customer care programme which aims to promote the highest standards of service and a warm welcome. Parks taking part in this initiative are indicated by the WH symbol.

FILEY

North Yorkshire
Map ref 6D3

Resort with elegant Regency buildings along the front and 6 miles of sandy beaches bounded by natural breakwater, Filey Brigg. Starting point of the Cleveland Way. St Oswald's church, overlooking a ravine, belonged to Augustinian canons until the Dissolution.

Orchard Farm Holiday Village ▲▲
★★★★★
Holiday, Touring and Camping Park
Stonegate, Hunmanby, Filey
YO14 0PU
T: (01723) 891582
F: (01723) 891582
Take A165 Scarborough/Bridlington road. Two miles from Filey. Signpost to Hunmanby, site is 1.5 miles down road. Signposted.
5.6 hectares (14 acres). Level, grassy, hard, sheltered.
85 touring pitches.

60	🚐	£7.00—£10.00
60	🚍	£7.00—£10.00
25	▲	£7.00—£10.00

Open all year round

🛒 P 🏪 🌳 🛡 🍴 🎱 🛍 🍴
📺 🛍 💈 🛟 🎡 ⛰ 🎣 🏊 ↻
🎵 🎶 🎱 T

The symbols in each entry give information about services and facilities. A key to these symbols appears at the back of this guide.

FLAMBOROUGH

East Riding of Yorkshire
Map ref 6D3

Village with strong seafaring tradition, high on chalk headland dominated by cliffs of Flamborough Head, a fortress for over 2000 years. St Oswald's Church is in the oldest part of Flamborough. A nature trail follows the Iron Age earthworks known as Danes Dyke.

Thornwick & Sea Farm Holiday Centre ▲▲
★★★★
Holiday, Touring and Camping Park
Member BH&HPA
Flamborough Holidays Ltd,
Flamborough, Bridlington, East Riding of Yorkshire YO15 1AU
T: (01262) 850369 & 850372
F: (01262) 851550
E: enquiries@thornwickbay.co.uk
I: www.thornwickbay.co.uk
Follow the B1255 from Bridlington to Flamborough, the park is approximately 1 mile farther towards North Landing. Signposted.
32 hectares (80 acres). Level, sloping, grassy, hard.
200 touring pitches.

200	🚐	£8.00—£12.50
	🚍	£8.00—£10.50
100	▲	£8.00—£10.50
70	🏕	£120.00—£340.00

1000 units privately owned
Open March—October
Cards accepted: Amex, Barclaycard, Delta, JCB, Mastercard, Switch, Visa

🍴 🛒 P 🏪 🌳 🛡 🍴 🎱 🛍 ✕ 🍴
📺 🛍 💈 🛟 🎡 ⛰ 🎣 🎵 🎱
T

Please mention this guide when making your booking.

HARROGATE

North Yorkshire
Map ref 5B1

Major conference, exhibition and shopping centre, renowned for its spa heritage and award-winning floral displays, spacious parks and gardens. Famous for antiques, toffee, fine shopping and excellent tea shops, also its Royal Pump Rooms and Baths. Annual Great Yorkshire Show in July.
Tourist Information Centre
T: (01423) 537300

Rudding Holiday Park ⚠
★ ★ ★ ★ ★
Holiday, Touring and Camping Park
Rose Award
Member BH&HPA
Rudding Park, Follifoot, Harrogate
HG3 1JH
T: (01423) 870439
F: (01423) 870859
E: hpreception@rudding-park.co.uk
I: www.rudding-park.co.uk
Three miles south of Harrogate, to the north of the A658 between its jct with the A61 to Leeds and the A661 to Wetherby. Signposted.
12 hectares (30 acres). Level, sloping, grassy, hard, sheltered.
141 touring pitches.

141	🚐	£10.00—£22.00
141	🚙	£10.00—£22.00
141	⛺	£7.50—£10.50

90 units privately owned
Open March—October
Cards accepted: Barclaycard, Delta, Mastercard, Solo, Switch, Visa

🔌🚗Ｐ🔲📶🏠🔥🛁🍴♿📞⛽
✕🍽📠🚫♿☉🔍⛰🔌U📍
🅐 Ｔ ᴴ

HATFIELD

South Yorkshire
Map ref 5C1

Hatfield Water Park ⚠
★ ★ ★ ★
Touring Park
Hatfield, Doncaster DN7 6EQ
T: (01302) 841572
F: (01302) 846368
Leave the M18 at jct 5. From M180, 1st jct onto A18. Signposted.
4 hectares (10 acres). Level, grassy, sheltered.
75 touring pitches.

75	🚐	£6.80
75	🚙	£6.80
75	⛺	£4.00

Open all year round

🚗Ｐ🔲📶🏠🔥🛁🍴✕🚫♿☉
⛰🔍✕🔥🔌☉

HELMSLEY

North Yorkshire
Map ref 6C3

Delightful small market town with red roofs, warm stone buildings and cobbled market square, on the River Rye at the entrance to Ryedale and the North York Moors. Remains of 12th C castle, several inns and All Saints' Church.

Foxholme Touring Caravan Park ⚠
★ ★ ★ ★ ★
Touring and Camping Park
Member BH&HPA
Harome, York YO62 5JG
T: (01439) 770416 & 771696
F: (01439) 771744
Leave Helmsley on the A170 in the direction of Scarborough. After 0.5 miles turn right for Harome. Turn left at the church, through the village and then follow the caravan signs. Signposted.
2.4 hectares (6 acres). Level, grassy, sheltered.
60 touring pitches.

60	🚐	£7.00—£7.50
60	🚙	£7.00—£7.50
60	⛺	£7.00—£7.50

Open March—October
Ｐ🔲📶🏠🔥🛁🔥📞📠📠🔌🚫🔌
☉🅐

Golden Square Caravan and Camping Park ⚠
★ ★ ★ ★ ★
Touring and Camping Park
Member BH&HPA
Oswaldkirk, York YO62 5YQ
T: (01439) 788269
F: (01439) 788236
E: barbara@goldensquarecaravanpark.com
I: www.goldensquare caravanpark.com
From Helmsley A170 to Thirsk take the 1st left onto the B1257 to York. Take the 1st right to Ampleforth and the turning is after 0.5 miles on the right. Signposted.
4 hectares (10 acres). Level, grassy, hard, sheltered.
129 touring pitches.

129	🚐	£6.50—£9.00
129	🚙	
129	⛺	

Open March—October
🔌🚗🔲📶🏠🔥🛁🔥📞⛽📶
🔲🚫🔌☉🔍⛰🚲U🅐Ｔ

All accommodation in this guide has been rated, or is awaiting a rating, by a trained Tourist Board assessor.

HOLMFIRTH

West Yorkshire
Map ref 5B1

Village on the edge of the Peak District National Park, famous as the location for the filming of the TV series "Last of the Summer Wine".
Tourist Information Centre
T: (01484) 222444

Holme Valley Camping and Caravan Park ⚠
★ ★ ★ ★
Touring and Camping Park
Member BH&HPA
Thongsbridge, Holmfirth, Huddersfield HD7 2TD
T: (01484) 665819
F: (01484) 663870
E: pmpeaker@hotmail.com
I: www.holme-valley.co.uk
The entrance to our lane is off the A6024, 0.5 miles south of Huddersfield. One mile north of Holmfirth, halfway between Honley and Holmfirth. Signposted.
1.6 hectares (4 acres). Level, grassy, stony, hard, sheltered.
59 touring pitches.

59	🚐	£7.50—£9.00
59	🚙	£6.50—£8.00
59	⛺	£6.50—£8.00
3	🏠	£90.00—£180.00

Open all year round
Cards accepted: Amex, Barclaycard, Delta, Maestro, Mastercard, Solo, Switch, Visa, Visa Electron

🚗Ｐ📶🏠🔥🛁🔥📞♿🔲📠🔌
🔌☉⛰U🔍🅐 ᴴ

HORSFORTH

West Yorkshire
Map ref 5B1

St Helena's Caravan Site ⚠
★ ★ ★ ★
Touring and Camping Park
Member BH&HPA
Wardens Bungalow, Otley Old Road, Horsforth, Leeds LS18 5HZ
T: (0113) 284 1142
Follow the A65 to the A658 past the airport to Carlton crossroads, then turn right at sign for Cookridge and Horsforth down Otley Old Road for 0.75 miles. Signposted.
4.8 hectares (12 acres). Level, grassy, hard, sheltered.
60 touring pitches.

40	🚐	£6.00—£8.00
10	🚙	£6.00—£8.00
10	⛺	£5.00—£5.00

40 units privately owned
Open all year round

🚗🔲📶🏠🔥🛁🔥📶🔲🔌🔌☉🅐

HUMBERSTON

North East Lincolnshire
Map ref 5D1

Thorpe Park Holiday Centre ⚏

★★★

Holiday, Touring and Camping Park
Member BH&HPA/NCC
Cleethorpes, North East
Lincolnshire DN36 4HG
T: 0870 2425678
F: (01442) 254956
I: www.british-holidays.co.uk
*Leave the M180 to A180 and follow
signs for holiday parks. Signposted.*
104 hectares (260 acres). Level,
grassy.
99 touring pitches.

40	🚐	£7.30—£26.00
99	🚛	£7.30—£26.00
120	⛺	£139.00—£583.00

2350 units privately owned
Open March—October
Cards accepted: Amex, Barclaycard,
Delta, Eurocard, Mastercard, Solo,
Switch, Visa

🚗 P 🅿 🐕 🦽 🛁 🍴 🛒 ✕ 🍽
🔲 🚿 🛢 ☺ ⚓ ⛰ ♨ ⛵ ∪ ⚲ ♪
♫ ⚘ Ⓣ ᵂᴴ
[Ad] See display advertisement on
page 10

MASHAM

North Yorkshire
Map ref 6C3

Famous market town on the River
Ure, with a large market square. St
Mary's Church has Norman tower
and 13th C spire. Theakston's "Old
Peculier" ale is brewed here, also
home of the Black Sheep Brewery.
Druids Temple, a replica of
Stonehenge.

Black Swan Caravan & Campsite ⚏

★★★

Touring Park
Member BH&HPA
Rear Black Swan Hotel, Fearby,
Ripon HG4 4NF
T: (01765) 689477
F: (01765) 689477
*The park is 2 miles from Masham on
left at rear of Black Swan Hotel.
Signposted.*
1.2 hectares (3 acres). Level,
sheltered.
47 touring pitches.

47	🚐	£9.00—£10.00
47	🚛	£9.00—£10.00
47	⛺	£8.00—£10.00
2	⛺	£95.00—£195.00

Open March—October

Cards accepted: Barclaycard, JCB,
Mastercard, Switch, Visa

🚗 🅿 P 🔲 🚿 🐕 🦽 🛁 🍴 🛒
✕ 🍽 📺 🈺 🔲 🚿 ⚓ 🛢 ☺ ⚓ ⛰ ∪ ⛵
♫ ⚘ Ⓣ

PICKERING

North Yorkshire
Map ref 6D3

Market town and tourist centre on
edge of North York Moors. Parish
church has complete set of 15th C
wall paintings depicting lives of
saints. Part of 12th C castle still
stands. Beck Isle Museum. The
North York Moors Railway begins
here.
Tourist Information Centre
T: (01751) 473791

Wayside Caravan Park ⚏

★★★★

Holiday, Touring and Camping Park
Member BH&HPA
Wrelton, Pickering YO18 8PG
T: (01751) 472608
F: (01751) 472608
E: waysideparks@talk21.com
I: www.waysideparks.co.uk
*Situated 2.5 miles west of Pickering,
250yds off the A170 by the village of
Wrelton. For correct turning watch for
signs. Signposted.*
4 hectares (10 acres). Level, grassy,
sheltered.
72 touring pitches.

40	🚐	£8.50
5	🚛	£8.00
32	⛺	£8.00

80 units privately owned
Open March—September
Cards accepted: Barclaycard, Delta,
JCB, Mastercard, Solo, Switch, Visa

P 🔲 🈺 🐕 🦽 🛁 🍴 🛒 🚿 🔲 🚿
🛢 ☺ ∪ ⛵ ✕ ⚘

ROOS

East Riding of Yorkshire
Map ref 5D1

Sand-le-Mere Caravan & Leisure Park ⚏

★★★

Holiday, Touring and Camping Park
Seaside Lane, Tunstall, Roos, Hull
East Yorkshire HU12 0JQ
T: (01964) 670403 & 0800 068 0407
F: (01964) 671099
E: info@sand-le-mere.co.uk
I: www.sand-le-mere.co.uk
*From Hull to Hedon take the B1362 at
Withernsea, B1242 to Roos. Look for
brown signs marked Sand-le-Mere.
Level, grassy.*
50 touring pitches.

40	🚐	£8.00—£14.00
10	🚛	£8.00—£14.00
	⛺	£8.00—£14.00
20	⛺	£100.00—£300.00

400 units privately owned
Open March—December
Cards accepted: Delta, Maestro,
Mastercard, Solo, Switch, Visa, Visa
Electron

🚗 P 🈺 🐕 🦽 🛁 🍴 🛒 ✕ 🍽
📺 🔲 🚿 🛢 ☺ ⚓ ⛰ ♨ ∪ ⛵ ⚲
⛵ ♫ ⚘

SCARBOROUGH

North Yorkshire
Map ref 6D3

Large, popular East Coast seaside
resort, formerly a spa town.
Beautiful gardens and two splendid
sandy beaches. Castle ruins date
from 1100; fine Georgian and
Victorian houses. Scarborough
Millennium depicts 1,000 years of
town's history. Sea Life Centre.
Tourist Information Centre
T: (01723) 373333

Cayton Village Caravan Park ⚏

★★★★

Touring and Camping Park
Member BH&HPA
D16 Mill Lane, Cayton Bay,
Scarborough YO11 3NN
T: (01723) 583171 & (01904)
624630 (Winter only)
*From the A64 take the B1261
signposted Filey. In Cayton village turn
2nd left after Blacksmiths Arms onto
Mill Lane. The Park is 200yds on left.
Or, from A165 turn inland at Cayton
Bay, onto Mill Lane at lights, on right.
Signposted.*
4.4 hectares (11 acres). Level,
grassy, hard, sheltered.
200 touring pitches.

125	🚐	£6.00—£10.00
125	🚛	£6.00—£10.00
75	⛺	£6.00—£10.00

Open March—October

🚗 P 🔲 🈺 🐕 🦽 🛁 🍴 🛒 🔲 🚿
🚿 🛢 ☺ ⛰ ⛺ ᵂᴴ

SLINGSBY

North Yorkshire
Map ref 6C3

Large, attractive village with ruined
castle and village green, on Castle
Howard estate.

Robin Hood Caravan & Camping Park ⚏

★★★★

Holiday, Touring and Camping Park
Green Dyke Lane, Slingsby, York
YO62 4AP
T: (01653) 628391
F: (01656) 628391
E: rebeccapalmer@tesco.net
*The caravan park is situated on the
edge of the village of Slingsby, with*

access off the B1257 Malton to Helmsley road. Signposted.
1.4 hectares (3.5 acres). Level, grassy, hard, sheltered.
39 touring pitches.

39	🚐	£9.00—£15.00
39	🚏	£9.00—£15.00
39	⛺	£9.00—£15.00
7	🏠	£160.00—£400.00

Open March–October

🚗🚐🔌📻🍴🔥🍳🛁⚡📺 ⚡🔌☉⛰️↻🔍⚓

THIRSK

North Yorkshire
Map ref 6C3

Thriving market town with cobbled square surrounded by old shops and inns. St Mary's Church is probably the best example of Perpendicular work in Yorkshire. House of Thomas Lord - founder of Lord's Cricket Ground - is now a folk museum.

Quernhow Caravan & Campsite
★★★

Holiday, Touring and Camping Park
Member BH&HPA
Great North Road, Sinderby, Thirsk
YO7 4LG
T: (01845) 567221
Adjacent to the A1 northbound. Three miles north of the jct of the A1 and the A61. Signposted.
1.6 hectares (4 acres). Level, grassy.
40 touring pitches.

30	🚐	£7.50—£9.00
5	🚏	£6.50—£8.00
5	⛺	£6.50—£8.00
	🏠	£145.00—£185.00

Open all year round

🔥🚗🔌📻🍳🛁⚡🔥🗙⚡🛁 ☉🔍⛰️🔍⚓

WELCOME HOST

This is a nationally recognised customer care programme which aims to promote the highest standards of service and a warm welcome. Parks taking part in this initiative are indicated by the [WH] symbol.

All accommodation in this guide has been rated, or is awaiting a rating, by a trained Tourist Board assessor.

WAKEFIELD

West Yorkshire
Map ref 5B1

Thriving city with cathedral church of All Saints boasting 247-ft spire. Old Bridge, a 9-arched structure, has fine medieval chantry chapels of St Mary's. Fine Georgian architecture and good shopping centre (The Ridings). National Coal Mining Museum for England nearby.
Tourist Information Centre
T: (01924) 305000 or 305001

Nostell Priory Holiday Home Park
★★★★

Holiday, Touring and Camping Park
Member BH&HPA
Top Park Wood, Nostell, Wakefield
WF4 1QD
T: (01924) 863938
F: (010924) 862226
Five miles east of Wakefield on A638 Doncaster road. Signposted.
12.4 hectares (31 acres). Level, grassy, hard, sheltered.
60 touring pitches.

60	🚐	£8.00—£8.50
7	🚏	£8.00—£8.50
60	⛺	£8.00—£8.50
5	🏠	£140.00—£245.00

75 units privately owned
Open March–October

🚗🅿️🔌📻🍳🛁⚡🔥⚡📺 ☉⛰️🔍⚓

WHITBY

North Yorkshire
Map ref 6D3

Quaint holiday town with narrow streets and steep alleys at the mouth of the River Esk. Captain James Cook, the famous navigator, lived in Grape Lane. 199 steps lead to St Mary's Church and St Hilda's Abbey overlooking harbour. Dracula connections. Gothic weekend every April.
Tourist Information Centre
T: (01947) 602674

Flask Holiday Home Park
★★★★

Holiday Park
Rose Award
Member BH&HPA
Robin Hoods Bay, Fylingdales, Whitby, North Yorkshire
YO22 4QH
T: (01947) 880592
F: (01947) 880592
E: flaskinn@aol.com
I: www.ukparks.com.co.uk/flask
Situated on the A171, 7 miles to Whitby and 12 miles to Scarborough. Signposted.
2.8 hectares (7 acres). Grassy.

| 10 | 🏠 | £150.00—£300.00 |

42 units privately owned
Open March–October
Cards accepted: Barclaycard, Mastercard, Switch, Visa, Visa Electron

🚗🅿️🔌📻🍳🛁⚡🍴🗙⚡🍽️📺⚡🛁 ☉⛰️↻🌀⚓

Middlewood Farm Holiday Park
★★★★★

Holiday, Touring and Camping Park
Rose Award
Member BH&HPA
Middlewood Lane, Fylingthorpe, Whitby, North Yorkshire
YO22 4UF
T: (01947) 880414
F: (01947) 880414
E: info@ middlewoodfarm.fsnet.co.uk
I: www.middlewoodfarm.fsnet.co.uk
From Scarborough take the A171, turn right for Fylingthorpe and right after the 30mph sign. Right again into Middlewood Lane. From Whitby take the A171 then the B1447 through Fylingthorpe onto Middlewood Lane. Park 500m on the left. Signposted.
2.8 hectares (7 acres). Level, grassy, hard, sheltered.
50 touring pitches.

20	🚐	£6.50—£10.50
50	🚏	£6.50—£10.50
50	⛺	£6.50—£10.50
30	🏠	£109.00—£417.00

Open March–December
Cards accepted: Barclaycard, Delta, Mastercard, Solo, Switch, Visa, Visa Electron

🚗🔌📻🍳🛁⚡🔥📺⚡🛁 ☉⛰️[WH]

Northcliffe Holiday Park
★★★★★

Holiday, Touring and Camping Park
Rose Award
Member BH&HPA
Bottoms Lane, High Hawsker, Whitby, North Yorkshire YO22 4LL
T: (01947) 880477 (Answerphone/ evenings)
F: (01947) 880972
E: enquiries@northcliffe.com
I: www.northcliffe.com
Three miles south from Whitby. Turn left onto the B1447 to Robin Hood's Bay. Through Hawsker village. Go left at the top of the hill at the Park sign. Follow the private road for 0.5 miles. Signposted.
10.4 hectares (26 acres). Level, grassy, hard.
30 touring pitches.

30	🚐	£6.00—£11.00
30	🚏	£6.00—£11.00
30	⛺	£6.00—£11.00
14	🏠	£140.00—£399.00

151 units privately owned
Open all year round

Continued ▶

WHITBY
Continued

Cards accepted: Barclaycard, Delta, Eurocard, JCB, Mastercard, Solo, Switch, Visa, Visa Electron

Partridge Nest Farm
★★★
Holiday Park
Eskdaleside, Sleights, Whitby, North Yorkshire YO22 5ES
T: (01947) 810450 & 811412
F: (01947) 811413
E: pnfarm@aol.com
I: www.tmis.uk.com/partridge-nest/
Travel along A169 Pickering to Sleights road. At Sleights take the Grosmont and North York Moors Railway sign at the bottom of bank. On to Eskdale. Follow road for 1.5 miles, farm is on the left.
18 hectares (45 acres). Sloping, grassy, sheltered.

6	🏕	£130.00—£255.00

Open January–October

YORK
North Yorkshire
Map ref 5C1

Ancient walled city nearly 2000 years old, containing many well-preserved medieval buildings. Its Minster has over 100 stained glass windows and is the largest Gothic cathedral in England. Attractions include Castle Museum, National Railway Museum, Jorvik Viking Centre and York Dungeon.
Tourist Information Centre
T: (01904) 621756 or 554488

Alders Caravan Park
★★★★★
Touring Park
Home Farm, Alne, York YO61 1TB
T: (01347) 838722
F: (01347) 838722
Situated 2 miles west of the A19 and 9 miles north of York. In the centre of the village. Signposted.
152 hectares (380 acres). Level, grassy, hard.
40 touring pitches.

40	🚐	£6.75—£9.50
40	🚎	£6.75—£8.50
	⛺	£6.50

Open March–October

You are advised to confirm your booking in writing.

Allerton Park Caravan Park
★★★★★
Holiday, Touring and Camping Park
Rose Award
Member BH&HPA
Allerton Park, Knaresborough, North Yorkshire HG5 0SE
T: (01423) 330569
F: (01759) 371377
Site is 0.25 miles east of the A1(M) leading from the A59 York to Harrogate road. Signposted.
4.8 hectares (12 acres). Level, grassy, hard, sheltered.
45 touring pitches.

45	🚐	£8.50—£11.00
45	🚎	£8.50—£11.00
45	⛺	£8.50—£11.00
5	🏕	£190.00—£490.00

100 units privately owned
Open February–December

Cawood Holiday Park
★★★★★
Holiday, Touring and Camping Park
Member BH&HPA
Ryther Road, Cawood, Selby, North Yorkshire YO8 3TT
T: (01757) 268450
F: (01757) 268537
Take the B1222 from the A1 or York and turn at Cawood traffic lights onto the B1223, signposted Tadcaster. Site is 1 mile farther on. Signposted.
3.6 hectares (9 acres). Level, grassy, hard, sheltered.
57 touring pitches.

57	🚐	£8.50—£12.00
57	🚎	£8.50—£12.00
57	⛺	£8.50—£12.00
4	🏕	£165.00—£395.00

Open January, March–December
Cards accepted: Amex, Barclaycard, Delta, Diners, Eurocard, JCB, Maestro, Mastercard, Solo, Switch, Visa, Visa Electron

Goosewood Caravan Park
★★★★★
Touring Park
Member BH&HPA
Sutton-on-the-Forest, York YO61 1ET
T: (01347) 810829
From the A1237 take the B1363 signed Helmsley. Past Haxby and Wigginton and take next right and follow signs.

Map references apply to the colour maps at the back of this guide.

8 hectares (20 acres). Level, grassy, hard, sheltered.
75 touring pitches.

75	🚐	£9.00—£11.00
75	🚎	£9.00—£11.00

Open March–October

Mount Pleasant Holiday Park and Park Home Estate
★★★
Holiday, Touring and Camping Park
Member BH&HPA
Acaster Malbis, York YO23 2UA
T: (01904) 707078 & 700088
F: (01904) 700888
E: mountpleasant.york@virgin.net
I: www.holgates.com
Exit A64 at the A1036. Go straight through lights towards Bishopthorpe. turn right at T-junction then left at next T-junction and left again. Signposted.
7.2 hectares (18 acres). Level, grassy.
49 touring pitches.

40	🚐	£8.50—£11.00
40	🚎	£8.50—£11.00
20	⛺	£8.50—£11.00
20	🏕	£110.00—£400.00

84 units privately owned
Open all year round
Cards accepted: Barclaycard, Delta, Eurocard, Mastercard, Solo, Switch, Visa

Weir Caravan Park
★★★★★
Holiday, Touring and Camping Park
Rose Award
Member BH&HPA
Stamford Bridge, York YO41 1AN
T: (01759) 371377
F: (01759) 371377
From York on the A166 turn left before bridge. Signposted.
3.2 hectares (8 acres). Level, grassy, hard.
67 touring pitches.

67	🚐	£8.50—£11.00
67	🚎	£8.50—£11.00
67	⛺	£8.50—£11.00
8	🏕	£150.00—£360.00

102 units privately owned
Open March–October

If you book by telephone and are asked for your credit card number, it is advisable to check the proprietor's policy should you cancel your reservation.

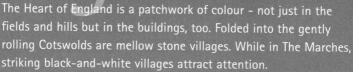
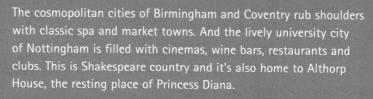

HEART OF ENGLAND

The Heart of England is a patchwork of colour - not just in the fields and hills but in the buildings, too. Folded into the gently rolling Cotswolds are mellow stone villages. While in The Marches, striking black-and-white villages attract attention.

The cosmopolitan cities of Birmingham and Coventry rub shoulders with classic spa and market towns. And the lively university city of Nottingham is filled with cinemas, wine bars, restaurants and clubs. This is Shakespeare country and it's also home to Althorp House, the resting place of Princess Diana.

If you happen to be in the Staffordshire village of Wetton, be sure to time your visit for the annual World Toe-Wrestling Championships in June!

The counties of Derbyshire, Gloucestershire, Herefordshire, Leicestershire, Lincolnshire Northamptonshire, Nottinghamshire, Rutland, Shropshire, Staffordshire, Warwickshire, Worcestershire and West Midlands

FOR MORE INFORMATION CONTACT:
Heart of England Tourist Board
Larkhill Road, Worcester WR5 2EZ
Tel: (01905) 761100
Fax: (01905) 763450

The Pictures:
1 Darwin Statue, Shrewsbury;
2 Anne Hathaway's Cottage, Warwickshire;
3 Warwick Castle.

Where to Go in the Heart of England - see pages 84–88
Where to Stay in the Heart of England - see pages 89-93

Whilst in the
HEART OF ENGLAND ...

You will find hundreds of interesting places to visit during your stay, just some of which are listed in these pages.

Contact any Tourist Information Centre in the region for more ideas on days out in the Heart of England.

Acton Scott Historic Working Farm

Acton Scott Church, Stretton, Warwickshire SY6 6QN
Tel: (01694) 781306
Demonstrates farming and rural life in south Shropshire at the close of the 19thC.

Alton Towers Theme Park

Alton, Stoke-on-Trent, Staffordshire ST10 4DB
Tel: 0870 5204060
Theme Park with over 125 rides and attractions including Oblivion, Nemesis, Haunted House, Runaway Mine Train, Congo River Rapids, Log Flume and many children's rides.

The American Adventure

Ilkeston, Derbyshire DE7 5SX
Tel: (01773) 531521
The American Adventure has action and entertainment for all ages. The Missile white-knuckle rollercoaster, Europe's tallest skycoaster and the world's wettest log flume.

Belton House, Park and Gardens

Belton, Grantham, Lincolnshire NG32 2LS
Tel: (01476) 566116
The crowning achievement of restoration country house architecture, built in 1685-1688 for Sir John Brownlow with alterations by James Wyatt in 1777.

Belvoir Castle

Belvoir, Grantham, Lincolnshire NG32 1PD
Tel: (01476) 870262
The present castle is the fourth to be built on this site and dates from 1816. Art treasures include works by Poussin, Rubens, Holbein and Reynolds. Queen's Royal Lancers display.

Birmingham Botanical Gardens and Glasshouses

Edgbaston, Birmingham, West Midlands B15 3TR
Tel: (0121) 454 1860
Fifteen acres of ornamental gardens and glasshouses. Widest range of plants in the Midlands from tropical rainforest to arid desert. Aviaries with exotic birds, child's play area.

Black Country Living Museum

Dudley, West Midlands DY1 4SQ
Tel: (0121) 557 9643
One of Britain's best open-air museums. Wander around original shops and houses, ride on fair attractions and take a look down a mine.

Museum of British Road Transport

Coventry, West Midlands CV1 1PN
Tel: (024) 7683 2425
Two hundred cars and commercial vehicles, 200 cycles and 75 motorcycles from the 19thC to date, plus the 'Thrust 2' land speed story.

Butlins Family Entertainment Resort

Roman Bank, Skegness, Lincolnshire PE25 1NJ
Tel: (01754) 762311
New skyline pavilion, toyland, sub tropical waterworld, tenpin bowling and entertainment's centre. Live shows.

Cadbury World

Bournville, Birmingham, West Midlands B30 2LD
Tel: (0121) 451 4180
The story of Cadbury's chocolate. Includes chocolate-making demonstration and childrens attractions.

Chatsworth House and Garden

Bakewell, Derbyshire DE45 1PP
Tel: (01246) 582204
Built in 1687–1707 with a collection of fine pictures, books, drawings and furniture. Garden laid out by 'Capability' Brown with fountains, cascades, a farmyard and playground.

Cotswold Farm Park

Guiting Power, Cheltenham, Gloucestershire GL54 5UG
Tel: (01451) 850307
Collection of rare breeds of British farm animals. Pets' corner, adventure playground, farm trail, picnic area, gift shop and cafe. Lambing and other seasonal farming displays.

Drayton Manor Family Theme Park

Tamworth, Staffordshire B78 3TW
Tel: (01827) 287979
A major theme park and zoo, with 100 rides and attractions. Set in 250 acres of countryside with lakes, nature trail, farmyard, restaurants and bars.

The Heights of Abraham Cable Cars, Caverns and Country Park

Matlock Bath, Matlock, Derbyshire DE4 3PD
Tel: (01629) 582365
A spectacular cable car ride takes you to the summit where there are a wide variety of attractions for young and old alike. Gift shop and coffee shop.

Ironbridge Gorge Museum

Ironbridge, Telford, Shropshire TF8 7AW
Tel: (01952) 433522
World's first cast-iron bridge. Museum of the River Visitor Centre, Tar Tunnel, Jackfield Tile Museum, Coalport China Museum, Rosehill House, Blists Hill Museum and Museum of Iron.

Lincoln Castle

Castle Hill, Lincoln, Lincolnshire LN1 3AA
Tel: (01522) 511068
A medieval castle including towers and ramparts with a Magna Carta exhibition, a prison chapel experience, reconstructed Westgate and popular events throughout the summer.

Midland Railway Centre

Butterley Station, Ripley, Derbyshire DE5 3QZ
Tel: (01773) 747674
Over 50 locomotives and over 100 items of historic rolling stock of Midland and LMS origin with a steam-hauled passenger service, a museum site, country and farm park.

National Sea Life Centre

Brindleyplace, Birmingham, West Midlands B1 2HL
Tel: (0121) 633 4700
Over 55 fascinating displays. The opportunity to come face-to-face with hundreds of sea creatures, from sharks to shrimps.

The National Tramway Museum

Crich, Matlock, Derbyshire DE4 5DP
Tel: (01773) 852565
A collection of over 70 trams from Britain and overseas dating from 1873-1957. Tram rides on a 1.6 km (1-mile) route, a period street scene, depots, a power station, workshops and exhibition.

The Pictures:
1 Rockingham Castle, Northamptonshire;
2 Chatsworth House, Derbyshire;
3 South Shropshire Hills;
4 New Place, Stratford–upon–Avon;
5 Brindley Place, Birmingham;
6 Robin Hood Statue, Nottingham;
7 Alderton, Gloucestershire;
8 Rutland Water.

Severn Valley Railway

Bewdley, Worcestershire DY12 1BG
Tel: (01299) 403816
Preserved standard gauge steam railway running 2.6 km (16 miles) between Kidderminster, Bewdley and Bridgnorth. Collection of locomotives and passenger coaches.

Shakespeare's Birthplace

Stratford-upon-Avon, Warwickshire CV37 6QW
Tel: (01789) 204016
The world famous house where William Shakespeare was born in 1564 and where he grew up. See the highly acclaimed exhibition 'Shakespeare's World'.

Nottingham Industrial Museum

Wollaton Park, Nottingham, Nottinghamshire NG8 2AE
Tel: (0115) 915 3910
An 18thC stables presenting the history of Nottingham's industries: printing, pharmacy, hosiery and lace. There is also a Victorian beam engine, a horse gin and transport.

Ye Olde Pork Pie Shoppe and the Sausage Shop

Melton Mowbray. Leicestershire LE13 1NW
Tel: (01664) 562341
Oldest and only remaining pork pie bakery producing authentic Melton Mowbray pork pies. Learn why Melton Mowbray became the original home to the pork pie industry. Demonstrations and tastings. Adjacent Dickinson & Morris Sausage Shop.

Peak District Mining Museum

Matlock Bath, Matlock, Derbyshire DE4 3NR
Tel: (01629) 583834
Explore 3,500 years of lead mining history with displays, hands-on exhibits and climbing shafts. Go underground and learn to pan for gold. Plus 'Hazards of Mining' display.

Rugby School Museum

Little Church Street, Rugby, Warwickshire CV21 3AW
Tel: (01788) 556109
Rugby School Museum tells the story of the school, scene of Tom Brown's Schooldays, and contains the earlier memorabilia of the game invented on the school close.

The Shrewsbury Quest

Abbey Foregate, Shrewsbury, Shropshire SY2 6AH
Tel: (01743) 243324
Twelfth-century medieval visitor attraction. Solve mysteries, create illuminated manuscripts, play medieval games and relax in the unique herb gardens. Gift shop and cafe.

Shugborough Estate

Shugborough, Milford, Staffordshire ST17 0XB
Tel: (01889) 881388
Eighteenth-century mansion house with fine collection of furniture. Gardens and park contain beautiful neo-classical monuments.

Skegness Natureland Seal Sanctuary

The Promenade, Skegnes, Lincolnshire PE25 1DB
Tel: (01754) 764345
Collection of performing seals, baby seals, penguins, aquarium, crocodiles, snakes, terrapins, scorpions, tropical birds, butterflies (May-October) and pets.

Snibston Discovery Park

Coalville, Leicester, Leicestershire LE67 3LN
Tel: (01530) 510851
An all-weather and award-winning science and industrial heritage museum.

Spode Visitor Centre

Spode, Stoke-on-Trent, Staffordshire ST4 1BX
Tel: (01782) 744011
Visitors are shown the various processes in the making of bone china. Samples can be bought at the Spode Shop.

The Tales of Robin Hood

Maid Marian Way, Nottingham NG1 6GF
Tel: (0115) 948 3284
Join the world's greatest medieval adventure. Ride through the magical green wood and play the Silver Arrow game, in the search for Robin Hood.

Three Choirs Vineyards

Baldwins Farm, Newent, Gloucestershire GL18 1LS
Tel: (01531) 890223
Internationally award-winning wines are available for tasting and for sale. Winery gallery shows you how wine is made. Restaurant with magnificent views of the vines. Peaceful ponds, plus vineyard walks.

Twycross Zoo

Twycross, Atherstone, Warwickshire CV9 3PX
Tel: (01827) 880250
Gorillas, orang-utans, chimpanzees, a modern gibbon complex, elephants, lions, giraffes, a reptile house, pets' corner and rides.

Walsall Arboretum

Lichfield Street, Walsall, West Midlands
Tel: (01922) 653148
Picturesque Victorian park with over 79 acres of gardens, lakes and parkland.

Warwick Castle

Warwick CV34 4QU
Tel: (01926) 406600
Set in 60 acres of grounds. State rooms, armoury, dungeon, torture chamber, clock tower. A Royal Weekend Party 1898, and Kingmaker — a preparation for battle attractions.

Wedgwood Visitor Centre

Barlaston, Stoke-on-Trent, Staffordshire ST12 9ES
Tel: (01782) 204141
The visitor centre is located in the Wedgwood factory which lies within a 500 acre country estate. You can see potters and decorators at work. Also museum and shop

The Wildfowl and Wetlands Trust

Slimbridge, Gloucester, Gloucestershire GL2 7BT
Tel: (01453) 890333
Tropical house, hides, heated observatory, exhibits, children's playground and pond zone. Shop and restaurant.

Worcester Cathedral

10A College Green, Worcester, Worcestershire WR1 2LH
Tel: (01905) 611002
Norman crypt and chapter house, King John's Tomb, Prince Arthur's Chantry, medieval cloisters and buildings. Touch and hearing control, visually impaired facilities available.

The Pictures:
1 Symonds Yat, Wye Valley;
2 Fords Hospital, Coventry;
3 Alford Craft Market, Lincolnshire;
4 Shrewsbury Castle;
5 River Avon and Warwick Castle, Warwick;
6 Stratford-upon-Avon;
7 Nr. Chapel-en-le-Frith, Peak District;
8 Lamport Hall, Northamptonshire.

Find out more about the
HEART OF ENGLAND ...

Further information about holidays and attractions
in the Heart of England is available from:

HEART OF ENGLAND TOURIST BOARD

Larkhill Road, Worcester WR5 2EZ.

Tel: (01905) 761100

Fax: (01905) 763450

The following publications are available free from the Heart of England Tourist Board:

Bed & Breakfast Touring Map including Caravan and Camping

Escape & Explore

Events list

Great Places to Visit

Activity Holidays in the Heart of England

Food & Drink

Also available

Places to Visit in the Heart of England 1999
featuring over 850 varied attractions, places to visit and things to do. Includes discount vouchers, map of the region and a comprehensive index - £2.95

The Pictures:
1   Packwood House, Warwickshire;
2   Black Country Museum, Dudley;
3   Ye Olde Trip to Jerusalem Inn,
    Nottingham;
4   Mary Arden's house, Wilmcote;
5   Burghley Horse Trials, Stamford.

Getting to the
HEART OF ENGLAND ...

BY ROAD: Britain's main motorways (M1/M6/M5) meet in the Heart of England; the M40 links with the M42 south of Birmingham while the M4 provides fast access from London to the south of the region. These road links ensure that the Heart of England is more accessible by road than any other region in the UK.

BY RAIL: The Heart of England lies at the centre of the country's rail network. There are direct trains from London and other major cities to many towns and cities within the region.

WHERE TO STAY (HEART OF ENGLAND)

Parks in this region are listed in alphabetical order by place name, and then by park.
As West Oxfordshire and Cherwell are promoted in both Heart of England
and South of England, places in these areas with parks are listed in this section.
See South of England for full West Oxfordshire and Cherwell entries.

Map references refer to the colour location maps at the back of this guide.
The first number indicates the map to use; the letter and number
which follow refer to the grid reference on the map.

At-a-glance symbols can be found inside the back cover flap. Keep this open for easy reference.

ASTON CANTLOW

Warwickshire
Map ref 3B1

Attractive village on the River Alne,
with a black and white timbered
guild house and a fine old inn.

Island Meadow Caravan Park ⚠
★★★
Holiday, Touring and Camping Park
Member BH&HPA
The Mill House, Aston Cantlow
B95 6JP
T: (01789) 488273
F: (01789) 488273
I: www.ukparks.co.uk/islandmeadow
*From the A3400 between Stratford and
Henley-in-Arden or from the A46
between Stratford and Alcester follow
the signs for Aston Cantlow. The park is
0.25 miles west of the village.
Signposted.*
2.8 hectares (7 acres). Level, grassy,
sheltered.
34 touring pitches.

24	🚐	£10.50
24	🚚	£10.50
10	▲	£8.00
6	🏠	£190.00—£320.00

51 units privately owned
Open March–October

🚗🏕🐕🛒🧺🛗🚻⚡🛗📵🛆 ☺🏔🛶🛖

BOSTON

Lincolnshire
Map ref 4A1

Historic town famous for its church
tower, the Boston Stump, 272 ft
high. Still a busy port, the town is full
of interest and has links with Boston,
Massachusetts, through the Pilgrim
Fathers. The cells where they were
imprisoned can be seen in the
medieval Guildhall.
*Tourist Information Centre
T: (01205) 356656*

Orchard Caravan Park ⚠
★★★
Holiday Park
Member BH&HPA
Frampton Lane, Hubberts Bridge,
Boston PE20 3QU
T: (01205) 290328
F: (01205) 290247
*From A17 take the A1121 towards
Boston and at the jct with the B1192
take the Hubberts Bridge turn.
Frampton Lane is 1st on the left and
the park is 0.25 miles down the lane.
Signposted.*
14.8 hectares (37 acres). Level,
grassy, sheltered.
60 touring pitches.

60	🚐	£10.00—£10.00
60	🚚	£10.00—£10.00
60	▲	£10.00—£10.00
3	🏠	£160.00—£180.00

125 units privately owned
Open March–October

🚗🏕🐕🛒🧺🛗🚻⚡🛗📺📵🛆☺🔍🏔🛶🛶🎵🛆

BRIDGNORTH

Shropshire
Map ref 5A3

Red sandstone riverside town in 2
parts - High and Low - linked by a
cliff railway. Much of interest
including a ruined Norman keep,
half-timbered 16th C houses,
Midland Motor Museum and Severn
Valley Railway.
*Tourist Information Centre
T: (01746) 763257*

Park Grange Holidays
★★★★
Holiday Park
Member BH&HPA
Morville, Bridgnorth WV16 4RN
T: (01746) 714285
F: (01746) 714145
E: parkgrangeholidays@hotmail.com
I: www.virtual-shropshire.co.uk/
park-grange-holidays
*On the A458 Bridgnorth to Shrewsbury
road, 1.5 miles beyond Morville towards
Shrewsbury, look for the signs to Park
Grange Holiday Luxury Caravans.
Signposted.*
4.8 hectares (12 acres). Sloping,
grassy, hard, sheltered.

	🚐	£4.00—£6.00
	🚚	£4.00—£6.00
4	🏠	£119.00—£294.00

Open all year round

🚗P📵🛗🛆⚡🛆☺🏔🛶🛶 ▶🚻🛗📵T

BRIDGNORTH

Continued

Stanmore Hall Touring Park

★★★★★
Touring and Camping Park
Member BH&HPA
Stourbridge Road, Bridgnorth
WV15 6DT
T: (01746) 761761
F: (01746) 768069
E: stanmore@morris-leisure.co.uk
I: www.morris-leisure.co.uk
Located to the east of Bridgnorth on the Stourbridge road, next to the Midland Motor Museum (A458). Signposted.
Wheelchair access category 2
4.8 hectares (12 acres). Level, grassy, hard, sheltered.
131 touring pitches.

121	£10.60—£12.60
10	£10.60—£12.60

Open all year round
Cards accepted: Barclaycard, Delta, Eurocard, Maestro, Mastercard, Solo, Switch, Visa, Visa Electron
WH

BUXTON

Derbyshire
Map ref 5B2

The highest market town in England and one of the oldest spas, with an elegant Crescent, Poole's Cavern, Opera House and attractive Pavilion Gardens. An excellent centre for exploring the Peak District.
Tourist Information Centre
T: (01298) 25106

Cottage Farm Caravan Park

★★★
Touring and Camping Park
Member BH&HPA
Blackwell in the Peak, Blackwell, Buxton SK17 9TQ
T: (01298) 85330
I: www.ukparks.co.uk/cottagefarm
North off A6 signposted with site name.
1.2 hectares (3 acres). Grassy, hard.
30 touring pitches.

30	£6.00
30	£6.00
30	£6.00

Open all year round

Lime Tree Park

★★★★
Holiday, Touring and Camping Park
Rose Award
Member BH&HPA
Dukes Drive, Buxton SK17 9RP
T: (01298) 22988
I: www.ukparks.co.uk/limetree
One mile south of Buxton centre between A6 and A515. Signposted.
4.8 hectares (12 acres). Level, sloping, grassy, stony, hard, sheltered.
99 touring pitches.

64	£8.00—£10.50
64	£8.00—£10.50
35	£8.00—£10.50
10	£120.00—£350.00

37 units privately owned
Open March–October
Cards accepted: Barclaycard, Delta, Mastercard, Switch, Visa
TV

Newhaven Caravan and Camping Park

★★★
Holiday, Touring and Camping Park
Member BH&HPA
Newhaven, Buxton SK17 0DT
T: (01298) 84300
Halfway between Ashbourne and Buxton on A515 at the jct with the A5012. Signposted.
12 hectares (30 acres). Level, sloping, grassy.
125 touring pitches.

95	£7.00—£8.50
95	£7.00—£8.50
30	£7.00—£8.50

73 units privately owned
Open March–October

CASTLE DONINGTON

Leicestershire
Map ref 5C3

A Norman castle once stood here. The world's largest collection of single-seater racing cars is displayed at Donington Park alongside the racing circuit, and an Aeropark Visitor Centre can be seen at nearby East Midlands International Airport.

Donington Park Farmhouse Hotel

★★★
Touring Park
Melbourne Road, Isley Walton, Castle Donington, Derby DE74 2RN
T: (01332) 862409
F: (01332) 862364
E: info@parkfarmhouse.co.uk
I: www.parkfarmhouse.co.uk
M1 exit 23a or 24, pass East Midlands airport to Isley Walton. Turn right and the park is 0.5 miles on the right- hand side. Signposted.
2.8 hectares (7 acres). Grassy, hard, sheltered.
75 touring pitches.

75	£9.00—£14.00
75	£9.00—£14.00
75	£9.00—£12.00

Open March–December
Cards accepted: Amex, Barclaycard, Delta, Diners, JCB, Mastercard, Switch, Visa
WH

CHARLBURY

Oxfordshire
Map ref 3C1

Cotswold View Caravan & Camping Site

See South of England region for full entry details

CIRENCESTER

Gloucestershire
Map ref 3B1

"Capital of the Cotswolds", Cirencester was Britain's second most important Roman town with many finds housed in the Corinium Museum. It has a very fine Perpendicular church and old houses around the market place.
Tourist Information Centre
T: (01285) 654180

Mayfield Touring Park

★★★★
Touring Park
Member BH&HPA
Cheltenham Road, Perrotts Brook, Cirencester GL7 7BH
T: (01285) 831301
F: (01285) 831301
E: jhutson@btclick.com
On the A435 2 miles north of Cirencester, 13 miles south of Cheltenham. Signposted.
4.8 hectares (12 acres). Level, sloping, grassy, hard, sheltered.
72 touring pitches.

36	£7.30—£9.80
25	£6.50—£9.80
36	£6.00—£9.80

Open all year round
Cards accepted: Barclaycard, Delta, Mastercard, Solo, Switch, Visa

WELCOME HOST

This is a nationally recognised customer care programme which aims to promote the highest standards of service and a warm welcome. Parks taking part in this initiative are indicated by the WH symbol.

ELLESMERE

Shropshire
Map ref 5A2

Small market town with old streets and houses and situated close to 9 lakes. The largest, the Mere, has many waterfowl and recreational facilities and some of the other meres have sailing and fishing.

Fernwood Caravan Park ▲▲
★★★★

Holiday and Touring Park
Member BH&HPA/NCC
Lyneal, Ellesmere, Shropshire
SY12 0QF
T: (01948) 710221
F: (01948) 710324
Ellesmere A495 road at Welshampton B5063, after canal follow signs. Signposted.
26.4 hectares (66 acres). Level, grassy.
60 touring pitches.

	🚐	£10.50—£14.50
	🚙	£10.50—£14.50
1	⛺	£210.00—£330.00

165 units privately owned
Open March–November

EVESHAM

Worcestershire
Map ref 3B1

Market town in the centre of a fruit-growing area. There are pleasant walks along the River Avon and many old houses and inns. A fine 16th C bell tower stands between 2 churches near the medieval Almonry Museum.
Tourist Information Centre
T: (01386) 446944

The Ranch Caravan Park ▲▲
★★★★

Holiday Park
Member BH&HPA/NCC
Station Road, Honeybourne,
Evesham WR11 5QG
T: (01386) 830744
F: (01386) 833503
I: www.ranch.co.uk
From Evesham take B4035 to Badsey and Bretforton. Left to Honeybourne. Signposted.
19.2 hectares (48 acres). Level, grassy.
120 touring pitches.

120	🚐	£7.75—£15.50
120	🚙	£7.75—£15.50
4	⛺	£190.00—£350.00

176 units privately owned
Open March–November

Cards accepted: Barclaycard, Delta, Eurocard, Mastercard, Switch, Visa

LINCOLN

Lincolnshire
Map ref 5C2

Ancient city dominated by the magnificent 11th C cathedral with its triple towers. A Roman gateway is still used and there are medieval houses lining narrow, cobbled streets. Other attractions include the Norman castle, several museums and the Usher Gallery.
Tourist Information Centre
T: (01522) 529828 or 579056

Hartsholme Country Park
★★

Touring Park
Skellingthorpe Road, Lincoln
LN6 0EY
T: (01522) 686264 & 873578
F: (01522) 686264
Signposted from A46 Lincoln bypass, brown signs.
.8 hectare (2 acres). Level, sheltered.
50 touring pitches.

50	🚐	£7.30—£12.00
50	🚙	£7.30—£12.00
18	⛺	£4.50—£8.50

Open March–October

MATLOCK

Derbyshire
Map ref 5B2

The town lies beside the narrow valley of the River Derwent surrounded by steep wooded hills. Good centre for exploring Derbyshire's best scenery.
Tourist Information Centre
T: (01629) 583388

Darwin Forest Country Park ▲▲
★★★★

Holiday and Touring Park
Member BH&HPA
Darley Moor, Two Dales, Matlock
DE4 5LN
T: (01629) 732428
F: (01629) 735015
E: admin@darwinforest.co.uk
I: darwinforest.co.uk
Take jct 29 of the M1 to Chesterfield then follow A632 towards Matlock. Turn off the B5057 towards Darley Dale Park; 3 miles on the right. Signposted.
Wheelchair access category 3 ♿
17.6 hectares (44 acres). Level, grassy, hard, sheltered.
48 touring pitches.

48	🚐	£10.00—£12.00
48	🚙	£10.00—£12.00

Open March–December
Cards accepted: Barclaycard, Delta, Eurocard, Mastercard, Switch, Visa

MOLLINGTON

Oxfordshire
Map ref 3C1

Mollington Touring Caravan Park
See South of England region for full entry details

RUGELEY

Staffordshire
Map ref 5B3

Town close to Cannock Chase which has over 2000 acres of heath and woodlands with forest trails and picnic sites. Nearby is Shugborough Hall (National Trust) with a fine collection of 18th C furniture and interesting monuments in the grounds.

Silvertrees Caravan Park ▲▲
★★★★

Rose Award
Holiday and Touring Park
Member BH&HPA
Stafford Brook Road, Penkridge Bank, Rugeley WS15 2TX
T: (01889) 582185
F: (01889) 582185
I: www.ukparks.co.uk/silvertrees
From Rugeley Western Springs Road turn west at traffic lights for Penkridge, after 2 miles turn right into Stafford Brook Road (unclassified). Signposted.
12 hectares (30 acres). Level, sloping, grassy, hard, sheltered.
50 touring pitches.

50	🚐	£7.00—£9.00
50	🚙	£7.00—£9.00
8	⛺	£199.00—£369.00

43 units privately owned
Open March–October
Cards accepted: Barclaycard, Mastercard, Visa

SHREWSBURY

Shropshire
Map ref 5A3

Beautiful historic town on the River
Severn retaining many fine old
timber-framed houses. Its
attractions include Rowley's
Museum with Roman finds, remains
of a castle, Clive House Museum, St
Chad's 18th C round church, rowing
on the river and the Shrewsbury
Flower Show in August.
Tourist Information Centre
T: (01743) 281200 or 281210

Oxon Hall Touring Park ⚠
★★★★★
Holiday and Touring Park
Member BH&HPA
Welshpool Road, Bicton Heath,
Shrewsbury SY3 5FB
T: (01743) 340868
E: oxon@morris-leisure.co.uk
I: www.morris-leisure.co.uk
On A458 to Welshpool, 1.5 miles from
Shrewsbury town centre, adjacent to
Oxon park and ride. Signposted.
Wheelchair access category 2 ♿
10 hectares (25 acres). Level, grassy,
hard, sheltered.
130 touring pitches.

130	🚐	£10.60—£12.60
130	🚚	£10.60—£12.60
130	▲	

12 units privately owned
Open all year round
Cards accepted: Barclaycard,
Diners, Mastercard, Switch, Visa

🚗 P 🖾 🍴 🛇 🛁 🍵 🛒 🎮 🔊
🥤 🚮 ☉ ♿

WELCOME HOST

This is a nationally recognised
customer care programme
which aims to promote
the highest standards of
service and a warm welcome.
Parks taking part in this
initiative are indicated
by the WH symbol.

Please check prices and other
details at the time of booking.

SOUTH CERNEY

Gloucestershire
Map ref 3B2

The 15,000 acres of lakes and ponds
and several Country Parks are being
developed at South Cerney as the
Cotswold Water Park, for sailing,
fishing, bird-watching and other
recreational activities.

Cotswold Hoburne
Limited ⚠
★★★★
Holiday, Touring and Camping Park
Member BH&HPA/NCC
Broadway Lane, South Cerney,
Cirencester GL7 5UQ
T: (01285) 860216
F: (01285) 862106
I: www.hoburne.co.uk
From the A419 take exit towards South
Cerney on to Spine Road. After 1 mile
turn right into Broadway Lane. The park
is 400 yards on the left. Signposted.
28 hectares (70 acres). Level, grassy,
hard.
302 touring pitches.

302	🚐	£11.00—£24.00
302	🚚	£11.00—£24.00
302	▲	£11.00—£24.00
20	🏠	£130.00—£450.00

155 units privately owned
Open March–October
Cards accepted: Barclaycard, Delta,
Eurocard, Mastercard, Solo, Switch,
Visa

🚗 🖾 P 🖾 🍴 🛇 🛁 🍵 🛒 ✕ 🍷
📺 🎮 🔊 🥤 🚮 ☉ ♨ ⛰ 🎣 🏕 🕈
🎱 🏌 🎿 🎵 🎯

A key to symbols can be
found inside the back
cover flap.

All accommodation in this
guide has been rated, or is
awaiting a rating, by a trained
Tourist Board assessor.

For ideas on places to visit
refer to the introduction at
the beginning of this section.

STRATFORD-UPON-AVON

Warwickshire
Map ref 3B1

Famous as Shakespeare's home
town, Stratford's many attractions
include his birthplace, New Place
where he died, the Royal
Shakespeare Theatre and Gallery
and Hall's Croft (his daughter's
house).
Tourist Information Centre
T: (01789) 293127

Dodwell Park ⚠
★★★★
Touring and Camping Park
Member BH&HPA
Evesham Rd, (B439), Stratford-
upon-Avon CV37 9ST
T: (01789) 204957
F: (01926) 336476
On the B439 2 miles south west of
Stratford-upon-Avon. Signposted.
.8 hectare (2 acres). Level, sloping,
grassy, hard, sheltered.
50 touring pitches.

50	🚐	£9.00—£10.00
50	🚚	£9.00—£10.00
50	▲	£7.00—£10.00

Open all year round
Cards accepted: Barclaycard, Delta,
Mastercard, Switch, Visa

🚗 P 🖾 🍴 🛇 🛁 🍵 🛒 🎮 🔊 🥤
🚮 ☉ ♿ T
Ad See display advertisement on this
page

For an explanation of
the Quality Assurance
Scheme, represented
by Stars, please refer
to the front of the guide.

COLOUR MAPS

Colour maps at the back
of this guide pinpoint all
places in which you will
find parks listed.

TELFORD

Shropshire
Map ref 5A3

New Town named after Thomas Telford, the famous engineer who designed many of the country's canals, bridges and viaducts. It is close to Ironbridge with its monuments and museums to the Industrial Revolution, including restored 18th C buildings.
Tourist Information Centre
T: (01952) 238008

Severn Gorge Park ⚐
★★★★
Touring and Camping Park
Bridgnorth Road, Tweedale, Telford, Shropshire TF7 4JB
T: (01952) 684789 (Answerphone)
F: (01952) 684789
From M54 jct 4 or 5 take the A442 south signposted Kidderminster (approximately 3 miles). Follow signs for Madeley then Tweedale. Signposted.
6.4 hectares (16 acres). Level, grassy, hard, sheltered.
110 touring pitches.

110	🚐	£9.00—£11.00
110	🚍	£9.00—£11.00
60	▲	£9.00—£11.00

Open all year round
Cards accepted: Barclaycard, Delta, Eurocard, JCB, Mastercard, Solo, Switch, Visa, Visa Electron

🚗 P 🖵 🅰 🅿 🛁 🚿 🚻 🅾 🍴 🔌 🎱 ⚐
⚡ 🧺 ☺ ⚠ 🔱 🛡 WH

DAVID BELLAMY CONSERVATION AWARDS

If you are looking for a site that's environmentally friendly look for those that have achieved the David Bellamy Conservation Award. Recently launched in conjunction with the British Holiday & Home Parks Association, this award is given to sites which are committed to protecting and enhancing the environment – from care of the hedgerows and wildlife to recycling waste – and are members of the Association. More information about this award scheme can be found at the front of the guide.

USE YOUR *i*s

There are more than 550 Tourist Information Centres throughout England offering friendly help with accommodation and holiday ideas as well as suggestions of places to visit and things to do. There may well be a centre in your home town which can help you before you set out. You'll find addresses in the local Phone Book.

EAST OF ENGLAND

Open skies, rich Fenland, gorgeous villages and miles of sandy beaches - welcome to the East of England where life ticks slowly by.

Barge your way through the Norfolk Broads, punt along the River Cam, or walk over water on the pier at Southend.

Woburn Abbey, Sandringham and Kentwell Hall are just a few of the fabulous houses and gardens in the area. And if you fancy a day at the races, you can bet on Newmarket.

Graceful cathedrals pierce the skies at Ely, Norwich, Cambridge and Colchester. While beautiful Walsingham is dubbed 'England's Nazareth' and attracts an annual Pilgrimage in the remains of the Medieval Priory.

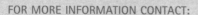

The counties of
Bedfordshire, Cambridgeshire,
Essex, Hertfordshire, Norfolk and Suffolk

FOR MORE INFORMATION CONTACT:
East of England Tourist Board
Toppesfield Hall, Hadleigh, Suffolk IP7 5DN
Tel: (01473) 822922
Fax: (01473) 823063
Email: eastofenglandtouristboard@compuserve.com
Internet: www.visitbritain.com/east-of-england/

Where to Go in the East of England - see pages 96-100
Where to Stay in the East of England - see pages 101-105

The Pictures:
1 Hunstanton, Norfolk;
2 King's College, Cambridge.

Whilst in the
EAST OF ENGLAND ...

You will find hundreds of interesting places to visit during your stay, just some of which are listed in these pages.

Contact any Tourist Information Centre in the region for more ideas on days out in the East of England.

Audley End House and Park

Audley End, Saffron Walden, Essex CB11 4JF
Tel: (01799) 522399
Palatial Jacobean house remodelled in the 18th-19thC. Magnificent Great Hall with 17thC plaster ceilings. Rooms and furniture by Robert Adam and park by 'Capability' Brown.

Banham Zoo

The Grove, Banham, Norwich, Norfolk NR16 2HE
Tel: (01953) 887771
Wildlife spectacular which will take you on a journey to experience at close quarters some of the world's most exotic, rare and endangered animals.

Barleylands Farm Museum and Visitor Centre

Billericay, Essex CM11 2UD
Tel: (01268) 532253
Visitor centre with a rural museum, animal centre, craft studios, blacksmith's shop, glass-blowing studio with viewing gallery, miniature steam railway. Restaurant.

Blickling Hall

Blickling, Norwich, Norfolk NR11 6NF
Tel: (01263) 738030
Jacobean redbrick mansion with garden, orangery, parkland and lake. Displays of fine tapestries and furniture. Picnic area, shop, restaurant and plant centre.

Bressingham Steam Museum and Gardens

Bressingham, Diss, Norfolk IP22 2AB
Tel: (01379) 687386
Steam rides through 8 km (5 miles) of woodland. Mainline locomotives, the Victorian Gallopers and over 50 steam engines. Plant centre.

Bure Valley Railway

Aylsham, Norwich, Norfolk NR11 6BW
Tel: (01263) 733858
A 15 inch narrow-gauge steam railway covering 14.4 km (9 miles) of track from Wroxham in the heart of the Norfolk Broads to Aylsham, a bustling market town.

Colchester Castle

Colchester, Essex CO1 1TJ
Tel: (01206) 282931
A Norman keep on the foundations of a Roman temple. The archaeological material includes much on Roman Colchester (Camulodunum).

Colchester Zoo

Stanway, Colchester, Essex CO3 5SL
Tel: (01206) 331292
Zoo with 200 species and some of the best cat collections in the UK, 40 acres of gardens and lakes, plus award-winning animal enclosures. Picnic areas, road train and four play areas.

Ely Cathedral

Ely, Cambridgeshire CB7 4DL
Tel: (01353) 667735
One of England's finest cathedrals. Monastic precinct, brass rubbing centre and stained glass museum. Guided tours.

Fritton Lake Country World

Fritton, Great Yarmouth, Norfolk NR31 9HA
Tel: (01493) 488208
A 250-acre centre with children's assault course, putting, an adventure playground, golf, fishing, boating, wildfowl, heavy horses, cart rides, falconry and flying displays.

The Gardens of the Rose

The Royal National Rose Society, Chiswell Green, St Albans, Hertfordshire AL2 3NR
Tel: (01727) 850461
The Royal National Rose Society's Garden with 27 acres of garden and trial grounds for new varieties of rose. Roses of all types displayed with 1,700 different varieties.

Hatfield House and Gardens

Hatfield, Hertfordshire AL9 5NQ
Tel: (01707) 262823
Magnificent Jacobean house, home of the Marquess of Salisbury. Exquisite gardens, model soldiers and park trails. Childhood home of Queen Elizabeth I.

Hedingham Castle

Castle Hedingham, Halstead, Essex C09 3DJ
Tel: (01787) 460261
The finest Norman keep in England, built in 1140 by the deVeres, Earls of Oxford. Visited by Kings Henry VII and VIII and Queen Elizabeth I. Besieged by King John.

The Pictures:
1 Holkham Beach, Norfolk;
2 Globe Inn, Linslade, Bedfordshire;
3 Thorpeness, Suffolk;
4 Nene Valley Railway, Stibbington, Cambridgeshire;
5 Punting on the River Cam, Cambridge.

Holkham Hall

Wells-next-the-Sea, Norfolk NR23 1AB
Tel: (01328) 710227
A classic 18thC Palladian-style mansion. Part of a great agricultural estate and a living treasure-house of artistic and architectural history. Bygones collection.

Ickworth House, Park and Gardens

Horringer, Bury St Edmunds, Suffolk IP29 5QE
Tel: (01284) 735270
An extraordinary oval house with flanking wings, begun in 1795. Fine paintings, a beautiful collection of Georgian silver, an Italian garden and stunning parkland.

Imperial War Museum

Duxford, Cambridgeshire CB2 4QR
Tel: (01223) 835000
Over 150 aircraft on display with tanks, vehicles and guns. Simulator ride and an adventure playground. Shops and restaurant.

Kentwell Hall

Long Melford, Sudbury, Suffolk CO10 9BA
Tel: (01787) 310207
A mellow redbrick Tudor manor surrounded by a moat. This family home has been interestingly restored with Tudor costume displays, a 16thC house and mosaic Tudor rose maze.

Knebworth House, Gardens and Park

Knebworth, Stevenage, Hertfordshire SG3 6PY
Tel: (01438) 812661
Tudor manor house, re-fashioned in the 19thC, housing a collection of manuscripts. Portraits, Jacobean banquet hall. Formal gardens and adventure playground.

Leighton Buzzard Railway

Page's Park Station, Leighton Buzzard, Bedfordshire LU7 8TN
Tel: (01525) 373888
An authentic narrow-gauge light railway, built in 1919, offering a 65-minute return journey into the Bedfordshire countryside.

Marsh Farm Country Park

South Woodham, Ferrers, Chelmsford, Essex CM3 5WP
Tel: (01245) 321552
Farm centre with sheep, a pig unit, free-range chickens, milking demonstrations, indoor and outdoor adventure play areas, nature reserve, walks, picnic area and pets' corner.

Melford Hall

Long Melford, Sudbury, Suffolk CO10 9AA
Tel: (01787) 880286
Turreted brick Tudor mansion with 18thC and Regency interiors. Collection of Chinese porcelain, gardens and a walk in the grounds.

Minsmere Nature Reserve

Westleton, Saxmundham, Suffolk IP17 3BY
Tel: (01728) 648281
Purpose-built visitor centre situated on the Suffolk coast. Information areas, nature trails, bird-watching and wildlife. Shop and tearoom.

National Horseracing Museum and Tours

Newmarket, Suffolk CB8 8JL
Tel: (01638) 667333
A museum displaying the development of horse-racing. A display of sporting art includes loans from the Tate gallery. Also a hands-on gallery.

National Stud

Newmarket, Suffolk CB8 0XE
Tel: (01638) 663464
A visit to the National Stud consists of a conducted tour which includes top thoroughbred stallions, mares and foals.

Norfolk Lavender

Caley Mill, Heacham, King's Lynn, Norfolk PE31 7JE
Tel: (01485) 570384
Lavender is distilled from the flowers and the oil made into a wide range of gifts. There is a slide show when the distillery is not working.

Norwich Cathedral

The Close, Norwich, Norfolk NR1 4EH
Tel: (01603) 764385
A Norman cathedral from 1096 with 14thC roof bosses depicting bible scenes from Adam and Eve to the Day of Judgement. Cloisters, cathedral close, shop and restaurant.

Oliver Cromwell's House

St Marys Street, Ely, Cambridgeshire CB7 4HF
Tel: (01353) 662062
The family home of Oliver Cromwell with a 17thC kitchen, parlour and haunted bedroom. Tourist Information Centre, souvenirs and a craft shop.

Peter Beales Roses

Attleborough, Norfolk NR17 1AY
Tel: (01953) 454707
A large display garden featuring a world famous collection of classic roses. Mainly old-fashioned roses plus rare and those of historic value.

Pleasure Beach

Great Yarmouth, Norfolk NR30 3EH
Tel: (01493) 844585
Rollercoaster, Terminator, log flume, Twister, monorail, breakdance, galloping horses, caterpillar, go-karts, ghost train, fun house and sheer terror show.

Pleasurewood Hills Family Leisure Park

Corton, Lowestoft, Suffolk NR32 5DZ
Tel: (01502) 586000
Log flume, chairlift, Horror Dome, two railways, pirate ship, fort, Aladdin's cave, parrot, sealion shows, rollercoaster, waveswinger.

The Pictures:
1 St Alban's Cathedral;
2 South of Ipswich, Suffolk;
3 The Norfolk Broads;
4 'A day at the races', Newmarket;
5 Thurne, Norfolk Broads;
6 Cromer, Norfolk;
7 Imperial War Museum, Duxford.

Sainsbury Centre for Visual Arts

University of East Anglia, Norwich, Norfolk NR4 7TJ
Tel: (01603) 456060
Housing the Sainsbury collection of works by Picasso, Bacon and Henry Moore alongside many objects of pottery and art. Cafe and art bookshop with monthly activities.

Sandringham

Sandringham, King's Lynn, Norfolk PE35 6EN
Tel: (01553) 772675
The country retreat of HM The Queen. A delightful house and 60 acres of grounds and lakes, plus museum of royal vehicles and royal memorabilia.

Shuttleworth Collection

Old Warden Aerodrome, Biggleswade,
Bedfordshire SG18 9EP
Tel: (01767) 627288
A unique historical collection of aircraft from a 1909 Bleriot to a 1942 Spitfire in flying condition. Cars dating from an 1898 Panhard in running order.

Somerleyton Hall and Gardens

Somerleyton, Lowestoft, Suffolk NR32 5QQ
Tel: (01502) 730224
Anglo Italian-style mansion with state rooms, a maze, 12-acre garden with azaleas and rhododendrons. Miniature railway, shop and tearooms.

Stondon Museum

Lower Stondon, Henlow Camp, Bedfordshire SG16 6JN
Tel: (01462) 850339
The largest private collection in England of bygone vehicles from the beginning of the century. Transport exhibits from the early 1900s to the 1980s.

Thursford Collection

Thursford Green, Fakenham, Norfolk NR21 0AS
Tel: (01328) 878477
Musical evenings some Tuesdays from mid-July to the end of September. A live musical show with nine mechanical organs and a Wurlitzer show starring Robert Wolfe daily April to October.

Whipsnade Wild Animal Park

Dunstable, Bedfordshire LU6 2LF
Tel: (01582) 872171
Over 2,500 animals set in 600 acres of beautiful parkland. Free animal demonstrations, plus the Great Whipsnade Railway.

Wimpole Hall and Home Farm

Arrington, Royston, Hertfordshire SG8 0BW
Tel: (01223) 207257
An 18thC house in a landscaped park with a folly and Chinese bridge. Plunge bath and yellow drawing room in the house, the work of John Soane. Rare breeds centre at Home Farm.

Woburn Abbey

Woburn, Milton Keynes, Bedfordshire MK43 0TP
Tel: (01525) 290666
An 18thC Palladian mansion, altered by Henry Holland, the Prince Regent's architect. Contains a collection of English silver, French and English furniture and art.

Woburn Safari Park

Woburn, Milton Keynes, Bedfordshire MK17 9QN
Tel: (01525) 290407
Drive through the safari park with 30 species of animals in natural groups just a windscreen's width away. Action-packed Wild World Leisure Area with shows for all.

Find out more about the
EAST OF ENGLAND ...

Further information about holidays and attractions
in the East of England is available from:

EAST OF ENGLAND TOURIST BOARD
Toppesfield Hall, Hadleigh, Suffolk IP7 5DN.
Tel: (01473) 822922
Fax: (01473) 823063
Email: eastofenglandtouristboard@compuserve.com
Internet: www.visitbritain.com/east-of-england/

The following publications are available free from the East of England Tourist Board:

Bed & Breakfast Touring Map 2001
England's Cycling Country
Travel Trade Directory
Places to Stay

Also available (price includes postage and packaging):
East of England – The Official Guide 2001 – £4.99

The Pictures:
1 South Raynham, Norfolk;
2 Ely Cathedral, Cambridge;
3 Cromer, Norfolk;
4 Cley next the Sea, Norfolk.

Getting to the
EAST OF ENGLAND ...

BY ROAD: The region is easily accessible. From London and the south via the A1, M11, M25, A10, M1, A46 and A12. From the north via the A17, A1, A15, A5, M1 and A6. From the west via the A14, A47, A421, A428, A418, A41 and A427.

BY RAIL: Regular fast trains run to all major cities and towns in the region. London stations which serve the region are Liverpool Street, Kings Cross, Fenchurch Street, Moorgate, St Pancras, London Marylebone and London Euston. Bedford, Luton and St Albans are on the Thameslink line which runs to Kings Cross and onto London Gatwick Airport. There is also a direct link between London Stansted Airport and Liverpool Street. Through the Channel Tunnel, there are trains direct from Paris and Brussels to Waterloo Station, London. A short journey on the Underground will bring passengers to those stations operating services into the East of England. Further information on rail journeys in the East of England can be obtained on (0845) 748 4950.

WHERE TO STAY (EAST OF ENGLAND)

Parks in this region are listed in alphabetical order of place name, and then in alphabetical order of park.

Map references refer to the colour location maps at the back of this guide. The first number indicates the map to use; the letter and number which follow refer to the grid reference on the map.

At-a-glance symbols can be found inside the back cover flap. Keep this open for easy reference.

BUNGAY

Suffolk
Map ref 4C1

Market town and yachting centre on the River Waveney with the remains of a great 12th C castle. In the market-place stands the Butter Cross, rebuilt in 1689 after being largely destroyed by fire. Nearby at Earsham is the Otter Trust.

Outney Meadow Caravan Park 𝗔

★★★

Touring and Camping Park
Member BH&HPA
Outney Meadow, Bungay
NR35 1HG
T: (01986) 892338
F: (01986) 896627
Signposted from roundabout at jct off the A144 and A143.
3.2 hectares (8 acres). Level, grassy, hard, sheltered.
45 touring pitches.

45	🚐	£7.00—£12.00
45	🏕	£6.50—£11.50
45	▲	£7.00—£12.00

20 units privately owned

Open April—October
🚗🚐🚑🏠🛆🌡🛎🏕🏧📺 ∥
🛏☉🚲✈🎣🏹☂🛗 WH

CAMBRIDGE

Cambridgeshire
Map ref 3D1

A most important and beautiful city on the River Cam with 31 colleges forming one of the oldest universities in the world. Numerous museums, good shopping centre, restaurants, theatres, cinema and fine bookshops.
Tourist Information Centre
T: (01223) 322640

Highfield Farm Touring Park 𝗔

★★★★★

Touring and Camping Park
Member BH&HPA
Long Road, Comberton, Cambridge
CB3 7DG
T: (01223) 262308
F: (01223) 262308
From Cambridge, take A1303, A428 to Bedford. After 3 miles, turn left at roundabout, sign to Comberton. From M11, take A603 to Sandy at jct 12 for

0.5 miles. Then take B1046 to Comberton. Signposted.
3.2 hectares (8 acres). Level, grassy, hard, sheltered.
120 touring pitches.

60	🚐	£7.50—£9.00
60	🏕	£7.25—£8.75
60	▲	£7.25—£8.75

Open April—October
🚗P🚐🚑🏠🛆🌡🛎🏕🛗📺
∥🛏☉🏧🚲☂ WH
Ad See display advertisement on this page

WELCOME HOST

This is a nationally recognised customer care programme which aims to promote the highest standards of service and a warm welcome. Parks taking part in this initiative are indicated by the WH symbol.

COLCHESTER

Essex
Map ref 4B2

Britain's oldest recorded town standing on the River Colne and famous for its oysters. Numerous historic buildings, ancient remains and museums. Plenty of parks and gardens, extensive shopping centre, theatre and zoo.
Tourist Information Centre
T: (01206) 282920

Colchester Camping and Caravanning Park 🔺
★★★★
Touring and Camping Park
Cymbeline Way, Lexden,
Colchester CO3 4AG
T: (01206) 545551
F: (01206) 710443
E: enquiries@
colchestercamping.co.uk
I: www.colchestercamping.co.uk
A12 then A133 slip road to Colchester central, follow tourist road signs. Signposted.
4.8 hectares (12 acres). Level, grassy, hard.
168 touring pitches.

168	🚐	£8.00—£13.00
168	🚐	£8.00—£13.00
	▲	£8.00—£13.00

Open all year round
Cards accepted: Barclaycard, Delta, Eurocard, Maestro, Mastercard, Solo, Switch, Visa, Visa Electron

🚗 P 🖥 📶 📞 🍴 🛁 🔔 🕐 💪 🏧 📟
〰 🚲 ☉ ⛰ ⛰ ▶ 🔥

CROMER

Norfolk
Map ref 4C1

Once a small fishing village and now famous for its fishing boats that still work off the beach and offer freshly caught crabs. Excellent bathing on sandy beaches fringed by cliffs. The town boasts a fine pier, theatre, museum and a lifeboat station.
Tourist Information Centre
T: (01263) 512497

Forest Park Caravan Site
★★★
Holiday Park
Member BH&HPA
Northrepps Road, Northrepps,
Cromer, Norfolk NR27 0JR
T: (01263) 513290
F: (01263) 511992
E: forestpark@netcom.co.uk
I: www.forest-park.co.uk
Turn right off A140 at Northrepps, turn immediately left under railway bridge to T-junction and turn left. Forest Park entrance on right. Signposted.

34 hectares (85 acres). Sloping, grassy, stony, sheltered.
338 touring pitches.

338	🚐	£8.50—£13.00
55	🚐	£8.50—£13.00
85	▲	£8.50—£13.50

402 units privately owned
Open March—October
Cards accepted: Barclaycard, Eurocard, Mastercard, Visa

🚗 P 🖥 📶 📞 🍴 🛁 🔔 🕐 💪 🏧 ✕ 🍴
〰 🖥 🚲 🚲 ☉ ⛰ 🔉 ∪ ▶ 🎵 🔥 [WH]

DUNWICH

Suffolk
Map ref 4C2

Due to sea erosion Dunwich is now just a small quiet village, but it was once the capital of East Anglia and a thriving port. The main street, containing a museum and inn, leads to the beach. To the south of the village is Dunwich Common (National Trust).

Cliff House (Dunwich) 🔺
★★★★
Holiday Park
Member BH&HPA
Minsmere Road, Dunwich,
Saxmundham IP17 3DQ
T: (01728) 648282
F: (01728) 648282
A12 to Yoxford. Turn right signposted Westleton/Dunwich, after 3 miles turn left in Westleton at T-junction. Follow signs for Dunwich Heath. Signposted.
12 hectares (30 acres). Level, grassy, hard, sheltered.
87 touring pitches.

87	🚐	£9.00—£14.00
1	🚐	£9.00—£14.00

88 units privately owned
Open April—October
Cards accepted: Barclaycard, Delta, Mastercard, Switch, Visa

🔔 🚗 P 🖥 📶 📞 🍴 🛁 🔔 🕐 💪
✕ 🍴 🖥 🚲 🚲 ☉ 🔉 ⛰ 🎵 ▶ 🔥
[WH]

GREAT YARMOUTH

Norfolk
Map ref 4C1

One of Britain's major seaside resorts with 5 miles of seafront and every possible amenity including an award winning leisure complex offering a huge variety of all-weather facilities. Busy harbour and fishing centre.

The Grange Touring Park
★★★★
Touring Park
Member BH&HPA
Ormesby St Margaret, Great
Yarmouth NR29 3QG
T: (01493) 730306 & 730023
F: (01493) 730188
E: john.groat@virgin.net
Three miles north of Great Yarmouth on the B1159 off the A149. Signposted.
1.4 hectares (3.5 acres). Level, grassy, sheltered.
70 touring pitches.

70	🚐	£7.00—£11.50
70	🚐	£7.00—£11.50
70	▲	£7.00—£11.50

Open March—September

🔔 P 📶 📞 🍴 🛁 🔔 🕐 💪 🖥 📟 〰
🚲 ☉ ⛰ ▶ 🔥

Grasmere Caravan Park (T.B.) 🔺
★★★
Holiday and Touring Park
Member BH&HPA
Bultitudes Loke, Yarmouth Road,
Caister-on-Sea, Great Yarmouth
NR30 5DH
T: (01493) 720382
Take the A149 from Great Yarmouth and enter Caister at the roundabout by Yarmouth Stadium. After 0.5 miles, turn left 100yds past the petrol station. Signposted.
2 hectares (5 acres). Level, grassy, stony, hard.
46 touring pitches.

46	🚐	£5.95—£8.25
46	🚐	£5.95—£8.25
9	🚐	£90.00—£280.00

53 units privately owned
Open April—October
Cards accepted: Barclaycard, Delta, Mastercard, Switch, Visa

🔔 🚗 📶 📞 🍴 🛁 🔔 🕐 📟 📟 〰
🚲 ☉ ⛰ 🐾 🔥

Hopton Holiday Village 🔺
★★★★
Holiday Park
Rose Award
Member BH&HPA/NCC
Warren Lane, Hopton-on-Sea,
Great Yarmouth NR31 9BW
T: 0870 2425678
F: (01442) 254956

From the A12, turn off at the sign for Hopton Holiday Village.
26 hectares (65 acres). Sloping, grassy.

350	🏠	£149.00—£622.00

605 units privately owned
Open April–October
Cards accepted: Amex, Barclaycard, Delta, Mastercard, Solo, Switch, Visa, Visa Electron

🚗📶🏠🏋️✕📺🛒🅿️🍴🔌
☺️⛰️♨️↻◡🔍🐾🎵🎣🛗Ⓣ|WH|

|Ad| See display advertisement on page 10

Liffens Holiday Park 🅰️
★★★★
Holiday Park
Member BH&HPA
Burgh Castle, Great Yarmouth
NR31 9QB
T: (01493) 780357
F: (01493) 782383
From Great Yarmouth, follow signs for Beccles and Lowestoft. Watch for left turn sign for Burgh Castle, follow for 2 miles to T-junction and turn right. Then follow signs to holiday park.
12 hectares (30 acres). Level, grassy.
150 touring pitches.

100	🚐	£8.50—£15.00
100	🚲	£8.50—£15.00
50	⛺	£8.50—£15.00
35	🏠	£120.00—£425.00

85 units privately owned
Open April–October
Cards accepted: Delta, Mastercard, Switch, Visa

🚗🅿️📶🛒🏋️🍴🔌🛒📺🛗✕🍴
📺🅿️🔌♨️🛒☺️🍷⛰️↻◡
🎵🎣🛗Ⓣ|WH|

Liffens Welcome Holiday Centre 🅰️
★★★
Holiday Park
Member BH&HPA
Butt Lane, Burgh Castle, Great Yarmouth NR31 9PY
T: (01493) 780481
F: (01493) 781627
On the main A143 from Great Yarmouth to Beccles road. Proceed through the village of Bradwell to the start of a small dual carriageway. Take 1st right turn, next turning on right and Liffens Holiday Centre is along on right. Signposted.
Level, grassy, sheltered.
150 touring pitches.

150	🚐	£8.50—£15.00
150	🚲	£8.50—£15.00
150	⛺	£8.50—£15.00
10	🏠	£120.00—£425.00

50 units privately owned
Open April–October
Cards accepted: Barclaycard, Delta, JCB, Maestro, Mastercard, Solo, Switch, Visa, Visa Electron

🚗🅿️📶🛒🏋️🍴🔌🛒🍷🛗
📺♨️🔌☺️🔍⛰️♨️🎵🎣🛗Ⓣ

Vauxhall Holiday Park 🅰️
★★★★
Holiday Park
Rose Award
Member BH&HPA
Acle New Road, Great Yarmouth
NR30 1TB
T: (01493) 857231
F: (01493) 331122
E: vauxhall.holidays@virgin.net
I: www.vauxhall-holiday-park.co.uk
On the A47 as you approach Great Yarmouth from Norwich. Signposted.
18.8 hectares (47 acres). Level, grassy.
252 touring pitches.

252	🚐	£13.00—£24.00
252	🚲	£13.00—£24.00
	⛺	£13.00—£24.00
373	🏠	£172.00—£545.00

Open April–September
Cards accepted: Barclaycard, Delta, Mastercard, Switch, Visa, Visa Electron

🚐🚗🅿️📶🛒🏋️🍴🔌🛒🏋️
✕📺🛒🔌♨️🛒☺️🍷⛰️🐾
♨️🔍🐾🎵🎣🛗Ⓣ|WH|

|Ad| See display advertisement on this page

Hertfordshire
Map ref 3D1

Several old buildings survive in this modern town including the 17th C Rawdon House, the medieval Chapel of St Katherine and Hogges Hall with its 15th C beams.

Lee Valley Caravan Park 🅰️
★★★★
Touring and Camping Park
Essex Road, Hoddesdon EN11 0AS
T: (01992) 462090
F: (01992) 462090
I: caravanpark@leevalleypark.org.uk

Off the A10 at the jct for Hoddesdon and turn left at the 2nd roundabout. Signposted.
9.6 hectares (24 acres). Level, grassy, sheltered.
100 touring pitches.

100	🚐	£10.40—£10.40
100	🚲	£10.40—£10.40
100	⛺	£10.40—£10.40

100 units privately owned
Open February–October
Cards accepted: Barclaycard, Delta, Maestro, Mastercard, Switch, Visa, Visa Electron

🚗🅿️📶🛒🏋️🍴🔌🛒🍷🔌♨️🛒
☺️⛰️🎵🎣🛗|WH|

|Ad| See display advertisement on page 45

Suffolk
Map ref 4C2

Seaside village whose church tower has served as a landmark to sailors for generations. Nearby is the Suffolk Wildlife and Country Park.

Heathland Beach Caravan Park 🅰️
★★★★
Holiday, Touring and Camping Park
Rose Award
Member BH&HPA
London Road, Kessingland, Lowestoft NR33 7PJ
T: (01502) 740337
F: (01502) 742355
E: heathlandbeach@btinternet.com
I: www.heathlandbeach.co.uk
One mile north of Kessingland village, off old B1437, now B1437 and 3 miles from Lowestoft. Signposted.
12 hectares (30 acres). Level, grassy, sheltered.
106 touring pitches.

106	🚐	£10.50—£13.50
106	🚲	£10.50—£13.50
106	⛺	£10.50—£13.50
10	🏠	£190.00—£400.00

165 units privately owned
Open April–October
Cards accepted: Barclaycard, Delta, Mastercard, Solo, Switch, Visa

🚗🅿️📶🛒🏋️🍴🔌🛒🏋️✕🍴
📺🔌♨️🛒☺️⛰️♨️🔍🐾
🛗|WH|

KING'S LYNN

Norfolk
Map ref 4B1

A busy town with many outstanding buildings. The Guildhall and Town Hall are both built of flint in a striking chequer design. Behind the Guildhall in the Old Gaol House the sounds and smells of prison life 2 centuries ago are recreated.
Tourist Information Centre
T: (01553) 763044

Bank Farm Caravan Park
★★★
Touring Park
Bank Farm, Fallow Pipe Road, Saddle Bow, King's Lynn PE34 3AS
T: (01553) 617305
F: (01553) 617648
Turn off King's Lynn southern bypass (A47) via slip road signposted Saddlebow. Once in the village, cross the river bridge and after 1 mile, fork right into Fallow Pipe Road. The farm is 0.66 miles, by the River Great Ouse. Signposted.
120 hectares (300 acres). Level, grassy, sheltered.
15 touring pitches.

15	🚐	£5.00—£5.00
15	🚗	£5.00—£5.00
2	▲	£3.00—£4.00

Open March—October

LITTLE CORNARD

Suffolk
Map ref 4B2

Willowmere Caravan Park
★★★
Touring and Camping Park
Member BH&HPA
Bures Road, Little Cornard, Sudbury CO10 0NN
T: (01787) 375559
F: (01787) 375559
From Sudbury B1508 to Colchester, 1.5 miles, site on left. Signposted.
1.2 hectares (3 acres). Level, grassy.
40 touring pitches.

30	🚐	£9.00—£9.00
15	🚗	£9.00—£9.00
15	▲	£8.00—£9.00

Open March—September

All accommodation in this guide has been rated, or is awaiting a rating, by a trained Tourist Board assessor.

MERSEA ISLAND

Essex
Map ref 4B3

Waldegraves Holiday Park
★★★
Holiday, Touring and Camping Park
Member BH&HPA
Mersea Island, Colchester, Essex CO5 8SE
T: (01206) 382898
F: (01206) 385359
E: holidays@waldegraves.co.uk
I: www.waldegraves.co.uk
Take the B1025 from Colchester then left to East Mersea, 2nd right then follow the brown tourist signs. Signposted.
10 hectares (25 acres). Level, grassy, sheltered.
60 touring pitches.

40	🚐	£9.00—£14.00
40	🚗	£9.00—£14.00
20	▲	£9.00—£14.00
14	🏠	£130.00—£300.00

195 units privately owned
Open March—November
Cards accepted: Amex, Barclaycard, Delta, Eurocard, Mastercard, Switch, Visa

MUNDESLEY

Norfolk
Map ref 4C1

Small seaside resort with a superb sandy beach and excellent bathing. Nearby is a smock-mill still with cap and sails.

Sandy Gulls Caravan Park
★★
Holiday and Touring Park
Member BH&HPA
Cromer Road, Mundesley Norwich NR11 8DF
T: (01263) 720513 (Answerphone)
From Cromer drive south along coast road for 5 miles. Signposted.
8 hectares (20 acres). Level, sloping, grassy.
160 touring pitches.

40	🚐	£7.00—£14.00
20	🚗	£6.00—£14.00
2	🏠	£170.00—£260.00

96 units privately owned
Open March—November

Map references apply to the colour maps at the back of this guide.

NORWICH

Norfolk
Map ref 4C1

Beautiful cathedral city and county town on the River Wensum with many fine museums and medieval churches. Norman castle, Guildhall and interesting medieval streets. Good shopping centre and market.
Tourist Information Centre
T: (01603) 666071

Reedham Ferry Touring and Camping Park
★★★
Touring and Camping Park
Reedham, Norwich NR13 3HA
T: (01493) 700429 & 07909 780747 (Mobile)
F: (01493) 700999
B1140 from Acle (A47) or B1140 from Beccles over ferry. Signposted.
1.6 hectares (4 acres). Level, grassy, sheltered.
20 touring pitches.

20	🚐	£8.00—£12.00
20	🚗	£8.00—£12.00
20	▲	£6.50—£9.00

Open April—October
Cards accepted: Barclaycard, Delta, Mastercard, Solo, Switch, Visa, Visa Electron

SAHAM HILLS

Norfolk
Map ref 4B1

Lowe Caravan Park ∧∧
★★★★
Touring and Camping Park
Ashdale, Hills Road, Saham Hills, Thetford IP25 7EW
T: (01953) 881051
F: (01953) 881051
From A11 Thetford, take Watton road and go through Watton High Street. Take 2nd turning on right, Saham Road, past Richmond Golf Club, take 2nd turning on right. At T-junction turn right and then 1st drive on the right.
20 touring pitches.

20	🚐	£5.00—£7.00
20	🚗	£5.00—£7.00
20	▲	£5.00—£7.00
	🏠	£195.00—£295.00

Open all year round

The ∧∧ symbol after a park name indicates that it is a Regional Tourist Board member.

ST OSYTH

Essex
Map ref 4B3

St Osyth was the daughter of the first Christian King of East Anglia. The priory gatehouse and gardens are open to the public during the summer.

The Orchards Holiday Village
★★★
Holiday, Touring and Camping Park
Member BH&HPA/NCC
Point Clear, St Osyth, Clacton-on-Sea CO16 8LJ
T: 0870 2425678
F: (01442) 254956
I: www.british-holidays.co.uk
From Clacton-on-Sea, take A133 towards Colchester. Approximately 4 miles from Clacton turn left following signs for St Osyth. At crossroads in St Osyth continue across and follow road for 2 miles, park is at the end of the road. Signposted.
66 hectares (165 acres). Sloping, grassy.
71 touring pitches.

71	🚐	£7.30—£20.60
71	🚏	£7.30—£20.60
150	🏕	£136.00—£563.00

1000 units privately owned
Open April–October
Cards accepted: Amex, Barclaycard, Delta, Mastercard, Solo, Switch, Visa, Visa Electron

🚗🅿️🗼🍴🏊🛎️🎣🏏🛒♿📺📶📱🔌⛱️😊🏕🚲🛶🎯🎾🎱 🏹🚬🛶🚩🎯Ⓣ🚾
Ad See display advertisement on page 10

SCRATBY

Norfolk
Map ref 4C1

Scratby Hall Caravan Park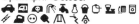
★★★★
Touring and Camping Park
Member BH&HPA
Scratby, Great Yarmouth NR29 3PH
T: (01493) 730283
Great Yarmouth A149 to Caister. Onto B1159 Scratby, site signed. Signposted.
2 hectares (5 acres). Level, grassy, sheltered.
108 touring pitches.

108	🚐	£4.95—£10.50
108	🚏	£4.95—£10.50
108	🏕	£4.95—£10.50

Open April–October

🚗🔌🗼🍴🏊🛎️🎣🏏🛒📶 🚬🛶😊🎯🏹🎾♿

SHOEBURYNESS

Essex
Map ref 4B3

East Beach Caravan Park
★★
Holiday, Touring and Camping Park
East Beach, Shoeburyness, Southend-on-Sea SS3 9SG
T: (01702) 292466
F: (01702) 290634
E: east.beach@care4free.net
From Southend follow Shoeburyness signs, then car park and camping signs. From A143 and A127 follow Shoeburyness signs and tourist signs.
3.6 hectares (9 acres). Level, grassy.
54 touring pitches.

44	🚐	£7.50
	🚏	£7.00
10	🏕	£6.50—£8.50

100 units privately owned
Open March–October

🚗🔌🗼🍴🏊🛎️🎣🏏🛒♿📶📱🔌 🛶😊⛱️

STANHOE

Norfolk
Map ref 4B1

The Rickels Caravan Site
★★★★
Touring Park
The Rickels, Bircham Road, Stanhoe, King's Lynn PE31 8PU
T: (01485) 518671
F: (01485) 518969
From King's Lynn, take the A148 to Hillington and turn left onto the B1153 to Great Bircham. Fork right onto the B1155. Go to the crossroads and straight over. The site is 100yds on the left. Signposted.
3.2 hectares (8 acres). Level, sloping, grassy, sheltered.
30 touring pitches.

15	🚐	£7.00—£8.50
10	🚏	£7.00—£8.50
5	🏕	£7.00—£8.50

Open March–October

🚗🅿️🔌🗼🍴🏊🛎️🎣🏏📶🔌😊 🏕⛱️

A key to symbols can be found inside the back cover flap.

Please mention this guide when making your booking.

WOODBRIDGE

Suffolk
Map ref 4C2

Once a busy seaport, the town is now a sailing centre on the River Deben. There are many buildings of architectural merit including the Bell and Angel Inns. The 18th C Tide Mill is now restored and open to the public.
Tourist Information Centre
T: (01394) 382240

Forest Camping
★★★
Touring and Camping Park
Tangham, Rendelsham Forest, Butley, Woodbridge IP12 3NF
T: (01394) 450707
F: (01394) 450707
E: camping@anglianet.co.uk
I: www.forestcamping.co.uk
Six miles east of Woodbridge off B1084 to Orford. Signposted.
2.8 hectares (7 acres). Level, sloping, grassy.
90 touring pitches.

90	🚐	£8.00—£10.00
90	🚏	£8.00—£10.00
90	🏕	£8.00—£10.00

Open April–October
Cards accepted: Barclaycard, Delta, Maestro, Mastercard, Solo, Switch, Visa, Visa Electron

🚗🅿️🔌🗼🍴🏊🛎️🎣🏏🛒📶📱🔌 🛶😊🏕⛱️

COLOUR MAPS

Colour maps at the back of this guide pinpoint all places in which you will find parks listed.

For ideas on places to visit refer to the introduction at the beginning of this section.

All accommodation in this guide has been rated, or is awaiting a rating, by a trained Tourist Board assessor.

You are advised to confirm your booking in writing.

On-line Information

In-depth information about travelling in **Britain** is now available on **BTA's VisitBritain** website.

Covering everything from castles to leisure parks and from festivals to road and rail links, the site complements Where to Stay perfectly, giving you up-to-the-minute details to help you with your travel plans.

BRITAIN on the internet
www.visitbritain.com

DAVID BELLAMY CONSERVATION AWARDS

If you are looking for a site that's environmentally friendly look for those that have achieved the David Bellamy Conservation Award. Recently launched in conjunction with the British Holiday & Home Parks Association, this award is given to sites which are committed to protecting and enhancing the environment – from care of the hedgerows and wildlife to recycling waste – and are members of the Association. More information about this award scheme can be found at the front of the guide.

SOUTH WEST

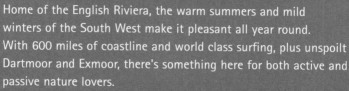

Home of the English Riviera, the warm summers and mild winters of the South West make it pleasant all year round. With 600 miles of coastline and world class surfing, plus unspoilt Dartmoor and Exmoor, there's something here for both active and passive nature lovers.

Step back 2000 year's in Bath's Roman Baths. Other great cities include Bristol, Plymouth and Wells. Clovelly, with its cobbled, car-free streets, and the little fishing village of Mousehole (which really is the cat's whiskers!) are just two of the many quaint places to visit.

The two-week Bath International Music Festival is on from mid May with something for everyone — from contemporary to classical, including jazz and more.

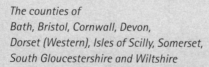

The counties of
Bath, Bristol, Cornwall, Devon,
Dorset (Western), Isles of Scilly, Somerset,
South Gloucestershire and Wiltshire

FOR MORE INFORMATION CONTACT:
South West Tourism
Admail 3186, Exeter EX2 7WH
Tel: (0870) 442 0880
Fax: (0870) 442 0881
Email: info@westcountryholidays.com
Internet: www.westcountryholidays.com

The Pictures:
1 Isles of Scilly;
2 Fingle Bridge, Dartmoor, Devon;
3 Cotehele, Cornwall.

Where to Go in the South West - see pages 108-112
Where to Stay in the South West - see pages 113-130

Whilst in the
SOUTH WEST ...

You will find hundreds of interesting places to visit during your stay, just some of which are listed in these pages.

Contact any Tourist Information Centre in the region for more ideas on days out in the South West.

At Bristol Harbourside

Bristol BS1 5DB

A new international, waterfront, leisure, education and entertainment complex. Including two visitor attractions – Wildscreen@Bristol, featuring wildlife and the environment, and Explore@Bristol, focusing on science and technology.

Atwell-Wilson Motor Museum Trust

Calne, Wiltshire SN11 0NF
Tel: (01249) 813119
Motor museum with vintage, post-vintage and classic cars, including American models. Classic motorbikes. A 17thC water meadow walk and play area.

Babbacombe Model Village

Babbacombe, Devon TQ1 3LA
Tel: (01803) 315315
Over 400 models many with sound and animation in four acres of award-winning gardens. See modern towns, villages and rural areas. Stunning illuminations.

Bristol City Museum & Art Gallery

Queen's Road, Bristol BS8 1RL
Tel: (0117) 922 3571
Collection representing applied, oriental and fine art, archaeology, geology, natural history, ethnography and Egyptology.

Bristol Zoo Gardens

Clifton, Bristol BS8 3HA
Tel: (0117) 973 8951
Enjoy an exciting real life experience and see over 300 species of wildlife in beautiful gardens.

Buckland Abbey

Yelverton, Devon PL20 6EY
Tel: (01822) 853607
Originally a Cistercian monastery, then home of Sir Francis Drake. Ancient buildings, exhibitions, herb garden, craft workshops and estate walks.

Cheddar Caves and Gorge

Cheddar, Somerset BS27 3QF
Tel: (01934) 742343
Beautiful caves located in Cheddar Gorge. Gough's Cave with cathedral-like caverns and Cox's Cave with stalagmites and stalactites. Also 'The Crystal Quest' fantasy adventure.

The Combe Martin Motor Cycle Collection

Combe Martin, Ilfracombe, Devon EX34 0DH
Tel: (01271) 882346
Collection of British motorcycles displayed against a background of old petrol pumps, signs and garage equipment. Motoring nostalgia in an old world atmosphere.

Combe Martin Wildlife and Dinosaur Park

Combe Martin, Ilfracombe, Devon EX34 0NG
Tel: (01271) 882486
Wildlife park and life-size models of dinosaurs.

Crealy Park

Clyst St Mary, Exeter, Devon EX5 1DR
Tel: (01395) 233200
One of Devon's largest animal farms. Milk a cow, feed a lamb and pick up a piglet. Adventure playgrounds. Dragonfly Lake and farm trails.

Dairyland Farm World

Tresillian, Barton, Newquay, Cornwall TR8 5AA
Tel: (01872) 510246
One hundred and seventy cows milked in a rotary parlour. Heritage centre. Farm nature trail. Farm park with animals, pets and wildfowl. Daily events.

Exmoor Falconry & Animal Farm

West Lynch Farm, Allerford, Somerset TA24 8HJ
Tel: (01643) 862816
Farm animals, rare breeds, pets' corner, birds of prey and owls. Flying displays daily. Historic farm buildings.

Flambards Village

Culdrose Manor, Helston, Cornwall TR13 0QA
Tel: (01326) 573404
Life-size Victorian village with fully stocked shops, carriages and fashions. 'Britain in the Blitz' life-size wartime street, historic aircraft. Exploratorium.

Heale Garden & Plant Centre

Middle Woodford, Salisbury, Wiltshire SP4 6NT
Tel: (01722) 782504
Mature, traditional garden with shrubs, musk and other roses, plus kitchen garden. Authentic Japanese teahouse in water garden. Magnolias. Snowdrops and aconites in winter.

International Animal Rescue Animal Tracks

Ash Mill, South Molton, Devon EX36 4QW
Tel: (01769) 550277
A 60-acre animal sanctuary with a wide range of rescued animals from monkeys to chinchillas. Shire horses and ponies. Also rare plant nursery.

Jamaica Inn Museums (Potters Museum of Curiosity)

Bolventor, Launceston, Cornwall PL15 7TS
Tel: (01566) 86838
Museums contain lifetime work of Walter Potter, a Victorian taxidermist. Exhibits include Kittens' Wedding, Death of Cock Robin and The Story of Smuggling.

Longleat

Warminster, Wiltshire BA12 7NW
Tel: (01985) 844400
Great Elizabethan house with lived-in atmosphere. Important libraries and Italian ceilings. 'Capability' Brown designed parkland. Safari Park.

The Lost Gardens of Heligan

Heligan, Pentewan, St Austell, Cornwall PL26 6EN
Tel: (01726) 845100
The largest garden restoration project undertaken since the war. New for 2000: The Lost Valley, covering 35 acres.

Lyme Regis Philpot Museum

Lyme Regis, Dorset DT7 3QA
Tel: (01297) 443370
Fossils, geology, local history and lace exhibitions. Museum shop.

The Pictures:
1 Selworthy, Somerset;
2 The interior of Salisbury Cathedral;
3 Land's End, Cornwall;
4 Wells Cathedral, Somerset;
5 Clifton Suspension Bridge, Bristol.

National Marine Aquarium

Plymouth, Devon PL4 0LF
Tel: (01752) 600301
The UK's only world-class aquarium. Visitor experiences include a mountain stream and Caribbean reef complete with sharks.

Paignton Zoo Environmental Park

Paignton, Devon TQ4 7EU
Tel: (01803) 557479
One of England's largest zoos with over 1200 animals in the beautiful setting of 75 acres of botanical gardens. A popular family day out.

Plant World

Newton Abbot, Devon TQ12 4SE
Tel: (01803) 872939
Four acres of gardens including the unique 'map of the world' gardens. Cottage garden. Panoramic views. Comprehensive nursery of rare and more unusual plants.

Plymouth Dome

The Hoe, Plymouth, Devon PL1 2NZ
Tel: (01752) 603300
Purpose-built visitor interpretation centre showing the history of Plymouth and its people from Stone Age beginnings to satellite technology.

Powderham Castle

Kenton, Exeter, Devon EX6 8JQ
Tel: (01626) 890243
Built in 1390 and restored in 18thC. Georgian interiors, china, furnishings and paintings. Family home of the Courtenays for over 600 years. Fine views across the deer park and River Exe.

Quaywest

Goodrington Sands, Paignton, Devon TQ4 6LN
Tel: (01803) 555550
Wettest and wildest fun at this outdoor waterpark. Eight flumes. Adult and children's swimming pool with water heated to 26°C. Grand-Prix go karts, amusement rides, bumper boats and crazy golf.

Railway Village Museum

Swindon, Wiltshire SN1 5BJ
Tel: (01793) 466555
Foreman's house in original Great Western Railway village. Furnished to re-create a Victorian working-class home.

Roman Baths Museum

Abbey Church Yard, Bath BA1 1LZ
Tel: (01225) 477785
Roman baths, hot springs and Roman temple. Jewellery, coins, curses and votive offerings from the sacred spring.

St Michael's Mount

Marazion, Cornwall TR17 0HT
Tel: (01736) 710507
Originally the site of a Benedictine chapel, the castle on its rock dates from 14thC. Fine views towards Land's End and the Lizard. Reached by foot, or ferry at high tide in the summer.

Steam – Museum of the Great Western Railway

Swindon, Wiltshire
Tel: (01793) 466646
Historic Great Western Railway locomotives, wide range of nameplates, models, illustrations, posters and tickets.

Stourhead House and Garden

Stourton, Warminster, Wiltshire BA12 6QH
Tel: (01747) 841152
Landscaped garden laid out in 1741-1780, with lakes, temples, rare trees and plants. The house, begun in 1721 by Colen Campbell, contains fine paintings and Chippendale furniture.

Tate Gallery St Ives

Porthmeor Beach, St Ives, Cornwall TR26 1TG
Tel: (01736) 796226
Opened in 1993 and offering a unique introduction to modern art. Changing displays focus on the modern movement St Ives is famous for.

Teignmouth Museum

French Street, Teignmouth, Devon TQ14 8ST
Tel: (01626) 777041
Exhibits include 16thC cannon and artefacts from Armada wreck and local history, 1920s pier machines and 1877 cannon.

The Time Machine

Weston-super-Mare, North Somerset BS23 1PR
Tel: (01934) 621028
Edwardian gaslight company building with central glazed courtyard. Seaside gallery, costume, Victorian cottage. Doll collection, local archaeology and natural history. Art gallery, people's collection.

Tintagel Castle

Tintagel, Cornwall PL34 0HE
Tel: (01840) 770328
Medieval ruined castle on wild, wind-swept coast. Famous for associations with Arthurian legend. Built largely in 13thC by Richard, Earl of Cornwall. Used as a prison in 14thC.

Tithe Barn Children's Farm

New Barn Road, Abbotsbury, Dorset DT3 4JF
Tel: (01305) 871817
Extensive children's farm for children under 11 years. Activities include hand-feeding milk to lambs and kids by bottle. Replicas of Terracotta Warriors on display in barn.

Totnes Costume Museum – Devonshire Collection of Period Costume

High Street, Totnes, Devon TQ9 5NP
Tel: (01803) 863821
New exhibition of costumes and accessories each season, displayed in one of the historic merchant's houses of Totnes.

Underground Passages

Exeter, Devon EX4 3PZ
Tel: (01392) 265887
Remarkable city passageways built during medieval times to carry water into the city centre. Now the only one's in Britain open to the public. Exhibition, video and guided tour.

West Somerset Railway

Minehead, Somerset TA24 5BG
Tel: (01643) 704996
Preserved steam railway operating between Minehead and Bishops Lydeard, near Taunton. Model railway and museums enroute. Longest independent railway in Britain, 32 km (20 miles).

Woodlands Leisure Park

Blackawton, Totnes, Devon TQ9 7DQ
Tel: (01803) 712598
A full day of variety set in 60 acres of countryside. Twelve venture playzones including 500-metre (1,640 ft) toboggan run, commando course, large indoor play area, toddlers' area and animals.

Wookey Hole Caves and Papermill

Wookey Hole, Wells, Somerset BA5 1BB
Tel: (01749) 672243
Spectacular caves and legendary home of the Witch of Wookey. Working Victorian papermill including Old Penny Arcade, Magical Mirror Maze and Cave Diving Museum.

The Pictures:
1   Dartmoor Ponies;
2   Torquay, Devon;
3   Bath;
4   Tarr Steps, Exmoor National Park;
5   Sunset at Stonehenge;
6   Shaftesbury Hill, Dorset;
7   Salisbury Cathedral, Wiltshire.

Find out more about the
SOUTH WEST ...

Further information about holidays and attractions
in the South West is available from:

SOUTH WEST TOURISM
Admail 3186, Exeter EX2 7WH.
Tel: **(0870) 442 0880**
Fax: **(0870) 442 0881**
Email: **info@westcountryholidays.com**
Internet: www.westcountryholidays.com

The following publications are available free from South West Tourism:

Bed & Breakfast Touring Map

West Country Holiday Homes & Apartments

West Country Hotels and Guesthouses

Glorious Gardens of the West Country

Camping and Caravan Touring Map

Tourist Attractions Touring Map

Trencherman's West Country, Restaurant Guide

The Pictures:
1   Stonehenge;
2   Newquay, Cornwall.

Getting to the
SOUTH WEST ...

BY ROAD: Somerset, Devon and Cornwall are well served from the North and Midlands
by the M6/M5 which extends just beyond Exeter, where it links in with the dual
carriageways of the A38 to Plymouth, A380 to Torbay and the A30 into Cornwall.
The North Devon Link Road A361 joins Junction 37 with the coast of north Devon
and A39, which then becomes the Atlantic Highway into Cornwall.

BY RAIL: The main towns in the South West are served throughout the year by fast,
direct and frequent rail services from all over the country. InterCity 125 trains operate
from London (Paddington) to Chippenham, Swindon, Bath, Bristol, Weston-super-Mare,
Taunton, Exeter, Plymouth and Penzance, and also from Scotland, the North East and the
Midlands to the South West. A service runs from London (Waterloo) to Exeter, via
Salisbury, Yeovil and Crewkerne. Sleeper services operate between Devon and Cornwall
and London as well as between Bristol and Glasgow and Edinburgh. Motorail services
operate from strategic points to key South West locations.

WHERE TO STAY (SOUTH WEST)

Parks in this region are listed in alphabetical order of place name, and then in alphabetical order of park.

Map references refer to the colour location maps at the back of this guide. The first number indicates the map to use; the letter and number which follow refer to the grid reference on the map.

At-a-glance symbols can be found inside the back cover flap. Keep this open for easy reference.

ASHBURTON

Devon
Map ref 2C2

Formerly a thriving wool centre and important as one of Dartmoor's four stannary towns. Today's busy market town has many period buildings. Ancient tradition is maintained in the annual ale-tasting and bread-weighing ceremony. Good centre for exploring Dartmoor or the south Devon coast.

Parkers Farm Holiday Park ♙
★★★
Holiday Park
Member BH&HPA
Higher Mead Farm, Alston,
Ashburton, Newton Abbot
TQ13 7LJ
T: (01364) 652598
F: (01364) 654004
E: parkersfarm@hotmail.com
*Take A38 from Exeter to Plymouth.
When you see sign 26 miles to
Plymouth, take 2nd left marked
Woodland and Denbury. At Alston
Cross. Signposted.*
148 hectares (370 acres). Level,
grassy, hard.
60 touring pitches.

60	🚐	£5.00—£10.50
60	🚚	£5.00—£10.50
60	⛺	£5.00—£10.50
25	🏠	£150.00—£400.00

Open March–November
Cards accepted: Barclaycard, Delta,
JCB, Maestro, Mastercard, Solo,
Switch, Visa, Visa Electron

🔌🚶P🚐🏧🎣🛝🛁🛒🖲♿
✕🍴📺📠🖥🚿🚪☺🔍⚱🪨♨
🎵🔥🅣
Ad See display advertisement on
page 15

AXMINSTER

Devon
Map ref 2D2

This tree-shaded market town on the banks of the River Axe was one of Devon's earliest West Saxon settlements, but is better known for its carpet making. Based on Turkish methods, the industry began in 1755, declined in the 1830s and was revived in 1937.

Andrewshayes Caravan Park ♙
★★★
Holiday Park
Member BH&HPA
Dalwood, Axminster EX13 7DY
T: (01404) 831225
F: (01404) 831893
E: enquiries@andrewhayes.co.uk
I: www.andrewhayes.co.uk
*One hundred and fifty yds off A35
signposted Dalwood, Stockland, at
Taunton Cross. Three miles Axminster,
6 miles Honiton. Signposted.*
4 hectares (10 acres). Sloping,
grassy, hard.
90 touring pitches.

60	🚐	£7.00—£9.50
10	🚚	£8.00—£9.50
20	⛺	£7.00—£8.00
22	🏠	£90.00—£400.00

58 units privately owned
Open January, March–December
Cards accepted: Barclaycard, Delta,
Eurocard, JCB, Mastercard, Solo,
Switch, Visa

🔌🚐🚶🏧🎣🛝🛁🛒🖲♿✕📺
🖥📠🔥🚿🚪☺🔍⚱⛩🚴🪨♨🅣

Map references apply to the colour maps at the back of this guide.

Hunters Moon Holiday Park ♙
★★★
Holiday Park
Member BH&HPA
Hawkchurch, Axminster EX13 5UL
T: (01297) 678402
F: (01297) 678402
*The park lies approximately 2 miles
east of Axminster. Turn off the main
A35 onto the B3165 towards
Crewkerne then follow the caravan and
camping signs. Signposted.*
5.2 hectares (13 acres). Level,
sloping, grassy, hard.
170 touring pitches.

170	🚐	£4.50—£10.00
170	🚚	£4.50—£10.00
170	⛺	£4.50—£10.00
10	🏠	£120.00—£420.00

20 units privately owned
Open March–November
& Christmas
Cards accepted: Barclaycard, Delta,
Mastercard, Visa, Visa Electron

🚐🔌🏧🎣🛝🛁🛒🖲🛞✕🍴⚱📹
🔥🛁☺🔍♨

WELCOME HOST

This is a nationally recognised customer care programme which aims to promote the highest standards of service and a warm welcome. Parks taking part in this initiative are indicated by the WH symbol.

Please check prices and other details at the time of booking.

113

BATH

Bath & North East Somerset
Map ref 3B2

Georgian spa city beside the River Avon. Important Roman site with impressive reconstructed baths, uncovered in 19th C. Bath Abbey built on site of monastery where first king of England was crowned (AD 973). Fine architecture in mellow local stone. Pump Room and museums.
Tourist Information Centre
T: (01225) 477101

Bath Marina and Caravan Park ⋒
★★★★
Touring Park
Brassmill Lane, Bath BA1 3JT
T: (01225) 428778
F: (01225) 428778
M4 jct 18, follow A46 to Bath. One and a half miles from city centre, opposite Newbridge park-and-ride bus terminus on the A4 Bristol road. Signposted.
1.6 hectares (4 acres). Level, grassy, hard, sheltered.
88 touring pitches.

64	⊞	£12.00—£15.00
88	⊞	£12.00—£15.00

Open all year round
Cards accepted: Barclaycard, Delta, Eurocard, Maestro, Mastercard, Solo, Switch, Visa, Visa Electron

BICKINGTON

Devon
Map ref 2C2

The Dartmoor Halfway ⋒
★★★★
Touring Park
Bickington, Newton Abbot
TQ12 6JW
T: (01626) 821270
F: (01626) 821820
M5 junction 31 onto A38 signposted Plymouth. After 10 miles on the A38 past Exeter, leave the A38 at the A382 signposted Newton Abbot. Take 3rd roundabout exit for Liverton, stay on this road for 3 miles, when you reach T-junction turn left.
Level, grassy, hard.
22 touring pitches.

22	⊞	£6.00—£8.50
22	⊞	

Open all year round
Cards accepted: Amex, Barclaycard, Delta, Diners, Eurocard, JCB, Maestro, Mastercard, Solo, Switch, Visa, Visa Electron

BLACKWATER

Cornwall
Map ref 2B3

Trevarth Holiday Park
★★★★
Holiday Park
Member BH&HPA
Blackwater, Truro TR4 8HR
T: (01872) 560266
F: (01872) 560266
Three hundred metres from Blackwater exit off Chiverton roundabout on A30. Four and a half miles north east of Redruth. Signposted.
1.8 hectares (4.5 acres). Level, grassy, sheltered.
30 touring pitches.

30	⊞	£5.00—£8.50
30	⊞	£5.00—£8.50
30	▲	£5.00—£8.50
20	⊞	£90.00—£420.00

Open April–October
Cards accepted: Barclaycard, Delta, Eurocard, Mastercard, Visa

[Ad] See display advertisement on this page

A key to symbols can be found inside the back cover flap.

BLUE ANCHOR

Somerset
Map ref 2D1

Small resort on the Bristol Channel, a station on the West Somerset Railway. Exmoor National Park, Quantocks and Brendon Hills are nearby.

Blue Anchor Bay Caravan Park ⋒
★★★★
Holiday and Touring Park
Rose Award
Member BH&HPA/NCC
Blue Anchor, Minehead TA24 6JT
T: (01643) 821360
F: (01643) 821572
E: enquiries@hoburne.co.uk
I: www.hoburne.co.uk
Exit M5 at jct 25 and take A358 for Minehead. After 12 miles turn left onto A39 to Williton. Approximately 4 miles later turn right onto B3191 Carhampton. Follow signs to Blue Anchor Park for 1.5 miles. Park is on the right-hand side. Signposted.
12 hectares (30 acres). Level, grassy, hard.
103 touring pitches.

103	⊞	£9.00—£17.00
103	⊞	£9.00—£17.00
37	⊞	£90.00—£410.00

263 units privately owned
Open March–October
Cards accepted: Barclaycard, Delta, Maestro, Mastercard, Switch, Visa

BODMIN

Cornwall
Map ref 2B2

County town south-west of Bodmin Moor with a ruined priory and church dedicated to St Petroc. Nearby are Lanhydrock House and Pencarrow House.
Tourist Information Centre
T: (01208) 76616

Ruthern Valley Holidays ⋒
★★★
Holiday and Touring Park
Ruthernbridge, Bodmin PL30 5LU
T: (01208) 831395
F: (01208) 832324
I: www.bookcornwall.com

A389 Bodmin to St Austell road.follow sign for Ruthernbridge Ruthern, at the bridge turn left,site is 300 yds on the left. Signposted.
2.8 hectares (7 acres). Sloping, grassy.
30 touring pitches.

30	🚐	£7.75—£11.25
30	🚍	£7.75—£11.25
30	▲	£7.75—£9.75
6	⛺	£125.00—£350.00

Open March–December

BRIDPORT

Dorset
Map ref 3A3

Market town and chief producer of nets and ropes just inland of dramatic Dorset coast. Old, broad streets built for drying and twisting and long gardens for rope-walks. Grand arcaded Town Hall and Georgian buildings. Local history museum has Roman relics.
Tourist Information Centre
T: (01308) 424901

Freshwater Beach Holiday Park ⚠
★★★★
Holiday Park
Member BH&HPA
Burton Bradstock, Bridport
DT6 4PT
T: (01308) 897317
F: (01308) 897336
E: enquiries@fbhp.co.uk
I: www.fphp.co.uk
From Bridport take B3157, situated 2 miles on the right. Signposted.
12 hectares (30 acres). Level, grassy.
425 touring pitches.

425	🚐	£8.00—£18.00
425	🚍	£8.00—£18.00
425	▲	£8.00—£18.00
60	⛺	£125.00—£480.00

215 units privately owned
Open April–October

Cards accepted: Barclaycard, Delta, Eurocard, JCB, Mastercard, Solo, Switch, Visa, Visa Electron

Ad See display advertisement on this page

Highlands End Holiday Park ⚠
★★★★★
Holiday and Touring Park
Rose Award
Member BH&HPA
Eype, Bridport DT6 6AR
T: (01308) 422139
F: (01308) 425672
E: highlands@wdlh.co.uk
I: www.wdlh.co.uk
One mile west of Bridport turn south for Eype, park signposted.
11.2 hectares (28 acres). Level, grassy, hard.
195 touring pitches.

120	🚐	£8.00—£12.50
120	🚍	£8.00—£12.50
75	▲	£8.00—£12.50
17	⛺	£180.00—£440.00

144 units privately owned
Open March–October
Cards accepted: Mastercard, Switch, Visa

IMPORTANT NOTE

Information on accommodation listed in this guide has been supplied by the proprietors. As changes may occur you are advised to check details at the time of booking.

BUDE

Cornwall
Map ref 2C2

Resort on dramatic Atlantic coast. High cliffs give spectacular sea and inland views. Golf-course, cricket pitch, folly, surfing, coarse-fishing and boating. Mother-town Stratton was base of Royalist Sir Bevil Grenville.
Tourist Information Centre
T: (01288) 354240

Budemeadows Touring Holiday Park
★★★★★
Touring Park
Bude EX23 0NA
T: (01288) 361646
F: (01288) 361646
E: wendyjo@globalnet.co.uk
I: www.budemeadows.com
Signposted on A39, 3 miles south of Bude, 200 yds past crossroads to Widemouth Bay. Signposted.
3.8 hectares (9.5 acres). Level, sloping, grassy, hard, sheltered.
145 touring pitches.

145	🚐	£9.50—£12.00
50	🚍	£9.50—£12.00
145	▲	£9.50—£12.00

Open all year round
Cards accepted: Barclaycard, Delta, Eurocard, JCB, Mastercard, Solo, Switch, Visa

Upper Lynstone Caravan and Camping Site ⚠
★★★
Holiday and Touring Park
Member BH&HPA
Lynstone, Bude EX23 0LP
T: (01288) 352017
F: (01288) 359034
E: reception@upperlynstone.co.uk
I: www.upperlynstone.co.uk
Half a mile south of Bude on coastal road to Widemouth Bay. Signposted.
2.4 hectares (6 acres). Level, sloping, grassy.

Continued ▶

BUDE

Continued

90 touring pitches.

90		£7.00—£10.50
90		£7.00—£10.50
90		£7.00—£10.50
16		£126.00—£305.00

30 units privately owned
Open April–September
Cards accepted: Barclaycard, Delta,
Eurocard, Mastercard, Switch, Visa,
Visa Electron

Wooda Farm Park

★★★★★
Holiday and Touring Park
Member BH&HPA
Poughill, Bude EX23 9HJ
T: (01288) 352069
E: enquiries@wooda.co.uk
I: www.wooda.co.uk
From A39 north of Stratton, take coast road to Poughill and Combe Valley. Wooda is 1 mile from A39. Signposted.
44 hectares (110 acres). Level,
sloping, grassy, hard, sheltered.
200 touring pitches.

200		£7.50—£11.00
200		£7.50—£11.00
200		£7.50—£11.00
55		£100.00—£480.00

Open April–October
Cards accepted: Barclaycard, Delta,
Diners, Eurocard, Mastercard,
Switch, Visa

BURNHAM-ON-SEA

Somerset
Map ref 2D1

Small Victorian resort famous for
sunsets and sandy beaches, a few
minutes from junction 22 of the M5.
Ideal base for touring Somerset,
Cheddar and Bath. Good sporting
facilities, championship golf-course.
Tourist Information Centre
T: (01278) 787852

Burnham-on-Sea Holiday Village

★★★★
Holiday Park
Member BH&HPA/NCC
Marine Drive, Burnham-on-Sea
TA8 1LA
T: 0870 2425678
F: (01442) 254956
Off M5 junction 22, A38 to Highbridge, right over railway bridge, B3139 to Burnham-on-Sea, turn left after Elf garage onto Marine Drive. Park situated 400 yards on the left. Signposted.
38 hectares (95 acres). Level, grassy.

75 touring pitches.

10		£9.50—£29.00
47		£9.50—£29.00
18		£9.50—£19.50
272		£149.00—£711.00

Open March–November
Cards accepted: Barclaycard, Delta,
Mastercard, Solo, Switch, Visa, Visa
Electron

[Ad] See display advertisement on
page 10

CHARD

Somerset
Map ref 2D2

Market town in hilly countryside.
The wide main street has some
handsome buildings, among them
the Guildhall, court house and
almshouses. Modern light industry
and dairy produce have replaced
19th C lace making which came at
decline of cloth trade.
Tourist Information Centre
T: (01460) 67463

Alpine Grove Touring Park

★★★
Touring Park
Alpine Grove, Forton, Chard
TA20 4HD
T: (01460) 63479
Turn off A303, follow signposts for Chard, turn off before Chard on the left, follow signs for Cricket St Thomas, turn off onto B3167. After 1 mile see signpost Alpine Grove, turn right, 0.5 mile on your right.
3.6 hectares (9 acres). Level, sloping,
grassy, hard, sheltered.
40 touring pitches.

40		£5.50—£7.50
40		£5.50—£7.50
40		£5.50—£7.50

Open April–September

CHEDDAR

Somerset
Map ref 2D1

Large village at foot of Mendips just
south of the spectacular Cheddar
Gorge. Close by are Roman and
Saxon sites and famous show caves.
Traditional Cheddar cheese is still
made here.

Broadway House Holiday Touring Caravan and Camping Park

★★★★
Holiday Park
Rose Award
Member BH&HPA
Cheddar, Somerset BS27 3DB
T: (01934) 742610
F: (01934) 744950
E: enquiries@
broadwayhouse.uk.com
I: www.broadwayhouse.uk.com
M5 jct 22. Midway betwen Cheddar and Axbridge on A371. Signposted.
12 hectares (30 acres). Level,
sloping, grassy, hard, sheltered.
200 touring pitches.

		£5.00—£13.50
		£5.00—£10.50
		£5.00—£13.50
35		£125.00—£540.00

Open March–November
Cards accepted: Amex, Barclaycard,
Delta, Diners, Eurocard, JCB,
Mastercard, Solo, Switch, Visa, Visa
Electron

CROYDE BAY

Devon
Map ref 2C1

Hamlet on the North Devon coast,
west of Croyde village, with fine
surfing beaches and magnificent cliff
scenery.

Ruda Holiday Park and Croyde Burrows

★★★★
Holiday Park
Member BH&HPA
Croyde Bay, Braunton EX33 1NY
T: (01271) 890671
F: (01271) 890656
E: enquiries@ruda.co.uk
I: www.ruda.co.uk
M5 jct 27, take the A361 to Barnstaple. From Barnstaple continue on A361 to Braunton. In the centre of Braunton, turn left after 2nd set of traffic lights onto the B3231. Enter Croyde Village and Ruda and Cascades are signposted.
88 hectares (220 acres). Sloping,
grassy.

306 touring pitches.

91	🚐	£9.00—£28.00
91	🚎	£6.00—£20.00
215	⛺	£6.00—£20.00
280	🏠	£119.00—£599.00

Open all year round
Cards accepted: Barclaycard, Delta,
Eurocard, Mastercard, Switch, Visa

DAWLISH

Devon
Map ref 2D2

Small resort, developed in Regency
and Victorian periods beside
Dawlish Water. Town centre has
ornamental riverside gardens with
black swans. One of England's most
scenic stretches of railway was built
by Brunel alongside jagged red cliffs
between the sands and the town.
Tourist Information Centre
T: (01626) 863589

Cofton Country Holiday Park ⚶
★★★★
Holiday Park
Member BH&HPA
Starcross, Exeter EX6 8RP
T: (01626) 890111
F: (01626) 891572
E: enquiries@
cofton-holidays-devon.co.uk
I: www.cofton-holidays-devon.co.uk
A379 Exeter to Dawlish road, 3 miles
Exeter side of Dawlish. Signposted.
6.4 hectares (16 acres). Level,
grassy, sheltered.
450 touring pitches.

450	🚐	£6.50—£11.00
450	🚎	£6.50—£11.00
450	⛺	£6.50—£11.00
62	🏠	£200.00—£580.00

Open April—October

Please mention this guide
when making your booking.

Cards accepted: Barclaycard, Delta,
Eurocard, Maestro, Mastercard,
Solo, Switch, Visa, Visa Electron

Ad See display advertisement on this
page

DAWLISH WARREN

Devon
Map ref 2D2

Popular with campers and
caravanners, a sandy spit of land at
the mouth of the River Exe. The
sand dunes with river golf links are
rich in plant and bird life. Brunel's
atmospheric railway once ran along
the dramatic line between jagged red
cliffs and sandy shore.

Welcome Family Holiday Park ⚶
★★★★
Holiday Park
Rose Award
Warren Road, Dawlish Warren,
Dawlish EX7 0PH
T: (01626) 862070 (Reservations &
enquiries) & 888323
F: (01626) 888157
From M5 follow A379 for
approximately 8 miles, signposted
Dawlish, then to Dawlish Warren.
10.4 hectares (26 acres). Level,
grassy.

200	🏠	£70.00—£500.00

140 units privately owned
Open April—October
Cards accepted: Barclaycard, Delta,
Mastercard, Solo, Switch, Visa

Ad See display advertisement on
page 15

The ⚶ symbol after a
park name indicates that
it is a Regional Tourist
Board member.

DORCHESTER

Dorset
Map ref 3B3

Busy medieval county town
destroyed by fires in 17th and 18th
C. Cromwellian stronghold and
scene of Judge Jeffreys' Bloody
Assize after Monmouth Rebellion of
1685. Tolpuddle Martyrs were tried
in Shire Hall. Museum has Roman
and earlier exhibits and Hardy relics.
Tourist Information Centre
T: (01305) 267992

Giants Head Caravan and Camping Park
★★
Touring Park
Member BH&HPA
Old Sherborne Road, Cerne Abbas,
Dorchester DT2 7TR
T: (01300) 341242
Into Dorchester, avoiding bypass, at top
of town roundabout, take Sherborne
road, after 500 yds take right-hand fork
at Loder garage. From Cerne Abbas
take Buckland Newton road.
Signposted.
1.6 hectares (4 acres). Level, grassy,
sheltered.
50 touring pitches.

50	🚐	£6.50—£8.00
50	🚎	£6.00—£7.50
50	⛺	£6.50—£8.00

Open March—October

IMPORTANT NOTE

Information on
accommodation listed in this
guide has been supplied by
the proprietors. As changes
may occur you are advised
to check details at the
time of booking.

DREWSTEIGNTON

Devon
Map ref 2C2

Pretty village of thatched cottages overlooking the steep, wooded Teign valley at the northern edge of Dartmoor. The tree-shaded square shelters a fine 15th C church. To the west is Sir Edwin Lutyens' dramatic Castle Drogo in a romantic setting high over the Teign Gorge.

Clifford Bridge Park ⋀

★★★
Touring Park
Member BH&HPA
Clifford, Drewsteignton, Exeter
EX6 6QE
T: (01647) 24226
F: (01647) 24116
E: info@clifford-bridge.co.uk
I: www.clifford-bridge.co.uk
M5 jct 31 west along A30 to Woodleigh jct and turn left signed Cheriton Bishop. At Old Thatch Inn follow 'brown tent' signs to Clifford Bridge. Signposted.
3.2 hectares (8 acres). Level, grassy, sheltered.
64 touring pitches.

24	🚐	£7.40—£11.50
64	🚏	£6.60—£11.50
40	⛺	£6.60—£11.50
	🏠	£209.00—£499.00

Open April–September

🔌🚗🔲⊙🦽🔥💧🛁🕐🛒🏕
📺✂️🛒⊙🔍⚑🎣∪🐾🅰️🅃
🆆🅷
🅰️🅳 See display advertisement on this page

EXETER

Devon
Map ref 2D2

University city rebuilt after the 1940s around its cathedral. Attractions include 13th C cathedral with fine west front; notable waterfront buildings; Guildhall; Royal Albert Memorial Museum; underground passages; Northcott Theatre.
Tourist Information Centre
T: (01392) 265700

Kennford International Caravan Park ⋀

Member BH&HPA
Kennford, Exeter EX6 7YN
T: (01392) 833046
F: (01392) 833046
Half a mile from end of M5 on A38, 4 miles south of Exeter. Signposted.
3.2 hectares (8 acres). Level, grassy, hard, sheltered.
120 touring pitches.

120	🚐	£10.50
120	🚏	£10.50
120	⛺	£10.50
3	🏠	£170.00—£300.00

Open all year round
Cards accepted: Barclaycard, Delta, Eurocard, Mastercard, Switch, Visa

🔌🚗🔲⊙🦽🔥💧🛁🕐✕🍽
📺📞🛒✂️🛒⊙🔍⚑∪🐾

For ideas on places to visit refer to the introduction at the beginning of this section.

Map references apply to the colour maps at the back of this guide.

The symbols in each entry give information about services and facilities. A key to these symbols appears at the back of this guide.

GLASTONBURY

Somerset
Map ref 3A2

Market town associated with Joseph of Arimathea and the birth of English Christianity. Built around its 7th C abbey said to be the site of King Arthur's burial. Glastonbury Tor with its ancient tower gives panoramic views over flat country and the Mendip Hills.
Tourist Information Centre
T: (01458) 832954

The Old Oaks Touring Park ⋀

★★★★★
Touring Park
Member BH&HPA
Wick Farm, Wick, Glastonbury
BA6 8JS
T: (01458) 831437
F: (01458) 833238
E: info@theoldoaks.co.uk
I: www.theoldoaks.co.uk
From Glastonbury 2 miles towards Shepton Mallet on A361, signed for Wick, site in 1 mile. From Wells left after roundabout entering Glastonbury at sign for Wick. Site 1.5 miles. Signposted.
40 hectares (100 acres). Level, sloping, grassy, hard, sheltered.
40 touring pitches.

20	🚐	£7.50—£10.00
20	🚏	£7.50—£10.00
20	⛺	£7.50—£10.00

Open March–October
Cards accepted: Barclaycard, Delta, Eurocard, JCB, Mastercard, Switch, Visa

🚗🔲🦽🔥💧🛁🕐🛒📺🔲✂️
🛒⊙🔍⚑🚶🆆🅷

GOONHAVERN

Cornwall
Map ref 2B2

Silverbow Park ⋀

★★★★★
Holiday Park
Rose Award
Member BH&HPA
Goonhavern, Truro TR4 9NX
T: (01872) 572347
Travel westward along A30. Turn right onto the B3285 Perranporth road. When in Goodhavern village turn left onto A3075 for 0.5 miles. Silverbow

Park entrance is on the left- hand side. Signposted.
9.6 hectares (24 acres). Sloping, grassy, hard, sheltered.
90 touring pitches.

90	🚐	£6.00—£14.00
90	🚎	£6.00—£14.00
14	⛺	£6.00—£14.00
	⛺	£180.00—£460.00

Open May–October

🚐🔌🍴📶🔥🔋💂🛒🔦💻📺
🚿🚗☀️⛰️�️🎣🛶🐾🐕🐾 WH

Cornwall
Map ref 2B3

Former mining town with modern light industry on the Hayle Estuary. Most buildings are Georgian or early Victorian, with some Regency houses along the canal.

Beachside Holiday Park ▲▲
★★★★
Holiday Park
Member BH&HPA
Hayle TR27 5AW
T: (01736) 753080
F: (01736) 757252
E: reception@
beachside.demon.co.uk
I: www.beachside.co.uk
Leave A30 at the large roundabout at the approach to Hayle, take the Hayle road, turn right beside the putting green and signpost showing 'Beachside'. Situated approximately 0.5 mile on right. Signposted.
16 hectares (40 acres). Sloping, grassy.
90 touring pitches.

90	🚐	£6.00—£18.00
90	🚎	£6.00—£18.00
90	⛺	£6.00—£18.00
	⛺	£85.00—£520.00

Open April–September
Cards accepted: Barclaycard, Delta, Eurocard, Mastercard, Solo, Switch, Visa, Visa Electron

🔌🚐📶🔥🔋💂🛒🔦💻📺💻
🚿☀️🎣�️🏹🎵🐾📺

All accommodation in this guide has been rated, or is awaiting a rating, by a trained Tourist Board assessor.

St Ives Bay Holiday Park ▲▲
★★★★
Holiday Park
Member BH&HPA
73 Loggans Road, Upton Towans,
Hayle TR27 5BH
T: (01736) 752274
F: (01736) 754523
E: stivesbay@pipex.com
I: www.stivesbay.co.uk
Exit A30 at Hayle, turn immediately right. Park entrance 500 m on the left. Signposted.
40 hectares (100 acres). Level, grassy.
300 touring pitches.

300	🚐	£6.00—£17.00
300	🚎	£6.00—£17.00
300	⛺	£6.00—£17.00
250	⛺	£99.00—£557.00

Open May–September
Cards accepted: Barclaycard, Delta, Mastercard, Solo, Switch, Visa, Visa Electron

🔌🚐P📶🔌📶🔥🔋💂🛒🔦🛒📺
📺💻📺🚿🚗☀️🎣⛰️🔫🎣🐾🐾
🎵🐾📺WH

Cornwall
Map ref 2B3

Handsome town with steep, main street and narrow alleys. In medieval times it was a major port and stannary town. Most buildings date from Regency and Victorian periods. The famous May dance, the Furry, is thought to have pre- Christian origins. A museum occupies the old Butter Market.
Tourist Information Centre
T: (01326) 565431

Poldown Caravan Park
★★★
Holiday and Touring Park
Poldown, Carleen, Helston
TR13 9NN
T: (01326) 574560
F: (01326) 574560
E: poldown@poldown.co.uk
I: www.poldown.co.uk
From Helston take A394 to Penzance. After 1 mile turn right onto B3302 then 2nd left towards Carleen, 1 mile down lane on the right. Signposted.
.8 hectare (2 acres). Level, grassy, sheltered.
13 touring pitches.

13	🚐	£6.50—£9.50
13	🚎	£6.50—£9.50
13	⛺	£6.50—£9.50
7	⛺	£95.00—£295.00

Open April–October

🚐P🔌🔌📶🔥🔋💂🛒🔦
🚗☀️⛰️🐾

Devon
Map ref 2D2

Pretty village at the foot of the Blackdown Hills. The church has a magnificent carved 15th C screen, and nearby is a medieval priest's house with a minstrels' gallery and oak screens.

Forest Glade Holiday Park ▲▲
★★★★
Holiday Park
Rose Award
Member BH&HPA
Kentisbeare, Cullompton EX15 2DT
T: (01404) 841381
F: (01404) 841593
E: forestglade@cwcom.net
I: www.forestglade.mcmail.com
From Honiton take Dunkerswell road and follow Forest Glade signs. From M5 A373, 2.5 miles at Keepers Cottage Inn then 2.5 miles on Sheldon Road. Signposted.
6 hectares (15 acres). Level, grassy, hard, sheltered.
80 touring pitches.

80	🚐	£6.25—£11.75
80	🚎	£6.25—£11.75
80	⛺	£6.25—£11.75
24	⛺	£93.00—£360.00

16 units privately owned
Open April–October
Cards accepted: Barclaycard, Delta, Mastercard, Switch, Visa

🔌🚐📶📶🔥🔋💂🛒🔦💻📺
🚗☀️⛰️🔫🎣🐾🐾📺WH
Ad See display advertisement on this page

IMPORTANT NOTE
Information on accommodation listed in this guide has been supplied by the proprietors. As changes may occur you are advised to check details at the time of booking.

FREE HEATED INDOOR POOL
Sheltered country park surrounded by forest in an area of outstanding natural beauty.
Large pitches with short mown grass and electric hook-ups. Some hard standings.
Luxury holiday homes for hire. Forest and hill walks.
David Bellamy Silver Award. See entry under Kentisbeare.

FOREST GLADE HOLIDAY PARK, CULLOMPTON, DEVON EX15 2DT
TEL: (01404) 841381 FAX: (01404) 841593 E-MAIL: forestglade@cwcom.net WEB: www.forestglade.mcmail.com

LACOCK

Wiltshire
Map ref 3B2

Village of great charm. Medieval buildings of stone, brick or timber-frame have jutting storeys, gables, oriel windows. Magnificent church has perpendicular fan-vaulted chapel with grand tomb to benefactor who, after Dissolution, bought Augustinian nunnery, Lacock Abbey.

Piccadilly Caravan Site ⚠
★★★★★
Touring Park
Member BH&HPA
Folly Lane (West), Lacock,
Chippenham SN15 2LP
T: (01249) 730260
Turn right off A350 Chippenham to Melksham road, signposted to Gastard (Folly Lane West), with caravan symbol, situated 300 yds on the left. Signposted.
1.2 hectares (3 acres). Level, grassy, hard.
43 touring pitches.

40	🚐	£8.50—£10.00
40	🚙	£8.50—£10.00
3	⛺	£8.50—£10.00

Open April–October
🚗🚐🏕🏕🛁🍴🛒📷💷 🔌 ⚡ ☺ ⚠ ⚓

LANDS END

Cornwall
Map ref 2A3

The most westerly point of the English mainland, 8 miles south-west of Penzance. Spectacular cliffs with marvellous views. Exhibitions and multi-sensory Last Labyrinth Show.

Cardinney Caravan and Camping Park
★★★
Touring Park
Main A30, Lands End TR19 6HJ
T: (01736) 810880 (Ansaphone)
F: (01736) 810998
On the main A30, signposted 5 miles past Penzance. Large name board on right-hand side.
1.8 hectares (4.5 acres). Level, grassy, hard.
105 touring pitches.

50	🚐	£5.00—£8.00
25	🚙	£5.00—£8.00
30	⛺	£5.00—£8.00
2	⛺	£84.00—£98.00

Open February–November
Cards accepted: Barclaycard, Delta, Eurocard, Mastercard, Solo, Switch, Visa
🚗🚐🔌🏕🛁🍴🛒⚡✕ 📺 🔌 📷 ⚡ 🛒 ☺ ⚓ ⚓

LOOE

Cornwall
Map ref 2C3

Small resort developed around former fishing and smuggling ports occupying the deep estuary of the East and West Looe Rivers. Narrow winding streets, with old inns; museum and art gallery are housed in interesting old buildings. Shark fishing centre, boat trips; busy harbour.

Tregoad Farm Touring Caravan and Camping Park ⚠
★★★
Touring and Camping Park
Member BH&HPA
St Martin's, Looe PL13 1PB
T: (01503) 262718 (Ansaphone)
F: (01503) 264777
E: tregoadfarmtccp@aol
I: www.cornwall-online.co.uk/tregoad
M5/A38 Plymouth. After crossing the Tamar Bridge into Cornwall, follow A38 for about 6 miles. At "Trerulefoot" roundabout turn left onto the A374, turn right to Looe A387, at Widegates follow road to left onto B3253, 3 miles on left. Signposted.
22 hectares (55 acres). Level, grassy, hard, sheltered.
150 touring pitches.

100	🚐	£6.50—£10.50
100	🚙	£6.50—£10.50
50	⛺	£4.00—£10.50
3	⛺	£125.00—£340.00

Open April–October
Cards accepted: Amex, Barclaycard, Delta, Eurocard, JCB, Mastercard, Switch, Visa, Visa Electron
🚗P🔌🏕🛁🍴🛒✕🍴 📺📷⚡🛒☺⚡⚓⚓⚓🔌
WH

MALMESBURY

Wiltshire
Map ref 3B2

Overlooking the River Avon, an old town dominated by its great church, once a Benedictine abbey. The surviving Norman nave and porch are noted for fine sculptures, 12th C arches and musicians' gallery.
Tourist Information Centre
T: (01666) 823748

Burton Hill Caravan and Camping Park ⚠
★★
Touring Park
Member BH&HPA
Burton Hill, Malmesbury SN16 0EH
T: (01666) 826880

Off A429 0.25 mile south, Malmesbury to Chippenham road, opposite hospital, Arches Lane. Signposted.
.8 hectare (2 acres). Level, grassy, sheltered.
30 touring pitches.

30	🚐	£7.50—£9.50
30	🚙	£7.50—£9.50
30	⛺	£7.50—£9.50

Open April–November
🚐🔌🏕🛁🍴🛒📷⚓🔌☺⚓⚓

MARTOCK

Somerset
Map ref 3A3

Large village with many handsome buildings of hamstone and a beautiful old church with tie-beam roof. Medieval treasurer's house where a 10' x 6' medieval mural has recently been discovered during National Trust restoration work. Georgian market house, 17th C manor.

Southfork Caravan Park ⚠
★★★★★
Touring Park
Member BH&HPA/NCC
Parrett Works, Martock TA12 6AE
T: (01935) 825661
F: (01935) 825122
E: southfork.caravans@virgin.net
A303 east of Ilminster. At roundabout take road signposted to South Petherton. Follow camping signs. A303 west of Ilchester. Take exit signposted Martock after jct to A3088. Follow camping signs. Signposted.
1 hectare (2.5 acres). Level, grassy.
30 touring pitches.

23	🚐	£6.00—£9.00
23	🚙	£6.00—£9.00
7	⛺	£6.00—£9.00
3	⛺	£115.00—£250.00

Open all year round
Cards accepted: Barclaycard, Delta, Eurocard, JCB, Mastercard, Switch, Visa, Visa Electron
🚗P🔌🏕🛁🍴🛒⚡📷⚡ 🚗☺⚓⚓⚓🔢T🔌WH

WELCOME HOST

This is a nationally recognised customer care programme which aims to promote the highest standards of service and a warm welcome. Parks taking part in this initiative are indicated by the WH symbol.

MEVAGISSEY

Cornwall
Map ref 2B3

Small fishing town, a favourite with holidaymakers. Earlier prosperity came from pilchard fisheries, boat-building and smuggling. By the harbour are fish cellars, some converted, and a local history museum is housed in an old boat-building shed. Handsome Methodist chapel; shark fishing, sailing.

Sea View International
★★★★★
Holiday Park
Rose Award
Member BH&HPA
Boswinger, St Austell PL26 6LL
T: (01726) 843425
F: (01726) 843358
E: gary@gmichell.freeserve.co.uk
I: www.gmichell.freeserve.co.uk
From St Austell roundabout take B3273 to Mevagissey. Prior to village turn right and follow signs to Gorran and Gorran Haven and brown tourism signs to park. Signposted.
11.2 hectares (28 acres). Level, grassy, hard, sheltered.
161 touring pitches.

161	🚐	£5.00—£16.90
161	🚚	£5.00—£16.90
158	⛺	£5.00—£16.90
38	🏠	£100.00—£530.00

Open April–September
Cards accepted: Barclaycard, Delta, Eurocard, Mastercard, Solo, Switch, Visa, Visa Electron

If you book by telephone and are asked for your credit card number, it is advisable to check the proprietor's policy should you cancel your reservation.

MINEHEAD

Somerset
Map ref 2D1

Victorian resort with spreading sands developed around old fishing port on the coast below Exmoor. Former fishermen's cottages stand beside the 17th C harbour; cobbled streets climb the hill in steps to the church. Boat trips, steam railway. Hobby Horse festival 1 May.
Tourist Information Centre
T: (01643) 702624

Beeches Holiday Park
★★★★
Holiday Park
Rose Award
Member BH&HPA
Blue Anchor Bay, Minehead
TA24 6JW
T: (01984) 640391
F: (01984) 640361
E: info@beeches-park.co.uk
I: www.beeches-park.co.uk
From M5 jct 23, A39 to Minehead. First right after West Quantoxhead and follow signs to Blue Anchor on B3191.
4 hectares (10 acres). Sloping.

30	🏠	£99.00—£350.00

110 units privately owned
Open April–October
Cards accepted: Barclaycard, Delta, Eurocard, JCB, Mastercard, Solo, Switch, Visa, Visa Electron

IMPORTANT NOTE

Information on accommodation listed in this guide has been supplied by the proprietors. As changes may occur you are advised to check details at the time of booking.

NEWQUAY

Cornwall
Map ref 2B2

Popular resort spread over dramatic cliffs around its old fishing port. Many beaches with abundant sands, caves and rock pools; excellent surf. Pilots' gigs are still raced from the harbour and on the headland stands the stone Huer's House from the pilchard-fishing days.
Tourist Information Centre
T: (01637) 854020

Hendra Holiday Park
★★★★
Holiday Park
Member BH&HPA
Newquay TR8 4NY
T: (01637) 875778
F: (01637) 879017
E: hendra.uk@dial.pipex.com
I: www.hendra-holidays.com
Take A30 to the Highgate Hill jct, follow the signs for the A392 to Newquay. At Quintrell Downs go straight across the roundabout, Hendra is 0.5 mile on the left. Signposted.
19.2 hectares (48 acres). Level, sloping, grassy, hard, sheltered.
588 touring pitches.

588	🚐	£7.60—£12.00
588	🚚	£7.60—£12.00
588	⛺	£7.60—£12.00
188	🏠	£119.00—£590.00

Open February–October
Cards accepted: Amex, Barclaycard, Delta, Mastercard, Switch, Visa

Ad See display advertisement on this page

The  symbol after a park name indicates that it is a Regional Tourist Board member.

Newperran Tourist Park
★★★★
Touring Park
Member BH&HPA
Rejerrah, Newquay TR8 5QJ
T: (01872) 572407
F: (01872) 571254
E: trevella@compuserve.com
I: www.chycor.co.uk/newperran
From A30 take B3285 Perranporth road, 2 miles past Mitchell village. Right onto A3075 Newquay road at Goonhavern. Site is 400 yds on left. Signposted.
10 hectares (25 acres). Level, grassy.
270 touring pitches.

270	🚐	£6.60—£11.80
270	🚏	£6.00—£11.00
270	⛺	£6.60—£11.80

Open May–September
Cards accepted: Amex, Barclaycard, Delta, Eurocard, Mastercard, Solo, Switch, Visa, Visa Electron

[Ad] See display advertisement on this page

Porth Beach Tourist Park
★★★★
Touring Park
Rose Award
Member BH&HPA
Alexandra Road, Porth, Newquay TR7 3NH
T: (01637) 876531
F: (01637) 871227
E: info@porthbeach.co.uk
I: www.porthbeach.co.uk
Take A392 from Indian Queens A30. At mini-roundabout turn right, B3276. Signposted.

2.4 hectares (6 acres). Level, grassy.
201 touring pitches.

	🚐	£6.20—£13.25
	🚏	£6.20—£13.25
	⛺	£5.50—£9.90
18	🏠	£160.00—£550.00

Open March–October
Cards accepted: Barclaycard, Delta, Eurocard, Mastercard, Solo, Switch, Visa, Visa Electron

[Ad] See display advertisement on this page

Treloy Tourist Park
★★★★
Touring and Camping Park
Member BH&HPA
Newquay TR8 4JN
T: (01637) 872063 & 876279
F: (01637) 871710
E: rpaull@treloy.co.uk
I: www.treloy.co.uk
Just off the A3059 St Columb Major to Newquay road. Signposted.
4.6 hectares (11.5 acres). Level, sloping, grassy, hard.
140 touring pitches.

140	🚐	£6.00—£10.40
140	🚏	£6.00—£10.40
140	⛺	£6.00—£10.40

Open April–September
Cards accepted: Barclaycard, Delta, Eurocard, Mastercard, Switch, Visa, Visa Electron

Map references apply to the colour maps at the back of this guide.

Trevella Caravan and Camping Park
★★★★★
Holiday, Touring and Camping Park
Rose Award
Member BH&HPA
Crantock, Newquay TR8 5EW
T: (01637) 830308
F: (01872) 571254
E: trevella@compuserve.com
I: www.chycor.co.uk/trevella
Take A3075 Redruth road from Newquay. After 1.5 miles turn right into road signposted Crantock. Signposted.
8 hectares (20 acres). Level, sloping, grassy, hard.
270 touring pitches.

230	🚐	£6.80—£11.80
230	🚏	£6.00—£11.00
40	⛺	£6.80—£11.80
56	🏠	£145.00—£495.00

Open April–October
Cards accepted: Amex, Barclaycard, Delta, Mastercard, Solo, Switch, Visa, Visa Electron

[Ad] See display advertisement on this page

WELCOME HOST
This is a nationally recognised customer care programme which aims to promote the highest standards of service and a warm welcome. Parks taking part in this initiative are indicated by the [WH] symbol.

NEWTON ABBOT

Devon
Map ref 2D2

Lively market town at the head of the Teign Estuary. A former railway town, well placed for moorland or seaside excursions. Interesting old houses nearby include Bradley Manor, dating from the 15th C, and Forde House, visited by Charles I and William of Orange.
Tourist Information Centre
T: (01626) 367494

Dornafield
★★★★★
Touring Park
Member BH&HPA
Dornafield Farm, Two Mile Oak,
Newton Abbot TQ12 6DD
T: (01803) 812732
F: (01803) 812032
E: enquiries@dornafield.com
I: www.dornafield.com
Take A381 Newton Abbot to Totnes road. In 2.5 miles at Two Mile Inn turn right. In 0.5 mile 1st turn to left. Site 200 yds on right. Signposted.
12 hectares (30 acres). Level, grassy, hard, sheltered.
135 touring pitches.

135	🚐	£8.00—£12.70
135	🚚	£8.00—£12.70
135	▲	£8.00—£12.70

Open March–October
Cards accepted: Barclaycard, Delta, Eurocard, Mastercard, Switch, Visa

🚗🅿️💷📞📶🎣🛁💧🛒🔱📺
📠📷🚿🐶⊙🔥⛰️⋔🔍►🛠️ WH

OWERMOIGNE

Dorset
Map ref 3B3

Sandyholme Holiday Park
★★★★
Holiday Park
Member BH&HPA
Moreton Road, Owermoigne,
Dorchester DT2 8HZ
T: (01305) 852677
F: (01305) 854677
One mile inland off A352. Through village of Owermoigne, 1 mile. Signposted.
2.4 hectares (6 acres). Level, grassy, sheltered.
61 touring pitches.

61	🚐	£7.00—£12.00
61	🚚	£7.00—£12.00
61	▲	£7.00—£12.00
25	🚐	£125.00—£375.00

19 units privately owned
Open April–October
Cards accepted: Barclaycard, Delta, Mastercard, Switch, Visa, Visa Electron

🅿️💷📞📶🎣🛁💧🛒🔱⚡️🛠️
📷🚿⊙🔥🎵►⛰️ T

PADSTOW

Cornwall
Map ref 2B2

Old town encircling its harbour on the Camel Estuary. The 15th C church has notable bench-ends. There are fine houses on North Quay and Raleigh's Court House on South Quay. Tall cliffs and golden sands along the coast and ferry to Rock. Famous 'Obby 'Oss Festival on 1 May.
Tourist Information Centre
T: (01841) 533449

Carnevas Farm Holiday Park
★★★★
Holiday Park
Rose Award
Member BH&HPA
Carnevas Farm, St Merryn, Padstow
PL28 8PN
T: (01841) 520230
F: (01841) 520230
At end of Bodmin bypass, on A30 carry on under iron bridge turn right onto A3059, St Columb road. Turn onto A39, then left onto B3271, Padstow. At St Merryn turn left onto B3276. Two miles, towards Porthcothan Bay, opposite Tredrea Inn. Signposted.
3.2 hectares (8 acres). Level, sloping, grassy.
198 touring pitches.

198	🚚	£6.00—£10.00
198	▲	£6.00—£10.00
9	🚐	£125.00—£400.00

Open April–October

⚡️🅿️💷📶🎣🛁💧🛒🔱⚡️🛒📷
🚿⊙🔥⛰️▲⊙

The Laurels Caravan and Camping Site
★★★★
Holiday and Camping Park
Whitecross, Wadebridge PL27 7JQ
T: (01208) 813341 (Ansaphone)
Corner of A39/A389 Padstow fork. Signposted.
1.6 hectares (4 acres). Level, grassy, sheltered.
30 touring pitches.

30	🚐	£9.00—£12.00
30	🚚	
30	▲	

Open April–October

🚗🅿️💷📶🎣🛁💧🛒📷🖥️⚡️🛒⊙
⛰️∪ T

A key to symbols can be found inside the back cover flap.

PAIGNTON

Devon
Map ref 2D2

Lively seaside resort with a pretty harbour on Torbay. Bronze Age and Saxon sites are occupied by the 15th C church, which has a Norman door and font. The beautiful Chantry Chapel was built by local landowners, the Kirkhams.
Tourist Information Centre
T: 0906 680 1268
(calls cost 25p per minute)

Beverley Park
★★★★
Holiday and Touring Park
Member BH&HPA/NCC
Goodrington Road, Paignton, Devon
TQ4 7JE
T: (01803) 843887
F: (01803) 845427
E: enquiries@
beverley-holidays.co.uk
I: www.beverley-holidays.co.uk
From end of M5 take A380 to Torbay. Then A3022 for 2 miles south of Paignton. Turn left into Goodrington Road.
9.2 hectares (23 acres). Level, sloping, grassy, hard.
189 touring pitches.

189	🚐	£9.00—£20.00
50	🚚	£9.00—£20.00
120	▲	£7.00—£18.00
197	🚐	£98.00—£599.00

19 units privately owned
Open February–December
Cards accepted: Barclaycard, Delta, Eurocard, Mastercard, Solo, Switch, Visa, Visa Electron

⚡️🅿️💷📶🎣🛁💧🛒🔱❌🍽️📷📷
🚿⊙🔥⛰️🔍🔍►✈️🎵
🛁 T WH
[Ad] See display advertisement on page 124

Grange Court Holiday Centre
★★★★
Holiday Park
Rose Award
Member BH&HPA/NCC
Grange Road, Goodrington, Paignton, Devon TQ4 7JP
T: (01803) 558010
F: (01803) 663336
E: enquiries@hoburne.co.uk
I: www.hoburne.co.uk
Turn off Paignton ring road at Nortel into Goodrington Road. After 0.5 mile at bottom of hill turn left into Grange Road. Signposted.
26 hectares (65 acres). Level, sloping, grassy, hard, sheltered.
157 touring pitches.

157	🚐	£9.00—£24.00
157	🚚	£9.00—£24.00
165	🚐	£100.00—£510.00

Continued ►

PAIGNTON
Continued

335 units privately owned
Open all year round
Cards accepted: Barclaycard, Delta, Eurocard, Mastercard, Solo, Switch, Visa

Higher Well Farm Holiday Park ▲▲
★★
Holiday Park
Member BH&HPA
Stoke Gabriel, Totnes, Devon
TQ9 6RN
T: (01803) 782289
From Paignton, A385 to Totnes turn left at Parkers Arms for Stoke Gabriel, 1.5 miles turn left to Waddeton, situated 200 yards down the road. Signposted.
3.2 hectares (8 acres). Level, sloping, grassy, sheltered.
80 touring pitches.

80	⊟	£6.00—£8.50
80	⊞	£6.00—£8.50
80	▲	£6.00—£8.50
18	⊡	£120.00—£350.00

Open April—October

Ramslade Touring Park ▲▲
★★★★★
Touring Park
Member BH&HPA
Stoke Road, Stoke Gabriel, Totnes, Devon TQ9 6QB
T: (01803) 782575
F: (01803) 782828
E: ramslade@compuserve.com
I: www.ramslade.co.uk
From M5 follow A380 towards Torquay. Turn right onto Paignton ring road. At traffic lights turn right (A385). Second left at Parkers Arms, signposted Stoke Gabriel. Signposted.
3.4 hectares (8.5 acres). Level, sloping, grassy, hard.
135 touring pitches.

135	⊟	£7.50—£13.80
135	⊞	£7.50—£13.80
135	▲	£7.50—£13.80

Open March—October
Cards accepted: Barclaycard, Delta, Eurocard, Mastercard, Solo, Switch, Visa

PAR
Cornwall
Map ref 2B3

Scattered coastal village and clayport. Lovely hills and woods surround the coast here, notably the beautiful Luxulyan Valley a little way inland.

Par Sands Holiday Park ▲▲
★★★★
Holiday Park
Rose Award
Member BH&HPA
Par Beach, Par PL24 2AS
T: (01726) 812868 & 07831 461403 (Mobile.)
F: (01726) 817899
E: holidays@parsands.co.uk
I: www.parsands.co.uk
Turn right off A3082 1 mile east of Par, heading to Fowey, signposted Par Sands Holiday Park.
9.2 hectares (23 acres). Level, grassy, sheltered.
150 touring pitches.

150	⊟	£6.00—£14.00
150	⊞	£6.00—£14.00
150	▲	£6.00—£14.00
38	⊡	£135.00—£460.00

173 units privately owned
Open April—October

Cards accepted: Barclaycard, Delta, Eurocard, Mastercard, Switch, Visa

PENZANCE

Cornwall
Map ref 2A3

Resort and fishing port on Mount's Bay with mainly Victorian promenade and some fine Regency terraces. Former prosperity came from tin trade and pilchard fishing. Grand Georgian style church by harbour. Georgian Egyptian building at head of Chapel Street and Morrab Gardens.
Tourist Information Centre
T: (01736) 362207

Tower Park Caravans and Camping
★★★
Touring Park
Member BH&HPA
St Buryan, Penzance TR19 6BZ
T: (01736) 810286
F: (01736) 810954
E: caravans&camping@
towerpark97.freeserve.co.uk
Off A30 3 miles west of Penzance, B3283 to St Buryan, fork right and keep right for 400 yds. Signposted.
2.4 hectares (6 acres). Level, grassy, sheltered.
102 touring pitches.

102	🚐	£6.50—£9.00
102	🚏	£6.50—£9.00
102	▲	£4.50—£9.00
5	🏠	£122.00—£280.00

Open March–December

POLPERRO

Cornwall
Map ref 2C3

Picturesque fishing village clinging to steep valley slopes about its harbour. A river splashes past cottages and narrow lanes twist between. The harbour mouth, guarded by jagged rocks, is closed by heavy timbers during storms.

Killigarth Caravan Park △
★★★★
Holiday Park
Member BH&HPA
Polperro, Looe PL13 2JQ
T: (01503) 272216 & 272409
F: (01503) 272065
From Tamar Bridge A38 to roundabout at Trerulefoot, left onto A387 to Looe. Cross bridge to Polperro 3.5 miles turn left at jct just past bus shelter. Signposted.
12 hectares (30 acres). Level.
202 touring pitches.

202	🚐	£9.50—£14.00
202	🚏	£9.50—£14.00
202	▲	£9.50—£14.00
146	🏠	£95.00—£630.00

Open April–October
Cards accepted: Barclaycard, Delta, Eurocard, Mastercard, Switch, Visa, Visa Electron

Ad See display advertisement on this page

POLRUAN-BY-FOWEY

Cornwall
Map ref 2B3

Old village linked to Fowey across its estuary by a passenger ferry. Twin medieval forts guard village and town at the river's mouth.

Polruan Holidays (Camping & Caravanning) △
★★★★
Holiday Park
Member BH&HPA
Townsend Road, Polruan-by-Fowey, Fowey PL23 1QH
T: (01726) 870263
F: (01726) 870263
E: polholiday@aol.com
A38 to Dobwalls, left on A390 to East Taphouse. Left on B3359 after 4.5 miles turn right signposted Polruan. Signposted.
1.2 hectares (3 acres). Level, sloping, grassy, hard, sheltered.
32 touring pitches.

7	🚐	£7.00—£10.50
7	🚏	£7.00—£10.50
25	▲	£4.50—£10.50
11	🏠	£110.00—£330.00

Open April–October

PORLOCK

Somerset
Map ref 2D1

Village set between steep Exmoor hills and the sea at the head of beautiful Porlock Vale. The narrow street shows a medley of building styles. South westward is Porlock Weir with its old houses and tiny harbour and further along the shore at Culbone is England's smallest church.

Porlock Caravan Park ▲▲
★★★
Holiday and Touring Park
Member BH&HPA
Highbanks, Porlock, Minehead
TA24 8ND
T: (01643) 862269
F: (01643) 862239
E: ADHPCP@aol.com
I: www.exmoortourism.org/
porlockcaravanpark.htm
A39 from Minehead to Lynton. In Porlock village take B3225 to Porlock Weir, site signposted.
2 hectares (5 acres). Level, grassy, sheltered.
40 touring pitches.

40	🚐	£8.00—£8.00
40	🚚	£7.00—£7.00
40	⛺	£8.00—£8.00
11	🏠	£176.00—£329.00

44 units privately owned
Open March—October

🔌 🚐 P 🔲 🏮 ♨ 🛒 🍼 🎡 🔩 📺 🖂
⚡ 🗑 ⊙ ▶ ⚑

PORTREATH

Cornwall
Map ref 2B3

Formerly developed as a mining port, small resort with some handsome 19th C buildings. Cliffs, sands and good surf.

Cambrose Touring Park ▲▲
★★★
Touring Park
Portreath Road, Redruth TR16 4HT
T: (01209) 890747
F: (01209) 891665
From new A30, 3 miles north on B3300 Portreath/Redruth road. Turn right, 100 yards on left. Signposted.
2.4 hectares (6 acres). Level, grassy, hard, sheltered.
60 touring pitches.

60	🚐	£7.00—£10.50
10	🚚	£7.00—£10.50
60	⛺	£7.00—£10.50
2	🏠	£80.00—£165.00

Open April—October

🚐 🔲 🏮 ♨ 🛒 🍼 🎡 🔩 📀 🖂 ⚡
🗑 ⊙ ⛰ 🥢 ⚑

Tehidy Holiday Park ▲▲
★★★
Touring Park
Member BH&HPA
Harris Mill, Illogan, Portreath, Redruth TR16 4JQ
T: (01209) 216489 & 314558
F: (01209) 216489
South on A30 take Porthtowan exit. Right 1st roundabout, 1st left to Portreath. Signposted.
Wheelchair access category 2 ♿
1.8 hectares (4.5 acres). Level, sloping, grassy, sheltered.
18 touring pitches.

10	🚐	£6.50—£8.00
3	🚚	£6.50—£8.00
15	⛺	£6.50—£8.00
20	🏠	£95.00—£350.00

Open April—October
Cards accepted: Barclaycard, Delta, JCB, Mastercard, Solo, Switch, Visa, Visa Electron

🔌 🚐 P 🔲 🏮 ♨ 🛒 🍼 🎡 🔩 📺
🖂 🔲 ⚡ 🗑 ⊙ 🔍 ⛰ ▶ 🥢 ⚑ T 🖂

RELUBBUS

Cornwall
Map ref 2B3

River Valley Country Park ▲▲
★★★★★
Holiday Park
Rose Award
Member BH&HPA
Relubbus, Penzance TR20 9ER
T: (01736) 763398
F: (01736) 763398
E: rivervalley@surfbay.dircon.co.uk
I: www.rivervalley.co.uk
A30 St Michael's Mount roundabout, left A394 Helston road, left next roundabout B3280. Straight through to Relubbus. Signposted.
7.2 hectares (18 acres). Level, grassy, hard, sheltered.
150 touring pitches.

90	🚐	£6.00—£11.00
20	🚚	£6.00—£11.00
40	⛺	£6.00—£11.00
27	🏠	£126.00—£440.00

Open March—December
Cards accepted: Mastercard, Switch, Visa

🚐 🔲 🏮 ♨ 🛒 🍼 🎡 🔩 📀 🖂 ⚡
🗑 ⊙ 🎵 ▶ ⚑

For an explanation of the Quality Assurance Scheme, represented by Stars, please refer to the front of the guide.

ST AGNES

Cornwall
Map ref 2B3

Small town in a once-rich mining area on the north coast. Terraced cottages and granite houses slope to the church. Some old mine workings remain, but the attraction must be the magnificent coastal scenery and superb walks. St Agnes Beacon offers one of Cornwall's most extensive views.

Beacon Cottage Farm Touring Park
★★★★
Touring Park
Member BH&HPA
Beacon Drive, St Agnes TR5 0NU
T: (01872) 552347 & 553381 (Evenings)
From A30 take B3277 to St Agnes, follow signs to park. Signposted.
48 hectares (120 acres). Level, grassy, sheltered.
50 touring pitches.

50	🚐	£5.00—£14.00
50	🚚	£5.00—£14.00
50	⛺	£5.00—£14.00

Open April—September

🚐 P 🔲 🏮 ♨ 🛒 🍼 🎡 📀 🖂 ⚡
🗑 ⊙ ⛰ ⚑

ST IVES

Cornwall
Map ref 2B3

Old fishing port, artists' colony and holiday town with good surfing beach. Fishermen's cottages, granite fish cellars, a sandy harbour and magnificent headlands typify a charm that has survived since the 19th C pilchard boom. Tate Gallery opened in 1993.
Tourist Information Centre
T: (01736) 796297

Polmanter Tourist Park ▲▲
★★★★★
Touring Park
Member BH&HPA
St Ives TR26 3LX
T: (01736) 795640
F: (01736) 795640
E: philip_osbourne@hotmail.com
I: www.polmanter.com
A3074 to St Ives from A30, 1st left at mini roundabout take route to St Ives (Halsetown) turn right at inn, signposted.
5.2 hectares (13 acres). Level, sloping, grassy.
240 touring pitches.

75	🚐	£9.00—£14.50
75	🚚	£9.00—£14.50
165	⛺	£9.00—£14.50

Open April—October

Cards accepted: Barclaycard, Delta, Eurocard, Maestro, Mastercard, Solo, Switch, Visa, Visa Electron

Trevalgan Holiday Farm ⋒
★★★★
Touring Park
Member BH&HPA
St Ives TR26 3BJ
T: (01736) 796433
F: (01736) 796433
E: holiday@trevalgan.demon.co.uk
From A30 take holiday route to St Ives, jct B3306 turn left, park sign 0.25 mile signposted.
2 hectares (4.9 acres). Level, grassy.
120 touring pitches.

40	🚐	£7.00—£12.00
40	🚏	£7.00—£12.00
40	▲	£7.00—£12.00
	🏠	£280.00—£500.00

Open April–September
Cards accepted: Amex, Barclaycard, Eurocard, Mastercard, Switch, Visa

---

Devon
Map ref 2C3

Sheltered yachting resort of whitewashed houses and narrow streets in a balmy setting on the Salcombe Estuary. Palm, myrtle and other Mediterranean plants flourish. There are sandy bays and creeks for boating.
Tourist Information Centre
T: (01548) 843927

Bolberry House Farm
★★★
Touring and Camping Park
Bolberry, Malborough, Kingsbridge
TQ7 3DY
T: (01548) 561251 & 560926
E: bolberry.house@virgin.net
I: www.bolberryparks.co.uk
A381 from Totnes to Kingsbridge. Between Kingsbridge and Salcombe is the village of Malborough. Take sharp right through the village following the signs to Bolberry which is approximately 1 mile. Signposted.
2.4 hectares (6 acres). Level, sloping, grassy.
70 touring pitches.

15	🚐	£7.50—£10.00
5	🚏	£7.50—£10.00
50	▲	£6.00—£9.00
5	🏠	£95.00—£325.00

Open April–October

Karrageen Caravan and Camping Park
★★★★
Touring and Camping Park
Karrageen, Bolberry, Malborough, Kingsbridge TQ7 3EN
T: (01548) 561230
F: (01548) 560192
E: phil@karrageen.co.uk
I: www.karrageen.co.uk
Take A381 Kingsbridge to Salcombe road, turn sharp right through Malborough village, following signs to Bolberry, for 0.6 mile. Turn right to Bolberry then after 0.9 mile the park is on the right. Signposted.
4 hectares (10 acres). Level, sloping, grassy.
75 touring pitches.

25	🚐	£7.50—£12.00
65	🚏	£7.00—£11.00
65	▲	£7.00—£11.00

20 units privately owned
Open March–November

Devon
Map ref 2D2

Charming resort set amid lofty red cliffs where the River Sid meets the sea. The wealth of ornate Regency and Victorian villas recalls the time when this was one of the south coast's most exclusive resorts. Museum; August International Festival of Folk Arts.
Tourist Information Centre
T: (01395) 516441

Salcombe Regis Camping and Caravan Park ⋒
★★★★★
Holiday and Touring Park
Rose Award
Member BH&HPA
Salcombe Regis, Sidmouth EX10 0JH
T: (01395) 514303
F: (01395) 514303
E: info@salcombe-regis.co.uk
I: www.salcombe-regis.co.uk
One and a half miles east of Sidmouth signposted off the A3052 road.
6.4 hectares (16 acres). Level, grassy, hard, sheltered.
100 touring pitches.

40	🚐	£7.00—£10.00
40	🚏	£7.00—£10.00
60	▲	£7.00—£10.00
10	🏠	£125.00

Open April–October
Cards accepted: Barclaycard, Delta, Eurocard, JCB, Mastercard, Solo, Switch, Visa, Visa Electron

---

Devon
Map ref 2C2

Old market town beside the River Tavy on the western edge of Dartmoor. Developed around its 10th C abbey, of which some fragments remain, it became a stannary town in 1305 when tin-streaming thrived on the moors. Tavistock Goose Fair, October.
Tourist Information Centre
T: (01822) 612938

Harford Bridge Holiday Park ⋒
★★★★
Holiday Park
Rose Award
Member BH&HPA
Peter Tavy, Tavistock PL19 9LS
T: (01822) 810349
F: (01822) 810028
E: enquiry@harfordbridge.co.uk
I: www.harfordbridge.co.uk
Two miles north of Tavistock off A386 Okehampton road take the Peter Tavy turning. Signposted.
6.4 hectares (16 acres). Level, grassy, hard, sheltered.
120 touring pitches.

40	🚐	£6.50—£10.50
40	🚏	£6.50—£10.50
40	▲	£6.50—£10.50
13	🏠	£120.00—£350.00

45 units privately owned
Open all year round
Cards accepted: Barclaycard, Mastercard, Switch, Visa

Cornwall
Map ref 2B3

Cornwall's administrative centre and cathedral city, set at the head of Truro River on the Fal Estuary. A medieval stannary town, it handled mineral ore from west Cornwall; fine Georgian buildings recall its heyday as a society haunt in the second mining boom.
Tourist Information Centre
T: (01872) 274555

Liskey Touring Park
★★★★★
Touring Park
Member BH&HPA
Greenbottom, Truro TR4 8QN
T: (01872) 560274
F: (01872) 560274
E: enquiries@liskey.com
I: www.liskey.com
Turn left off the A30 onto A390 at Chiverton Cross roundabout, at next

Continued ▶

TRURO
Continued

roundabout turn right, signposted
Threemilestone, right at mini
roundabout, site 600 yds on the right.
Signposted.
3.2 hectares (8 acres). Level, sloping,
grassy, hard, sheltered.
60 touring pitches.

46	🚐	£6.50—£10.50
4	🚃	£6.50—£10.50
10	▲	£6.50—£10.50

Open April—September
Cards accepted: Barclaycard, Delta,
Eurocard, JCB, Mastercard, Solo,
Switch, Visa, Visa Electron

🚗 🔌 🦮 🛠 🛎 🍴 🕒 TV ⊞ 🗑 🦯
🚿 ⊙ 🔍 ⚠ ♿ WH

Ringwell Valley Holiday Park 𝗔𝗔
★★★★★
Holiday Park
Rose Award
Member BH&HPA
Bissoe Road, Carnon Downs, Truro
TR3 6LQ
T: (01872) 862194
F: (01872) 864343
E: keith@ringwell.co.uk
I: www.ringwell.co.uk
A39 from Truro to Falmouth at the
Carnon Downs roundabout turn into
Carnon Downs village, turn right just
after filling station. We are 0.75 mile
down this road. Signposted.
4.6 hectares (11.5 acres). Sloping,
grassy, sheltered.
34 touring pitches.

34	🚐	£8.00—£14.00
14	🚃	£8.00—£14.00
25	▲	£8.00—£14.00
44	🏠	£160.00—£560.00

Open April—October
Cards accepted: Barclaycard, Delta,
Diners, Mastercard, Switch, Visa

P 🔌 🦮 🛠 🛎 🍴 🕒 🦯 ✗ 🍴 ⊞ 🗑
🦯 🚿 ⊙ 🔍 ⚠ ⚲ ∪ 🎵 ♿ WH

Summer Valley Touring Park
★★★★
Touring Park
Member BH&HPA
Shortlanesend, Truro TR4 9DW
T: (01872) 277878
I: summervalley.co.uk
One and a half miles from A30 on the
B3284 Truro to Perranporth road.
Signposted.

1.2 hectares (3 acres). Level, sloping,
grassy, sheltered.
60 touring pitches.

60	🚐	£6.50—£9.00
20	🚃	£6.50—£9.00
40	▲	£6.50—£9.00

Open April—October
Cards accepted: Visa

🚗 P 🔌 🦮 🛠 🛎 🍴 🕒 🦯 ⊞ 🗑 🦯
🚿 ⊙ ⚠ ♿ WH

WADEBRIDGE
Cornwall
Map ref 2B2

Old market town with Cornwall's
finest medieval bridge, spanning the
Camel at its highest navigable point.
Twice widened, the bridge is said to
have been built on woolpacks sunk
in the unstable sands of the river
bed.
Tourist Information Centre
T: (01208) 813725

Little Bodieve Holiday Park 𝗔𝗔
★★★★
Holiday Park
Bodieve Road, Wadebridge
PL27 6EG
T: (01208) 812323
I: www.chycor.co.uk/parks/little-
bodieve
Situated on B3314 towards Rock/Port
Isaac 0.5 mile from A39 trunk road, 1
mile north of Wadebridge town centre.
Signposted.
8.8 hectares (22 acres). Level,
grassy.
195 touring pitches.

195	🚐	£7.00—£10.00
195	🚃	£7.00—£10.00
195	▲	£7.00—£10.00
16	🏠	£115.00—£475.00

53 units privately owned
Open April—October
Cards accepted: Barclaycard, Delta,
Eurocard, Mastercard, Switch, Visa

🚗 P 🔌 🦮 🦮 🛠 🛎 🍴 🕒 🦯 ✗ 🍴
⊞ 🗑 🦯 🚿 ⊙ 🔍 ⚠ ⚲ ∪ 🎵 ♿

Star ratings were correct
at the time of going
to press but are subject
to change.
Please check at the time
of booking.

WARMWELL
Dorset
Map ref 3B3

Warmwell Country Touring Park 𝗔𝗔
★★★★
Touring Park
Member BH&HPA
Warmwell, Weymouth DT2 8JD
T: (01305) 852313
F: (01305) 851824
I: welcome.to/warmwell
From Dorchester A352 towards
Wareham turn left at roundabout on
B3390 2.5 miles on right. From Bere
Regis on A31 to Dorchester. Turn left
on B3390 6 miles on left. Signposted.
6 hectares (15 acres). Level, sloping,
grassy, stony, hard, sheltered.
190 touring pitches.

165	🚐	£10.00—£14.90
	🚃	£10.00—£14.90
25	▲	£10.00—£14.90

Open all year round
Cards accepted: Barclaycard, Delta,
Mastercard, Switch, Visa

🚗 P 🔌 🔌 🦮 🛠 🛎 🍴 🕒 🦯 🍴
TV ⊞ 🗑 🦯 🚿 ⊙ 🔍 ⚠ ♿ T

WELLS
Somerset
Map ref 3A2

Small city set beneath the southern
slopes of the Mendips. Built between
1180 and 1424, the magnificent
cathedral is preserved in much of its
original glory and with its ancient
precincts forms one of our loveliest
and most unified groups of medieval
buildings.
Tourist Information Centre
T: (01749) 672552

Mendip Heights Camping and Caravan Park 𝗔𝗔
★★★★
Touring Park
Member BH&HPA
Townsend, Priddy, Wells BA5 3BP
T: (01749) 870241 (0800-2200)
F: (01749) 870368
E: bta@mendipheights.co.uk
I: www.mendipheights.co.uk
Wells north along A39 for 3 miles. Left
along B3135 towards Cheddar for 4.5
miles. Park 200 yds on left (signed).
1.8 hectares (4.5 acres). Level,
sloping, grassy, hard.
90 touring pitches.

40	🚐	£6.50—£7.90
40	🏕	£6.50—£7.90
80	⛺	£6.50—£7.90
1	🏠	£195.00—£350.00

Open March–November

🚗 P 🏪 📺 📶 🛁 💧 ☕ 🛒 🧺 🔲 📷 ∥
🚙 ☉ ⚠ ♿ ♨ WH

Ad See display advertisement on page 128

WEST QUANTOXHEAD

Somerset
Map ref 2D1

Home Farm Holiday Centre
★★★
Holiday Park
Member BH&HPA
St Audries Bay, Williton, Taunton
TA4 4DP
T: (01984) 632487
F: (01984) 634687
Off M5 at Bridgwater, A39 towards Minehead for 17 miles to West Quantoxhead, 1st right after St Audries Garage, entrance on right after 0.5 mile, after mock Tudor lodge. Signposted.
14 hectares (35 acres). Level, sloping, grassy, hard, sheltered.
40 touring pitches.

30	🚐	£8.00—£10.00
5	🏕	£8.00—£10.00
5	⛺	£8.00—£10.00
4	🏠	£115.00—£200.00

230 units privately owned
Open all year round

🚂 🚗 P 📺 ⚡ 📶 🛁 💧 ☕ 🛒 ♔
🔲 📷 ∥ 🚙 ☉ ⚠ ⚑ ♪ ▶ ♨

St Audries Bay Holiday Club ⚠
★★★
Holiday Park
Member BH&HPA
West Quantoxhead, Taunton
TA4 4DY
T: (01984) 632515
F: (01984) 632785
M5 junction 23 take A39 signposted Minehead. St Audries is 15 miles from Bridgwater. Entrance from A39. Signposted.
Level, grassy, hard.
20 touring pitches.

20	🚐	£9.00—£15.00
20	🏕	£9.00—£15.00
20	⛺	£9.00—£15.00
10	🏠	£130.00—£305.00

50 units privately owned
Open April–October
Cards accepted: Barclaycard, Delta, Mastercard, Solo, Switch, Visa

🚂 🚗 P 📺 ⚡ 📶 🛁 💧 ☕ 🛒 ✕ ♔
TV 🔲 📷 ∥ 🚙 ☉ ⚫ ⚠ ⚑ ♪
♨ T

WIDEMOUTH BAY

Cornwall
Map ref 2C2

Small resort on the north Cornwall coast, with spectacular beaches. Good surfing centre.

Penhalt Farm Holiday Park ⚠
★★★
Holiday Park
Widemouth Bay, Bude EX23 0DG
T: (01288) 361210
F: (01288) 361210
I: www.holidaybank.co.uk
Travelling south 4.5 miles from Bude on A39. Take 2nd right into Widemouth Bay, left at bottom. Our sign is just over 0.5 mile on left. Signposted.
3.2 hectares (8 acres). Level, sloping, grassy, some hard standing.
100 touring pitches.

33	🚐	£6.00—£10.00
33	🏕	£6.00—£10.00
34	⛺	£5.00—£8.00
2	🏠	£80.00—£280.00

Open April–October

🚗 P 📺 ⚡ 📶 🛁 💧 ☕ 🛒 TV
🔲 📷 ∥ 🚙 ☉ ⚫ ⚠ ♨

WINSFORD

Somerset
Map ref 2D1

Small village in Exmoor National Park, on the River Exe in splendid walking country under Winsford Hill. On the other side of the hill is a Celtic standing stone, the Caratacus Stone, and nearby across the River Barle stretches an ancient packhorse bridge, Tarr Steps.

Halse Farm Caravan & Tent Park ⚠
★★★★
Touring Park
Member BH&HPA
Winsford, Minehead TA24 7JL
T: (01643) 851259
F: (01643) 851592
E: brown@halsefarm.co.uk
I: www.halsefarm.co.uk
Signposted from A396 Minehead to Tiverton road. Turn off A396 for Winsford. In the village turn left and bear left in front of the Royal Oak Inn. Keep up hill for 1 mile; our entrance is immediately after the cattle grid on the left. Signposted.
Wheelchair access category 2 ♿
77.2 hectares (193 acres). Level, sloping, grassy, hard, sheltered.
44 touring pitches.

22	🚐	£6.00—£8.00
22	🏕	£6.00—£8.00
22	⛺	£6.00—£8.00

Open March–October

🚗 P 📺 ⚡ 📶 🛁 💧 ☕ ☉ 🔲 📷 ∥
🚙 ☉ ⚠ ♨ T

WOOLACOMBE

Devon
Map ref 2C1

Between Morte Point and Baggy Point, Woolacombe and Mortehoe offer 3 miles of the finest sand and surf on this outstanding coastline. Much of the area is owned by the National Trust.
Tourist Information Centre
T: (01271) 870553

Golden Coast Holiday Village ⚠
★★★★
Holiday Park
Member BH&HPA
Station Road, Woolacombe
EX34 7HW
T: (01271) 870343
F: (01271) 870089
E: goodtimes@
woolacombe-bay.co.uk
I: www.woolacombe-bay.co.uk
M5 jct 27. A361 to Ilfracombe. At Mullacott Cross take the B3343 towards Woolacombe. Situated on this road on left, approximately 2 miles past "once upon a time". Signposted.
4 hectares (10 acres). Level, sloping, grassy, hard.
30 touring pitches.

30	🚐	£11.50—£33.00
30	🏕	£11.50—£33.00
30	⛺	£8.00—£22.00
80	🏠	£90.00—£700.00

Open March–December
Cards accepted: Barclaycard, Delta, JCB, Mastercard, Solo, Switch, Visa, Visa Electron

🚂 P 📺 ⚡ 📶 🛁 💧 ☕ 🛒 ✕ ♔
TV 🔲 📷 ∥ 🚙 ☉ ⚫ ⚠ ♨ ⚑ ♪
∥ ♪ ♿ ∪ ♔ ♪ ▶ ✈ ♪ ♨ T WH

Continued ▶

WOOLACOMBE

Continued

Woolacombe Sands Holiday Park

★★★
Holiday Park
Member BH&HPA
Beach Road, Woolacombe
EX34 7AF
T: (01271) 870569
F: (01271) 870606
E: lifesabeach@
woolacombe-sands.co.uk
I: www.woolacombe-sands.co.uk
*M5 jct 27 to Barnstaple. A361 to
Mullacott Cross then B3343 to
Woolacombe. Left just before
Woolacombe. Signposted.*
Level, sloping, grassy, sheltered.
250 touring pitches.

150	🚐	£8.00—£27.50
100	🚏	£8.00—£27.50
60	🏕	£8.00—£27.50
	🏠	£99.00

14 units privately owned
Open April–October
Cards accepted: Barclaycard, Delta,
Eurocard, JCB, Maestro, Mastercard,
Solo, Switch, Visa, Visa Electron

[icons]

[Ad] See display advertisement on this page

YEOVIL

Somerset
Map ref 3A3

Lively market town, famous for glove making, set in dairying country beside the River Yeo. Interesting parish church. Museum of South Somerset at Hendford Manor.
*Tourist Information Centre
T: (01935) 471279*

Long Hazel International Caravan and Camping Park

★★★★
Touring Park
Member BH&HPA
High Street, Sparkford, Yeovil
BA22 7JH
T: (01963) 440002
F: (01963) 440002
I: www.sparkford.f9.co.uk/lhi.htm
Four hundred yds from roundabout on A303/A359 at Sparkford. Proceed into village along the High Street, entrance on the left just before Sparkford Inn. Signposted.
Wheelchair access category 2
1.4 hectares (3.5 acres). Level, grassy, hard, sheltered.
75 touring pitches.

75	🚐	£8.00—£10.00
75	🚏	£8.00—£10.00
75	🏕	£8.00—£10.00
3	🏠	£170.00—£320.00

Open March–December

[icons]

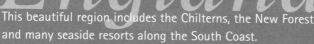

SOUTH OF ENGLAND

This beautiful region includes the Chilterns, the New Forest and many seaside resorts along the South Coast.

For cream teas and sightseeing, Windsor is an olde worlde delight. And nearby Runnymede, where the Magna Carta was signed, is a beautiful spot for a picnic. Oxford, Winchester and Salisbury offer shopping, nightlife and culture. While Southampton and Portsmouth are awash with maritime museums. But if you're mainly interested in sun, sea and sand, hire a deckchair in the seaside resorts of Bournemouth, Poole, Swanage or Weymouth.

The annual regatta at Cowes on the Isle of Wight, starting at the end of July, is something even land lubbers will enjoy.

*The counties of
Berkshire, Buckinghamshire,
Dorset (Eastern), Hampshire,
Isle of Wight and Oxfordshire*

FOR MORE INFORMATION CONTACT:
Southern Tourist Board
40 Chamberlayne Road, Eastleigh,
Hampshire SO50 5JH
Tel: (023) 8062 0555
Fax: (023) 8062 0010
Email: stbinfo@bta.org.uk
Internet: www.visitbritain.com

The Pictures:
1 HMS Victory, Portsmouth;
2 Deer at Bolderwood, New Forest;
3 Blenheim Palace, Oxfordshire.

Where to Go in the South of England - see pages 132-135
Where to Stay in the South of England - see pages 136-143

Whilst in the
SOUTH OF ENGLAND ...

You will find hundreds of interesting places to visit during your stay, just some of which are listed in these pages.

Contact any Tourist Information Centre in the region for more ideas on days out in the South of England.

Beale Park

Lower Basildon, Reading, Berkshire RG8 9NH
Tel: (0118) 9845172
An extraordinary collection of rare birds and animals. Narrow gauge railway, adventure playground, splash pools. Also nature trails and fishing on day tickets.

Beaulieu National Motor Museum

Beaulieu, Brockenhurst, Hampshire SO42 7ZN
Tel: (01590) 612345
Motor museum with over 250 exhibits showing the history of motoring from 1896. Also Palace House, Wheels Experience, Beaulieu Abbey ruins and a display of monastic life.

Bekonscot Model Village

Beaconsfield, Buckinghamshire HP9 2PL
Tel: (01494) 672919
The oldest model village in the world, Bekonscot depicts rural England in the 1930s where time has stood still for 70 years.

Blenheim Palace

Woodstock, Oxfordshire OX20 1PX
Tel: (01993) 811325
Home of the 11th Duke of Marlborough. Birthplace of Sir Winston Churchill. Designed by Vanbrugh in the English baroque style. Landscaped by 'Capability' Brown.

Breamore House

Breamore, Fordingbridge, Hampshire SP6 2DF
Tel: (01725) 512233
Elizabethan manor house of 1583 with fine collection of works of art. Furniture, tapestries, needlework, paintings mainly 17th and 18thC Dutch School.

Buckinghamshire County Museum

Aylesbury, Buckinghamshire HP20 2QP
Tel: (01296) 331441
Lively, hands-on, innovative museum complex consisting of county heritage displays, regional art gallery and Roald Dahl Children's Gallery in lovely garden setting.

Carisbrooke Castle

Newport, Isle of Wight PO30 1X
Tel: (01983) 522107
A splendid Norman castle where Charles I was imprisoned. The governor's lodge houses the county museum. Wheelhouse with wheel operated by donkeys.

Compton Acres

Canford Cliffs, Poole, Dorset BH13 7ES
Tel: (01202) 700778
Ten separate and distinct gardens of the world including Italian, Japanese, subtropical glen, rock and water gardens. Country crafts and 'Off the Beaten Track Trail'.

Cotswold Wild Life Park

Burford, Oxford, Oxfordshire OX18 4JW
Tel: (01993) 823006
Wildlife park in 200 acres of gardens and woodland. Includes a variety of animals from all over the world.

The D Day Museum and Overlord Embroidery

Clarence Esplanade, Portsmouth, Hampshire PO5 3NT
Tel: (023) 9282 7261
The magnificent 83 metre long 'Overlord Embroidery' depicts the allied invasion of Normandy on 6 June 1944. Soundguides available in three languages.

Didcot Railway Centre

Didcot, Oxfordshire OX11 7NJ
Tel: (01235) 817200
Living museum re-creating the golden age of the Great Western Railway. Steam locomotives and trains, engine shed and small relics museum.

Exbury Gardens

Exbury, Southampton SO45 1AZ
Tel: (023) 8089 1203
Over 200 acres of woodland garden, including the Rothschild collection of rhododendrons, azaleas, camellias and magnolias.

Flagship Portsmouth

HM Naval Base, Portsmouth, Hampshire PO1 3LJ
Tel: (023) 9283 9766
The world's greatest historic ships - Mary Rose, HMS Victory, HMS Warrior 1860, plus Royal Naval Museum, 'Warships by Water' tours, and Dockyard Apprentice exhibition.

Gilbert White's House and Garden and The Oates Museum

Selborne, Alton, Hampshire GU34 3JH
Tel: (01420) 511275
Historic house and garden, home of Gilbert White, author of 'The Natural History of Selborne'. Exhibition on Frank Oates, explorer and Captain Lawrence Oates of Antarctic fame.

The Hawk Conservancy

Andover, Hampshire SP11 8DY
Tel: (01264) 772252
Unique to Great Britain - 'Valley of the Eagles' held here daily at 1400.

Jane Austen's House

Chawton, Alton, Hampshire GU34 1SD
Tel: (01420) 83262
The 17thC house where Jane Austen lived from 1809-1817, and wrote or revised her six great novels. Letters, pictures, memorabilia, garden with old-fashioned flowers.

The Pictures:
1 Poole, Dorset;
2 Swan Green, New Forest;
3 Oxford;
4 Lulworth Cove, Dorset;
5 Windsor, Berkshire;
6 Winchester Cathedral, Hampshire;
7 Hertford and New College, Oxford.

Legoland Windsor

Windsor, Berkshire SL4 4AY
Tel: 0870 5040404
A family park with hands-on activities, rides, themed playscapes and more Lego bricks than you ever dreamed possible.

Manor Farm

Manor Farm Country Park, Bursledon, Hampshire SO30 2ER
Tel: (01489) 787055
Traditional Hampshire farmstead - buildings, farm animals, machinery and equipment, pre-1950's farmhouse and 13thC church set for 1900.

Newport Roman Villa

Newport, Isle of Wight PO36 1EY
Tel: (01983) 529720
Underfloor heated bath system, tessellated floors displayed in reconstructed rooms, corn-drying kiln plus small site museum of objects recovered.

Osborne House

East Cowes, Isle of Wight PO32 6JY
Tel: (01983) 200022
Queen Victoria and Prince Albert's seaside holiday home. Swiss Cottage where royal children learnt cooking and gardening. Victorian carriage service to Swiss Cottage.

The Oxford Story

Broad Street, Oxford, Oxfordshire OX1 3AJ
Tel: (01865) 728822
An excellent introduction to Oxford - experience 800 years of University history in one hour. From scientists to poets, astronomers to comedians.

River and Rowing Museum

Mill Meadows, Henley-on-Thames, Oxfordshire RG9 1BF
Tel: (01491) 415600
A spectacular journey through over 250,000 years of life on the river. Discover the river's role in feeding the nation, its navigation and wildlife.

Royal Marines Museum

Southsea, Hampshire PO4 9PX
Tel: (023) 9281 9385
History of the Royal Marines from 1664 to present day. Jungle and trench warfare sight and sound exhibitions. Supporting exhibitions and memorial gardens.

Royal Navy Submarine Museum

Jetty Road, Gosport PO12 2AS
Tel: (023) 9252 9217
HM Submarine Alliance, HM Submarine No 1 (Holland 1) under restoration. Midget submarines and models of every type from earliest days to present nuclear age submarines.

The Sir Harold Hillier Gardens and Arboretum

Ampfield, Romsey, Hampshire SO51 0QA
Tel: (01794) 368787
Established in 1953, The Sir Harold Hillier Gardens and Arboretum comprises the greatest collection of wild and cultivated woody plants in the world.

Staunton Country Park

Havant, Hampshire PO9 5HB
Tel: (023) 9245 3405
Restored Victorian glasshouses with displays of exotic plants in the charming setting of the historic walled gardens. Ornamental farm with a wide range of animals.

Swanage Railway

Swanage, Dorset BH19 1HB
Tel: (01929) 425800
Enjoy a nostalgic steam-train ride on the Purbeck line. Steam trains run every weekend throughout the year, and daily at peak times.

The Tank Museum

Bovington, Wareham, Dorset BH20 6JG
Tel: (01929) 405096
The world's finest display of armoured fighting vehicles. Experimental vehicles, interactive displays, disabled access and facilities.

Tudor House Museum

Bugle Street, Southampton SO14 2AD
Tel: (023) 8033 2513
Large half-timbered Tudor house with exhibitions on Tudor, Georgian and Victorian domestic and local history. Unique Tudor garden.

The Vyne

Sherborne St John, Hampshire RG24 9HL
Tel: (01256) 881337
Original house dating back to Henry VIII's time. Extensively altered in the mid 17thC. Tudor chapel, beautiful gardens and lake.

Waterperry Gardens

Waterperry, Oxford, Oxfordshire OX33 1JZ
Tel: (01844) 339254
Ornamental gardens covering six acres of the 83-acre estate. Saxon village church, garden shop, teashop, art and craft gallery.

4

Whitchurch Silk Mill

Whitchurch, Hampshire RG28 7AL
Tel: (01256) 892065
A unique Georgian silk-weaving watermill still producing fine silk fabrics on Victorian machinery. Riverside garden, tearoom for light meals, silk gift shop.

Winchester Cathedral

Winchester, Hampshire SO23 9LS
Tel: (01962) 857200
Originally Norman, with nave converted to perpendicular. 16thC additions. Old Saxon site adjacent. Tombs, library, medieval wall paintings and Close.

Windsor Castle

Windsor, Berkshire SL4 1NJ
Tel: (01753) 869898
Official residence of HM The Queen and royal residence for nine centuries. State apartments, Queen Mary's Doll's House.

Find out more about the
SOUTH OF ENGLAND ...

Further information about holidays and attractions in the South of England is available from:

SOUTHERN TOURIST BOARD

40 Chamberlayne Road, Eastleigh, Hampshire SO50 5JH.

Tel: (023) 8062 0555

Fax: (023) 8062 0010

Email: stbinfo@bta.org.uk

Internet: www.visitbritain.com

The Pictures:
1 Alum Bay, Isle of Wight;
2 Beaulieu, Hampshire;
3 Bucklers Hard, New Forest;
4 Broughton Castle, Oxfordshire;
5 Corfe, Dorset;
6 Cheyney Court, Winchester;
7 Radcliffe Camera, Oxford;
8 Chawton Church, Hampshire;
9 New Forest, Hampshire.

Getting to the
SOUTH OF ENGLAND ...

BY ROAD: A good road network links London and the rest of the UK with major Southern destinations. The M27 provides a near continuous motorway route along the south coast and the M25/M3/A33 provides a direct route from London to Winchester and Southampton. The scenic A31 stretches from London, through Hampshire and to mid Dorset, whilst the M40/A34 have considerably cut travelling times from the West Midlands to the South. The M25 has speeded up access to Berkshire on the M4, Buckinghamshire and Oxfordshire on the M40.

BY RAIL: From London's Waterloo, trains travel to Portsmouth, Southampton and Bournemouth approximately three times an hour. From these stations, frequent trains go to Poole, Salisbury and Winchester. Further information on rail journeys in the South of England can be obtained from 08457 484950.

WHERE TO STAY (SOUTH OF ENGLAND)

Parks in this region are listed in alphabetical order of place name, and then in alphabetical order of park.

Map references refer to the colour location maps at the back of this guide. The first number indicates the map to use; the letter and number which follow refer to the grid reference on the map.

At-a-glance symbols can be found inside the back cover flap.
Keep this open for easy reference.

ANDOVER

Hampshire
Map ref 3C2

Town that achieved importance from the wool trade and now has much modern development. A good centre for visiting places of interest.
Tourist Information Centre
T: (01264) 324320

Wyke Down Touring Caravan & Camping Park ⚠
★★★

Touring and Camping Park
Picket Piece, Andover SP11 6LX
T: (01264) 352048
F: (01264) 324661
E: wykedown@ukonline.co.uk
I: www.ukonline.co.uk/wykedown
Follow international camping signs from A303 trunk road, Andover ring road, then through village. Picket Piece is signposted, approximately 2 miles.
2.8 hectares (7 acres). Level, sloping, grassy, hard, sheltered.
200 touring pitches.

100	🚐	£9.00—£11.00
100	🚚	£9.00—£11.00
100	▲	£9.00—£11.00

Open all year round
Cards accepted: Barclaycard, Delta, Diners, Eurocard, Maestro, Mastercard, Solo, Switch, Visa, Visa Electron

🅿️ P 🖥️ 🔌 🍴 🚿 🛁 ♨ ☕ ✕ 🍽️ 📺 📶 ☉ 🔍 🐕 ⚲

BEACONSFIELD

Buckinghamshire
Map ref 3D2

Former coaching town with several inns still surviving. The old town has many fine houses and an interesting church. Beautiful countryside and beech woods nearby.

Highclere Farm Country Touring Park ⚠
★★★★

Touring and Camping Park
Member BH&HPA
Newbarn Lane, Seer Green, Beaconsfield HP9 2QZ
T: (01494) 874505
F: (01494) 875238
A40 to Potkiln Lane and follow signs up to site. M40 jct 2 to Beaconsfield, A355 signed Amersham 1 mile, right to Seer Green. Signposted.
1 hectare (2.5 acres). Level, grassy, hard, sheltered.
60 touring pitches.

45	🚐	£10.00—£14.00
45	🚚	£10.00—£14.00
15	▲	£8.00—£14.00

Open January, March–December
Cards accepted: Amex, Barclaycard, Delta, Diners, Eurocard, JCB, Mastercard, Solo, Switch, Visa, Visa Electron

🅿️ P 🖥️ 🔌 🍴 🚿 🛁 ♨ ☕ 🍽️ 📶 📱
🚗 🔔 ☉ ⚠ 🔧 WH

Ad See display advertisement on this page

BERE REGIS

Dorset
Map ref 3B3

This watercress-growing village was in the Middle Ages famed for its fairs and being a resort of kings on their way to the south-west; its former splendour is well commemorated by the medieval church.

Rowlands Wait Touring Park
★★★

Touring Park
Member BH&HPA
Rye Hill, Bere Regis, Wareham BH20 7LP
T: (01929) 472727
F: (01929) 472727
E: info@rowlandswait.co.uk
I: www.rowlandswait.co.uk
From A35 (Poole/Dorchester road) at Bere Regis take Wool/ Bovington Tank Museum road. About 0.5 miles up Rye Hill turn right, site 300 yds. Signposted.
3.2 hectares (8 acres). Level, sloping, grassy, hard, sheltered.
71 touring pitches.

30	🚐	£6.40—£9.40
6	🚚	£6.40—£9.40
35	▲	£6.40—£9.40

Open all year round
Cards accepted: Barclaycard, Delta, JCB, Mastercard, Switch, Visa

🅿️ 🖥️ 🔌 🍴 🚿 🛁 ♨ ☕ 🍽️ 📶 📱
🚗 🔔 ☉ 🔍 ⚠ 🚲 ∪ Γ ⚲

CHARLBURY

Oxfordshire
Map ref 3C1

Large Cotswold village with beautiful views of the Evenlode Valley just outside the village and close to the ancient Forest of Wychwood.

Cotswold View Caravan & Camping Site
★★★★
Touring and Camping Park
Enstone Road, Charlbury, Oxford
OX7 3JH
T: (01608) 810314
F: (01608) 811891
Two miles off A44 on B4022.
Signposted.
21.6 hectares (54 acres). Level, sloping, grassy, hard.
140 touring pitches.

140	🚐	£8.00—£11.00
140	🚕	£8.00—£11.00
140	⛺	£8.00—£11.00

Open April–October

🍴 P 🚐 🅿 🛍 🛁 🎣 🏪 🕐 🛒 📼 🗑 ✂ 🔥 ⊙ ⚘ 🐾 🔍 🅰

CHRISTCHURCH

Dorset
Map ref 3B3

Tranquil town lying between the Avon and Stour just before they converge and flow into Christchurch Harbour. A fine 11th C church and the remains of a Norman castle and house can be seen.
Tourist Information Centre
T: (01202) 471780

Hoburne Park
★★★★★
Holiday and Touring Park
Member BH&HPA/NCC
Hoburne Lane, Christchurch
BH23 4HU
T: (01425) 273379
F: (01425) 270705
E: enquiries@hoburne.co.uk
I: www.hoburne.co.uk

A35 then A337, 0.5 miles from A35 at Somerford roundabout. Signposted.
24 hectares (60 acres). Level, grassy, hard, sheltered.
232 touring pitches.

232	🚐	£11.00—£28.00
232	🚕	£11.00—£28.00

322 units privately owned
Open March–October
Cards accepted: Barclaycard, Mastercard, Switch, Visa

🍴 P 🚐 🅿 🛍 🎣 🛁 🎣 🏪 🕐 🛒 ✂ 🍽
📼 📻 🗑 ✂ 🔥 ⊙ ⚘ 🐾 🎵 🔍 🅰
🏹 🐾 🎵 🔍 📶

GOSPORT

Hampshire
Map ref 3C3

From a tiny fishing hamlet, Gosport has grown into an important centre with many naval establishments, including HMS Dolphin, the submarine base, with the Naval Submarine Museum which preserves HMS Alliance and Holland I.
Tourist Information Centre
T: (023) 92522944

Kingfisher Caravan Park
★★★★
Holiday, Touring and Camping Park
Rose Award
Member BH&HPA/NCC
Browndown Road, Stokes Bay,
Gosport PO13 9BE
T: (023) 9250 2611
F: (023) 9258 3583
E: info@
kingfisher-caravan-park.co.uk
I: www.kingfisher-caravan-park.co.uk
M27 jct 11, A32 to Gosport (3 miles approximately) and follow signs to Stokes Bay. Midway between Gosport and Lee on Solent on coast road. Signposted.
5.6 hectares (14 acres). Level, grassy, hard, sheltered.
110 touring pitches.

90	🚐	£13.00—£16.00
20	🚕	£13.00—£16.00
20		£6.00—£16.00
-20	⛺	£120.00—£350.00

Open March–October & Christmas
Cards accepted: Amex, Barclaycard, Delta, Diners, Eurocard, Mastercard, Solo, Switch, Visa

P 🚐 📻 🛍 🛁 🎣 🏪 🕐 🛒 ✂ 📼 📻
🗑 ✂ 🚐 ⊙ ⚘ 🎵 🔥 🔍 🎵 🅰
🅰 See display advertisement on this page

HAMBLE

Hampshire
Map ref 3C3

Set almost at the mouth of the River Hamble, this quiet fishing village has become a major yachting centre.

Riverside Park
★★★★
Holiday and Touring Park
Rose Award
Member BH&HPA
Satchell Lane, Hamble, Southampton
SO31 4HR
T: (023) 8045 3220 (Answerphone)
F: (023) 8045 3611
E: enquiries@
riversideholidays.co.uk
I: www.riversideholidays.co.uk
Junction 8 off M27, take B3397 south to Hamble. Signposts from Hamble Lane to Riverside Park, via Satchell Lane Signposted.
2.2 hectares (5.6 acres). Level, sloping, grassy, sheltered.
40 touring pitches.

40	🚐	£8.00—£11.00
40	🚕	£8.00—£11.00
40		£8.00—£11.00
8	⛺	£205.00—£500.00

17 units privately owned
Open all year round
Cards accepted: Barclaycard, Delta, Mastercard, Switch, Visa

🔥 🍴 P 🚐 📻 🛍 🛁 🎣 🏪 🕐 📼 🗑 ✂
🚐 ⊙ 🐾 🔥 ⚘ 🅰 📶
🅰 See display advertisement on this page

HAYLING ISLAND

Hampshire
Map ref 3C3

Small island of historic interest, surrounded by natural harbours and with fine sandy beaches, linked to the mainland by an attractive bridge under which boats sail. Birthplace of windsurfing and home to many international sailing events.

Fishery Creek Caravan & Camping Park
★★★
Camping Park
Fishery Lane, Hayling Island
PO11 9NR
T: (023) 9246 2164
F: (023) 9246 2164
Follow brown tourist signs for Fishery Creek.
3 hectares (7.5 acres). Level, grassy.
165 touring pitches.

165	🚐	£8.00—£11.00
165	🚚	£8.00—£11.00
165	▲	£8.00—£11.00

Open March–October
Cards accepted: Barclaycard, Delta, Eurocard, Mastercard, Switch, Visa

🚗P🅿♿🌲🔥🚰♨🅰🛒🌀😊♨⛗🔼♨
Ad See display advertisement on this page

HIGHCLIFFE

Dorset
Map ref 3B3

Seaside district of Christchurch some 3 miles to the east. Highcliffe Castle is of interest.

Cobb's Holiday Park
★★★★
Holiday Park
Rose Award
Member BH&HPA
32 Gordon Road, Highcliffe,
Christchurch BH23 5HN
T: (01425) 273301
F: (01425) 276090
Leave A35 near Christchurch, take A337 to Highcliffe, follow brown tourist signs, turn left at traffic lights in village centre. Park is situated 200yds on the left. Signposted.
1.4 hectares (3.5 acres). Level, grassy, sheltered.

45	⬜	£150.00—£410.00

17 units privately owned
Open March–October
Cards accepted: Barclaycard, Eurocard, Mastercard, Solo, Switch, Visa

🔲🚗P🅿🌲🔥🅰🚰♨💷⛗♨🔼
😊🌀🎵♨

IMPORTANT NOTE

Information on accommodation listed in this guide has been supplied by the proprietors. As changes may occur you are advised to check details at the time of booking.

HURLEY

Berkshire
Map ref 3C2

Hurley Farm Caravan & Camping Park
★★★
Holiday, Touring and Camping Park
Member BH&HPA
Shepherds Lane, Hurley,
Maidenhead, Berkshire SL6 5NE
T: (01628) 823501 (Bookings) &
824493 (Warden)
F: (01628) 825533
I: www.henley.on.thames.com/hurley
From M4 jct 8/9, take A404M, then A4130 towards Henley. Travel north for 5 miles and turn right, 1 mile past East Arms pub, into Shepherds Lane. From M40 jct 4, take A404 south, then A4130 towards Henley and as above. Signposted.
160 hectares (400 acres). Level, grassy, sheltered.
200 touring pitches.

138	🚐	£8.50—£13.50
138	🚚	£8.50—£13.50
62	▲	£6.50—£11.50
6	⬜	£150.00—£360.00

450 units privately owned
Open March–October
Cards accepted: Barclaycard, Delta, Eurocard, JCB, Mastercard, Switch, Visa, Visa Electron

🚗P🔲♿🌲🔥🅰🚰♨🛒⛗💷
♨😊✕🎵🅰Ⓣ🚿
Ad See display advertisement on this page

The symbols in each entry give information about services and facilities. A key to these symbols appears at the back of this guide.

For ideas on places to visit refer to the introduction at the beginning of this section.

Set in a beautiful, quiet location adjoining a tidal creek of Chichester Harbour. Two children's play areas, indoor games room, well-stocked shop, constant de luxe hot showers. Facilities for disabled. Rallies welcome. Five minutes to beach, shops, restaurants, pubs and clubs.
Fishery Lane, Hayling Island, PO11 9NR. Tel/Fax: (023) 9246 2164

MILFORD-ON-SEA

Hampshire
Map ref 3C3

Victorian seaside resort with shingle beach and good bathing, set in pleasant countryside and looking out over the Isle of Wight. Nearby is Hurst Castle, built by Henry VIII.

Lytton Lawn Touring Park
★★★★
Touring and Camping Park
Member BH&HPA
Lymore Lane, Milford-on-Sea,
Lymington SO41 0TX
T: (01590) 643339
F: (01590) 643339
E: holidays@shorefield.co.uk
I: www.shorefield.co.uk
On B3058 coast road midway between Everton and Milford-on-Sea. Signposted.
2.8 hectares (7 acres). Level, sloping, grassy, hard, sheltered.
126 touring pitches.

126	🚐	£5.10—£23.00
126	�caravan	£5.10—£23.00
126	⛺	£5.10—£23.00

Open March–August, October–December
Cards accepted: Barclaycard, Delta, Maestro, Mastercard, Solo, Switch, Visa
🚐P🅿🏠♨♿☕🅿🛒⚽🎮📺 💺☉🔍⛰♿🚲🚾☎🐕🎵⛱T
Ad See display advertisement on page 14

Shorefield Country Park
★★★★★
Holiday Park
Rose Award
Member BH&HPA
Shorefield Road, Milford-on-Sea,
Lymington SO41 0LH
T: (01590) 642513
F: (01590) 645610
E: holidays@shorefield.co.uk
I: www.shorefield.co.uk
From M27 take Lyndhurst exit 1 onto A337 to Downton, turn left at Royal Oak public house. Signposted.
40 hectares (100 acres). Level, grassy, stony.

50	🚐	£160.00—£615.00

610 units privately owned
Open February–December

Cards accepted: Barclaycard, Delta, Mastercard, Solo, Switch, Visa
🚐�caravanP🏠♨♿☕🅿🛒✖💺🎮📺 💤🅰T🚾
Ad See display advertisement on page 14

MOLLINGTON

Oxfordshire
Map ref 3C1

Mollington Touring Caravan Park
★★★
Touring and Camping Park
Member BH&HPA
The Yews, Mollington, Banbury
OX17 1AZ
T: (01295) 750731 & 07966 171959
I: www.ukparks.co.uk/mollington
Site situated directly off A423 main Banbury/Southam road. Travelling northerly direction, the site is on left just past the Mollington turn. Signposted.
40 hectares (100 acres). Level, sloping, grassy, hard, sheltered.
24 touring pitches.

24	🚐	£6.00—£7.00
24	🚐caravan	£6.00—£7.00
10	⛺	£5.00—£6.00

Open all year round
🚐🔌🏠♨♿☕☉🅰
Ad See display advertisement on this page

NEW MILTON

Hampshire
Map ref 3B3

New Forest residential town on the mainline railway.

Glen Orchard Holiday Park
★★★★
Holiday Park
Member BH&HPA
Walkford Lane, New Milton
BH25 5NH
T: (01425) 616463
F: (01425) 638655
E: enquiries@glenorchard.co.uk
I: glenorchard.co.uk
A35 Lyndhurst to Bournemouth approximately 8 miles, at Hinton turn left into Walkford after 0.75 miles turn left into Walkford Lane. Signposted.
.5 hectare (1.15 acres). Sloping, grassy, sheltered.

19	🚐	£140.00—£440.00

Open March–October
Cards accepted: Barclaycard, Delta, Mastercard, Solo, Switch, Visa
🚐P🅿🏠♨♿☕📺🎮📺 🚐☉🔍⛰🎋🅰T🚾

Naish Estate (Hoburne) Ltd 🚐
★★★★★
Holiday Park
Rose Award
Member BH&HPA/NCC
Christchurch Road, New Milton
BH25 7RE
T: (01425) 273586 & 273786
F: (01425) 270923
E: enquiries@hoburne.co.uk
I: www.hoburne.co.uk
Off A377 between Highcliffe and New Milton Signposted.
40 hectares (100 acres). Level, grassy, hard.

53	🚐	£120.00—£550.00

806 units privately owned
Open March–October
& Christmas
Cards accepted: Barclaycard, Mastercard, Switch, Visa
🚐P♨☕🛒✖💺📺🎮📺 ☉🔍⛰🚲🛶🚾☎🐕►🎋🎵 🅰🚾

OLNEY

Buckinghamshire
Map ref 3C1

Emberton Country Park 🚐
★★★
Touring and Camping Park
Emberton, Olney, Buckinghamshire
MK46 5DB
T: (01234) 711575 (Bookings & Enquiries)
F: (01234) 711575
E: embertonpark@ milton-keynes.gov.uk
M1 jct 14, follow A509 north, 10 miles to Emberton, just before Olney. Signposted.
70 hectares (175 acres). Level, sloping, grassy, sheltered.
200 touring pitches.

200	🚐	£6.00—£11.00
200	🚐caravan	£6.00—£11.00
200	⛺	£4.50—£8.50

115 units privately owned
Open April–October

Cards accepted: Barclaycard, Delta, Mastercard, Switch, Visa

OWER

Hampshire
Map ref 3C3

New Forest hamlet lying close to the important road junction of the A36 and the M27.

Green Pastures Caravan Park ⚑
★★★
Touring Park
Member BH&HPA
Green Pastures Farm, Ower, Romsey SO51 6AJ
T: (023) 8081 4444
I: www.ukparks.co.uk/ greenpasturesfarm
Between Cadnam and Romsey just off A31/A3090 west of junction with A36, exit 2 off M27. Initially follow signs for Paultons Park. Signposted.
2 hectares (5 acres). Level, grassy.
45 touring pitches.

45	🚐	£9.00—£9.00
45	🚛	£9.00—£9.00
10	▲	£9.00—£9.00

Open March—October

OXFORD

Oxfordshire
Map ref 3C1

Beautiful university town with many ancient colleges, some dating from the 13th C, and numerous buildings of historic and architectural interest. The Ashmolean Museum has outstanding collections. Lovely gardens and meadows with punting on the Cherwell.
Tourist Information Centre
T: (01865) 726871

Cassington Mill Caravan Park ⚑
★★
Touring and Camping Park
Member BH&HPA
Eynsham Road, Cassington, Witney OX8 1DB
T: (01865) 881081
F: (01865) 884167

Take the 2nd turn left, 2.5 miles west of Oxford on the A40 towards Witney. Signposted.
1.6 hectares (4 acres). Level, grassy, sheltered.
83 touring pitches.

83	🚐	£8.50—£10.50
83	🚛	£8.50—£10.50
83	▲	£8.50—£10.50
6	🏠	£170.00—£200.00

29 units privately owned
Open April—October
Cards accepted: Barclaycard, Delta, Diners, Eurocard, Mastercard, Switch, Visa

POOLE

Dorset
Map ref 3B3

Tremendous natural harbour makes Poole a superb boating centre. The harbour area is crowded with historic buildings including the 15th C Town Cellars housing a maritime museum.
Tourist Information Centre
T: (01202) 253253

Beacon Hill Touring Park ⚑
★★★
Touring Park
Member BH&HPA
Blandford Road North, Near Lytchett Minster, Poole, Dorset BH16 6AB
T: (01202) 631631
On A350, 0.25 miles from junction of A35 and A350 towards Blandford. Approximately 3 miles north of Poole. Signposted.
Wheelchair access category 2
12 hectares (30 acres). Level, grassy, hard, sheltered.
170 touring pitches.

120	🚐	£9.00—£17.00
120	🚛	£8.50—£17.00
50	▲	£8.50—£17.00

Open April—September

Map references apply to the colour maps at the back of this guide.

Pear Tree Touring Park ⚑
★★★★★
Touring Park
Member BH&HPA
Organford Road, Holton Heath, Poole, Dorset BH16 6LA
T: (01202) 622434
F: (01202) 631985
E: info@visitpeartree.co.uk
I: www.visitpeartree.co.uk
Between A351 and A35. Turn right off A351 (Wareham Road) at Holton Heath, signposted Organford, the park entrance is 0.5 miles on the left. Signposted.
3 hectares (7.5 acres). Level, sloping, grassy, hard, sheltered.
125 touring pitches.

76	🚐	£7.00—£10.00
66	🚛	£7.00—£10.00
49	▲	£7.00—£10.00

Open April—October
Cards accepted: Barclaycard, Delta, Eurocard, Mastercard, Solo, Switch, Visa

Rockley Park Holiday Park ⚑
★★★★★
Holiday Park
Rose Award
Member BH&HPA/NCC
Napier Road, Hamworthy, Poole, Dorset BH15 4LZ
T: (0870) 2425678
F: (01442) 254956
I: www.british-holidays.co.uk
Leave M27 and join A31. Follow signs for Poole town centre, follow signs for Rockley Park. Alternatively take Dorchester bypass into Poole and follow signs for Rockley Park. Signposted.
29.6 hectares (74 acres). Level, sloping, grassy.
98 touring pitches.

71	🚐	£13.40—£29.00
71	🚛	£13.40—£29.00
332	🏠	£164.00—£820.00

745 units privately owned
Open March—October
Cards accepted: Amex, Barclaycard, Delta, Mastercard, Solo, Switch, Visa, Visa Electron

See display advertisement on page 10

RINGWOOD

Hampshire
Map ref 3B3

Market town by the River Avon comprising old cottages, many of them thatched. Although just outside the New Forest, there is heath and woodland nearby and it is a good centre for horse-riding and walking.

Red Shoot Camping Park ▲▲
★★★★
Camping Park
Linwood, Ringwood BH24 3QT
T: (01425) 473789 & 478940
F: (01425) 471558
E: redshoot@fsnet.co.uk
Two miles north of Ringwood on A338 and follow signs to Linwood or off M27 jct 1, follow signs for Linwood. Signposted.
1.6 hectares (4 acres). Level, grassy.
105 touring pitches.

30	🚐	£8.60—£11.80
70	🚎	£8.60—£11.80
70	⛺	£8.60—£11.80

Open March—October

🚗 P ▣ ◉ ⛺ ♨ ☕ 🛒 📞 ⚲ 🔌 📺
⚵ 🚗 ⊙ 🎡 ♿ 🔔

Ad See display advertisement on page 141

ROMSEY

Hampshire
Map ref 3C3

Town grew up around the important abbey and lies on the banks of the River Test, famous for trout and salmon. Broadlands House, home of the late Lord Mountbatten, is open to the public.
Tourist Information Centre
T: (01794) 512987

Hill Farm Caravan Park ▲▲
★★★★
Holiday, Touring and Camping Park
Member BH&HPA
Branches Lane, Sherfield English, Romsey SO51 6FH
T: (01794) 340402
F: (01794) 340402
A27 from Romsey towards Salisbury 3rd turn right, called Branches Lane, which is 4 miles from Romsey. Signposted.
5 hectares (12.5 acres). Level, sloping, grassy, sheltered.
45 touring pitches.

45	🚐	£8.00—£12.00
45	🚎	£8.00—£12.00
45	⛺	£8.00—£11.00
2	🏠	£140.00—£300.00

Open February—December

🚗 P ▣ ◉ ⛺ ♨ ☕ 🛒 📞 ⚲ 📺 🔌
⚵ ⊙ 🎡 ♿ ▶

ST LEONARDS

Dorset
Map ref 3B3

Oakdene Forest Park ▲▲
★★★
Holiday Park
Member BH&HPA
St Leonards, Ringwood, Hampshire
BH24 2RZ
T: (01202) 875422
F: (01202) 894152
E: holidays@shorefield.co.uk
I: www.shorefield.co.uk
Turn off next to St Leonards hospital westbound on the A31. Signposted.

22.8 hectares (57 acres). Level, grassy.
330 touring pitches.

200	🚐	£3.30—£21.00
50	🚎	
80	⛺	
127	🏠	£95.00—£595.00

127 units privately owned
Open February—December
Cards accepted: Barclaycard, Delta, Mastercard, Solo, Switch, Visa

🚗 ▣ 🛒 ♿ ♨ ☕ 🔌 🛒 ✕ 🍴
▣ ▣ 🚗 ◉ ⚲ 🎡 ♿ 🔔 📺 ⊙
🎵 ♿ T WH

Ad See display advertisement on page 14

SHANKLIN

Isle of Wight
Map ref 3C3

Set on a cliff with gentle slopes leading down to the beach, esplanade and marine gardens. The picturesque, old thatched village nestles at the end of the wooded chine.
Tourist Information Centre
T: (01983) 862942

Landguard Camping Park
★★★★
Touring and Camping Park
Member BH&HPA
Landguard Manor Road, Shanklin, Isle of Wight PO37 7PH
T: (01983) 865988
E: landguard@fsbdial.co.uk
I: www.landguard-camping.co.uk
From Newport follow the A3056 towards Sandown. Turn right after Safeway into White Cross Lane. Follow signs.
2.8 hectares (7 acres). Level, grassy.
150 touring pitches.

150	🚐	£7.50—£11.50
150	🚎	£7.50—£11.50
150	⛺	£7.50—£11.50

Open April—September

Cards accepted: Barclaycard, Delta, Eurocard, JCB, Mastercard, Solo, Switch, Visa, Visa Electron

Cards accepted: Barclaycard, Delta, Mastercard, Switch, Visa

Ad See display advertisement on page 142

Cards accepted: Barclaycard, Delta, Eurocard, Mastercard, Switch, Visa

Ad See display advertisement on this page

SWANAGE

Dorset
Map ref 3B3

Began life as an Anglo-Saxon port, then a quarrying centre of Purbeck marble. Now the safe, sandy beach set in a sweeping bay and flanked by downs is good walking country, making it an ideal resort.
Tourist Information Centre
T: (01929) 422885

Ulwell Cottage Caravan Park ⚑
★★★★
Holiday, Touring and Camping Park
Rose Award
Member BH&HPA
Ulwell, Swanage, Dorset BH19 3DG
T: (01929) 422823
F: (01929) 421500
E: enq@ulwellcottagepark.co.uk
I: www.ulwellcottagepark.co.uk
Studland Road, 1.5 miles on left. On Swanage to Studland Road. Signposted.
5.2 hectares (13 acres). Level, sloping, grassy, hard, sheltered.
77 touring pitches.

80	🚐	£10.50—£23.00
	🏕	£10.50—£23.00
	▲	£10.50—£23.00
	🏠	£130.00—£490.00

60 units privately owned
Open January, March–December

WAREHAM

Dorset
Map ref 3B3

This site has been occupied since pre-Roman times and has a turbulent history. In 1762 fire destroyed much of the town, so the buildings now are mostly Georgian.
Tourist Information Centre
T: (01929) 552740

The Lookout Holiday Park ⚑
★★★★
Holiday Park
Member BH&HPA
Stoborough, Wareham BH20 5AZ
T: (01929) 552546
F: (01929) 556662
E: enquiries@caravan-sites.co.uk
I: www.harrowwood.co.uk
bournemouth-net.co.uk
From Wareham take the A351 for 1.25 miles towards Corfe Castle. Site on left-hand side. Signposted.
6 hectares (15 acres). Level, grassy, hard, sheltered.
150 touring pitches.

150	🚐	£9.50—£12.50
150	🏕	£9.50—£12.50
100	▲	£9.50—£12.50
30	🏠	£99.00—£450.00

55 units privately owned
Open February–November

You are advised to confirm your booking in writing.

Wareham Forest Tourist Park ⚑
★★★★★
Touring Park
Member BH&HPA/NCC
Bere Road, North Trigon, Wareham BH20 7NZ
T: (01929) 551393
F: (01929) 551393
E: holiday@wareham-forest.co.uk
I: www.wareham-forest.co.uk
Located off A35. Signposted.
17.4 hectares (43.5 acres). Level, grassy, stony, hard, sheltered.
200 touring pitches.

200	🚐	£6.50—£12.00
200	🏕	£6.50—£12.00
200	▲	£6.50—£12.00

Open all year round
Cards accepted: Barclaycard, Delta, Mastercard, Switch, Visa

Ad See display advertisement on this page

For an explanation of the Quality Assurance Scheme, represented by Stars, please refer to the front of the guide.

WIMBORNE MINSTER

Dorset
Map ref 3B3

Market town centred on the twin-towered Minster Church of St Cuthberga which gave the town the second part of its name. Good touring base for the surrounding countryside, depicted in the writings of Thomas Hardy.
Tourist Information Centre
T: (01202) 886116

Merley Court Touring Park ⚠
★★★★★
Touring and Camping Park
Member BH&HPA
Merley House Lane, Merley,
Wimborne Minster BH21 3AA
T: (01202) 881488
F: (01202) 881484
E: holidays@merley-court.co.uk
I: www.merley-court.co.uk
Wimborne 1.5 miles. Off Wimborne bypass A31 junction A349 Poole road, signposted.
8 hectares (20 acres). Level, grassy, hard, sheltered.
160 touring pitches.

160	🚐	£7.00—£12.00
160	🚏	£7.00—£12.00
80	▲	£7.00—£12.00

Open March–December
Cards accepted: Barclaycard, Delta, Maestro, Mastercard, Solo, Switch, Visa, Visa Electron

🚗 P 🖥 📷 🍴 🔥 🛉 🍵 🏧 ⛽ ✕ 🍷 📺 📠 ⚡ 🛁 ☉ 🐕 ⚠ 🎣 🔌 🪅

Springfield Touring Park ⚠
★★★★★
Touring and Camping Park
Member BH&HPA
Candys Lane, Corfe Mullen,
Wimborne Minster BH21 3EF
T: (01202) 881719
Close to main A31 trunk road, 1.5 miles west of Wimborne. Signposted.
1.4 hectares (3.5 acres). Level, sloping, grassy, hard, sheltered.
45 touring pitches.

45	🚐	£7.50—£8.50
45	🚏	£7.50—£8.50
45	▲	£6.00—£8.50

Open April–October

🚗 📷 🍴 🔥 🛉 🍵 🏧 ⛽ 📠 📺 ⚡ 🛁 ☉ ⚠ 🪅

Wilksworth Farm Caravan Park ⚠
★★★★★
Holiday Park
Member BH&HPA
Cranborne Road, Wimborne
Minster BH21 4HW
T: (01202) 885467
One mile north of Wimborne and A31 on B3078 to Cranborne. Signposted.
4.4 hectares (11 acres). Level, grassy, hard, sheltered.
85 touring pitches.

60	🚐	£6.00—£14.00
60	🚏	£6.00—£14.00
25	▲	£6.00—£14.00

77 units privately owned
Open March–October

🚗 P 🖥 📷 🍴 🔥 🛉 🍵 🏧 ⛽ ✕ 📺 📠 ⚡ 🛁 ☉ 🐕 ⚠ 🎣 🔌 🪅 WH

Dorset
Map ref 3B3

On the River Frome with a mainline station. Woolbridge Manor is of interest and occupies a prominent position.

Whitemead Caravan Park
★★★
Camping Park
East Burton Road, Wool, Wareham
BH20 6HG
T: (01929) 462241
E: nadinechurch@aol.com
On A352 from Wareham turn right before Wool level crossing 350 yds. Signposted.
2 hectares (5 acres). Level, grassy, hard, sheltered.
95 touring pitches.

95	🚐	£6.25—£10.25
95	🚏	£6.25—£10.25
95	▲	£6.25—£10.25

Open March–October

🚗 🖥 📷 🍴 🔥 🛉 🍵 🏧 ⛽ 📠 📺 🔌 🛁 ☉ ⚠ 🪅

AT-A-GLANCE SYMBOLS

Symbols at the end of each accommodation entry give useful information about services and facilities.

A key to symbols can be found inside the back cover flap.

Keep this open for easy reference.

📷 🍵 🔌 🏧 🏭 🏠 🐕 🔥 🍴 ☉ 🍷

USE YOUR *i*s

There are more than 550 Tourist Information Centres throughout England offering friendly help with accommodation and holiday ideas as well as suggestions of places to visit and things to do. There may well be a centre in your home town which can help you before you set out. You'll find addresses in the local Phone Book.

On-line Information

In-depth information about travelling in Britain is now available on BTA's VisitBritain website.

Covering everything from castles to leisure parks and from festivals to road and rail links, the site complements Where to Stay perfectly, giving you up-to-the-minute details to help you with your travel plans.

BRITAIN on the internet
www.visitbritain.com

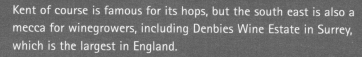

SOUTH EAST ENGLAND

The North and South Downs straddle the South East in a roller coaster of countryside delight. You'll also find over 270 miles of coastline with dramatic chalk cliffs and traditional seaside fun.

Whether you're a shopper or a bopper, Brighton is full of designer stores and nightclubs. While more sedate pleasures such as a Sussex cream tea can be enjoyed in the many picturesque villages.

Kent of course is famous for its hops, but the south east is also a mecca for winegrowers, including Denbies Wine Estate in Surrey, which is the largest in England.

Oyez! Oyez! If you're in Hastings in August, listen out for the National Town Criers Championship.

The counties of
East Sussex, Kent, Surrey
and West Sussex

FOR MORE INFORMATION CONTACT:
South East England Tourist Board,
The Old Brew House, Warwick Park,
Tunbridge Wells, Kent TN2 5TU
Tel: (01892) 540766
Fax: (01892) 511008
Email: enquiries@seetb.org.uk
Internet: www.SouthEastEngland.uk.com

The Pictures:
1   Chiddingfold Village, Surrey;
2   Broadstairs Harbour, Kent;
3   Arundel Castle, West Sussex.

Where to Go in South East England - see pages 146-149
Where to Stay in South East England - see pages 150-153

Whilst in
SOUTH EAST ENGLAND ...

You will find hundreds of interesting places to visit during your stay, just some of which are listed in these pages.

Contact any Tourist Information Centre in the region for more ideas on days out in South East England.

A Smugglers Adventure at St Clements Caves

West Hill, Hastings, East Sussex TN34 3HY
Tel: (01424) 422964
An extensive exhibition of 18thC smuggling, housed in 2,000 sq m (6,562 sq ft) of caves. Exhibition, museum, video theatre, extensive Adventure Walk incorporating dramatic special effects.

Bateman's

Burwash, East Sussex TN19 7DS
Tel: (01435) 882302
A 17thC Ironmaster's house which was the home of Rudyard Kipling between 1902-1935. His study and Rolls Royce can be seen. Garden with working watermill.

The Bluebell Railway

Sheffield Park, Uckfield, East Sussex TN22 3QL
Tel: (01825) 722370
The Bluebell Railway runs standard-gauge steam trains through 14 km (9 miles) of Sussex countryside and has the largest collection of engines in the South.

Bodiam Castle

Bodiam, East Sussex TN32 5UA
Tel: (01580) 830436
A well-preserved ruin of a castle built in 1385. Exterior walls almost complete. Good views of surrounding area. Wide moat. Museum. Audio visual display on medieval life.

The Body Shop Tour

Watersmead, Littlehampton, West Sussex BN17 6LS
Tel: (01903) 844044
A guided tour of the Body Shop's headquarters. Discover how natural ingredients are used in products and how it campaigns for social and environmental change.

Clandon Park

West Clandon, Guildford, Surrey GU4 7RQ
Tel: (01483) 222482
A Palladian-style house built for Lord Onslow circa 1730. Marble Hall, Gubbay collection of furniture, needlework and porcelain. Royal Surrey Regiment Museum. Parterre in garden.

Claremont Landscape Garden

Esher, Surrey KT10 9JG
Tel: (01372) 467806
One of the earliest surviving English landscape gardens by Vanbourgh and Bridgeman. Lake, island, view points and avenues with pavilion grotto and turf amphitheatre.

Denbies Wine Estate

Dorking, Surrey RH5 6AA
Tel: (01306) 876616
England's largest wine estate, 250 acres in beautiful countryside plus winery and visitor centre featuring 3-D time lapse film of vine growing. Viewing and picture galleries.

Dover Castle and Secret Wartime Tunnels

Dover, Kent CT16 1HU
Tel: (01304) 201628
One of the most powerful medieval fortresses in Western Europe. St Mary-in-Castro Saxon church. Roman lighthouse, secret wartime tunnels, Henry II Great Keep.

Fishbourne Roman Palace and Museum

Fishbourne, West Sussex PO19 3QR
Tel: (01243) 785859
The remains of the largest Roman residence in Britain. Many beautiful mosaics, now under cover. Hypocaust and restored formal garden. Museum of finds. Model.

The Gardens of Gaia

Cranbrook, Kent TN17 3NS
Tel: (01580) 715289
Twenty-two acres of gardens and woodland in the spirit of 'Eden'. The historic and magical Lake Chad lies at its heart complimented by enviro-sculptures.

Great Dixter House and Gardens

Northiam, Kent TN31 6PH
Tel: (01797) 252878
An example of a 15thC manor house with antique furniture and needlework. Home of gardening writer Christopher Lloyd. The house is restored and the gardens were designed by Lutyens.

Guildford Boat House

Millbrook, Guildford, Surrey GU1 3XJ
Tel: (01483) 504494
Regular trips from Guildford to St Catherine's Lock and Godalming along the River Wey. Also 'Alfred Leroy' cruising restaurant. Rowing boats, canoes and holiday narrow boats.

Hever Castle and Gardens

Hever, Kent TN8 7NG
Tel: (01732) 865224
Moated castle once the childhood home of Anne Boleyn. Restored by the Astor family, it contains furniture, paintings and panelling. Set in award-winning gardens.

Howletts Wild Animal Park

Bekesbourne, Canterbury, Kent CT4 5EL
Tel: (01303) 264647
Mature parkland containing John Aspinall's animals, famous for its gorilla and tiger collections. Many other animals including elephants, deer and cats.

Knockhatch Adventure Park

Hailsham, East Sussex BN27 3PR
Tel: (01323) 442051
Birds of prey centre, laser adventure game, off-road go-karting, paintball, children's farm and crazy golf.

Leonardslee Gardens

Lower Beeding, Horsham, West Sussex RH13 6PP
Tel: (01403) 891212
Rhododendrons and azaleas in a romantic 240-acre valley with seven lakes. Rock garden, bonsai, wallabies and wildfowl. Victorian motorcars and doll's house exhibition.

Marle Place Gardens

Brenchley, Tonbridge, Kent TN12 7HS
Tel: (01892) 722304
Romantic, peaceful gardens with topiary, unusual shrubs and plants, ponds, Edwardian rockery and Victorian gazebo. Walled scented garden and sculptures.

Michelham Priory

Upper Dicker, Hailsham, East Sussex BN27 3QS
Tel: (01323) 844224
An Augustinian priory incorporated into a Tudor mansion. Seven acres of gardens, a working watermill, an Elizabethan Great Barn, smithy and a rope museum.

The Pictures:
1 Southover Grange Gardens, Lewes, East Sussex;
2 Leeds Castle, Kent;
3 Chichester Cathedral, West Sussex;
4 Smallhythe Place, Kent;
5 Brighton Marina, East Sussex;
6 Guildford Castle, Surrey;
7 Sheffield Park, East Sussex.

Paddle Steamer Kingswear Castle

The Historic Dockyard, Chatham, Kent ME4 4TQ
Tel: (01634) 827648
A part of Britain's maritime heritage, the award-winning coal-fired paddle steamer, Kingswear Castle, offers morning, afternoon, evening and full day excursions on the Medway.

Penshurst Place and Gardens

Penshurst, Tonbridge, Kent TN11 8DG
Tel: (01892) 870307
A medieval manor house with Baron's Hall, portraits, tapestries, armour, park, lake, venture playground and toy museum. Tudor gardens. Visitor and plant centres.

Petworth House and Park

Petworth, West Sussex GU28 0AE
Tel: (01798) 342207
A late 17thC mansion set in 'Capability' Brown landscaped deer park. The house is noted for its paintings, Gibbons carvings and fine collection of furniture and sculpture.

Polesden Lacey

Great Bookham, Dorking, Surrey RH5 6BD
Tel: (01372) 458203
A Regency villa, re-modelled after 1906 with collections of paintings, porcelain, tapestries and furniture. Walled rose garden and extensive grounds with fine trees and views.

The RHS Garden, Wisley

Wisley, Woking, Surrey GU23 6QB
Tel: (01483) 224234
Stretching over 240 acres of glorious garden, Wisley demonstrates the best in British gardening practices, whatever the season. Plant centre, gift shop and restaurant.

Romney, Hythe and Dymchurch Railway

New Romney, Kent TN28 8PL
Tel: (01797) 362353
The world's only main line in miniature. Fourteen miles (22.5kms) of 15 inch gauge across Romney Marsh. Steam and diesel locomotives, engine sheds and a Toy and Model Museum.

St Mary's House and Gardens

Bramber, Steyning, West Sussex BN44 3WE
Tel: (01903) 816205
A medieval timber-framed Grade I house with rare 16thC wall-leather, fine panelled rooms and a unique painted room. Topiary gardens.

Sheffield Park Garden

Sheffield Park, Uckfield, East Sussex TN22 3QX
Tel: (01825) 790231
One-hundred acres of 'Capability' Brown designed landscaped gardens and woodland with four lakes on different levels. Noted for its rhododendrons, rare trees and azaleas.

Sussex Falconry Centre

Birdham, Chichester, West Sussex PO20 7BS
Tel: (01243) 512472
Aviaries containing birds of prey including hawks, falcons, and owls. Flying displays of birds throughout the day, weather permitting.

Wakehurst Place Gardens

Ardingly, Haywards Heath, West Sussex RH17 6TN
Tel: (01444) 894000
Extensive 202-hectare estate gardens administered by Royal Botanic Gardens, Kew with lakes, ponds and an important collection of exotic trees, plants and shrubs.

The Whitstable Oyster and Fishery Exhibition

The Harbour, Whitstable, Kent CT5 1AB
Tel: (01227) 280753
An exhibition of unique artefacts, memorabilia and photographs depicting oyster fishing. Live fish display and 'hands-on' seashore experience.

Find out more about
SOUTH EAST
ENGLAND ...

Further information about holidays and attractions in
South East England is available from:

SOUTH EAST ENGLAND TOURIST BOARD
The Old Brew House, Warwick Park,
Tunbridge Wells, Kent TN2 5TU.

Tel: (01892) 540766
Fax: (01892) 511008
Email: enquiries@seetb.org.uk
Internet: www.SouthEastEngland.uk.com

The following publications are available free from the South East England Tourist Board:

Guide to the Guides

Bed and Breakfast Touring Map

Relaxation
featuring the green, rural areas of the region. For those
seeking rest and relaxation in a rural setting

Lively
for those seeking heritage and history combined with
the entertainment possibilities of a city or coastal break

Walk South East England

Glorious Gardens of South East England

Camping and Caravanning in the South of England

Outstanding Churches and Cathedrals

Golfing in the South East

Eating and Drinking in the South East

The Pictures:
1 Bateman's,
   East Sussex;
2 The Pantiles, Royal
   Tunbridge Wells, Kent;
3 Port Lympne Wild
   Animal Park, Kent;
4 Great Dixter House &
   Gardens, Northiam,
   East Sussex;
5 Bodiam Castle,
   East Sussex;
6 Chichester Cathedral
   Gardens, West Sussex.

Getting to
SOUTH EAST ENGLAND ...

BY ROAD: From the north of England – M1/M25; the west and Wales – M4/M25; the
east of England – M25; the south of England M3/M25; London – M20 or M2.

BY RAIL: Regular services from London's Charing Cross, Victoria and Waterloo East
stations to all parts of South East England.

WHERE TO STAY (SOUTH EAST ENGLAND)

Parks in this region are listed in alphabetical order of place name, and then in alphabetical order of park.

Map references refer to the colour location maps at the back of this guide. The first number indicates the map to use; the letter and number which follow refer to the grid reference on the map.

At-a-glance symbols can be found inside the back cover flap. Keep this open for easy reference.

ARUNDEL

West Sussex
Map ref 3D3

Picturesque, historic town on the River Arun, dominated by Arundel Castle, home of the Dukes of Norfolk. There are many 18th C houses, the Wildfowl and Wetlands Centre and Museum and Heritage Centre.
Tourist Information Centre
T: (01903) 882268

Ship & Anchor Marina
★★★
Touring Park
Heywood & Bryett Ltd, Ford,
Arundel BN18 0BJ
T: (01243) 551262
From A27 at Arundel take road south signposted Ford. Site 2 miles on the left, after level crossing. Also signposted from A259 between Littlehampton and Bognor Regis.
4.8 hectares (12 acres). Level, grassy.
160 touring pitches.

160	🚐	£10.00—£12.00
160	🚗	£10.00—£12.00
160	⛺	£10.00—£12.00

Open March–October

Please check prices and other details at the time of booking.

ASHFORD

Kent
Map ref 4B4

Once a market centre for the farmers of the Weald of Kent and Romney Marsh. The town centre has a number of Tudor and Georgian houses and a museum. Eurostar trains stop at Ashford International station.
Tourist Information Centre
T: (01233) 629165

Broadhembury Caravan & Camping Park
★★★★★
Holiday, Touring and Camping Park
Member BH&HPA
Steeds Lane, Kingsnorth, Ashford
TN26 1NQ
T: (01233) 620859
F: (01233) 620859
E: holidays@broadhembury.co.uk
I: www.broadhembury.co.uk
From M20 jct 10 take A2070 for 3 miles, then follow signs for Kingsnorth. Turn left at 2nd crossroads in Kingsnorth. Signposted.
2 hectares (5 acres). Level, grassy, hard, sheltered.
60 touring pitches.

60	🚐	£10.00—£13.00
60	🚗	£10.00—£13.00
60	⛺	£8.00—£13.00
3	🏠	£110.00—£340.00

20 units privately owned
Open all year round

Cards accepted: Barclaycard, Eurocard, Mastercard, Switch, Visa

BATTLE

East Sussex
Map ref 4B4

The Abbey at Battle was built on the site of the Battle of Hastings, when William defeated Harold II and so became the Conqueror in 1066. The museum has a fine collection relating to the Sussex iron industry and there is a social history museum - Buckleys Yesterday's World.
Tourist Information Centre
T: (01424) 773721

Crowhurst Park
★★★★★
Holiday and Touring Park
Rose Award
Member BH&HPA/NCC
Crowhurst Park, Telham Lane,
Battle TN33 0SL
T: (01424) 773344
F: (01424) 775727
E: enquiries@crowhurstpark.co.uk
I: www.crowhurstpark.co.uk
Two miles south of Battle on A2100. Signposted.
12.8 hectares (32 acres). Level, sloping, grassy.
40 touring pitches.

32	🚐	£15.00
8	🚗	£15.00
	🏠	£225.00—£695.00

135 units privately owned

Open March–December
Cards accepted: Barclaycard,
Mastercard, Visa

[icons]

Ad See display advertisement on
page 150

BEXHILL

East Sussex
Map ref 4B4

Popular resort with beach of shingle
and firm sand at low tide. The
impressive 1930s designed De la
Warr Pavilion has good
entertainment facilities. Costume
Museum in Manor Gardens.
Tourist Information Centre
T: (01424) 732208

Cobbs Hill Farm Caravan & Camping Park M
★★★★
Holiday, Touring and Camping Park
Member BH&HPA
Watermill Lane, Sidley, Bexhill
TN39 5JA
T: (01424) 213460 & 221358
F: (01424) 213460
*Turning off the A269 into Watermill
Lane, 1 mile on the left. Signposted.*
2.8 hectares (7 acres). Level, grassy,
sheltered.
45 touring pitches.

45	🚐	£4.60—£5.30
45	🚏	£4.40—£5.10
45	⛺	£4.60—£5.30
2	🛖	£87.00—£215.00

Open April–October

[icons]

BIDDENDEN

Kent
Map ref 4B4

Perfect village with black and white
houses, a tithe barn and a pond. Part
of the village is grouped around a
green with a village sign depicting the
famous Biddenden Maids. It was an
important centre of the Flemish
weaving industry, hence the beautiful
Old Cloth Hall. Vineyard nearby.

Woodlands Park M
★★★★
Touring Park
Member BH&HPA
Tenterden Road, Biddenden,
Ashford TN27 8BT
T: (01580) 291216
F: (01580) 291216
E: woodlandsp@aol.com
I: www.campingsite.co.uk
*Take A28 from Ashford to Tenterden.
Approximately 3 miles before
Tenterden take right turn, A262,*

signposted Tunbridge Wells. Park is
approximately 1.5 miles on the right-
hand side. Signposted.
2.8 hectares (7 acres). Level, grassy.
200 touring pitches.

200	🚐	£8.50—£10.00
200	🚏	£8.50—£10.00
200	⛺	£8.50—£10.00

Open March–October

[icons]

BOGNOR REGIS

West Sussex
Map ref 3D3

Five miles of firm, flat sand have
made the town a popular family
resort. Well supplied with gardens.
Tourist Information Centre
T: (01243) 823140

The Lillies Nursery & Caravan Park M
★★★
Holiday, Touring and Camping Park
Yapton Road, Barnham, Bognor
Regis PO22 0AY
T: (01243) 552081
F: (01243) 552081
*3 miles north of Bognor Regis. Take
A29 to Westergate, bearing right at
Labour in Vain pub to Eastergate and
onto B2233. From A27 Fontwell
roundabout onto A29 then B2233 to
park. Signposted.*
1.2 hectares (3 acres). Level, grassy,
sheltered.
32 touring pitches.

21	🚐	£8.00—£10.00
21	🚏	£8.00—£10.00
16	⛺	£8.00—£10.00
6	🛖	£140.00—£230.00

Open March–October

[icons]

WELCOME HOST

This is a nationally recognised
customer care programme
which aims to promote
the highest standards of
service and a warm welcome.
Parks taking part in this
initiative are indicated
by the WH symbol.

All accommodation in this
guide has been rated, or is
awaiting a rating, by a trained
Tourist Board assessor.

CANTERBURY

Kent
Map ref 4B3

Place of pilgrimage since the
martyrdom of Becket in 1170 and
the site of Canterbury Cathedral.
Visit St Augustine's Abbey, St
Martin's (the oldest church in
England), Royal Museum and Art
Gallery and the Canterbury Tales.
Nearby is Howletts Wild Animal
Park. Good shopping centre.
Tourist Information Centre
T: (01227) 766567

Yew Tree Caravan Park M
★★★★
Holiday, Touring and Camping Park
Member BH&HPA
Stone Street, Petham, Canterbury
CT4 5PL
T: (01227) 700306
F: (01227) 700306
I: www.ukparks.co.uk/yewtreepark
*On B2068 7 miles from M20 jct 11.
Signposted.*
Wheelchair access category 2 ♿
1.6 hectares (4 acres). Level, sloping,
grassy, sheltered.
45 touring pitches.

15	🚐	£8.00—£12.50
5	🚏	£7.50—£12.00
25	⛺	£7.20—£11.50
7	🛖	£99.00—£350.00

Open March–October
Cards accepted: Barclaycard, Delta,
Eurocard, JCB, Mastercard, Solo,
Switch, Visa

[icons]

CHICHESTER

West Sussex
Map ref 3C3

The county town of West Sussex
with a beautiful Norman cathedral.
Noted for its Georgian architecture
but also has modern buildings like
the Festival Theatre. Surrounded by
places of interest, including
Fishbourne Roman Palace, Weald
and Downland Open-Air Museum
and West Dean Gardens.
Tourist Information Centre
T: (01243) 775888

Wicks Farm Camping Park M
★★★★★
Holiday and Touring Park
Member BH&HPA
Redlands Lane, West Wittering,
Chichester PO20 8QD
T: (01243) 513116
F: (01243) 511296
*From A27 at Chichester take A286/
B2179 for 6 miles, Wicks Park is 2nd
on the right just past Lamb pub.
Signposted.*

Continued ▶

CHICHESTER
Continued

5.6 hectares (14 acres). Level, grassy, sheltered.
42 touring pitches.

42	🚐	£9.50—£11.50
42	⛺	£9.50—£11.50

Open March–October
Cards accepted: Barclaycard, Delta, Mastercard, Switch, Visa

🚗📶🍴🔥🕯🍼🔌🎿🛒💻📺✎🗝
☺🏴🚲🔍⛳ WH

EASTBOURNE
East Sussex
Map ref 4B4

One of the finest, most elegant resorts on the south-east coast situated beside Beachy Head. Long promenade, well known Carpet Gardens on the seafront, Devonshire Park tennis and indoor leisure complex, theatres, Towner Art Gallery, "How We Lived Then" Museum of Shops and Social History.
Tourist Information Centre
T: (01323) 411400

Fairfields Farm Caravan & Camping Park ⚠
★★★
Touring and Camping Park
Eastbourne Road, Westham, Pevensey BN24 5NG
T: (01323) 763165
F: (01323) 469175
E: fairfields.farm@btinternet.com
I: www.btinternet.com/~fairfields.farm
Signposted off A27 Pevensey roundabout. Straight through Pevensey and Westham villages. Then B2191 to Eastbourne east, left turn, over level crossing on the left. Signposted.
1.2 hectares (3 acres). Level, grassy, sheltered.
60 touring pitches.

60	🚐	£7.00—£7.00
60	🚏	£7.00—£7.00
60	⛺	£6.50—£6.50

Open April–October

🚗📶🍴🔥🕯🍼🔌🎿🛒✎☺
🔍🛁⛳

If you book by telephone and are asked for your credit card number, it is advisable to check the proprietor's policy should you cancel your reservation.

HASTINGS
East Sussex
Map ref 4B4

Ancient town which became famous as the base from which William the Conqueror set out to fight the Battle of Hastings. Later became one of the Cinque Ports, now a leading resort. Castle, Hastings Embroidery inspired by the Bayeux Tapestry and Sea Life Centre.
Tourist Information Centre
T: (01424) 781111

Shear Barn Holiday Park ⚠
★★★
Holiday, Touring and Camping Park
Member BH&HPA/NCC
Barley Lane, Hastings TN35 5DX
T: (01424) 423583 (Answerphone available.) & 716474 & 07970 788028 (mobile).)
F: (01424) 718740
E: shearbarn@pavilion.co.uk
I: www.shearbarn.co.uk
From Hastings old town take A259 to Rye/Folkestone. Turn into Harold Road, Gurth Road and Barley Lane signposts on A252.
13.6 hectares (34 acres). Level, sloping, grassy.
450 touring pitches.

150	🚐	£10.00—£18.00
150	🚏	£7.50—£18.00
300	⛺	£6.00—£18.00
30	🏠	£160.00—£475.00

187 units privately owned
Open March–December
Cards accepted: Barclaycard, Delta, Mastercard, Switch, Visa

🚗📶🍴🔥🕯🍼🔌🎿🛒🍽💻📺✎🗝☺🔍🏴🎵⛳

HENFIELD
West Sussex
Map ref 3D3

Ancient village with many old houses and good shopping facilities, on a ridge of high ground overlooking the Adur Valley. Views to the South Downs.

Downsview Caravan Park
★★★★
Holiday, Touring and Camping Park
Member BH&HPA
Bramlands Lane, Woodmancote, Henfield BN5 9TG
T: (01273) 492801
F: (01273) 495214
Signed from A281 in village of Woodmancote 2.5 miles east of Henfield and 6.5 miles north west of Brighton.
1.8 hectares (4.5 acres). Level, grassy, hard, sheltered.
27 touring pitches.

12	🚐	£8.50—£10.50
12	🚏	£8.50—£10.50
15	⛺	£7.50—£9.50

27 units privately owned
Open February–December
Cards accepted: Barclaycard, Delta, Eurocard, Mastercard, Visa

🚗📶🍴🔥🕯🍼🔌🎿🛒💻📺✎🗝
🛁☺🔍⛳

HORAM
East Sussex
Map ref 3D3

Horam Manor Touring Park ⚠
★★★★
Touring and Camping Park
Member BH&HPA
Horam, Heathfield TN21 0YD
T: (01435) 813662
E: horam.manor@virgin.net
I: www.handbooks.co.uk/horam-manor
On A267 south of Horam village. Ten miles north of Eastbourne, 3 miles south of Heathfield. Signposted.
2.8 hectares (7 acres). Level, sloping, grassy, sheltered.
90 touring pitches.

60	🚐	£11.85—£11.85
10	🚏	£11.85—£11.85
30	⛺	£11.85—£11.85

Open March–October

🚗📶🍴🔥🕯🍼🔌🎿💻📺✎🗝
☺🔍🎵▶⛳

LEYSDOWN ON SEA
Kent
Map ref 4B3

Priory Hill Holiday Park ⚠
★★★★
Holiday, Touring and Camping Park
Member BH&HPA
Wing Road, Leysdown on Sea, Sheerness ME12 4OT
T: (01795) 510267 & 07979 530600/1 (Mobiles)
F: (01795) 510267
E: info@prioryhill.co.uk
I: www.prioryhill.co.uk
M2/M20 onto A249 signposted Sheerness, roundabout on Sheppey turn right onto B2231 to Leysdown, right into Wing Road. Signposted.
6.2 hectares (15.5 acres). Level, grassy, sheltered.
54 touring pitches.

54	🚐	£9.50—£16.00
	🚏	£9.00—£15.00
	⛺	£9.00—£15.00
3	🏠	£200.00—£400.00

243 units privately owned
Open March–October
Cards accepted: Barclaycard, Delta, Eurocard, Mastercard, Switch, Visa

🚗📶🍴🔥🕯🍼🔌🎿🍽📺📺💻🗝✎☺🔍🍺⛳🛁🎵⛳🗝

LINGFIELD

Surrey
Map ref 3D2

Wealden village with many buildings dating back to the 15th C. Nearby there is year-round horse racing at Lingfield Park.

Long Acres Caravan & Camping Park ▲▲
★★★★
Touring and Camping Park
Member BH&HPA
Newchapel Road, Lingfield RH7 6LE
T: (01342) 833205
F: (01622) 735038
From M25 jct 6 south on A22 for 6 miles towards East Grinstead. At Newchapel roundabout turn left onto B2028 to Lingfield. Site is 700yds on the right. Signposted.
16 hectares (40 acres). Level, sloping, grassy, hard, sheltered.
60 touring pitches.

60	🚐	£9.50—£9.50
60	🚌	£9.50—£9.50
60	▲	£9.50—£9.50

Open all year round

MAIDSTONE

Kent
Map ref 4B3

Busy county town of Kent on the River Medway has many interesting features and is an excellent centre for excursions. Museum of Carriages, Museum and Art Gallery, Mote Park.
Tourist Information Centre
T: (01622) 602169 or 739029
(M20, jct 8)

Pine Lodge Touring Park ▲▲
★★★★★
Touring and Camping Park
Member BH&HPA
A20 Ashford Road, Hollingbourne, Maidstone ME17 1XH
T: (01622) 730018
F: (01622) 734498
From M20 jct 8 onto A20, take turning to Maidstone/Bearsted, site is 0.5 miles on left. Signposted.
2.8 hectares (7 acres). Level, sloping, grassy, hard, sheltered.
100 touring pitches.

60	🚐	£9.00—£11.00
20	🚌	£9.00—£11.00
20	▲	£8.00—£11.00

Open all year round

Cards accepted: Barclaycard, Delta, JCB, Maestro, Mastercard, Solo, Switch, Visa, Visa Electron

MARDEN

Kent
Map ref 4B4

The village is believed to date back to Saxon times, though today more modern homes surround the 13th C church.

Tanner Farm Touring Caravan & Camping Park ▲▲
★★★★★
Touring and Camping Park
Member BH&HPA
Goudhurst Road, Marden, Tonbridge TN12 9ND
T: (01622) 832399
F: (01622) 832472
E: tannerfarmpark@cs.com
From A21 or A229 onto B2079 midway between Marden and Goudhurst. Signposted.
Wheelchair access category 2 ♿
60 hectares (150 acres). Level, grassy, hard, sheltered.
100 touring pitches.

100	🚐	£6.50—£11.00
20	🚌	£6.50—£11.00
20	▲	£5.50—£11.00

Open all year round
Cards accepted: Barclaycard, Delta, Maestro, Mastercard, Solo, Switch, Visa, Visa Electron

PAGHAM

West Sussex
Map ref 3C3

Church Farm Holiday Village ▲▲
★★★★
Holiday Park
Rose Award
Member BH&HPA/NCC
Pagham, Chichester PO21 4NR
T: 0870 2425678
F: (01442) 254956
Where A27 roundabout crosses the A259 on the outskirts of Chichester, take the Pagham exit and follow this road for 1 mile to roundabout. Turn left and follow road to end. Signposted.
24.8 hectares (62 acres). Level, grassy, sheltered.

166	🏠	£153.00—£755.00

750 units privately owned
Open March–October

Cards accepted: Barclaycard, Delta, Mastercard, Switch, Visa

Ad See display advertisement on page 10

UCKFIELD

East Sussex
Map ref 3D3

Once a medieval market town and centre of the iron industry, Uckfield is now a busy country town on the edge of the Ashdown Forest.

Honeys Green Farm Caravan Park ▲▲
★★★
Holiday, Touring and Camping Park
Member BH&HPA
Easons Green, Framfield, Uckfield TN22 5RE
T: (01825) 840334
Turn off A22 at Halland roundabout onto B2192, Heathfield. Site 0.25 miles on left. Signposted.
.8 hectare (2 acres). Level, grassy, sheltered.
22 touring pitches.

18	🚐	£6.50—£9.00
4	🚌	£6.50—£9.00
	▲	£5.50—£6.50
6	🏠	£150.00—£210.00

Open April–October

WASHINGTON

West Sussex
Map ref 3D3

Near the village is the famous Chanctonbury Ring, an Iron Age camp on a rise nearly 800 ft above sea-level.

Washington Caravan & Camping Park ▲▲
★★★★
Touring and Camping Park
London Road, Washington, Pulborough RH20 4AJ
T: (01903) 892869
F: (01903) 893252
A24 - A283. Signposted.
1.8 hectares (4.5 acres). Hard.
60 touring pitches.

21	🚐	£9.00—£9.00
21	🚌	£9.00—£9.00
40	▲	£9.00—£9.00

Open all year round
Cards accepted: Barclaycard, Eurocard, Mastercard, Visa

USE YOUR *i*s

There are more than 550 Tourist Information Centres throughout England offering friendly help with accommodation and holiday ideas as well as suggestions of places to visit and things to do. There may well be a centre in your home town which can help you before you set out. You'll find addresses in the local Phone Book.

DAVID BELLAMY CONSERVATION AWARDS

If you are looking for a site that's environmentally friendly look for those that have achieved the David Bellamy Conservation Award. Recently launched in conjunction with the British Holiday & Home Parks Association, this award is given to sites which are committed to protecting and enhancing the environment – from care of the hedgerows and wildlife to recycling waste – and are members of the Association. More information about this award scheme can be found at the front of the guide.

Scotland
SCOTLAND

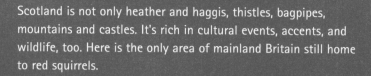

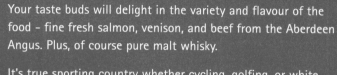

Scotland is not only heather and haggis, thistles, bagpipes, mountains and castles. It's rich in cultural events, accents, and wildlife, too. Here is the only area of mainland Britain still home to red squirrels.

Your taste buds will delight in the variety and flavour of the food - fine fresh salmon, venison, and beef from the Aberdeen Angus. Plus, of course pure malt whisky.

It's true sporting country whether cycling, golfing, or white water rafting. And from the lowlands to the highlands and islands, the seasons are dramatic with long summer nights, rich autumn days, white winters and crisp springs.

Why not have a fling while you're here, at one of the many Highland Festivals!

FOR MORE INFORMATION ON SCOTLAND, CONTACT:
Scottish Tourist Board
Central Information Department
23 Ravelston Terrace,
Edinburgh EH4 3TP
Tel: (0131) 332 2433
Fax: (0131) 315 4545
Internet: www.visitscotland.com

Where to Go in Scotland - see pages 156-161
Where to Stay in Scotland - see pages 162-171

The Pictures:
1 Highland Cow;
2 Blairgowrie Pipe Band;
3 Castle Menzies;
4 Killiecrankie Pass.

Whilst in
SCOTLAND ...

You will find hundreds of interesting places to visit during your stay in Scotland, just some of which are listed in these pages. Contact any Tourist Information Centre in Scotland for more ideas on days out.

Aberdeen Maritime Museum
Shiprow, Aberdeen AB11 2BY
Tel: (01224) 337700
Maritime museum with large exhibition area, including hands-on and interactive displays. The North Sea oil and gas industry is featured. Historic ship models.

Archaeolink Prehistory Park
Archaeolink, Oyne, Insch AB52 6QP
Tel: (01464) 851500
Ancient history recreated - triple screen film presentation, Myths and Legends Gallery, interactive displays and outdoor reconstruction park with working Iron Age farm.

Baxters Visitor Centre
Fochabers IV32 7LD
Tel: (01343) 820666
The Great Hall charts the history of the food company Baxters of Speyside since 1868. Audiovisual demonstration theatre.

The Big Idea
The Harbourside, Irvine KA12 8XX
Tel: (08708) 403100
New permanent millennium exhibition celebrating a thousand years of invention, but most importantly, the Big Ideas of the visitor.

Brodick Castle, Garden and Country Park
Brodick KA27 8HY
Tel: (01770) 302202
The castle was built on the site of a Viking fortress and parts of it date from the 13thC. It contains superb silver, porcelain, paintings and fine 18thC furniture.

Burrell Collection
Pollockshaws Road, Glasgow G43 1AT
Tel: (0141) 649 7151
The award-winning building welcomes visitors to the riches of Sir William Burrell's unique collection. There are art objects from Iraq, Egypt, Greece and Italy.

Caithness Glass Factory and Visitor Centre
Airport Industrial Estate, Harrowhill, Wick KW1 5BP
Tel: (01955) 602286
Marvel at close quarters the skilled glassmakers transforming fine Scottish sand into exquisite glassware using the heat of the furnace and the skill of hand and eye.

Calanais Standing Stones Visitor Centre

Callanish, Isle of Lewis HS2 9DY
Tel: (01851) 621422
These standing stones are older than Stonehenge and are one of the most remote and ancient monuments in Europe. Visitor centre with multi-lingual interpretation.

Chatelherault Country Park

Ferniegair, Hamilton ML3 7UE
Tel: (01698) 426213
Country park with visitor centre exhibits on natural history and history of the restored William Adam lodge (open to the public). River gorge, woodland walks and nature trails.

Cruachan Power Station

Scottish Power, Dalmally PA33 1AN
Tel: (01866) 822618
A unique 30-minute guided tour inside a hollow mountain to discover a reversible pumped storage scheme hidden 1km (0.6 miles) inside a granite mountain.

Dawyck Botanic Garden

Stobo, Peebles EH45 9JU
Tel: (01721) 760254
Spectacular woodland garden, with a history of tree planting of over 300 years. Landscaped walks with stunning views of the garden and countryside of the Scottish Borders.

Deep-Sea World

North Queensferry, Inverkeithing KY11 1JR
Tel: (01383) 411880
Discover Scotland's triple award-winning aquarium. Enjoy a spectacular divers-eye view of our marine environment in the world's longest underwater acrylic tunnel.

The Pictures:
1 Edinburgh Skyline and Castle;
2 Eileean Donan Castle;
3 Glencoe;
4 River Tay;
5 Blaven, Isle of Skye;
6 Walking, Wester Ross;
7 Cailaverock Castle;
8 Crail Harbour.

Discovery Point and RRS Discovery

Discovery Quay, Dundee DD1 4XA
Tel: (01382) 201245
Discovery Point Centre contains audiovisual displays about Captain Scott's ship 'Discovery' and includes a spectacular film show. Exhibits also depict Antarctic exploration.

Drum Castle

Drumoak, Banchory AB31 5EY
Tel: (01330) 811204
The combination over the years of a 13thC square tower, a very fine Jacobean mansion and additions by Victorian lairds makes Drum Castle unique among Scottish castles.

Dynamic Earth

Holyrood Road, Edinburgh EH8 8AS
Tel: (0131) 550 7800
See, hear and smell the planet as it was thousands of years ago. Experience everything from boiling volcanoes to freezing ice age and travel to the future itself.

Edinburgh Castle

Royal Mile, Edinburgh
Tel: (0131) 225 9846
Dominating Scotland's capital, parts of this famous castle date from the Norman period. Mons Meg, the enormous 500-year-old siege cannon is located here.

Edinburgh Crystal Visitor Centre

Eastfield Industrial Estate, Penicuik EH26 8HB
Tel: (01968) 675128
A stunning exhibition and video presentation reveals the heritage of Edinburgh Crystal. Join a guided tour of the factory and watch the craftsmen at work.

Eilean Donan Castle

Dornie, Kyle of Lochalsh IV40 8DX
Tel: (01599) 555202
The castle of dreams. Romantic, photogenic, lots to see, not to be missed. Great fun and great coffee too.

Gallery of Modern Art

Queen Street, Glasgow G1 3AZ
Tel: (0141) 229 1996
Four floors each offering a gallery themed on one of the four elements: fire, air, earth, water. Fashionable roof-top cafe with panoramic views across the city.

Glenfiddich Distillery

WM Grant & Sons, Dufftown Keith AB55 4DH
Tel: (01340) 820373
Guided tours around the distillery and bottling hall with a complimentary dram at the end of the tour. Picnic area, shop and car park. Audio-visual display in six languages.

Glenturret Distillery

The Hosh, Crieff PH7 4HA
Tel: (01764) 656565
Scotland's oldest Highland distillery. Guided tours, free tasting, award-winning visitor heritage centre, audiovisual presentation, 3-dimensional exhibition museum. Restaurant.

Highland and Rare Breeds Farm

Scottish Farm Animal Visitor Centre,
Elphin, Lairg IV27 4HH
Tel: (01854) 666204
An educational highland farm with over 30 breeds of animals and poultry in a beautiful open setting. Highland cattle, rare breeds of Scottish sheep, goats, pigs and fowl.

Highland Mysteryworld

Glencoe, Ballachulish PA35 4HL
Tel: (01855) 811660
Prepare to become involved. Learn as you laugh, explore as you touch, see as you sense the fantastic mysteries around you. Five fabulous indoor attractions.

Inveraray Jail

Church Square, Inveraray PA32 8TX
Tel: (01499) 302381
Scotland's living 19thC prison featuring an exhibition on torture, death and damnation. Sit and listen to trials in the 1820s courtroom.

James Pringle Weavers of Inverness

Holm Woollen Mill, Dores Road, Inverness IV2 4RB
Tel: (01463) 223311
A 200-year-old woollen mill with a new weaving exhibition which includes interactive displays and a have-a-go area.

Jarlshof Prehistoric and Norse Settlement

Sumburgh Head, Shetland
Tel: (01950) 460112
Three acres spanning 3,000 years from the stone age including bronze age houses and Viking long houses.

Johnstons of Elgin – Cashmere Visitor Centre

Newmill, Elgin IV30 4AF
Tel: (01343) 554099
Be guided around the only British mill still to transform cashmere from fibre to garment and enjoy an audiovisual presentation. Shop and coffee shop.

Landmark Forest Heritage Park

Carrbridge PH23 3AJ
Tel: (01479) 841614
Amazing range of attractions: Microworld exhibition, Wildwater Coaster, Treetop Trail, steam-powered sawmill, Wild Forest Maze and Clydesdale horse demonstrations.

The Mill on the Fleet

Gatehouse of Fleet, Castle Douglas DG7 2HS
Tel: (01577) 814099
An 18thC cotton mill, rebuilt as a heritage centre, telling the story of the building of Gatehouse. Model of town, craft and art exhibitions, cafe with riverside terrace.

Mount Stuart House and Gardens

Mount Stuart, Rothesay PA20 9LR
Tel: (01700) 503877
A magnificent Victorian Gothic house, the architectural fantasy of the 3rd Marquess of Bute. The profusion of astrological designs and stained glass is breathtaking.

6

National Wallace Monument

Abbey Craig, Hillfoots Road, Causewayhead,
Stirling FK9 5LF
Tel: (01786) 472140
Spectacular 67m-high (220ft) 19thC tower built to commemorate Scotland's 'Braveheart', William Wallace. Experience his life through a series of exhibitions.

New Lanark Visitor Centre

New Lanark Mills, New Lanark, Lanark ML11 9DB
Tel: (01555) 661345
A two hundred-year-old nominated World Heritage Site. The birth place of Robert Owen's radical vision for the future, featuring a new ride called the 'New Millennium Experience'.

Ortak Visitor Centre

Ortak Jewellery, Hatston, Kirkwall KW15 1RH
Tel: (01856) 872224
The visitor centre, next to the jewellery workshops, houses a permanent exhibition with a video presentation describing how modern jewellery is made.

4

Rob Roy & Trossachs Visitor Centre

Ancaster Square, Callander FK17 8ED
Tel: (01877) 330342
Exhibition of the life and times of Rob Roy McGregor, including a Highland cottage, cinematic tour of the Trossachs plus play area, gift shop and entertainment.

The Royal Yacht Britannia

Ocean Drive, Leith Docks, Edinburgh EH6 6JJ
Tel: (0131) 555 5566
The Royal Yacht Britannia is permanently moored in Edinburgh and is open all year round as a visitor attraction and hospitality venue. Voted Best New Attraction 1999.

St Andrews Castle and Visitor Centre

The Scores, St Andrews KY16 9AR
Tel: (01334) 477196
See the fascinating mine and counter-mine - rare examples of medieval siege techniques and the bottle dungeon.

Scone Palace

Scone, Perth PH2 6BD
Tel: (01738) 552300
This historic house, home of the Earls of Mansfield, is situated at the heart of Scottish history on the site of the crowning place of the Kings of Scotland.

The Pictures:
1   Loch Torridon;
2   West Highland Line;
3   Princes Street Gardens,
    Edinburgh;
4   Glenfinnan Monument;
5   Orchardardton Tower;
6   Forth Rail Bridge.

5

Museum of Scotland

Chambers Street, Edinburgh EH1 1JF
Tel: (0131) 225 7534
A new museum which tells the story of Scotland's past, its land, its people and their achievements over 3,000 million years.

Scottish Seabird Centre

The Harbour, North Berwick EH39 4SS
Tel: (01620) 890202
Located in a spectacular location, attractions include interactive displays, a sound and light show, an observation deck, auditorium, cafe and shop.

Shaping a Nation

Fountainpark, Dundee Street, Edinburgh EH11 1AW
Tel: (0131) 22901706
Explore the innovative and creative energy of the people of Scotland through the use of interactive technology.

Stirling Castle

Stirling, Stiringshire
Tel: (01786) 450000
A grand castle with outstanding architecture. Many royal connections including strong links with Mary Queen of Scots. Exhibition on life in the royal palace.

The Tall Ship at Glasgow Harbour

Clyde Maritime Centre, Stobcross Road,
Glasgow G3 8QQ
Tel: (0141) 339 0631
Visit the tall ship at Glasgow Harbour. Principal attraction is the chance to go aboard the 103-year-old tall ship Glenlee. Exhibitions and children's activities.

Thirlestane Castle

Lauder TD2 6RU
Tel: (01578) 722430
Rebuilt in the 16thC, the castle is famed for its 17thC plasterwork ceilings, fine furniture and newly-restored picture collection. Parkland and picnic areas.

Museum of Transport

Kelvin Hall, Bunhouse Road, Glasgow G3 8DP
Tel: (0141) 287 2720
A unique collection of transport and technology which reflects Glasgow's history as the second city of the British Empire.

Verdant Works

West Henderson's Wynd, Dundee DD1 5BT
Tel: (01382) 225282
Verdant Works takes you on a tour of the jute trade from its beginnings in the Indian subcontinent to the end product.

Whithorn Cradle of Christianity

George Street, Whithorn, Newton Stewart
Tel: (01988) 500508
Nowhere in Scotland will you find more periods of history associated with one site. Archaeologists have pieced together evidence to reveal the story of Whithorn.

The Pictures:
1 Loch Lomond;
2 Edinburgh Festival Street Theatre;
3 Piper at Glamis Castle;
4 Highland Games;
5 Tay Valley;
6 Queen's View, Loch Tummel;
7 Italian Centre, Glasgow.

Find out more about
SCOTLAND ...

Further information about holidays and attractions
in Scotland is available from:

SCOTTISH TOURIST BOARD
Central Information Department,
23 Ravelston Terrace,
Edinburgh EH4 3TP
Tel: (0131) 332 2433
Fax: (0131) 315 4545
Internet: www.visitscotland.com

SCOTTISH TOURIST BOARD
19 Cockspur Street (off Trafalgar Square), London SW1Y 5BL

BRITISH VISITOR CENTRE
Scotland Desk, No. 1 Regent Street, London SW1Y 4XT

Getting to
SCOTLAND ...

BY ROAD: The A1 and M6 bring you quickly over the border and immerse you in beautiful scenery. Scotland's network of excellent roads span out from Edinburgh – Glasgow takes approximately $1^1/_4$ hours by car, Aberdeen $2^1/_2$ hours and Inverness 3 hours.

BY RAIL: The cross-border service from England and Wales to Scotland is fast and efficient, and Scotrail trains offer overnight Caledonian sleepers to make the journey even easier. Telephone (08457) 484950 for further details.

WHERE TO STAY (SCOTLAND)

Parks in Scotland are listed in alphabetical order of place name,
and then in alphabetical order of park.

Map references refer to the colour location maps at the back of this guide.
The first number indicates the map to use; the letter and number which follow refer to the
grid reference on the map.

At-a-glance symbols can be found inside the back cover flap.
Keep this open for easy reference.

ABERFOYLE

Central
Map ref 7B1

Village on the River Forth. Nearby are the Loch Ard forests and Menteith Hills.

Trossachs Holiday Park
★ ★ ★ ★ ★
Holiday Park
Thistle Award
Member BH&HPA
Aberfoyle, Stirling FK8 3SA
T: (01877) 382614
F: (01877) 382732
On east side of A81 3 miles south of Aberfoyle. Signposted.
6 hectares (15 acres). Grassy, hard.
45 touring pitches.

45	🚐	£9.00—£12.00
45	🚚	£9.00—£12.00
20	⛺	£9.00—£12.00
12	🏠	£149.00—£449.00

Open March–October
Cards accepted: Barclaycard, Delta, Eurocard, Mastercard, Switch, Visa

ALYTH

Tayside
Map ref 7C1

Small holiday centre in the Grampian foothills overlooking Strathmore. Popular destination for trout fishing.

Nether Craig Caravan Park
★ ★ ★ ★ ★
Touring Park
Member BH&HPA
Alyth, Blairgowrie, Perthshire
PH11 8HN
T: (01575) 560204
F: (01575) 560315

South of Alyth, join B954, signposted Glenisla. After 4 miles (5km) turn right onto unclassified road, signposted Nether Craig Caravan Park. Park is 0.5 miles (1km) on left. Signposted.
1.6 hectares (4 acres). Level, grassy, hard, sheltered.
40 touring pitches.

40	🚐	£10.00—£11.00
40	🚚	£10.00—£11.00
40	⛺	£6.00

Open March–October

AUCHENMALG

Dumfries & Galloway
Map ref 7B3

Cock Inn Caravan Park
★ ★ ★ ★
Holiday Park
Thistle Award
Member BH&HPA
Auchenmalg, Newton Stewart,
Wigtownshire DG8 0JT
T: (01581) 500227
On the A747 Glenluce to Port William road, 5 miles (8km) from the A75 Newton Stewart to Stranraer road. Signposted.
2.8 hectares (7 acres). Level, sloping, grassy, hard.
30 touring pitches.

30	🚐	£7.00—£12.50
30	🚚	£7.00—£12.50
30	⛺	£6.00—£8.70
5	🏠	£170.00—£260.00

70 units privately owned
Open March–October

Please mention this guide when making your booking.

AVIEMORE

Highland
Map ref 8C3

Popular centre for exploring Speyside and the Cairngorms. Winter sports, fishing, walking and climbing.
Tourist Information Centre
T: (01479) 810363

Rothiemurchus Camping & Caravan Park
★ ★ ★ ★ ★
Holiday Park
Member BH&HPA/NCC
Coylumbridge Aviemore, Inverness-shire PH22 1QU
T: (01479) 812800
F: (01479) 812800
E: Rothie@enterprise.net
From A9 take B970. The park is 1.5 miles from Aviemore on the right hand side. Signposted.
Level, sloping, grassy, hard, sheltered.
39 touring pitches.

17	🚐	£10.00—£13.00
17	🚚	£10.00—£13.00
22	⛺	£7.00—£9.00
5	🏠	£275.00—£400.00

40 units privately owned
Open all year round
Cards accepted: JCB, Mastercard, Solo, Switch, Visa

COLOUR MAPS

Colour maps at the back of this guide pinpoint all places in which you will find parks listed.

BALMACARA

Highland
Map ref 8B3

Small village on the north shore of Loch Alsh with views towards the Sound of Sleat and Skye.

Reraig Caravan Site
★★★★
Touring Park
Balmacara, Kyle of Lochalsh, Ross-shire IV40 8DH
T: (01599) 566215
1.75 miles (3km) west of junction of A87 and A890 behind Balmacara Hotel. Signposted. No youth groups. .8 hectare (2 acres). Level, grassy, hard.
45 touring pitches.

40		£7.80
40		£7.80
5		£7.80

Open May–September
Cards accepted: Delta, Eurocard, Mastercard, Visa

BLAIR ATHOLL

Tayside
Map ref 7C1

Highland village at the foot of the Grampian mountains.
Tourist Information Centre
T: (01796) 472215 or 472751

Blair Castle Caravan Park
★★★★★
Holiday Park
Thistle Award
Member BH&HPA/NCC
Blair Atholl, Perthshire PH18 5SR
T: (01796) 481263
F: (01796) 481587
Take A9 north from Pitlochry. Turn off for Blair Atholl after 6 miles. Signposted. 12.8 hectares (32 acres). Level, sloping, grassy, hard, sheltered.
241 touring pitches.

140		£8.50—£10.50
15		£8.50—£10.50
82		£7.00—£10.50
27		£170.00—£370.00

74 units privately owned
Open April–October

Cards accepted: Barclaycard, Eurocard, Mastercard, Switch, Visa

Ad See display advertisement on this page

CALLANDER

Central
Map ref 7C1

A favourite centre for exploring the Trossachs and the Highlands, beautifully situated at the entrance to the Pass of Leny.
Tourist Information Centre
T: (01877) 330342

Keltie Bridge Caravan Park ▲▲
★★★★
Touring Park
Member BH&HPA
Callander, Perthshire FK17 8LQ
T: (01877) 330606
F: (01877) 330075
On A84 between Doune and Callander. Signposted.
Wheelchair access category 3
Level, grassy, sheltered.
50 touring pitches.

50		£7.50—£9.50
50		£7.50—£9.50
50		£6.00—£9.50

30 units privately owned
Open April–October

CROCKETFORD

Dumfries & Galloway
Map ref 7C3

Small village in the valley of the River Urr.
Tourist Information Centre
T: (01387) 253862

Park of Brandedleys
★★★★
Holiday Park
Thistle Award
Member BH&HPA
Crocketford, Dumfries DG2 8RG
T: (01556) 690250
F: (01556) 690681
Turn south from A75, at west end of Crocketford village, and continue for 150 yards. Signposted. 9.6 hectares (24 acres). Level, sloping, grassy, hard, sheltered.
80 touring pitches.

80		£9.00—£15.00
30		£9.00—£15.00
20		£9.00—£15.00
10		£145.00—£365.00

18 units privately owned
Open all year round
Cards accepted: Barclaycard, Delta, Eurocard, Mastercard, Solo, Switch, Visa

DUMFRIES

Dumfries & Galloway
Map ref 7C3

Fascinating town with old five-arched bridge spanning the River Nith. County capital and Royal Burgh with associations with Robert Burns, James Barrie and Robert Bruce. Burns died here and the house he occupied contains interesting personal relics. His tomb is in St Michaels.
Tourist Information Centre
T: (01387) 253862

Barnsoul Farm and Wild Life Area
★★★
Holiday Park
Member BH&HPA
Shawhead, Dumfries DG2 9SQ
T: (01387) 730249
F: (01387) 730249
E: barnsouldg@aol.com
I: www.barnsoulfarm.co.uk
Off A75 at sign for Shawhead. At Shawhead take right, then within 50m bear left. After 1.5 miles Barnsoul is on left. Signposted. 100 hectares (250 acres). Level, sloping, grassy, hard, sheltered.
20 touring pitches. Also, "Sheiling" family bothies.

20		£7.00—£10.00
20		£7.00—£10.00
20		£7.00—£10.00
4		£130.00—£200.00

Open April–October

The ▲▲ symbol after a park name indicates that it is a Regional Tourist Board member.

BLAIR CASTLE CARAVAN PARK
Blair Atholl, Perthshire PH18 5SR. Tel: (01796) 481263
Stay at our glorious highland park set amidst spectacular mountain scenery. Top quality facilities, tourist board rating "excellent". Thistle Award for our hire caravan holiday homes. Spacious central park and recreation areas, extensive woodland, hill and riverside walks. Water, drainage. Electric hook-ups and flat pitches are available. Blair Castle (open to the public) is a ten minute walk away. Pony trekking, mountain bikes, fishing and golf, all from Blair Atholl village (100 yds).
Write or telephone today for full colour brochure

DUNBAR

Lothian
Map ref 7D2

Popular seaside resort at the foot of the Lammermuir Hills. Good bathing from extensive sands. On the rock above the harbour are the remains of Dunbar Castle. Mary Queen of Scots fled here with Darnley in 1566, immediately after the murder of Rizzio, her secretary.
*Tourist Information Centre
T: (01368) 863353*

Belhaven Bay Caravan Park ⚑
★★★★
Holiday Park
Thistle Award
Member BH&HPA
Belhaven Bay, Dunbar, East Lothian
EH42 1TU
T: (01368) 865956
F: (01368) 865022
E: enquiries@
belhavenbay.demon.co.uk
*From the A1 north or south exit at roundabout west of Dunbar. Park is approx .5 mile along the A1087 on left. From south do not take the first exit on the A1087.
Level, grassy, sheltered.
52 touring pitches.*

52	🚐	£6.75—£10.50
52	🚗	£6.75—£10.50
52	▲	£6.75—£10.50
5	🏠	£155.00—£390.00

23 units privately owned
Open March—October
Cards accepted: Barclaycard, Delta, Mastercard, Switch, Visa
⚑ P 🅿 🚗 🐕 🛏 🍴 ✏ 🖭 ✦ ⊙ 🗻 🛁 Ⓣ WH

DUNDONNELL

Highland
Map ref 8B2

Locality of scattered crofting hamlets round the shores of Little Loch Broom, dominated by the magnificent ridge of An Teallach. Glorious scenery, mountaineering and sea angling.

Badrallach Bothy & Camping Site
★★★
Camping Park
Croft No 9, Badrallach, Dundonnell, Garve, Ross-shire IV23 2QP
T: (01854) 633281
*Off A832. One mile east of Dundonnell Hotel take single track road 7 miles to lochside site. Signposted.
16 hectares (40 acres). Level, grassy.
15 touring pitches.*

3	🚐	£7.50—£7.50
3	🚗	£7.50—£7.50
12	▲	£7.50—£7.50

Open all year round
🏕 ⚑ P 🐕 🛏 🍴 ✦ ⚄ 🌿 ⚓ 🛁 Ⓣ

DUNKELD

Tayside
Map ref 7C1

Picturesque cathedral town beautifully situated in the richly wooded valley of the River Tay on the edge of the Perthshire Highlands. Salmon and trout fishing.
*Tourist Information Centre
T: (01350) 727688*

Invermill Farm Caravan Park
★★★★
Touring Park
Inver Dunkeld, Perthshire PH8 0JR
T: (01350) 727477
F: (01350) 727477
*Turn off the A9 onto the A822 (signposted Crieff). Immediately turn right following the sign to Inver for 0.5 mile past the static site and cross the bridge. We are the first on the left. Signposted.
4 hectares (10 acres). Level, grassy, sheltered.
65 touring pitches.*

50	🚐	£8.00—£9.00
50	🚗	£8.00—£9.00
15	▲	£8.00—£9.00

Open April—October
🚗 🐕 🛏 🍴 🖭 🖥 ✦ ⚓ ⊙ ✦ 🌿 WH

DUNOON

Strathclyde
Map ref 7B2

Popular Clyde Coast resort and excursion centre on the Firth of Clyde. Wonderful walks in Argyll National Forest Park. Steamer trips, good sailing, golf and fishing.
*Tourist Information Centre
T: (01369) 703785*

Cowal Caravan Park ⚑
★★★
Holiday Park
Thistle Award
Member BH&HPA
Hunters Quay, Dunoon, Argyll
PA23 8JY
T: (01369) 704259
E: cowalpark@LineOne.net
Site off A815 coast road, signposted at Clyde-Argyll ferry terminal, Hunters Quay, Dunoon. Signposted. Landscaped, sheltered, quiet.

| 3 | 🏠 | £175.00—£250.00 |

23 units privately owned
Open all year round
⚑ 🐕 🛏 🖒 🖭 ✦ ⚓ ⊙ 🗻 🛁 Ⓣ

ECCLEFECHAN

Dumfries & Galloway
Map ref 7C3

Cressfield Caravan Park ⚑
★★★★★
Holiday Park
Ecclefechan, Lockerbie,
Dumfriesshire DG11 3DR
T: (01576) 300702
F: (01576) 300702
*Leave A74 (M) at Ecclefechan (Junction 19). Follow B7076 for 0.25 miles to south side of village. Signposted.
15.2 hectares (38 acres). Level, grassy, hard.
90 touring pitches.*

60	🚐	£6.50—£8.50
30	🚗	£6.50—£8.50
20	▲	£6.50—£7.00

48 units privately owned
Open all year round
⚑ P 🚗 🐕 🛏 🍴 🖒 🖭 🖥 ✦ ⚓ ⊙ 🗻 WH

EDINBURGH

Lothian
Map ref 7C2

Scotland's capital and international festival city. Dominated by its ancient fortress, the city is surrounded by hills, woodlands and rivers. Good shopping on Princes Street.
*Tourist Information Centre
T: (0131) 473 3600*

Linwater Caravan Park ⚑
★★★★
Touring Park
Member BH&HPA
West Clifton, East Calder,
Livingston, West Lothian EH53 0HT
T: (0131) 333 3326
F: (0131) 333 1952
*At junction of M8/A8/M9 at Newbridge, take B7030 signposted Wilkieston for 2 miles. Park signposted on right, 1 mile on. Signposted.
20 hectares (50 acres). Level, grassy.
60 touring pitches.*

50	🚐	£8.00—£10.00
50	🚗	£8.00—£10.00
10	▲	£8.00—£10.00

Open April—October
🖭 🐕 🛏 🍴 🖒 🖭 🖥 ⊙ 🗻 ∪ 🌿 🛁

Map references apply to the colour maps at the back of this guide.

Mortonhall Caravan Park
★★★★
Holiday Park
Thistle Award
Member BH&HPA
38 Mortonhall Gate, Frogston Road
East, Edinburgh EH16 6TJ
T: (0131) 664 1533 & 664 2104
F: (0131) 664 5387
E: enquiries@mortonhallcp.demon.
co.uk
*From the city bypass at Lothianburn
junction, follow signs for Mortonhall.
From city centre take the east or west
ends of Princes Street. Signposted.*
10 hectares (25 acres). Level,
sloping, grassy, hard, sheltered.
250 touring pitches.

150		£9.00—£13.25
150		£9.00—£13.25
100		£9.00—£13.25
18		£180.00—£450.00

Open March–October
Cards accepted: Amex, Barclaycard,
Delta, Eurocard, Mastercard, Switch,
Visa

EYEMOUTH

Borders
Map ref 7D2

Eyemouth Holiday Park
★★★★
Holiday Park
Thistle Award
Member BH&HPA
Fort Road, Eyemouth Berwickshire
TD14 5BE
T: (01890) 751050
F: (01890) 751462
*Five miles north of Scottish Border take
A1107 from A1 to Eyemouth then
clearly signposted.*

Level, grassy, hard.
17 touring pitches.

17		£10.50—£12.50
17		£8.50—£10.50
7		£180.00—£350.00

273 units privately owned
Open mid March–mid November
Cards accepted: Barclaycard, Delta,
Mastercard, Switch, Visa

FORT WILLIAM

Highland
Map ref 7B1

One of the finest touring centres in
the Western Highlands. A busy
holiday town set on the shores of
Loch Linnhe at the western end of
the Great Glen almost in the
shadow of Ben Nevis, the highest
mountain in the British Isles. Nearby
are fishing, climbing, walking and
steamer trips to the islands.
*Tourist Information Centre
T: (01397) 703781*

Glen Nevis Caravan and Camping Park
★★★★★
Holiday Park
Member BH&HPA
Glen Nevis, Fort William, Inverness-
shire PH33 6SX
T: (01397) 702191 & 705181
F: (01397) 703904
E: holidays@glen-nevis.co.uk
I: www.glen-nevis.co.uk
*From A82 north of Fort William, turn
east at roundabout signed Glen Nevis.
Park is 2.5 miles up glen from A82.*
11.6 hectares (29 acres). Level,
sloping, grassy, stony, hard,
sheltered.
380 touring pitches.

250		£7.80—£11.50
250		£7.50—£11.20
130		£7.10—£11.20
28		£195.00—£370.00

Open March–October
Cards accepted: Barclaycard, Delta,
Mastercard, Switch, Visa

See display advertisement on this page

Linnhe Lochside Holidays
★★★★★
Holiday Park
Member BH&HPA/NCC
Corpach, Fort William, Inverness-
shire PH33 7NL
T: (01397) 772376
F: (01397) 772007
*On A830 1.5 miles (3km) west of
Corpach village, 5 miles from Fort
William. Signposted.*
8 hectares (20 acres). Level, hard,
sheltered.
75 touring pitches.

65		£11.50—£13.50
65		£11.50—£13.50
10		£8.50—£10.50
68		£170.00—£435.00

21 units privately owned
Open February–October &
Christmas
Cards accepted: Barclaycard, Delta,
Eurocard, Mastercard, Switch, Visa

See display advertisement on this page

A key to symbols can be
found inside the back
cover flap.

GAIRLOCH

Highland
Map ref 8B2

Scattered village at the head of Loch Gairloch with superb beaches and glorious scenery.
Tourist Information Centre
T: (01445) 712130

Sands Holiday Centre
★★★★
Holiday Park
Thistle Award
Member NCC
Gairloch, Ross-shire IV21 2DL
T: (01445) 712152
F: (01445) 712518
At Gairloch turn on to B8021 (Melvaig).
Site 3 miles on, beside sandy beach.
Signposted.
Level, sloping, grassy.
360 touring pitches.

120	🚐	£8.50—£9.60
40	🚙	
200	▲	£8.00—£9.60
5	⛺	£230.00—£400.00

15 units privately owned
Open April–October
Cards accepted: Amex, Eurocard, Mastercard, Solo, Switch, Visa
🚗🅿🏍🛶♨💧🍴🏪🔌🛒🛢🔵 ⚡
🛅☉🎢🎣🏸🚶▶🔥

GARTOCHARN

Strathclyde
Map ref 7B2

Lagganbeg Caravan Park
Member BH&HPA
Gartocharn, Dunbartonshire
G83 8NQ
T: (01389) 830281
F: (01389) 830367
From Glasgow take the A82 west to Balloch and then the A811 to Gartocharn. From Stirling head south to Drymen and then to Gartocharn. Signposted.
1.4 hectares (3.5 acres). Level, grassy, hard, sheltered.
37 touring pitches.

12	🚐	£10.00—£12.00
	🚙	£10.00—£12.00
25	▲	£8.00—£9.00

Open January, March–December
🅿🏍♨💧🍴🏪🔌🛒🛢🔵☉🎢🔥

GLASGOW

Strathclyde
Map ref 7B2

Scotland's largest city, whose shipyards have built many of the world's most famous vessels. Although a commercial city it has also become a famous centre for the arts and was the European City of Culture for 1990. Excellent shopping facilities and nightlife.
Tourist Information Centre
T: (0141) 204 4400

Craigendmuir Park
★★★
Holiday Park
Member BH&HPA
Campsie View, Stepps, Glasgow
G33 6AF
T: (0141) 779 2973 & 779 4159
F: (0141) 779 4057
E: info@craigendmuir.co.uk
I: www.craigendmuir.co.uk
From south or west exit at junction 11 on M8 and take A80 (Cumbernauld and Sterling). From north continue on A80 to Stepps. Signposted.
Wheelchair access category 3 ♿
Level, grassy, hard.
20 touring pitches.

18	🚐	£8.00
6	🚙	£8.00
	▲	£8.00
6	⛺	£175.00—£225.00

Open all year round
Cards accepted: Mastercard, Visa
🚗🅿🏍🛶♨💧🍴🏪🔌🛒🛢
⚡🛅☉🎢🚶▶🔥 WH

GLENCOE

Highland
Map ref 7B1

Village at the foot of Glen Coe, a deep and rugged defile enclosed by towering mountains. Scene of massacre of MacDonalds of Glencoe by the Campbells of Glen Lyon in 1692. A valley of haunting beauty offering winter sports.

Invercoe Caravan & Camping Park
★★★★★
Holiday Park
Thistle Award
Member BH&HPA
Invercoe, Glencoe, Argyll PH49 4HP
T: (01855) 811210
F: (01855) 811210
E: invercoe@sol.co.uk
Site is 0.25 mile from Glencoe crossroads (A82) on the Kinlochleven road B863. Signposted.
2 hectares (5 acres). Level, hard.
55 touring pitches.

55	🚐	£10.00—£12.00
55	🚙	£10.00—£12.00
55	▲	£8.00—£10.00
5	⛺	£230.00—£350.00

Open March–October
⚡🅿🏍🏍♨💧🍴🏪🔌🛒🛢🔵⚡
🛅☉🎣🚶 T WH

HADDINGTON

Lothian
Map ref 7D2

County capital and birthplace of John Knox, the religious reformer. Well situated on the River Tyne with old houses and 14th C church.

The Monks' Muir ♨
★★★★
Holiday Park
Thistle Award
Member BH&HPA/NCC
Haddington, East Lothian EH41 3SB
T: (01620) 860340
F: (01620) 861770
E: d@monksmuir.co.uk
I: www.monksmuir.com
Site entrance on A1, 2.5 miles (4km) east of Haddington. Signposted.
2.8 hectares (7 acres). Level, grassy, sheltered.
35 touring pitches.

45	🚐	£6.00—£12.00
45	🚙	£6.00—£12.00
45	▲	£4.25—£12.00
8	⊞	£120.00—£440.00

30 units privately owned
Open all year round

🚐 P 🔌 🐕 🏕 🛇 📶 ⚲ ✕ 🛒 🔲
⚡ 🛎 ⊙ ⚠ ⛲ ↯ 🔲 Ⓣ ᵂᴴ
Ad See display advertisement on page 166

INVERUGLAS

Strathclyde
Map ref 7B1

Tourist Information Centre
T: (01301) 702260

Loch Lomond Holiday Park
★★★★★
Holiday Park
Thistle Award
Member NCC
Inveruglas, Tarbet, Argyll G83 7DW
T: (01301) 704224
F: (01301) 704206
E: enquiries@lochlomond-lodges.
co.uk
From Glasgow A82 north 30 miles
(48km) to Tarbet Hotel. Turn right on
A82 Oban road for 3 miles (5km) and
site on right. Signposted.
5.2 hectares (13 acres). Sloping,
grassy, stony, sheltered.
18 touring pitches.

15	🚐	£8.50—£13.50
18	🚙	£8.50—£13.50
8	⊞	£140.00—£365.00

46 units privately owned
Open January, March–October,
December
Cards accepted: Barclaycard,
Mastercard, Switch

🚐 🔌 ⊙ 🐕 🏕 🛇 📶 ⚲ 🔲 ᵀⱽ 🛒
🔲 ⚡ 🛎 ⊙ ⚬ ⚠ ⚒ ↯ 🔲 ⛲

KIPPFORD

Dumfries & Galloway
Map ref 7C3

Beautiful seaside village, part of the
Colvend Coast Heritage Trail, with
sailing centre, spectacular beach
views and pubs. National Trust and
Forestry Commission walks and
cycle tracks, game and coarse fishing
trips and cycle hire.

Kippford Holiday Park
★★★★
Holiday Park
Thistle Award
Member BH&HPA/NCC
Kippford, Dalbeattie,
Kirkcudbrightshire DG5 4LF
T: (01556) 620636
F: (01556) 620607
I: www.kippfordsholidaypark.co.uk
From A711 Dalbeattie take Solway
coast road A710. After 3.5 miles
continue straight ahead at junction with
Kippford Road. Entrance to park is 200
yards on right. Signposted.
8 hectares (18 acres). Level, sloping,
grassy, hard, sheltered.
45 touring pitches.

30	🚐	£9.00—£11.00
5	🚙	£9.00—£11.00
10	▲	£7.00—£11.00
10	⊞	£90.00—£350.00

105 units privately owned
Open March–October

🛇 🚐 🔌 🐕 🏕 🛇 📶 ⊙ 🛒 🔲
⚡ 🛎 ⊙ ⚠ 🚲 ↯ ⚓
Ad See display advertisement on this page

LAUDER

Borders
Map ref 7C2

Royal Burgh with quaint old
tolbooth, 16th C church and
medieval Thirlstane Castle.

Thirlestane Castle Caravan and Camping Site
★★★★
Touring Park
Member BH&HPA
Thirlestane Castle, Lauder,
Berwickshire TD2 6RU
T: (01578) 722254 & 07976 231032
F: (01578) 718749
0.25 miles (0.5km) south of Lauder,
just off A68 and A697. Edinburgh 28
miles (45km), Newcastle 68 miles
(109km). Signposted.

1.8 hectares (4.5 acres). Level,
sloping, grassy.
50 touring pitches.

50	🚐	£8.00—£8.00
50	🚙	£8.00—£8.00
50	▲	£8.00—£8.00

Open April–September

🚐 🔌 🐕 🏕 🛇 📶 ⊙ 🛒 🔲 ⚡ ⊙ ↯

LAURENCEKIRK

Grampian
Map ref 7D1

Dovecot Caravan Park
★★★★
Holiday Park
Member BH&HPA
North Water Bridge, Laurencekirk,
Kincardineshire AB30 1QL
T: (01674) 840630
F: (01674) 840630
From Laurencekirk (A90) 5 miles south
at Northwater Bridge, turn right to
Edzell. Site is 300m on left. Signposted.
2.4 hectares (6 acres). Grassy,
sheltered.
25 touring pitches.

25	🚐	£7.00—£8.00
25	🚙	£7.00—£8.00
25	▲	
2	⊞	£190.00—£210.00

40 units privately owned
Open April–October

🚐 🔌 🐕 🏕 🛇 📶 ⊙ 🛒 ᵀⱽ 🔲 🔲
⚡ 🛎 ⊙ ⚬ ⚠ ᵂᴴ

LINLITHGOW

Lothian
Map ref 7C2

Historic town west of Edinburgh
whose industries include
electronics, distilling and
manufacturing. Close by stand the
ruins of Linlithgow Palace, birthplace
of Mary Queen of Scots.
Tourist Information Centre
T: (01506) 844600

Beecraigs Caravan and Camping Site ⚇
★★★★
Touring Park
Beecraigs Country Park, The Park
Centre, Linlithgow, West Lothian
EH49 6PL
T: (01506) 844516
F: (01506) 846256
E: mail@beecraigs.com
From Linlithgow, follow Beecraigs
Country Park or international caravan
Continued ▶

LINLITHGOW
Continued

park signposts. Park is 2 miles south of Linlithgow. From M8, follow B792. Signposted.
400 hectares (1000 acres). Level, grassy, hard, sheltered.
59 touring pitches.

39	🚐	£10.50
39	🚏	£10.50
20	⛺	£9.50

Open all year round

🚗 P 🔌 📶 🏕 🛁 🍴 📞 🚻 ✕ 📶 ⊘ ⚡
📺 ⊙ 🎱 🛟 ⛱ 🏑 ⛳ WH

LOCHGILPHEAD
Strathclyde
Map ref 7B2

Town at the head of Loch Gilphead.

Lochgilphead Caravan Park
★★★★
Holiday Park
Thistle Award
Member BH&HPA
Bank Park, Lochgilphead, Argyll
PA31 8NE
T: (01546) 602003
F: (01546) 603699
Adjacent to junction of A83/A816 within town of Lochilphead. Signposted. Signposted.
2.8 hectares (7 acres). Level, grassy, hard, sheltered.
40 touring pitches.

30	🚐	£8.00
30	🚏	£8.00
10	⛺	£8.00
15	⛴	£125.00

15 units privately owned
Open April–October

🚗 📶 🏕 🛁 📞 🚻 📶 ⊘ ⚡ 📺 ⊙
🎱 ⛱ 🛟 ⛳
Ad See display advertisement on this page

LOCHRANZA
Ayrshire
Map ref 7B2

Tourist Information Centre
T: (01770) 302395

Lochranza Golf Caravan and Camping Site
★★★
Touring Park
Member BH&HPA
Lochranza, Brodick, Isle of Arran
KA27 8HL
T: (0177083) 273
At the golf course.
Level, grassy.
60 touring pitches.

60	🚐	£10.00—£12.00
60	🚏	£9.00—£12.00
60	⛺	£8.00—£15.00

Open April–October
📶 🏕 🛁 📞 🚻 📶 ⊘ ⊙ 🏑 ⛱ ⛳

LOCKERBIE
Dumfries & Galloway
Map ref 7C3

Market town in the beautiful Valley of Annandale.

Hoddom Castle Caravan Park
★★★★★
Holiday Park
Hoddom, Lockerbie, Dumfriesshire
DG11 1AS
T: (01576) 300251
From A74 turn off at Junction 19. Follow signs to Hoddom Castle from A75. Take B723 west of Annan to Lockerbie. Follow signs to Hoddom Castle. Signposted.
11.2 hectares (28 acres). Level, sloping, grassy, hard, sheltered.
170 touring pitches.

170	🚐	£6.00—£11.00
170	🚏	£6.00—£11.00
170	⛺	£5.00—£11.00

29 units privately owned
Open March–October
Cards accepted: Barclaycard, Mastercard, Switch, Visa

🚗 🔌 📶 🏕 🛁 📞 🚻 🛒 ✕ 🍴
📺 📶 ⊘ ⚡ 📺 ⊙ 🎱 ⛱ ⛳ 🏑 ⛳
⛴

LONGNIDDRY
Lothian
Map ref 7C2

Small village on the Firth of Forth.
Tourist Information Centre
T: (0131) 653 6172

Seton Sands Holiday Village
★★★
Holiday Park
Thistle Award
Member BH&HPA/NCC
Longniddry, East Lothian EH32 0QF
T: 0870 2425678
F: (01442) 254956
Take A1 until approximately 10 miles south of Edinburgh. Take exit signposted Seton Sands, follow signs through Port Seton. Park is 1 mile along on right hand side. Signposted.
Level, grassy.
50 touring pitches.

	🚐	£8.30—£21.70
	🚏	£8.30—£21.70
250	⛴	£134.00—£580.00

300 units privately owned
Open March–October
Cards accepted: Barclaycard, Delta, Mastercard, Solo, Switch, Visa

🚗 📶 🏕 🛁 📞 🚻 🛒 ✕ 🍴 📺 📶
⊘ ⚡ 📺 ⊙ 🔍 ⛱ 🏑 🛟 ⛳ 🎵 ⛳ T
WH
Ad See display advertisement on page 10

MUSSELBURGH
Lothian
Map ref 7C2

Tourist Information Centre
T: (0131) 653 6172

Drummohr Caravan Park
★★★★★
Touring Park
Member BH&HPA/NCC
Levenhall, Musselburgh, Edinburgh
EH21 8JS
T: (0131) 665 6867
F: (0131) 653 6859
From south on A1, take A199 Musselburgh, then B1361. Follow park signs. From the north on the A1, come off at Wallyford slip road and follow Caravan Park and Mining Museum signs. Signposted.
4 hectares (10 acres). Level, grassy, hard, sheltered.
120 touring pitches.

120	🚐	£8.00—£10.00
40	🚏	£8.00—£10.00
60	⛺	£8.00—£10.00

Open March–October
Cards accepted: Barclaycard, Delta,
Eurocard, Mastercard, Switch, Visa

🚗🖥️🔌🎣🍴🔥🛁🍼♿🛒📻🖨️
🚿🔌☺⚠️🦺
Ad See display advertisement on this
page

NAIRN

Highland
Map ref 8C3

Royal Burgh, county town and
popular holiday resort on the
southern shore of the Moray Firth
and at the mouth of the River Nairn.

Spindrift Caravan and Camping Park
★★★★
Touring Park
Member BH&HPA
Little Kildrummie, Nairn,
Invernesshire IV12 5QU
T: (01667) 453992
*From Nairn take B9090 south for 1.5
miles, signposted Little Kildrummie.
Turn right at sharp left-hand bend
signposted Little Kildrummie. Follow
left-hand bend on to unclassified road,
site is 400 yards on the left. Signposted.*
1.2 hectares (3 acres). Level, grassy,
sheltered.
40 touring pitches.

40	🚐	£6.50—£9.50
40	🚏	£6.50—£9.50
40	⛺	£6.50—£9.50

Open April–October
🚗🔌🎣🔥🛁🍼♿📻🖨️🚗☺🦺
WH

WELCOME HOST
This is a nationally recognised
customer care programme
which aims to promote
the highest standards of
service and a warm welcome.
Parks taking part in this
initiative are indicated
by the WH symbol.

NORTH BERWICK

Lothian
Map ref 7D2

Holiday resort on the Firth of Forth
with sandy beaches, golf and a
picturesque harbour.
*Tourist Information Centre
T: (01620) 892197*

Tantallon Caravan Park 🅼
★★★★★
Holiday Park
Thistle Award
Member BH&HPA
Dunbar Road, North Berwick, East
Lothian EH39 5NJ
T: (01620) 893348
F: (01620) 895623
E: enquiries@tantalloncp.demon.
co.uk
*From North Berwick take A198
towards Dunbar. Situated on east side
of town overlooking golf course and
Firth of Forth. From A1 turn onto A198
3 miles west of Dunbar. Signposted.*
Level, sloping, grassy.
147 touring pitches.

147	🚐	£7.25—£11.50
147	🚏	£7.25—£11.50
147	⛺	£7.25—£11.50
10	🏠	£155.00—£450.00

45 units privately owned
Open March–October
Cards accepted: Barclaycard, Delta,
Eurocard, Mastercard, Switch, Visa
🚗P🖥️🔌🎣🍴🛁🍼♿🛒📻
🖨️🔌🚿🗑️☺⚠️🦺T WH

PEEBLES

Borders
Map ref 7C2

County capital and market town in
the Tweed Valley. A favourite
holiday centre popular with anglers.
*Tourist Information Centre
T: (01721) 720138*

Rosetta Caravan and Camping Park 🅼
★★★★
Holiday Park
Member NCC
Rosetta Road, Peebles EH45 8PG
T: (01721) 720770
F: (01721) 720623
E: mprosetta@aol.com
*Travelling west from centre of Peebles
on A72, turn right in town on to
unclassified road signposted Rosetta.*

Site half a mile (1km) on left.
Signposted.
10.8 hectares (27 acres). Grassy.
130 touring pitches.

100	🚐	£10.50—£11.00
100	🚏	£10.50—£11.00
30	⛺	£9.00—£10.00
1		

Open April–October
🚗P🖥️🔌🎣🛁🍼♿🛒📻🍴TV🖨️
🗑️🚿🚗☺🔍⚠️⛵🦺T

PITLOCHRY

Tayside
Map ref 7C1

A favourite holiday resort and
touring centre in the valley of the
Tummel. Points of interest are
Pitlochry Dam and Salmon Ladder.
*Tourist Information Centre
T: (01796) 474046*

Milton of Fonab Caravan Park
★★★★
Holiday Park
Thistle Award
Member BH&HPA
Pitlochry, Perthshire PH16 5NA
T: (01796) 472882
F: (01796) 474363
*From south take Pitlochry filter road.
Site is half a mile south of Pitlochry.
Signposted.*
6 hectares (15 acres). Level, grassy,
sheltered.
154 touring pitches.

154	🚐	£10.00—£10.50
154	🚏	£10.00—£10.50
154	⛺	£10.00—£10.50
36	🏠	£210.00—£360.00

Open March–October
🚗🔌🎣🍴🛁🍼♿🛒📻🖨️🗑️
🚗☺⛵🦺

For ideas on places to visit
refer to the introduction at
the beginning of this section.

All accommodation in this
guide has been rated, or is
awaiting a rating, by a trained
Tourist Board assessor.

ST ANDREWS

Fife
Map ref 7D1

Historic university city known to golfers world-wide as the home of the Royal and Ancient Club. Old harbour, priory and 13th C castle.
Tourist Information Centre
T: (01334) 472021

Craigtoun Meadows Holiday Park
★★★★★
Holiday Park
Thistle Award
Member BH&HPA
Mount Melville, St Andrews, Fife
KY16 8PQ
T: (01334) 475959
F: (01334) 476424
E: craigtoun@aol.com
I: www.craigtounmeadows.co.uk
From M90 junction 8 take A91 to St Andrews. Turn right 436 yards (400m) after Guardbridge, sign Strathkinness. Turn left at second crossroads after Strathkinness. Signposted.
12.8 hectares (32 acres). Level, sloping, grassy, hard, sheltered.
98 touring pitches.

95	🚐	£14.00—£21.50
95	🚏	£14.00—£21.50
98	▲	£11.50—£21.50
32	⊡	£200.00—£450.00

111 units privately owned
Open March—October
Cards accepted: Barclaycard, Delta, Eurocard, Mastercard, Switch, Visa

SANDHEAD

Dumfries & Galloway
Map ref 7B3

Tourist Information Centre
T: (01776) 702595

Sands of Luce Caravan Park 🅜
★★★★
Holiday Park
Member BH&HPA
Sandhead, Stranraer, Wigtownshire
DG9 9JR
T: (01776) 830456
F: (01776) 830456
From Stranraer take A77 to the A716 signposted to Drummore. Park is 7 miles south of Stranraer, 1 mile past the village of Stoneykirk. Signposted.
4.8 hectares (12 acres). Level, grassy.
60 touring pitches.

50	🚐	£7.50—£9.50
20	🚏	£7.00—£9.00
10	▲	£7.50—£9.50
6	⊡	£150.00—£310.00

37 units privately owned

Open March—October

🚗🅿🎱🚿🏕♨🔥🍳🔥⛽🚮💻

SKELMORLIE

Ayrshire
Map ref 7B2

Firth of Clyde resort opposite Bute.
Tourist Information Centre
T: (01475) 673765

Mains Caravan Park
★★★
Holiday Park
Member BH&HPA
Skelmorlie Mains, Skelmorlie, Ayrshire PA17 5EU
T: (01475) 520794
F: (01475) 520794
Off A78, 4 miles north of Largs. Signposted.
96 hectares (240 acres). Level, sloping, grassy, stony, hard, sheltered.
96 touring pitches.

26	🚐	£9.00—£12.00
26	🚏	£9.00—£12.00
70	▲	£8.00—£10.00
10	⊡	£210.00—£450.00

72 units privately owned
Open March—October

🏕🚗🅿🎱🍳🏕♨🔥🍳🔥📺💻🚮⊙🔍⛽⛄🔥

SOUTHERNESS

Dumfries & Galloway
Map ref 7C3

Lighthouse Leisure 🅜
★★★
Holiday Park
Member BH&HPA
Southerness, Dumfries DG2 8AZ
T: (01387) 880277
F: (01387) 880298
E: lighthouseleis@aol.com
15 miles Dumfries on A710. After Kirkbean, follow Southerness signs (to left) to the sea. Park office by 1st house in village on right (black, steep-pitched roof).
3.5 hectares (8.5 acres). Level, grassy .

	🚐	£7.00—£10.50
	🚏	£7.00—£10.50
	▲	
10	⊡	£105.00—£290.00

190 units privately owned
Open March—October
Credit cards accepted

🚗🅿🍳🏕♨🔥🍳🔥⛽🚮✕🚮💻🚮⊙🔥⛄🔥🎵⛄🚮

Please check prices and other details at the time of booking.

STIRLING

Central
Map ref 7C2

Ancient town with a long and turbulent history. The famous castle perched on its towering rock was a vital stronghold which became the scene of several battles, notably the Battle of Bannockburn in 1314.
Tourist Information Centre
T: (01786) 475019

Witches Craig Caravan Park
★★★★★
Touring Park
Member BH&HPA
Blairlogie, Stirling FK9 5PX
T: (01786) 474947
Leave Stirling on St Andrews road, A91. Site 3 miles (5km) east of Stirling. Signposted.
2 hectares (5 acres). Level, grassy, hard, sheltered.
60 touring pitches.

60	🚐	£9.75—£13.00
60	🚏	£9.75—£13.00
60	▲	£9.75—£13.00

Open April—October

🚗🎱🍳🏕♨🔥🍳🔥⛽💻🚮⊙🔥⛄🚮

ULLAPOOL

Highland
Map ref 8B2

Picturesque fishing village and holiday resort on a promontory in sheltered Loch Broom. Glorious scenery, angling and boating.

Ardmair Point Caravan Park 🅜
★★★★
Touring Park
Member BH&HPA
Ardmair Point, Ullapool, Ross-shire
IV26 2TN
T: (01854) 612054
F: (01854) 612757
Situated 3.5 miles north of Ullapool on A835. Entrance next to telephone kiosk. Signposted.
2 hectares (5 acres). Level, grassy
45 touring pitches.

45	🚐	£8.50
45	🚏	£8.00
45	▲	£8.00

Open May—September
Cards accepted: Barclaycard, Delta, Eurocard, Mastercard, Switch, Visa

Please mention this guide when making your booking.

Broomfield Holiday Park
Member BH&HPA
Shore Street, Ullapool, Ross-shire
IV26 2SX
T: (01854) 612020 & 612664
In Ullapool, take 2nd right past harbour. Signposted.
4.4 hectares (11 acres). Level, grassy.
140 touring pitches.

140	🚐	£11.00—£12.00
140	🚎	£9.00—£10.00
140	⛺	£8.00—£11.00

Open April–September

P ⚘ ⛺ ♣ ↻ ☎ ⊙ ▣ ⛽ ☺ ⚲ ⚱ 🔧 ▶

Strathclyde
Map ref 7B2

Wemyss Bay Holiday Park
★★★★
Holiday Park
Thistle Award
Member BH&HPA/NCC
Wemyss Bay, Renfrewshire
PA18 6BA
T: 0870 2425678
F: (01442) 254956
From Glasgow follow the M8 to Greenock and take the A78 to Wemyss Bay. Entrance opposite railway station and Wemyss Steamer terminal. Signposted.

🛏	£134.00—£593.50

480 units privately owned
Open March–October

P 🏋 ✕ ♟ 📺 🗄 ⚡ ⛽ 🔍 ⚱ 🔧 ↻ ♫ ♨ T WH
Ad See display advertisement on page 10

On-line Information

In-depth information about travelling in Britain is now available on BTA's VisitBritain website.

Covering everything from castles to leisure parks and from festivals to road and rail links, the site complements Where to Stay perfectly, giving you up-to-the-minute details to help you with your travel plans.

BRITAIN on the internet
www.visitbritain.com

On-line Information

In-depth information about travelling in **Britain** is now available on **BTA's VisitBritain website**.

Covering everything from castles to leisure parks and from festivals to road and rail links, the site complements Where to Stay perfectly, giving you up-to-the-minute details to help you with your travel plans.

BRITAIN on the internet
www.visitbritain.com

DAVID BELLAMY CONSERVATION AWARDS

If you are looking for a site that's environmentally friendly look for those that have achieved the David Bellamy Conservation Award. Recently launched in conjunction with the British Holiday & Home Parks Association, this award is given to sites which are committed to protecting and enhancing the environment – from care of the hedgerows and wildlife to recycling waste – and are members of the Association. More information about this award scheme can be found at the front of the guide.

Wales
WALES

Sparkling rivers weave through woodland, and the hills and valleys of Wales are mirrored in the softly undulating dunes of her beaches. Wales is a land of myths and ancient legends - a bewitching landscape studded with castles.

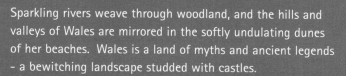

Home to the ancient Celts, you can explore their history at 'Celtica' in Machynlleth which includes a re-creation of a Celtic village. Discover the dark secrets of Blaenau Ffestiniog where you can take a ride underground on Britain's steepest passenger railway to see the conditions endured by Victorian slate miners.

Or for a more contemporary insight into Welsh life, the Tydfil Arts Festival in October includes concerts, drama, music, dance, prose and poetry.

FOR MORE INFORMATION ON WALES, CONTACT:

Wales Tourist Board
Brunel House, 2 Fitzalen Road,
Cardiff CF24 0UY
Tel: (029) 2049 9909
Fax: (029) 2048 5031
Email: info@tourism.wales.gov.uk

Where to Go in Wales - see pages 174–179
Where to Stay in Wales - see pages 180–184

The Pictures:
1 Criccieth Castle;
2 Caernarfon Castle;
3 Craig-goch reservoir;
4 Nant Gwynant.

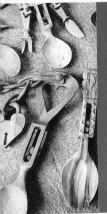

Whilst in
WALES

You will find hundreds of interesting places to visit during your stay in Wales, just some of which are listed in these pages. Contact any Tourist Information Centre in Wales for more ideas on days out.

Aberaeron Sea Aquarium

Quay Parade, Aberaeron SA46 0BT
Tel: (01545) 570142
Sea aquarium reflecting fish, fishing interests and conservation in Cardigan Bay. Voyages on a jet boat to discover the marine ecology of Cardigan Bay.

Aberystwyth Arts Centre

Penglais, Aberystwyth SY23 3DE
Tel: (01970) 622882
The centre offers a range of events including performances, cinema, exhibitions and courses.

Afan Argoed Country Centre

Afan Forest Park, Cynonville, Port Talbot SA13 3HG
Tel: (01639) 850564
Forest trails, picnic sites, barbecue, mountain bike trails, cycle hire, camping, disabled access.

Alice in Wonderland Centre

The Rabbit Hole, Trinity Square,
Llandudno LL30 2PY
Tel: (01492) 860082
Experience the timeless world of Lewis Carroll's Alice down a rabbit hole. Walk through beautiful life-size scenes with many models, some animated. An ideal indoor adventure!

Anglesey Sea Zoo

The Oyster Hatchery, Brynsiencyn LL61 6TQ
Tel: (01248) 430411
See the beautiful marine inhabitants of Wales and beyond.

Bala Lake Railway

Llanuwchllyn Station, Llanuwchllyn, Bala LL23 7DD
Tel: (01678) 540666
A 14.5 km (9 mile) return journey by narrow gauge steam train through the scenery of the Snowdonia National Park - riding along the shoreline of the largest natural lake in Wales.

Big Pit Mining Museum

Blaenavon NP4 9XP
Tel: (01495) 790311
Preserved working colliery offering underground tours of Victorian workings by experienced miner guides.

Bodnant Garden

Tal-y-cafn, Colwyn Bay LL28 5RE
Tel: (01492) 650460
A garden with interest and colour all year. Rhododendrons in spring, laburnum arch in late May. Terraces, ponds and giant trees.

Borth Animalarium

Ynys Fergi, Borth SY24 5NA
Tel: (01970) 871224
A unique collection of mammals, reptiles, birds and invertebrates which are of interest to all age groups.

Brecknock Museum

Captain's Walk, Brecon LD3 7DW
Tel: (01874) 624121
Regional museum and art gallery. Displays include prehistory to dark ages, country life plus major new townlife gallery. Natural History including Edwardian Naturalists Study.

Brecon Cathedral

Cathedral Close, Brecon LD3 9DP
Tel: (01874) 623344
Cathedral, heritage centre, shop, restaurant.

Carew Castle & Tidal Mill

Carew, Tenby SA70 8SL
Tel: (01646) 651782
A magnificent castle which later became an Elizabethan residence. Royal links with Henry Tudor and setting for the Great Tournament of 1507. One of four restored tidal mills.

Castell Coch

Tongwynlais, Cardiff CF4 7JS
Tel: (029) 2081 0101
Rarely used and still perfectly preserved, this Victorian extravaganza must be seen to be believed. A fairytale castle in the woods.

The Pictures:
1 Welsh Love Spoons;
2 Sheep Dog Trials;
3 Walking near Machynlleth;
4 Royal National Eisteddfod;
5 Carreg Samson;
6 Llangollen;
7 Snowdonia;
8 Swansea Marina, Gower Peninsula.

Castell Henllys Iron Age Fort

Meline, Crymych SA41 3UT
Tel: (01239) 891319
Castell Henllys is a partially reconstructed iron age hillfort. Set in 26 acres of woodland, river meadows and grassland.

Caws Cenarth Welsh Cheese

Fferm Glyneithinog, Pontseli, Boncath SA37 0LH
Tel: (01239) 710432
The making of traditional handmade Caerphilly cheese.

Celtica

Y Plas, Aberystwyth Road, Machynlleth SY20 8ER
Tel: (01654) 702702
Celtica is an unique heritage centre that interprets the history and culture of the Celts.

Centre for Alternative Technology

Llwyngwern Quarry, Pantperthog, Machynlleth SY20 9AZ
Tel: (01654) 702400
A water balanced cliff railway provides the entrance to Europe's leading Eco-Centre. Displays of wind, water and solar power, self-build and energy conservation.

Museum of Childhood

1 Castle Street, Beaumaris LL58 8AP
Tel: (01248) 871498
A visit of joyful nostalgia. Unlimited viewing of items that have brought pleasure to families over the past 200 years.

Chirk Castle

Chirk, Wrexham LL14 5AF
Tel: (01691) 777701
A magnificent Marcher Fortress, completed 1310, now owned by the National Trust.

Cilgwyn Candles

Trefelin, Cilgwyn, Newport SA42 0QN
Tel: (01239) 820470
A small craft workshop where Inger John specialises in the production of traditional hand-dipped and scented candles. Shop.

Colby Woodland Garden

Narberth, Stepaside, Narberth SA67 8PP
Tel: (01834) 811885
Tranquil and secluded valley, walled garden, tearooms, arts and crafts, gift shop, events.

Conwy Butterfly Jungle

Bodlondeb Park, Bangor Road, Conwy LL32 8DU
Tel: (01492) 593149
A living educational attraction with over 300 tropical butterflies flying freely around the visitor in a jungle environment of exotic plants and flowers.

Corris Craft Centre

Corris, Machynlleth SY20 9RF
Tel: (01654) 761584
Skilled craftsmen can be seen at work and their products purchased. The cafe offers a wide range of meals and snacks in the wooded valley setting.

Craig-y-nos Country Park

Pen-y-cae, Swansea SA9 1GL
Tel: (01639) 730395
Water, woodland and meadows to enjoy in varying seasons.

Dan-yr-Ogof Showcaves

Glyntawe, Abercraf, Swansea SA9 1GJ
Tel: (01639) 730284
The largest showcave complex in Northern Europe, including three award-winning showcaves. Latest attraction is the Shire Horse Centre.

Doctor Who Exhibition and International Model Railway World

Lower Dee Exhibition Centre, Llangollen LL20 8RX
Tel: (01978) 860584
The BBC Doctor Who exhibition tells the story of the well known television programme. An award-winning site.

Egypt Centre

University of Wales, Singleton Park, Swansea SA2 8PP
Tel: (01792) 295960
The largest collection of Egyptian antiquities in Wales.

Erdigg

Wrexham LL13 0XT
Tel: (01978) 355314
A unique family home capturing the life of a bustling household during the early 1900s. The walled garden is one of the most important surviving 18thC gardens in Britain.

Ffestiniog Railway

Harbour Station, Porthmadog LL49 9NF
Tel: (01766) 512340
The Ffestiniog Railway operates a narrow gauge steam and diesel service from Porthmadog to Blaenau Ffestiniog, and also between Caernarfon and Waunfawr.

Glynn Vivian Art Gallery

Alexandra Road, Swansea SA1 5DZ
Tel: (01792) 655006
Large collection of 20thC painting and Swansea pottery, plus full programme of temporary exhibitions.

Great Orme Copper Mines

Great Orme, Pyllau Road, Llandudno LL30 2XG
Tel: (01492) 870447
Visitor centre, film and displays, underground trip and surface walkway.

Gwili Railway

Bronwydd Arms Station, Carmarthen SA33 6HT
Tel: (01267) 230666
A reminder of a former Great Western Railway branch line. Steam hauled services geared to the holidaymaker take a 2.4km (1.5 mile) journey beside the River Gwili.

King Arthur's Labyrinth

Corris Craft Centre, Corris SY20 9RF
Tel: (01654) 761584
An underground boat takes visitors into spectacular caverns where Welsh tales of King Arthur are told with tableaux and stunning sound and light effects.

Llanberis Lake Railway

Gilfach Ddu, Llanberis LL55 4TY
Tel: (01286) 870549
*A 40 minute ride on one of the steam hauled Great
Little Trains of Wales along the shores of Llyn Padarn.*

Llanerch Vineyard

Hensol, Pontyclun CF72 8JU
Tel: (01443) 225877
*Largest vineyard in Wales producing estate bottled
wines marketed under the Cariad label. Six acres of
vines planted on the gentle south facing slopes of the
Vale of Glamorgan.*

Llangloffan Cheese Centre

Llangloffan Farm, Castle Morris,
Haverfordwest SA62 5ET
Tel: (01348) 891241
*The cheesemaking process from milk to cheese provides a
fascinating excursion for the whole family.*

Llechwedd Slate Caverns

Blaenau Ffestiniog LL41 3NB
Tel: (01766) 830306
*Two underground rides, plus the Victorian Village which
has reminted Victorian coins from the 'Old Bank' in
shops and pub.*

National Museum & Gallery

Cathays Park, Cardiff CF10 3NP
Tel: (029) 2039 7951
*A remarkable range of treasures which are sure to
surprise every visitor. 'Evolution of Wales' permanent
exhibition. Original paintings from Monet and Cezanne.*

New Quay Honey Farm

Cross Inn, Llandysul SA44 6NN
Tel: (01545) 560822
*Discover the fascinating world of bees in this live
exhibition. Relax in the tea room, visit the meadery and
explore the honey shop.*

Oakwood Adventure Park

Canaston Bridge, Narberth SA67 8DE
Tel: (01834) 891373
*Oakwood is Wales' largest theme park set in 80 acres of
beautiful Pembrokeshire countryside with over 40 rides
and attractions.*

Powis Castle and Garden

Welshpool SY21 8RF
Tel: (01938) 554338
*World famous terraced garden. Medieval castle with
fine collection of paintings and furniture plus a
collection of treasures from India.*

Rheidol Hydro Electric Station

Cwm Rheidol, Aberystwyth SY23 3NF
Tel: (01970) 880667
*Free guided tours of the largest Hydro Electrical Scheme
in England and Wales plus a working Fish Farm. Visitor
centre with interactivities and refreshments.*

Rhiannon Jewellery

Canolfan Aur Cymru, Main Square, Tregaron SY25 6JL
Tel: (01974) 298415
*Craft design centre and jewellery workshop specialising
in the Welsh and Celtic heritage. Established since 1971.*

Rhondda Heritage Park

Lewis Merthyr Colliery, Coed Cae Road, Trehafod,
Pontypridd CF37 7NP
Tel: (01443) 682036
*A unique living history attraction situated in the
South Wales Valleys. Visitors can take a cage ride to
the 'Pit Bottom'.*

The Pictures:
1 Marloes;
2 Cambrian Mountains;
3 St Davids Cathedral;
4 Pony Trekking, Cader Idris;
5 Harlech Castle;
6 Llanberis Lake Railway.

WALES

Scolton Visitor Centre

Spittal, Haverfordwest SA62 5QL
Tel: (01437) 760460
Victorian manor house, museum and award-winning visitor centre set in 60 acres of country park and woodlands.

Skomer Island Nature Reserve

c/o Dyfed Wildlife Trust, 7 Market Street, Haverfordwest SA61 1NF
Tel: (01437) 765462
Discover the most important seabird colony in Southern Britain.

Snowdon Mountain Railway

Llanberis, Caernarfon LL55 4TY
Tel: (01286) 870223
Britain's only rack and pinion mountain railway running from the lakeside village of Llanberis to the summit of Snowdon.

Sygun Copper Mine

Beddgelert LL55 4NE
Tel: (01766) 510100
Sygun Copper Mine is an example of industrial heritage reclaimed and restored into a family attraction.

Techniquest

Stuart Street, Cardiff CF10 5BW
Tel: (029) 2047 5475
Launch a hot air balloon, create your own shadow in colour or film your own animation! All this and more in the UK's leading hands-on science discovery centre.

Trefriw Woollen Mills

Trefriw LL27 0NQ
Tel: (01492) 640462
A family business established 1859. The mill manufactures traditional Welsh bedspreads from raw wool. Weaving and hydro-electric turbines can be seen.

Vale of Rheidol Railway

Park Avenue, Aberystwyth SY23 1PG
Tel: (01970) 625819
Narrow gauge steam railway running from Aberystwyth to Devil's Bridge, a distance of 18.5 km (11.5 miles).

Museum of Welsh Life

St Fagans, Cardiff CF5 6XB
Tel: (029) 2057 3500
Take a walk round Wales at Europe's leading open air museum. Displays by traditional craftsmen and special events at Midsummer and Christmas.

Welsh Royal Crystal

Brynberth Industrial Estate, Rhayader LD6 5EN
Tel: (01597) 811005
Welsh Royal Crystal is Wales' only manufacturer of handcrafted crystalware. Visitors have the opportunity to tour the manufacturing process.

Museum of the Welsh Woollen Industry

Drefach Felindre, Llandysul SA44 5UP
Tel: (01559) 370929
A museum of carving, spinning, weaving and dyeing which shows the processes of fleece to fabric from the middle ages to the present day.

The Pictures:
1 Tenby Harbour;
2 Dolbadarn Castle;
3 Porth Dinllaen;
4 Walking in Snowdonia;
5 Pen-y-fan;
6 Llyn Nantlle;
7 Llangollen International Eisteddfod;
8 World Harp Festival;
9 Llangollen.

Find out more about
WALES

Further information about holidays and attractions in Wales is available from:

WALES TOURIST BOARD
Brunel House, 2 Fitzalan Road, Cardiff CF24 1UY
Tel: (029) 2049 9909
Fax: (029) 2048 5031
Email: info@tourism.wales.gov.uk

The following publications are available from the Wales Tourist Board:

The Complete Guides to South, Mid and North Wales - £5.60 each
Wales Tourist Map - £2.90
Travelmaster Guide to South Wales - £8.75
A Journey Through Wales - £4.99
Exploring Snowdonia, Anglesey and the Llyn Peninsula - £5.85
Ghosts and Legends of Wales - £5.95
By Car' Guides - £2.40 each
Ordnance Survey Pathfinder Guides - £9.75 each
Castles Guide - £7.25
All prices include post and packing.

Free publications:

Activity Wales
Discovering Accessible Wales (holidays for disabled people, covering everything from accommodation to activities)
Wales Touring Camping and Caravanning
Beaches Guide
Wales Bus, Rail and Tourist Map and Guide
Wales Countryside Holidays
Cycling, Walking, Fishing and Golfing Wales (4 separate guides)
Freedom Holiday Parks Wales
Wales Farm Holidays
Riding and Trekking Wales

Getting to
WALES

BY ROAD: Travelling to South and West Wales is easy on the M4 and the dual carriageway network. The new Second Severn Crossing gives two ways to enter Wales, but those wishing to visit Chepstow and the Wye Valley should use the original Severn Bridge and the M48 (originally part of the M4).

In North Wales the A55 'Expressway' has made travelling speedier, whilst mid Wales is accessible via the M54 which links with the M6, M5 and M1.

BY RAIL: Fast and frequent Great Western Intercity trains travel between London Paddington and Cardiff, departing hourly and half-hourly at peak times, and taking only two hours. Newport, Bridgend, Port Talbot, Neath and Swansea are also accessible through this service, which encompasses most of West Wales. London Euston links to the North Wales coast via Virgin trains, who also run a service between the North East of England and South Wales. In addition, Wales and West Passenger Trains run Alphaline services from London Waterloo, Manchester and the North East, Brighton and the South, and Nottingham and the Heart of England.

For further rail enquiries, please telephone (08457) 484950.

WHERE TO STAY (WALES)

Parks in Wales are listed in alphabetical order of place name,
and then in alphabetical order of park.

Map references refer to the colour location maps at the back of this guide.
The first number indicates the map to use; the letter and number which follow refer to the
grid reference on the map.

At-a-glance symbols can be found inside the back cover flap.
Keep this open for easy reference.

ABERYSTWYTH

Ceredigion
Map ref 1A2

The county town of Dyfed. Popular seaside resort with harbour and good bathing beaches. Its central position on Cardigan Bay makes it a good touring centre. Home of University College and National Library of Wales.
Tourist Information Centre
T: (01970) 612125

Ocean View Caravan Park 🚐
★ ★ ★ ★
Holiday Park
Member BH&HPA
Clarach Bay, Clarach, Aberystwyth, Dyfed SY23 3DT
T: (01970) 828425
F: (01970) 820215
E: alan@grover10.freeserve.co.uk
At Bow Street from A487, 2 miles north of Aberystwyth turn for Clarach and Llangorwen. Follow road—Ocean View is on right near beach.
Wheelchair access category 3 🧍
Level, grassy, hard.
30 touring pitches.

20	🚐	£7.00—£9.50
5	🚎	£7.00—£9.50
5	▲	£6.50—£9.00
4	🚐	£145.00—£325.00

46 units privately owned
Open April—November
🚐 P 🚐 🛝 🔥 🕯 🍴 🖙 📻 📺 ☺
⚱ ∪ WH

A key to symbols can be found inside the back cover flap.

BALA

Gwynedd
Map ref 1B1

Small market town on Bala Lake, the largest natural sheet of water in Wales. Mountain scenery, fishing, walking and boating.
Tourist Information Centre
T: (01678) 521021

Pen Y Garth Caravan and Camping Park 🚐
★ ★ ★ ★
Holiday, Touring and Camping Park
Dragon Award
Member BH&HPA
Bala, Gwynedd LL23 7ES
T: (01678) 520485
F: (01678) 520401
E: stay@penygarth.co.uk
I: www.penygarth.co.uk
By road, take B4391 Bala to Llangynog road. 1 mile from Bala fork right at sign to Rhosygwaliau. Site is 600 yds on the right. Signposted.
Level, grassy, sheltered.
63 touring pitches.

30	🚐	£7.25—£8.95
5	🚎	£8.25—£9.95
28	▲	£7.25—£8.95
5	🚐	£135.00—£285.00

49 units privately owned
Open March—October
Cards accepted: Delta, Mastercard, Switch, Visa
🚐 P 🚐 🛝 🔥 🕯 🍴 🖙 📻 📺 ∅
🛒 ☺ ⚱ ⚱ ∪ ⚓

All accommodation in this guide has been rated, or is awaiting a rating, by a trained Tourist Board assessor.

Penybont Touring and Camping Park
★ ★ ★ ★
Touring and Camping Park
Member BH&HPA
Llangynog Road, Bala, Gwynedd LL23 7PH
T: (01678) 520549
F: (01678) 520006
E: penybont@tinyonline.co.uk
I: www.penybont-bala.co.uk
By road, take main A494 Bala road, turn onto B4391 and we are 0.45 miles on the right hand side. Signposted.
Wheelchair access category 2 🦽
Level, grassy, hard, sheltered.
85 touring pitches.

35	🚐	£8.45—£10.45
35	🚎	£7.75—£9.75
50	▲	£7.45—£10.45

Open all year round
🚐 🛝 🍴 🕯 🔥 🖙 📻 📺 ∅ ∪ ⚓ ⚓ ⚓
WH

BARMOUTH

Gwynedd
Map ref 1A2

Popular seaside resort at the mouth of the beautiful Mawddach estuary, on the edge of the Snowdonia National Park.
Tourist Information Centre
T: (01341) 280787

Hendre Mynach Barmouth Touring Caravan and Camping Park 🚐
★ ★ ★ ★ ★
Touring and Camping Park
Llanaber Road, Barmouth, Gwynedd LL42 1YR
T: (01341) 280262
F: (01341) 280586
E: mynach@lineone.net
1/2 mile north of Barmouth on the A496 Barmouth - Harlech coastal road, seaward side. Signposted.

Level, grassy, hard, sheltered.
180 touring pitches.

60	�

| £6.00—£14.00 |
| 60 | | £6.00—£13.00 |
| 180 | A | £5.00—£14.00 |

Open January, March–December
Cards accepted: Delta, Switch,
Mastercard, Visa

BRECON

Powys
Map ref 1B3

Market town situated at the junction
of the rivers Usk and Honddu.
Excellent base for exploring the
Brecon Beacons National Park.
Tourist Information Centre
T: (01874) 622485

Anchorage Caravan Park ⚠
★★★★
Holiday, Touring and Camping Park
Member BH&HPA
Bronllys, Brecon, Powys LD3 0LD
T: (01874) 711246
F: (01874) 711711
*Situated 8 miles North East of Brecon
on A438 in the village of Bronllys.
Signposted.*
Wheelchair access category 2 ♿
Level, sloping, grassy, sheltered.
110 touring pitches.

60	🚐	£8.00
10	🚍	£8.00
40	A	£8.00

Open all year round

COLOUR MAPS

Colour maps at the back
of this guide pinpoint all
places in which you will
find parks listed.

Brynich Caravan Park ⚠
★★★★★
Touring and Camping Park
Member BH&HPA
Brecon, Brecon, Powys LD3 7SH
T: (01874) 623325
F: (01874) 623325
E: Brynich@aol.com
I: www.brynich.co.uk
*The caravan park is situated on A470,
200 yards from jct with A40 2 km east
of Brecon. Signposted.*
Wheelchair access category 1 ♿
Level, grassy.
130 touring pitches.

50	🚐	£8.50—£10.00
20	🚍	£8.50—£10.00
60	A	£8.50—£10.00

Open April–October
Cards accepted: Delta, Mastercard,
Solo, Switch, Visa

BRYN-CRUG

Gwynedd
Map ref 1A2

Tynllwyn Caravan Site
★★★
Holiday, Touring and Camping Park
Bryn-crug, Tywyn, Gwynedd
LL36 9RD
T: (01654) 710370
F: (01654) 710370
*From Tywyn on A493, take right turn
onto B4405, then take first right by the
grass island. Signposted.*
Level, grassy, sheltered.
68 touring pitches.

50	🚐	£8.00—£10.00
8	🚍	£8.00—£10.00
10	A	£5.50—£7.00
7	🛖	£160.00—£290.00

49 units privately owned
Open March–October

You are advised to confirm
your booking in writing.

CAERNARFON

Gwynedd
Map ref 1A1

Ancient county town famous for its
magnificent and well preserved
medieval castle, the birthplace of
Edward I and scene of the
investiture of the Prince of Wales in
1969.
Tourist Information Centre
T: (01286) 672232

Bryn Gloch Caravan & Camping Park
★★★★
Holiday Park
Dragon Award
Betws Garmon, Caernarfon,
Gwynedd LL54 7YY
T: (01286) 650216
F: (01286) 650591
E: eurig@easynet.co.uk
I: www.bryngloch.co.uk
*Located on A4085 Caernarfon to
Beddgelert road 5 miles from
Caernarfon and 7 miles from
Beddgelert. Signposted.*
Level, grassy.
160 touring pitches.

80	🚐	£9.00—£10.00
80	🚍	£9.00—£10.00
80	A	£9.00—£10.00
8	🛖	£100.00—£300.00

Open all year round
Cards accepted: Mastercard, Switch,
Visa

Ad See display advertisement on this
page

Star ratings were correct
at the time of going
to press but are subject
to change.
Please check at the time
of booking.

CARDIGAN

Ceredigion
Map ref 1A2

Tourist Information Centre
T: (01239) 613230

Cenarth Falls Holiday Park
★★★★★
Touring and Holiday Park
Dragon Award
Member BH&HPA
Cenarth, Newcastle Emlyn,
Ceredigion SA38 9JS
T: (01239) 710345
F: (01239) 710344
E: enquiries@cenarth-holipark.co.uk
I: www.cenarth-holipark.co.uk
After 0.25 mile from Cenarth bridge
turn right at park signs. Situated off
A484 Cardigan-Carmarthen Road.
Signposted.
Wheelchair access category 3 ⟨⟩
Level, grassy, sheltered.
30 touring pitches.

26	🚐	£8.00—£15.00
	🚌	£8.00—£15.00
10	▲	£8.00—£15.00
6	⌂	£130.00—£485.00

83 units privately owned
Open March–December
Cards accepted: Delta, JCB,
Mastercard, Switch, Visa

COLWYN BAY

Conwy
Map ref 1B1

Popular seaside resort with sands,
bathing and a pier. Ideal centre for
touring Snowdonia.
Tourist Information Centre
T: (01492) 530478

Bron-Y-Wendon Touring Caravan Park
★★★★★
Touring Park
Dragon Award
Wern Road, Llanddulas, Colwyn
Bay, Conwy, LL22 8HG
T: (01492) 512903
F: (01492) 512903
E: bron-y-wendon@
northwales-holidays.co.uk
I: www.northwales-holidays.co.uk
Leave the A55 at the Llanddulas
junction (A547) and follow the Tourist
Information signs to the Park.
Signposted.
Wheelchair access category 2 ⟨⟩
Level, sloping, grassy, hard,
sheltered.
130 touring pitches.

| 120 | 🚐 | £9.00—£11.00 |
| 10 | 🚌 | £9.00—£11.00 |

Open March–October

Cards accepted: Visa

COWBRIDGE

Vale of Glamorgan
Map ref 1B3

Small, old-world borough with an
Edwardian gatehouse. Parts of
13th-14th C walls are still standing.
Good shops.

Llandow Caravan Park
★★★★
Touring and Camping Park
Member BH&HPA
Marcross Farm, Marcross, Llantwit
Major, South Glamorgan CF61 1ZG
T: (01446) 792462
F: (01446) 792462
E: marcross@farmline.com
I: come.to/llandow
Leave M4 at jct33. To A48, bypass
Cowbridge, follow brown signs on
B4268, towards Llantwit Major.
Signposted.
Level, grassy, sheltered.
100 touring pitches.

70	🚐	£7.00—£9.00
10	🚌	£7.00—£9.00
20	▲	£5.00—£9.00

Open February–November

CWMCARN

Caerphilly
Map ref 1B3

Cwmcarn Forest Drive Campsite
★★★★
Touring and Camping Park
Nantcarn Road, Cwmcarn,
Newport, Gwent NP11 7FA
T: (01495) 272001
F: (01495) 272001
E: tic@caerphilly.gov.uk
I: www.caerphilly.gov.uk
M4, jct 28 follow A467 for 7 miles to
Cwmcarn, follow brown tourism signs.
Signposted.
Wheelchair access category 3 ⟨⟩
Level, sloping, grassy, hard.
40 touring pitches.

30	🚐	£7.00—£11.00
5	🚌	£7.00—£11.00
5	▲	£4.50—£8.00

Open all year round
Cards accepted: Mastercard, Visa

> The **ᐱ** symbol after a
> park name indicates that
> it is a Regional Tourist
> Board member.

FISHGUARD

Pembrokeshire
Map ref 1A2

Picturesque little town perched high
above its harbour. Fine cliff scenery.
Tourist Information Centre
T: (01348) 873484

Fishguard Bay Caravan and Camping Park
★★★★
Touring and Holiday Park
Dragon Award
Member BH&HPA
Garn Gelli, Fishguard,
Pembrokeshire SA65 9ET
T: (01348) 811415
F: (01348) 811425
E: neil@fishguardbay.com
I: www.fishguardbay.com
Take A487 Cardigan Road from
Fishguard, 3 miles outside Fishguard,
turning on left. Signposted.
Sloping, grassy.
50 touring pitches.

20	🚐	£9.50—£11.50
	🚌	£9.50—£11.50
30	▲	£8.50—£10.50
11	⌂	£145.00—£360.00

39 units privately owned
Open March–November
Cards accepted: Amex, Delta,
Diners, Mastercard, Switch, Visa

Gwaun Vale Touring Park
★★★★
Touring Park
Member BH&HPA
Llanychaer, Fishguard, Dyfed
SA65 9TA
T: (01348) 874698
From Fishguard, take B4313 for 1.5
miles. The site is on the right.
Signposted.
Level, grassy, hard, sheltered.
30 touring pitches.

	🚐	£7.00—£8.00
	🚌	£7.00—£8.00
	▲	£7.00—£8.00

Open March–October

LLANGADOG

Carmarthenshire
Map ref 1B3

Abermarlais Caravan Park
★★★★
Touring and Camping Park
Member BH&HPA
Llangadog, Carmarthenshire
SA19 9NG
T: (01550) 777868
F: (01550) 77797

Situated on A40, 6 miles west of Llandovery or 6 miles east of Llandeilo. Signposted.
Level, sloping, grassy, hard, sheltered.
88 touring pitches.

60		£7.50—£7.50
60		£7.50—£7.50
28	A	£7.50—£7.50

Open March–November

LLANGORSE

Powys
Map ref 1B3

Lakeside Caravan and Camping Park ⚲
★★★
Holiday, Touring and Camping Park
Member BH&HPA
Llangorse, Brecon, Powys LD3 7TR
T: (01874) 658226
F: (01874) 658430
E: holidays@lakeside.zx3.net
I: www.lakeside-holidays.net
From Abergavenny A40 to Bwlch, turn right onto B4560 to Llangorse. Head for the lake.
Level, grassy, sheltered.
150 touring pitches.

50		£7.00—£9.00
50		£7.00—£9.00
50	A	£7.00—£9.00
10		£140.00—£305.00

72 units privately owned
Open March–October
Cards accepted: Amex, Delta, Mastercard, Switch, Visa

MONMOUTH

Monmouthshire
Map ref 1B3

Historic market town, birthplace of Henry V, with unique 13th C gateway built across the Monnow.

Glen Trothy Caravan Park ⚲
★★★
Touring and Camping Park
Member BH&HPA
Mitchel Troy, Monmouth,
Monmouthshire NP25 4BD
T: (01600) 712295
F: (01600) 712295
E: glentrothy@mresources.co.uk
I: www.mresources.co.uk/glentrothy/
In the village of Mitchel Troy, 1.5 miles SW of Monmouth, off A40. Free colour brochure gives more information and directions.
Level, grassy, hard, sheltered.
140 touring pitches.

80		£7.00
6		£7.00
54	A	£7.00

Open March–October

OXWICH

Swansea
Map ref 1A3

Oxwich Camping Park
★★★
Camping Park
Gower, Oxwich, Swansea SA3 1LS
T: (01792) 390777
Take A4118 from Swansea. Turn left at Oxwich signpost. First right, campsite on right.
Level, sloping, grassy, hard, sheltered.
180 touring pitches.

90		£10.00—£10.00
90	A	£10.00—£10.00

Open April–September

PENMAENMAWR

Conwy
Map ref 1B1

Holiday resort at the foot of Penmaenmawr Mountain, with excellent sands and bathing, sailing and golf.

Woodlands Camping Park ⚲
★
Holiday, Touring and Camping Park
Pendyffren Hall, Penmaenmawr,
Penmaenmawr, Gwynedd LL34 6UF
T: (01492) 623219
Off A55 between Conwy and Penmaemawr, signposted Dwygyfylchi.
Level, grassy, stony, sheltered.
100 touring pitches.

25		£7.00—£13.00
		£7.00—£13.00
100	A	£7.00—£13.00

200 units privately owned
Open March–October

PORTHMADOG

Gwynedd
Map ref 1A1

Delightful seaside resort with a good harbour and some fine sandy bays. Wonderful views across the estuary to the mountains beyond. Trips into the hills on the narrow gauge Festiniog Railway.
Tourist Information Centre
T: (01766) 512981

Black Rock Camping & Touring Park ⚲
★★★
Touring and Camping Park
Member BH&HPA
Pensyflog, Morfa Bychan,
Porthmadog, Porthmadog, Gwynedd
LL49 9LD
T: (01766) 513919
Signposted.
Level, grassy, sheltered.
150 touring pitches.

20		£12.00—£15.50
20		£12.00—£15.50
130	A	£10.00—£10.50

Open April–September

Greenacres Holiday Park
★★★★
Holiday Park
Dragon Award
Member NCC
Morfa Bychan, Porthmadog,
Gwynedd LL49 9YB
T: 0870 2425678
F: (01442) 254956
I: www.british-holidays.co.uk
Porthmadog High Street, take road to Black Rock Sands. Follow into village of Morfa Bychan, Greenacres is situated on the left hand side at the end of the village. Signposted.
Wheelchair access category 3 ⚲
Level, grassy.
51 touring pitches.

51		£8.50—£23.70
		£8.50—£23.70
161		£149.00—£552.00

758 units privately owned
Open April–October
Cards accepted: Delta, Mastercard, Switch, Visa

See display advertisement on page 10

See display advertisement on page 10

COLOUR MAPS

Colour maps at the back of this guide pinpoint all places in which you will find parks listed.

PRESTATYN

Denbighshire
Map ref 1B1

Tourist Information Centre
T: (01745) 889092

Tan y Don Caravan Park
★ ★ ★ ★
Touring and Holiday Park
263 Victoria Road, Prestatyn,
Prestatyn, Clwyd LL19 7UT
T: (01745) 853749
F: (01745) 854147
Main A548 Coast road between
Prestatyn and Rhyl. Entrance in
Sandhurst road. Signposted.
Wheelchair access category 3 🧍
Level, grassy, hard, sheltered.
8 touring pitches.

8	🚐	£10.00—£12.00
8	🚏	£10.00—£12.00
3	🏠	£75.00—£375.00

61 units privately owned
Open January, March–December
Cards accepted: Delta, Mastercard,
Switch, Visa

🚗 P 🅿 🎣 🍴 🔥 📺 📟 🚿 🐾 ⛺ 🅣
🆎 See display advertisement on this
page

ST DAVIDS

Pembrokeshire
Map ref 1A3

A place of pilgrimage for over eight
centuries, situated on the rugged
western peninsula within easy reach
of some of Britain's finest cliffs and
bays. Interesting cathedral.
Tourist Information Centre
T: (01437) 720392

Caerfai Bay Caravan Park
★ ★ ★
Holiday and Touring Park
Member BH&HPA
St Davids, Haverfordwest,
Pembrokeshire SA62 6QT
T: (01437) 720274
F: (01437) 720274
Turn off A487 (Haverfordwest to St
Davids) in St Davids at visitor centre
signposted. Caerfai Park is at road end,
1 mile, on the right. Signposted.
Level, sloping, grassy.
120 touring pitches.

28	🚐	£7.50—£11.50
15	🚏	£5.50—£11.50
77	⛺	£5.50—£6.50
5	🏠	£150.00—£350.00

27 units privately owned
Open April–October

🚗 P 🅿 🎣 🔥 ⛄ 🍴 🔥 📟 📺 🚿 🔌
☺ ⛽ 🆆🅷

TENBY

Pembrokeshire
Map ref 1A3

Town with colourful harbour,
superb sands, cliff-top hotels and
ancient walls and gateways. It stands
on a rocky promontory on
Carmarthen Bay and is an ideal
centre for exploring the coast.
Tourist Information Centre
T: (01834) 842402

Kiln Park Holiday Centre
★ ★ ★
Holiday Park
Marsh Road, Tenby, Tenby, Dyfed
SA34 0NS
T: 0870 2425678
F: (01442) 254956
E: www.british-holidays.co.uk
Follow signs to Tenby. At mini
roundabout follow signs for Penally. 1
mile on left hand side. Signposted.
Wheelchair access category 3 🧍
Level, grassy.
350 touring pitches.

200	🚐	£9.40—£26.00
	🚏	£9.40—£26.00
200	⛺	£8.30—£19.60
350	🏠	£163.00—£758.00

290 units privately owned
Open April–October
Cards accepted: Delta, Mastercard,
Switch, Visa

🅿 🍴 🔥 ☺ 🛒 ✕ 📟 📺 🚿 📶 ⚡ ∪
⛽ 🅣 🆆🅷
🆎 See display advertisement on
page 10

WREXHAM

Map ref 1B1

Busy market town with medieval
church.
Tourist Information Centre
T: (01978) 292015

The Plassey Leisure Park
★ ★ ★ ★
Touring and Camping Park
Member BH&HPA
Eyton, Wrexham, Clwyd LL13 0SP
T: (01978) 780277
F: (01978) 780019
E: jbrookshaw@aol.com
I: www.theplassey.co.uk
Take Bangor-on-Dee exit off the A483,
and 2.5 miles along B5426 to the
Plassey. Signposted.
Level, grassy, hard, sheltered.
120 touring pitches.

100	🚐	£11.00—£13.50
10	🚏	£11.00—£13.50
10	⛺	£11.00—£13.50

Open March–November
Cards accepted: Delta, Diners,
Switch, Visa

P 🅿 🍴 🔥 ☺ 🛒 ✕ 📟 📺 🚿 📶 ∪
⛽ 🅣 ⛽

British Graded Holiday Parks Scheme
Quality Assessed Parks

For the very first time we are publishing a complete listing of all camping and caravan parks in England that have been assessed for quality under the British Graded Holiday Parks Scheme.

On the following pages you will find brief contact details for each park, together with its Star rating and type of site. The listing also shows if an establishment is taking part in the Welcome Host scheme [WH], and if it has a National Accessible rating (see the information pages for further information).

More detailed information on all the places shown in green can be found in the regional sections (where establishments have paid to have their details included). To find these entries please refer to the appropriate regional section, or look in the town index at the back of this guide.

The list which follows was complied slightly later than the regional sections. For this reason you may find that, in a few instances, a Star rating may differ between the two sections. This list contains the most up-to-date information and was correct at the time of going to press. Please note that it does not include parks in Scotland and Wales.

LONDON

CHINGFORD

Lee Valley Campsite ★★★★
Touring and Camping Park
Sewardstone Road, Chingford,
London E4 7RA
T: (020) 8529 5689
F: (020) 8559 4070
E: scs@leevalleypark.org.uk
I: www.leevalleypark.org.uk
|WH|

CRYSTAL PALACE

Crystal Palace C C Site ★★★★★
Touring and Camping Park
Crystal Palace Parade, London
SE19 1UF
T: (020) 8778 7155
F: (020) 8676 0980
|WH|

EDMONTON

Lee Valley Leisure Centre ★★★★
Touring and Camping Park
Meridian Way, London N9 0AS
T: (020) 8345 6666 & 8803 6900
F: (020) 8884 4975
E: leisurecentre@leevalleypark.
org.uk
I: www.leevalleypark.org.uk
|WH|

LOUGHTON

Debden House Camp Site ★★
Touring and Camping Park
Debden Green, Loughton, Essex
IG10 2PA
T: (020) 8508 3008 & 85083008
F: (020) 8508 0284

The Elms Caravan and Camping Park ★★★
Touring and Camping Park
Lippitts Hill, High Beech,
Loughton, IG10 4AW
T: (020) 8508 3749 & 8508 1000
F: (020) 8502 0016
E: elmscar@aol.com
I: members.aol.com/elmscar

STANSTED

Thriftwood Caravan & Camping Park ★★★★★
Holiday, Touring and Camping Park
Rose Award
Plaxdale Green Road, Stansted,
Wrotham, Sevenoaks, Kent
TN15 7PB
T: (01732) 822261
F: (01732) 822261
I: www.ukparks.co.uk/thriftwood

CUMBRIA

ALLONBY
Cumbria

Manor House Caravan Park ★★
Holiday, Touring and Camping Park
Edderside Road, Allonby,
Maryport, Cumbria CA15 6RA
T: (01900) 881236
F: (01900) 881199
E: holidays@manorhousepark.
co.uk
I: www.manorhousepark.co.uk
|WH|

Spring Lea Caravan Park ★★★
Holiday, Touring and Camping Park
Allonby, Maryport, Cumbria
CA15 6QF
T: (01900) 881331
F: (01900) 881209

AMBLESIDE
Cumbria

Greenhowe Caravan Park
★★★
Holiday Park
Great Langdale, Ambleside,
Cumbria LA22 9JU
T: (015394) 37231
F: (015394) 37464

Skelwith Fold Caravan Park ★★★★★
Holiday and Touring Park
Skelwith Fold, Ambleside,
Cumbria LA22 0HX
T: (015394) 32277
F: (015394) 34344
|WH|

APPLEBY-IN-WESTMORLAND
Cumbria

Wild Rose Park ★★★★★
Holiday, Touring and Camping Park
Ormside, Appleby-in-
Westmorland, Cumbria
CA16 6EJ
T: (017683) 51077
F: (017683) 52551
E: hs@wildrose.co.uk
I: www.wildrose.co.uk
|WH|

BASSENTHWAITE
Cumbria

Bassenthwaite Lakeside Lodges ★★★★★
Holiday Park
Rose Award
Scarness, Bassenthwaite,
Keswick, Cumbria CA12 4QZ
T: (017687) 76641
F: (017687) 76919
E: enquiries@bll.ac
I: www.bll.ac
|WH|

BEETHAM
Cumbria

Beetham Caravan Park ★★★★★
Holiday Park
Beetham, Milnthorpe, Cumbria
LA7 7AL
T: (015395) 62552

BOUTH
Cumbria

Black Beck Caravan Park ★★★★★
Holiday, Touring and Camping Park
Bouth, Ulverston, Cumbria
LA12 8JN
T: (01229) 861274
F: (01229) 861041
E: ribble@netcomuk.co.uk
|WH|

BRAMPTON
Cumbria

Cairndale Caravan Park ★★★
Holiday and Touring Park
Cumwhitton, Headsnook,
Brampton, Carlisle, Cumbria
CA8 9BZ
T: (01768) 896280

BRAYSTONES
Cumbria

Tarnside Caravan Park ★★★
Holiday and Touring Park
Braystones, Beckermet, Cumbria
CA21 2YL
T: (01946) 841308
E: ann@hotmail.com
I: www.ukparks.co.uk/tarnside

CARLISLE
Cumbria

Dalston Hall Caravan Park ★★★★
Touring and Camping Park
Dalston Hall, Dalston, Carlisle
CA5 7JX
T: (01228) 710165

Dandy Dinmont Caravan and Camping Site ★★★★
Touring and Camping Park
Blackford, Carlisle CA6 4EA
T: (01228) 674611

Orton Grange Caravan Park ★★★★
Holiday, Touring and Camping Park
Wigton Road, Carlisle, CA5 6LA
T: (01228) 710252
F: (01228) 710252
E: chris@ortongrange.flyer.co.
uk

COCKERMOUTH
Cumbria

Violet Bank Holiday Home Park Ltd ★★
Holiday, Touring and Camping Park
Simonscales Lane, Cockermouth,
Cumbria CA13 9TG
T: (01900) 822169

CONISTON
Cumbria

Crake Valley Holiday Park ★★★★★
Holiday Park
Rose Award
Water Yeat, Blawith, Ulverston,
Cumbria LA12 8DL
T: (01229) 885203
F: (01229) 885203

Park Coppice Caravan Club Site ★★★★★
Touring and Camping Park
Coniston, Cumbria LA21 8AU
T: (01539) 441555
|WH|

CROOK
Cumbria

Ratherheath Lane Camping and Caravan Park★★★★
Holiday, Touring and Camping Park
Chain House, Bonningate,
Kendal, Cumbria LA8 8JU
T: (01539) 821154 & 0797 163
0226
E: djwilson@ndirect.co.uk
I: www.ndirect.co.uk/Sdjwilson

CROOKLANDS
Cumbria

Millness Hill Park ★★★★
Holiday, Touring and Camping Park
Crooklands, Milnthorpe,
Cumbria LA7 7NU
T: (015395) 67306
F: (015395) 67306
E: holidays@millness.demon.co.
uk

ENDMOOR
Cumbria

Gatebeck Park ★★★★★
Holiday Park
Endmoor, Kendal, Cumbria
LA8 0HL
T: (015395) 67875
F: (015395) 67875
|WH|

ESKDALE
Cumbria

Fisherground Farm Campsite ★★
Camping Park
Fisherground, Eskdale,
Holmrook, Cumbria CA19 1TF
T: (019467) 23319
E: holidays@fisherground.co.uk
I: www.fisherground.campsite.
co.uk

FLOOKBURGH
Cumbria
Lakeland Leisure Park ★★★★
Holiday, Touring and Camping Park
Moor Lane, Flookburgh, Grange-over-Sands, Cumbria LA11 7LT
T: 0870 2425678
F: (01442) 234956
I: www.british-holidays.co.uk
[WH]

GRANGE-OVER-SANDS
Cumbria
Greaves Farm Caravan Park ★★★★
Holiday and Touring Park
Field Broughton, Grange-over-Sands, Cumbria LA11 6HR
T: (015395) 36329 & 36587
[WH]

Meathop Fell Caravan Club Site ★★★★★
Touring Park
Grange-over-Sands, Cumbria LA11 6RB
T: (01539) 532912
[WH]

Old Park Wood Caravan Park ★★★★
Holiday and Touring Park
Holker, Grange-over-Sands, Cumbria LA11 7PP
T: (015395) 58266
F: (015395) 58101
[WH]

HAWKSHEAD
Cumbria
The Croft Caravan and Camp Site ★★★
Touring and Camping Park
North Lonsdale Road, Hawkshead, Ambleside, Cumbria LA22 0NX
T: (015394) 36374
F: (015394) 36544
E: enquiries@hawkshead-croft.com
I: www.hawkshead-croft.com

Grizedale Hall Camping and Caravanning Club Site ★★★
Camping Park
Grizedale Hall, Hawkshead, Ambleside, Cumbria LA22 0GL
T: (01229) 860257
I: www.campingandcaravanningclub.co.uk

KENDAL
Cumbria
Camping and Caravanning Club Kendal ★★★★
Touring and Camping Park
Millcrest, Shap Road, Kendal, Cumbria LA9 6NY
T: (01539) 741363
I: www.campingandcaravanningclub.co.uk

Waters Edge Caravan Park ★★★★
Touring and Camping Park
Crooklands, Kendal, Cumbria LA7 7NN
T: (015395) 67708 & 67527
F: (015395) 67610
E: cromoco@aol.com

KESWICK
Cumbria
Castlerigg Farm Camp Site ★★
Touring and Camping Park
Keswick, Cumbria CA12 4TE
T: (017687) 72479 & 74718
F: (017687) 74718
E: info@castleriggfarm.freeserve.co.uk
I: www.kesnet.co.uk/castlerigg.htm
[WH]

Castlerigg Hall Caravan and Camping Park ★★★★
Holiday, Touring and Camping Park
Castlerigg Hall, Keswick, Cumbria CA12 4TE
T: (017687) 72437
F: (017687) 72437
I: www.castlerigg.co.uk

Derwentwater Caravan Park ★★★★
Holiday and Touring Park
Crowe Park Road, Keswick, Cumbria CA12 5EN
T: (017687) 72579

Keswick Camping and Caravanning Club Site ★★★★
Touring and Camping Park
Derwentwater, Keswick, Cumbria CA12 5EP
T: (017687) 772392
I: www.campingandcaravanningclub.co.uk

Lakeside Holiday Park ★★★★
Holiday and Touring Park
Norman Garner Ltd, Crow Park Road, Keswick, Cumbria CA12 5EW
T: (017687) 72878
F: (017687) 72017
E: welcome@lakesideholidaypark.co.uk
I: www.lakesideholidaypark.co.uk
[WH]

Low Briery Holiday Village ★★★★
Holiday Park
Penrith Road, Keswick, Cumbria CA12 4RN
T: (017687) 72044
I: www.keswick.uk.com

Scotgate Holiday Park ★★★★
Holiday, Touring and Camping Park
Braithwaite, Keswick, Cumbria CA12 5TF
T: (017687) 78343
F: (017687) 78099

KIRKBY STEPHEN
Cumbria
Pennine View Caravan Park ★★★★★
Touring and Camping Park
Station Road, Kirkby Stephen, Cumbria CA17 4SZ
T: (017683) 71717

LAMPLUGH
Cumbria
Inglenook Caravan Park ★★★★
Holiday, Touring and Camping Park
Lamplugh, Workington, Cumbria CA14 4SH
T: (01946) 861240
F: (01946) 861240

LOUGHRIGG
Cumbria
Neaum Crag ★★★★★
Holiday Park
Loughrigg, Ambleside, Cumbria LA22 9HG
T: (015394) 33221
F: (015394) 33735

MILNTHORPE
Cumbria
Fell End Caravan Park ★★★★★
Holiday, Touring and Camping Park
Slack Head Road, Hale, Milnthorpe, Cumbria LA7 7BS
T: (015395) 62122
F: (015395) 63810

NEW HUTTON
Cumbria
The Ashes Exclusively Adult Caravan Park★★★★
Touring Park
New Hutton, Kendal, Cumbria LA8 0AS
T: (01539) 731833 & 07974 058296
F: (01539) 731833
E: ashes-new-hutton@cwcom.net
I: www.ashes-new-hutton.cwc.net
[WH]

NEWBY BRIDGE
Cumbria
Newby Bridge Caravan Park ★★★★★
Holiday Park
Rose Award
Canny Hill, Newby Bridge, Ulverston, Cumbria LA12 8NF
T: (015395) 31030
F: (015395) 30105
E: newbybridge@hopps.freeserve.co.uk
[WH]

ORTON
Cumbria
Tebay Caravan Site ★★★★
Holiday and Touring Park
Orton, Penrith, Cumbria CA10 3SB
T: (015396) 24511
F: (015396) 24511
E: julie@rheged.com

PENRITH
Cumbria
Lowther Holiday Park ★★★★
Holiday, Touring and Camping Park
Eamont Bridge, Penrith, Cumbria CA10 2JB
T: (01768) 863631
F: (01768) 868126
E: holiday.park@lowther.co.uk
I: www.lowther.co.uk

Melmerby Caravan Park ★★★★
Holiday and Touring Park
Melmerby, Penrith, Cumbria CA10 1HE
T: (01768) 881311
F: (01768) 881311

POOLEY BRIDGE
Cumbria
Waterside House Campsite ★★★
Touring and Camping Park
Waterside House, Howtown Road, Pooley Bridge, Penrith, Cumbria CA10 2NA
T: (017684) 86332
F: (017684) 86332

ST BEES
Cumbria
Seacote Park ★★★
Holiday, Touring and Camping Park
The Beach, St Bees, Cumbria CA27 0ES
T: (01946) 822777
F: (01946) 824442

SEDGWICK
Cumbria
Low Park Wood Caravan Club Site ★★★★
Touring Park
Sedgwick, Kendal, Cumbria LA8 0JZ
T: (01539) 560186
[WH]

SILECROFT
Cumbria
Silecroft Caravan and Camping Park ★★★
Holiday, Touring and Camping Park
Silecroft, Millom, Cumbria LA18 4NX
T: (01229) 772659
F: (01229) 772659
E: silecroftpark@aol.com
I: www.caravanholidayhomes.com

SILLOTH
Cumbria
Seacote Caravan Park ★★★★
Holiday and Touring Park
Skinburness Road, Silloth, Carlisle, Cumbria CA5 4QJ
T: (016973) 31121
F: (016973) 31121

The Solway Holiday Village ★★
Holiday, Touring and Camping Park
Skinburness Drive, Silloth, Carlisle CA5 4QQ
T: (016973) 31236
F: (016973) 32553

Stanwix Park Holiday Centre ★★★★★
Holiday, Touring and Camping Park
Rose Award
Greenrow, West Silloth, Silloth, Carlisle, Cumbria CA7 4HH
T: (016973) 32666
F: (016973) 32555
E: stanwix.park@btinternet.com
I: www.stanwix.com
[WH]

Tanglewood Caravan Park
★★★
Holiday, Touring and Camping Park
Causewayhead, Silloth, Cumbria
CA5 4PE
T: (016973) 31253

STAVELEY
Cumbria

Ashes Lane Caravan and Camping Park★★★★
Touring and Camping Park
Ashes Lane, Staveley, Kendal, Cumbria LA8 9JS
T: (01539) 821119
F: (01539) 821282
I: www.asheslane.com

ULLSWATER
Cumbria

The Quiet Camping Site
★★★★★
Touring and Camping Park
Ullswater, Penrith, Cumbria
CA11 0LS
T: (017684) 86337
F: (017684) 86610

Ullswater Caravan Camping and Marine Park★★★
Holiday, Touring and Camping Park
Watermillock, Penrith, Cumbria
CA11 0LR
T: (017684) 86666
F: (017684) 86095

Waterfoot Caravan Park
★★★★★
Holiday and Touring Park
Pooley Bridge, Penrith, Cumbria
CA11 0JF
T: (017684) 86302
F: (01784) 86728

ULVERSTON
Cumbria

Brook Hollow Caravan Park
★★★★★
Holiday Park
Alpine Road, Newland Bottom, Ulverston, Cumbria LA12 7QD
T: (01229) 582582

WATERMILLOCK
Cumbria

Cove Caravan and Camping Park ★★★★★
Touring and Camping Park
Ullswater, Penrith, Cumbria
CA11 0LS
T: (017684) 86549
WH

WESTWARD
Cumbria

Clea Hall Holiday Park ★★★★
Holiday, Touring and Camping Park
Westward, Wigton, Cumbria
CA7 8NQ
T: (016973) 42880

WINDERMERE
Cumbria

Fallbarrow Park ★★★★★
Holiday and Touring Park
Rose Award
Rayrigg Road, Windermere, Cumbria LA23 3DL
T: (015394) 44427 & 44428
F: (015394) 88736
I: www.fallbarrow.co.uk
WH

Hill of Oaks and Blakeholme Caravan Estate★★★★★
Holiday and Touring Park
Tower Wood, Windermere, Cumbria LA23 3PJ
T: (015395) 31578
F: (015395) 30431
WH

Limefitt Park ★★★★★
Holiday, Touring and Camping Park
Rose Award
Windermere, Cumbria LA23 1PA
T: (015394) 32300
I: www.limefitt.co.uk
WH

Park Cliffe Caravan and Camping Estate★★★★★
Holiday, Touring and Camping Park
Birks Road, Windermere, Cumbria LA23 3PG
T: (015395) 31344
F: (015395) 31971
E: info@parkcliffe.co.uk
I: www.parkcliffe.co.uk
WH

White Cross Bay Holiday Park and Marina★★★★★
Holiday and Touring Park
Ambleside Road, Troutbeck Bridge, Windermere, Cumbria LA23 1LF
T: (015394) 43937
F: (015394) 88704
E: wxb@windermere.uk.com
I: www.windermere.uk.com

<h1>NORTHUMBRIA</h1>

ASHINGTON
Northumberland

Wansbeck Riverside Park
★★★
Holiday, Touring and Camping Park
Green Lane, Ashington, Northumberland NE63 8TX
T: (01670) 812323
F: (01670) 812323

BAMBURGH
Northumberland

Bradford Kaims Caravan Park
★★
Holiday, Touring and Camping Park
Bamburgh, Northumberland NE70 7JT
T: (01668) 213432 & 213595
F: (01668) 213891

Glororum Caravan Park ★★★
Holiday and Touring Park
Glororum, Bamburgh, Northumberland NE69 7AW
T: (01668) 214457 & 214205
F: (01668) 214622

Waren Caravan Park ★★★★
Holiday, Touring and Camping Park
Rose Award
Waren Mill, Belford, Northumberland NE70 7EE
T: (01668) 214366
F: (01668) 214224
E: enquiries@warencp.demon.co.uk
I: www.meadowhead.co.uk/waren
WH

BARDON MILL
Northumberland

Winshields Camp Site ★★
Camping Park
Winshields, Bardon Mill, Hexham, Northumberland NE47 7AN
T: (01434) 344243

BARNARD CASTLE
Durham

Bend Holm Farm Caravan Park
★★
Touring and Camping Park
Egglestone, Barnard Castle, County Durham DL12 0AX
T: (01833) 650457

BARRASFORD PARK
Northumberland

Barrasford Park Caravan and Camping Site★★★
Touring and Camping Park
1 Front Drive, Barrasford Park, Hexham, Northumberland NE48 4BE
T: (01434) 681210

BEADNELL
Northumberland

Beadnell ★★★★
Touring and Camping Park
Camping & Caravanning Club Site, Beadnell, Chathill, Northumberland NE67 5BX
T: (01665) 720586
I: www.campingandcaravanningclub.co.uk

Beadnell Links Caravan Park
★★★★
Holiday and Touring Park
Beadnell Harbour, Beadnell, Chathill, Northumberland NE67 5BN
T: (01665) 720993
E: jameshall@beadnell.freeserve78.co.uk
I: www.ukparks.co.uk/beadnell

BEAL
Northumberland

Haggerston Castle ★★★★
Holiday and Touring Park
Rose Award
Beal, Berwick-upon-Tweed, Northumberland TD15 2PA
T: 0870 2425678
F: (01442) 254956
I: www.british-holidays.co.uk
WH

BEAMISH
Durham

Bobby Shafto Caravan Park
★★★
Holiday, Touring and Camping Park
Beamish, Stanley, County Durham DH9 0RY
T: (0191) 370 1776
F: (0191) 370 1776

BELLINGHAM
Northumberland

Brown Rigg Caravan & Camping Park ★★★★
Touring and Camping Park
Bellingham, Hexham, Northumberland NE48 2JY
T: (01434) 220175
F: (01434) 220175
WH

BERWICK-UPON-TWEED
Northumberland

Beachcomber Campsite ★★★
Touring and Camping Park
Goswick, Berwick-upon-Tweed, Northumberland TD15 2RW
T: (01289) 381217

Berwick Holiday Centre ★★★
Holiday Park
Magdalene Fields, Berwick-upon-Tweed, Northumberland TD15 1NE
T: 0870 2425678
F: (01442) 254956
I: www.british-holidays.co.uk
WH

Marshall Meadows Farm
★★★
Holiday, Touring and Camping Park
Berwick-upon-Tweed, Northumberland TD15 1UT
T: (01289) 307375

Ord House Country Park
★★★★★
Holiday, Touring and Camping Park
Rose Award
East Ord, Berwick-upon-Tweed, Northumberland TD15 2NS
T: (01289) 305288
F: (01289) 330832
E: enquiries@ordhouse.co.uk
I: www.ordhouse.co.uk
WH

Salutation Caravan Park
Rating Applied For
Salutation Inn, Shoreswood (A698), Berwick-upon-Tweed, Northumberland TD15 2NL
T: (01289) 382291

BIRLING
Northumberland
Rose Cottage Camp Site ★★★
Touring and Camping Park
Rose Cottage, Birling, Morpeth,
Northumberland NE65 0XS
T: (01665) 711459

CASTLESIDE
Durham
**Manor Park Caravan Park
(Manor Park Ltd)★★★★**
*Holiday, Touring and Camping
Park*
Broadmeadows, Rippon Burn,
Castleside, Consett, County
Durham DH8 9HD
T: (01207) 501000
F: (01207) 509271
WH

COTHERSTONE
Durham
Doe Park Caravan Site ★★★★
Touring Park
Doe Park, Cotherstone, Barnard
Castle, County Durham
DL12 9UQ
T: (01833) 650302 &
07710 069682
F: (01833) 650302

CRASTER
Northumberland
**Proctors Stead Caravan Site
★★★**
*Holiday, Touring and Camping
Park*
Proctors Stead, Craster, Alnwick,
Northumberland NE66 3TF
T: (01665) 576613
F: (01665) 576311

CRESSWELL
Northumberland
**Cresswell Towers Holiday Park
★★★**
Holiday Park
Cresswell, Morpeth,
Northumberland NE61 5JT
T: (01670) 860411
F: (01670) 860226
I: www.leisuregb.co.uk

DUNSTAN
Northumberland
Dunstan Hill ★★★★
Touring and Camping Park
Camping & Caravanning Club
Site, Dunstan, Alnwick,
Northumberland NE66 3TQ
T: (01665) 576310
I: www.
campingandcaravanningclub.co.
uk

DURHAM
Durham
**Finchale Abbey Caravan Park
★★★**
*Holiday, Touring and Camping
Park*
Finchale Abbey Farm, Finchale
Abbey, Durham, County Durham
DH1 5SH
T: (0191) 386 6528 &
(01388) 720271
F: (0191) 386 8593
E: finchaleabbey@talk21.com
I: www.finchaleabbey@co.uk

**Grange Caravan Club Site
★★★★**
Touring and Camping Park
Meadow Lane, Durham, DH1 1TL
T: (0191) 384 4778
F: (0191) 383 9161

EBCHESTER
Durham
Byreside Caravan Site ★★★★
Touring and Camping Park
Hamsterley, Ebchester,
Newcastle upon Tyne NE17 7RT
T: (01207) 560280
WH

FALSTONE
Northumberland
**Kielder Water Caravan Club
Site★★★★**
Touring and Camping Park
Leaplish Waterside Park,
Falstone, Hexham,
Northumberland NE48 1AX
T: (01434) 250278
WH

GREENHEAD
Northumberland
**Roam-n-Rest Caravan Park
★★★**
Touring and Camping Park
Raylton House, Greenhead,
Northumberland CA8 7HA
T: (016977) 47213

HALTWHISTLE
Northumberland
**Camping & Caravanning Club
Site ★★★★**
Touring and Camping Park
Burnfoot Park Village,
Haltwhistle, Northumberland
NE49 0JP
T: (01434) 320106
I: www.
campingandcaravanningclub.co.
uk

HARTLEPOOL
Tees Valley
**Ash Vale Homes & Holiday
Park ★★**
Holiday and Touring Park
Easington Road, Hartlepool,
Cleveland TS24 9RF
T: (01429) 862111
E: ashvale@compuserve.com
I: www.ashvalepark.demon.co.uk

HAYDON BRIDGE
Northumberland
**Poplars Riverside Caravan Park
★★★★**
*Holiday, Touring and Camping
Park*
East Lands Ends, Haydon Bridge,
Hexham, Northumberland
NE47 6BY
T: (01434) 684427

HEXHAM
Northumberland
**Causey Hill Caravan Park
★★★**
*Holiday, Touring and Camping
Park*
Causey Hill, Hexham,
Northumberland NE46 2JN
T: (01434) 604647

**Fallowfield Dene Caravan and
Camping Park★★★★**
Touring and Camping Park
Acomb, Hexham,
Northumberland NE46 4RP
T: (01434) 603553

**Hexham Racecourse Caravan
Site ★★★**
Touring and Camping Park
High Yarridge, Hexham,
Northumberland NE46 2JP
T: (01434) 606847
E: hexrace@aol.com

Riverside Leisure ★★★★★
*Holiday, Touring and Camping
Park*
Rose Award
Tyne Green, Hexham,
Northumberland NE46 3RY
T: (01434) 604705
F: (01434) 606217
E: riverleis@aol.com

KIELDER
Northumberland
**Forestry Commission – Kielder
Caravan and Camping Site
★★★**
Touring and Camping Park
Kielder, Hexham,
Northumberland NE48 1EP
T: (01434) 250291

LARTINGTON
Durham
**Barnard Castle Camping and
Caravanning Club★★★★**
Touring and Camping Park
Dockenflatts Lane, Lartington,
Barnard Castle, County Durham
DL12 9DG
T: (01833) 630228
I: www.
campingandcaravanningclub.co.
uk

Pecknell Farm ★★★★
Touring and Camping Park
Lartington, Barnard Castle,
County Durham DL12 9DF
T: (01833) 638357

LONGHORSLEY
Northumberland
**Forget-me-not Caravan Park
★★★**
Touring and Camping Park
Longhorsley, Morpeth,
Northumberland NE65 8QY
T: (01670) 788364
F: (01670) 788715

LOWICK
Northumberland
Barmoor South Moor ★★★★
Holiday Park
Lowick, Berwick-upon-Tweed,
Northumberland TD15 2QF
T: (01289) 388205
E: barrgold@farming.co.uk

NEWTON
Northumberland
Well House Farm ★★★
Touring and Camping Park
Newton, Stocksfield,
Northumberland NE43 7UY
T: (01661) 842193

NEWTON-BY-THE-SEA
Northumberland
**Newton Hall Caravan Park
★★★★**
Holiday and Touring Park
Newton Hall, Newton-by-the-
Sea, Alnwick, Northumberland
NE66 3DZ
T: (01665) 576239
F: (01665) 576239
E: patterson@newtonhall.
prestel.co.uk
I: www.commercepark.co.
uk/newtonhall

NORTH SEATON
Northumberland
Sandy Bay Holiday Park ★★★
Holiday and Touring Park
North Seaton, Ashington,
Northumberland NE63 9YD
T: (01670) 815055
F: (01670) 812705
I: www.leisuregb.co.uk

OTTERBURN
Northumberland
**Border Forest Caravan Park
★★★★**
*Holiday, Touring and Camping
Park*
Cottonshopeburnfoot,
Otterburn, Newcastle upon Tyne,
Northumberland NE19 1TF
T: (01830) 520259

OVINGHAM
Northumberland
**The High Hermitage Caravan
Park ★★★**
Holiday and Touring Park
The Hermitage, Ovingham,
Prudhoe, Northumberland
NE42 6HH
T: (01661) 832250
F: (01661) 834848

ROTHBURY
Northumberland
**Coquetdale Caravan Park
★★★**
*Holiday, Touring and Camping
Park*
Whitton, Rothbury, Morpeth,
Northumberland NE65 7RU
T: (01669) 620549
I: www.coquetdalecaravanpark.
co.uk

SEAHOUSES
Northumberland
Seafield Caravan Park ★★★★
Holiday and Touring Park
Rose Award
Seafield Road, Seahouses,
Northumberland NE68 7SP
T: (01665) 720628
F: (01665) 720088
E: info@seafield-caravan.
demon.co.uk
I: www.seafieldpark.co.uk

SOUTH SHIELDS
Tyne and Wear
**Lizard Lane Camping &
Caravan Site★★★**
*Holiday, Touring and Camping
Park*
Lizard Lane, South Shields, Tyne
and Wear NE34 7AB
T: (0191) 454 4982

**Sandhaven Caravan and
Camping Park★★★**
*Holiday, Touring and Camping
Park*
Sea Road, Bents Park Road,
South Shields, Tyne and Wear
NE33 2LD
T: (0191) 4247988

SPITTAL
Northumberland
**Seaview Caravan Club Site
★★★★**
Touring and Camping Park
Billendean Road, Spittal,
Berwick-upon-Tweed,
Northumberland TD15 1QU
T: (01289) 305198
WH

STOCKTON-ON-TEES
Tees Valley

White Water Caravan Club Park ★ ★ ★ ★
Touring and Camping Park
Tees Barrage, Stockton-on-Tees,
Cleveland TS18 2QW
T: (01642) 634880

SWARLAND
Northumberland

Percy Wood Caravan Park ★ ★ ★ ★
Holiday and Touring Park
Rose Award
Swarland, Morpeth,
Northumberland NE65 9JW
T: (01670) 787649
F: (01670) 787034
I: www.ukparks.co.
uk/percywood
WH

WHITLEY BAY
Tyne and Wear

**Whitley Bay Holiday Park
Leisure Great Britain Plc★ ★ ★**
Holiday and Touring Park
The Links, Whitley Bay, Tyne and
Wear NE26 4RR
T: (0191) 253 1216
F: (0191) 297 1033
E: whitley@leisuregb.co.uk
WH

WINSTON
Durham

Winston Caravan Park ★ ★ ★ ★
*Holiday, Touring and Camping
Park*
The Old Forge, Winston,
Darlington, County Durham
DL2 3RH
T: (01325) 730228
F: (01325) 730228
E: m.willetts@ic24.net
I: www.touristnetuk.
com/ne/winston

WOOLER
Northumberland

Riverside Holiday Village ★ ★ ★ ★
*Holiday, Touring and Camping
Park*
Rose Award
Brewery Road, Wooler,
Northumberland NE71 6QG
T: (01668) 281447
F: (01668) 282142

NORTH WEST

AINSDALE
Merseyside

Willowbank Holiday Home and Touring Park★ ★ ★ ★
*Holiday, Touring and Camping
Park*
Coastal Road, Ainsdale,
Southport, Merseyside PR8 3ST
T: (01704) 571566
F: (01704) 571566
E: willowbankcp@yahooo.com.

BAY HORSE
Lancashire

Wyreside Lakes Fishery ★ ★ ★
Touring and Camping Park
Sunnyside Farmhouse, Gleaves
Hill Road, Bay Horse, Lancaster
LA2 9DQ
T: (01524) 792093
F: (01524) 792093
I: www.wyresidelakes.co.uk

BLACKPOOL
Lancashire

Gillett Farm Caravan Park Ltd ★ ★ ★
Touring and Camping Park
Peel Road, Peel, Blackpool,
Lancashire FY4 5JU
T: (01253) 761676

Marton Mere Holiday Village ★ ★ ★ ★
Holiday and Touring Park
Mythop Road, Blackpool,
FY4 4XN
T: 0870 2425678
F: (01442) 254956
WH

Newton Hall Caravan Park ★ ★ ★
Holiday and Touring Park
Staining Road, Staining,
Blackpool FY3 0AX
T: (01253) 882512 & 885465
F: (01253) 893101
E: parthols@netcomuk.co.uk

Sunset Park ★ ★ ★ ★
*Holiday, Touring and Camping
Park*
Hambleton, Poulton-le-Fylde,
FY6 9EQ
T: (01253) 701757
F: (01253) 701756
E: sunset@caravans.com
I: www.caravans.
com/parks/sunset
WH

Windy Harbour Holiday Centre ★ ★ ★
*Holiday, Touring and Camping
Park*
Little Singleton, Blackpool,
FY6 8NB
T: (01253) 883064

CABUS
Lancashire

Claylands Caravan Park ★ ★ ★ ★
Holiday and Touring Park
Claylands Farm, Cabus, Preston
PR3 1AJ
T: (01524) 791242
F: (01524) 792406
I: www.claylands-caravan-park.
co.uk

CAPERNWRAY
Lancashire

Old Hall Caravan Park ★ ★ ★ ★ ★
Holiday and Touring Park
Capernwray, Carnforth,
Lancashire LA6 1AD
T: (01524) 733276
F: (01524) 734488
E: oldhall@charis.co.uk
I: www.oldhall.com

CARNFORTH
Lancashire

Netherbeck Holiday Home Park ★ ★ ★ ★ ★
Holiday Park
North Road, Carnforth,
Lancashire LA5 9NG
T: (01524) 735133 &
07967 112961
F: (01524) 735133
E: info@netherbeck.co.uk
I: www.netherbeck.co.uk

CLEVELEYS
Lancashire

Kneps Farm Holiday Park ★ ★ ★ ★
*Holiday, Touring and Camping
Park*
River Road, Stanah, Cleveleys,
Blackpool FY5 5LR
T: (01253) 823632
F: (01253) 863967
I: www.kneps-farm.co.uk
WH

CLITHEROE
Lancashire

The Camping and Caravanning Club Site Clitheroe★ ★ ★
Touring and Camping Park
Edisford Road, Clitheroe,
Lancashire BB7 3LA
T: (01200) 425294
I: www.
campingandcaravanningclub.co.
uk

COCKERHAM
Lancashire

Cockerham Sands Country Park ★ ★ ★ ★
Holiday and Touring Park
Cockerham, Lancaster LA2 0BB
T: (01524) 751387
F: (01524) 752275

Moss Wood Caravan Park ★ ★ ★ ★ ★
Holiday and Touring Park
Crimbles Lane, Cockerham,
Lancaster LA2 0ES
T: (01524) 791041
F: (01524) 792444
I: www.mosswood.co.uk
WH

FLEETWOOD
Lancashire

Cala Gran ★ ★ ★
Holiday Park
Fleetwood Road, Fleetwood,
Lancashire FY7 8JX
T: 0870 2425678
F: (01442) 254956
WH

GLASSON DOCK
Lancashire

Marina Caravan Park ★ ★ ★ ★
Holiday Park
Conder Green, Glasson Dock,
Lancaster LA2 0BP
T: (01524) 751787 & 751436
F: (01524) 751436

HEYSHAM
Lancashire

Ocean Edge Leisure Park ★ ★
Holiday and Touring Park
Moneyclose Lane, Heysham,
LA3 3DL
T: (01524) 855657 & 858828
F: (01524) 855884

HEYWOOD
Greater Manchester

Gelder Wood Country Park ★ ★ ★ ★
Touring and Camping Park
Oak Leigh Cottage, Ashworth
Road, Heywood, Rochdale,
Lancashire OL11 5UP
T: (01706) 364858 & 620300
F: (01706) 364858

KIRKHAM
Lancashire

Mowbreck Holiday and Residential Park★ ★ ★ ★
Holiday Park
Mowbreck Lane, Wesham,
Preston PR4 3HA
T: (01772) 682494
F: (01772) 672986

LANCASTER
Lancashire

New Parkside Farm Caravan Park ★ ★ ★
Touring Park
Denny Beck, Caton Road,
Lancaster, LA2 9HH
T: (01524) 770723 & 770337
I: www.ukparks.co.
uk/newparkside

Establishments printed in green have a detailed entry in this guide

LEYLAND
Lancashire

Royal Umpire Caravan Park
★★★★
Touring and Camping Park
Southport Road, Croston,
Leyland, Preston PR5 7JB
T: (01772) 600257
F: (01772) 600662
WH

LITTLE STANNEY
Cheshire

Chester Fairoaks Caravan Club Site ★★★★★
Touring Park
Rake Lane, Little Stanney,
Chester CH2 4HS
T: (0151) 355 1600
WH

LITTLEBOROUGH
Greater Manchester

Hollingworth Lake Caravan Park ★★★
Touring and Camping Park
Rakewood, Littleborough,
Lancashire OL15 0AT
T: (01706) 378661

LONGRIDGE
Lancashire

Beacon Fell View Holiday Park ★★★
Holiday, Touring and Camping Park
110 Higher Road, Longridge,
Preston PR3 2TF
T: (01772) 785434
F: (01772) 784204
WH

LYTHAM ST ANNES
Lancashire

Eastham Hall Caravan Park ★★
Holiday and Touring Park
Saltcotes Road, Lytham St
Annes, Lancashire FY8 4LS
T: (01253) 737907

MIDDLETON
Lancashire

Melbreak Caravan Park ★★★
Touring and Camping Park
Carr Lane, Middleton,
Morecambe, Lancashire LA3 3LH
T: (01524) 852430

MORECAMBE
Lancashire

Bungalow Camp Site ★★★
Holiday, Touring and Camping Park
272 Oxcliffe Road, Morecambe,
Lancashire LA3 3EH
T: (01524) 411273

Regent Leisure Park ★★★★★
Holiday Park
Westgate, Morecambe,
Lancashire LA3 3DF
T: (01524) 413940
F: (01524) 832247

Summerville Caravan Park ★★★
Holiday Park
Westgate, Morecambe,
Lancashire LA3 3DE
T: (01524) 422891 &
07831 395107

Venture Caravan Park ★★★
Holiday and Touring Park
Langridge Way, Westgate,
Morecambe, Lancashire LA4 4TQ
T: (01524) 412986
F: (01524) 422029
E: mark@venturecaravanpark.co.uk
I: www.venturecaravanpark.co.uk
WH

Westgate Caravan Park ★★★
Holiday and Touring Park
Westgate, Morecambe,
Lancashire LA3 3DE
T: (01524) 411448 & 414226
F: (01524) 414226
I: www.ukparks.co.uk/westgate

NATEBY
Lancashire

Bridge House Marina and Caravan Park ★★★
Holiday and Touring Park
Nateby Crossing Lane, Nateby,
Preston PR3 0JJ
T: (01995) 603207
F: (01995) 601612

ORMSKIRK
Lancashire

Abbey Farm Caravan Park ★★★★★
Holiday, Touring and Camping Park
Dark Lane, Ormskirk, Lancashire L40 5TX
T: (01695) 572686
F: (01695) 572686
E: abbeyfarm@yahoo.com
I: www.abbeyfarmcaravanpark.co.uk

PEEL
Lancashire

Pipers Height Caravan & Camping Park ★★★★
Holiday, Touring and Camping Park
Peel Road, Peel, Blackpool,
Lancashire FY4 5JT
T: (01253) 763767

PREESALL
Lancashire

Willowgrove Caravan Park ★★★
Holiday and Touring Park
Sandy Lane, Preesall, FY6 0EJ
T: (01253) 811306

PRESTON
Lancashire

Ribby Hall Holiday Village ★★★★★
Holiday Park
Ribby Road, Wrea Green,
Preston PR4 2PA
T: (01772) 671111
F: (01772) 673113
E: enquiries@ribbyhall.co.uk
I: www.ribbyhall.co.uk

RIMINGTON
Lancashire

Rimington Caravan Park ★★★★★
Holiday, Touring and Camping Park
Hardcacre Lane, Rimington,
Clitheroe, Lancashire BB7 4EE
T: (01200) 445355
F: (01200) 447235

SCARISBRICK
Lancashire

Hurlston Hall Country Caravan Park ★★★★
Holiday, Touring and Camping Park
Southport Road, Scarisbrick,
Ormskirk, Lancashire L40 8HB
T: (01704) 841064
F: (01704) 841700

SCORTON
Lancashire

Six Arches Caravan Park ★★★
Holiday and Touring Park
Scorton, Preston PR3 1AL
T: (01524) 791683
F: (01524) 792926

SILVERDALE
Lancashire

Far Arnside Caravan Park ★★★★★
Holiday Park
Holgates Caravan Parks Ltd,
Middlebarrow Plain, Silverdale,
Carnforth, Lancashire LA5 0SH
T: (01524) 701508
F: (01524) 701580
E: caravan@holgates.co.uk
I: www.holgates.co.uk

Holgates Caravan Park Ltd ★★★★★
Holiday and Touring Park
Rose Award
Cove Road, Silverdale, Carnforth,
Lancashire LA5 0SH
T: (01524) 701508
F: (01524) 701580
E: caravan@holgates.co.uk
I: www.holgates.co.uk

TARLETON
Lancashire

Leisure Lakes Ltd ★★
Touring and Camping Park
Mere Brow, Tarleton, Preston,
Lancashire PR9 7TW
T: (01772) 813446 & 814502
F: (01772) 816250
E: gab@leisurelakes.co.uk

THURSTASTON
Merseyside

Wirral Country Park Caravan Club Site ★★★★★
Touring Park
Station Road, Thurstaston,
Wirral, Merseyside LH61 0HN
T: (0151) 648 5228
WH

TOSSIDE
Lancashire

Crowtrees Park ★★★★
Holiday Park
Rose Award
Tosside, Skipton, North Yorkshire
BD23 4SD
T: (01729) 840278
F: (01729) 840278
I: www.holidaysyorkshiredales.com

WARRINGTON
Cheshire

Holly Bank Caravan Park ★★★★
Touring and Camping Park
Warburton Bridge Road, Rixton,
Warrington, WA3 6HU
T: (0161) 775 2842

WEST BRADFORD
Lancashire

Three Rivers Woodland Park ★★★★
Holiday, Touring and Camping Park
Eaves Hall Lane, West Bradford,
Clitheroe, Lancashire BB7 3JG
T: (01200) 423523
F: (01200) 442383

WINSFORD
Cheshire

Lakeside Caravan Park ★★★★
Holiday Park
Stockhill, Winsford, Cheshire
CW7 4EF
T: (01606) 861043
F: (01606) 861043

YORKSHIRE

ACASTER MALBIS
North Yorkshire

Chestnut Farm Caravan Park ★★★★★
Holiday, Touring and Camping Park
Rose Award
Acaster Malbis, York YO23 2UQ
T: (01904) 704676
F: (01904) 704676

Moor End Farm ★★★★
Holiday, Touring and Camping Park
Acaster Malbis, York YO23 2UQ
T: (01904) 706727
F: (01904) 706727

YORKSHIRE

ALLERSTON
North Yorkshire
Vale of Pickering Caravan Park
★★★★★
Touring and Camping Park
Carr House Farm, Allerston,
Pickering, North Yorkshire
YO18 7PQ
T: (01723) 859280
F: (01723) 850060
E: uopcp@netscapeonline.co.uk
I: www.ukparks.co.
uk/valeofpickering

BARDSEY
West Yorkshire
Moor Lodge Caravan Park
★★★★
Holiday and Touring Park
Blackmoor Lane, Bardsey, Leeds
LS17 9DZ
T: (01937) 572424

BARMBY MOOR
East Riding of Yorkshire
**The Sycamores Touring
Caravan Park** ★★★★
Touring and Camping Park
Feoffe Common Lane, Barmby
Moor, York YO42 4HS
T: (01759) 388838
E: sycamores@york.camping.
freeserve.co.uk

BARMSTON
East Riding of Yorkshire
Barmston Beach Holiday Park
★★★
Holiday and Touring Park
Sands Lane, Barmston, Driffield,
East Riding of Yorkshire
YO25 8PJ
T: (01262) 468202
F: (01262) 468670
WH

BEDALE
North Yorkshire
Pembroke Caravan Park
★★★★
Touring and Camping Park
19 Low Street, Leeming Bar,
Northallerton, North Yorkshire
DL7 9BW
T: (01677) 422608 & 422652

BOLTON ABBEY
North Yorkshire
Howgill Lodge ★★★★★
*Holiday, Touring and Camping
Park*
Barden, Bolton Abbey, Skipton,
North Yorkshire BD23 6DJ
T: (01756) 720655
I: www.ukrivernet.co.
uk/stayat/howgill

BRANDESBURTON
East Riding of Yorkshire
Dacre Lakeside Park ★★★★
Touring and Camping Park
New Road, Brandesburton,
Driffield, North Humberside
YO25 8RT
T: (01964) 543704 &
07785 922478
F: (01964) 544040
E: dacresurf@aol.com
I: www.bridlington.
net/accommodation/camp/
dacre/index.html

BRIDLINGTON
East Riding of Yorkshire
Park Estate Caravan Park
★★★★
Holiday and Touring Park
Rose Award
Lime Kiln Lane, Bridlington, East
Riding of Yorkshire YO16 6TG
T: (01262) 673733
F: (01262) 401851
E: 'admin'@park-estates.co.uk
I: park-estates.co.uk

BURTON-IN-LONSDALE
North Yorkshire
Gallaber ★★★★
*Holiday, Touring and Camping
Park*
Gallaber Farm, Burton-in-
Lonsdale, Carnforth, Lancashire
LA6 3LU
T: (015242) 61361

CARLTON
North Yorkshire
Carlton Caravan Park ★★★
*Holiday, Touring and Camping
Park*
Blackwell Ox Inn, Carlton,
Middlesbrough, Cleveland
TS9 7DJ
T: (01642) 712287

CAYTON BAY
North Yorkshire
Cayton Bay Holiday Park
★★★★
Holiday Park
Cayton Bay, Scarborough, North
Yorkshire YO11 3NJ
T: (01723) 583111
F: (01723) 584863
WH

Cliff Farm Caravan Park
★★★★★
Holiday Park
Mill Lane, Cayton Bay,
Scarborough, North Yorkshire
YO11 3NN
T: (01723) 582239 & 583073

CONSTABLE BURTON
North Yorkshire
**Constable Burton Hall Caravan
Park**★★★★★
Touring and Camping Park
Constable Burton, Leyburn,
North Yorkshire DL8 5LJ
T: (01677) 450428
F: (01677) 450622

CROPTON
North Yorkshire
**Spiers House Caravan and
Camping Site**★★★★
Touring and Camping Park
Forestry Commission, Cropton,
Pickering, North Yorkshire
YO18 8ES
T: (01751) 417591
E: fe.holidays@forestry.gov.uk
I: www.forestry.co.uk

FARNHAM
North Yorkshire
**Kingfisher Caravan and
Camping Park** ★★★
*Holiday, Touring and Camping
Park*
Low Moor Lane, Farnham,
Knaresborough, North Yorkshire
HG5 9DQ
T: (01423) 869411
F: (01423) 869411
WH

FILEY
North Yorkshire
Crows Nest Caravan Park
★★★★★
*Holiday, Touring and Camping
Park*
Rose Award
Gristhorpe, Filey, North
Yorkshire YO14 9PS
T: (01723) 582206
F: (01723) 582206

**Filey Brigg Caravan & Country
Park**★★★
Touring and Camping Park
Church Cliff Drive, North Cliff,
Arndale, Filey, North Yorkshire
YO14 0XX
T: (01723) 513852
WH

Orchard Farm Holiday Village
★★★★★
*Holiday, Touring and Camping
Park*
Stonegate, Hunmanby, Filey,
North Yorkshire YO14 0PU
T: (01723) 891582
F: (01723) 891582

Primrose Valley Holiday Park
★★★★
Holiday and Touring Park
Primrose Valley, Filey, North
Yorkshire YO14 9RF
T: (01723) 513771
F: (01723) 513777
WH

FLAMBOROUGH
East Riding of Yorkshire
**Thornwick & Sea Farm Holiday
Centre**★★★★
*Holiday, Touring and Camping
Park*
Flamborough Holidays Ltd,
Flamborough, Bridlington, East
Riding of Yorkshire YO15 1AU
T: (01262) 850369 & 850372
F: (01262) 851550
E: enquiries@thornwickbay.co.
uk
I: www.thornwickbay.co.uk

GARGRAVE
North Yorkshire
Dalesway Caravan Park
★★★★★
Holiday Park
Rose Award
Dale View Bungalow, Marton
Road, Gargrave, Skipton, North
Yorkshire BD23 3NS
T: (01756) 749592
F: (01756) 749592
E: bfrrnda.bdcaravans@
btinternet.com
I: www.ukparks.co.uk/dalesway
WH

GILLING WEST
North Yorkshire
**Hargill House Caravan Club
Site** ★★★★
Touring and Camping Park
Gilling West, Richmond, North
Yorkshire DL10 5LJ
T: (01748) 822734
WH

GLAISDALE
North Yorkshire
Hollins Farm ★
Camping Park
Glaisdale, Whitby, North
Yorkshire YO21 2PZ
T: (01947) 897516

GRISTHORPE BAY
North Yorkshire
Blue Dolphin Holiday Park
★★★
*Holiday, Touring and Camping
Park*
Gristhorpe Bay, Filey, North
Yorkshire YO14 9PU
T: (01723) 515155
F: (01723) 512059
WH

HARDEN
West Yorkshire
Harden & Bingley Caravan Park
★★★★
Holiday and Touring Park
Goit Stock Private Estate, Goit
Stock Lane, Harden, Bingley,
West Yorkshire BD16 1DF
T: (01535) 273810
I: www.ukparks.co.uk/harden

HARROGATE
North Yorkshire
Bilton Park ★★★
*Holiday, Touring and Camping
Park*
Village Farm, Bilton Lane,
Harrogate, North Yorkshire
HG1 4DH
T: (01423) 863121 & 565070
E: tony@bilton-park.swinternet.
co.uk
WH

High Moor Farm Park ★★★★
*Holiday, Touring and Camping
Park*
Skipton Road, Harrogate, North
Yorkshire HG3 2LT
T: (01423) 563637 & 564955
F: (01423) 529449

Ripley Caravan Park ★★★★★
Touring and Camping Park
Ripley, Harrogate, North
Yorkshire HG3 3AU
T: (01423) 770050
F: (01423) 770050

Rudding Holiday Park
★★★★★
*Holiday, Touring and Camping
Park*
Rose Award
Rudding Park, Follifoot,
Harrogate, North Yorkshire
HG3 1JH
T: (01423) 870439
F: (01423) 870859
E: hpreception@rudding-park.
co.uk
I: www.rudding-park.co.uk
WH

Shaws Trailer Park ★★★
*Holiday, Touring and Camping
Park*
Knaresborough Road, Harrogate,
North Yorkshire HG2 7NE
T: (01423) 884432

192

Establishments printed in green have a detailed entry in this guide

Warren Forest Caravan Park
★★★★★
Holiday Park
Warsill, Ripley, Harrogate, North
Yorkshire HG3 3LH
T: (01765) 620683
F: (01765) 620683
WH

HATFIELD
South Yorkshire
Hatfield Water Park ★★★★
Touring Park
Hatfield, Doncaster, South
Yorkshire DN7 6EQ
T: (01302) 841572
F: (01302) 846368

HAWES
North Yorkshire
**Bainbridge Ings Caravan and
Camping Site★★**
*Holiday, Touring and Camping
Park*
Hawes, North Yorkshire
DL8 3NU
T: (01969) 667354
I: www.bainbridge-ings.co.uk

Honeycott Caravan Park ★★★
*Holiday, Touring and Camping
Park*
Ingleton Road, Hawes, North
Yorkshire DL8 3LH
T: (01969) 667310
WH

HELMSLEY
North Yorkshire
**Foxholme Touring Caravan
Park ★★★★★**
Touring and Camping Park
Harome, York YO62 5JG
T: (01439) 770416 & 771696
F: (01439) 771744

**Golden Square Caravan and
Camping Park★★★★★**
Touring and Camping Park
Oswaldkirk, York YO62 5YQ
T: (01439) 788269
F: (01439) 788236
E: barbara@
goldensquarecaravanpark.com
I: www.
goldensquarecaravanpark.com

HIGH BENTHAM
North Yorkshire
Riverside Caravan Park
★★★★
*Holiday, Touring and Camping
Park*
High Bentham, Lancaster
LA2 7HS
T: (015242) 61272 &
07711 587428
F: (015242) 62163

HIGH HAWSKER
North Yorkshire
Seaview Caravan Park
★★★★★
Holiday Park
Rose Award
High Hawsker, Whitby, North
Yorkshire YO22 4LL
T: (01947) 880584
F: (01947) 880590

HOLMFIRTH
West Yorkshire
**Holme Valley Camping and
Caravan Park★★★★**
Touring and Camping Park
Thongsbridge, Holmfirth,
Huddersfield HD7 2TD
T: (01484) 665819
F: (01484) 663870
E: pmpeaker@hotmail.com
I: www.holme-valley.co.uk
WH

HORNSEA
East Riding of Yorkshire
Longbeach Leisure Park
★★★★
*Holiday, Touring and Camping
Park*
South Cliff, Hornsea, East Riding
of Yorkshire HU18 1TL
T: (01964) 532506
F: (01964) 536846
I: www.longbeach-leisure.co.uk

HORSFORTH
West Yorkshire
St Helena's Caravan Site
★★★★
Touring and Camping Park
Wardens Bungalow, Otley Old
Road, Horsforth, Leeds LS18 5HZ
T: (0113) 284 1142

HUMBERSTON
Lincolnshire
Thorpe Park Holiday Centre
★★★
*Holiday, Touring and Camping
Park*
Cleethorpes, North East
Lincolnshire DN36 4HG
T: 0870 2425678
F: (01442) 254956
I: www.british-holidays.co.uk
WH

INGLETON
North Yorkshire
Parkfoot Holiday Homes
★★★★★
Holiday Park
Bentham Road, Ingleton,
Carnforth, Lancashire LA6 3HR
T: (015242) 61833 &
(01253) 890854
F: (015242) 61961

KEARBY WITH NETHERBY
North Yorkshire
Maustin Caravan Park
★★★★★
*Holiday, Touring and Camping
Park*
Kearby With Netherby,
Wetherby, West Yorkshire
LS22 4DA
T: (0113) 288 6234
F: (0113) 288 6234
E: enquiries@maustinpark.
demon.co.uk
I: www.yorkshirenet.co.
uk/accgde/maustin
WH

KILLINGHALL
North Yorkshire
Pinemoor Caravan Park
★★★★
Holiday Park
Burley Bank Road, Killinghall,
Harrogate, North Yorkshire
HG3 2RZ
T: (01423) 503980

LANGTHORPE
North Yorkshire
Old Hall Caravan Park ★★★★
*Holiday, Touring and Camping
Park*
Skelton Road, Langthorpe,
Boroughbridge, York YO51 9BZ
T: (01423) 322130
F: (01423) 322130

LEBBERSTON
North Yorkshire
Lebberston Touring Park
★★★★★
Touring Park
Home Farm, Filey Road,
Lebberston, Scarborough, North
Yorkshire YO11 3PF
T: (01723) 585723

LOFTHOUSE
North Yorkshire
**Studfold Farm Caravan and
Camping Park★★★**
*Holiday, Touring and Camping
Park*
Studfold Farm, Lofthouse,
Harrogate, North Yorkshire
HG3 5SG
T: (01423) 755210

MASHAM
North Yorkshire
**Black Swan Caravan &
Campsite ★★★**
Touring Park
Rear Black Swan Hotel, Fearby,
Ripon, North Yorkshire HG4 4NF
T: (01765) 689477
F: (01765) 689477

NAWTON
North Yorkshire
**Wrens of Ryedale Caravan and
Camp Site★★★★**
Touring and Camping Park
Gale Lane, Nawton, York
YO62 7SD
T: (01439) 771260
F: (01439) 771260

NORTHALLERTON
North Yorkshire
**Otterington Touring Caravan
and Camping Park★★★**
Touring and Camping Park
Station Farm, South Otterington,
Northallerton, North Yorkshire
DL7 9JB
T: (01609) 780263 & 780656

PATRINGTON
East Riding of Yorkshire
**Patrington Haven Leisure Park
Ltd ★★★★**
Holiday Park
Rose Award
Patrington, Hull, East Yorkshire
HU12 0PT
T: (01964) 630071
F: (01964) 631060
E: info@
patringtonhavenleisurepark.co.
uk

PICKERING
North Yorkshire
**Upper Carr Chalet and Touring
Park★★★★★**
*Holiday, Touring and Camping
Park*
Upper Carr Lane, Malton Road,
Black Bull, Pickering, North
Yorkshire YO18 7JP
T: (01751) 473115
F: (01751) 475325
E: green@uppercarr.demon.co.
uk
I: www.upercarr.demon.co.uk
WH

Wayside Caravan Park ★★★★
*Holiday, Touring and Camping
Park*
Wrelton, Pickering, North
Yorkshire YO18 8PG
T: (01751) 472608
F: (01751) 472608
E: waysideparks@talk21.com
I: www.waysideparks.co.uk

POCKLINGTON
East Riding of Yorkshire
South Lea Caravan Park
★★★★
Touring Park
South Lea, The Balk, Pocklington,
York YO42 2NX
T: (01759) 303467

REIGHTON GAP
North Yorkshire
Reighton Sands Holiday Park
★★★
*Holiday, Touring and Camping
Park*
Reighton Gap, Filey, North
Yorkshire YO14 9SJ
T: (01723) 890476
F: (01723) 891043
WH

RICHMOND
North Yorkshire
**Brompton-on-Swale Caravan
and Camping Park★★★★★**
*Holiday, Touring and Camping
Park*
Brompton-on-Swale, Richmond,
North Yorkshire DL10 7EZ
T: (01748) 824629
F: (01748) 826383
E: brompton.caravan@virgin.
net

RIPON
North Yorkshire
River Laver Holiday Park
★★★★★
Holiday and Touring Park
Studley Road, Ripon, North
Yorkshire HG4 2QR
T: (01765) 690508
F: (01765) 690508

**Sleningford Watermill Caravan
and Camping Park★★★★**
Touring and Camping Park
North Stainley, Ripon, North
Yorkshire HG4 3HQ
T: (01765) 635201
WH

Woodhouse Farm Caravan &
Camping Park★★★★
Holiday, Touring and Camping
Park
Winksley, Ripon, North Yorkshire
HG4 3PG
T: (01765) 658309
F: (01765) 658882
E: woodhouse.farm@btinternet.
com
WH

ROECLIFFE
North Yorkshire
Camping & Caravanning Club
Site ★★★★
Touring Park
Bar Lane, Roecliffe, York
YO51 9LS
T: (01423) 322683
I: www.
campingandcaravanningclub.co.
uk

ROOS
East Riding of Yorkshire
Sand-le-Mere Caravan &
Leisure Park ★★★
Holiday, Touring and Camping
Park
Seaside Lane, Tunstall, Roos,
Hull, East Yorkshire HU12 0JQ
T: (01964) 670403 & 0800 068
0407
F: (01964) 671099
E: info@sand-le-mere.co.uk
I: www.sand-le-mere.co.uk

ROUNDHAY
West Yorkshire
Roundhay Park Caravan &
Campsite ★★★
Touring and Camping Park
Elmete Lane, Roundhay, Leeds,
West Yorkshire LS8 2LG
T: (0113) 265 2354
F: (0113) 237 0077

RUDSTON
East Riding of Yorkshire
Thorpe Hall Caravan and
Camping Site★★★★
Touring and Camping Park
Thorpe Hall, Rudston, Driffield,
East Riding of Yorkshire
YO25 4JE
T: (01262) 420393 & 420574
F: (01262) 420588
E: caravansite@thorpehall.co.uk
I: www.thorpehall.co.uk

SALTWICK BAY
North Yorkshire
Whitby Holiday Park ★★★
Holiday, Touring and Camping
Park
Saltwick Bay, Whitby, North
Yorkshire YO22 4JX
T: (01947) 602664

SCARBOROUGH
North Yorkshire
Cayton Village Caravan Park
★★★★
Touring and Camping Park
D16 Mill Lane, Cayton Bay,
Scarborough, North Yorkshire
YO11 3NN
T: (01723) 583171 &
(01904) 624630
WH

Flower of May Holiday Park
★★★★★
Holiday, Touring and Camping
Park
Lebberston Cliff, Scarborough,
North Yorkshire YO11 3NU
T: (01723) 584311
F: (01723) 581361
WH

Jacob's Mount Caravan Park &
Camping Site★★★★★
Holiday, Touring and Camping
Park
Rose Award
Bell Elliott Construction Ltd,
Stepney Road, Scarborough,
North Yorkshire YO12 5NL
T: (01723) 361178
F: (01723) 361178

Scalby Close Camping ★★★★
Touring and Camping Park
Burniston Road, Scarborough,
North Yorkshire YO13 0DA
T: (01723) 365908
E: scalbyclose@hotmail.com
I: www.angelfire.
com/b124/scalbyclose

Scalby Manor Touring Caravan
& Camp Park★★★
Touring and Camping Park
Burniston Road, Scarborough,
North Yorkshire YO13 0DA
T: (01723) 366212
WH

SCOTTON
North Yorkshire
Knaresborough Caravan Club
Site ★★★★
Touring and Camping Park
New Road, Scotton,
Knaresborough, North Yorkshire
HG5 9HH
T: (01423) 860196
WH

SEAMER
North Yorkshire
Arosa Caravan & Camping Park
★★★
Touring and Camping Park
Ratten Row, Seamer,
Scarborough, North Yorkshire
YO12 4QB
T: (01723) 862166
E: neilcherry@
lineonenetarose-seamer
I: www.mywebpage.net/arosa

SHERIFF HUTTON
North Yorkshire
Sheriff Hutton Camping &
Caravanning Club Site★★★★★
Touring and Camping Park
Bracken Hill, Sheriff Hutton,
York YO60 6QG
T: (01347) 878660
I: www.
campingandcaravanningclub.co.
uk

SILSDEN
West Yorkshire
Dales Bank Holiday Park ★★
Touring Park
Low Lane, Silsden, Keighley,
West Yorkshire BD20 9JH
T: (01535) 653321 & 656523
E: m.preston@btclick.com
I: home.btclick.com/rm.preston

SKIPSEA
East Riding of Yorkshire
Far Grange Park Ltd ★★★★★
Holiday, Touring and Camping
Park
Rose Award
Skipsea, Driffield, East Riding of
Yorkshire YO25 8SY
T: (01262) 468293 & 468248
F: (01262) 468648
E: enquiries@fargrangepark.co.
uk
I: www.fargrangepark.co.uk
WH

Skipsea Sands Holiday Village
★★★★
Holiday, Touring and Camping
Park
Rose Award
Mill Lane, Skipsea, Driffield, East
Riding of Yorkshire YO25 8TZ
T: (01262) 468210
F: (01262) 468454

Skirlington Caravan Park
★★★★
Holiday, Touring and Camping
Park
Low Skirlington, Skipsea,
Driffield, East Riding of
Yorkshire YO25 8SY
T: (01262) 468213 & 468466
F: (01262) 468105
E: info@skirlington.com
I: www.skirlington.com

SKIPWITH
North Yorkshire
Oakmere Caravan Park and
Fishery ★★★
Holiday, Touring and Camping
Park
Hill Farm, Skipwith, Selby, North
Yorkshire YO8 5SN
T: (01757) 288910 & 288430
F: (01757) 288910

SKIRLAUGH
East Riding of Yorkshire
Burton Constable Country Park
★★★★
Holiday, Touring and Camping
Park
Old Lodges, Skirlaugh, Hull
HU11 4LN
T: (01964) 562508
F: (01964) 563420

SLINGSBY
North Yorkshire
Robin Hood Caravan &
Camping Park★★★★
Holiday, Touring and Camping
Park
Green Dyke Lane, Slingsby, York,
North Yorkshire YO62 4AP
T: (01653) 628391
F: (01656) 628391
E: rebeccapalmer@tesco.net

Slingsby Camping &
Caravanning Club Site
★★★★★
Touring and Camping Park
Railway Street, Slingsby, York
YO62 4AA
T: (01653) 628335
I: www.
campingandcaravanningclub.co.
uk

SNAINTON
North Yorkshire
Jasmine Caravan Park
★★★★★
Touring and Camping Park
Cross Lane, Snainton,
Scarborough, North Yorkshire
YO13 9BE
T: (01723) 859240
F: (01723) 859240
I: www.touristnetuk.
com/ne/jasmine
WH

STAINFORTH
North Yorkshire
Knight Stainforth Hall Caravan
and Camping Park★★★
Touring and Camping Park
Stainforth, Settle, North
Yorkshire BD24 0DP
T: (01729) 822200 & 823387
E: info@knightstainforth.co.uk
I: www.knightstainforth.co.uk

STAXTON
North Yorkshire
Spring Willows Touring
Caravan Park ★★★★
Touring and Camping Park
Main Road, Staxton,
Scarborough, North Yorkshire
YO12 4SB
T: (01723) 891505
E: enquiries@springwillows.co.
uk
I: www.springwillows.co.uk
WH

STRENSALL
North Yorkshire
Moorside Caravan Park
★★★★★
Touring Park
Moorside Park, Lords Moor Lane,
Strensall, York YO32 5XF
T: (01904) 491208 & 491865

THIRSK
North Yorkshire
Nursery Garden Caravan Park
★★★★
Holiday and Touring Park
Baldersby Park, Rainton, Thirsk,
North Yorkshire YO7 3PG
T: (01845) 577277 &
07979 543337
F: (01845) 577277

Quernhow Caravan & Campsite
★★★
Holiday, Touring and Camping
Park
Great North Road, Sinderby,
Thirsk, North Yorkshire YO7 4LG
T: (01845) 567221

York House Caravan Park
★★★
Holiday, Touring and Camping
Park
Balk, Thirsk, North Yorkshire
YO7 2AQ
T: (01845) 597495
F: (01845) 597495

THORNE
South Yorkshire
Elder House Touring Park
★★★★
Touring Park
Elder House Farm, Sandtoft
Road, Thorne, Doncaster, South
Yorkshire DN8 5TD
T: (01405) 813173

Establishments printed in green have a detailed entry in this guide

THRESHFIELD
North Yorkshire
Long Ashes Park ★★★★
Holiday Park
Warfield Park Homes Ltd, Long
Ashes Park, Threshfield, Skipton,
North Yorkshire BD23 5PN
T: (01756) 752261
F: (01756) 752876
[WH]

Wood Nook Caravan Park
★★★★
*Holiday, Touring and Camping
Park*
Rose Award
Skirethorns, Threshfield, Skipton,
North Yorkshire BD23 5NU
T: (01756) 752412
F: (01756) 752412
E: bookings@wood-nook.
demon.co.uk
I: www.ukparks.co.uk/woodnook

WAKEFIELD
West Yorkshire
**Nostell Priory Holiday Home
Park** ★★★★
*Holiday, Touring and Camping
Park*
Top Park Wood, Nostell,
Wakefield, West Yorkshire
WF4 1QD
T: (01924) 863938
F: (010924) 862226

WHITBY
North Yorkshire
Flask Holiday Home Park
★★★★
Holiday Park
Rose Award
Robin Hoods Bay, Fylingdales,
Whitby, North Yorkshire
YO22 4QH
T: (01947) 880592
F: (01947) 880592
E: flaskinn@aol.com
I: www.ukparks.com.co.uk/flask

**Ladycross Plantation Caravan
Park** ★★★★★
Touring and Camping Park
Egton, Whitby, North Yorkshire
YO21 1UA
T: (01947) 895502

**Middlewood Farm Holiday
Park** ★★★★★
*Holiday, Touring and Camping
Park*
Rose Award
Middlewood Lane, Fylingthorpe,
Whitby, North Yorkshire
YO22 4UF
T: (01947) 880414
F: (01947) 880414
E: info@middlewoodfarm.fsnet.
co.uk
I: www.middlewoodfarm.fsnet.
co.uk
[WH]

Northcliffe Holiday Park
★★★★★
*Holiday, Touring and Camping
Park*
Rose Award
Bottoms Lane, High Hawsker,
Whitby, North Yorkshire
YO22 4LL
T: (01947) 880477
F: (01947) 880972
E: enquiries@northcliffe.com
I: www.northcliffe.com
[WH]

Partridge Nest Farm ★★★
Holiday Park
Eskdaleside, Sleights, Whitby,
North Yorkshire YO22 5ES
T: (01947) 810450 & 811412
F: (01947) 811413
E: pnfarm@aol.com
I: www.tmis.uk.
com/partridge-nest/

**Sandfield House Farm Caravan
Park** ★★★★
Touring and Camping Park
Sandsend Road, Whitby, North
Yorkshire YO21 3SR
T: (01947) 602660
F: (01947) 606274
E: sandfieldw@aol.com
[WH]

WILSTHORPE
East Riding of Yorkshire
South Cliff Caravan Park
★★★★
*Holiday, Touring and Camping
Park*
Wilsthorpe, Bridlington, East
Riding of Yorkshire YO15 3QN
T: (01262) 671051
F: (01262) 605639
[WH]

The White House Caravan Park
★★★★★
Holiday Park
The White House, Wilsthorpe,
Bridlington, North Humberside
YO15 3QN
T: (01262) 673894
F: (01262) 401350

WOMBLETON
North Yorkshire
Wombleton Caravan Park
★★★★★
Touring and Camping Park
Moorfield Lane, Wombleton,
York YO62 7RY
T: (01751) 431684
I: www.europage.co.
uk/wombeltonpark

YORK
North Yorkshire
Alders Caravan Park ★★★★★
Touring Park
Rose Award
Home Farm, Alne, York YO61 1TB
T: (01347) 838722
F: (01347) 838722
[WH]

Allerton Park Caravan Park
★★★★★
*Holiday, Touring and Camping
Park*
Allerton Park, Knaresborough,
North Yorkshire HG5 0SE
T: (01423) 330569
F: (01759) 371377

**Beechwood Grange Caravan
Club Site** ★★★★★
Touring Park
Malton Road, York, YO3 9TH
T: (01904) 424637
[WH]

**Castle Howard Caravan and
Camping Site** ★★★
*Holiday, Touring and Camping
Park*
Coneysthorpe, York YO60 7DD
T: (01653) 648366 & 648316
E: wjmonks1@aol.com
I: www.castlehoward.co.uk

Cawood Holiday Park
★★★★★
*Holiday, Touring and Camping
Park*
Ryther Road, Cawood, Selby,
North Yorkshire YO8 3TT
T: (01757) 268450
F: (01757) 268537
[WH]

Goosewood Caravan Park
★★★★★
Touring Park
Sutton-on-the-Forest, York
YO61 1ET
T: (01347) 810829
[WH]

**Mount Pleasant Holiday Park
and Park Home Estate** ★★★
*Holiday, Touring and Camping
Park*
Acaster Malbis, York YO23 2UA
T: (01904) 707078 & 700088
F: (01904) 700888
E: mountpleasant.york@virgin.
net
I: www.holgates.com

Rawcliffe Manor Caravan Park
★★★★★
Touring and Camping Park
Manor Lane, Shipton Road, York,
YO30 5TZ
T: (01904) 624422
F: (01904) 640845
E: bill.herbert@
rawcliffecaravans.sagehost.co.
uk
I: www.ukparks.co.
uk/rawcliffemanor

**Rowntree Park Caravan Club
Site** ★★★★★
Touring Park
Terry Avenue, York, YO2 1JQ
T: (01904) 658997
[WH]

**The Shieling Adult Caravan
Park** ★★★★
Touring Park
Wheldrake Lane, Crockey Hill,
York YO19 4SH
T: (01904) 659271

Weir Caravan Park ★★★★★
*Holiday, Touring and Camping
Park*
Rose Award
Stamford Bridge, York YO41 1AN
T: (01759) 371377
F: (01759) 371377

HEART OF ENGLAND

ALDERTON
Gloucestershire
**Winchcombe Camping and
Caravanning Site** ★★★★
Touring and Camping Park
Brooklands Farm, Alderton,
Tewkesbury, Gloucestershire
GL20 8NX
T: (01242) 620259
I: www.
campingandcaravanningclub.co.
uk

ALSOP-EN-LE-DALE
Derbyshire
**Rivendale Caravan and Leisure
Park** ★★★
Touring and Camping Park
Buxton Road, Alsop-en-le-Dale,
Ashbourne, Derbyshire DE6 1QU
T: (01335) 310311 & 310441
F: (01335) 310441
E: ALSOPDALE@AOL.COM

AMBERGATE
Derbyshire
**The Firs Farm Caravan and
Camping Park** ★★★★
Touring Park
Crich Lane, Nether Heage,
Ambergate, Belper, Derbyshire
DE56 2JH
T: (01773) 852913

ANDERBY CREEK
Lincolnshire
**Anderby Springs Caravan
Estate** ★★★
Holiday Park
Anderby Creek, Skegness,
Lincolnshire PE24 5XW
T: (01754) 72265 &
(01507) 441333
F: (01507) 441333
[WH]

ASHBOURNE
Derbyshire
Callow Top Holiday Park
★★★★
Holiday, Touring and Camping Park
Callow Top Farm, Buxton Road,
Ashbourne, Derbyshire DE6 2AQ
T: (01335) 344020

ASTON CANTLOW
Warwickshire
Island Meadow Caravan Park
★★★
Holiday, Touring and Camping Park
The Mill House, Aston Cantlow,
Warwickshire B95 6JP
T: (01789) 488273
F: (01789) 488273
I: www.ukparks.co.
uk/islandmeadow

BAKEWELL
Derbyshire
**Chatsworth Park Caravan Club
Site** ★★★★★
Touring Park
Chatsworth, Bakewell,
Derbyshire DE45 1PN
T: (01246) 582226

Greenhills Caravan Park ★★
Holiday, Touring and Camping Park
Crow Hill Lane, Bakewell,
Derbyshire DE45 1PX
T: (01629) 813467 & 813052
F: (01629) 815131

BODYMOOR HEATH
West Midlands
**Kingsbury Water Park
Camping & Caravanning Club
Site**★★★
Touring Park
Bodymoor Heath, Sutton
Coldfield, West Midlands
B76 0DY
T: (01827) 874101

BOSTON
Lincolnshire
Orchard Caravan Park ★★★
Holiday Park
Frampton Lane, Hubberts Bridge,
Boston, Lincolnshire PE20 3QU
T: (01205) 290328
F: (01205) 290247

BREWOOD
Staffordshire
Homestead Caravan Park
★★★★
Holiday Park
Shutt Green Lane, Shutt Green,
Brewood, Stafford ST19 9LX
T: (01902) 851302
F: (01902) 850099

BRIDGNORTH
Shropshire
Park Grange Holidays ★★★★
Holiday Park
Morville, Bridgnorth, Shropshire
WV16 4RN
T: (01746) 714285
F: (01746) 714145
E: parkgrangeholidays@
hotmailcom
I: www.virtual-shropshire.co.
uk/park-grange-holidays

Stanmore Hall Touring Park
★★★★★
Touring and Camping Park
Stourbridge Road, Bridgnorth,
Shropshire WV15 6DT
T: (01746) 761761
F: (01746) 768069
E: stanmore@morris-leisure.co.
uk
I: www.morris-leisure.co.uk
WH 🖧

BRINKLEY
Nottinghamshire
**The Orchards
Rating Applied For**
Brinkley, Southwell NG25 0TP
T: (01636) 812257

BUXTON
Derbyshire
Cottage Farm Caravan Park
★★★
Touring and Camping Park
Blackwell in the Peak, Blackwell,
Buxton, Derbyshire SK17 9TQ
T: (01298) 85330
I: www.ukparks.co.
uk/cottagefarm

Lime Tree Park ★★★★
Holiday, Touring and Camping Park
Rose Award
Dukes Drive, Buxton, Derbyshire
SK17 9RP
T: (01298) 22988
I: www.ukparks.co.uk/limetree

**Newhaven Caravan and
Camping Park**★★★
Holiday, Touring and Camping Park
Newhaven, Buxton, Derbyshire
SK17 0DT
T: (01298) 84300

CASTLE DONINGTON
Leicestershire
**Donington Park Farmhouse
Hotel** ★★★
Touring Park
Melbourne Road, Isley Walton,
Castle Donington, Derby
DE74 2RN
T: (01332) 862409
F: (01332) 862364
E: info@parkfarmhouse.co.uk
I: www.parkfarmhouse.co.uk
WH

CASTLETON
Derbyshire
Losehill Caravan Club Site
★★★★★
Touring Park
Castleton, Hope Valley,
Derbyshire S33 8WB
T: (01433) 620636
WH

CHAPEL ST LEONARDS
Lincolnshire
Robin Hood Leisure Park
★★★★
Holiday and Touring Park
Rose Award
South Road, Chapel St Leonards,
Skegness, Lincolnshire PE24 5TR
T: (01754) 874444
F: (01754) 874648

CHARLESWORTH
Derbyshire
Woodseats Holiday Home Park
★★★
Holiday Park
Woodseats Lane, Charlesworth,
Glossop, Derbyshire SK13 5DR
T: (01457) 863415
F: (01457) 863415
E: woodseatspark@btinternet.
com
I: www.btinternet.
com/§woodseatspark

CHEDDLETON
Staffordshire
Glencote Caravan Park
★★★★
Holiday and Touring Park
Station Road, Cheddleton, Leek,
Staffordshire ST13 7EE
T: (01538) 360745
F: (01538) 361788
WH

CHELTENHAM
Gloucestershire
**Briarfields Caravan and
Camping** ★★★★
Touring and Camping Park
Gloucester Road, Cheltenham,
Gloucestershire GL51 0SX
T: (01242) 235324 &
07836 274440
F: (01242) 235324

CIRENCESTER
Gloucestershire
Mayfield Touring Park ★★★★
Touring Park
Cheltenham Road, Perrotts
Brook, Cirencester,
Gloucestershire GL7 7BH
T: (01285) 831301
F: (01285) 831301
E: jhutson@btclick.com

COLEFORD
Gloucestershire
Forest Holidays ★★
Touring and Camping Park
Reception Site Office,
Bracelands Drive, Christchurch,
Coleford, Gloucestershire
GL16 7NN
T: (01594) 833376

EARDISLAND
Herefordshire
Arrow Bank Caravan Park
★★★★
Holiday and Touring Park
Rose Award
Nun House Farm, Eardisland,
Leominster, Herefordshire
HR6 9BG
T: (01544) 388312
F: (01544) 388312

EAST FIRSBY
Lincolnshire
**Manor Farm Caravan and
Camping Site** ★★
Touring and Camping Park
Manor Farm, East Firsby, Market
Rasen, Lincolnshire LN8 2DB
T: (01673) 878258 &
07850 679189
F: (01673) 878258
E: lincolnshirelanes@tesco.com
WH

ELLESMERE
Shropshire
Fernwood Caravan Park
★★★★
Holiday and Touring Park
Lyneal, Ellesmere, Shropshire
SY12 0QF
T: (01948) 710221
F: (01948) 710324

EVESHAM
Worcestershire
The Ranch Caravan Park
★★★★
Holiday Park
Station Road, Honeybourne,
Evesham, Worcestershire
WR11 5QG
T: (01386) 830744
F: (01386) 833503
I: www.ranch.co.uk

FISHTOFT
Lincolnshire
Pilgrims Way ★★★
Touring Park
Church Green Road, Fishtoft,
Boston, Lincolnshire PE21 0QY
T: (01205) 366646
F: (01205) 366646
E: pilgrimswaylincs@yahoo.com
I: travel.to/pilgrimsway

FLAGG
Derbyshire
Pomeroy Caravan Park ★★
Touring and Camping Park
Street House Farm, Pomeroy,
Flagg, Buxton, Derbyshire
SK17 9QG
T: (01298) 83259

FLEET HARGATE
Lincolnshire
**Delph Bank Touring Caravan &
Camping Park**★★★★
Touring and Camping Park
Main Street, Fleet Hargate,
Holbeach, Spalding, Lincolnshire
PE12 8LL
T: (01406) 422910
F: (01406) 422910
I: www.ukparks.co.uk/delphbank

FOLKINGHAM
Lincolnshire
Low Farm Touring Park ★★★
Touring Park
Spring Lane, Folkingham,
Sleaford, Lincolnshire NG34 0SJ
T: (01529) 497322

GREAT BILLING
Northamptonshire
Billing Aquadrome ★★★
Holiday Park
Crow Lane, Great Billing,
Northampton NN3 9DA
T: (01604) 408181 & 784948
F: (01604) 784412
E: brochure@aquadrome.co.uk
I: www.aquadrome.co.uk

HADFIELD
Derbyshire
**Camping & Caravanning Club
Site** ★★★
Camping Park
Crowden, Hadfield, Glossop,
Derbyshire SK13 1HZ
T: (01457) 866057

HANLEY SWAN
Worcestershire
Camping & Caravanning Club Site ★★★★
Holiday, Touring and Camping Park
Blackmore Camp No. 2, Hanley Swan, Worcester, Worcestershire WR8 0EE
T: (01684) 310280

HAUGHTON
Shropshire
Camping and Caravanning Site Ebury Hill ★★★★
Touring and Camping Park
Ring Bank, Haughton, Telford, Shropshire TF6 6BU
T: (01743) 709334
I: www.campingandcaravanningclub.co.uk

HAYFIELD
Derbyshire
Camping & Caravanning Club Site ★★★
Camping Park
Kinder Road, Hayfield, High Peak, Derbyshire SK22 2LE
T: (01663) 745394

HOPTON HEATH
Shropshire
Ashlea Pools Country Park Holiday Homes ★★★★★
Holiday Park
Rose Award
Ashlea, Hopton Heath, Craven Arms, Shropshire SY7 0QD
T: (01547) 530430
I: www.go2.co.uk/ashleapools

HORNCASTLE
Lincolnshire
Elmhirst Lakes Caravan Park ★★★★
Holiday Park
Elmhirst Road, Horncastle, Lincolnshire LN9 5LU
T: (01507) 527533

INGOLDMELLS
Lincolnshire
Coastfield Caravan Park ★★★
Holiday Park
Vickers Point, Roman Bank, Ingoldmells, Skegness, Lincolnshire PE25 1JU
T: (01754) 872592 & 872356
F: (01754) 874450
WH

Country Meadows Touring Park ★★★
Holiday Park
Anchor Lane, Ingoldmells, Skegness, Lincolnshire PE25 1LZ
T: (01754) 874455 & 873351
F: (01754) 874125
I: geoff@countrymeadows.co.uk

KIRK IRETON
Derbyshire
Blackwall Plantation Caravan Club Site ★★★★★
Touring Park
Kirk Ireton, Ashbourne, Derbyshire DE6 3JL
T: (01335) 370903
WH

KIRKBY-ON-BAIN
Lincolnshire
Camping & Caravanning Club Site ★★★★
Holiday, Touring and Camping Park
Woodhall Spa Club Site, Wellsyke Lane, Kirkby-on-Bain, Woodhall Spa, Lincolnshire LN10 6YU
T: (01526) 352911
I: www.campingandcaravanningclub.co.uk

LADMANLOW
Derbyshire
Grin Low Caravan Club Site ★★★★★
Touring Park
Grin Low Road, Ladmanlow, Buxton, Derbyshire SK17 6UJ
T: (01298) 77735
WH

LEEK
Staffordshire
The Camping and Caravanning Club ★★★★
Touring Park
Blackshaw Grange, Blackshaw Moor, Leek, Staffordshire ST13 8TL
T: (01538) 300285
I: www.campingandcaravanningclub.co.uk

LINCOLN
Lincolnshire
Hartsholme Country Park ★★
Touring Park
Skellingthorpe Road, Lincoln, LN6 0EY
T: (01522) 686264 & 873578
F: (01522) 686264
WH

Hazelwood Tourer Caravan Park ★
Touring and Camping Park
Moor Lane, Thorpe-on-the-Hill, Lincoln, LN6 9OA
T: (01522) 688245 & 688887
F: (01522) 688891
E: hazelwood@dial.pipex.com

LITTLE TARRINGTON
Herefordshire
Little Tarrington Fishing and Leisure ★★★★
Touring and Camping Park
The Millpond, Little Tarrington, Hereford, Herefordshire HR1 4JD
T: (01432) 890243
T: (01432) 890243
E: enquiries @millpond.co.uk
I: www.millpond.co.uk

LUDLOW
Shropshire
Orleton Rise Holiday Home Park ★★★★★
Holiday and Touring Park
Green Lane, Orleton, Ludlow, Shropshire SY8 4JE
T: (01584) 831617
F: (01584) 831617

MABLETHORPE
Lincolnshire
Camping & Caravanning Club Site ★★★★
Touring and Camping Park
Highfield, 120 Church Lane, Mablethorpe, Lincolnshire LN12 2NU
T: (01507) 472374

Golden Sands Holiday Park ★★★
Holiday Park
Quebec Road, Mablethorpe, Lincolnshire LN12 1QJ
T: (01507) 477871
F: (01507) 472066
E: GeneralGoldenSands/Haven/HOL/Rank@Rank
WH

Kirkstead Holiday Park ★★★
Holiday and Touring Park
North Road, Trusthorpe, Mablethorpe, Lincolnshire LN12 2QD
T: (01507) 441483
F: (01507) 443447
E: mark@kirkstead.force9.net
I: www.kirkstead.force9.co.uk

Trusthorpe Springs Leisure Park ★★
Holiday and Touring Park
Trusthorpe Hall, Mile Lane, Mablethorpe, Lincolnshire LN12 2QQ
T: (01507) 441384 & 07711 829908
F: (01507) 443334
E: d.brailsford@ukonline.co.uk

MATLOCK
Derbyshire
Darwin Forest Country Park ★★★★
Holiday and Touring Park
Darley Moor, Two Dales, Matlock, Derbyshire DE4 5LN
T: (01629) 732428
F: (01629) 735015
E: admin@darwinforest.co.uk
I: darwinforest.co.uk
WH

MERIDEN
West Midlands
Somers Wood Caravan and Camping Park ★★★★
Touring and Camping Park
Somers Road, Meriden, Coventry CV7 7PL
T: (01676) 522978
F: (01676) 522978

MINSTERLEY
Shropshire
The Old School Caravan Park ★★★
Touring Park
Shelve, Minsterley, Shrewsbury SY5 0JQ
T: (01588) 650410 & 0777 173 1631

MORDIFORD
Herefordshire
Luck's All Caravan and Camping Park ★★★★
Holiday and Touring Park
Lucksall, Mordiford, Hereford HR1 4LP
T: (01432) 870213
WH

MORETON-IN-MARSH
Gloucestershire
Moreton-in-Marsh Caravan Club Site ★★★★★
Touring Park
Bourton Road, Moreton-in-Marsh, Gloucestershire GL56 0BT
T: (01608) 650519
WH

NEWARK
Nottinghamshire
Milestone Caravan Park ★★★★★
Touring Park
Milestone House, North Road, Cromwell, Newark, Nottinghamshire NG23 6JE
T: (01636) 821244 & 822256
E: milestone.cp@pgen.net

NORTON
Gloucestershire
Red Lion Camping and Caravan Park ★★
Touring and Camping Park
Wainlode Hill, Norton, Gloucester GL2 9LW
T: (01452) 730251

OLLERTON
Nottinghamshire
The Shannon Caravan & Camping Park ★★★★
Touring and Camping Park
Wellow Road, Ollerton, Newark, Nottinghamshire NG24 1DW
T: (01636) 703820 & (01623) 836193

PETERCHURCH
Herefordshire
Poston Mill Park ★★★★★
Holiday and Touring Park
Poston Mill Park, Golden Valley, Peterchurch, Hereford HR2 0SF
T: (01981) 550225
F: (01981) 550885
E: Enquiries@poston-mill.co.uk
I: www.ukparks.co.uk/postonmill
WH

ROMSLEY
Worcestershire
Camping & Caravanning Club Site, Clent Hills ★★★★
Touring Park
Fieldhouse Lane, Romsley, Halesowen, West Midlands B62 0NH
T: (01562) 710015
I: www.campingandcaravanningclub.co.uk

ROSS-ON-WYE
Herefordshire
Broadmeadow Caravan Park ★★★★★
Holiday, Touring and Camping Park
Broadmeadows, Ross-on-Wye, Herefordshire HR9 7BH
T: (01989) 768076
F: (01989) 566030

RUGELEY
Staffordshire
Camping and Caravanning Club Site, Cannock Chase
★★★★
Touring and Camping Park
Old Youth Hostel, Wandon,
Rugeley, Staffordshire
WS15 1QW
T: (01889) 582166

Silvertrees Caravan Park
★★★★
Holiday and Touring Park
Rose Award
Stafford Brook Road, Penkridge
Bank, Rugeley, Staffordshire
WS15 2TX
T: (01889) 582185
F: (01889) 582185
I: www.ukparks.co.uk/silvertrees
WH

SHOBDON
Herefordshire
Pearl Lake Leisure Park Ltd
★★★★
Holiday and Touring Park
Shobdon, Leominster,
Herefordshire HR6 9NQ
T: (01568) 708326
F: (01568) 708408
E: enquiries@pearl-lake.
freeserve.co.uk

SHREWSBURY
Shropshire
Beaconsfield Farm Caravan Park★★★★★
Holiday and Touring Park
Battlefield, Shrewsbury, SY4 4AA
T: (01939) 210370 & 210399
F: (01939) 210349
I: members.aol.com/beacfield

Oxon Hall Touring Park
★★★★★
Holiday and Touring Park
Welshpool Road, Bicton Heath,
Shrewsbury, SY3 5FB
T: (01743) 340868
E: oxon@morris-leisure.co.uk
I: www.morris-leisure.co.uk

SKEGNESS
Lincolnshire
Manor Farm Caravan Park ★★
Touring and Camping Park
Sea Road, Anderby, Skegness,
Lincolnshire PE24 5YB
T: (01507) 490372
WH

Richmond Holiday Centre
★★★
Holiday Park
Richmond Drive, Skegness,
Lincolnshire PE25 3TQ
T: (01754) 762097
F: (01754) 765631
E: richmond.leisure1@virgin.net
I: freespace.virgin.net/richmond.
leisure1

SOUTH CERNEY
Gloucestershire
Cotswold Hoburne Limited
★★★★
Holiday, Touring and Camping Park
Broadway Lane, South Cerney,
Cirencester, Gloucestershire
GL7 5UQ
T: (01285) 860216
F: (01285) 862106
I: www.hoburne.co.uk

STOKE-ON-TRENT
Staffordshire
The Star Caravan and Camping Park★★★
Holiday, Touring and Camping Park
Star Road, Cotton, Oakamoor,
Stoke-on-Trent, ST10 3BN
T: (01538) 702256 & 702564

STONEY MIDDLETON
Derbyshire
Peakland Caravans ★★★
Holiday Park
High Street, Stoney Middleton,
Hope Valley S32 4TL
T: (01433) 631414
E: peakland2000@aol.com

STOURPORT-ON-SEVERN
Worcestershire
Lickhill Manor Caravan Park
★★★★★
Holiday, Touring and Camping Park
Lickhill Road, Stourport-on-
Severn, Worcestershire
DY13 8RL
T: (01299) 822024 & 871041
F: (01299) 824998
E: excellent@lickhillmanor.co.uk
I: www.lickhillmanor.co.uk
WH

Lincomb Lock Caravan Park
★★★★
Holiday and Touring Park
Worcester Road, Titton,
Stourport-on-Severn,
Worcestershire DY13 9QR
T: (01299) 823836 & 822024
F: (01299) 827527
WH

STRATFORD-UPON-AVON
Warwickshire
Dodwell Park ★★★★
Touring and Camping Park
Evesham Rd, (B439), Stratford-
upon-Avon, Warwickshire
CV37 9ST
T: (01789) 204957
F: (01926) 336476

SUTTON ST EDMUND
Lincolnshire
Orchard View Caravan & Camping Park★★★
Holiday, Touring and Camping Park
102 Broadgate, Sutton St
Edmund, Spalding, Lincolnshire
PE12 0LT
T: (01945) 700482

SUTTON ST JAMES
Lincolnshire
Foreman's Bridge Caravan Park
★★★★
Holiday, Touring and Camping Park
Sutton Road, Sutton St James,
Spalding, Lincolnshire PE12 0HU
T: (01945) 440346 &
07885 788857
F: (01945) 440346
E: FOREMANSBRIDGE@
BTINTERNET.COM
I: www.foremans-bridge.co.uk
WH

SWINDERBY
Lincolnshire
Oakhill Leisure ★★★
Touring and Camping Park
Oakhill Farm, Butt Lane, Thurlby
Moor, Swinderby, Lincoln
LN6 9QG
T: (01522) 868771
F: (01522) 868771

SYMONDS YAT WEST
Herefordshire
Doward Park Camp Site ★★★
Camping Park
Great Doward, Symonds Yat
West, Ross-on-Wye,
Herefordshire HR9 6BP
T: (01600) 890438

Sterretts Caravan Park ★★★
Holiday and Touring Park
Symonds Yat West, Ross-on-
Wye, Herefordshire HR9 6BY
T: (01594) 832888 & 833162

Symonds Yat Camping and Caravan Park Ltd.★★
Touring Park
Premier Leisure Park, Symonds
Yat West, Ross-on-Wye,
Herefordshire HR9 6BY
T: (01600) 890883 & 891069
F: (01600) 890883

SYWELL
Northamptonshire
Overstone Lakes Caravan Park Ltd ★★
Holiday Park
Ecton Lane, Sywell,
Northampton NN6 0BD
T: (01604) 645255
F: (01604) 645979

TANSLEY
Derbyshire
Packhorse Farm Bungalow
★★★
Touring Park
Tansley, Matlock, Derbyshire
DE4 5LF
T: (01629) 582781

TELFORD
Shropshire
Severn Gorge Park ★★★★
Touring and Camping Park
Bridgnorth Road, Tweedale,
Telford, Shropshire TF7 4JB
T: (01952) 684789
F: (01952) 684789
WH

TEVERSAL
Nottinghamshire
Shardaroba Caravan Park
★★★★
Touring and Camping Park
Shardaroba, Silverhill Lane,
Teversal, Sutton in Ashfield,
Nottinghamshire NG17 3JJ
T: (01623) 551838 &
07940 936712
F: (01623) 551838
E: stay@shardaroba.co.uk
I: www.shardaroba.co.uk

TEWKESBURY
Gloucestershire
Tewkesbury Abbey Caravan Club Site★★★★
Touring Park
Gander Lane, Tewkesbury,
Gloucestershire GL20 5PG
T: (01684) 294035
WH

TRENTHAM
Staffordshire
Trentham Gardens Caravan Park ★★
Touring Park
Stone Road, Trentham, Stoke-
on-Trent, Staffordshire ST4 8AX
T: (01782) 657341 &
07966 247393
F: (01782) 644536
E: Enquiry@trenthamgardens.
co.uk
I: Trenthamgardens.co.uk

TRUSTHORPE
Lincolnshire
Sutton Springs Holiday Estate
★★★★
Holiday Park
Sutton Road, Trusthorpe,
Mablethorpe, Lincolnshire
LN12 2PZ
T: (01507) 441333 &
07774 829908
F: 07711 443334
E: d.brailsford@ukonline.co.uk

TUXFORD
Nottinghamshire
Greenacres Touring Park ★★★
Holiday and Touring Park
Lincoln Road, Tuxford, Newark,
Nottinghamshire NG22 0JN
T: (01777) 870264
F: (01777) 872512
E: bailey-security@freezone.co.
uk
I: www.freezone.co.
uk/bailey-security/

UTTOXETER
Staffordshire
Uttoxeter Racecourse Caravan Club Site★★★
Touring Park
Uttoxeter Racecourse, Wood
Lane, Uttoxeter, Staffordshire
ST14 8BD
T: (01889) 564172
WH

WATERHOUSES
Staffordshire
The Cross Inn Caravan Park
★★
Holiday, Touring and Camping Park
Cauldon Low, Waterhouses,
Stoke-on-Trent ST10 3EX
T: (01538) 308338 & 308767
F: (01538) 308767
E: adrian-weaver@hotmail.com
I: www.crossinn.co.uk

WEM
Shropshire
Lower Lacon Caravan Park ★★
Holiday, Touring and Camping Park
Wem, Shrewsbury SY4 5RP
T: (01939) 232376
F: (01939) 233606
WH

WHATSTANDWELL
Derbyshire
Birchwood Farm Caravan Park
★★
Holiday, Touring and Camping Park
Wirksworth Road,
Whatstandwell, Matlock,
Derbyshire DE4 5HS
T: (01629) 822280
F: (01629) 822280

Merebrook Caravan Park
★★★
Touring and Camping Park
Derby Road, Whatstandwell,
Derbyshire DE4 5HH
T: (01773) 852154 & 857010

WICHENFORD
Worcestershire
The Coppice Leisure Park
★★★★
Holiday Park
Ockeridge Wood, Wichenford,
Worcester WR6 6YP
T: (01886) 888305 &
07774 737106

WOLVERLEY
Worcestershire
**Camping and Caravanning
Club Site** ★★★★
Touring Park
Brown Westhead Park,
Wolverley, Kidderminster,
Worcestershire DY10 3PX
T: (01562) 850909

WOODHALL SPA
Lincolnshire
Bainland Country Park Ltd
★★★★
Holiday and Touring Park
Rose Award
Horncastle Road, Woodhall Spa,
Lincolnshire LN10 6UX
T: (01526) 352903 & 353572
F: (01526) 353730
E: bookings@bainland.com
I: www.bainland.com

**Jubilee Park Camping &
Caravan Park**★★★
Touring and Camping Park
Stixwould Road, Woodhall Spa,
Lincolnshire LN10 6SP
T: (01526) 352448
I: www.skegness-resort.co.uk

WORKSOP
Nottinghamshire
**Camping & Caravanning Club
Site** ★★★
Touring Park
The Walled Garden, Clumber
Park, Worksop, Nottinghamshire
S80 3BD
T: (01909) 482303

**Clumber Park Caravan Club
Site** ★★★★
Touring Park
Lime Tree Avenue, Clumber Park,
Worksop, Nottinghamshire
S80 3AE
T: (01909) 484758
WH

Riverside Caravan Park
★★★★
Touring Park
Worksop Cricket Club, Central
Avenue, Worksop,
Nottinghamshire S80 1ER
T: (01909) 474118

WYRE PIDDLE
Worcestershire
Rivermead Holiday Home Park
★★★★★
Holiday Park
Church Street, Wyre Piddle,
Pershore, Worcestershire
WR10 2JD
T: (01386) 555566 & 561250

WYTHALL
Worcestershire
Chapel Lane Caravan Club Site
★★★★★
Touring Park
Wythall, Birmingham B47 6JX
T: (01564) 826483
WH

YARWELL
Northamptonshire
Yarwell Mill Caravan Park ★★
Holiday Park
Yarwell, Peterborough PE8 6PS
T: (01780) 782344 & 782247
F: (01708) 221860

YOULGREAVE
Derbyshire
**Camping & Caravanning Club
Site** ★★★
Touring and Camping Park
c/o Hopping Farm, Youlgreave,
Bakewell, Derbyshire DE45 1NA
T: (01629) 636555

EAST OF ENGLAND

ALDEBY
Norfolk
Waveney Lodge Caravan Site
★★★
Touring Park
Elms Road, Aldeby, Beccles,
Suffolk NR34 0EJ
T: (01502) 677445
F: (01502) 677445
E: waveneylodge25@hotmail.com

ASHILL
Norfolk
Brick Kiln Farm ★★★★
Touring and Camping Park
Swaffham Road, Ashill, Thetford,
Norfolk IP25 7BT
T: (01760) 441300
E: brick.kiln@btclick.com
I: www.home.btclick.com/brick.kiln
WH

ATTLEBOROUGH
Norfolk
Oak Tree Caravan Park ★★★★
Touring Park
Norwich Road, Attleborough,
Norfolk NR17 2JX
T: (01953) 455565
F: (01953) 455565
E: oaktree.cp@virgin.net

BACTON-ON-SEA
Norfolk
Cable Gap Caravan Park
★★★★★
Holiday Park
Rose Award
Coast Road, Bacton-on-Sea,
Norwich NR12 0EW
T: (01692) 650667 &
0800 0686870
F: (01692) 651388
E: cablegap@freenet.co.uk
WH

BANHAM
Norfolk
**Applewood Caravan and
Camping Park** ★★★★
Touring and Camping Park
Banham Zoo, The Grove,
Banham, Norwich NR16 2HE
T: (01953) 888370
F: (01953) 887384
WH

BAWBURGH
Norfolk
**Norfolk Showground Caravan
Club Site**★★★★
Holiday Park
Royal Norfolk Showground,
Long Lane, Bawburgh, Norwich
NR9 3LX
T: (01603) 742708

BELTON
Norfolk
Wild Duck Holiday Park ★★★
Holiday Park
Howards Common, Belton,
Great Yarmouth, Norfolk
NR31 9NE
T: (01493) 780268
F: (01493) 782308

BENHALL
Suffolk
**Whitearch (Touring Caravan)
Park** ★★★
Touring Park
Main Road, Benhall,
Saxmundham, Suffolk IP17 1NA
T: (01728) 604646 & 603773

BLAKENEY
Norfolk
Friary Farm Caravan Park
★★★★
Holiday Park
Cley Road, Blakeney, Holt,
Norfolk NR25 7NW
T: (01263) 740393
WH

BRENTWOOD
Essex
**Camping and Caravanning
Club Site Kelvedon Hatch Site**
★★★
Touring and Camping Park
Warren Lane, Doddinghurst,
Brentwood, Essex CM15 0JG
T: (01277) 372773
I: www.campingandcaravanningclub.co.uk

BUNGAY
Suffolk
Outney Meadow Caravan Park
★★★
Touring and Camping Park
Outney Meadow, Bungay,
Suffolk NR35 1HG
T: (01986) 892338
F: (01986) 896627
WH

BURGH CASTLE
Norfolk
**Burgh Castle Marina and
Caravan Park**★★★
Holiday, Touring and Camping Park
Butt Lane, Burgh Castle, Great
Yarmouth, Norfolk NR31 9PZ
T: (01493) 780331
F: (01493) 780163
E: rdw_chesham@compuserve.com

Cherry Tree Holiday Park
★★★★
Holiday and Touring Park
Mill Road, Burgh Castle, Great
Yarmouth, Norfolk NR31 9QR
T: (01493) 780229 & 780024
F: (01493) 780457
E: admin_cherrytree@rank.com

Kingfisher Holiday Park
★★★★
Holiday Park
Butt Lane, Burgh Castle, Great
Yarmouth, Norfolk NR31 9PY
T: (01493) 781412 & 728990
F: (01493) 780039
E: kingfisher@freezone.co.uk
I: www.ukparks.
uk/kingfisherholidaypark
WH

Stanford Park ★★★
Touring and Camping Park
Weirs Drove, Burwell, Cambridge
CB5 0BP
T: (01638) 741547 &
07802 439997

Caister Beach Holiday Park
★★★★★
Holiday Park
Rose Award
Branford Road, Caister-on-Sea,
Great Yarmouth, Norfolk
NR30 5NE
T: (01493) 720278
F: (01493) 728947
WH

Caister Holiday Centre ★★★
Holiday Park
Ormesby Road, Caister-on-Sea,
Great Yarmouth, Norfolk
NR30 5NQ
T: (01493) 728931
F: (01493) 722016
WH

Elm Beach Caravan Park
★★★★
Holiday Park
Manor Road, Caister-on-Sea,
Great Yarmouth, Norfolk
NR30 5HG
T: (01493) 721630 &
0500 400462
F: (01493) 721630
E: elmbch@bohemian.freeserve.
co.uk

Old Hall Leisure Park ★★★★
Holiday and Touring Park
High Street, Caister-on-Sea,
Great Yarmouth, Norfolk
NR30 5JL
T: (01493) 720400
F: (01493) 720261
E: oldhall.caister@virgin.net
I: www.norfolk-holidays.co.uk

Wakefield Court Holidays
★★★★
Holiday Park
Beachside, Rottenstone Lane,
California, Great Yarmouth,
Norfolk NR29 3QT
T: (01493) 730279 &
07879 416172
F: (01493) 730279
E: info@beachside-holidays.co.
uk
I: www.beachside-holidays.co.uk
WH

Highfield Farm Touring Park
★★★★★
Touring and Camping Park
Long Road, Comberton,
Cambridge CB3 7DG
T: (01223) 262308
F: (01223) 262308
WH

**Cherry Hinton Caravan Club
Site** ★★★★★
Touring and Camping Park
Lime Kiln Road, Cherry Hinton,
Cambridge CB1 8NQ
T: (01223) 244088
WH

Highfield Holiday Park ★★
Holiday and Touring Park
London Road, Clacton-on-Sea,
Essex CO16 9QY
T: (01255) 424244
F: (01255) 689805
E: highfield'leisuregb.co.uk
WH

Valley Farm Caravan Park
★★★
Holiday and Touring Park
Valley Farm Camping Ground
Ltd, Valley Road, Clacton-on-
Sea, Essex CO15 6LY
T: (01255) 422484
F: (01255) 422484
E: valley.farm@virgin.net
I: www.valleyfarm.co.uk

Clippesby Holidays ★★★★
Holiday Park
Clippesby, Great Yarmouth,
Norfolk NR29 3BL
T: (01493) 367800
F: (01493) 367809
E: holidays@clippesby.ndirect.
co.uk
I: www.clippesby.ndirect.co.uk
WH

**Colchester Camping and
Caravanning Park** ★★★★
Touring and Camping Park
Cymbeline Way, Lexden,
Colchester, CO3 4AG
T: (01206) 545551
F: (01206) 710443
E: enquiries@
colchestercamping.co.uk
I: www.colchestercamping.co.uk

Broadland Sands Holiday Park
★★★
Holiday Park
Coast Road, Corton, Lowestoft,
Suffolk NR32 5LG
T: (01502) 730939
F: (01502) 730071
I: www.broadlandsands.co.
uk/holidaypark.htm

Corton Adult Holiday Village
★★★★
Holiday Park
Corton, Lowestoft, Suffolk
NR32 5HR
T: (01502) 730226
F: (01502) 732334

Forest Park Caravan Site ★★★
Holiday Park
Northrepps Road, Northrepps,
Cromer, Norfolk NR27 0JR
T: (01263) 513290
F: (01263) 511992
E: forestpark@netcom.co.uk
I: www.forest-park.co.uk
WH

Seacroft Caravan Park ★★★★
Touring and Camping Park
Runton Road, Cromer, Norfolk
NR27 9NJ
T: (01263) 511722
F: (01263) 511512
E: seacroft@lc24net
I: www.seacroftcamping.co.uk

Cliff House (Dunwich) ★★★★
Holiday Park
Minsmere Road, Dunwich,
Saxmundham, Suffolk IP17 3DQ
T: (01728) 648282
F: (01728) 648282
WH

The Grange Country Park
★★★★
*Holiday, Touring and Camping
Park*
Rose Award
East End, East Bergholt,
Colchester, Suffolk CO7 6UX
T: (01206) 298567 & 298912
F: (01206) 298770

The Dower House Touring Park
★★★★
Touring and Camping Park
East Harling, Norwich NR16 2SE
T: (01953) 717314
F: (01953) 717843
E: info@dowerhouse.co.uk
I: www.dowerhouse.co.uk/

Cosway Holiday Home Park
★★★★
Holiday Park
Fen Lane, East Mersea,
Colchester CO5 8UA
T: (01206) 383252
F: (01206) 385524
E: comersea@aol.com
I: www.cosways.co.uk

**Fen Farm Caravan and
Camping Site** ★★★
Touring and Camping Park
East Mersea, Colchester
CO5 8UA
T: (01206) 383275
F: (01206) 386316

Woodhill Park ★★★★
*Holiday, Touring and Camping
Park*
Rose Award
Cromer Road, East Runton,
Cromer, Norfolk NR27 9PX
T: (01263) 512242
F: (01263) 515326
E: info@woodhill-park.com
I: www.woodhill-park.com

Fakenham Racecourse ★★★
Touring Park
The Racecourse, Fakenham,
Norfolk NR21 7NY
T: (01328) 862388
F: (01328) 855908
WH

**The Old Brick Kilns Caravan
and Camping Park** ★★★★★
Touring and Camping Park
Little Barney Lane, Barney,
Fakenham, Norfolk NR21 0NL
T: (01328) 878305
F: (01328) 878948
E: enquire@old-brick-kilns.co.
uk
I: www.old-brick-kilns.co.uk
WH 🏠

The Paddocks ★★★★★
Touring Park
Little Barney, Fakenham, Norfolk
NR21 0NL
T: (01328) 878803
F: (01328) 878802
E: gent.paddocks@btinternet.
com

Felixstowe Beach Holiday Park
★★★
Holiday Park
Walton Avenue, Felixstowe,
Suffolk IP11 2HA
T: (01394) 283393
F: (01394) 671315

Peewit Caravan Park ★★★★
Touring and Camping Park
Walton Avenue, Felixstowe,
Suffolk IP11 2HB
T: (01394) 284511
F: (01473) 659824

Suffolk Sands Holiday Park
★★★
*Holiday, Touring and Camping
Park*
Carr Road, Languard Common,
Felixstowe, Suffolk IP11 2TS
T: (01394) 273434
F: (01394) 671269

**Crystal Lakes Touring Caravan
Park** ★★
Touring and Camping Park
Fenstanton, Huntingdon,
Cambridgeshire PE18 9HU
T: (01480) 497728 &
07976 840765

FOXHALL
Suffolk

Low House Touring Caravan Centre ★★★
Holiday and Camping Park
Low House, Bucklesham Road,
Foxhall, Ipswich IP10 0AU
T: (01473) 659437
F: (01473) 659880
E: john.e.booth@talk21.com

GOLDHANGER
Essex

Osea Leisure Park ★★★
Holiday Park
Goldhanger, Maldon, Essex
CM9 4SA
T: (01621) 854695
F: (01621) 854695
I: jamie@osea.freeserve.co.uk

GRAFHAM
Cambridgeshire

Old Manor Caravan Park ★★★★
Touring and Camping Park
Church Road, Grafham,
Huntingdon, Cambridgeshire
PE18 0BB
T: (01480) 810264
F: (01480) 819099
E: camping@old-manor.
freeserve.co.uk
I: www.old-manor.freeserve.co.
uk

GREAT SHELFORD
Cambridgeshire

Camping and Caravanning Club Site Cambridge★★★★
Touring Park
19 Cabbage Moor, Great
Shelford, Cambridge CB2 5NB
T: (01223) 841185
I: www.
campingandcaravanningclub.co.
uk

GREAT YARMOUTH
Norfolk

The Grange Touring Park ★★★★
Touring Park
Ormesby St Margaret, Great
Yarmouth, Norfolk NR29 3QG
T: (01493) 730306 & 730023
F: (01493) 730188
E: john.groat@virgin.net

Grasmere Caravan Park (T.B.) ★★★
Holiday and Touring Park
Bultitudes Loke, Yarmouth Road,
Caister-on-Sea, Great Yarmouth,
Norfolk NR30 5DH
T: (01493) 720382

Great Yarmouth Caravan Club Site ★★★★
Touring Park
Great Yarmouth Racecourse,
Jellicoe Road, Great Yarmouth,
Norfolk NR30 4AU
T: (01493) 855223
WH

Hopton Holiday Village ★★★★
Holiday Park
Rose Award
Warren Lane, Hopton-on-Sea,
Great Yarmouth, Norfolk
NR31 9BW
T: 0870 2425678
F: (01442) 254956
WH

Liffens Holiday Park ★★★★
Holiday Park
Burgh Castle, Great Yarmouth,
Norfolk NR31 9QB
T: (01493) 780357
T: (01493) 782383
WH

Liffens Welcome Holiday Centre ★★★
Holiday Park
Butt Lane, Burgh Castle, Great
Yarmouth, Norfolk NR31 9PY
T: (01493) 780481
F: (01493) 781627

Seashore Holiday Park ★★★
Holiday Park
North Denes, Great Yarmouth,
Norfolk NR30 4HG
T: (01493) 851131
F: (01493) 332267
WH

Summerfields Holiday Village ★★★★
Holiday Park
Rose Award
Beach Road, Scratby, Great
Yarmouth, Norfolk NR29 3NW
T: (01493) 731419 & 733733
F: (01493) 730292
WH

Vauxhall Holiday Park ★★★★
Holiday Park
Rose Award
Acle New Road, Great Yarmouth,
Norfolk NR30 1TB
T: (01493) 857231
F: (01493) 331122
E: vauxhall.holidays@virginnet
I: www.vauxhall-holiday-park.
co.uk
WH

HEACHAM
Norfolk

Heacham Beach Holiday Park ★★★
Holiday Park
South Beach Road, Heacham,
King's Lynn, Norfolk PE31 7BD
T: (01485) 570270
F: (01485) 572055
WH

HEMINGFORD ABBOTS
Cambridgeshire

Quiet Waters Caravan Park ★★★★
Holiday, Touring and Camping Park
Hemingford Abbots,
Huntingdon, Cambridgeshire
PE18 9AJ
T: (01480) 463405
F: (01480) 463405

HEMSBY
Norfolk

Newport Caravan Park (Norfolk) Ltd★★★
Holiday, Touring and Camping Park
Newport Road, Hemsby, Great
Yarmouth, Norfolk NR29 4NW
T: (01493) 730405
F: (01493) 733122
E: enquiries@
newportcaravanpark.co.uk
I: www.newportcaravanpark.co.
uk

HERTFORD
Hertfordshire

Camping and Caravanning Club Site Hertford★★★★
Touring and Camping Park
Mangrove Road, Hertford,
SG13 8QF
T: (01992) 586696
I: www.
campingandcaravanningclub.co.
uk

HEYBRIDGE
Essex

Barrow Marsh Caravan and Chalet Park★
Holiday, Touring and Camping Park
Goldhanger Road, Heybridge,
Maldon, Essex CM9 4RA
T: (01621) 852859

HODDESDON
Hertfordshire

Lee Valley Caravan Park ★★★★
Touring and Camping Park
Essex Road, Hoddesdon,
Hertfordshire EN11 0AS
T: (01992) 462090
F: (01992) 462090
I: caravanpark@leevalleypark.
org.uk
WH

HOLLESLEY
Suffolk

The Sandlings Centre ★★
Holiday, Touring and Camping Park
Lodge Road, Hollesley,
Woodbridge, Suffolk IP12 3RR
T: (01394) 411202 & 411422
F: (01394) 411422
E: sales@sandlings.co.uk
I: www.sandlings.co.uk

HOLME NEXT THE SEA
Norfolk

Sunnymead Holiday Park ★★★★
Holiday Park
Rose Award
Sunnymead Corner, 2 Kirkgate
Street, Holme next the Sea,
Hunstanton, Norfolk PE36 6LH
T: (01485) 525381 & 571838
F: (01485) 525381
E: sunnymeadholpark@aol.com
I: www.sunnymead-holidays.co.
uk

HUNSTANTON
Norfolk

Manor Park Holiday Village ★★★
Holiday and Touring Park
Manor Road, Hunstanton,
Norfolk PE36 5AZ
T: (01485) 532300
T: (01485) 533881
E: info@manor-park.co.uk
I: www.manor-park.co.uk

Searles Holiday Centre ★★★★
Holiday, Touring and Camping Park
Rose Award
South Beach, Hunstanton,
Norfolk PE36 5BB
T: (01485) 534211
F: (01485) 533815
E: bookings@searles.co.uk
I: www.searles.co.uk.
WH

IPSWICH
Suffolk

Orwell Meadows Leisure Park ★★★★
Holiday, Touring and Camping Park
Priory Lane, Nacton Road,
Ipswich, IP10 0JS
T: (01473) 726666
T: (01473) 721441
E: recept@orwellmeadows.co.uk

JAYWICK
Essex

Tower Holiday Park ★★★
Holiday, Touring and Camping Park
Jaywick, Clacton-on-Sea, Essex
CO15 2LF
T: (01255) 820372
F: (01255) 820060
WH

KESSINGLAND
Suffolk

Camping and Caravanning Club ★★★★
Touring and Camping Park
Suffolk Wildlife Park, Whites
Lane, Kessingland, Lowestoft,
Suffolk NR33 7SL
T: (01502) 742040
I: www.
campingandcaravanningclub.co.
uk

Heathland Beach Caravan Park ★★★★
Holiday, Touring and Camping Park
Rose Award
London Road, Kessingland,
Lowestoft, Suffolk NR33 7PJ
T: (01502) 740337
F: (01502) 742355
E: heathlandbeach@btinternet.
com
I: www.heathlandbeach.co.uk
WH

Kessingland Beach Holiday Village★★★
Holiday, Touring and Camping Park
Kessingland Beach, Beach Road,
Kessingland, Lowestoft, Suffolk
NR33 7RN
T: (01502) 740636
F: (01502) 740907

KING'S LYNN
Norfolk

Bank Farm Caravan Park ★★★
Touring Park
Bank Farm, Fallow Pipe Road,
Saddle Bow, King's Lynn, Norfolk
PE34 3AS
T: (01553) 617305
F: (01553) 617648

LITTLE CORNARD
Suffolk

Willowmere Caravan Park ★★★
Touring and Camping Park
Bures Road, Little Cornard,
Sudbury, Suffolk CO10 0NN
T: (01787) 375559
F: (01787) 375559

LOWESTOFT
Suffolk
Beach Farm Residential and Holiday Park Limited★★★
Holiday, Touring and Camping Park
1 Arbor Lane, Pakefield,
Lowestoft, Suffolk NR33 7BD
T: (01502) 572794 & 519398
F: (01502) 537460
E: beachfarmpark@aol.com
I: www.beachfarmpark.co.uk
WH

Gunton Hall Classic Resort ★★★★
Holiday Park
Gunton Avenue, Gunton,
Lowestoft, Suffolk NR32 5DF
T: (01502) 730288
F: (01502) 732319

MARCH
Cambridgeshire
Floods Ferry Touring Park ★★
Touring and Camping Park
Staffurths Bridge, Floods Ferry
Road, March, Cambridgeshire
PE15 0YP
T: (01354) 677302
WH

MERSEA ISLAND
Essex
Waldegraves Holiday Park ★★★
Holiday, Touring and Camping Park
Mersea Island, Colchester, Essex
CO5 8SE
T: (01206) 382898
F: (01206) 385359
E: holidays@waldegraves.co.uk
I: www.waldegraves.co.uk
WH

MUNDESLEY
Norfolk
Sandy Gulls Caravan Park ★★
Holiday and Touring Park
Cromer Road, Mundesley,
Norwich NR11 8DF
T: (01263) 720513
WH

MUTFORD
Suffolk
Beulah Hall Caravan Park ★★★
Touring and Camping Park
Beulah Hall, Dairy Lane,
Mutford, Beccles, Suffolk
NR34 7QJ
T: (01502) 476609
F: (01502) 476453
E: beulah.hall@fsmail.net

NEWMARKET
Suffolk
Camping and Caravanning Club Site ★★
Touring Park
Rowley Mile Racecourse,
Newmarket, Suffolk CB8 8JL
T: (01638) 663235
I: www.campingandcaravanningclub.co.uk

NORTH WALSHAM
Norfolk
North Walsham Caravan and Chalet Park★★★
Holiday Park
Bacton Road, North Walsham,
Norfolk NR28 0RA
T: (01692) 500526

Two Mills Touring Park ★★★★★
Touring Park
Old Yarmouth Road,
Scarborough Hill, North
Walsham, Norwich, Norfolk
NR28 9NA
T: (01692) 405829
F: (01692) 405829
E: enquiries@twomills.co.uk
I: www.twomills.co.uk

NORWICH
Norfolk
Camping and Caravanning Club Site ★★★
Touring Park
Martineau Lane, Norwich,
Norfolk NR1 2HX
T: (01603) 620060
I: www.campingandcaravanningclub.co.uk

Reedham Ferry Touring and Camping Park★★★
Touring and Camping Park
Reedham, Norwich NR13 3HA
T: (01493) 700429 &
07909 780747
F: (01493) 700999

OULTON BROAD
Suffolk
Broadland Holiday Village ★★★★★
Holiday Park
Rose Award
Marsh Road, Oulton Broad,
Lowestoft, Suffolk NR33 9JY
T: (01502) 573033
F: (01502) 512681
E: broadlandhv@hotmail.com
I: www.broadlandvillage.co.uk

OVERSTRAND
Norfolk
Ivy Farm Caravan Park ★★★
Holiday, Touring and Camping Park
No 1 High Street, Overstrand,
Cromer, Norfolk NR27 0PS
T: (01263) 579239
WH

PAKEFIELD
Suffolk
Pakefield Caravan Park ★★★
Holiday, Touring and Camping Park
Arbor Lane, Pakefield, NR33 7BQ
T: (01502) 561136 & 511884
F: (01502) 539264

PENTNEY
Norfolk
Pentney Park Caravan Site ★★★
Touring and Camping Park
Pentney, King's Lynn, Norfolk
PE32 1HU
T: (01760) 337479
F: (01760) 338118
E: holidays@pentney.demon.co.uk
I: www.pentney-park.co.uk

PETERBOROUGH
Cambridgeshire
Ferry Meadows Caravan Club Site ★★★★★
Touring Park
Ferry Meadows, Ham Lane,
Peterborough, PE2 5UU
T: (01733) 233526
WH

POLSTEAD
Suffolk
Polstead Touring Park ★★★★
Touring and Camping Park
Holt Road, Polstead, Colchester
CO6 5BZ
T: (01787) 211969
F: (01787) 211969

ROYDON
Essex
Roydon Mill Leisure Park ★★★
Holiday, Touring and Camping Park
Roydon, Harlow, Essex CM19 5EJ
T: (01279) 792777
F: (01279) 792695
E: info@roydonpark.com
I: www.roydonpark.com

SAHAM HILLS
Norfolk
Lowe Caravan Park ★★★★
Touring and Camping Park
Ashdale, Hills Road, Saham Hills,
Thetford, Norfolk IP25 7EW
T: (01953) 881051
F: (01953) 881051

ST NEOTS
Cambridgeshire
Camping and Caravanning Club Site St Neots★★★★
Touring Park
Rush Meadow, St Neots,
Cambridgeshire PE19 2UD
T: (01480) 474404
I: www.campingandcaravanningclub.co.uk

ST OSYTH
Essex
The Orchards Holiday Village ★★★
Holiday, Touring and Camping Park
Point Clear, St Osyth, Clacton-on-Sea, Essex CO16 8LJ
T: 0870 2425678
F: (01442) 254956
I: www.british-holidays.co.uk
WH

St Osyth Holiday Park ★★★
Holiday Park
Haven Leisure, Beach Road, St
Osyth, Clacton-on-Sea, Essex
CO16 8SG
T: (01255) 820247
F: (01255) 821381
WH

SANDRINGHAM
Norfolk
Camping and Caravanning Club Site ★★★★★
Touring Park
Sandringham Estate, Double
Lodges, Sandringham, Norfolk
PE36 6EA
T: (01485) 542555
I: www.campingandcaravanningclub.co.uk

The Sandringham Estate Caravan Club Site★★★★
Touring Park
Glucksburg Woods,
Sandringham, Norfolk PE35 6EZ
T: (01553) 631614
WH

SAXMUNDHAM
Suffolk
Lakeside Leisure Park Rendham Road★★★★
Touring and Camping Park
Saxmundham, Suffolk IP17 2QP
T: (01728) 603344
F: (01728) 603344

SCRATBY
Norfolk
California Cliffs Holiday Park ★★★
Holiday Park
Rottenstone Lane, Scratby, Great
Yarmouth, Norfolk NR29 3QU
T: (01493) 730584
F: (01493) 733146

Green Farm Caravan Park ★★★★
Holiday and Touring Park
Beach Road, Scratby, Great
Yarmouth, Norfolk NR29 3NW
T: (01493) 730440
F: (01493) 733500

Scratby Hall Caravan Park ★★★★
Touring and Camping Park
Scratby, Great Yarmouth,
Norfolk NR29 3PH
T: (01493) 730283

SEA PALLING
Norfolk
Golden Beach Holiday Centre ★★★
Holiday and Touring Park
Beach Road, Sea Palling,
Norwich NR12 0AL
T: (01692) 598269
F: (01692) 598693

SHOEBURYNESS
Essex
East Beach Caravan Park ★★
Holiday, Touring and Camping Park
East Beach, Shoeburyness,
Southend-on-Sea SS3 9SG
T: (01702) 292466
F: (01702) 290634
E: east.beach@care4free.net

SNETTISHAM
Norfolk
Diglea Caravan and Camping Park★★★
Holiday, Touring and Camping Park
Beach Road, Snettisham, King's
Lynn, Norfolk PE31 7RA
T: (01485) 541367

STANHOE
Norfolk
The Rickels Caravan Site ★★★★
Touring Park
The Rickels, Bircham Road,
Stanhoe, King's Lynn, Norfolk
PE31 8PU
T: (01485) 518671
F: (01485) 518969

STEEPLE
Essex
Steeple Bay Holiday Park ★★
Holiday, Touring and Camping Park
Steeple, Southminster, Essex
CM0 7RS
T: (01621) 773991
F: (01621) 773967

TATTERSETT
Norfolk
Manor Park Touring Caravans ★★★
Touring Park
Manor Farm, Tattersett, King's Lynn, Norfolk PE31 8RS
T: (01485) 528310

TRIMINGHAM
Norfolk
Woodland Caravan Park ★★★
Holiday and Touring Park
Trimingham, Norwich NR11 8AL
T: (01263) 579208 & 07768 720109
F: (01263) 833071
WH

UPPER SHERINGHAM
Norfolk
Woodlands Caravan Park ★★★★
Camping Park
Holt Road, Upper Sheringham, Sheringham, Norfolk NR26 8TU
T: (01263) 823802

WALTHAM CROSS
Hertfordshire
Camping and Caravanning Club Site ★★
Touring and Camping Park
Theobalds Park, Bulls Cross Ride, Waltham Cross, Hertfordshire EN7 5HS
T: (01992) 620604
I: www.campingandcaravanningclub.co.uk

WALTON-ON-THE-NAZE
Essex
Naze Marine Holiday Park ★★
Holiday and Touring Park
Hall Lane, Walton-on-the-Naze, Essex CO14 8HL
T: (01255) 676633 & 678980
F: (01255) 671615
E: enquiries@nazemarine.com
I: www.nazemarine.com
WH

WEELEY
Essex
Weeley Bridge Holiday Park ★★★
Holiday and Touring Park
Weeley, Clacton-on-Sea CO16 9DH
T: (01255) 830403
F: (01255) 831544
E: info@weeleybridge.fsnet.co.uk
I: www.leisuregb.co.uk

WELLS–NEXT–THE–SEA
Norfolk
Pinewood Holiday Park ★★★
Holiday, Touring and Camping Park
Beach Road, Wells-next-the-Sea, Norfolk NR23 1DR
T: (01328) 710439
F: (01328) 711060
E: holiday@pinewoods.co.uk
I: www.pinewoods.co.uk
WH

WEST RUNTON
Norfolk
Camping and Caravanning Club Site ★★★★
Touring and Camping Park
Holgate Lane, West Runton, Cromer, Norfolk NR27 9NW
T: (01263) 837544
I: www.campingandcaravanningclub.co.uk

Laburnum Caravan Park ★★★
Holiday Park
Water Lane, West Runton, Cromer, Norfolk NR27 9QP
T: (01263) 837473
E: laburnum.park.@bt.internet.com

WEYBOURNE
Norfolk
Kelling Heath Holiday Park ★★★★★
Holiday, Touring and Camping Park
Rose Award
Sandy Hill Lane, Weybourne, Holt, Norfolk NR25 7HW
T: (01263) 588181
F: (01263) 588599
E: info@kellingheath.co.uk
I: www.kellingheath.co.uk

WISBECH
Cambridgeshire
Virginia Lake Caravan Park ★★★
Holiday and Touring Park
Virginia House, St John's Fen End, Wisbech, Cambridgeshire PE14 8JF
T: (01945) 430332
F: (01945) 430128

WOODBRIDGE
Suffolk
Forest Camping ★★★
Touring and Camping Park
Tangham, Rendelsham Forest, Butley, Woodbridge, Suffolk IP12 3NF
T: (01394) 450707
F: (01394) 450707
E: camping@anglianet.co.uk
I: www.forestcamping.co.uk

WORTWELL
Norfolk
Little Lakeland Caravan Park ★★★★
Holiday and Touring Park
Wortwell, Harleston, Norfolk IP20 0EL
T: (01986) 788646
F: (01986) 788646
I: www.ukparks.co.uk/littlelakeland

SOUTH WEST

ASHBURTON
Devon
Ashburton Caravan Park ★★★★
Holiday and Touring Park
Rose Award
Waterleat, Ashburton, Newton Abbot, Devon TQ13 7HU
T: (01364) 652552
F: (01364) 652552

Parkers Farm Holiday Park ★★★
Holiday Park
Higher Mead Farm, Alston, Ashburton, Newton Abbot, Devon TQ13 7LJ
T: (01364) 652598
F: (01364) 654004
E: parkersfarm@hotmail.com

River Dart Country Park ★★★★
Holiday Park
Holne Park, Ashburton, Newton Abbot, Devon TQ13 7NP
T: (01364) 652511
F: (01364) 652020

AVONWICK
Devon
Webland Farm Holiday Park ★★
Holiday Park
Avonwick, South Brent, Devon TQ10 9EX
T: (01364) 73273

AXMINSTER
Devon
Andrewshayes Caravan Park ★★★
Holiday Park
Dalwood, Axminster, Devon EX13 7DY
T: (01404) 831225
F: (01404) 831893
E: enquiries@andrewhayes.co.uk
I: www.andrewhayes.co.uk

Hunters Moon Holiday Park ★★★
Holiday Park
Hawkchurch, Axminster, Devon EX13 5UL
T: (01297) 678402
F: (01297) 678402

BARTON
Devon
Torquay Holiday Park ★★★★
Holiday Park
Kingskerswell Road, Barton, Torquay TQ2 8JU
T: (01803) 323077
F: (01803) 323503

BATH
Bath & North East Somerset
Bath Marina and Caravan Park ★★★★
Touring Park
Brassmill Lane, Bath, BA1 3JT
T: (01225) 428778
F: (01225) 428778

Newton Mill Camping ★★★★
Touring Park
Newton Road, Bath, BA2 9JF
T: (01225) 333909
F: (01225) 461556
E: newtonmillenium@email.com
I: www.newtonmill.co.uk

BATHPOOL
Somerset
Tanpits Cider Farm Camping and Caravan Park★★
Touring Park
Bathpool, Taunton, Somerset TA2 8BZ
T: (01823) 270663
F: (01823) 270663

BAWDRIP
Somerset
Fairways International Touring Caravan and Camping Park ★★★
Touring Park
Bath Road, Bawdrip, Bridgwater, Somerset TA7 8PP
T: (01278) 685569
F: (01278) 685569

BEETHAM
Somerset
Five Acres Caravan Club Site ★★★★
Touring Park
Beetham, Chard, Somerset TA20 3QA
T: (01460) 234519
WH

BERROW
Somerset

Sandyglade Caravan Park Ltd
★★★★
Holiday Park
Rose Award
Coast Road, Berrow, Burnham-
on-Sea, Somerset TA8 2QX
T: (01278) 751271
F: (01278) 751036
E: admin@sandygla.demon.co.
uk

BERRY HEAD
Devon

Landscove Holiday Village
★★★★
Holiday Park
Rose Award
Gillard Road, Berry Head,
Brixham, Devon TQ5 9EP
T: (01803) 859759 & 853176
F: (01803) 851139

BERRYNARBOR
Devon

Sandaway Beach Holiday Park
★★★
Holiday Park
Berrynarbor, Ilfracombe, Devon
EX34 9ST
T: (01271) 883155 & 866766
F: (01271) 866791
I: www.jfhols.co.uk
`WH`

**Watermouth Cove Holiday
Park** ★★★
Touring Park
Berrynarbor, Ilfracombe, Devon
EX34 9SJ
T: (01271) 862504
I: www.
watermouthcoveholidays.co.uk

BICKINGTON
Devon

The Dartmoor Halfway
★★★★
Touring Park
Bickington, Newton Abbot,
Devon TQ12 6JW
T: (01626) 821270
F: (01626) 821820

Lemonford Caravan Park
★★★★
Holiday Park
Bickington, Newton Abbot,
Devon TQ12 6JR
T: (01626) 821242
F: (01626) 821242
E: lemonford@dartmoor.co.uk
I: www.dartmoor.co.
uk/lemonford

BIDEFORD
Devon

Bideford Bay Holiday Park
★★★
Holiday Park
Buck's Cross, Bideford, Devon
EX39 5DU
T: (01237) 431331
F: (01237) 431624
E: gm_bideford@rank.com
I: www.haven-holidays.co.uk
`WH`

BISHOP SUTTON
Bath & North East Somerset

Bath Chew Valley Caravan Park
★★★★★
Touring Park
Ham Lane, Bishop Sutton, Bristol
BS39 5TZ
T: (01275) 332127
F: (01275) 332664

BLACKAWTON
Devon

Woodlands Leisure Park
★★★★
Holiday Park
Blackawton, Totnes, Devon
TQ9 7DQ
T: (01803) 712598
F: (01803) 712680
E: fun@woodlands-leisure-park
I: www.woodlandspark.com

BLACKWATER
Cornwall

Trevarth Holiday Park ★★★★
Holiday Park
Blackwater, Truro, Cornwall
TR4 8HR
T: (01872) 560266
F: (01872) 560266

BLUE ANCHOR
Somerset

Blue Anchor Bay Caravan Park
★★★★
Holiday and Touring Park
Rose Award
Blue Anchor (Hoburne), Blue
Anchor, Minehead, Somerset
TA24 6JT
T: (01643) 821360
F: (01643) 821572
E: enquiries@hoburne.co.uk
I: www.hoburne.co.uk
`WH`

BODMIN
Cornwall

**Camping and Caravanning
Club Site** ★★★★
Touring Park
Old Callywith Road, Bodmin,
Cornwall PL31 2DZ
T: (01208) 73834
I: www.
campingandcaravanningclub.co.
uk

Glenmorris Park ★★★
Holiday Park
Longstone Road, St Mabyn,
Bodmin, Cornwall PL30 3BY
T: (01208) 841677
F: (01208) 841677
E: gmpark@dircon.co.uk
I: www.gmpark.dircon.co.uk
`WH`

Ruthern Valley Holidays ★★★
Holiday and Touring Park
Ruthernbridge, Bodmin,
Cornwall PL30 5LU
T: (01208) 831395
F: (01208) 832324
I: www.bookcornwall.com

BOVISAND
Devon

Bovisand Lodge Estate Ltd
★★★★
Holiday Park
Rose Award
Bovisand, Plymouth, Devon
PL9 0AA
T: (01752) 403554
F: (01752) 482646
E: blodge@netcomuk.co.uk
I: www.bovisand.com

BRATTON FLEMING
Devon

**Greenacres Farm Touring
Caravan Par** ★★★★
Touring Park
Bratton Fleming, Barnstaple,
Devon EX31 4SG
T: (01598) 763334

BRAUNTON
Devon

**Lobb Fields Caravan and
Camping Park** ★★★
Touring Park
Saunton Road, Braunton, Devon
EX33 1EB
T: (01271) 812090
E: lobbfields@compuserve.com

BREAN
Somerset

Brean Beach Holiday Parks
★★★★
Holiday Park
Coast Road, Brean, Burnham-
on-Sea, Somerset TA8 2RH
T: (01278) 751349
F: (01278) 751666
E: icj@breanbeach.co.uk
I: www.breanbeach.co.uk

Brightholme Holiday Park
★★★
Holiday Park
Coast Road, Brean, Burnham-
on-Sea, Somerset TA8 2QY
T: (01278) 751327
F: (01278) 751327
E: brightholme@
burnham-on-sea.co.uk
I: www.burnham-on-sea.co.
uk/brightholme

Diamond Farm ★★★
Touring Park
Weston Road, Brean, Burnham-
on-Sea, Somerset TA8 2RL
T: (01278) 751263 & 751041
E: diamond@crosswaysnet.
freeserve.co.uk

Dolphin Caravan Park ★★★★
Holiday Park
Coast Road, Brean, Burnham-
on-Sea, Somerset TA8 2QY
T: (01278) 751258
F: (01278) 751258

Embelle Holiday Park ★★★★
Holiday Park
Coast Road, Brean Sands, Brean,
Burnham-on-Sea, Somerset
TA8 2QZ
T: (01278) 751346 &
0800 190322
F: (01278) 751683
E: embelle@breansands.fsnet.
co.uk

Holiday Resort Unity ★★★
Holiday Park
Coast Road, Brean Sands, Brean,
Burnham-on-Sea, Somerset
TA8 2RB
T: (01278) 751235 & 752100
F: (01278) 751539
E: admin@holidayunity.demon.
co.uk
I: www.holidayunity.demon.co.
uk

Isis Park ★★★★
Holiday Park
Rose Award
Warren Road, Brean, Burnham-
on-Sea, Somerset TA8 2RP
T: (01278) 751227

Northam Farm Touring Park
★★★★
Touring Park
Brean Sands, Brean, Burnham-
on-Sea, Somerset TA8 2SE
T: (01278) 751244 & 751222
F: (01278) 751150

Warren Farm Holiday Park
★★★
Holiday Park
Warren Road, Brean, Burnham-
on-Sea, Somerset TA8 2RP
T: (01278) 751227
F: (01278) 751033

BRIDESTOWE
Devon

Glebe Park ★★★
Holiday Park
Bridestowe, Okehampton, Devon
EX20 4ER
T: (01837) 861261

BRIDGETOWN
Somerset

Exe Valley Caravan Park ★★★
Touring Park
The Mill House, Bridgetown,
Dulverton, Somerset TA22 9JR
T: (01643) 851432

BRIDPORT
Dorset

**Binghams Farm Touring
Caravan Park** ★★★★
Touring Park
Binghams Farm, Melplash,
Bridport, Dorset DT6 3TT
T: (01308) 488234
F: (01308) 488234
E: royphilpott@msn.com

Freshwater Beach Holiday Park
★★★★
Holiday Park
Burton Bradstock, Bridport,
Dorset DT6 4PT
T: (01308) 897317
F: (01308) 897336
E: enquiries@fbhp.co.uk
I: www.fphp.co.uk

Golden Cap Holiday Park
★★★★
Holiday and Touring Park
Rose Award
Seatown, Chideock, Bridport,
Dorset DT6 6JX
T: (01308) 422139
F: (01308) 425672
E: highlands@wdlh.co.uk
I: www.wdlh.co.uk
`WH`

Highlands End Holiday Park ★★★★★
Holiday and Touring Park
Rose Award
Eype, Bridport, Dorset DT6 6AR
T: (01308) 422139
F: (01308) 425672
E: highlands@wdlh.co.uk
I: www.wdlh.co.uk
[WH]

BRISTOL

Baltic Wharf Caravan Club Site ★★★★
Touring Park
Cumberland Road, Bristol,
BS1 6XG
T: (0117) 9268030
[WH]

BRIXHAM
Devon

Brixham Holiday Park ★★★★
Holiday Park
Rose Award
Fishcombe Cove, Brixham,
Devon TQ5 8RB
T: (01803) 853324
F: (01803) 853569

Centry Touring Caravans and Tents ★
Touring Park
Mudberry House, Centry Road,
Brixham, Devon TQ5 9EY
T: (01803) 853215
E: jlacentry.touring@talk21.com
I: www.english-riviera.co.uk

St Mary's Bay Holiday Village ★★★★
Holiday Park
Mudstone Lane, Brixham, Devon
TQ5 9EJ
T: (01803) 856335
F: (01803) 883855
E: admin@weststarholidays.co.uk
I: www.weststarholidays.co.uk

South Bay Holiday Park ★★★★
Holiday Park
St Mary's Road, Brixham, Devon
TQ5 9QW
T: (01803) 853004
F: (01803) 882738
[WH]

BRYHER
Isles of Scilly

Bryher Campsite ★★★
Camping Park
Jenford, Bryher, Isles of Scilly
TR23 0PR
T: (01720) 422886
F: (01720) 423092

BUDE
Cornwall

Budemeadows Touring Holiday Park ★★★★★
Touring Park
Bude, Cornwall EX23 0NA
T: (01288) 361646
F: (01288) 361646
E: wendyjo@globalnet.co.uk
I: www.budemeadows.com

Penstowe Park Holiday Village ★★★★
Holiday Park
Penstowe Park, Kilkhampton,
Bude, Cornwall EX23 9QY
T: (01288) 321354 & 321282
F: (01288) 321273

Sandymouth Bay Holiday Park ★★★
Holiday Park
Sandymouth Bay, Bude,
Cornwall EX23 9HW
T: (01288) 352563 &
07831 213932
F: (01288) 352563
E: sandymouth@aol.com
I: www.sandymouthbay.co.uk

Upper Lynstone Caravan and Camping Site ★★★
Holiday and Touring Park
Lynstone, Bude, Cornwall
EX23 0LP
T: (01288) 352017
F: (01288) 359034
E: reception@upperlynstone.co.uk
I: www.upperlynstone.co.uk

Wooda Farm Park ★★★★★
Holiday and Touring Park
Poughill, Bude, Cornwall
EX23 9HJ
T: (01288) 352069
E: enquiries@wooda.co.uk
I: www.wooda.co.uk
[WH]

BURNHAM-ON-SEA
Somerset

Burnham-on-Sea Holiday Village ★★★★
Holiday Park
Marine Drive, Burnham-on-Sea,
Somerset TA8 1LA
T: 0870 2425678
F: (01442) 254956
[WH]

Home Farm Holiday Park ★★★★★
Holiday Park
Edithmead, Burnham-on-Sea,
Somerset TA9 4HD
T: (01278) 788888
F: (01278) 780113

Lakeside Holiday Park ★★★★
Holiday Park
Westfield Road, Burnham-on-Sea, Somerset TA8 2AE
T: (01278) 792222
F: (01278) 795592

The Retreat Caravan Park ★★★★
Holiday Park
Berrow Road, Burnham-on-Sea,
Somerset TA8 2ES
T: (01458) 860504
F: (01458) 860330

BURTON BRADSTOCK
Dorset

Coastal Caravan Park ★★★
Holiday Park
Annings Lane, Burton Bradstock,
Bridport, Dorset DT6 4QP
T: (01308) 422139 & 897361
F: (01308) 425672
E: highlands@wdlh.co.ulc
I: www.wdlh.co.uk
[WH]

CAMELFORD
Cornwall

Juliot's Well Holiday Park ★★★
Holiday Park
Camelford, Cornwall PL32 9RF
T: (01840) 213302
F: (01840) 212700
E: juliot.well@bun.com
I: www.holidaysincornwall.net

Carlyon Bay Caravan and Camping Park ★★★★★
Holiday and Camping Park
Bethesda, Cypress Avenue,
Carlyon Bay, St Austell, Cornwall
PL25 3RE
T: (01726) 812735
F: (01726) 815496

CARNON DOWNS
Cornwall

Carnon Downs Caravan and Camping Park ★★★★
Touring Park
Carnon Downs, Truro, Cornwall
TR3 6JJ
T: (01872) 862283
F: (01872) 862800
E: park@carnon-downs.co.uk
I: www.carnon-downs.co.uk
[WH]

CHACEWATER
Cornwall

Chacewater Park ★★★★
Touring Park
Cox Hill, Chacewater, Truro,
Cornwall TR4 8LY
T: (01209) 820762
F: (01209) 820544
E: ajpeterken@aol.com
[WH]

CHARD
Somerset

Alpine Grove Touring Park ★★★
Touring Park
Alpine Grove, Forton, Chard,
Somerset TA20 4HD
T: (01460) 63479

CHARMOUTH
Dorset

The Camping and Caravanning Club Site ★★★★
Touring Park
Monkton Wylde Farm,
Charmouth, Bridport, Dorset
DT6 6DB
T: (01297) 32965
I: www.campingandcaravanningclub.co.uk

Dolphins River Park ★★★★
Holiday Park
Berne Lane, Charmouth, Dorset
DT6 6RD
T: 0800 074 6375
F: (01308) 868 180

Manor Farm Holiday Centre ★★★
Holiday Park
Charmouth, Bridport, Dorset
DT6 6QL
T: (01297) 560226
F: (01297) 560429

Monkton Wylde Farm Caravan and and Camping Park ★★★★
Touring Park
Charmouth, Bridport, Dorset
DT6 6DB
T: (01297) 34525 & 631131
F: (01297) 33594

Newlands Holidays ★★★★
Holiday Park
Charmouth, Bridport, Dorset
DT6 6RB
T: (01297) 560259
F: (01297) 560787
I: www.newlandsholidays.co.uk

Seadown Holiday Park ★★★★
Holiday Park
Bridge Road, Charmouth,
Bridport, Dorset DT6 6QS
T: (01297) 560154
E: www.seadowncaravanpark.co.uk

Wood Farm Caravan and Camping Park ★★★★★
Holiday and Touring Park
Axminster Road, Charmouth,
Bridport, Dorset DT6 6BT
T: (01297) 560697
F: (01297) 560697
E: holidays@woodfarm.co.uk
I: www.woodfarm.co.uk
[WH]

CHEDDAR
Somerset

Broadway House Holiday Touring Caravan and Camping Park ★★★★
Holiday Park
Rose Award
Cheddar, Somerset BS27 3DB
T: (01934) 742610
F: (01934) 744950
E: enquiries@broadwayhouse.uk.com
I: www.broadwayhouse.uk.com
[WH]

CHIPSTABLE
Somerset

Oxenleaze Farm Caravans ★★★★
Holiday Park
Chipstable, Taunton, Somerset
TA4 2QH
T: (01984) 623427
F: (01984) 623427
I: www.somerset-farm-holidays.co.uk/oxenleazefarmcaravans homepag.htm

CHUDLEIGH
Devon

Holmans Wood Touring Park ★★★★
Touring Park
Harcombe Cross, Chudleigh,
Newton Abbot, Devon TQ13 0DZ
T: (01626) 853785

COLYTON
Devon

Leacroft Touring Park ★★★★
Touring Park
Colyton Hill, Colyton, Devon
EX24 6HY
T: (01297) 552823
[WH]

COMBE MARTIN
Devon

Combe Martin Beach Holiday Park ★★★★
Holiday Park
Woodlands, Combe Martin,
Ilfracombe, Devon EX34 0AS
T: (01271) 866766
F: (01271) 866791
I: www.jfhols.co.uk
[WH]

Manleigh Holiday Park ★★★★
Holiday Park
Rectory Road, Combe Martin,
Ilfracombe, Devon EX34 0NS
T: (01271) 883353
E: info@manleighpark.co.uk
I: www.manleighpark.co.uk

Newberry Farm Touring Caravans and Camping ★★★
Touring Park
Woodlands, Combe Martin, Ilfracombe, Devon EX34 0AT
T: (01271) 882333 & 882334
F: (01271) 882880
WH

Stowford Farm Meadows ★★★★
Touring Park
Berry Down, Combe Martin, Ilfracombe, Devon EX34 0PW
T: (01271) 882476
F: (01271) 883053
E: enquiries@stowford.co.uk
I: www.stowford.co.uk
WH

CONNOR DOWNS
Cornwall
Higher Trevaskis Caravan and Camping Park ★★★★
Touring and Camping Park
Gwinear Road, Connor Downs, Hayle, Cornwall TR27 5JQ
T: (01209) 831736

COOMBE BISSETT
Wiltshire
Summerlands Caravan Park ★★★
Touring Park
College Farm, Rockbourne Road, Coombe Bissett, Salisbury, Wiltshire SP5 4LP
T: (01722) 718259

CROSSWAYS
Dorset
Crossways Caravan Club Site ★★★★
Touring Park
Crossways, Dorchester, Dorset DT2 8BE
T: (01305) 852032
WH

CROWCOMBE
Somerset
Quantock Orchard Caravan Park ★★★★★
Touring Park
Crowcombe, Taunton, Somerset TA4 4AW
T: (01984) 618618
F: (01984) 618618
E: QOCP@FLAXPOOL.FREESERVE.CO.UK
I: www.flaxpool.freeserve.co.uk

CROYDE BAY
Devon
Ruda Holiday Park and Croyde Burrows ★★★★
Holiday Park
Croyde Bay, Braunton, Devon EX33 1NY
T: (01271) 890671
F: (01271) 890656
E: enquiries@ruda.co.uk
I: www.ruda.co.uk

CUBERT
Cornwall
Treworgans Holiday Park Pennros Cottage ★★★★
Holiday Park
Cubert, Newquay, Cornwall TR8 5HH
T: (01637) 830200

DARTMOUTH
Devon
Hillfield Holiday Park ★★★★
Holiday Park
Hillfield, Dartmouth, Devon TQ6 0LX
T: (01803) 712322
F: (01803) 712322

Little Cotton Caravan Park ★★★★★
Touring Park
Little Cotton, Dartmouth, Devon TQ6 0LB
T: (01803) 832558
F: (01803) 834887

DAWLISH
Devon
Cofton Country Holiday Park ★★★★
Holiday Park
Starcross, Exeter, Devon EX6 8RP
T: (01626) 890111
F: (01626) 891572
E: enquiries@cofton-holidays-devon.co.uk
I: www.cofton-holidays-devon.co.uk

Golden Sands Holiday Park ★★★★
Holiday Park
Week Lane, Dawlish, Devon EX7 0LZ
T: (01626) 863099
F: (01626) 867149
E: info@goldensands.co.uk
I: www.goldensands.co.uk

Leadstone Camping ★★★
Camping Park
Warren Road, Dawlish, Devon EX7 0NG
T: (01626) 872239 & 864411
F: (01626) 873833
E: info@leadstonecamping.co.uk
I: www.leadstonecamping.co.uk

DAWLISH WARREN
Devon
Dawlish Sands Holiday Park ★★★★
Holiday Park
Warren Road, Dawlish Warren, Dawlish, Devon EX7 0PG
T: (01626) 862038
F: (01626) 866298

Oakcliff Holiday Park ★★★★
Holiday Park
Rose Award
Mount Pleasant Road, Dawlish Warren, Dawlish, Devon EX7 0ND
T: (01626) 863347
F: (01626) 866636

Peppermint Park ★★★★
Holiday Park
Warren Road, Dawlish Warren, Dawlish, Devon EX7 0PQ
T: (01626) 863436
E: www.peppermintpark.co.uk

Welcome Family Holiday Park ★★★★
Holiday Park
Rose Award
Warren Road, Dawlish Warren, Dawlish, Devon EX7 0PH
T: (01626) 862070 & 888323
F: (01626) 888157

DEVIZES
Wiltshire
The Bell Caravan and Camping Park ★★★
Touring Park
Andover Road, Lydeway, Devizes, Wiltshire SN10 3PS
T: (01380) 840230
F: (01380) 840137

DOBWALLS
Cornwall
Doublebois Park ★★★★
Holiday Park
Rose Award
Dobwalls, Liskeard, Cornwall PL14 6LD
T: (01579) 320049
F: (01579) 321415
E: mail@hoseasons.co.uk
I: www.hoseasons.co.uk
WH

DONIFORD
Somerset
Doniford Bay Holiday Park ★★★★
Holiday and Touring Park
Doniford, Watchet, Somerset TA23 0TJ
T: (01984) 632423
F: (01984) 633649
WH

Sunnybank Caravan Park ★★★★★
Holiday Park
Doniford, Watchet, Somerset TA23 0UD
T: (01984) 632237
F: (01984) 634834
E: sunnybankmtb@compuserve.com
WH

DORCHESTER
Dorset
Giants Head Caravan and Camping Park ★★
Touring Park
Old Sherborne Road, Cerne Abbas, Dorchester, Dorset DT2 7TR
T: (01300) 341242

Morn Gate Caravan Park ★★★
Holiday Park
Bridport Road, Dorchester, Dorset DT2 9DS
T: (01305) 250348 & 889284

DOUBLEBOIS
Cornwall
Pine Green Caravan Park ★★★★
Holiday Park
Doublebois, Liskeard, Cornwall PL14 6LE
T: (01271) 328981 & (01579) 320183
E: mary.ruhleman@talk21.com
I: www.jpr1994sagehost.co.uk/pine.htm

DOWNDERRY
Cornwall
Downderry Beach Holiday Park ★★★★
Holiday Park
Downderry, Torpoint, Cornwall PL11 3LY
T: (01503) 250410 & (01271) 866766
I: www.jfhols.co.uk
WH

DREWSTEIGNTON
Devon
Clifford Bridge Park ★★★
Touring Park
Clifford, Drewsteignton, Exeter, Devon EX6 6QE
T: (01647) 24226
F: (01647) 24116
E: info@clifford-bridge.co.uk
I: www.clifford-bridge.co.uk
WH

DULVERTON
Somerset
Exmoor House Caravan Club Site ★★★★
Touring Park
Dulverton, Somerset TA22 9HL
T: (01398) 323268
WH

Lakeside Touring Caravan Park ★★★★
Touring Park
Higher Grants, Exbridge, Dulverton, Somerset TA22 9BE
T: (01398) 324068

EAST WORLINGTON
Devon
Yeatheridge Farm Caravan Park ★★★
Holiday Park
East Worlington, Crediton, Devon EX17 4TN
T: (01884) 860330
F: (01884) 860330

EXETER
Devon
Kennford International Caravan Park
Kennford, Exeter, Devon EX6 7YN
T: (01392) 833046
F: (01392) 833046

EXMINSTER
Devon
Three Farm Cottages Camping ★★★★
Holiday Park
Deepway Lane, Exminster, Exeter EX6 8BG

EXMOUTH
Devon
St John's Farm Caravan and Camping Park ★★★
Holiday Park
St John's Road, Withycombe, Exmouth, Devon EX8 5EG
T: (01395) 263170

EYPE
Dorset
Eype House Caravan Park ★★★
Holiday Park
Eype, Bridport, Dorset DT6 6AL
T: (01308) 424903
F: (01308) 424903
E: enquires@eypehouse.co.uk
I: www.eypehouse.co.uk

FALMOUTH
Cornwall

Maen Valley Holiday Park
★★★
Holiday Park
Falmouth, Cornwall TR11 5BJ
T: (01326) 312190
F: (01326) 211120
E: maenvalley@aol.com
I: www.chycor.co.
uk/maen-valley

Pennance Mill Farm Touring Park ★★
Touring Park
Maenporth, Falmouth, Cornwall
TR11 5HJ
T: (01326) 312616 & 317431
F: (01326) 317431

FIDDINGTON
Somerset

Mill Farm Caravan and Camping Park★★★★
Touring Park
Fiddington, Bridgwater,
Somerset TA5 1JQ
T: (01278) 732286

FOWEY
Cornwall

Penhale Caravan and Camping Park★★★
Holiday Park
Fowey, Cornwall PL23 1JU
T: (01726) 833425
F: (01726) 833425
E: penhale@farmersweekly.net

GALMPTON
Devon

Galmpton Touring Park
★★★★
Touring Park
Greenway Road, Galmpton,
Brixham, Devon TQ5 OEP
T: (01803) 842066

GLASTONBURY
Somerset

The Isle of Avalon Touring Caravan Park★★★★★
Touring Park
Godney Road, Glastonbury,
Somerset BA6 9AF
T: (01458) 833618
F: (01458) 833618

The Old Oaks Touring Park
★★★★★
Touring Park
Wick Farm, Wick, Glastonbury,
Somerset BA6 8JS
T: (01458) 831437
F: (01458) 833238
E: info@theoldoaks.co.uk
I: www.theoldoaks.co.uk

GOONHAVERN
Cornwall

Penrose Farm Touring Park
★★★★
Touring Park
Goonhavern, Truro, Cornwall
TR4 9QF
T: (01872) 573185
E: col@penrose99.freeserve.co.
uk
I: members.xoom.
com/penrosefarm/

Silverbow Park ★★★★★
Holiday Park
Rose Award
Goonhavern, Truro, Cornwall
TR4 9NX
T: (01872) 572347

GORRAN
Cornwall

Tregarton Park ★★★★
Touring Park
Gorran, Mevagissey, St Austell,
Cornwall PL26 6NF
T: (01726) 843666
F: (01726) 844481
E: holidays@tregarton.co.uk
I: www.tregarton.co.uk

Trelispen Caravan and Camping Park★
Touring Park
Gorran, St Austell, Cornwall
PL26 6HT
T: (01726) 843501
F: (01726) 843501

GULVAL
Cornwall

Kenegie Manor Holiday Park
★★★★
Holiday Park
Gulval, Penzance, Cornwall
TR20 8YN
T: (01736) 369174
F: (01736) 369174
I: www.jfhols.co.uk

GWINEAR
Cornwall

Parbola Holiday Park ★★★★
Holiday Park
Wall, Gwinear, Hayle, Cornwall
TR27 5LE
T: (01209) 831503
F: (01209) 831503
E: bookings@parbola.demon.co.
uk
I: www.parbola.demon.co.uk

HAYLE
Cornwall

Beachside Holiday Park
★★★★
Holiday Park
Hayle, Cornwall TR27 5AW
T: (01736) 753080
F: (01736) 757252
E: reception@beachside.demon.
co.uk
I: www.beachside.co.uk

Riviere Sands Holiday Park
★★★
Holiday Park
Riviere Towans, Hayle, Cornwall
TR27 5AF
T: (01736) 752132
F: (01736) 756368

St Ives Bay Holiday Park
★★★★
Holiday Park
73 Loggans Road, Upton
Towans, Hayle, Cornwall
TR27 5BH
T: (01736) 752274
F: (01736) 754523
E: stivesbay@pipex.com
I: www.stivesbay.co.uk

Tolroy Manor Holiday Park
★★★★
Holiday Park
Tolroy Road, Hayle, Cornwall
TR27 6HG
T: (01736) 753082
F: (01736) 756530

HELSTON
Cornwall

Boscrege Caravan Park
★★★★
Holiday and Camping Park
Ashton, Helston, Cornwall
TR13 9TG
T: (01736) 762231 &
07850 722909
F: (01736) 762231

Poldown Caravan Park ★★★
Holiday and Touring Park
Poldown, Carleen, Helston,
Cornwall TR13 9NN
T: (01326) 574560
F: (01326) 574560
E: poldown@poldown.co.uk
I: www.poldown.co.uk

HIGHBRIDGE
Somerset

Greenacre Place Touring Caravan Park★★★
Touring Park
Bristol Road, Edithmead,
Highbridge, Somerset TA9 4HA
T: (01278) 785227
F: (01278) 785227

HONITON
Devon

Camping and Caravanning Club Site★★★
Touring Park
Otter Valley Park, Northcote,
Honiton, Devon EX14 4PX
T: (01404) 44546
I: www.
campingandcaravanningclub.co.
uk

ILFRACOMBE
Devon

Beachside Holiday Park
★★★★
Holiday Park
Hele Bay, Ilfracombe, Devon
EX34 9QZ
T: (01271) 863006
F: (01271) 867296
E: enquiries@beachsidepark.co.
uk
I: www.beachsidepark.co.uk

Devon Coast Holiday Park
★★★★
Holiday Park
Marlborough Road, Ilfracombe,
Devon EX34 9JA
T: (01271) 866766
F: (01271) 866791
I: www.jfhols.co.uk

Golden Coast Holiday Park
★★★★
Holiday Park
Worth Road, Ilfracombe, Devon
EX34 9JA
T: (01271) 866766
F: (01271) 866791
I: www.jfhols.co.uk

Hidden Valley Coast and Country Touring and Camping Park★★★★
Touring Park
Ilfracombe, Ilfracombe, Devon
EX34 8NU
T: (01271) 813837

Ilfracombe Holiday Park
★★★★
Holiday Park
John Fowler Holidays,
Marlborough Road, Ilfracombe,
Devon EX34 8PF
T: (01271) 866766
F: (01271) 866791
I: www.jfhols.co.uk

Mullacott Cross Caravan Park
★★★
Holiday Park
Mullacott Cross, Ilfracombe,
Devon EX34 8NB
T: (01271) 862212
F: (01271) 862979

IPPLEPEN
Devon

Ross Park ★★★★★
Touring Park
Park Hill Farm, Moor Road,
Ipplepen, Newton Abbot, Devon
TQ12 5TT
T: (01803) 812983
F: (01803) 812983
E: enquiries@
rossparkcaravanpark.co.uk

Woodville Touring Park
★★★★
Touring Park
Totnes Road, Ipplepen, Newton
Abbot, Devon TQ12 5TN
T: (01803) 812240
F: (01803) 813984
E: woodvillepark@lineone.net
I: www.caravan-sitefinder.co.
uk/sthwest/devon/woodville.
html

ISLES OF SCILLY

Saint Martins Campsite ★★★
Camping Park
St Martin's, Isles of Scilly
TR25 0QN
T: (01720) 422888
F: (01720) 422888
E: chris@stmartinscampsite.
freeserve.co.uk

KENTISBEARE
Devon

Forest Glade Holiday Park
★★★★
Rose Award
Holiday Park
Kentisbeare, Cullompton, Devon
EX15 2DT
T: (01404) 841381
F: (01404) 841593
E: forestglade@cwcom.net
I: www.forestglade.mcmail.com

KEWSTOKE
North Somerset

Ardnave Holiday Park ★★★
Holiday Park
Kewstoke, Weston-super-Mare
BS22 9XJ
T: (01934) 622319

Kewgardens Chalet and Caravan Park★★
Holiday Park
Off Crooks Lane, Sand Bay, Kewstoke, Weston-super-Mare BS22 9XL
T: (01934) 622598 & 645733

Kewside Caravans ★★
Holiday Park
Royal Oak Stores, Kewstoke, Weston-super-Mare BS22 9XF
T: (01934) 623237

KINGSBRIDGE
Devon

Haven Leisure Challaborough Bay Holiday Park★★
Holiday Park
Challaborough Beach, Kingsbridge, Devon TQ7 4HU
T: (01548) 810771
F: (01548) 810842
WH

KINGTON LANGLEY
Wiltshire

Plough Lane Caravan Site
★★★★★
Touring Park
Plough Lane, Kington Langley, Chippenham, Wiltshire SN15 5PS
T: (01249) 750795
F: (01249) 750795
E: ploughnursery@lineone.net
WH

LACOCK
Wiltshire

Piccadilly Caravan Site
★★★★★
Touring Park
Folly Lane (West), Lacock, Chippenham, Wiltshire SN15 2LP
T: (01249) 730260

LANDRAKE
Cornwall

Dolbeare Caravan and Camping Park ★★★★
Holiday and Camping Park
St Ive Road, Landrake, Saltash, Cornwall PL12 5AF
T: (01752) 851332
E: dolbeare@compuserve.com
I: www.dolbeare.co.uk

LANDS END
Cornwall

Cardinney Caravan and Camping Park★★★
Touring Park
Main A30, Lands End, Cornwall TR19 6HJ
T: (01736) 810880
F: (01736) 810998

LANGPORT
Somerset

Bowdens Crest Caravan and Camping Park★★
Holiday Park
Bowdens, Langport, Somerset TA10 0DD
T: (01458) 250553
F: (01458) 253360
E: bowcrest@aol.com
I: www/scoot.co.uk/bowcrest

LANSALLOS
Cornwall

Valleybrook ★★★
Holiday Park
Peakswater, Lansallos, Looe, Cornwall PL13 2QE
T: (01503) 220493
F: (01503) 220455
E: admin@valleybrookholidays.co.uk
I: www.valleybrookholidays.co.uk
WH

LEEDSTOWN
Cornwall

Calloose Caravan and Camping Park★★★★★
Holiday Park
Rose Award
Leedstown, Hayle, Cornwall TR27 5ET
T: (01736) 850431
F: (01736) 850431
I: www.calloose.co.uk

LELANT
Cornwall

St Ives Holiday Village ★★★★
Holiday Park
Lelant, St Ives, Cornwall TR26 3HX
T: (01736) 752000
F: (01736) 756880
WH

LITTLE TORRINGTON
Devon

Smytham Manor Leisure ★★★
Holiday Park
Little Torrington, Torrington, Devon EX38 8PU
T: (01805) 622110
F: (01805) 625451

LOOE
Cornwall

Looe Bay Holiday Park ★★★★
Holiday Park
St Martins, Looe, Cornwall PL13 1NX
T: (01503) 263737
F: (01503) 264511
E: admin@weststarholidays.co.uk
I: www.weststarholidays.co.uk

Millendreath Holiday Village ★★
Holiday Park
Millendreath, Looe, Cornwall PL13 1NY
T: (01503) 263281
F: (01503) 264467
WH

Polborder House Caravan and Camping Park★★★★
Holiday and Touring Park
Bucklawren Road, St Martins by, Looe, Cornwall PL13 1QR
T: (01503) 240265
F: (01503) 240700
E: rlf.polborder@virgin.net
I: www.cornwallexplore.co.uk/Polborder

Tencreek Caravan Park ★★★★
Holiday Park
Looe, Cornwall PL13 2JR
T: (01503) 262447 & 07831 411843
F: (01503) 262760
E: tencreek@aol.com
I: www.tencreel.co.uk

Tregoad Farm Touring Caravan and Camping Park★★★
Touring and Camping Park
St Martin's, Looe, Cornwall PL13 1PB
T: (01503) 262718
F: (01503) 264777
E: tregoadfarmtccp@aol
I: www.tregoad-online.co.uk/tregoad
WH

Trelawne Manor Holiday Village ★★★★
Holiday Park
Looe, Cornwall PL13 2NA
T: (01503) 272151
F: (01503) 272176
WH

LOWER METHERELL
Cornwall

Trehorner Farm Holiday Park ★★★★★
Holiday Park
Rose Award
Lower Metherell, Callington, Cornwall PL17 8BJ
T: (01579) 351122
F: (01579) 351239
E: woodfawood@cs.com
WH

LUXULYAN
Cornwall

Croft Farm Holiday Park ★★★★
Holiday Park
Luxulyan, Bodmin, Cornwall PL30 5EQ
T: (01726) 850228
F: (01726) 850498
E: lynpick@globalnet.co.uk
I: www.chycor.co.uk/parks/croft-farm
WH

LYDFORD
Devon

Camping and Caravanning Club Site ★★★★
Touring Park
Lydford, Okehampton, Devon EX20 4BE
T: (01822) 820275
I: www.campingandcaravanningclub.co.uk

LYMPSHAM
Somerset

Dulhorn Farm Camping Site ★★
Holiday and Touring Park
Weston Road, Lympsham, Weston-super-Mare BS24 0JQ
T: (01934) 750298

LYNTON
Devon

Camping and Caravanning Club Site ★★★★
Touring Park
Caffyn's Cross, Lynton, Devon EX35 6JS
T: (01598) 752379
I: www.campingandcaravanningclub.co.uk

Channel View Caravan Park ★★★★
Holiday Park
Manor Farm, Barbrook, Lynton, Devon EX35 6LD
T: (01598) 753349 & 752777
I: www.ukparks.co.uk/channelview

MALMESBURY
Wiltshire

Burton Hill Caravan and Camping Park★★
Touring Park
Burton Hill, Malmesbury, Wiltshire SN16 0EH
T: (01666) 826880

MARLDON
Devon

Widend Touring Park ★★★★
Touring Park
Berry Pomeroy Road, Marldon, Paignton, Devon TQ3 1RT
T: (01803) 550116
F: (01803) 550116

MARTOCK
Somerset

Southfork Caravan Park ★★★★★
Touring Park
Parrett Works, Martock, Somerset TA12 6AE
T: (01935) 825661
F: (01935) 825122
E: southfork.caravans@virgin.net
WH

MAWGAN PORTH
Cornwall

Mawgan Porth Holiday Park ★★★★
Holiday Park
Mawgan Porth, Newquay, Cornwall TR8 4BD
T: (01637) 860322
E: mawganporthhp@fsbdial.co.uk
I: www.mawganporth.co.uk

Sun Haven Valley Caravan Park and Camping Park★★★★★
Holiday and Camping Park
Rose Award
Mawgan Porth, Newquay, Cornwall TR8 4BQ
T: (01637) 860373
F: (01637) 860373

Trevarrian Holiday Park ★★★★
Holiday Park
Trevarrian, Mawgan Porth, Newquay, Cornwall TR8 4AQ
T: (01637) 860381

MEVAGISSEY
Cornwall

Penhaven Touring Park ★★★★
Touring Park
Pentewan, St Austell, Cornwall PL26 6DL
T: (01726) 843687
F: (01726) 843870
E: penhaven.cornwall@virgin.net
I: www.penhaventouring.co.uk
WH

Establishments printed in green have a detailed entry in this guide

Sea View International ★★★★★
Holiday Park
Rose Award
Boswinger, St Austell, Cornwall
PL26 6LL
T: (01726) 843425
F: (01726) 843358
E: gary@gmichell.freeserve.co.uk
I: www.gmichell.freeserve.co.uk

MINEHEAD
Somerset

Beeches Holiday Park ★★★★
Holiday Park
Rose Award
Blue Anchor Bay, Minehead,
Somerset TA24 6JW
T: (01984) 640391
F: (01984) 640361
E: info@beeches-park.co.uk
I: www.beeches-park.co.uk

Camping and Caravanning Club Site ★★★★
Touring Park
Hill Road, North Hill, Minehead,
Somerset TA24 5SF
T: (01643) 704138
I: www.campingandcaravanningclub.co.uk

MODBURY
Devon

Camping and Caravanning Club Site ★★★★
Touring Park
California Cross, Modbury,
Ivybridge, Devon PL21 0SG
T: (01548) 821297
I: www.campingandcaravanningclub.co.uk

Moor View Touring Park ★★★
Touring Park
California Cross, Modbury,
Ivybridge, Devon PL21 0SG
T: (01548) 821485
F: (01548) 821485
I: www.ukparks.co.uk/moorview

Pennymoor Camping and Caravan Park ★★★★
Holiday Park
Modbury, Ivybridge, Devon
PL21 0SB
T: (01548) 830269 & 830542
F: (01548) 830542
I: www.pennymoor-camping.co.uk

MOORTOWN
Devon

Langstone Manor Caravan and Camping Park ★★★
Holiday Park
Moortown, Tavistock, Devon
PL19 9JZ
T: (01822) 613371
F: (01822) 613371
E: jane@langstone-manor.freeserve.co.uk

MORTEHOE
Devon

Easewell Holiday Park ★★★★
Holiday Park
Easewell Farm, Mortehoe,
Woolacombe, Devon EX34 7EH
T: (01271) 870225

North Morte Farm Caravan and Camping Park ★★★
Holiday Park
North Morte Road, Mortehoe,
Woolacombe, Devon EX34 7EG
T: (01271) 870381
F: (01271) 870115
WH

Twitchen Park ★★★★
Holiday Park
Rose Award
Mortehoe, Woolacombe, Devon
EX34 7ES
T: (01271) 870476
F: (01271) 870498
E: enquiries@hoburne.co.uk
I: www.hoburne.co.uk
WH

Warcombe Farm Camping Park ★★★
Touring Park
Station Road, Mortehoe,
Woolacombe, Devon EX34 7EJ
T: (01271) 870690 & 07774 428770
F: (01271) 871070

MUCHELNEY
Somerset

Thorney Lakes and Caravan Park ★★★
Touring Park
Thorney West Farm, Muchelney,
Langport, Somerset TA10 0DW
T: (01458) 250811
WH

MULLION
Cornwall

Criggan Mill ★★★★
Holiday Park
Rose Award
Mullion Cove, Mullion, Helston,
Cornwall TR12 7EU
T: (01326) 240496
F: 0870 1640 549
E: info@criggan-mill.demon.co.uk

Franchis Farm Ltd ★★★★
Holiday and Touring Park
Cury Cross Lanes, Helston,
Cornwall TR12 7AZ
T: (01326) 240301

Mullion Holiday Park ★★★★
Holiday Park
Mullion, Helston, Cornwall
TR12 7LJ
T: (01392) 447447 & (01326) 240000
F: (01392) 445202
E: admin@weststarholidays.co.uk
I: www.weststarholidays.co.uk

NEWQUAY
Cornwall

Crantock Beach Holiday Park ★★★★
Holiday Park
Crantock, Newquay, Cornwall
TR8 5RH
T: (01637) 871111
F: (01637) 850818
E: bookings@newquay-hol-park.demon.co.uk
I: www.newquay-holiday-parks.co.uk
WH

Hendra Holiday Park ★★★★
Holiday Park
Newquay, Cornwall TR8 4NY
T: (01637) 875778
F: (01637) 879017
E: hendra.uk@dial.pipex.com
I: www.hendra-holidays.com

Holywell Bay Holiday Park ★★★★
Holiday Park
Holywell Bay, Newquay,
Cornwall TR8 5PR
T: (01637) 871111
F: (01637) 850818
E: bookings@newquay-hol-park.demon.co.uk
I: www.newquay-holiday-parks.co.uk
WH

Nancolleth Farm Caravan Gardens ★★★★
Holiday Park
Rose Award
Newquay, Cornwall TR8 4PN
T: (01872) 510236
F: (01872) 510948
WH

Newperran Tourist Park ★★★★
Touring Park
Rejerrah, Newquay, Cornwall
TR8 5QJ
T: (01872) 572407
F: (01872) 571254
E: trevella@compuserve.com
I: www.chycor.co.uk/newperran

Newquay Holiday Park ★★★★
Holiday Park
Rose Award
Newquay, Cornwall TR8 4HS
T: (01637) 871111
F: (01637) 850818
E: bookings@newquay-hol-park.demon.co.uk
I: www.newquay-holiday-parks.co.uk
WH

Porth Beach Tourist Park ★★★★
Touring Park
Rose Award
Alexandra Road, Porth,
Newquay, Cornwall TR7 3NH
T: (01637) 876531
F: (01637) 871227
E: info@porthbeach.co.uk
I: www.porthbeach.co.uk

Resparva House Touring Park ★★★★
Touring Park
Summercourt, Newquay,
Cornwall TR8 5AH
T: (01872) 510332
E: daveknight1@compuserve.com

Riverside Holiday Park ★★★
Holiday Park
Gwills Lane, Newquay, Cornwall
TR8 4PE
T: (01637) 873617
F: (01637) 877051

Trekenning Tourist Park ★★★★
Touring Park
Newquay, Cornwall TR8 4JF
T: (01637) 880462
F: (01637) 880462

Treloy Tourist Park ★★★★
Touring and Camping Park
Newquay, Cornwall TR8 4JN
T: (01637) 872063 & 876279
F: (01637) 871710
E: rpaull@treloy.co.uk
I: www.treloy.co.uk

Trenance Holiday Park ★★★
Holiday Park
Edgcumbe Avenue, Newquay,
Cornwall TR7 2JY
T: (01637) 873447
F: (01637) 852677
E: tony.hoyte@virgin.net
I: www.mywebpage.net/trenance

Trethiggey Touring Park ★★★★
Touring Park
Quintrell Downs, Newquay,
Cornwall TR8 4LG
T: (01637) 877672
E: suttonjw@m.s.n.com
I: www.trethiggey.co.uk

Trevella Caravan and Camping Park ★★★★★
Holiday, Touring and Camping Park
Rose Award
Crantock, Newquay, Cornwall
TR8 5EW
T: (01637) 830308
F: (01637) 571254
E: trevella@compuserve.com
I: www.chycor.co.uk/trevella

Trevornick Holiday Park ★★★★★
Holiday Park
Holywell Bay, Newquay,
Cornwall TR8 5PW
T: (01637) 830531
F: (01637) 831000
E: info@trevornick.co.uk
I: www.trevornick.co.uk

NEWTON ABBOT
Devon

Dornafield ★★★★★
Touring Park
Dornafield Farm, Two Mile Oak,
Newton Abbot, Devon TQ12 6DD
T: (01803) 812732
F: (01803) 812032
E: enquiries@dornafield.com
I: www.dornafield.com
WH

OARE
Wiltshire

Hill-View Park ★★★
Touring Park
Oare, Marlborough, Wiltshire
SN8 4JE
T: (01672) 563151 & 562271

OKEHAMPTON
Devon

Yertiz Caravan and Camping Park ★★
Holiday and Camping Park
Exeter Road, Okehampton,
Devon EX20 1QF
T: (01837) 52281
E: yertiz@dial.pipex.com
I: www.dspace.dial.pipex.com/yertiz
WH

ORCHESTON
Wiltshire

Stonehenge Touring Park
★★★
Touring Park
Orcheston, Salisbury, Wiltshire
SP3 4SH
T: (01980) 620304
F: (01980) 621121
E: stp@orcheston.freeserve.co.
uk
I: www.orcheston.freeserve.co.
uk

OSMINGTON
Dorset

White Horse Holiday Park
★★★
Holiday Park
Osmington Hill, Osmington,
Weymouth, Dorset DT3 6ED
T: (01305) 832164
F: (01305) 832164
E: whitehorsepark@
whitehorsepark.co.uk
I: www.whitehorsepark.co.uk

OWERMOIGNE
Dorset

Sandyholme Holiday Park
★★★★
Holiday Park
Moreton Road, Owermoigne,
Dorchester, Dorset DT2 8HZ
T: (01305) 852677
F: (01305) 854677

PADSTOW
Cornwall

Carnevas Farm Holiday Park
★★★★
Holiday Park
Rose Award
Carnevas Farm, St Merryn,
Padstow, Cornwall PL28 8PN
T: (01841) 520230
F: (01841) 520230

**The Laurels Caravan and
Camping Site★★★★**
Holiday and Camping Park
Whitecross, Wadebridge,
Cornwall PL27 7JQ
T: (01208) 813341

**Mother Ivey's Bay Caravan
Park★★★★**
Holiday and Touring Park
Rose Award
Trevose Head, Padstow,
Cornwall PL28 8SL
T: (01841) 520990
F: (01841) 520550
E: info@motheriveysbay.com
I: www.motheriveysbay.com
WH

Trerethern Touring Park
★★★★
Touring Park
Padstow, Cornwall PL28 8LE
T: (01841) 532061
F: (01841) 532061
E: camping.trerethern@
btinternet.com
I: www.btinternet.
com/§camping.trerethern

PAIGNTON
Devon

Ashvale Holiday Park ★★★★
Holiday Park
Rose Award
Goodrington Road, Paignton,
Devon TQ4 7JD
T: (01803) 843887
F: (01803) 845427
E: enquiries@beverley-holidays.
co.uk
I: www.beverley-holidays.co.uk
WH

Beverley Park ★★★★
Holiday and Touring Park
Goodrington Road, Paignton,
Devon TQ4 7JE
T: (01803) 843887
F: (01803) 845427
E: enquiries@beverley-holidays.
co.uk
I: www.beverley-holidays.co.uk
WH

Bona Vista Holiday Park ★★★
Holiday Park
Totnes Road, Paignton, Devon
TQ4 7PZ
T: (01803) 551971
E: user@bonavista.softnet.co.uk

**Byslades International Touring
and Camping Park★★★**
Touring Park
Totnes Road, Paignton, Devon
TQ4 7PY
T: (01803) 555072

Grange Court Holiday Centre
★★★★
Holiday Park
Rose Award
Grange Road, Goodrington,
Paignton, Devon TQ4 7JP
T: (01803) 558010
F: (01803) 663336
E: enquiries@hoburne.co.uk
I: www.hoburne.co.uk
WH

Higher Well Farm Holiday Park
★★
Holiday Park
Stoke Gabriel, Totnes, Devon
TQ9 6RN
T: (01803) 782289

Marine Park Holiday Centre
★★★★
Holiday and Touring Park
Grange Road, Paignton, Devon
TQ4 7JR
T: (01803) 843887
F: (01803) 845427
E: enquiries@beverley-holidays.
co.uk
I: www.beverley-holidays.co.uk
WH

Ramslade Touring Park
★★★★★
Touring Park
Stoke Road, Stoke Gabriel,
Totnes, Devon TQ9 6QB
T: (01803) 782575
F: (01803) 782828
E: ramslade@compuserve.com
I: www.ramslade.co.uk

PAR
Cornwall

Par Sands Holiday Park
★★★★
Holiday Park
Rose Award
Par Beach, Par, Cornwall
PL24 2AS
T: (01726) 812868 &
07831 461403
F: (01726) 817899
E: holidays@parsands.co.uk
I: www.parsands.co.uk

PELYNT
Cornwall

Trelay Farm Park ★★★★
Touring Park
Pelynt, Looe, Cornwall PL13 2JX
T: (01503) 220900
F: (01503) 220900

PENTEWAN
Cornwall

Pentewan Sands Holiday Park
★★★★
Holiday Park
Pentewan, St Austell, Cornwall
PL26 6BT
T: (01726) 843485
F: (01726) 844142
E: info@pentewan.co.uk
I: www.pentewan.co.uk

PENZANCE
Cornwall

**Tower Park Caravans and
Camping★★★**
Touring Park
St Buryan, Penzance, Cornwall
TR19 6BZ
T: (01736) 810286
F: (01736) 810954
E: caravans&camping@
towerpark97.freeserve.co.uk

PERRANPORTH
Cornwall

**Perran Sands Holiday Centre
Haven Holidays★★★**
Holiday Park
Perranporth, Cornwall TR6 0AQ
T: (01872) 573551
F: (01872) 571158
E: Amin_Perran_Sands@rank.
com
I: www.Haven-Holidays.co.uk
WH

POLGOOTH
Cornwall

**Saint Margaret's Holiday
Bungalows ★★★★★**
Holiday Park
Tregongeeves Lane, Polgooth, St
Austell, Cornwall PL26 7AX
T: (01726) 74283
F: (01726) 71680
E: sunvalley_holidays@yahoo.
com
I: www/sunvalley_holidays.co.uk

POLPERRO
Cornwall

Killigarth Caravan Park
★★★★
Holiday Park
Polperro, Looe, Cornwall
PL13 2JQ
T: (01503) 272216 & 272409
F: (01503) 272065

POLRUAN-BY-FOWEY
Cornwall

**Polruan Holidays (Camping &
Caravanning)★★★★**
Holiday Park
Townsend Road, Polruan-by-
Fowey, Fowey, Cornwall
PL23 1QH
T: (01726) 870263
F: (01726) 870263
E: polholiday@aol.com
WH

PORLOCK
Somerset

**Burrowhayes Farm Caravan
and Camping Site and Riding
Stables★★★★**
Touring and Camping Park
West Luccombe, Porlock,
Minehead, Somerset TA24 8HT
T: (01643) 862463

Porlock Caravan Park ★★★
Holiday and Touring Park
Highbanks, Porlock, Minehead,
Somerset TA24 8ND
T: (01643) 862269
F: (01643) 862239
E: ADHPCP@aol.com
I: www.exmoortourism.
org/porlockcaravanpark.htm

PORTHTOWAN
Cornwall

Rose Hill Touring Park ★★★★
Touring Park
Porthtowan, Truro, Cornwall
TR4 8AR
T: (01209) 890802
E: johnbarrow@compuserve.
com
I: www.rosehillcamping.co.uk

PORTREATH
Cornwall

Cambrose Touring Park ★★★
Touring Park
Portreath Road, Redruth,
Cornwall TR16 4HT
T: (01209) 890747
F: (01209) 891665

Tehidy Holiday Park ★★★
Touring Park
Harris Mill, Illogan, Portreath,
Redruth, Cornwall TR16 4JQ
T: (01209) 216489 & 314558
F: (01209) 216489
WH

PRESTON
Dorset

Seaview Holiday Park ★★★
Holiday Park
Preston, Weymouth, Dorset
DT3 6DZ
T: (01305) 833037
F: (01305) 833169
WH

Weymouth Bay Holiday Park
★★★
Holiday Park
Preston Road, Preston,
Weymouth, Dorset DT3 6BQ
T: (01305) 832271
F: (01305) 835101
WH

REDHILL

Brook Lodge Farm Touring Caravan and Tent Park★★
Touring Park
Cowslip Green, Redhill, Bristol BS40 5RD
T: (01934) 862311
F: (01934) 862311

REDRUTH
Cornwall

Lanyon Holiday Park ★★★
Losombe Lane, Four Lanes, Redruth, Cornwall TR
T: (01209) 313474 &
07775 782249
F: (01209) 313422

RELUBBUS
Cornwall

River Valley Country Park ★★★★★
Holiday Park
Rose Award
Relubbus, Penzance, Cornwall TR20 9ER
T: (01736) 763398
F: (01736) 763398
E: rivervalley@surfbay.dircon.co.uk
I: www.rivervalley.co.uk

RODNEY STOKE
Somerset

Bucklegrove Caravan & Camping Park ★★★★
Holiday Park
Rose Award
Wells Road, Rodney Stoke, Cheddar, Somerset BS27 3UZ
T: (01749) 870261
F: (01749) 870101
E: bucklegrove@u.genie.co.uk

ROSUDGEON
Cornwall

Kenneggy Cove Holiday Park ★★★
Holiday Park
Higher Kenneggy, Rosudgeon, Penzance, Cornwall TR20 9AU
T: (01736) 763453
F: (01736) 763453
E: enquiries@kenneggycove.co.uk
I: www.kenneggycove.co.uk

ROUSDON
Devon

Pinewood Homes ★★★★
Holiday Park
Rousdon, Lyme Regis, Dorset DT7 3RD
T: (01297) 22055
F: (01297) 22055

Westhayes Caravan Park ★★★★
Holiday Park
Sidmouth Road, Rousdon, Lyme Regis, Dorset DT7 3RD
T: (01297) 23456
F: (01297) 625079
I: welome.to/westhayes
WH

RUAN MINOR
Cornwall

Sea Acres Holiday Park ★★★★
Holiday Park
Kennack Sands, Ruan Minor, Helston, Cornwall TR12 7LT
T: (01326) 290064
F: (01326) 290063
E: seaacres1.@aol.com

Silver Sands Holiday Park ★★★
Holiday Park
Gwendreath, Kennack Sands, Ruan Minor, Helston, Cornwall TR12 7LZ
T: (01326) 290631
F: (01326) 290631
E: silversnds@aol.com
I: www.cornwall-online.co.uk/silversands
WH

ST AGNES
Cornwall

Beacon Cottage Farm Touring Park★★★★
Touring Park
Beacon Drive, St Agnes, Cornwall TR5 0NU
T: (01872) 552347 & 553381
WH

Troytown Farm Campsite ★★★
Camping Park
Troytown Farm, St Agnes, Isles of Scilly TR22 0PL
T: (01720) 422360
E: troytown@talk21.com
I: www.isles-of-scilly.co.uk

ST AUSTELL
Cornwall

Duporth Holiday Park ★★★
Holiday Park
St Austell Bay, St Austell, Cornwall PL26 6AJ
T: (01726) 65511
F: (01726) 68497
E: duporth@aol.com
WH

River Valley Holiday Park ★★★★
Holiday Park
Rose Award
Pentewan Road, London Apprentice, St Austell, Cornwall PL26 7AP
T: (01726) 73533
F: (01726) 73533
E: JohnClemo@aol.com
I: river-valley.co.uk
WH

Sun Valley Holiday Park ★★★★★
Holiday Park
Rose Award
Pentewan Road, St Austell, Cornwall PL26 6DJ
T: (01726) 843266 & 843842
E: sunvalley_holidays@yahoo.com
I: www.sunvalley-holidays.co.uk
WH

Trewhiddle Holiday Estate ★★★★
Holiday Park
Pentewan Road, Trewhiddle, St Austell, Cornwall PL26 7AD
T: (01726) 67011
F: (01726) 67010
E: mcclelland@btinternet.com
I: www.trewhiddle.co.uk

ST BURYAN
Cornwall

Camping and Caravanning Club Site★★★★
Touring Park
Sennen Cove Club Site, Higher Tregiffian Farm, St Buryan, Penzance, Cornwall TR19 6JB
T: (01736) 871588
I: www.camping&caravanningclub.co.uk

ST COLUMB MAJOR
Cornwall

Tregatillian Holiday Park ★★★★
Holiday Park
Rose Award
St Columb Major, Cornwall TR9 6JH
T: (01637) 880482
F: (01637) 880482
E: tregattillian@fsbdial.co.uk
I: www.chycor.co.uk/parks/tregatillian

ST GENNYS
Cornwall

Camping and Caravanning Club Site ★★★★
Touring and Camping Park
Bude Club Site, Gillards Moor, St Gennys, Bude, Cornwall EX23 0BG
T: (01840) 230650
I: www.campingandcaravanningclub.co.uk

ST IVES
Cornwall

Ayr Holiday Park ★★★★
Holiday Park
Rose Award
Higher Ayr, Ayr, St Ives, Cornwall TR26 1EJ
T: (01736) 795855
F: (01736) 798797
E: andy@ayr-holiday-park.demon.co.uk
WH

Little Trevarrack Touring Park ★★★
Touring Park
Laity Lane, Carbis Bay, St Ives, Cornwall TR26 3HW
T: (01736) 797580 & 795640
F: (01736) 797580
E: littletrevarrack@hotmail.com
WH

Polmanter Tourist Park ★★★★★
Touring Park
St Ives, Cornwall TR26 3LX
T: (01736) 795640
F: (01736) 795640
E: philip_osbourne@hotmail.com
I: www.polmanter.com
WH

Trevalgan Holiday Farm ★★★★
Touring Park
St Ives, Cornwall TR26 3BJ
T: (01736) 796433
F: (01736) 796433
E: holiday@trevalgan.demon.co.uk
WH

ST JUST-IN-PENWITH
Cornwall

Roselands Caravan Park ★★★
Holiday Park
Dowran, St Just-in-Penwith, Penzance, Cornwall TR19 7RS
T: (01736) 788571
F: (01736) 788571
E: camping@roseland84.freeserve.co.uk
I: www.roselands

ST JUST IN ROSELAND
Cornwall

Trethem Mill Touring Park ★★★★★
Touring Park
St Just in Roseland, Truro, Cornwall TR2 5JF
T: (01872) 580504
F: (01872) 580968
E: reception@trethem-mill.co.uk
I: www.trethem-mill.co.uk
WH

ST MARY'S
Isles of Scilly

Garrison Farm Campsite ★★
Camping Park
St Mary's, Isles of Scilly TR21 0LS
T: (01720) 422670
F: (01720) 422670
E: tedmoulson@cs.com
I: www.isles-of-scilly.co.uk

ST MERRYN
Cornwall

Higher Harlyn Park ★★
Holiday Park
St Merryn, Padstow, Cornwall PL28 8SG
T: (01841) 520022 & 520879
F: (01841) 520879

Trethias Farm Caravan Park ★★
Touring Park
Treyarnon Bay, St Merryn, Padstow, Cornwall PL28 8PL
T: (01841) 520323 & 520055
F: (01841) 520055

Trevean Farm ★★★
Holiday Park
St Merryn, Padstow, Cornwall PL28 8PR
T: (01841) 520772

ST MINVER
Cornwall

St Minver Holiday Park ★★★
Holiday Park
St Minver, Wadebridge, Cornwall PL27 6RR
T: (01208) 862305
F: (01208) 862265

ST TUDY
Cornwall

Hengar Manor ★★★★
Holiday Park
Rose Award
St Tudy, Bodmin, Cornwall PL30 3PL
T: (01208) 850382
F: (01208) 850722
E: holidays@hengarmanor.co.uk
I: www.hengarmanor.co.uk

SALCOMBE
Devon

Bolberry House Farm ★★★
Touring and Camping Park
Bolberry, Malborough,
Kingsbridge, Devon TQ7 3DY
T: (01548) 561251 & 560926
E: bolberry.house@virgin.net
I: www.bolberryparks.co.uk

Higher Rew Caravan & Camping Park ★★★★
Touring Park
Malborough, Salcombe, Devon
TQ7 3DW
T: (01548) 842681 & 843681
F: (01548) 843681

Karrageen Caravan and Camping Park ★★★★
Touring and Camping Park
Karrageen, Bolberry,
Malborough, Kingsbridge, Devon
TQ7 3EN
T: (01548) 561230
F: (01548) 560192
E: phil@karrageen.co.uk
I: www.karrageen.co.uk

SALCOMBE REGIS
Devon

Kings Down Tail Caravan and Camping Park★★★★
Touring Park
Salcombe Regis, Sidmouth,
Devon EX10 0PD
T: (01297) 680313
F: (01297) 680313
I: www.uk.parks.co.uk/kingsdowntail

SALISBURY
Wiltshire

Camping And Caravanning Club Site★★★★
Touring and Camping Park
Hudsons Field, Castle Road,
Salisbury, Wiltshire SP1 3RR
T: (01722) 320713
I: www.campingandcaravanningclub.co.uk

SANDY BAY
Devon

Devon Cliffs Holiday Park ★★★
Holiday Park
Sandy Bay, Exmouth, Devon
EX8 5BT
T: (01395) 226226
F: (01395) 223111
WH

SEATON
Devon

Axe Vale Caravan Park ★★★
Holiday Park
Colyford Road, Seaton, Devon
EX12 2DF
T: (01297) 21342 & 0800 0688826
F: (01297) 21712
E: info@axevale.co.uk
I: www.axevale.co.uk

Lyme Bay Holiday Park ★★★★
Holiday Park
87 Harbour Road, Seaton, Devon
EX12 2NE
T: (01297) 21816
F: (01297) 24688
I: www.renowned.co.uk
WH

SEEND
Wiltshire

Camping and Caravanning Club Site ★★★★★
Touring Park
Scout Lane, Seend, Melksham,
Wiltshire SN12 6RN
T: (01380) 828839
I: www.campingandcaravanningclub.co.uk
WH

SHALDON
Devon

Coast View Holiday Park ★★★★
Holiday Park
Torquay Road, Shaldon,
Teignmouth, Devon TQ14 0BG
T: (01626) 872392
F: (01626) 872719

Devon Valley Holiday Village ★★★★
Holiday Park
Rose Award
Coombe Road, Ringmore,
Shaldon, Teignmouth, Devon
TQ14 0EY
T: (01626) 872525 & (01803) 852600
F: (01626) 873634
E: devalley@aol.com

SIDBURY
Devon

Putts Corner Caravan Club Site ★★★★★
Touring Park
Sidbury, Sidmouth, Devon
EX10 0QQ
T: (01404) 42875
WH

SIDMOUTH
Devon

Salcombe Regis Camping and Caravan Park★★★★★
Holiday and Touring Park
Rose Award
Salcombe Regis, Sidmouth,
Devon EX10 0JH
T: (01395) 514303
F: (01395) 514303
E: info@salcombe-regis.co.uk
I: www.salcombe-regis.co.uk
WH

SLAPTON
Devon

Slapton Camping and Caravanning Club Site★★★★
Touring Park
Middle Grounds, Slapton,
Kingsbridge, Devon TQ7 1QW
T: (01548) 580538
I: www.campingandcaravanningclub.co.uk

STICKLEPATH
Devon

Olditch Farm Caravan and Camping Park★★★
Holiday Park
Sticklepath, Okehampton, Devon
EX20 2NT
T: (01837) 840734
F: (01837) 840877
E: info@olditch.co.uk
I: www.olditch.co.uk

STRATTON
Cornwall

Ivyleaf Combe ★★★★
Holiday Park
Ivyleaf Hill, Stratton, Bude,
Cornwall EX23 9LD
T: (01288) 321323
E: tony@ivyleafcombe.com
I: www.ivyleafcombe.com
WH

TAUNTON
Somerset

Ashe Farm Caravan and Campsite ★★★
Touring Park
Ashe, Thornfalcon, Taunton,
Somerset TA3 5NW
T: (01823) 442567
F: (01823) 443372
WH

Holly Bush Park ★★★★
Touring Park
Culmhead, Taunton, Somerset
TA3 7EA
T: (01823) 421515
F: (01823) 421885
E: beaumont@hollybushpark.ndo.co.uk
I: www.hollybushpark.co.uk

TAVISTOCK
Devon

Harford Bridge Holiday Park ★★★★
Holiday Park
Rose Award
Peter Tavy, Tavistock, Devon
PL19 9LS
T: (01822) 810349
F: (01822) 810028
E: enquiry@harfordbridge.co.uk
I: www.harfordbridge.co.uk
WH

Woodovis Park ★★★★
Holiday Park
Rose Award
Tavistock, Devon PL19 8NY
T: (01822) 832968
F: (01822) 832948
E: info@woodovis.com
I: www.woodovis.com
WH

TEDBURN ST MARY
Devon

Springfield Holiday Park ★★★★
Holiday Park
Rose Award
Tedburn Road, Tedburn St Mary,
Exeter, Devon EX6 6EW
T: (01647) 24242
F: (01647) 24131
E: springhol@aol.com

TEIGNGRACE
Devon

Twelve Oaks Farm Caravan Park ★★★★
Touring Park
Twelve Oaks Farm, Teigngrace,
Newton Abbot, Devon TQ12 6QT
T: (01626) 352769 & 335015
F: (01626) 352769

TINTAGEL
Cornwall

Bossiney Farm Caravan and Camping Park★★★★
Holiday Park
Tintagel, Cornwall PL34 0AY
T: (01840) 770481
F: (01840) 770025

TORQUAY
Devon

Widdicombe Farm Caravan Park ★★★★
Holiday Park
Ring Road (A380), Compton,
Paignton, Devon TQ3 1ST
T: (01803) 558325
F: (01803) 559526

TREGURRIAN
Cornwall

Camping and Caravanning Club Site★★★★
Touring Park
Tregurrian, Newquay, Cornwall
TR8 4AE
T: (01637) 860448
I: www.campingandcaravanningclub.co.uk

TREVELLAS
Cornwall

Perran View Holiday Park ★★★★
Holiday Park
Trevellas, St Agnes, Cornwall
TR5 0XS
T: (01872) 552623
F: (01872) 553813
I: www.jfhols.co.uk
WH

TRURO
Cornwall

Leverton Place ★★★★★
Camping Park
Rose Award
Greenbottom, Truro, Cornwall
TR4 8QW
T: (01872) 560462
F: (01872) 560668

Liskey Touring Park ★★★★★
Touring Park
Greenbottom, Truro, Cornwall
TR4 8QN
T: (01872) 560274
F: (01872) 560274
E: enquiries@liskey.com
I: www.liskey.com
WH

Ringwell Valley Holiday Park ★★★★★
Holiday Park
Rose Award
Bissoe Road, Carnon Downs,
Truro, Cornwall TR3 6LQ
T: (01872) 862194
F: (01872) 864343
E: keith@ringwell.co.uk
I: www.ringwell.co.uk
WH

Summer Valley Touring Park ★★★★
Touring Park
Shortlanesend, Truro, Cornwall
TR4 9DW
T: (01872) 277878
I: summervalley.co.uk
WH

UMBERLEIGH
Devon

Camping and Caravanning Club Site ★★★★
Touring Park
Over Weir, Umberleigh, Devon
EX37 9DU
T: (01769) 560009
I: www.campingandcaravanningclub.co.uk

UPHILL
North Somerset
Slimeridge Farm ★★★★
Touring Park
Links Road, Uphill, Weston-
super-Mare BS23 4XY
T: (01934) 641641

VERYAN
Cornwall
**Camping & Caravanning Club
Site ★★★★**
Touring Park
Tretheake Manor, Veryan, Truro,
Cornwall TR2 5PP
T: (01872) 501658
F: (01872) 501658
I: www.
campingandcaravanningclub.co.
uk

WADEBRIDGE
Cornwall
**Little Bodieve Holiday Park
★★★★**
Holiday Park
Bodieve Road, Wadebridge,
Cornwall PL27 6EG
T: (01208) 812323
I: www.chycor.co.
uk/parks/little-bodieve

**Trewince Farm Holiday Park
★★★★**
Holiday Park
Rose Award
St Issey, Wadebridge, Cornwall
PL27 7RL
T: (01208) 812830
F: (01208) 812835

WALTON
Somerset
**Bramble Hill Caravan &
Camping Park ★★**
Touring Park
Bramble Hill, Walton, Street,
Somerset BA16 9RQ
T: (01458) 442548 &
07711 893670

WARMINSTER
Wiltshire
**Longleat Caravan Club Site
★★★★**
Touring Park
Warminster, Wiltshire BA12 7NL
T: (01985) 844663
WH

WARMWELL
Dorset
**Warmwell Country Touring
Park ★★★★**
Touring Park
Warmwell, Weymouth, Dorset
DT2 8JD
T: (01305) 852313
F: (01305) 851824
I: welcome.to/warmwell

**Warmwell Leisure Resort
★★★**
Holiday Park
Warmwell, Dorchester, Dorset
DT2 8JE
T: (01305) 852911
F: (01305) 854588
I: www.parkdean.com
WH

WATCHET
Somerset
**Lorna Doone Caravan Park
★★★★★**
Holiday Park
Rose Award
Watchet, Somerset TA23 0BJ
T: (01984) 631206
F: (01984) 633537
E: mail@lornadoone.co.uk
I: www.lornadoone.co.uk

**West Bay Caravan Park
★★★★★**
Holiday Park
Rose Award
Cleeve Hill, Watchet, Somerset
TA23 0BJ
T: (01984) 631261
F: (01984) 634944

WATERROW
Somerset
**Waterrow Touring Park
★★★★**
Touring Park
Waterrow, Taunton, Somerset
TA4 2AZ
T: (01984) 623464 & 624280
F: (01984) 624280
E: taylor@waterrowpark.u-net.
com
I: www.waterrowpark.u-net.com

WELLS
Somerset
**Mendip Heights Camping and
Caravan Park ★★★★**
Touring Park
Townsend, Priddy, Wells,
Somerset BA5 3BP
T: (01749) 870241
F: (01749) 870368
E: bta@mendipheights.co.uk
I: www.mendipheights.co.uk
WH

WEMBURY
Devon
**Churchwood Valley Holiday
Cabins ★★★★**
Holiday Park
Wembury Bay, Wembury,
Plymouth PL9 0DZ
T: (01752) 862382
F: (01752) 863274
E: Churchwoodvalley@
btinternet.com
WH

WEST BAY
Dorset
West Bay Holiday Park ★★★
Holiday Park
West Bay, Bridport, Dorset
DT6 4HB
T: (01308) 422424
F: (01308) 421371
WH

WEST BEXINGTON
Dorset
**Gorselands Caravan Park
★★★★**
Holiday Park
Rose Award
West Bexington, Dorchester,
Dorset DT2 9DJ
T: (01308) 897232
F: (01308) 897239

WEST QUANTOXHEAD
Somerset
**Home Farm Holiday Centre
★★★**
Holiday Park
St Audries Bay, Williton,
Taunton, Somerset TA4 4DP
T: (01984) 632487
F: (01984) 634687

**St Audries Bay Holiday Club
★★★**
Holiday Park
West Quantoxhead, Taunton,
Somerset TA4 4DY
T: (01984) 632515
F: (01984) 632785

WESTON
Devon
**Oakdown Touring and Holiday
Home Park ★★★★★**
Rose Award
Holiday and Touring Park
Weston, Sidmouth, Devon
EX10 0PH
T: (01297) 680387
F: (01297) 680541
E: oakdown@btinternet.com
WH

**Stoneleigh Holiday and Leisure
Village ★★★★**
Holiday Park
Weston, Sidmouth, Devon
EX10 0PJ
T: (01395) 513619
F: (01395) 513629

WESTON-SUPER-MARE
North Somerset
**Brean Leisure Park Limited
★★★**
Holiday Park
Coast Road, Brean, Burnham-
on-Sea, Somerset TA8 2RF
T: (01278) 751595 & 752100
F: (01278) 752102
E: admin@hru.co.uk
I: www.hru.co.ukwww.
holidayunity.demon.co.uk

**Camping and Caravanning
Club Site ★★★**
Touring Park
West End Farm, Locking,
Weston-super-Mare, Somerset
BS24 8RH
T: (01934) 822548
I: www.
campingandcaravanningclub.co.
uk

**Carefree Holiday Park
★★★★★**
Holiday Park
Rose Award
12 Beach Road, Sand Bay,
Weston-super-Mare, BS22 9UZ
T: (01934) 624541
F: (01934) 613636

**Country View Caravan Park
★★★**
Holiday Park
Sand Road, Sand Bay, Weston-
super-Mare, BS22 9UJ
T: (01934) 627595 &
07785 245461
F: (01934) 627595

Purn International Holiday
Park ★★★★
Holiday Park
Bridgwater Road, A370 Bleadon,
Weston-super-Mare, BS24 0AN
T: (01934) 812342
F: (01934) 812342
E: gavin@purn-international.
freeserve.co.uk

**Sand Bay Caravan Park
★★★★**
Holiday Park
52 Beach Road, Sand Bay,
Weston-super-Mare, BS22 9UW
T: (01934) 633126
WH

**West End Farm/Caravan and
Camping Park ★★★**
Touring Park
Locking, Weston-super-Mare
BS24 8RH
T: (01934) 822529
F: (01934) 822529

**Weston Gateway Tourist
Caravan Park ★★★**
Holiday Park
West Wick, Weston-super-Mare,
BS24 7TF
T: (01934) 510344

WESTWARD HO!
Devon
**Beachside Holiday Park
★★★★**
Holiday Park
Rose Award
Merley Road, Westward Ho!,
Bideford, Devon EX39 1JX
T: (01237) 421163
F: (01237) 472100
E: beachside@surfbay.dircon.co.
uk
I: www.beachsideholidays.co.uk

Surf Bay Holiday Park ★★★★
Holiday Park
Rose Award
Golf Links Road, Westward Ho!,
Bideford, Devon EX39 1HD
T: (01237) 471833
F: (01237) 474387
E: surfbayholidaypark@surfbay.
dircon.co.uk
I: www.surfbay.co.uk

**Westward Ho! Beach Holiday
Park ★★★★**
Holiday Park
Nelson Road, Westward Ho!,
Bideford, Devon EX34 8PF
T: (01237) 478924 &
(01271) 866766
F: (01271) 866791
WH

WEYMOUTH
Dorset
**Bagwell Farm Touring Park
★★★★**
Touring Park
Chickerell, Weymouth, Dorset
DT3 4EA
T: (01305) 782575
F: (01305) 786987

**Chesil Beach Holiday Village
★★★**
Holiday Park
Chesil Beach, Weymouth, Dorset
DT4 9AG
T: (01305) 773233

East Fleet Farm Touring Park
★★★
Touring Park
Fleet Lane, Chickerell,
Weymouth, Dorset DT3 4DW
T: (01305) 785768
E: richard@eastfleetfc.freeserve.
co.uk
I: www.eastfleet.co.uk

Littlesea Holiday Park ★★★
Holiday Park
Lynch Lane, Weymouth, Dorset
DT4 9DT
T: (01305) 774414
F: (01305) 760038
[WH]

Pebble Bank Caravan Park
★★★
Camping Park
90 Camp Road, Wyke Regis,
Weymouth, Dorset DT4 9HF
T: (01305) 774844
F: (01305) 774844
E: ian@pebbank.freeserve.co.uk
I: www.westcountry.
nett/dorset/
pebble_bank_caravan_park.htm
[WH]

Waterside Holiday Park
★★★★★
Holiday Park
Rose Award
Bowleaze Cove, Weymouth,
Dorset DT3 6PP
T: (01305) 833103
F: (01305) 832830
E: whgewatside.demon.co.uk
I: www.watersideholidays.co.uk
[WH]

WHIDDON DOWN
Devon

Dartmoor View Holiday Park
★★★★★
Holiday and Touring Park
Whiddon Down, Okehampton,
Devon EX20 2QL
T: (01647) 231545
F: (01647) 231654
E: jo@dartmoorview.co.uk
I: www.dartmoorview.co.uk
[WH]

WHITE CROSS
Cornwall

Summer Lodge Holiday Park
★★★★
Holiday Park
White Cross, Newquay, Cornwall
TR8 4LW
T: (01726) 860415
F: (01726) 861490
E: reservations@summerlodge.
co.uk
I: www.summerlodge.co.uk

White Acres Holiday Park
★★★★★
Holiday Park
Rose Award
White Cross, Newquay, Cornwall
TR8 4LW
T: (01726) 860220
F: (01726) 860877
E: whiteacres.co.uk

WIDEMOUTH BAY
Cornwall

Penhalt Farm Holiday Park
★★★
Holiday Park
Widemouth Bay, Bude, Cornwall
EX23 0DG
T: (01288) 361210
F: (01288) 361210
I: www.holidaybank.co.uk

Widemouth Bay Caravan Park
★★★
Holiday Park
Widemouth Bay, Bude, Cornwall
EX23 0DW
T: (01288) 361208 &
(01271) 866766
F: (01271) 866791
I: www.jfhols.co.uk
[WH]

WINSFORD
Somerset

**Halse Farm Caravan & Tent
Park ★★★★**
Touring Park
Winsford, Minehead, Somerset
TA24 7JL
T: (01643) 851259
F: (01643) 851592
E: brown@halsefarm.co.uk
I: www.halsefarm.co.uk

WINSLEY
Wiltshire

**Church Farm
Rating Applied For**
Winsley, Bradford-on-Avon,
Wiltshire BA15 2JH
T: (01225) 722246 &
07831 421427
F: (01225) 722246
[WH]

WOODBURY
Devon

Castle Brake Holiday Park
★★★
Holiday Park
Castle Lane, Woodbury, Exeter,
Devon EX5 1HA
T: (01395) 232431

**Webbers Farm Caravan &
Camping Park ★★★★★**
Touring Park
Castle Lane, Woodbury, Exeter,
Devon EX5 1EA
T: (01395) 232276
F: (01395) 233389
E: reception@webbersfarm.co.
uk
I: www.webbersfarm.co.uk
[WH]

WOOLACOMBE
Devon

Cleavewood Holiday Park
★★★★
Holiday Park
Rose Award
Woolacombe, Devon EX34 7HT
T: (01271) 870277 & 870343
F: (01271) 871042
E: goodtimes@
woolacombe-bay.co.uk
I: www.woolacombe-bay.co.uk
[WH]

Golden Coast Holiday Village
★★★★
Holiday Park
Station Road, Woolacombe,
Devon EX34 7HW
T: (01271) 870343
F: (01271) 870089
E: goodtimes@
woolacombe-bay.co.uk
I: www.woolacombe-bay.co.uk
[WH]

**Woolacombe Bay Holiday
Village ★★★★**
Holiday Park
Rose Award
Seymour, Sandy Lane,
Woolacombe, Devon EX34 7AH
T: (01271) 870221
F: (01271) 871042
E: goodtimes@
woolacombe-bay.co.uk
I: www.woolacombe-bay.co.uk
[WH]

**Woolacombe Sands Holiday
Park ★★★**
Holiday Park
Beach Road, Woolacombe,
Devon EX34 7AF
T: (01271) 870569
F: (01271) 870606
E: lifesabeach@
woolacombe-sands.co.uk
I: www.woolacombe-sands.co.
uk

YEOVIL
Somerset

**Long Hazel International
Caravan and Camping Park**
★★★★
Touring Park
High Street, Sparkford, Yeovil,
Somerset BA22 7JH
T: (01963) 440002
F: (01963) 440002
I: www.sparkford.f9.co.uk/lhi.
htm
[♿]

SOUTH OF ENGLAND

ALDERHOLT
Dorset

**Hill Cottage Farm Caravan
Park ★★★★**
Touring Park
Sandleheath Road, Alderholt,
Fordingbridge, Hampshire
SP6 3EG
T: (01425) 650513
F: (01425) 652339

ANDOVER
Hampshire

**Wyke Down Touring Caravan &
Camping Park★★★**
Touring and Camping Park
Picket Piece, Andover,
Hampshire SP11 6LX
T: (01264) 352048
F: (01264) 324661
E: wykedown@ukonline.co.uk
I: www.ukonline.co.
uk/wykedown

APSE HEATH
Isle of Wight

Cheverton Farm Camping Site
★★★★
Touring and Camping Park
Newport Road, Apse Heath,
Sandown, Isle of Wight
PO36 9PJ
T: (01983) 866414 & (024) 7669
4995

Village Way Camping Site
★★★
*Holiday, Touring and Camping
Park*
Newport Road, Apse Heath,
Sandown, Isle of Wight
PO36 9PJ
T: (01983) 863279

ASHURST
Hampshire

**Forestry Commission Ashurst
Caravan & Camping Site**
★★★★
Camping Park
Lyndhurst Road, Ashurst,
Southampton, Hampshire
SO40 2AA
T: (0131) 3146505
E: fe.holidays@forestry.gov.uk
I: www.forestry.gov.uk

ATHERFIELD BAY
Isle of Wight

Chine Farm Camping Site ★★
Touring and Camping Park
Chine Farm, Military Road,
Atherfield Bay, Ventnor, Isle of
Wight PO38 2JH
T: (01983) 740228

BANBURY
Oxfordshire

Bo-Peep Caravan Park ★★★★
Touring Park
Aynho Road, Adderbury,
Banbury, Oxfordshire OX17 3NP
T: (01295) 810605
F: (01295) 810605
E: warden@bo-peep.co.uk
I: www.bo-peep.co.uk
[WH]

BEACONSFIELD
Buckinghamshire

**Highclere Farm Country
Touring Park★★★★**
Touring and Camping Park
Newbarn Lane, Seer Green,
Beaconsfield, Buckinghamshire
HP9 2QZ
T: (01494) 874505
F: (01494) 875238
[WH]

BEMBRIDGE
Isle of Wight
Sandhills Holiday Park ★★★
Holiday Park
Whitecliff Bay, Bembridge, Isle of Wight PO35 5QB
T: (01983) 872277
F: (01983) 874888

Whitecliff Bay Holiday Park Ltd ★★★★
Holiday Park
Rose Award
Hillway Road, Bembridge, Isle of Wight PO35 5PL
T: (01983) 872671
F: (01983) 872941
E: whitecliff-bay@
isle-of-wight.com
I: www.isle-of-wight.uk.
com/whitecliff-bay

BERE REGIS
Dorset
Rowlands Wait Touring Park ★★★
Touring Park
Rye Hill, Bere Regis, Wareham, Dorset BH20 7LP
T: (01929) 472727
F: (01929) 472727
E: info@rowlandswait.co.uk
I: www.rowlandswait.co.uk

BLANDFORD FORUM
Dorset
The Inside Park ★★★★
Touring and Camping Park
Blandford Forum, Dorset DT11 9AD
T: (01258) 453719 &
07778 313293
F: (01258) 459921
E: inspark@aol.com
I: members.aol.
com/inspark/inspark

BLETCHINGDON
Oxfordshire
Diamond Farm Caravan & Camping Park ★★★
Touring Park
Islip Road, Bletchingdon, Oxford, Oxfordshire OX5 3DR
T: (01869) 350909
F: (01869) 350918

BRIGHSTONE
Isle of Wight
Grange Farm Camping & Caravan ★★★
Camping Park
Military Road, Brighstone, Isle of Wight PO30 4DA
T: (01983) 740296
F: (01983) 741233
E: grangefarm@brighstonebay.
fsnet.co.uk
I: www.brighstonebay.fsnet.co.
uk/main.htm

Lower Sutton Farm ★★★
Holiday Park
Military Road, Brighstone, Newport, Isle of Wight PO30 4PG
T: (01983) 740401

BROCKENHURST
Hampshire
Forestry Commission Hollands Wood Caravan & Camping Site ★★★★
Camping Park
Lyndhurst Road, Brockenhurst, Hampshire SO42 7QH
T: (0131) 314 6505
E: fe.holidays@forestry.gov.uk
I: www.forestry.gov.uk

Forestry Commission Roundhill Caravan & Camping Site ★★★
Touring and Camping Park
Beaulieu Road, Brockenhurst, Hampshire SO42 7QL
T: (0131) 314 6505
F: (0131) 334 0849
E: fe.holidays@forestry.gov.uk
I: www.forestry.gov.uk

BROOK
Isle of Wight
Compton Farm ★★
Holiday and Camping Park
Brook, Newport, Isle of Wight PO30 4HF
T: (01983) 740215
F: (01983) 740215

BURFORD
Oxfordshire
Burford Caravan Club Site ★★★★★
Touring and Camping Park
Bradwell Grove, Burford, Oxfordshire OX18 4JJ
T: (01993) 823080
[WH]

CHADLINGTON
Oxfordshire
Camping & Caravanning Club Site ★★★★
Touring and Camping Park
Chipping Norton Road, Chadlington, Oxford, Oxfordshire OX7 3PE
T: (01608) 641993
I: www.
campingandcaravanningclub.co.
uk

CHARLBURY
Oxfordshire
Cotswold View Caravan & Camping Site ★★★★
Touring and Camping Park
Enstone Road, Charlbury, Oxford, Oxfordshire OX7 3JH
T: (01608) 810314
F: (01608) 811891

CHRISTCHURCH
Dorset
Beaulieu Gardens Holiday Park ★★★★★
Holiday Park
Rose Award
Beaulieu Avenue, Christchurch, Dorset BH23 2EB
T: (01202) 486215
F: (01202) 483878
E: enquiries@
meadowbank-holidays.co.uk
I: www.meadowbank-holidays.
co.uk
[WH]

Grove Farm Meadow Holiday Park ★★★★★
Holiday Park
Rose Award
Stour Way, Christchurch, Dorset BH23 2PQ
T: (01202) 483597
F: (01202) 483878
E: ashley@meadowbank-hols.
demon.co.uk
[WH]

Harrow Wood Farm Caravan Park ★★★★
Touring and Camping Park
Poplar Lane, Bransgore, Christchurch, Dorset BH23 8JE
T: (01425) 672487
F: (01425) 672487
E: harwood@caravan-sites.co.
uk
I: www.caravan-sites.co.uk

Hoburne Park ★★★★★
Holiday and Touring Park
Hoburne Lane, Christchurch, Dorset BH23 4HU
T: (01425) 273379
F: (01425) 270705
E: enquiries@hoburne.co.uk
I: www.hoburne.co.uk
[WH]

Mount Pleasant Touring Park ★★★★★
Touring Park
Matchams Lane, Hurn, Christchurch, Dorset BH23 6AW
T: (01202) 475474
E: enq@mount-pleasant-ec.co.
uk
I: www.mount-pleasant-cc.co.uk
[WH]

COWES
Isle of Wight
Sunnycott Caravan Park ★★★
Holiday Park
Rew Street, Cowes, Isle of Wight PO31 8NN
T: (01983) 292859
F: (01983) 292859

CRANMORE
Isle of Wight
Silver Glades Caravan Park ★★★★
Holiday Park
Solent Road, Cranmore, Yarmouth, Isle of Wight PO41 0XZ
T: (01983) 760172

EAST COWES
Isle of Wight
Waverley Park Holiday Centre ★★
Holiday Park
Old Road, East Cowes, Isle of Wight PO32 6AW
T: (01983) 293452
F: (01983) 200494
E: cowes@msn.com

FERNDOWN
Dorset
St Leonards Farm ★★★
Touring and Camping Park
Ringwood Road, West Moors, Ferndown, Dorset BH22 0AQ
T: (01202) 872637
F: (01202) 872637

FRESHWATER
Isle of Wight
Heathfield Farm Camping Site ★★★
Camping Park
Heathfield Road, Freshwater, Isle of Wight PO40 9SH
T: (01983) 756756
F: (01983) 752480
E: heathfield@netguides.co.uk
I: www.netguides.co.uk

Mountfield Holiday Park ★★★
Holiday Park
Norton Green, Freshwater, Isle of Wight PO40 9RU
T: (01983) 752993
F: (01983) 755664

FRITHAM
Hampshire
Forestry Commission Ocknell/ Longbeech Caravan & Camping Site ★★★
Camping Park
Fritham, Lyndhurst, Hampshire SO43 7HH
T: (0131) 314 6505
F: (0131) 3340849
E: fe.holidays@forestry.gov.uk
I: www.forestry.gov.uk

GILLINGHAM
Dorset
Thorngrove Caravan & Camping Park ★★★★
Camping Park
Common Mead Lane, Gillingham, Dorset SP8 4RE
T: (01747) 822242
F: (01747) 825966
♿

GODSHILL
Hampshire
Sandy Balls Holiday Centre ★★★★★
Holiday, Touring and Camping Park
Rose Award
Godshill, Fordingbridge, Hampshire SP6 2JY
T: (01425) 653042
F: (01425) 653067
E: post@sandy-balls.co.uk
I: www.sandy-balls.co.uk
[WH]

GOSPORT
Hampshire
Kingfisher Caravan Park ★★★★
Holiday, Touring and Camping Park
Rose Award
Browndown Road, Stokes Bay, Gosport, Hampshire PO13 9BE
T: (023) 9250 2611
F: (023) 9258 3583
E: info@
kingfisher-caravan-park.co.uk
I: www.kingfisher-caravan-park.
co.uk

SOUTH OF ENGLAND

GURNARD
Isle of Wight

Gurnard Pines Holiday Village ★★★★
Holiday Park
Rose Award
Cockleton Lane, Gurnard, Cowes,
Isle of Wight PO31 8QE
T: (01983) 292395
F: (01983) 299415
E: mail@pines.tcp.co.uk
I: www.netguides.co.uk
WH

Solent Lawn Holiday Park ★★★
Holiday Park
Shore Road, Gurnard, Cowes,
Isle of Wight PO31 8JX
T: (01983) 293243
E: info@isleofwightselfcatering.
co.uk
I: www.isleofwightselfcatering.
co.uk

HAMBLE
Hampshire

Riverside Park ★★★★
Holiday and Touring Park
Rose Award
Satchell Lane, Hamble,
Southampton, Hampshire
SO31 4HR
T: (023) 8045 3220
F: (023) 8045 3611
E: enquiries@riversideholidays.
co.uk
I: www.riversideholidays.co.uk
WH

HAYLING ISLAND
Hampshire

Fishers Caravan Park ★★★★
Holiday Park
31 Fishery Lane, Hayling Island,
Hampshire PO11 9NP
T: (023) 9246 3501

**Fishery Creek Caravan &
Camping Park★★★**
Camping Park
Fishery Lane, Hayling Island,
Hampshire PO11 9NR
T: (023) 9246 2164
F: (023) 9246 2164

Higworth Caravan Park ★★★
Holiday Park
Manor Road, Hayling Island,
Hampshire PO11 0QS
T: (023) 9246 5021
F: (023) 9246 4632

Mill Rythe Holiday Village ★★★★★
Holiday Park
Havant Road, Hayling Island,
Hampshire PO11 0PB
T: (023) 9246 3805
F: (023) 9246 4842
WH

Woodcot Caravan Park ★★★★
Holiday Park
29 Fishery Lane, Hayling Island,
Hampshire PO11 9NP
T: (023) 9246 3501

HENLEY-ON-THAMES
Oxfordshire

**Swiss Farm International
Camping ★★**
Touring and Camping Park
Swiss Farm, Marlow Road,
Henley-on-Thames, Oxfordshire
RG9 2HY
T: (01491) 573419
F: (01494) 573419
E: borlase@borlase.demon.uk

HIGHCLIFFE
Dorset

Cobb's Holiday Park ★★★★
Holiday Park
Rose Award
32 Gordon Road, Highcliffe,
Christchurch, Dorset BH23 5HN
T: (01425) 273301
F: (01425) 276090

HOLMSLEY
Hampshire

**Forestry Commission Holmsley
Caravan & Camping Site ★★★★**
Touring and Camping Park
Forest Road, Holmsley,
Christchurch, Dorset BH23 7EQ
T: (0131) 314 6505
E: fe.holidays@forestry.gov.uk
I: www.forestry.gov.uk

HOLTON HEATH
Dorset

Tanglewood Holiday Park ★★★★
Holiday Park
Organford Road, Holton Heath,
Poole, Dorset BH16 6JY
T: (01305) 780209 &
(01202) 632618
F: (01305) 777218

HURLEY
Berkshire

**Hurley Farm Caravan &
Camping Park ★★★**
*Holiday, Touring and Camping
Park*
Shepherds Lane, Hurley,
Maidenhead, Berkshire SL6 5NE
T: (01628) 823501 & 824493
F: (01628) 825533
I: www.henley.on.thames.
com/hurley
WH

HURN
Dorset

Tall Trees Holiday Caravan Park ★★★★
Holiday Park
Matchams Lane, Hurn,
Christchurch, Dorset BH23 6AW
T: (01202) 477144
F: (01202) 479546
E: talltrees.park@talk21.com
I: www.tall-trees.co.uk
WH

LIPHOOK
Hampshire

The Deer's Hut ★★★
Touring and Camping Park
Griggs Green, Longmoor Road,
Liphook, Hampshire GU30 7PD
T: (01428) 724406

MILFORD-ON-SEA
Hampshire

Carrington Park ★★★★★
Holiday Park
New Lane, Milford-on-Sea,
Lymington, Hampshire
SO41 0UU
T: (01590) 642654
F: (01590) 642951

Downton Holiday Park ★★★★
Holiday Park
Shorefield Road, Milford-on-
Sea, Lymington, Hampshire
SO41 0LH
T: (01425) 476131 &
(01590) 642515

Lytton Lawn Touring Park ★★★★
Touring and Camping Park
Lymore Lane, Milford-on-Sea,
Lymington, Hampshire SO41 0TX
T: (01590) 643339
F: (01590) 643339
E: holidays@shorefield.co.uk
I: www.shorefield.co.uk
WH

Shorefield Country Park ★★★★★
Holiday Park
Rose Award
Shorefield Road, Milford-on-
Sea, Lymington, Hampshire
SO41 0LH
T: (01590) 642513
F: (01590) 645610
E: holidays@shorefield.co.uk
I: www.shorefield.co.uk
WH

MOLLINGTON
Oxfordshire

**Mollington Touring Caravan
Park ★★★**
Touring and Camping Park
The Yews, Mollington, Banbury,
Oxfordshire OX17 1AZ
T: (01295) 750731 &
07966 171959
I: www.ukparks.co.
uk/mollington

MORETON
Dorset

**Camping & Caravanning Club
Site ★★★★**
Camping Park
Station Road, Moreton,
Dorchester, Dorset DT2 8BB
T: (01305) 853801
I: www.
campingandcaravanningclub.co.
uk

MUDEFORD
Dorset

Sandhills Holiday Park ★★★
Holiday Park
Avon Beach, Mudeford,
Christchurch, Dorset BH23 4AL
T: (01425) 274584
F: (01425) 270016
WH

NEW MILTON
Hampshire

Bashley Park Ltd ★★★★
Holiday and Touring Park
Sway Road, New Milton,
Hampshire BH25 5QR
T: (01425) 612340 & 616422
F: (01425) 612602
E: enquires@hobourne.co.uk
I: www.hobourne.co.uk
WH

**Forestry Commission Setthorns
Caravan and Camping Site. ★★★★**
Touring and Camping Park
Wootton, New Milton,
Hampshire BH25 5UA
T: (0131) 314 6505
E: fe.holidays@forestry.gov.uk
I: www.forestry.gov.uk

Glen Orchard Holiday Park ★★★★
Holiday Park
Walkford Lane, New Milton,
Hampshire BH25 5NH
T: (01425) 616463
F: (01425) 638655
E: enquiries@glenorchard.co.uk
I: glenorchard.co.uk
WH

Naish Estate (Hoburne) Ltd ★★★★★
Holiday Park
Rose Award
Christchurch Road, New Milton,
Hampshire BH25 7RE
T: (01425) 273586 & 273786
F: (01425) 270923
E: enquires@hoburne.co.uk
I: www.hoburne.co.uk
WH

NEWCHURCH
Isle of Wight

Southland Camping Park ★★★★★
Touring and Camping Park
Newchurch, Sandown, Isle of
Wight PO36 0LZ
T: (01983) 865385
F: (01983) 867663
E: info@southland.co.uk
I: www.southland.co.uk

NITON
Isle of Wight

Meadow View Caravan Site ★
Holiday Park
Hoyes Farm, Newport Lane,
Niton, Ventnor, Isle of Wight
PO38 2NS

NORTH BOARHUNT
Hampshire

South Hants Country Club ★★★★
Holiday Park
Stockers, North Boarhunt,
Fareham, Hampshire PO17 6JS
T: (01329) 832919
F: (01329) 834506
E: contact@southhants.
swinternet.co.uk
I: www.southhants.swinternet.
co.uk

OLNEY
Buckinghamshire
Emberton Country Park ★★★
Touring and Camping Park
Emberton, Olney,
Buckinghamshire MK46 5DB
T: (01234) 711575
F: (01234) 711575
E: embertonpark@
milton-keynes.gov.uk

OWER
Hampshire
Green Pastures Caravan Park
★★★
Touring Park
Green Pastures Farm, Ower,
Romsey, Hampshire SO51 6AJ
T: (023) 8081 4444
I: www.ukparks.co.
uk/greenpasturesfarm

OXFORD
Oxfordshire
**The Camping & Caravanning
Club Site ★★★★**
Touring and Camping Park
426 Abingdon Road, Oxford,
Oxfordshire OX1 4XN
T: (01865) 244088
I: www.
campingandcaravanningclub.co.
uk

Cassington Mill Caravan Park
★★
Touring and Camping Park
Eynsham Road, Cassington,
Witney, Oxfordshire OX8 1DB
T: (01865) 881081
F: (01865) 884167

PENNINGTON
Hampshire
Hurst View Caravan Park
★★★
Holiday Park
Lower Pennington Lane,
Pennington, Lymington,
Hampshire SO41 8AL
T: (01590) 671648 &
07798 938911
F: (01590) 689244
E: enquiries@hurstview.
freeserve.co.uk

POOLE
Dorset
Beacon Hill Touring Park
★★★
Touring Park
Blandford Road North, Near
Lytchett Minster, Poole, Dorset
BH16 6AB
T: (01202) 631631
WH

**Organford Manor Caravans &
Holidays ★★★**
*Holiday, Touring and Camping
Park*
The Lodge, Organford, Poole,
Dorset BH16 6ES
T: (01202) 622202 & 623278
F: (01202) 623278
E: organford@ids.co.uk
WH

Pear Tree Touring Park
★★★★★
Touring Park
Organford Road, Holton Heath,
Poole, Dorset BH16 6LA
T: (01202) 622434
F: (01202) 631985
E: info@visitpeartree.co.uk
I: www.visitpeartree.co.uk

Rockley Park Holiday Park
★★★★★
Holiday Park
Rose Award
Napier Road, Hamworthy, Poole,
Dorset BH15 4LZ
T: 0870 2425678
F: (01442) 254956
I: www.british-holidays.co.uk
WH

Sandford Holiday Park
★★★★
Holiday Park
Holton Heath, Poole, Dorset
BH16 6JZ
T: (01202) 631600 &
(01392) 447447
F: (01202) 625678
E: admin@weststarholidays.co.
uk
I: www.weststarholidays.co.uk

PORTSMOUTH & SOUTHSEA
Hampshire
**Harbour Side Holiday Caravan
& Camping Site★★★**
Holiday and Touring Park
Eastern Road, Portsmouth,
Hampshire PO3 6QB
T: (023) 9266 3867
I: www.portsmouthcc.gov.uk

Southsea Leisure Park ★★★
Holiday and Touring Park
Melville Road, Southsea,
Hampshire PO4 9TB
T: (023) 9273 5070
F: (023) 9282 1302

RINGWOOD
Hampshire
Red Shoot Camping Park
★★★★
Camping Park
Linwood, Ringwood, Hampshire
BH24 3QT
T: (01425) 473789 & 478940
F: (01425) 471558
E: redshoot@fsnet.co.uk

RISELEY
Hampshire
Wellington Country Park
★★★★
Touring and Camping Park
Riseley, Reading, Berkshire
RG7 1SP
T: (0118) 932 6444
F: (0118) 932 3445
I: www.
wellington-country-park.co.uk

ROMSEY
Hampshire
Hill Farm Caravan Park
★★★★
*Holiday, Touring and Camping
Park*
Branches Lane, Sherfield English,
Romsey, Hampshire SO51 6FH
T: (01794) 340402
F: (01794) 340402

ROOKLEY
Isle of Wight
Rookley Country Park ★★★★
Holiday Park
Rose Award
Main Road, Rookley, Ventnor,
Isle of Wight PO38 3RU
T: (01983) 721606
F: (01983) 721607
I: www.webwight.co.uk.
islandview

RYDE
Isle of Wight
Beaper Farm Camping Site
★★★
Camping Park
Beaper Farm, Ryde, Isle of Wight
PO30 1QJ
T: (01983) 615210
E: beaper@btinternet.com

Harcourt Sands Holiday Village
★★★★★
Holiday Park
Ryde, Isle of Wight PO33 1PJ
T: (01983) 567321
F: (01983) 611622
WH

Pondwell Holiday Park ★★★
Holiday Park
Pondwell Hill, Ryde, Isle of
Wight PO33 1QA
T: (01983) 612100
F: (01983) 613511
E: info@isleofwightselfcatering.
co.uk
I: www.isleofwightselfcatering.
co.uk

ST HELENS
Isle of Wight
Carpenters Farm ★★
Touring Park
St Helens, Ryde, Isle of Wight
PO33 1YL
T: (01983) 872450

Field Lane Holiday Park
★★★★
Holiday Park
Rose Award
St Helens, Ryde, Isle of Wight
PO33 1UX
T: (01983) 872779
F: (01983) 873000
E: fieldlane@freeuk.com

Hillgrove Park ★★★★
Holiday Park
Rose Award
Field Lane, St Helens, Ryde, Isle
of Wight PO33 1UT
T: (01983) 872802
F: (01983) 872100
E: info@hillgrove.co.uk
I: www.hillgrove.co.uk
WH

Nodes Point Holiday Park
★★★
Holiday Park
St Helens, Ryde, Isle of Wight
PO33 1YA
T: (01983) 872401 &
07802 466186
F: (01983) 874696
WH

Old Mill Holiday Park ★★★★
Holiday Park
Rose Award
Mill Road, St Helens, Ryde, Isle
of Wight PO33 1UE
T: (01983) 872507
E: oldmill@fsbdial.co.uk
I: www.oldmill.co.uk

ST LAWRENCE
Isle of Wight
Undercliff Glen Caravan Park
★★★
Holiday Park
The Undercliffe Drive, St
Lawrence, Ventnor, Isle of Wight
PO38 1XY
T: (01983) 730261

ST LEONARDS
Dorset
Camping International
★★★★
Touring and Camping Park
229 Ringwood Road, St
Leonards, Ringwood, Hampshire
BH24 2SD
T: (01202) 872817 & 872742
F: (01202) 893986
E: campint@globalnet.co.uk

Oakdene Forest Park ★★★
Holiday Park
St Leonards, Ringwood,
Hampshire BH24 2RZ
T: (01202) 875422
F: (01202) 894152
E: holidays@shorefield.co.uk
I: www.shorefield.co.uk
WH

Shamba Holiday Park ★★★
Touring Park
230 Ringwood Road, St
Leonards, Ringwood, Hampshire
BH24 2SB
T: (01202) 873302
F: (01202) 873302
E: tim@shamba.co.uk
I: ww.shamba.co.uk

SANDOWN
Isle of Wight
Adgestone Camping Park
★★★★★
Camping Park
Lower Road, Adgestone,
Sandown, Isle of Wight
PO36 0HL
T: (01983) 403432 & 403989
F: (01983) 404955

**Cheverton Copse Caravan &
Camping Park★★★**
Holiday Park
Newport Road, Sandown, Isle of
Wight PO36 0JP
T: (01983) 403161
F: (01983) 403161

Fairway Holiday Park Ltd
★★★
Holiday Park
The Fairway, Sandown, Isle of
Wight PO36 9PS
T: (01983) 403462
F: (01983) 405713

Fort Holiday Park ★★
Holiday Park
Avenue Road, Sandown, Isle of
Wight PO36 8BD
T: (01983) 402858

Fort Spinney Holiday Chalets ★★★★★
Holiday Park
Yaverland Road, Sandown, Isle
of Wight PO36 8QB
T: (01983) 402360 & 404025
F: (01983) 404025
E: clem@fortspinney.freeserve.
co.uk.

Sandown Holiday Chalets ★★★★
Holiday Park
Avenue Road, Sandown, Isle of
Wight PO36 8AP
T: (01983) 404025 & 402360
F: (01983) 404025
E: clem@fortspinney.freeserve.
co.uk.

SEAVIEW
Isle of Wight

Salterns Holidays ★★★
Holiday Park
Isle of Wight Self-Catering Ltd,
Seaview, Isle of Wight PO34 5AQ
T: (01983) 612330
F: (01983) 613511
E: info@isleofwightselfcatering.
co.uk
I: www.isleofwightselfcatering.
co.uk

Tollgate Holiday Park ★★★
Holiday Park
The Duver, Seaview, Isle of
Wight PO34 5AJ
T: (01983) 612107
E: info@isleofwightselfcatering.
co.uk
I: www.isleofwightselfcatering.
co.uk

SHANKLIN
Isle of Wight

Landguard Camping Park ★★★★
Touring and Camping Park
Landguard Manor Road,
Shanklin, Isle of Wight
PO37 7PH
T: (01983) 865988
E: landguard@fsbdial.co.uk
I: www.landguard-camping.co.
uk
WH

Landguard Holidays ★★★★
Holiday Park
Rose Award
Landguard Manor Road,
Shanklin, Isle of Wight PO37 7PJ
T: (01983) 863100
F: (01983) 867896
E: enquiries@
landguardholidays.co.uk
I: www.landguardholidays.co.uk
WH

Lower Hyde Holiday Village ★★★★
*Holiday, Touring and Camping
Park*
Landguard Road, Shanklin, Isle
of Wight PO37 7LL
T: (01983) 866131
F: (01983) 862532
WH

Ninham Country Holidays ★★★★
*Holiday, Touring and Camping
Park*
Shanklin, Isle of Wight PO37 7PL
T: (01983) 864243
F: (01983) 868881
E: office@ninham-holidays.co.
uk
I: www.ninham-holidays.co.uk

STANDLAKE
Oxfordshire

Hardwick Parks ★★★
*Holiday, Touring and Camping
Park*
Downs Road, Standlake, Witney,
Oxfordshire OX8 7PZ
T: (01865) 300501
F: (01865) 300037
E: info@hardwickparks.co.uk
I: www.hardwickparks.co.uk

Lincoln Farm Park Limited ★★★★★
Touring Park
High Street, Standlake, Witney,
Oxfordshire OX8 7RH
T: (01865) 300239
E: info@lincolnfarm-touristnet.
uk.com
I: www.lincolnfarm.touristnet.
uk.com

SWANAGE
Dorset

**Cauldron Barn Farm Caravan
Park ★★★★★**
Holiday Park
Rose Award
Landopen Ltd, Cauldron Barn
Road, Swanage, Dorset
BH19 1QQ
T: (01929) 422080
F: (01929) 427870
I: cauldronbarn@fsbdial.co.uk

Haycraft Caravan Club Site ★★★★★
Touring Park
Haycrafts Lane, Harmans Cross,
Swanage, Dorset BH19 3EB
T: (01929) 480572
WH

Priestway Holiday Park ★★★
Holiday Park
Priestway, Swanage, Dorset
BH19 2RS
T: (01929) 422747 & 424154
F: (01929) 421822
WH

Swanage Caravan Park ★★★
Holiday Park
Priests Road, Swanage, Dorset
BH19 2QS
T: (01929) 422130
F: (01929) 427952
WH

Ulwell Cottage Caravan Park ★★★★
*Holiday, Touring and Camping
Park*
Rose Award
Ulwell, Swanage, Dorset
BH19 3DG
T: (01929) 422823
F: (01929) 421500
E: enq@ulwellcottagepark.co.uk
I: www.ulwellcottagepark.co.uk
WH

Ulwell Farm Caravan Park ★★★★
Holiday and Touring Park
Ulwell, Swanage, Dorset
BH19 3DG
T: (01929) 422825
I: www.ukparks.co.uk/ulwellfarm

THORNESS BAY
Isle of Wight

Thorness Bay Holiday Park ★★★
Holiday Park
Thorness Bay, Cowes, Isle of
Wight PO31 8NJ
T: (01983) 523109
F: (01983) 822213
WH

THREE LEGGED CROSS
Dorset

**Woolsbridge Manor Farm
Caravan Park ★★★★**
Touring Park
Ringwood Road, Three Legged
Cross, Wimborne Minster,
Dorset BH21 6RA
T: (01202) 826369
F: (01202) 813172

TOTLAND BAY
Isle of Wight

Ivylands Holiday Park ★★★★
Holiday Park
Rose Award
The Broadway, Totland Bay, Isle
of Wight PO39 0AN
T: (01983) 752480
F: (01983) 752480
WH

Stoats Farm ★★
Camping Park
Weston Lane, Totland Bay, Isle of
Wight PO39 0HE
T: (01983) 755258

UPPER HEYFORD
Oxfordshire

**Heyford Leys Mobile Home
Park ★★**
Touring and Camping Park
Camp Road, Upper Heyford,
Bicester, Oxfordshire OX6 3LU
T: (01869) 232048
F: (01869) 232706
E: kbuxey3595@aol.com.au
I: www.oxlink.co.
uk/camping/djbuxey/

WAREHAM
Dorset

Birchwood Tourist Park ★★★★
Touring Park
Bere Road, North Trigon,
Wareham, Dorset BH20 7PA
T: (01929) 554763

The Lookout Holiday Park ★★★★
Holiday Park
Stoborough, Wareham, Dorset
BH20 5AZ
T: (01929) 552546
F: (01929) 556662
E: enquiries@caravan-sites.co.
uk
I: www.
harrowwood@bournemouth-
net.co.uk
WH

Wareham Forest Tourist Park ★★★★★
Touring Park
Bere Road, North Trigon,
Wareham, Dorset BH20 7NZ
T: (01929) 551393
F: (01929) 551393
E: holiday@wareham-forest.co.
uk
I: www.wareham-forest.co.uk

WARSASH
Hampshire

Dibles Park Company Ltd ★★★★
Touring Park
Dibles Park, Dibles Road,
Warsash, Southampton,
Hampshire SO31 9SA
T: (01489) 575232

Solent Breezes Holiday Village ★★★★
Holiday Park
Rose Award
Hook Lane, Warsash,
Southampton, Hampshire
SO31 9HG
T: (01489) 572084
F: (01489) 885045
WH

WEST LULWORTH
Dorset

Durdle Door Holiday Park ★★★★
Holiday Park
West Lulworth, Wareham,
Dorset BH20 5PU
T: (01929) 400200
F: (01929) 400260
I: www.lulworth.com
WH

WIMBORNE MINSTER
Dorset

**Charris Camping & Caravan
Park ★★★★**
Touring and Camping Park
Candy's Lane, Corfe Mullen,
Wimborne Minster, Dorset
BH21 3EF
T: (01202) 885970
F: (01202) 881281
E: jandjjcharris@iclway.co.uk
I: www.charris.co.uk

Merley Court Touring Park ★★★★★
Touring and Camping Park
Merley House Lane, Merley,
Wimborne Minster, Dorset
BH21 3AA
T: (01202) 881488
F: (01202) 881484
E: holidays@merley-court.co.uk
I: www.merley-court.co.uk

Springfield Touring Park ★★★★★
Touring and Camping Park
Candys Lane, Corfe Mullen,
Wimborne Minster, Dorset
BH21 3EF
T: (01202) 881719

Wilksworth Farm Caravan Park ★★★★★
Holiday Park
Cranborne Road, Wimborne
Minster, Dorset BH21 4HW
T: (01202) 885467
WH

WINCHESTER
Hampshire
Morn Hill Caravan Club Site
★★★★
Camping Park
Morn Hill, Winchester,
Hampshire SO21 1HL
T: (01962) 869877

WOKINGHAM
Berkshire
California Chalet & Touring Park ★★★★
Holiday and Touring Park
Nine Mile Ride, Finchampstead,
Wokingham, Berkshire
RG40 4HU
T: (0118) 973 3928
F: (0118) 932 8720

WOODLANDS
Dorset
Sutton Hill Camping & Caravanning Club Site★★★★
Camping Park
Sutton Hill, Woodlands,
Wimborne Minster, Dorset
BH21 6LF
T: (01202) 822763
I: www.
campingandcaravanningclub.co.
uk

WOOL
Dorset
Whitemead Caravan Park
★★★
Camping Park
East Burton Road, Wool,
Wareham, Dorset BH20 6HG
T: (01929) 462241
E: nadinechurch@aol.com

WOOTTON BRIDGE
Isle of Wight
Kite Hill Farm Caravan & Camping Park★★★★
Touring and Camping Park
Wootton Bridge, Ryde, Isle of
Wight PO33 4LE
T:
E: barry@kitehillfarm.freeserve.
co.uk
I: www.campingparkisleofwight.
com

WROXALL
Isle of Wight
Appuldurcombe Gardens Caravan & Camping Park
★★★★
Holiday, Touring and Camping Park
Rose Award
Appuldurcombe Road, Wroxall,
Ventnor, Isle of Wight PO38 3EP
T: (01983) 852597
F: (01983) 856225

YARMOUTH
Isle of Wight
The Orchards Holiday Caravan Park ★★★★★
Holiday and Touring Park
Rose Award
Main Road, Newbridge,
Yarmouth, Isle of Wight
PO41 0TS
T: (01983) 531331
F: (01983) 531666
E: info@orchards-holiday-park.
co.uk
I: www.orchards-holiday-park.
co.uk

Savoy Holiday Village ★★★
Holiday Park
Halletts Shute, Yarmouth, Isle of
Wight PO41 0RJ
T: (01983) 760355
F: (01983) 761277
[WH]

ARUNDEL
West Sussex
Ship & Anchor Marina ★★★
Touring Park
Heywood & Bryett Ltd, Ford,
Arundel, West Sussex BN18 0BJ
T: (01243) 551262
[WH]

ASHFORD
Kent
Broadhembury Caravan & Camping Park ★★★★★
Holiday, Touring and Camping Park
Steeds Lane, Kingsnorth,
Ashford, Kent TN26 1NQ
T: (01233) 620859
F: (01233) 620859
E: holidays@broadhembury.co.
uk
I: www.broadhembury.co.uk
[WH]

BATTLE
East Sussex
Crowhurst Park ★★★★★
Holiday and Touring Park
Rose Award
Crowhurst Park, Telham Lane,
Battle, East Sussex TN33 0SL
T: (01424) 773344
F: (01424) 775727
E: enquiries@crowhurstpark.co.
uk
I: www.crowhurstpark.co.uk
[WH]

Normanhurst Court Caravan Club Site ★★★★★
Touring Park
Stevens Crouch, Battle, East
Sussex TN33 9LR
T: (01424) 773808
[WH]

BEXHILL
East Sussex
Cobbs Hill Farm Caravan & Camping Park★★★★
Holiday, Touring and Camping Park
Watermill Lane, Sidley, Bexhill,
East Sussex TN39 5JA
T: (01424) 213460 & 221358
F: (01424) 213460

Kloofs Caravan Park ★★★★
Touring and Camping Park
Sandhurst Lane, Whydown,
Bexhill, East Sussex TN39 4RG
T: (01424) 842839
E: camping@kloofs.ndirect.co.
uk
I: www.kloofs.ndirect.co.uk

BIDDENDEN
Kent
Woodlands Park ★★★★
Touring Park
Tenterden Road, Biddenden,
Ashford, Kent TN27 8BT
T: (01580) 291216
F: (01580) 291216
E: woodlandsp@aol.com
I: www.campingsite.co.uk

BIRCHINGTON
Kent
Quex Caravan Park ★★★★★
Holiday and Touring Park
Park Road, Birchington, Kent
CT7 0BL
T: (01843) 841273
F: (01227) 740585
E: info@keatfarm.co.uk/
I: www.keatfarm.co.uk/

Two Chimneys Caravan Park
★★★★
Holiday, Touring and Camping Park
Shottendane Road, Birchington,
Kent CT7 0HD
T: (01843) 841068 & 843157
F: (01843) 843157
I: www.sews.co.uk/two.
-chimneys

BOGNOR REGIS
West Sussex
Bognor Regis Caravan Club Site ★★★★★
Touring and Camping Park
Rowan Way, Bognor Regis, West
Sussex PO22 9RP
T: (01243) 828515
[WH]

Copthorne Caravans ★★★★
Holiday Park
Rose Award
Rose Green Road, Bognor Regis,
West Sussex PO21 3ER
T: (01243) 262408
F: (01243) 262408

The Lillies Nursery & Caravan Park ★★★
Holiday, Touring and Camping Park
Yapton Road, Barnham, Bognor
Regis, West Sussex PO22 0AY
T: (01243) 552081
F: (01243) 552081

Riverside Caravan Centre (Bognor) Ltd★★★★★
Holiday Park
Shripney Road, Bognor Regis,
West Sussex PO22 9NE
T: (01243) 865823 & 865824
F: (01243) 841570
E: info@rivcentre.co.uk
I: www.rivcentre.co.uk

BRIGHTON & HOVE
East Sussex
Sheepcote Valley Caravan Club Site ★★★★★
Touring Park
East Brighton Park, Brighton,
East Sussex BN2 5TS
T: (01273) 626546
F: (01273) 682600

CAMBER
East Sussex
Camber Sands Holiday Park
★★★
Holiday and Touring Park
Lydd Road, Camber, Rye, East
Sussex TN31 7RT
T: (01797) 225555
F: (01797) 225756
[WH]

CANTERBURY
Kent
Canterbury Camping & Caravanning Club Site★★★★
Touring and Camping Park
Bekesbourne Lane, Canterbury,
Kent CT3 4AB
T: (01227) 463216

Yew Tree Caravan Park
★★★★
Holiday, Touring and Camping Park
Stone Street, Petham,
Canterbury, Kent CT4 5PL
T: (01227) 700306
F: (01227) 700306
I: www.ukparks.co.
uk/yewtreepark
[&]

CAPEL LE FERNE
Kent
Varne Ridge Caravan Park
★★★★★
Holiday and Touring Park
145 Old Dover Road, Capel le
Ferne, Folkestone, Kent
CT18 7HX
T: (01303) 251765
F: (01303) 251765
E: vrep@varne-ridge.freeserve.
co.uk

CHERTSEY
Surrey

**Chertsey Camping &
Caravanning Club Site★★★★**
Camping Park
Bridge Road, Chertsey, Surrey
KT16 8JX
T: (01932) 562405
I: www.
campingandcaravanningclub.co.
uk

CHICHESTER
West Sussex

Bell Caravan Park ★★
Holiday and Touring Park
Bell Lane, Birdham, Chichester,
West Sussex PO20 7HY
T: (01243) 512264

**Southern Leisure Lakeside
Village ★★**
Holiday and Touring Park
Vinnetrow Road, Chichester,
West Sussex PO20 6LB
T: (01243) 787715
F: (01243) 533643
[WH]

**Wicks Farm Camping Park
★★★★★**
Holiday and Touring Park
Redlands Lane, West Wittering,
Chichester, West Sussex
PO20 8QD
T: (01243) 513116
F: (01243) 511296
[WH]

CROWBOROUGH
East Sussex

**Crowborough Camping and
Caravanning Club Site★★★★**
Touring and Camping Park
Goldsmith Recreation Ground,
Crowborough, East Sussex
TN6 2TN
T: (01892) 664827
I: www.
campingandcaravanningclub.co.
uk

DIAL POST
West Sussex

Honeybridge Park ★★★★
Touring and Camping Park
Honeybridge Lane, Dial Post,
Horsham, West Sussex
RH13 8NX
T: (01403) 710923
F: (01403) 710923
E: enquiries@
honeybridgepark-free-online.co.
uk
I: www.honeybridgepark.co.uk

DOVER
Kent

**Hawthorn Farm Caravan &
Camping Park★★★★★★**
*Holiday, Touring and Camping
Park*
Station Road, Martin Mill, Dover,
Kent CT15 5LA
T: (01304) 852658 & 852914
F: (01304) 853417
E: info@keatfarm.co.uk/
I: www.keatfarm.co.uk/
[WH]

**Sutton Vale Country Club &
Caravan Park★★★★**
Holiday and Touring Park
Vale Road, Sutton-by-Dover,
Dover, Kent CT15 5DH
T: (01304) 374155
F: (01304) 381132
E: office@sutton-vale.v-net.
com

DYMCHURCH
Kent

**Dymchurch Caravan Park
★★★★**
Holiday Park
St Mary's Road, Dymchurch,
Romney Marsh, Kent TN29 0PW
T: (01303) 872303
F: (01303) 875179

**New Beach Holiday Village
★★★★**
Holiday Park
Hythe Road, Dymchurch,
Romney Marsh, Kent TN29 0JX
T: (01303) 872233
F: (01303) 872939

**New Beach Holiday Village
Touring Park★★★★**
Touring and Camping Park
Hythe Road, Dymchurch,
Romney Marsh, Kent TN29 0JX
T: (01303) 872234
F: (01303) 872939

EAST HORSLEY
Surrey

**Horsley Camping &
Caravanning Club ★★★★**
Camping Park
Ockham Road North, East
Horsley, Leatherhead, Surrey
KT24 6PE
T: (01483) 283273
I: www.
campingandcaravanningclub.co.
uk.

EASTBOURNE
East Sussex

**Fairfields Farm Caravan &
Camping Park★★★★**
Touring and Camping Park
Eastbourne Road, Westham,
Pevensey, East Sussex
BN24 5NG
T: (01323) 763165
F: (01323) 469175
E: fairfields.farm@btinternet.
com
I: www.btinternet.
com/§fairfields.farm

EASTCHURCH
Kent

Bramley Park ★★★
Holiday Park
Second Avenue, Warden Road,
Eastchurch, Sheerness, Kent
ME12 4EP
T: (01795) 880338
F: (01795) 880629
E: bramley.park@btinternet.com
I: www.ukparks.co.uk/bramley
[WH]

**Coconut Grove Holiday Park
★★★★**
Holiday Park
Warden Road, Eastchurch,
Sheerness, Kent ME12 4EN
T: (01795) 880353

**Palm Trees Holiday Park
★★★★**
Holiday Park
Second Avenue, Eastchurch,
Sheerness, Kent ME12 4ET
T: (01795) 880080

**Warden Springs Caravan Park
Ltd ★★★★**
*Holiday, Touring and Camping
Park*
Warden Point, Eastchurch,
Sheerness, Kent ME12 4HF
T: (01795) 880216 & 880217
F: (01795) 880218
E: jackie@wscp.freeserve.co.uk
I: www.ukparks.co.uk/warden

EWHURST GREEN
East Sussex

**Lordine Court Caravan &
Camping Park★★**
*Holiday, Touring and Camping
Park*
Lordine Court, Ewhurst Green,
Robertsbridge, East Sussex
TN32 5TS
T: (01580) 830209
F: (01580) 830091

FOLKESTONE
Kent

**Black Horse Farm Caravan Club
Site ★★★★★**
Touring and Camping Park
385 Canterbury Road, Densole,
Folkestone, Kent CT18 7BG
T: (01303) 892665

**Folkestone Camping &
Caravanning Club Site★★**
Touring and Camping Park
The Warren, Folkestone, Kent
CT19 6PT
T: (01303) 255093
I: www.
campingandcaravanningclub.co.
uk

GOODWOOD
West Sussex

**Goodwood Racecourse
Caravan Park ★★★**
Touring Park
Goodwood Racecourse,
Goodwood, Chichester, West
Sussex PO18 0PS
T: (01243) 755033
F: (01243) 755025

GRAFFHAM
West Sussex

**Camping & Caravanning Club
Site ★★★★**
Camping Park
Great Bury, Graffham, Petworth,
West Sussex GU28 0QJ
T: (01798) 867476
I: www.
campingandcaravanningclub.co.
uk

HASTINGS
East Sussex

**Combe Haven Holiday Park
★★★★**
Holiday Park
Harley Shute Road, St Leonards-
on-Sea, Hastings, East Sussex
TN38 8BZ
T: (01424) 427891
F: (01424) 442991
[WH]

**Rocklands Holiday Park
★★★★**
Holiday Park
Rocklands Lane, East Hill,
Hastings, East Sussex TN35 5DY
T: (01424) 423097

Shear Barn Holiday Park ★★★
*Holiday, Touring and Camping
Park*
Barley Lane, Hastings, East
Sussex TN35 5DX
T: (01424) 423583 & 716474
F: (01424) 718740
E: shearbarn@pavilion.co.uk
I: www.shearbarn.co.uk

**Stalkhurst Camping and
Caravan Site★★★**
*Holiday, Touring and Camping
Park*
Stalkhurst Cottage, Ivyhouse
Lane, Hastings, East Sussex
TN35 4NN
T: (01424) 439015
F: (01424) 439015

HENFIELD
West Sussex

**Downsview Caravan Park
★★★★**
Holiday Park
Bramlands Lane, Woodmancote,
Henfield, West Sussex BN5 9TG
T: (01273) 492801
F: (01273) 495214

HERNE BAY
Kent

**Keat Farm Holiday Park
★★★★★**
*Holiday, Touring and Camping
Park*
Reculver Road, Herne Bay, Kent
CT6 6SR
T: (01227) 374381
F: (01227) 740585
E: info@keatfarm.co.uk/
I: www.keatfarm.co.uk/
[WH]

HERSTMONCEUX
East Sussex

Orchard View Park ★★★★★
Holiday Park
Victoria Road, Windmill Hill,
Herstmonceux, Hailsham, East
Sussex BN27 4SY
T: (01323) 832335
F: (01323) 832335

HORAM
East Sussex

**Horam Manor Touring Park
★★★★**
Touring and Camping Park
Horam, Heathfield, East Sussex
TN21 0YD
T: (01435) 813662
E: horam.manor@virgin.net
I: www.handbooks.co.
uk/horam-manor

KINGSDOWN
Kent

**Kingsdown Park Holiday
Village ★★★★★**
Holiday Park
Upper Street, Kingsdown, Deal,
Kent CT14 8AU
T: (01304) 361205
F: (01304) 380125
E: info@kingsdownpark.co.uk
I: www.kingsdownpark.co.uk

LEYSDOWN ON SEA
Kent
Priory Hill Holiday Park
★★★★
Holiday, Touring and Camping Park
Wing Road, Leysdown on Sea, Sheerness, Kent ME12 4OT
T: (01795) 510267 &
07979 530600/1
F: (01795) 510267
E: info@prioryhill.co.uk
I: www.prioryhill.co.uk

LINGFIELD
Surrey
Long Acres Caravan & Camping Park ★★★★
Touring and Camping Park
Newchapel Road, Lingfield, Surrey RH7 6LE
T: (01342) 833205
F: (01622) 735038

MAIDSTONE
Kent
Pine Lodge Touring Park
★★★★★
Touring and Camping Park
A20 Ashford Road, Hollingbourne, Maidstone, Kent ME17 1XH
T: (01622) 730018
F: (01622) 734498

MARDEN
Kent
Tanner Farm Touring Caravan & Camping Park ★★★★★
Touring and Camping Park
Goudhurst Road, Marden, Tonbridge, Kent TN12 9ND
T: (01622) 832399
F: (01622) 832472
E: tannerfarmpark@cs.com
WH

MERSTHAM
Surrey
Alderstead Heath Caravan Club Site ★★★★★
Touring Park
Dean Lane, Merstham, Redhill, Surrey RH1 3AH
T: (01737) 644629
WH

MINSTER-IN-SHEPPEY
Kent
Ashcroft Holiday Park ★★★
Holiday Park
Plough Road, Minster-in-Sheppey, Sheerness, Kent ME12 4JE
T: (01795) 880324 & 880090
WH

Golden Leas Holiday Park
★★★★
Holiday Park
Bell Farm Lane, Minster-in-Sheppey, Sheerness, Kent ME12 4JA
T: (01795) 874874
F: (01795) 872086

Seacliff Holiday Estate Ltd
★★
Holiday, Touring and Camping Park
Oak Lane, Minster-in-Sheppey, Sheerness, Kent ME12 3QS
T: (01795) 872262

Willow Trees Holiday Park ★★
Holiday Park
Oak Lane, Minster-in-Sheppey, Sheerness, Kent ME12 3QR
T: (01795) 875833

MINSTER-IN-THANET
Kent
Wayside Caravan Park
★★★★★
Holiday and Touring Park
Way Hill, Minster-in-Thanet, Ramsgate, Kent CT12 4HP
T: (01843) 821272
F: (01843) 822668

MONKTON
Kent
The Foxhunter Park ★★★★★
Holiday Park
Rose Award
Monkton, Ramsgate, Kent CT12 4JG
T: (01843) 821311 & 821587
F: (01843) 821458
E: foxhunterpark@netscape.co.uk
I: www.saundersparkhomes.co.uk

NEW ROMNEY
Kent
Romney Sands Holiday Park
★★★
Holiday Park
The Parade, Greatstone On Sea, New Romney, Kent TN28 8RN
T: (01797) 363877
F: (01797) 367497

PAGHAM
West Sussex
Church Farm Holiday Village
★★★★
Holiday Park
Rose Award
Pagham, Chichester, West Sussex PO21 4NR
T: 0870 2425678
F: (01442) 254956
WH

PEVENSEY
East Sussex
Normans Bay Camping and Caravanning Club Site★★★★
Touring and Camping Park
Pevensey, East Sussex BN24 6PR
T: (01323) 761190
I: www.campingandcaravanningclub.co.uk

PEVENSEY BAY
East Sussex
Bay View Caravan & Camping Park ★★★★★
Holiday, Touring and Camping Park
Old Martello Road, Pevensey Bay, Eastbourne, East Sussex BN24 6DX
T: (01323) 768688
F: (01323) 769637
E: bayviewcaravanpark@tesco.net
I: www.bay-view.co.uk
WH

Martello Beach Park ★★★★
Holiday and Touring Park
Pevensey Bay, Pevensey, East Sussex BN24 6DH
T: (01323) 761424
F: (01323) 460433
I: www.m.smart@martellobeachpark.fsbusiness.co.uk
WH

POLEGATE
East Sussex
Peel House Farm Caravan Park
★★★★
Holiday, Touring and Camping Park
Polegate, East Sussex BN26 6QX
T: (01323) 845629
F: (01323) 845629
E: peelhocp@tesco.net

RAMSGATE
Kent
Manston Caravan & Camping Park ★★★★
Holiday, Touring and Camping Park
Manston Court Road, Manston, Ramsgate, Kent CT12 5AU
T: (01843) 823442
E: mccp.roy@virgin.net
WH

RECULVER
Kent
Blue Dolphin Park ★★★★
Holiday Park
Reculver, Herne Bay, Kent CT6 6SS
T: (01227) 375406
F: (01227) 375406

RINGMER
East Sussex
Bluebell Holiday Park ★★
Holiday, Touring and Camping Park
The Broyle, Shortgate, Ringmer, Lewes, East Sussex BN8 6PJ
T: (01825) 840407

ROCHESTER
Kent
Allhallows Leisure Park
★★★★
Holiday Park
Allhallows-on-Sea, Allhallows, Rochester, Kent ME3 9QD
T: (01634) 270385
F: (01634) 270081
I: www.british-holidays.co.uk
WH

Woolmans Wood Caravan Park
★★★★
Touring and Camping Park
Rochester/Maidstone Road, Bridgewood, Rochester, Kent ME5 9SB
T: (01634) 867685

ST NICHOLAS AT WADE
Kent
Frost Farm Thanet Way Caravan Co ★★★
Holiday and Touring Park
Thanet Way, St Nicholas at Wade, Birchington, Kent CT7 0NA
T: (01843) 847219

SANDWICH
Kent
Sandwich Leisure Park ★★★★
Holiday, Touring and Camping Park
Woodnesborough Road, Sandwich, Kent CT13 0AA
T: (01304) 612681
F: (01227) 273512
E: coastandcountry@btclick.com
I: www.coastcountryleisure.co.uk
WH

SEAFORD
East Sussex
Sunnyside Caravan Park ★★★
Holiday Park
Marine Parade, Seaford, East Sussex BN25 2QW
T: (01323) 892825
F: (01323) 892825

SEAL
Kent
Oldbury Hill Camping & Caravanning Club Site★★★★
Touring and Camping Park
Styants Bottom Road, Styants Bottom, Seal, Sevenoaks, Kent TN15 0ET
T: (01732) 762728
I: www.campingandcaravanningclub.co.uk

SEASALTER
Kent
Alberta Holiday Park ★★★★
Holiday Park
Faversham Road, Seasalter, Whitstable, Kent CT5 4BJ
T: (01227) 274485
F: (01227) 770785
WH

Homing Caravan Park ★★★★
Holiday Park
Church Lane, Seasalter, Whitstable, Kent CT5 4BU
T: (01227) 771777
F: (01227) 273512
E: coastandcountry@btclick.com
I: www.coastcountryleisure.co.uk
WH

SELSEY
West Sussex
Green Lawns Caravan Park
★★★★
Holiday Park
Rose Award
Paddock Lane, Selsey, Chichester, West Sussex PO20 9EJ
T: (01243) 604121
F: (01243) 602355
E: john.burn@btinternet.com
I: www.bunnleisure.co.uk

Warner Farm Touring Park
★★★★★
Touring Park
Warner Lane, Selsey, Chichester, West Sussex PO20 9EL
T: (01243) 608440 & 604499
F: (01243) 604499
E: warner.farm@bt internet.com
I: www.bunnleisure.co.uk
WH

West Sands Caravan Park
★★★★
Holiday Park
Rose Award
Mill Lane, Selsey, Chichester,
West Sussex PO20 9BH
T: (01243) 606080
F: (01243) 606068
E: west.sands@btinternet.com
I: www.westsands.co.uk

White Horse Caravan Park
★★★★
Holiday Park
Rose Award
Paddock Lane, Selsey,
Chichester, West Sussex
PO20 9EJ
T: (01243) 604121
F: (01243) 602355
E: john.bunn@btinternet.com
I: www.bunnleisure.co.uk

SHEERNESS
Kent

Riverbank Park ★★★
Holiday, Touring and Camping Park
The Broadway, Minster,
Sheerness, Kent ME12 2DB
T: (01795) 870300 & 875211

Sheerness Holiday Park ★★★
Holiday, Touring and Camping Park
Halfway Road, Sheerness, Kent
ME12 3AA
T: (01795) 662638
[WH]

SLINDON
West Sussex

**Slindon Camping &
Caravanning Club Site** ★★★
Touring and Camping Park
Slindon Park, Slindon, Arundel,
West Sussex BN18 0RG
T: (01243) 814387
I: www.
campingandcarvanningclub.co.
uk

SMALL DOLE
West Sussex

Southdown Caravan Park
★★★
Holiday Park
Henfield Road, Small Dole,
Henfield, West Sussex BN5 9XH
T: (01903) 814323
F: (01903) 812572
I: www.southdowncaravanpark.
co.uk

SOUTHBOURNE
West Sussex

**Camping & Caravanning Club
Site Chichester**★★★★
Touring Park
345 Main Road, Southbourne,
Emsworth, Hampshire PO10 8JH
T: (01243) 373202
I: www.
campingandcaravaningclub.co.
uk

SOUTHWATER
West Sussex

Raylands Park ★★★★
Holiday Park
Jackrells Lane, Southwater,
Horsham, West Sussex
RH13 7DH
T: (01403) 730218 & 731822
F: (01403) 732828
E: raylands@
roundstonecaravans.co.uk
I: www.roundstonecaravans.co.
uk
[WH]

ST-MARGARETS-AT-CLIFFE
Kent

St Margarets Holiday Park
★★★★
Holiday Park
Reach Road, St-Margarets-at-
Cliffe, Dover, Kent CT15 6AE
T: (01304) 853262 & 852255
F: (01304) 853434
I: www.leisuregb.co.uk

UCKFIELD
East Sussex

**Honeys Green Farm Caravan
Park**★★★
Holiday, Touring and Camping Park
Easons Green, Framfield,
Uckfield, East Sussex TN22 5RE
T: (01825) 840334

WALTON-ON-THAMES
Surrey

**Camping & Caravanning Club
Site**★★★
Camping Park
Fieldcommon Lane, Walton-on-
Thames, Surrey KT12 3QG
T: (01932) 220392
I: www.campingand
caravanningclub.co.uk

WASHINGTON
West Sussex

**Washington Caravan &
Camping Park** ★★★★
Touring and Camping Park
London Road, Washington,
Pulborough, West Sussex
RH20 4AJ
T: (01903) 892869
F: (01903) 893252

WINCHELSEA BEACH
East Sussex

Winchelsea Sands Holiday Park
★★★★
Holiday Park
Pett Level Road, Winchelsea
Beach, Winchelsea, East Sussex
TN36 4NB
T: (01797) 226442
F: (01797) 226630

WOODGATE
West Sussex

Willows Caravan Park
★★★★★
Holiday Park
Lidsey Road, Woodgate,
Chichester, West Sussex
PO20 6SU
T: (01243) 543124
F: (01243) 543124

WORTHING
West Sussex

**Northbrook Farm Caravan Club
Site** ★★★★
Touring Park
Titnore Way, Worthing, West
Sussex BN13 3RT
T: (01903) 502962
[WH]

Onslow Caravan Park ★★★★
Holiday Park
Onslow Drive, Ferring-by-Sea,
Worthing, West Sussex
BN12 5RX
T: (01903) 243170 &
(01243) 513084
F: (01243) 513053
E: islandmeadow@virgin.net
I: www.islandmeadow.co.uk

WROTHAM HEATH
Kent

**Gate House Wood Touring
Park** ★★★★★
Touring and Camping Park
Ford Lane, Wrotham Heath,
Sevenoaks, Kent TN15 7SD
T: (01732) 843062

Information

Useful Addresses

AUTOMOBILE ASSOCIATION

Routes can be prepared, avoiding unsuitable routes for caravans and steep gradients if specified. Please write to: AA Routes, Lambert House, Stockport Road, Cheadle, Staffordshire SK8 2DY.
Tel: 0990 500 600 (members only);
Internet: www.theaa.co.uk

BRITISH HOLIDAY & HOME PARKS ASSOCIATION LTD

Chichester House, 6 Pullman Court,
Great Western Road, Gloucester GL1 3ND
Enquiries and brochure requests (01452) 526911
Fax: (01452) 508508

The BH&HPA is recognised as the official representative body of the Parks Industry in the UK.

Member parks are located all over Britain. The parks are situated within some of the most spectacular locations that Britain can offer, from the breathtaking scenery of the Scottish Highlands, the beautiful coastal landscape of Cornwall, to the splendid mountains and lakes of North Wales and Northern Ireland. Parks can also be found nearby historic cities such as Oxford and Cambridge, and Shakespeare's city of Stratford-upon-Avon. Castles and historic sites are within reach of many BH&HPA parks.

Member parks offer pitches for touring caravans, tent and motor homes, caravan holiday homes and chalets to let, and holiday home ownership. The type of park ranges from the large multi-facility park to the smaller park run by a farm. So there is something to suit all needs.

BH&HPA jointly produces a set of full colour guides to holiday parks covering Scotland, Wales, Western England, Southern England, Northern England and Eastern England. These are available free-of-charge by calling (01452) 526911.

THE CAMPING AND CARAVANNING CLUB

Greenfields House, Westwood Way,
Coventry, West Midlands CV4 8JH
Tel: (02476) 856798

Operates a national network of over 90 camping and caravanning parks throughout Britain, most of which are open to non-members.

The club publishes a detailed guide to the above sites, a Big Sites book listing over 4000 parks in Britain and Ireland and an accompanying map with all these sites plotted on, useful for route planning. These are all available free to members.

Foreign visitors can obtain the above guides and map for £10.00 plus postage and by quoting their Camping Card International (CCI) number. Foreign visitors without a CCI may obtain the guide to the Club parks open to them through temporary membership at £10.00 plus postage for three months membership.

THE CARAVAN CLUB

East Grinstead House, East Grinstead,
West Sussex RH19 1UA
Tel: (01342) 326944 Fax: (01342) 410258
Internet: www.caravanclub.co.uk

The Caravan Club offers over 200 sites in the United Kingdom and Ireland. These include city locations such as London, Edinburgh, York and Chester, plus sites near leading heritage attractions such as Longleat, Sandringham, Chatsworth and Blenheim Palace. A further 20 are in National Parks. Over 90% of pitches have an electric hook-up point and most sites offer emptying points for motor caravanners. Foreign visitors are welcomed and holders of International Camping Cards (CCI's) qualify for pitch discounts on selected sites. Non member caravanners pay a supplement of £5 per pitch per night, refunded against the membership fee (£32.50 in 2000) which adds access to a further 3000 small 5-van sites. A 700-page Sites Directory and UK Location Map gives clear directions whilst towing. Tent campers are welcome on 70 sites.

FORESTRY COMMISSION

231 Corstorphine Road, Edinburgh EH12 7AT.
Tel: (0131) 334 0303 Fax: (0131) 334 3047

Forest Holidays, run by Forest Enterprise, an executive agency of the Forestry Commission, have almost 30 camping and caravan sites in the scenic forest locations throughout the UK. Choose from the Scottish Highlands, the New Forest, Snowdonia National Park, the Forest of Dean, or the banks of Loch Lomond. Some sites are open all year.

Advance bookings accepted for many sites. Dogs welcome on most sites. For a unique forest experience, call the Forestry Commission for a brochure on (0131) 334 0066.

THE MOTOR CARAVANNERS' CLUB LTD

22 Evelyn Close, Twickenham TW2 7BN
Tel: (020) 8893 3883

The Motor Caravanners' Club is authorised to issue the Camping Card International (CCI). It also produces a monthly magazine, 'Motor Caravanner' for all members.

Standards for
Caravan and Camping Parks

NORMES REQUISES POUR LES TERRAINS DE CAMPING ET POUR CARAVANES
REGELN FÜR CAMPING- UND CARAVANPLÄTZE
AAN CARAVAN EN CAMPINGPARKEN GESTELDE EISEN
NORME IMPOSTE AI CAMPEGGI PER TENDE E ROULOTTES

These standards should be read in conjunction, where applicable, with the Caravan Sites and Control of Development Act 1960, and, where applicable, the Public Health Act 1936.

A THE PARK

1 The park must have planning permission and site licence readily available, if applicable.

2 Facilities must be clean and in wholesome condition.

3 The park must be well managed and maintained and kept in a clean and presentable manner and attention paid to the road-side sign and entrance.

4 The park must have reception arrangements at appropriate times where advice and assistance can be obtained if necessary.

5 The park operator must be capable of arranging or carrying out repairs to caravans and equipment.

6 Supplies of gas and replacement bottles together with essential (where applicable) spares must be available at all reasonable times.

7 Where provided, all toilet blocks and washing facilities must be lit internally and externally during the hours of darkness, whilst the park is open.

8 All shower blocks must have internal lighting.

9 Where washing and/or shower facilities are provided, an adequate supply of hot and cold water must be available at all reasonable times.

10 A proprietary first-aid kit must be readily available. Emergency notices must be prominently displayed giving details and location of park, contact, telephone, doctor, fire service, local hospital and other essential services.

11 It is the park operator's responsibility to ensure that all caravans offered for hire on the park have insurance cover for public liability as letting caravans and comply with the Consumer Protection Act.

12 The park owner must have fire fighting equipment and notices which conform with the conditions of the site licence.

13 All electricity installations on the park both internally and externally must have the appropriate safety certification.

14 Parks providing pitches for touring units must provide facilities for chemical disposal unless specifically prohibited by local authorities.

15 Lighting should be appropriate to the size and type of park.

16 Adequate provision to be made for refuse disposal.

17 The intended use of facilities must be indicated by signage.

NB: Parks providing NO toilet facilities make this clear in all promotional literature and advertising.

B VISITOR INFORMATION

The booking form must be accompanied by details of the park, stating clearly:

1 A description of the park and its amenities, e.g:

a) Whether cars park by caravans or in a car park.

b) Whether or not pets are allowed.

c) Details of shower and bath facilities.

d) Whether a grocery shop is on site or the distance to nearest shop.

e) Licensed bar.

f) Laundry facilities.

g) Dancing, entertainments.

h) Television room.

i) Sports facilities.

j) Public transport to and from park.

k) Distance from sea and accessibility to beach (coastal parks only).

2 The prices for the pitch for the period booked and details of any further charges, e.g. electricity, gas, showers, awnings as well as any optional charges, e.g. holiday insurance.

Note: If Value Added Tax (VAT) is not included in the total charge, this must be clearly stated.

3 Any special conditions for payment of deposits or balance.

4 Wherever possible, a map showing the location of the park and its proximity to main centres and attractions.

5 If bookings in advance are necessary during the summer months.

C CARAVAN HOLIDAY HOMES AND CHALETS

1 All caravans must be of proprietary make.

2 All caravans/chalets must be in good state of internal and external repair and decoration with no internal dampness.

3 The caravans/chalets must not be occupied by more than the number of persons for which they are designed by the manufacturer ie four persons in a four-berth.

4 Equipment must be provided as listed opposite. An inventory of this equipment must be available for each caravan/chalet.

5 All caravans/chalets must have adequate storage space for luggage and food for the maximum number of occupants.

6 All doors, windows, skylights and all ventilation in the caravan/chalet must function correctly. All windows must be properly fitted with opaque curtains or blinds.

7 All caravans/chalets must have adequate internal lighting.

8 All caravans/chalets must be thoroughly cleaned and checked before every letting and equipment maintained and replaced as necessary.

9 Where linen is provided it must be changed on each change of occupier and as appropriate during lets of two weeks or more. All mattresses must be in sound condition.

10 The sink and its waste pipe must be in sound condition with a draining board. A fixed impervious work top for food preparation must be provided.

11 All caravans/chalets must have a fridge and a cooker with at least two boiling rings. The cooker must be in a sound and clean condition and functioning properly.

12 All caravans/chalets must have adequate heating.

13 All caravans must have safe steps or equivalent, to each external door.

14 All caravans must have a supply of hot and cold water.

D INVENTORY OF EQUIPMENT FOR CARAVAN HOLIDAY-HOMES AND CHALETS

The accommodation should contain the following:

● **One per caravan/chalet**

Kettle
Teapot
Tea caddy
Saucepan & lid (large, medium & small)
Frying pan
Colander
Oven roasting tray
Casserole dish
Carving knife and fork
Bread knife
Bread/cake container
Bread/chopping board
Fish slice
Small vegetable knife
Tin opener
Corkscrew/bottle opener
Potato peeler
Large fruit dish
Butter dish
Sugar dish
Tray
Milk jug
Condiment set (two-piece)
Washing-up bowl
Dustpan and brush
Broom
Floor cloth
Pot scourer/dish mop
Bucket
Mirror
Doormat
Covered kitchen refuse container
Fire extinguisher/blanket
Smoke detector

● **Two per caravan/chalet**

Table spoons
Mixing bowls or basins
Bread/cake plates
Dusters
Ash trays

● **Per bed**

Three blankets or one continental quilt and cover

(for winter lettings, or letting very early or late in the season the scale of bedding to be increased and adequate heating provided)
one pillow per person

● **One per person**

Knife (table & dessert)
Fork (table & dessert)
Spoon (dessert & tea)
Plate (large & small)
Tea cup and saucer
Cereal/soup plate
Tumbler
Egg cup

● **Four per person**

Coat-hangers

E INFORMATION FOR HIRERS

The booking form should be accompanied by details of the park and caravan(s)/chalet(s) stating clearly:

1   The accommodation size (length and width) of the caravan and the number of berths. This shall not exceed the maximum number of berths as defined by the manufacturer.

2   Whether caravans are connected to:
Mains water
Mains drainage
Mains sewerage
Electricity (stating voltage)
Piped gas (stating LPG or Natural)

3   Type of lighting: Electricity or Gas

4   Type of cooking: Electricity or Gas

5   A full description of park and its amenities.

6   Wherever possible a map showing the location of the park and its proximity to main centres and attractions.

7   The charges for the accommodation/pitch for the period booked and details of any further additional charges, for example, electricity, gas, showers etc, as well as any optional charges, eg holiday insurance.
Note: If VAT is payable it must be included in the quoted price.

F THE CARAVAN PARKS STANDARD FOR GUESTS WITH DISABILITIES

The National Accessible Scheme is operated by the English Tourism Council and the national and regional tourist boards throughout Britain. They assess places to stay that provide accommodation for wheelchair users or others who may have difficulty walking. The tourist organisations recognise three categories of accessibility:

 CATEGORY 1   Accessible to a wheelchair user travelling independently.

 CATEGORY 2   Accessible to a wheelchair user travelling with assistance.

 CATEGORY 3   Accessible to a wheelchair user able to walk a few paces and up a maximum of 3 steps.

For holiday home parks, the rating will depend upon access to reception, route to the caravan, food shop and telephone (where provided), and the holiday home itself.

For touring/camping parks, it will depend upon access to reception, routes to pitches, food shop and telephone (where provided), toilet and washing facilities.

Please contact individual park operators for more detailed information you may require.

A list of parks offering accessible accommodation featured in this guide can be found on page 239.

G CODE OF CONDUCT

In addition to fulfilling its statutory obligations, the park management undertakes to observe the following Code of Conduct:

1   To ensure high standards of courtesy, cleanliness, catering and service appropriate to the type of site.

2   To describe fairly to all visitors and prospective visitors, the amenities, facilities and service provided by the park, whether by advertisement, brochure, word of mouth, or any other means, and to allow visitors to see pitches, if requested, before booking.

3   To make clear to visitors exactly what is included in all prices quoted for pitches, meals and refreshments, including service charges, taxes and other surcharges. Details of cancellation procedures and charges for additional services or facilities available should also be made clear.

4   To adhere to, and not to exceed, prices current at the time of occupation for accommodation or other services.

5   To advise visitors at the time of booking and subsequent to any change, if the pitch offered is on another park and the location of the park and any difference in the comfort and amenities from the pitch previously booked.

6   To give each visitor, on request, details of payment due and receipt, if required.

7   To deal promptly and courteously with all enquiries, requests, reservations, correspondence and complaints from visitors.

8   To allow an English Tourism Council or national tourist board representative reasonable access to the establishment, on request, to confirm that the Code of Conduct is being observed.

9   The operator must also comply with the provisions of the caravan industry Codes of Practice.

A selection of events for
2001 in England

MANIFESTATIONS EN ANGLETERRE EN 2001
VERANSTALTUNGEN IN ENGLAND 2001
EVENEMENTEN IN ENGELAND IN 2001
CALENDARIO DEGLI AVVENIMENTI IN INGHILTERRA NEL 2001

This is a selection of the many cultural, sporting and other events that will be taking place throughout England during 2001. Please note, as changes often occur after press date, it is advisable to confirm the date and location before travelling.

- Vous trouverez ci-dessous un choix de manifestations devant se dérouler en Angleterre dans le courant de l'année. Etant donné que des modifications sont susceptibles de survenir après la date de mise sous presse, nous vous conseillons de vous faire confirmer, une fois arrivé en Angleterre, les reseignements donnés dans ce guide auprès du Centre d'Information Touristique de la région où vous séjournez.

- Nachstehend finden Sie eine Auswahl der 2001 in England stattfindenden Veranstaltungen. Da nach Redaktionsschluß oft Änderungen vorkommen, ist es ratsam, sich die Angaben bei Ihrer Ankunft in England vom jeweiligen Tourist Information Centre bestätigen zu lassen.

- Hieronder vindt u een keuze uit de evenementen die er het komende jaar in Engeland zullen plaatsvinden. Eventuele veranderingen vinden vaak pas na de persdatum plaats. Het is daarom raadzaam de gegeven informatie na aankomst in Engeland bij het plaatselijke Toeristen Informatie Bureau te controleren.

- Riportiamo una selezione degli avvenimenti che si svolgeranno in Inghilterra nel corso dell'anno prossimo. Dal momento che dopo la data di stampa si verificano spesso dei cambiamenti, si consiglia di verificare l'esattezza delle informazioni riportate in questa guida rivolgendosi, dopo l'arrivo in Inghilterra, al Tourist Information Centre del luogo.

January 2001

4-28 January
Holiday on Ice 2001: Xotica – A Journey to the Heart
Brighton Centre, Kings Road, Brighton, East Sussex
Contact: (0870) 900 9100

5-14 January
47th London International Boat Show
Earls Court Exhibition Centre, Warwick Road, London SW5
Contact: (01784) 473377

6 January
Old Custom: Haxey Hood Game
The Village, Haxey, Doncaster, South Yorkshire
Contact: (01427) 752845

20-21 January
Motorbike 2001
Springfields Exhibition Centre, Camelgate, Spalding, Lincolnshire
Contact: (01775) 724843

Feburary 2001

1-3 February
Wakefield Rhubarb Trail and Festival of Rhubarb
Various venues, Wakefield, West Yorkshire
Contact: (01924) 305841

3-4 February
The 22nd Bristol Classic Car Show
The Royal Bath and West Showground, Shepton Mallet, Somerset
Contact: (0117) 907 1000

15-17 February
Garrick Drama Festival
Civic Hall, Castle Dyke, Lichfield, Staffordshire
Contact: (01543) 308797

17-18 February*
Motorsport Day
Brooklands Museum, Brooklands Road, Weybridge, Surrey
Contact: (01932) 857381

* Provisional at time of going to press.

17-25 February
National Boat, Caravan and Leisure Show
National Exhibition Centre, Birmingham,
West Midlands
Contact: (024) 7622 1443

March 2001

1 March
Lancashire Food Festival
Accrington Town Hall, Accrington, Lancashire
Contact: (01254) 872595

8-11 March
Crufts 2001
National Exhibition Centre, Birmingham,
West Midlands

13-15 March
Cheltenham Gold Cup National Hunt Racing Festival
Cheltenham Racecourse, Prestbury Park,
Cheltenham, Gloucestershire
Contact: (01242) 513014

25-28 March
Diesel Gala – GWR (Gloucestershire/Warwickshire)
The Railway Station, Toddington,
Cheltenham, Gloucestershire
Contact: (01242) 621405

April 2001

*1 April-23 December**
Cornwall 2001 Festival of Steam and Invention
Various venues, Wakefield, West Yorkshire,
Contact: (01924) 305841

5-7 April
Grand National Festival
Aintree Racecourse, Ormskirk Road, Aintree,
Liverpool, Merseyside
Contact: (0151) 523 2600

7-8 April
Gateshead Spring Flower Show
Gateshead Central Nurseries, Lobley Hill,
Gateshead, Tyne & Wear
Contact: (0191) 477 1011

8 April
World Dock Pudding Championship
Mytholmroyd Community Centre, Elphaborough,
Mytholmroyd, Hebden Bridge, West Yorkshire
Contact: (01422) 883023

13-20 April
Harrogate International Youth Music Festival
Various venues, Harrogate, North Yorkshire
Contact: (01306) 744360

15-16 April
Easter Egg Hunt
Crealy Park, Clyst St Mary, Exeter, Devon
Contact: (01395) 233200

26-29 April
Harrogate Spring Flower Show
Great Yorkshire Showground,
Harrogate, North Yorkshire
Contact: (01423) 561049

*28-29 April**
South West Custom and Classic Bike Show
The Royal Bath and West Showground,
Shepton Mallet, Somerset
Contact: (01749) 822222

May 2001

4-7 May
Hastings Jack in the Green Morris Dance Festival
Various venues, Hastings, East Sussex
Contact: (01424) 716576

*4-7 May**
Lincoln Folk Festival
The Lawn, Union Road, Lincoln, Lincolnshire
Contact: (01522) 523000

6-7 May
Bexhill 100 Festival of Motoring
Seafront, De La Warr Parade, Bexhill, East Sussex
Contact: (01424) 730564

7 May
May Day Festival
Michelham Priory, Upper Dicker, Hailsham, East Sussex
Contact: (01323) 844224

*9-13 May**
Royal Windsor Horse Show
Windsor Home Park, Datchet Road, Windsor, Berkshire
Contact: (01753) 860633

13 May
South Suffolk Show
Ampton Park, Ingham, Bury St Edmunds, Suffolk
Contact: (01638) 750879

18 May-3 June
Bath International Music Festival
Various venues, Bath
Contact: (01225) 463362

26-27 May
Hertfordshire County Show
Hertfordshire County Showground, Redbourn,
St Albans, Hertfordshire
Contact: (01582) 792626

26-28 May
Window on the World International Music Festival
North Shields Fishquay and Town, Tyne & Wear
Contact: (0191) 200 8909

28 May
Luton International Carnival
Town Centre and nearby, Luton, Bedfordshire
Contact: (01582) 877282

28 May
Northumberland County Show
Tynedale Park, Corbridge, Northumberland
Contact: (01697) 747848

30-31 May
Suffolk Show
Suffolk Showground, Bucklesham Road,
Ipswich, Suffolk
Contact: (01473) 726847

June 2001

1 June
Robert Dover's Cotswold Olimpick Games
Dovers Hill, Weston Subedge,
Chipping Campden, Gloucestershire
Contact: (01384) 274041

1-30 June*
Royal Cornwall Show
Royal Cornwall Showground, Wadebridge, Cornwall
Contact: (01208) 812183

2-3 June*
Steam Fair
Bedford Square, Tavistock, Devon
Contact: (01822) 615526

7-9 June
South of England Agricultural Show
South of England Showground, Ardingly,
Haywards Heath, West Sussex
Contact: (01444) 892700

8-10 June*
Wimborne Folk Festival 2001
Town Centre, Wimborne Minster, Dorset
Contact: (01202) 743465

9 June*
Trooping the Colour – The Queen's Birthday Parade
Horse Guards Parade, London, SW1
Contact: (020) 7414 2479

10 June
Manchester to Blackpool Veteran Vintage and
Classic Car Run
Granada Studios, Manchester, Greater Manchester
Contact: (01925) 791922

12-14 June*
Three Counties Show
Three Counties Showground, The Showground,
Malvern, Worcestershire
Contact: (01684) 584900

13-19 June*
Grosvenor House Art and Antiques Fair
Le Meridien Grosvenor House, Park Lane, London, W1A
Contact: (020) 7399 8100

15-17 June
East of England Show
East of England Showground, Alwalton,
Peterborough, Cambridgeshire
Contact: (01733) 234451

16 June*
Firework Spectacular
Seafront, Ilfracombe, Devon
Contact: (01271) 863001

19-20 June*
Cheshire County Show
The Showground, Tabley, Knutsford, Cheshire
Contact: (01829) 760020

22 June-1 July
Newcastle Hoppings
Town Moor, Newcastle upon Tyne, Tyne & Wear
Contact: (07831) 458774

24-30 June
Alnwick Medieval Fair
Market Square, Alnwick, Northumberland
Contact: (01665) 602552

25 June-8 July*
Wimbledon Lawn Tennis Championships
All England Lawn Tennis and Croquet Club,
Church Road, London, SW19
Contact: (020) 8946 2244

27-28 June
Royal Norfolk Show 2001
The Showground, New Costessey, Norwich, Norfolk
Contact: (01603) 748931

29 June-1 July*
Milton Keynes International Festival
Milton Keynes Theatre & Gallery,
Central Milton Keynes, Buckinghamshire
Contact: (01908) 610564

30 June
Toe Wrestling
Wetton, Staffordshire
Contact: (01782) 283377

July 2001

1-31 July*
The Balloon and Flower Festival
Southampton Common, Southampton, Hampshire
Contact: (023) 8083 2525

4-8 July
Henley Royal Regatta
Henley-on-Thames, Oxfordshire
Contact: (01491) 572153

7-8 July
Sunderland International Kite Festival
Northern Area Playing Fields, District 12,
Washington, Tyne & Wear
Contact: (0191) 514 1235

7 July-11 August*
Cookson Country Festival
Various venues, South Shields, Tyne & Wear
Contact: (0191) 427 1717

10-12 July
Great Yorkshire Show
Great Yorkshire Showground, Harrogate,
North Yorkshire
Contact: (01423) 541000

12-14 July*
Kent County Show
Kent County Showground, Detling, Maidstone, Kent
Contact: (09068) 884591

14 July
The Big Day Out
Parker's Piece, Cambridge, Cambridgeshire
Contact: (01223) 457521

14 July
Tendring Hundred Show
Lawford House Park, Lawford, Manningtree, Essex
Contact: (01206) 571517

14-15 July
Tewkesbury Medieval Festival
The Gastons, Gloucester Road,
Tewkesbury, Gloucestershire
Contact: (01684) 297607

19-22 July
Golf: The Open Championship 2001
Royal Lytham St Annes Golf Club,
Lytham St Annes, Lancashire
Contact: (01253) 725610

20 July-15 September
Henry Wood Promenade Concerts
Royal Albert Hall, London, SW7
Contact: (020) 7765 5575

21-22 July*
Halton Show
Spike Island and West Bank, West Bank,
Widnes, Cheshire
Contact: (0151) 424 2061

24-26 July*
New Forest and Hampshire County Show
New Park, The Showground, Brockenhurst, Hampshire
Contact: (01590) 622409

25 July
Sandringham Flower Show
Sandringham Park, Sandringham, Norfolk
Contact: (01485) 540860

27 July-5 August*
Stockton International Riverside Festival
Various venues, Stockton-on-Tees, Cleveland
Contact: (0191) 276 9911

28 July-4 August
Cowes Week
Cowes, Isle of Wight
Contact: (01703) 620006

* Provisional at time of going to press.

EVENTS

August 2001

3-4 August
Living History Weekend
Northernhay Gardens, Exeter, Devon
Contact: (01392) 265118

4-11 August
Alnwick International Music and Dance Festival
Market Place, Alnwick, Northumberland
Contact: (01665) 606033

10-12 August
Saltburn International Festival of Folk Music,
Dance and Song
Various venues, Saltburn-by-the-Sea, Cleveland
Contact: (01947) 840928

11-18 August
Billingham International Folklore Festival
Town Centre, Queensway, Billingham, Cleveland
Contact: (01642) 553220

*12-18 August**
Falmouth Regatta Week
Helford River, Carrick Roads and Falmouth Bay,
Cornwall
Contact: (01326) 211555

19 August
Rare Breeds Show and Country Fair
South of England Rare Breeds Centre, Highlands Farm,
Woodchurch, Ashford, Kent
Contact: (01233) 861493

25-26 August
Saddleworth Rushcart Festival
Various venues, Uppermill, Saddleworth,
Greater Manchester
Contact: (01457) 834871

25-27 August
Herstmonceux Castle Medieval Festival
Herstmonceux, Hailsham, East Sussex
Contact: (0891) 172902

*25-27 August**
The Chelmsford Spectacular
Hylands Park, Writtle, Chelmsford, Essex
Contact: (01245) 606985

26 August
Grasmere Lakeland Sports and Show
Sports Field, Grasmere, Ambleside, Cumbria
Contact: (015394) 32127

*26-27 August**
Notting Hill Carnival
Streets around Ladbroke Grove, London, W11
Contact: (020) 8964 0544

31 August-2 September
The Long Weekend – Clevedon's Annual Jazz Festival
Prince's Hall, Clevedon, North Somerset
Contact: (01275) 343210

September 2001

1-2 September
Berwick Military Tattoo
Berwick Barracks, Berwick-upon-Tweed,
Northumberland
Contact: (01289) 307426

*1-2 September**
Lancashire Vintage and Country Show
Hamilton House Farm, St Michael's on Wyre,
Preston, Lancashire
Contact: (01772) 687259

*1-30 September**
New Brighton Classic Car Show
Fort Perch Rock Car Park, off Kings Parade,
New Brighton, Wirral, Merseyside
Contact: (0151) 647 6780

*1-30 September**
Great Dorset Steam Fair
South Down Farm, Tarrant Hinton,
Blandford Forum, Dorset
Contact: (01258) 860361

*1-30 September**
Ocean Race – Round the World Yacht Race
Mayflower Park, Town Quay, Southampton, Hampshire
Contact: (023) 8083 2453

*7-9 September**
Weald of Kent Craft Fair
Penshurst Place and Gardens, Penshurst,
Tonbridge, Kent
Contact: (01425) 272711

14-23 September*
Southampton International Boat Show
Western Esplanade, Southampton, Hampshire
Contact: (01784) 473377

16-17 September
Farming Festival
Farming World, Nash Court, Boughton, Faversham, Kent
Contact: (01227) 751144

26-30 September*
Horse of the Year Show
Wembley Arena, Middlesex
Contact: (020) 8900 9282

October 2001

1-31 October*
Great North Run, The World's Biggest Half Marathon
Various venues throughout Tyne & Wear,
Newcastle upon Tyne, Tyne & Wear
Contact: (0191) 402 0016

13-27 October
Canterbury Festival
Various venues, Canterbury, Kent
Contact: (01227) 452853

21 October*
Trafalgar Day Parade – The Sea Cadet Corps
Trafalgar Square, London, WC2
Contact: (020) 7928 8978

November 2001

3 November*
Alton Round Table's Magnificent Fireworks and
Bonfire
Bass Sports Ground, Anstey Road, Alton, Hampshire
Contact: (01420) 561460

4 November*
London to Brighton Veteran Car Run
Hyde Park, London, W2
Contact: (01753) 681736

4 November
Old Custom: Rolling of the Tar Barrels
Town Centre, Ottery St Mary, Devon
Contact: (01404) 813964

10 November*
Lord Mayor's Show
City of London, London
Contact: (020) 7606 3030

11 November*
Remembrance Day Service and Parade
Cenotaph, Whitehall, London, SW1
Contact: (020) 7273 3498

16-25 November
International Guitar Festival of Great Britain
Various venues, Wirral, Merseyside
Contact: (0151) 666 5060

17 November-23 December
Thursford Christmas Spectacular
Thursford Collection, Thursford Green,
Fakenham, Norfolk
Contact: (01328) 878477

21 November-2 December
Huddersfield Contemporary Music Festival
Various venues, Huddersfield
Contact: (01484) 425082

December 2001

6-13 December
Victorian Christmas in Maldon
High Street, Maldon, Essex

24 December
Old Custom: Tolling the Devil's Knell
All Saints Parish Church, Rishworth Road,
Dewsbury, West Yorkshire
Contact: (01484) 223200

31 December
The Snow Ball – New Years Eve Party
Sheffield Ski Village, Parkwood Springs, Sheffield,
South Yorkshire
Contact: (0114) 276 9459

* Provisional at time of going to press.

A selection of events for
2001 in Scotland

January 2001

30 January
Up Helly Aa
Lerwick Town Centre, Shetland
Contact: (01595) 693434

February 2001

17 February-10 March*
Inverness Music Festival
Various venues, Inverness
Contact: (01463) 716616

April 2001

April *
St Andrews Golf Week
Links Golf St Andrews
Contact: (01334) 478639

1-12 April
Edinburgh International Science Festival
Various venues, Edinburgh
Contact: (0131) 530 2001

20-30 April
Spirit of Speyside Whisky Festival
Various venues, Speyside
Contact: (01343) 542666

May 2001

24-27 May
Orkney Folk Festival
Various venues, Orkney
Contact: (01856) 851331

25 May-9 June*
The Highland Festival
Various venues over the Highlands
Contact: (01463) 711112 (information and ticket line)

July 2001

Mid July*
Hebridean Celtic Festival
Stornoway Castle, Stornoway
Contact: (07001) 878 787

4-8 July*
Glasgow Jazz Festival
Various venues, Glasgow
Contact: (0141) 287 5511 (ticket line)

August 2001

3-25 August
Edinburgh Military Tattoo
Edinburgh Castle, Esplanade, Edinburgh
Contact: (0131) 225 1188

12 August-1 September
Edinburgh International Festival
Various venues, Edinburgh
Contact: (0131) 473 2001 (information)
(0131) 473 2000 (tickets)

Mid August-24-25 August
Cowal Highland Gathering
Dunoon, Argylshire
Contact: (01369) 703206

Mid August - 1st week in October *
Gaelforce
Various venues, Dumfries & Galloway
Contact: (01387) 262084

September 2001

1 September
Braemar Highland Gathering
The Princess Royal and Duke of Fife Memorial Park,
Braemar
Contact: (01399) 755377

1-8 September
Borders Walking Festival
West Linton, Borders
Contact: (01835) 824632

November 2001

24-30 November*
St Andrews Week
Various venues, St Andrews
Contact: (01334) 477872

October 2001

12-19 October
Royal National Mod
Various venues, Stornoway
Contact: (01463) 231226

12-20 October*
Aberdeen Alternative Festival
Various venues, Aberdeen
Contact: (01224) 635822

15-20 October
Pitlochry Festival of Walking
Various venues, Pitlochry
Conact: (01796) 472 215

December 2001

31 December
Hogmanay
Various venues, throughout Scotland

Since changes often occur after press date, it is advisable to confirm the date and locations of events before travelling.

* provisional at time of going to press.

Britain
On-Line

In-depth information about travelling in Britain is now available on BTA's VisitBritain website.

Covering everything from castles to leisure parks and from festivals to road and rail links, the site complements Where to Stay perfectly, giving you up-to-the-minute details to help with your travel plans.

BRITAIN on the internet
www.visitbritain.com

A selection of events for
2001 in Wales

February 2001

3 February
Wales v England: 6 Nations Rugby International
Millennium Stadium, Westgate Street, Cardiff
Contact: (029) 2078 1700

March 2001

3 March
Wales v Ireland: 6 Nations Rugby International
Millennium Stadium, Westgate Street, Cardiff
Contact: (029) 2078 1700

May 2001

25 May-3 June
Hay Festival
Various venues, Hay-on-Wye, Hereford
Contact: (01497) 821217

26 May-3 June
Festival: Gwyl Beaumaris
Beaumaris Leisure Centre, Beaumaris, Gwynnedd
Contact: (01248) 810415

28 May-2 June
The Urdd Gobaith Cymru National Eisteddfod
Coopers Field Civic Centre, Cardiff
Contact: (01248) 672105

June 2001

1-30 June*
22nd Man v Horse Marathon
Various venues, Llanwrtyd Wells, Powys
Contact: (01591) 610236

July 2001

2-8 July
Llangollen International Musical Eisteddfod
Royal International Pavilion, Llangollen, Denbighshire
Contact: (01978) 860236

21-28 July
Fishguard International Music Festival
Various venues, Fishguard, Pembrokeshire
Contact: (01348) 873 612

23-26 July
Royal Welsh Show
Royal Welsh Showground, Llanelwedd,
Builth Wells, Powys
Contact: (01982) 553683

23 July-5 August*
Cardiff International Festival 2001
Various venues, Cardiff
Contact: (029) 2087 3936

27 July
The Great Cheese Race
Various venues, Caerphilly, Mid Glamorgan
Contact: (029) 2088 0011

August 2001

4-5 August
St Asaph Gala Day
Roe Plas Field, St Asaph, Clwyd
Contact: (01745) 582746

4-11 August
Eisteddfod Genedlaethol Frenhinol Cymru
– Royal National Eisteddfod
Denbeigh, Clwyd
Contact: (029) 2076 3777

9-10 August
United Counties Show
United Counties Showground, Nantyci,
Carmarthen, Carmarthenshire
Contact: (01267) 232141

10-13 August
Brecon Jazz Festival
Various venues, Brecon, Powys
Contact: (01874) 625557

12-14 August
Cardigan Bay Regatta
The Pier, South John Street, New Quay, Dyfed
Contact: (01545) 561019

18-26 August
Llandrindod Wells Victorian Festival
Old Town Hall, Llandrindod Wells, Powys
Contact: (01597) 823441

September 2001

1-8 September
Barmouth Arts Festival
Dragon Theatre, Barmouth, Gwynedd
Contact: (01341) 28039

Since changes often occur after press date, it is advisable to confirm the date and locations of events before travelling.

* provisional at time of going to press.

Ratings you can trust

When you're looking for a place to stay, you need a rating system you can trust. The British Graded Holiday Parks Scheme, operated jointly by the national tourist boards for England, Scotland and Wales, gives you a clear guide of what to expect. Based on the internationally recognised rating of One to Five Stars, the system puts great emphasis on quality and reflects customer expectations. Parks are visited annually by trained, impartial assessors who award a rating based on cleanliness, environment and the quality of services and facilities provided.

STAR QUALITY

★★★★★	Exceptional Quality
★★★★	Excellent Quality
★★★	Very Good Quality
★★	Good Quality
★	Acceptable Quality

Tourist Information in
Britain

INFORMATION POUR LES TOURISTES
EN GRANDE-BRETAGNE
TOURISTEN-INFORMATION IN GROSSBRITANNIEN
TOERISTISCHE INFORMATIE IN GROOT-BRITTANNIE
INFORMAZIONI PER TURISTI IN GRAN BRETAGNA

To help you explore Britain, to see both the major sites and the fascinating attractions off the beaten track, there is a country-wide service of Tourist Information Centres (TICs), each ready and able to give advice and directions on how best to enjoy your holiday in Britain. A comprehensive list can be obtained from BTA offices overseas.

Call in at these centres while travelling - you'll find them in most towns and many villages - and make use of the help that awaits you. Much development of Tourist Information Centre services has taken place in recent years and you should have no difficulty in locating them as most are well signposted and the use of the following international symbol is becoming more common:

You can rest assured that the Tourist Information Centres in the places you visit will be ready to give you all the help you need when you get to Britain, particularly on matters of detailed local information.

ACCOMMODATION RESERVATION SERVICES

Wherever you go in Britain, you will find TICs which can help and advise you about all types of accommodation. Details of Park Finding Services are outlined on page 18.

THE BRITAIN VISITOR CENTRE

The Britain Visitor Centre offers the most comprehensive information and booking service in London - and it's all under one roof, just two minutes walk from Piccadilly Circus.

The Britain Visitor Centre will book rail, air and car travel, reserve sightseeing tours, theatre tickets and accommodation, change currency and, of course, provide information in many languages on the whole of Britain and Ireland. There is also a bookshop within the Centre.

Open seven days a week, 0900 to 1830 Monday to Friday, 1000 to 1600 Saturday and Sunday (0900 to 1700 Saturdays June to September) at 1 Regent Street, London SW1Y 4XT.

TOURIST ORGANISATIONS

Here is an address list of official tourist organisations in all parts of Britain. All these offices welcome personal callers, except those marked.

LONDON

London Tourist Board and Convention Bureau
6th floor, Glen House, Stag Place, London SW1E 5LT
(no personal callers please).
Web site: www.LondonTown.com
For further information on London Tourist Information Centres please refer to pages 41-42.

Scottish Tourist Board
19 Cockspur Street, London SW1Y 5BL
(personal callers only)
Telephone enquiries: (0131) 332 2433

Wales Tourist Board
1 Regent Street, London SW1Y 4XT
Tel: (020) 7808 3838

British Tourist Authority
Thames Tower, Black's Road,
Hammersmith, London W6 9EL
(written enquiries only)

ENGLAND

Information is available from the 10 regional tourist boards in England (contact details can be found at the beginning of each regional section), and a network of around 600 Tourist Information Centres. Look out for the sign shown above.

SCOTLAND

The Scottish Tourist Board has a substantial network of local tourist boards, backed up by more than 140 information centres.

Scottish Tourist Board
23 Ravelston Terrace, Edinburgh EH4 3TP
Tel: (0131) 332 2433

WALES

There are three Regional Tourism Companies and over 84 information centres to help you.

Wales Tourist Board
Brunel House, 2 Fitzalan Road, Cardiff CF24 0UY
Tel: (029) 20499909
(telephone and written enquiries only)

INFORMATION ON THE INTERNET

Visit the BTA's website for a wealth of information including travel information, places to visit and events.
WWW.VISITBRITAIN.COM

National
Accessible Scheme

The English Tourism Council and the National and Regional Tourist Boards throughout Britain assess all types of places to stay, on holiday or business, that provide accessible accommodation for wheelchair users and others who may have difficulty walking.

Accommodation establishments taking part in the National Accessible Scheme, and which appear in this guide are listed below. Use the Town Index at the back to find the page numbers for their full entries.

The Tourist Boards recognise three categories of accessibility:

 CATEGORY 1   Accessible to all wheelchair users including those travelling independently.

 CATEGORY 2   Accessible to a wheelchair user with assistance.

 CATEGORY 3   Accessible to a wheelchair user able to walk short distances and up at least three steps.

If you have additional needs or special requirements of any kind, we strongly recommend that you make sure these can be met by your chosen establishment before you confirm your booking.

The criteria the English Tourism Council and the National and Regional Tourist Boards have adopted do not necessarily conform to British Standards or to Building Regulations. They reflect what the Boards understand to be acceptable to meet the practical needs of wheelchair users.

 CATEGORY 1

• Brecon, Powys, Wales - Brynich Caravan Park

 CATEGORY 2

• Bala, Gwynedd, Wales
  - Penybont Touring & Camping Park
• Brecon, Powys, Wales - Anchorage Caravan Park
• Bridgnorth, Shropshire - Stanmore Hall Touring Park
• Canterbury, Kent - Yew Tree Caravan Park
• Colwyn Bay, Conwy, Wales
  - Bron Y Wendon Caravan Park
• Marden, Kent - Tanner Farm Touring Caravan & Camping Park
• Poole, Dorset - Beacon Hill Touring Park
• Portreath, Cornwall - Tehidy Holiday Park
• Shrewbury, Shropshire - Oxon Hall Touring Park
• Telford, Shropshire - Severn Gorge Park

• Winsford, Somerset - Halse Farm Caravan & Tent Park
• Yeovil, Somerset - Long Hazel International Caravan & Camping Park

 CATEGORY 3

• Aberystwyth, Ceredigion, Wales
  - Ocean View Caravan Parks
• Cardigan, Ceredigion, Wales
  - Cenarth Falls Holiday Park
• Callander, Central - Keltie Bridge Caravan Park
• Cwmcarn, Gwent, Wales
  - Cwmcarn Forest Drive Campsite
• Glasgow, Strathclyde - Craigendmuir Park
• Matlock, Derbyshire - Darwin Forest Country Park
• Porthmadog, Gwynedd, Wales - Greenacres Holiday Park
• Prestatyn, Denbighshire, Wales - Tan y Don Caravan Park
• Tenby, Pembrokeshire, Wales - Kiln Park Holiday Centre

The National Accessible Scheme forms part of the Tourism for All Campaign that is being promoted by National and Regional Tourist Boards. Additional help and guidance on finding suitable holiday accommodation for those with special needs can be obtained from:

HOLIDAY CARE

Holiday Care, 2nd Floor, Imperial Buildings, Victoria Road, Horley, Surrey RH6 7PZ

Tel: (01293) 774535 Fax: (01293) 784647
Minicom: (01293) 776943

BTA Overseas Offices

ARGENTINA – Buenos Aires
BTA
Avenida Cordoba 645, 2nd Floor
1054 Buenos Aires
Tel: 00 54 (11) 4314 6735
Fax: 00 54 (11) 4315 3161
E-mail: btaarg@comnet.com.ar
(open to public Mon-Thu 1000-1700; Fri 1000-1300)

AUSTRALIA – Sydney
BTA
Level 16, Gateway
1 Macquarie Place
Sydney, NSW 2000
Tel: 00 61 (2) 9377 4400
Fax: 00 61 (2) 9377 4499
E-mail: visitbritainaus@bta.org.uk
Website: www.visitbritain.com/au

AUSTRIA – Vienna
Britain Visitor Centre
The British Council
Schenkestr. 4
A-1010 Vienna
Tel: 00 43 (1) 533 26 16 81
Fax: 00 43 (1) 533 26 16 85
E-mail: tourist.information@bc-vienna.at

BELGIUM – Brussels
Visit Britain Centre
Avenue Louise 140, 2nd Floor
1050 Brussels
Tel: 00 32 (2) 646 35 10
Fax: 00 32 (2) 646 39 86
Email: british.be@bta.org.uk
Website: www.visitbritain.com/be

BRAZIL – Rio de Janeiro
BTA
Rua da Assembleia 10, sala 3707
Rio de Janeiro-RJ 20119-900
Tel: 00 55 (21) 531 1717/0382
Fax: 00 55 (21) 531 0383
E-mail: btabras@vetor.com.br

CANADA – Toronto
BTA
5915 Airport Road, Suite 120
Mississauga, Ontario L4V 1T1
Fax: 00 1 (905) 405 1835
Email: travelinfo@bta.org.uk
Toll free: 1 888 VISIT UK
Website: www.visitbritain.com/ca

DENMARK – Copenhagen
BTA
Møntergade 3
1116 Copenhagen K
Tel: (00 45) 33 33 91 88
Fax: (00 45) 33 14 01 36
E-mail: dkweb@bta.org.uk

FINLAND – Helsinki
British Travel Centre
Mikonkatu 13A
00100 Helsinki
Tel: 00 358 (9) 681 2466
Fax: 00 358 (9) 622 1562
Email: finlandbtc@bta.org.uk

FRANCE – Paris
BTA
Maison de la Grande-Bretagne
19 rue des Mathurins
75009 Paris
Tel: 00 33 (1) 4451 5620
Fax: 00 33 (1) 4451 5621
Minitel: 3615 BRITISH
Website: www.grandebretagne.net

GERMANY – Frankfurt
BTA
Westendstr 16-22
60325 Frankfurt
Tel: 00 49 (69) 97 1123
Fax: 00 49 (69) 97 112 444
E-mail: gbinfo@bta.org.uk
Website: www.visitbritain.com.de

HONG KONG
BTA
Room 1504, Eton Tower
8 Hysan Avenue
Causeway Bay
Hong Kong
Tel: (00 852) 2882 9967
Fax: (00 852) 577 1443
Email: hko@bta.org.uk
Website: www.visitbritain.com/hk

IRELAND – Dublin
BTA
18/19 College Green
Dublin 2
Tel: 00 353 (1) 670 8000
Fax: 00 353 (1) 670 8244

ITALY – Milan
BTA
Corso Magenta 32
20123 Milano
Tel: 00 39 (02) 8808 151
Fax: 00 39 (02) 7201 0086

ITALY – Rome
BTA
Via Nazionale 230
00184 Rome
Tel: 00 39 (06) 462 0221
Fax: 00 39 (06) 474 2054

JAPAN – Tokyo
BTA
Akasaka Twin Tower 1F
2-17-22 Akasaka
Minato-ku
Tokyo
Tel: 00 81 (3) 5562 2550
Fax: 00 81 (3)5562 2551
Website: www.uknow.com.jp

NETHERLANDS – Amsterdam
BTA
Aurora Gebouw (5e)
Stadhouderskade 2
1054 ES Amsterdam
Tel: 00 31 (20) 689 0002
Fax: 00 31 (20) 689 0003
E-mail: BritInfo.NL@bta.org.uk
Website: www.visitbritain.com/nl

NEW ZEALAND – Auckland
BTA
17th Floor, NZI House
151 Queen Street
Auckland 1
Tel: 00 64 (9) 303 1446
Fax: 00 64 (9) 377 6965
Email: bta.nz@bta.org.uk

NORWAY – Oslo
BTA
Nedre Slottsgate 21, 4 etg
0157 Oslo
Tel: (00 47) 22 39 68 39
Fax: (00 47) 22 42 48 74
Email: britisketuristkontor@bta.org.uk
Website: www.storbritannia.no

SINGAPORE
BTA
108 Robinson Road
#01-00 GMG Building
Singapore 068900
Tel: (00 65) 227 5400
Fax: (00 65) 227 5411
Website: www.visitbritain.com/sg

SOUTH AFRICA – Johannesburg
BTA
Lancaster Gate
Hyde Park Lane
Hyde Park 2196 (public address)
PO Box 41896, Craighall 2024 (postal address)
Tel: 00 27 (11) 325 0343
Fax: 00 27 (11) 325 0344
Email: johannesburg@bta.org.uk

SPAIN – Madrid
British Tourist Authority/Turismo Britanico
Calle Santiago de Compostela 100, 2
28035 Madrid
Tel: 00 902 171 181
Fax: 00 34 (91) 386 10 88
E-mail: turismo.britanico@bta.org.uk
Website: www.visitbritain.com/es

SWEDEN – Stockholm
BTA
Box 3102, 103 62 Stockholm (postal address);
Klara Norra Kyrkogata 29, S 111 22 Stockholm (public address)
Tel: 00 46 (8) 4401 700
Fax: 00 46 (8) 21 31 29
E-mail: stockholm.internet@bta.org.uk
Website: www.visitbritain.com/sverige

SWITZERLAND – Zurich
BTA
Limmatquai 78
CH-8001 Zurich
Tel: 00 41 (1) 266 2166
Fax: 00 41 (1) 266 2161
Email: ch-info@bta.org.uk

UNITED ARAB EMIRATES – Dubai
BTA
Tariq Bin Zaid Street
Near Rashid Hospital
Al Maktoum Roundabout
PO Box 33342
Dubai
Tel: 00 971 (4) 3350088
Fax: 00 971 (4) 3355335

USA – Chicago
BTA
625 North Michigan Avenue
Suite 1001, Chicago
IL 60611
Toll free: 1 800 462 2748

USA – New York
BTA
7th Floor, 551 Fifth Avenue
New York, NY 10176-0799
Tel: 00 1 (212) 986 2266
Toll free: 1 800 GO 2 BRITAIN

The David Bellamy

CONSERVATION AWARD

Holiday Parks in Britain provide not only a perfect holiday, but many have created an absolute oasis for wildlife. Whether it is a small park with few facilities or a large park with all the amenities on offer, many are taking important steps to protect and enhance the environment.

If you are seeking a holiday, caravan or camping park for your next holiday why not try one of 211 British Parks who have recently received a conservation award from International conservation champion Professor David Bellamy.

Parks in the scheme are making a positive contribution to conservation and the environment through areas such as landscaping, recycling policies, waste management, the cultivation of flora and fauna, and the creation of habitats designed to encourage a variety of wildlife on to the park. Links with the local community and the use of local materials and craftsmen is also an important consideration.

Caravan and camping parks that participate in the award scheme are assessed by David Bellamy on the basis of postcards completed by holidaymakers and an independent inspection by a local conservation group. There are Gold, Silver and Bronze awards.

Parks with Bellamy Awards offer a variety of accommodation from pitches for touring caravans, motorhomes and tents to caravan holiday homes, holiday lodges and cottages for hire. A range of facilities and entertainment is also available.

Gold, Silver and Bronze award winning parks featured in this guide are listed opposite.

For further information please contact:

BH&HPA, 6 Pullman Court, Great Western Road, Gloucester GL1 3ND.

Tel: 01452 526911, Fax: 01452 508508

Internet: www.ukparks.com/bellamy.htm

The David Bellamy
Conservation Awards

The following parks, which are all featured in this guide, have received a Gold, Silver or Bronze David Bellamy Conservation Award.

LONDON

Thriftwood Caravan Park, Stansted	Silver

CUMBRIA

Castlerigg Hall Caravan & Camping Park, Keswick	Silver
Crake Valley Holiday Park, Coniston	Gold
Fallbarrow Park, Windermere	Gold
Greenhowe Caravan Park, Ambleside	Silver
Lakeland Leisure Park, Flookburgh	Silver
Wild Rose Park, Appleby-in-Westmoorland	Gold

NORTHUMBRIA

Beadnell Links Caravan Park, Beadnell	Gold
Haggerston Castle, Beal	Silver
Waren Caravan & Camping Park, Bamburgh	Silver

NORTH WEST

Cala Gran, Fleetwood	Bronze
Kneps Farm Holiday Park, Cleveleys	Gold
Marton Mere Holiday Village, Blackpool	Bronze

YORKSHIRE

Allerton Park Caravan Park, York	Silver
Cayton Village Caravan Park, Scarborough	Silver
Holme Valley Camping & Caravan Park, Holmefirth	Gold
Northcliffe Holiday Park, Whitby	Gold
Rudding Holiday Park, Harrogate	Silver
St Helena's Caravan Park, Horsforth	Silver
Thorpe Park Holiday Centre, Humberston	Silver
Weir Caravan Park, York	Silver

HEART OF ENGLAND

Darwin Forest Country Park, Matlock	Gold
Fernwood Caravan Park, Ellesmere	Silver
Island Meadow Caravan Park, Aston Cantlow	Gold
Ranch Caravan Park, Evesham	Silver

EAST OF ENGLAND

Cliff House Dunwich, Dunwich	Silver
Forest Park Caravan Site, Cromer	Gold
Hopton Holiday Village, Great Yarmouth	Silver
The Orchards Holiday Village, St Osyth	Silver
Waldegraves Holiday Park, Mersea Island	Silver

SOUTH WEST ENGLAND

Beverley Park, Paignton	Gold
Broadway House Caravan Park, Cheddar	Gold
Burnham-on-Sea Holiday Village, Burnham-on-Sea	Silver
Clifford Bridge Park, Drewsteignton	Silver
Dornafield, Newton Abbot	Silver
Forest Glade Holiday Park, Kentisbeare	Silver
Freshwater Beach Holiday Park, Bridport	Bronze
Halse Farm Caravan & Tent Park, Winsford	Gold
Harford Bridge Holiday Park, Tavistock	Gold
Highlands End Holiday Park, Bridport	Silver
Par Sands Holiday Park, Par	Gold
Parkers Farm Holiday Park, Ashburton	Silver
Polmanter Tourist Park, St Ives	Silver
Polruan Holiday Centre, Polruan-by-Fowey	Silver
Ramslade Touring Park, Paignton	Gold
Ringwell Valley Holiday Park, Truro	Gold
Rowlands Wait Touring Park, Bere Regis	Gold
Sea View International, Mevagissey	Gold
Silverbow Park, Goonhaven	Gold
The Old Oaks Touring Park, Glastonbury	Silver
Trevella Caravan & Camping Park, Newquay	Gold
Warmwell Country Touring Park, Warmwell	Silver

SOUTH OF ENGLAND

Beacon Hill Touring Park, Poole	Silver
Hurley Farm Caravan & Camping Park, Hurley	Gold
Merley Court Touring Park, Wimborne Minster	Silver
Rockley Park Holiday Park, Poole	Bronze
Shorefield Country Park, Milford-on-Sea	Gold
Ulwell Cottage Caravan Park, Swanage	Silver
Wilksworth Farm Caravan Park, Wimborne Minster	Silver

SOUTH EAST ENGLAND

Church Farm Holiday Village, Pagham	Silver
Crowhurst Park, Battle	Silver

SCOTLAND

Blair Castle Caravan Park, Blair Atholl	Silver
Craigtoun Meadows Holiday Park, St Andrews	Silver
Glen Nevis Caravan & Camping Park, Fort William	Gold
Kippford Caravan Park, Kippford	Gold
Linnhe Lockside Holidays, Fort William	Gold
Park of Brandedleys, Crocketford	Silver
Rothiemurchus Camp & Caravan Park, Aviemore	Gold
Sands of Luce Caravan Park, Sandhead	Silver
Seton Sands Holiday Village, Longniddry	Silver
Trossachs Holiday Park, Aberfoyle	Gold
Wemyss Bay Holiday Park, Wemyss Bay	Silver

WALES

Black Rock Camping & Touring Park, Porthmadog	Gold
Greenacres Holiday Park, Porthmadog	Silver

Ratings you can trust

When you're looking for a place to stay, you need a rating system you can trust. The British Graded Holiday Parks Scheme, operated jointly by the national tourist boards for England, Scotland and Wales, gives you a clear guide of what to expect. Based on the internationally recognised rating of One to Five Stars, the system puts great emphasis on quality and reflects customer expectations. Parks are visited annually by trained, impartial assessors who award a rating based on cleanliness, environment and the quality of services and facilities provided.

STAR QUALITY

★★★★★   Exceptional Quality

★★★★   Excellent Quality

★★★   Very Good Quality

★★   Good Quality

★   Acceptable Quality

The England for Excellence
Awards 2001

LA CREME DE LA CREME

If you are looking for somewhere truly outstanding, then why not try one of the following caravan parks listed below. Having proved their mettle at a regional level, each one has made it through to the semi-finals of the 1999 England for Excellence Awards. Run by the English Tourism Council in association with the Regional Tourist Boards, these highly competitive annual awards reward only the very best in English tourism. So if somewhere has made it through to the short-list, you can be sure that they really are the bees knees.

ENGLISH
TOURISM
COUNCIL

ENGLAND FOR
EXCELLENCE
AWARDS 2000

Sponsored by:

Warner

Dornafield, Newton Abbot, Devon	Tel: 01803 812732
Haven Lower Hyde Holiday Park, Isle of Wight	Tel: 01983 866131
Ord House Country Park, Berwick Upon Tweed, Northumberland `WINNER`	Tel: 01289 305288
Stanmore Hall Touring Park, Stanmore, Bridgnorth `SILVER`	Tel: 01746 761761
The Old Brick Kilns, Barney, Fakenham	Tel: 01328 878305
Upper Carr Chalet and Touring Park, Pickering, North Yorkshire `SILVER`	Tel: 01751 473115
Varne Ridge Caravan Park, Capel-le-Ferne, Kent	Tel: 01303 251765

Tourist Information
Centres

When it comes to your next break in Britain, the first stage of your journey could be closer than you think. You've probably got a Tourist Information Centre nearby which is there to serve the local community - as well as visitors. Knowledgeable staff will be happy to help you, wherever you're heading.

Many Tourist Information Centres can provide you with maps and guides, and sometimes it's even possible to book your accommodation, too.

Across Britain, there are nearly 800 Tourist Information Centres. You'll find the address of your nearest Tourist Information Centre in your local Phone Book.

Competition
Rules

See competition on page 16

1. One entry per household.

2. All entries must be received by 30 November 2001. Entries received after this date will not be accepted. The British Tourist Authority and British Holidays cannot accept responsibility for entries that are damaged, illegible or lost in the mail.

3. All correct entries received by 30 November 2001 will be entered into the draw which will take place by 14 December 2001.

4. The judges' decision is final and no correspondence will be entered into.

5. There will be one winner of the 7-day break and three runners up winning either a 3-night weekend break or a 4-night mid-week break. Winners can choose from any British Holidays Park excluding Rockley Park, Marton Mere and Lydstep Beach. All breaks are subject to availability and must be booked in either Spring 2002 (March-June) or Autumn 2002 (September-October) excluding Bank Holidays in England and Scotland. Towels, insurance, food and transport are not supplied. Parties must be over 21 years of age.

Subject to British Holidays Terms and Conditions. Call for a copy of the British Holidays brochure.

6. No cash alternative will be offered and prizes are non-transferable.

7. The winners will be notified within 28 days of the draw taking place.

8. Details of the winners may be obtained by sending an SAE to BTA Camping and Caravan Parks Competition, British Holidays, Normandy Court, 1 Wolsey Road, Hemel Hempstead, Hertfordshire HP2 4TU, England.

9. Any employee of the British Tourist Authority or Bourne Leisure Group (including British Holidays), their agents or immediate family are not eligible to enter.

10. All information is correct at time of printing. The British Tourist Authority and British Holidays cannot be held responsible for any changes made thereafter.

Distance Chart

The distances between towns on the chart below are given to the nearest mile, and are measured along routes based on the quickest travelling time, making maximum use of motorways or dual-carriageway roads. The chart is based upon information supplied by the Automobile Association.

Inverness
Fort William   Aberdeen
Perth
Glasgow   Edinburgh
Stranraer   Newcastle upon Tyne
          Carlisle   Middlesbrough
          Kendal
                York
          Leeds   Hull
          Manchester
Holyhead   Liverpool   Sheffield
          Lincoln
          Nottingham
                          Norwich
Aberystwyth   Birmingham   Cambridge
          Gloucester   Colchester
Carmarthen   Oxford
Cardiff   London
          Bristol   Guildford
Barnstaple   Taunton   Southampton   Maidstone   Dover
Exeter   Dorchester   Brighton
Plymouth
Penzance

To calculate the distance in kilometres multiply the mileage by 1.6

For example: Brighton to Dover
82 miles x 1.6
=131.2 kilometres

	Aberdeen	Aberystwyth	Barnstaple	Birmingham	Brighton	Bristol	Cambridge	Cardiff	Carlisle	Carmarthen	Colchester	Dorchester	Dover	Edinburgh	Exeter	Fort William	Glasgow	Gloucester	Guildford	Holyhead	Hull	Inverness	Kendal	Leeds	Lincoln	Liverpool	Maidstone	Manchester	Middlesbrough	Newcastle	Norwich	Nottingham	Oxford	Penzance	Perth	Plymouth	Sheffield	Southampton	Stranraer	Taunton	York
Aberystwyth	468
Barnstaple	603	214
Birmingham	431	124	180
Brighton	605	288	208	171
Bristol	513	128	99	90	169
Cambridge	462	215	267	97	120	170
Cardiff	531	110	127	109	201	44	203
Carlisle	231	236	372	199	375	282	257	300
Carmarthen	513	48	190	171	264	106	266	67	282
Colchester	516	289	292	112	112	195	48	227	310	290
Dorchester	595	206	94	172	119	62	179	119	363	182	206
Dover	587	325	273	207	82	206	124	238	400	301	116	200
Edinburgh	125	335	470	298	473	380	333	398	96	381	385	462	458
Exeter	585	196	53	162	175	82	249	109	353	172	274	55	245	453
Fort William	156	446	581	409	584	491	466	509	209	491	518	573	590	133	563
Glasgow	147	333	468	296	472	379	353	397	96	379	405	461	478	49	451	102
Gloucester	479	111	125	56	155	35	150	61	247	124	171	117	192	347	107	456	343
Guildford	563	224	175	128	44	106	91	138	332	201	103	97	97	432	147	541	428	99
Holyhead	459	101	339	167	343	250	259	201	227	149	333	332	369	327	322	436	323	215	300
Hull	375	228	321	140	258	231	138	249	170	312	191	313	262	247	303	379	266	196	239	219
Inverness	106	494	630	457	633	540	514	558	257	540	566	622	639	158	612	66	174	505	591	485	428
Kendal	279	190	325	153	329	236	245	254	47	236	319	318	355	147	308	256	181	286	181	164	305
Leeds	331	174	302	121	263	212	146	230	126	220	200	294	271	202	284	335	222	177	220	165	60	383	71
Lincoln	387	199	276	89	216	186	95	204	182	267	147	245	220	258	258	391	278	151	173	204	46	439	176	72
Liverpool	357	174	274	102	277	184	193	202	126	163	268	266	304	225	256	335	222	150	235	101	128	383	79	74	140
Maidstone	548	286	234	168	50	167	85	199	361	262	77	161	41	419	206	570	458	153	58	329	223	619	315	233	181	263
Manchester	356	134	261	89	264	171	160	189	123	180	212	253	291	223	243	332	219	137	222	125	97	381	77	44	85	35	251
Middlesbrough	276	245	357	177	318	268	198	286	95	291	251	350	322	147	340	280	191	233	276	236	89	308	84	63	123	145	283	115
Newcastle	234	276	388	208	349	299	229	317	60	322	282	381	353	106	371	239	154	264	307	267	142	266	102	94	154	176	314	146	38
Norwich	488	277	329	159	171	233	63	264	282	327	61	241	175	359	311	491	379	212	162	320	150	540	276	173	104	241	135	186	223	254
Nottingham	393	162	234	54	195	144	86	163	188	226	139	226	218	265	216	397	284	110	153	178	92	446	164	74	38	112	179	71	129	160	119
Oxford	503	159	170	68	109	73	81	105	271	168	124	115	146	371	152	480	367	48	67	239	189	529	225	171	130	173	106	161	226	257	144	103
Penzance	697	308	108	274	287	194	361	221	465	284	386	167	357	565	111	674	562	219	259	433	414	723	419	396	369	367	317	355	451	482	423	328	264
Perth	87	382	518	345	521	428	402	446	145	428	454	510	527	42	500	102	62	393	478	373	315	114	193	268	327	271	487	266	192	151	428	334	418	611
Plymouth	628	239	67	205	218	125	292	152	396	215	316	98	288	496	45	605	492	150	190	364	345	654	350	326	300	298	248	286	382	413	354	259	195	77	542
Sheffield	365	167	272	76	233	182	122	201	159	264	176	264	247	236	254	368	255	148	191	158	66	417	125	36	47	79	207	39	100	131	147	44	141	366	281	297
Southampton	570	225	142	135	66	106	131	138	339	201	159	53	152	439	109	548	435	100	49	307	257	596	292	238	197	241	112	228	293	324	193	171	67	221	484	152	208
Stranraer	232	342	478	305	481	388	363	406	106	388	415	470	487	133	460	188	86	354	439	333	276	258	153	228	288	231	448	226	201	163	388	294	378	572	146	503	265	446
Taunton	554	165	50	132	160	51	218	79	323	142	243	45	224	423	32	532	419	77	126	291	272	581	276	253	227	225	184	212	308	339	280	186	121	144	469	75	223	94	429
York	322	202	315	134	276	225	155	243	117	248	209	307	280	193	297	326	213	191	233	193	38	374	91	24	80	103	240	72	50	89	180	86	184	409	238	340	58	251	223	266
London	544	238	216	120	59	120	60	152	313	215	61	128	79	413	198	522	409	102	30	281	186	571	266	198	143	215	39	202	253	284	115	131	56	310	458	241	168	80	419	167	211

Calendar 2001

JANUARY
M	T	W	T	F	S	S
1	2	3	4	5	6	7
8	9	10	11	12	13	14
15	16	17	18	19	20	21
22	23	24	25	26	27	28
29	30	31				

FEBRUARY
M	T	W	T	F	S	S
			1	2	3	4
5	6	7	8	9	10	11
12	13	14	15	16	17	18
19	20	21	22	23	24	25
26	27	28				

MARCH
M	T	W	T	F	S	S
			1	2	3	4
5	6	7	8	9	10	11
12	13	14	15	16	17	18
19	20	21	22	23	24	25
26	27	28	29	30	31	

APRIL
M	T	W	T	F	S	S
30						1
2	3	4	5	6	7	8
9	10	11	12	13	14	15
16	17	18	19	20	21	22
23	24	25	26	27	28	29

MAY
M	T	W	T	F	S	S
	1	2	3	4	5	6
7	8	9	10	11	12	13
14	15	16	17	18	19	20
21	22	23	24	25	26	27
28	29	30	31			

JUNE
M	T	W	T	F	S	S
				1	2	3
4	5	6	7	8	9	10
11	12	13	14	15	16	17
18	19	20	21	22	23	24
25	26	27	28	29	30	

JULY
M	T	W	T	F	S	S
30	31					1
2	3	4	5	6	7	8
9	10	11	12	13	14	15
16	17	18	19	20	21	22
23	24	25	26	27	28	29

AUGUST
M	T	W	T	F	S	S
		1	2	3	4	5
6	7	8	9	10	11	12
13	14	15	16	17	18	19
20	21	22	23	24	25	26
27	28	29	30	31		

SEPTEMBER
M	T	W	T	F	S	S
					1	2
3	4	5	6	7	8	9
10	11	12	13	14	15	16
17	18	19	20	21	22	23
24	25	26	27	28	29	30

OCTOBER
M	T	W	T	F	S	S
1	2	3	4	5	6	7
8	9	10	11	12	13	14
15	16	17	18	19	20	21
22	23	24	25	26	27	28
29	30	31				

NOVEMBER
M	T	W	T	F	S	S
			1	2	3	4
5	6	7	8	9	10	11
12	13	14	15	16	17	18
19	20	21	22	23	24	25
26	27	28	29	30		

DECEMBER
M	T	W	T	F	S	S
31					1	2
3	4	5	6	7	8	9
10	11	12	13	14	15	16
17	18	19	20	21	22	23
24	25	26	27	28	29	30

Calendar 2002

JANUARY
M	T	W	T	F	S	S
	1	2	3	4	5	6
7	8	9	10	11	12	13
14	15	16	17	18	19	20
21	22	23	24	25	26	27
28	29	30	31			

FEBRUARY
M	T	W	T	F	S	S
				1	2	3
4	5	6	7	8	9	10
11	12	13	14	15	16	17
18	19	20	21	22	23	24
25	26	27	28			

MARCH
M	T	W	T	F	S	S
				1	2	3
4	5	6	7	8	9	10
11	12	13	14	15	16	17
18	19	20	21	22	23	24
25	26	27	28	29	30	31

APRIL
M	T	W	T	F	S	S
1	2	3	4	5	6	7
8	9	10	11	12	13	14
15	16	17	18	19	20	21
22	23	24	25	26	27	28
29	30					

MAY
M	T	W	T	F	S	S
		1	2	3	4	5
6	7	8	9	10	11	12
13	14	15	16	17	18	19
20	21	22	23	24	25	26
27	28	29	30	31		

JUNE
M	T	W	T	F	S	S
					1	2
3	4	5	6	7	8	9
10	11	12	13	14	15	16
17	18	19	20	21	22	23
24	25	26	27	28	29	30

JULY
M	T	W	T	F	S	S
1	2	3	4	5	6	7
8	9	10	11	12	13	14
15	16	17	18	19	20	21
22	23	24	25	26	27	28
29	30	31				

AUGUST
M	T	W	T	F	S	S
			1	2	3	4
5	6	7	8	9	10	11
12	13	14	15	16	17	18
19	20	21	22	23	24	25
26	27	28	29	30	31	

SEPTEMBER
M	T	W	T	F	S	S
30						1
2	3	4	5	6	7	8
9	10	11	12	13	14	15
16	17	18	19	20	21	22
23	24	25	26	27	28	29

OCTOBER
M	T	W	T	F	S	S
	1	2	3	4	5	6
7	8	9	10	11	12	13
14	15	16	17	18	19	20
21	22	23	24	25	26	27
28	29	30	31			

NOVEMBER
M	T	W	T	F	S	S
				1	2	3
4	5	6	7	8	9	10
11	12	13	14	15	16	17
18	19	20	21	22	23	24
25	26	27	28	29	30	

DECEMBER
M	T	W	T	F	S	S
30	31					1
2	3	4	5	6	7	8
9	10	11	12	13	14	15
16	17	18	19	20	21	22
23	24	25	26	27	28	29

Win a short break to Britain
- including flights and accommodation!

To enter into the Prize Draw for a four day/three night break, for two people, from a selection offered by BTA, just complete and return the questionnaire to the address overleaf.

Closing date for entries is 31 May 2001.

About this brochure
(Camping & Caravan Parks in Britain)

Q1 *What is your first impression of the brochure?*
- ☐ Very good
- ☐ Good
- ☐ Fair
- ☐ Poor
- ☐ Very poor

Q2 *How easy is it for you to use the brochure?*
- ☐ Very easy
- ☐ Easy
- ☐ Fair
- ☐ Difficult
- ☐ Very difficult

Q3 *How would you describe the design style?*
- ☐ Contemporary
- ☐ Traditional
- ☐ Dated

Q4 *How successfully does the cover reflect the content?*
- ☐ Very successfully
- ☐ Successfully
- ☐ Reasonably
- ☐ Poorly
- ☐ Very poorly

Q5 *How would you rate the way it was written?*
- ☐ Very well
- ☐ Well
- ☐ Fair
- ☐ Poor
- ☐ Very poorly

Q6 *How appropriate are the advertisements to you?*
- ☐ Useful
- ☐ Potentially useful
- ☐ Not very useful

Suggestions for improvements

Q7 *Would you like to see more or less photographs?*
- ☐ More
- ☐ Less

Q8 *How do you view the amount of information?*
- ☐ Too much
- ☐ About right
- ☐ Too little

Q9 *What extra information would you like to see?*
- ☐ Nightlife (clubs, eating, drinking)
- ☐ Britain's heritage
- ☐ Festivals, concerts, theatre
- ☐ Countryside
- ☐ Sport (watching and participating)
- ☐ Travel information
- ☐ Shopping
- ☐ Websites
- ☐ Contemporary lifestyle
- ☐ Accommodation
- ☐ Art/culture
- ☐ Prices/costs
- ☐ Views from other visitors to Britain

continued over

FEEDBACK QUESTIONNAIRE

Overall effectiveness of the brochure

Q10 *How would you rate the brochure in promoting Britain as an attractive destination for overseas visitors?*

- ☐ Very effective
- ☐ Quite effective
- ☐ Fair
- ☐ Not particularly effective
- ☐ Not at all effective

Q11 *How successful do you think it is in projecting an image of Britain as a whole?*

- ☐ Very good
- ☐ Good
- ☐ Fair
- ☐ Poor
- ☐ Very poor

Q12 *This brochure is produced by the British Tourist Authority. How important to you is it that information is produced by a non-commercial organisation?*

- ☐ Very important
- ☐ Important
- ☐ No view
- ☐ Not really important
- ☐ Not at all important

Q13 *How much has it influenced your decision to visit Britain?*

- ☐ Very much
- ☐ A little
- ☐ Possibly
- ☐ Not really
- ☐ Not at all

Q14 *How likely are you to visit Britain in the future?*

- ☐ In 2001
- ☐ In 2002
- ☐ In 2003
- ☐ Longer
- ☐ Not at all

Q15 *Have you ever visited Britain before for any reason (such as childhood, business, family, holiday)?*

- ☐ Yes
- ☐ No

About you

Q16 *Your gender*

- ☐ Male
- ☐ Female

Q17 *Your age*

- ☐ 18-24
- ☐ 25-34
- ☐ 35-54
- ☐ 55-70
- ☐ 70+

Q18 *Who do you usually go with on holidays abroad?*

- ☐ Alone
- ☐ With partner
- ☐ With dependant family
- ☐ With older family
- ☐ With friends
- ☐ Organised group
- ☐ Other

Q19 *What is your nationality?*

Many thanks for your help – we hope you consider coming to Britain, if not this year in the near future.

Winner to be selected at random in June 2001 (winner will be notified by post). Entrants must be 18 years old or over and submit a completed questionnaire to qualify - no questionnaires can be returned. Winners details can be obtained by sending a stamped address envelope, not before July 2001, to the address below.

Not open to staff employees of BTA or their families. There is no cash alternative.

Address for returning questionnaire and for obtaining winners details:

Head of Media Services,
British Tourist Authority,
Thames Tower, Black's Road,
London, W6 9EL, United Kingdom

INDEX TO PARKS
REPERTOIRE DES TERRAINS/PLATZVERZEICHNIS/
REGISTER VAN CAMPINGS/INDICE DEI CAMPEGGI

CHECK THE MAPS

The colour maps at the back of this guide show all the cities, towns and villages for which you will find park entries.

Refer to the town index to find the page on which they are listed.

Index to Advertisers

INDEX TO TOWNS
ANNUAIRE PAR VILLES/STÄDTEVERZEICHNIS/ INDEX VAN STEDEN/INDICE DELLE CITTA

CHECK THE MAPS

The colour maps at the back of this guide show
all the cities, towns and villages for which you will
find park entries.

Refer to the town index to find the page
on which they are listed.

Location

Maps

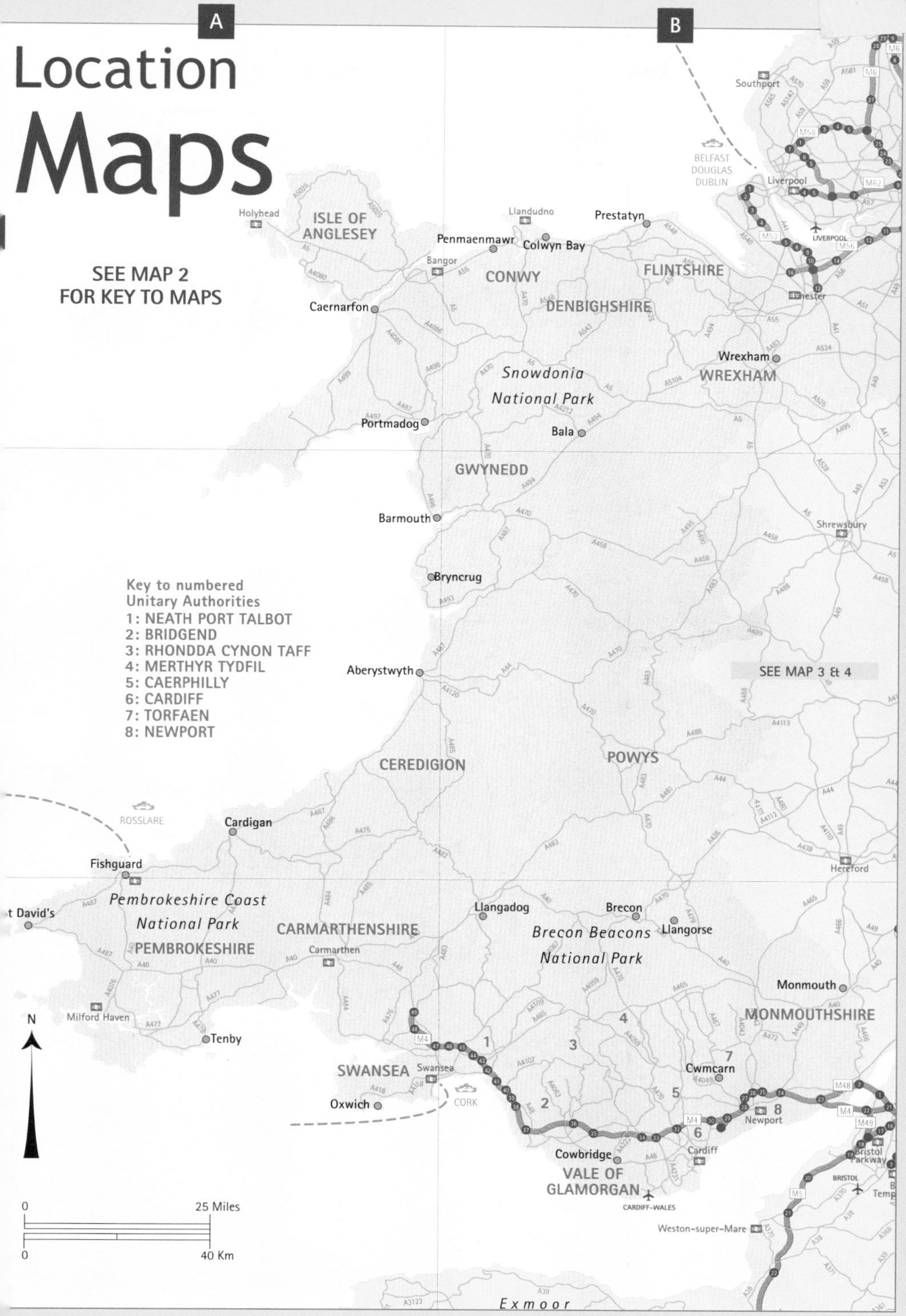

SEE MAP 2
FOR KEY TO MAPS

Key to numbered
Unitary Authorities
1: NEATH PORT TALBOT
2: BRIDGEND
3: RHONDDA CYNON TAFF
4: MERTHYR TYDFIL
5: CAERPHILLY
6: CARDIFF
7: TORFAEN
8: NEWPORT

SEE MAP 3 & 4

Holyhead

ISLE OF
ANGLESEY

Llandudno
Penmaenmawr Colwyn Bay
Bangor
Caernarfon

CONWY

Prestatyn

FLINTSHIRE

DENBIGHSHIRE

Wrexham
WREXHAM

Snowdonia

National Park

Portmadog
Bala

GWYNEDD

Barmouth

Shrewsbury

Bryncrug

Aberystwyth

CEREDIGION

POWYS

ROSSLARE

Cardigan

Fishguard

Hereford

t David's

Pembrokeshire Coast
National Park
PEMBROKESHIRE

Milford Haven

N

Tenby

Llangadog

Carmarthen

CARMARTHENSHIRE

Brecon

Brecon Beacons   Llangorse
National Park

Monmouth

MONMOUTHSHIRE

SWANSEA   Swansea

Oxwich

CORK

1

2

3

4

5

7

6

Cwmcarn

8
Newport

M48
M4
M49

Cowbridge

Cardiff

VALE OF
GLAMORGAN

CARDIFF-WALES

Bristol
Parkway
BRISTOL
Temp

Weston-super-Mare

Exmoor

BELFAST
DOUGLAS
DUBLIN

Southport

Liverpool

LIVERPOOL

Chester

0   25 Miles

0   40 Km

ey to regions: ☐ Wales

All place names in black offer parks in this guide.

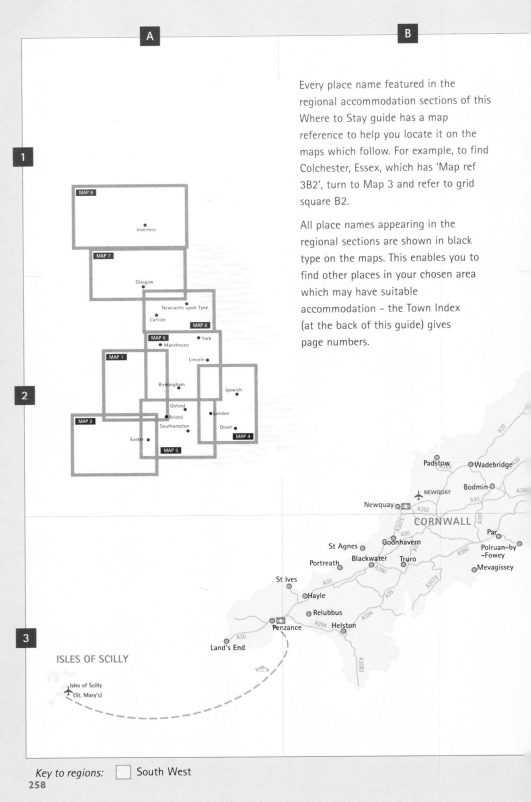

A

B

1

2

3

Every place name featured in the regional accommodation sections of this Where to Stay guide has a map reference to help you locate it on the maps which follow. For example, to find Colchester, Essex, which has 'Map ref 3B2', turn to Map 3 and refer to grid square B2.

All place names appearing in the regional sections are shown in black type on the maps. This enables you to find other places in your chosen area which may have suitable accommodation - the Town Index (at the back of this guide) gives page numbers.

MAP 8

Inverness

MAP 7

Glasgow

Newcastle upon Tyne

Carlisle

MAP 6

MAP 5

York

Manchester

MAP 1

Lincoln

Birmingham

Ipswich

Oxford

Bristol

London

MAP 2

Southampton

Dover

Exeter

MAP 4

MAP 3

Padstow

Wadebridge

Bodmin

NEWQUAY

Newquay

A392

A30

CORNWALL

Par

St Agnes

Goonhavern

Polruan-by
–Fowey

Portreath

Blackwater

Truro

Mevagissey

St Ives

Hayle

Relubbus

Penzance

Helston

ISLES OF SCILLY

Land's End

Isles of Scilly
(St. Mary's)

Key to regions: ☐ South West

MAP 2

C

D

A418 A418 A465 A4042 A470 A4232 M4 A4232 M48 M4

41 40 39 38 37 36 35 34 33 32 31 30 29 28 27 26 25 24 23

M4 Newport

Cardiff A48 A4232 A4232

✈ CARDIFF-WALES

Weston-super-Mare BRI BRISTOL 19 20

A370 A370 A38 A371 Ched

21

Burnham-on-Sea 22 A38 A372 A39

Porlock Minehead West Quantoxhead A39

Exmoor National Park Blue Anchor

Woolacombe A3123 A361 A39

Croyde Bay Winsford A396 A358 22 A39

A361 23

SOMERSET Taunton 24 M5

M5 25

Bude A388 A386 A377 A3072 A3072 A3072 26

Widemouth Bay A30 27

A3079 Kentisbeare A373 A303 A30 Chard A303 A3086

28 A30 A358 A35

DEVON A382 Axminster A35 Bri

A39 A386 A30 A35

Drewsteignton Exeter 29 ✈ EXETER A3052 A373 Bri

A395 A388 *Dartmoor National Park* 31 A376 Sidmouth A30

Bodmin Moor Tavistock A380 A379 Dawlish Warren Dawlish

A390 A386 Bickington A381 Newton Abbot

Ashburton A38 A381 A380 Torquay 🚉

PLYMOUTH ✈ A385 Paignton 🚉

Looe A387 A38 A379 A3121 A381 A379

Polperro Plymouth 🚉

ROSCOFF SANTANDER A38

Salcombe

N

0 _____ 25 Miles

0 _____ 40 Km

ll place names in black offer parks in this guide.

MAP 3

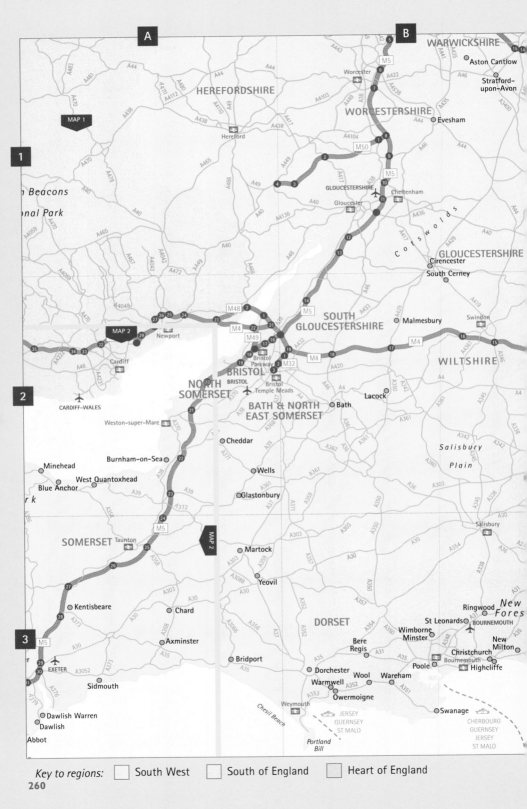

A

B

WARWICKSHIRE

Aston Cantlow

Stratford-upon-Avon

HEREFORDSHIRE

MAP 1

Worcester

WORCESTERSHIRE

Evesham

Hereford

Beacons

nal Park

M50

GLOUCESTERSHIRE

Gloucester

Cheltenham

Cotswolds

GLOUCESTERSHIRE

Cirencester

South Cerney

Malmesbury

Swindon

SOUTH GLOUCESTERSHIRE

MAP 2

Newport

M48

M4

M49

BRISTOL

Bristol Parkway

NORTH SOMERSET

Cardiff

CARDIFF–WALES

BRISTOL

Bristol Temple Meads

M4

WILTSHIRE

Lacock

BATH & NORTH EAST SOMERSET

Bath

Salisbury Plain

Weston-super-Mare

MAP 2

Cheddar

Minehead

Burnham-on-Sea

West Quantoxhead

Blue Anchor

Wells

Glastonbury

Salisbury

r k

M5

SOMERSET   Taunton

Martock

Yeovil

Kentisbeare

Chard

DORSET

Ringwood   New Forest

St Leonards

BOURNEMOUTH

Axminster

Wimborne Minster

New Milton

EXETER

Sidmouth

Bridport

Bere Regis

Dorchester

Wool   Wareham

Warmwell

Bournemouth   Highcliffe

Poole

Christchurch

Dawlish Warren

Dawlish

Abbot

Owermoigne

Weymouth

Chesil Beach

JERSEY
GUERNSEY
ST MALO

Swanage

CHERBOURG
GUERNSEY
JERSEY
ST MALO

Portland Bill

Key to regions: ☐ South West ☐ South of England ☐ Heart of England

260

MAP 3

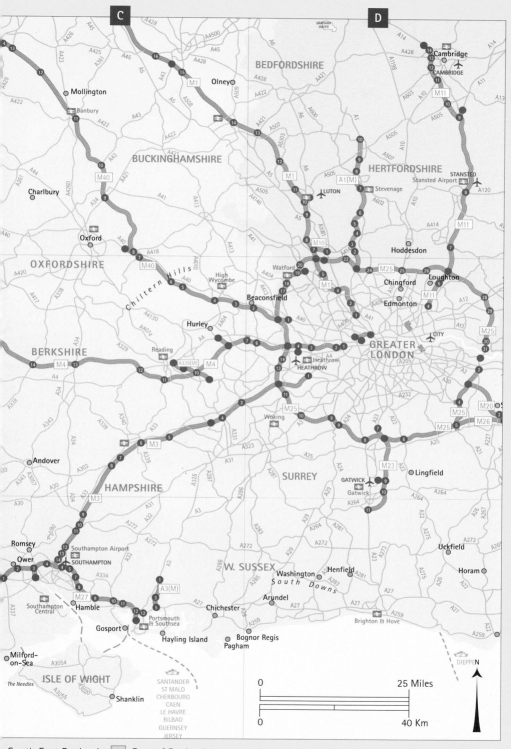

South East England | East of England

All place names in black offer parks in this guide.

MAP 4

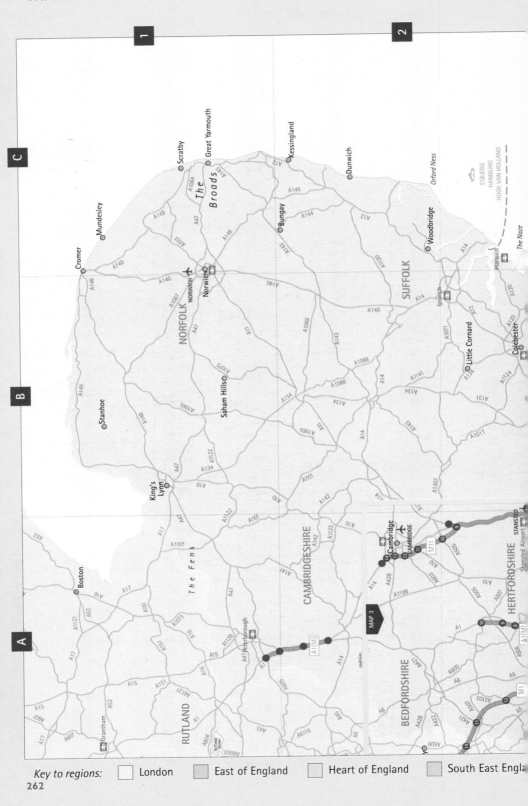

1

2

C

B

A

Mundesley

Cromer

A148

A149

A149

A1067

A140

A47

A149

A151

A148

A1065

A1065

Stanhoe

A149

A148

Scratby

Great Yarmouth

The Broads

A1064

A47

A146

A1075

A1066

A1064
NORWICH

Norwich

NORFOLK

A11

A47

A1122

A134

A47

King's Lynn

A10

A122

A1101

A10

A10

A1101

A17

A17

A1101

A1073

A16

A151

The Fens

Boston

A16

A52

A1121

A52

A15

A16

A15

A607

A17

A15

A52

Grantham

A606

RUTLAND

A1

A606

A605

A1139

A15

A47 Peterborough

A47

A1(M)

A14

A605

A1

A43

A6116

A6

A5

A605

A145

Kessingland

A12

A144

Bungay

A143

A140

A1066

A143

A1088

A1088

A134

A11

A1065

A142

A1123

A142

A1141

CAMBRIDGESHIRE

A134

A14

A14

A143

A142

A14

A1302

Dunwich

A12

A12

A120

SUFFOLK

A140

Ipswich

A14

A1141

A134

A1017

A131

A124

Little Cornard

Colchester

A120

A120

A12

Woodbridge

A14

A1152

A1120

Orford Ness

The Naze

Harwich

ESBJERG
HAMBURG
HOOK VAN HOLLAND

Cambridge

Cambridge

MAP 3

M11

A14

A428

A1198

A10

A505

A603

A10

A1307

A1

A600

A6

HERTFORDSHIRE

STANSTED

Stansted Airport

A120

A10

A505

A507

BEDFORDSHIRE

A6

A428

A422

A421

A507

A600

A1081

A6

A5

A505

M1

M11

9

10

11

12

13

8

9

10

11

12

A509

MAP 4

All place names in black offer parks in this guide.

MAP 5

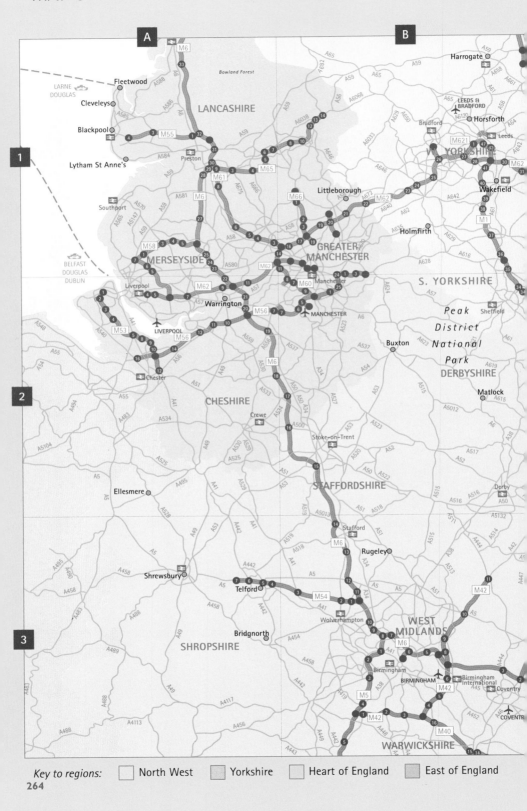

MAP 5

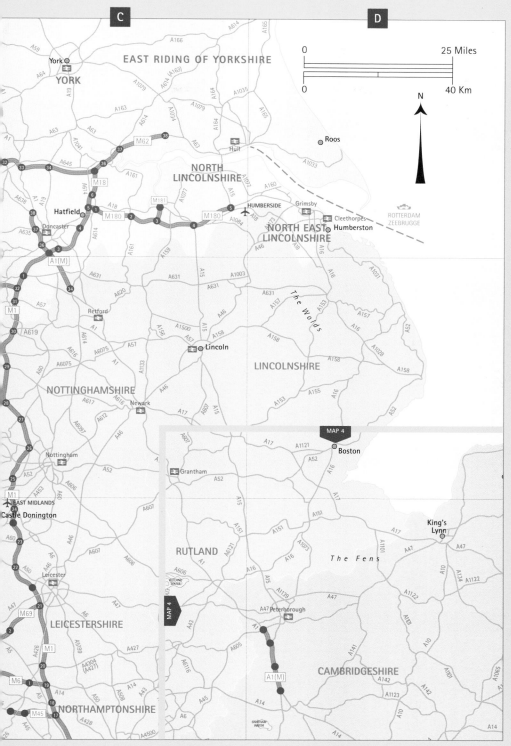

C

D

0   25 Miles

0   40 Km

N

EAST RIDING OF YORKSHIRE

York

YORK

Hull

NORTH LINCOLNSHIRE

HUMBERSIDE

Grimsby

Cleethorpes

NORTH EAST LINCOLNSHIRE

Humberston

ROTTERDAM ZEEBRUGGE

Roos

The Wolds

Hatfield

Doncaster

A1(M)

Retford

Lincoln

LINCOLNSHIRE

NOTTINGHAMSHIRE

Newark

M1

Nottingham

MAP 4

Boston

Grantham

EAST MIDLANDS

Castle Donington

RUTLAND

The Fens

King's Lynn

MAP 4

Leicester

M69

LEICESTERSHIRE

A47 Peterborough

A1(M)

CAMBRIDGESHIRE

M6

M45

NORTHAMPTONSHIRE

All place names in black offer parks in this guide.

MAP 6

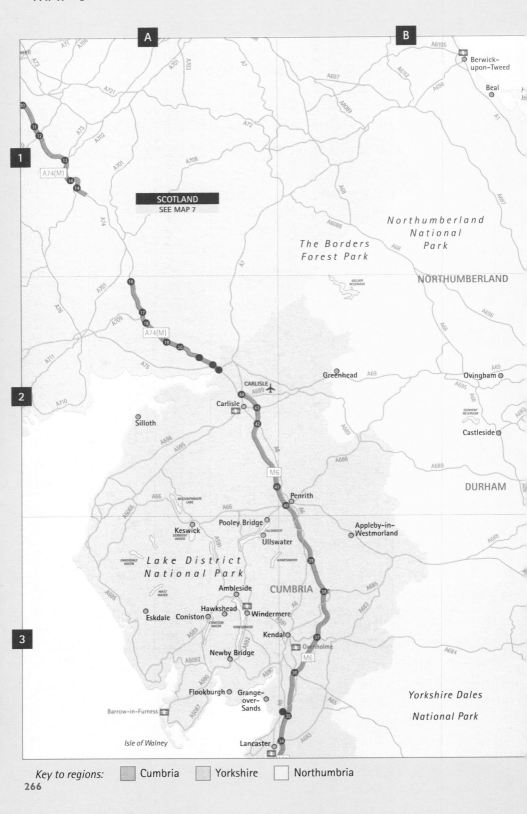

A

B

A6105

Berwick-
upon-Tweed

Beal

A1

10

11

12

A74(M)

13

14

SCOTLAND
SEE MAP 7

Northumberland
National
Park

The Borders
Forest Park

NORTHUMBERLAND

KIELDER
RESERVOIR

A696

16

17

18

A74(M)

19

20

Greenhead   A69   Ovingham

A695

CARLISLE

Carlisle   A689

Silloth

Castleside

DERWENT
RESERVOIR

M6

DURHAM

Penrith

A689

41

40

Keswick

Pooley Bridge

Appleby-in-
Westmorland

BASSENTHWAITE
LAKE

DERWENT
WATER

ULLSWATER

Ullswater

ENNERDALE
WATER   Lake District
National Park

HAWESWATER

39

CUMBRIA

38

Ambleside

WAST
WATER

Hawkshead

Eskdale   Coniston   Windermere

CONISTON
WATER

WINDERMERE

Kendal

37

Oxenholme

M6

Newby Bridge

36

Flookburgh   Grange-
over-
Sands

35

Barrow-in-Furness

Yorkshire Dales

National Park

Isle of Walney

Lancaster   34

MAP 6

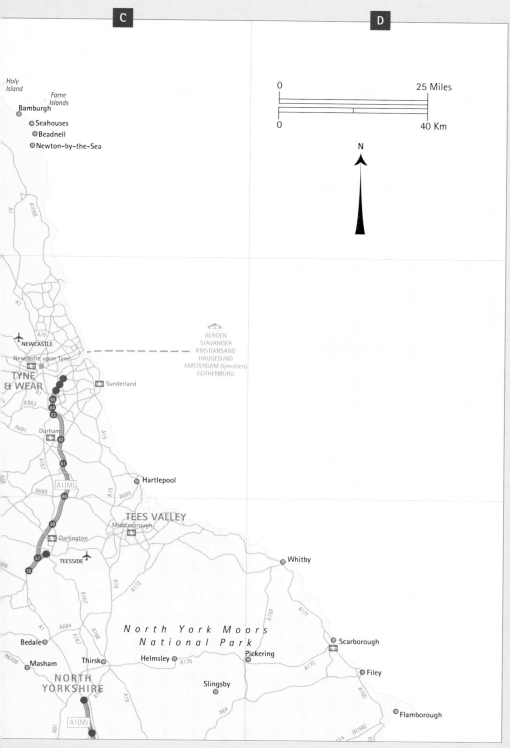

C D

Holy Island
Farne Islands
Bamburgh
Seahouses
Beadnell
Newton-by-the-Sea

0 — 25 Miles
0 — 40 Km

N

BERGEN
STAVANGER
KIRSTIANSAND
HAUGESUND
AMSTERDAM (Ijmulden)
GOTHENBURG

NEWCASTLE
Newcastle upon Tyne
TYNE & WEAR
Sunderland
Durham
Hartlepool
TEES VALLEY
Middlesbrough
Darlington
TEESSIDE
Whitby
North York Moors National Park
Bedale
Masham
Thirsk
Helmsley
Pickering
Scarborough
Filey
NORTH YORKSHIRE
Slingsby
Flamborough

All place names in black offer parks in this guide.

MAP 7

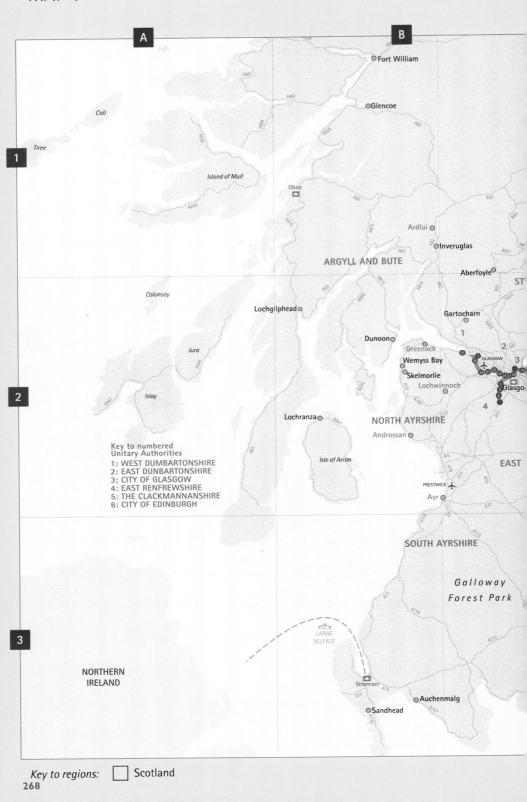

A

B

1

2

3

Fort William

Glencoe

Coll

Tiree

Island of Mull

Oban

Ardlui

Inveruglas

Aberfoyle

ST

ARGYLL AND BUTE

Colonsay

Lochgilphead

Gartocharn

Dunoon

Greenock

GLASGOW

Glasgo

Wemyss Bay

Skelmorlie

Lochwinnoch

Glasgo

Jura

Islay

Lochranza

NORTH AYRSHIRE

Androssan

EAST

Isle of Arran

Key to numbered
Unitary Authorities
1: WEST DUMBARTONSHIRE
2: EAST DUNBARTONSHIRE
3: CITY OF GLASGOW
4: EAST RENFREWSHIRE
5: THE CLACKMANNANSHIRE
6: CITY OF EDINBURGH

PRESTWICK

Ayr

SOUTH AYRSHIRE

Galloway
Forest Park

LARNE
BELFAST

NORTHERN
IRELAND

Stranraer

Auchenmalg

Sandhead

Key to regions: ☐ Scotland

MAP 7

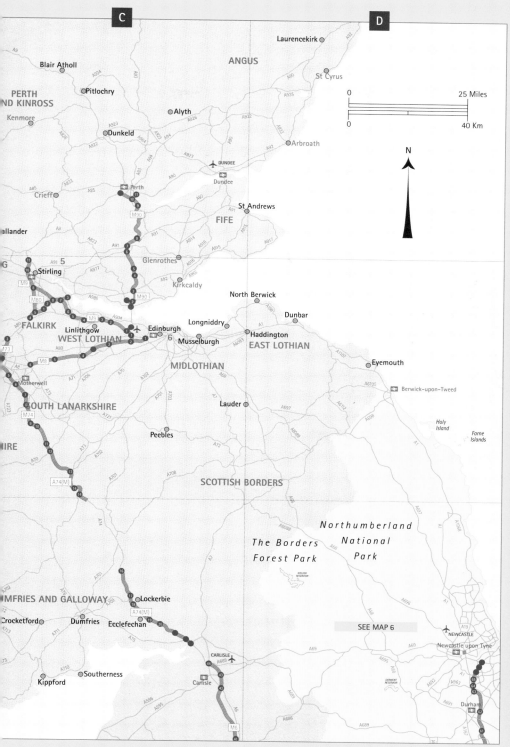

All place names in black offer parks in this guide.

MAP 8

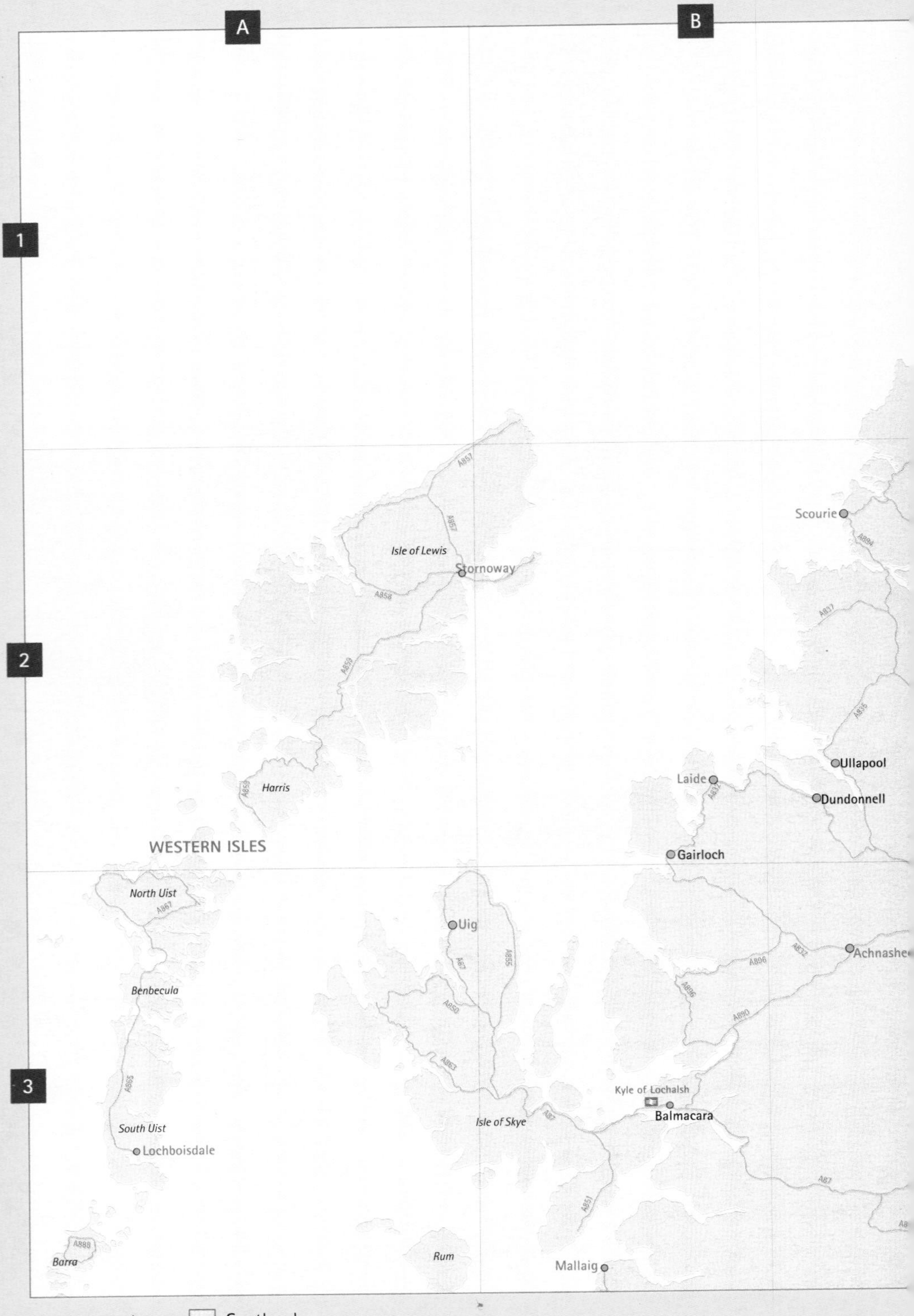
A
B
1
2
3
A857
Isle of Lewis
Stornoway
A858
A859
Harris
WESTERN ISLES
North Uist
A867
Benbecula
A865
South Uist
Lochboisdale
A888
Barra
Uig
A87
A855
A850
A863
Isle of Skye
Rum
A851
Mallaig
Kyle of Lochalsh
Balmacara
Scourie
A894
A837
A835
Ullapool
Laide
A832
Dundonnell
Gairloch
A896
Achnashe
A890
A87

Key to regions: Scotland

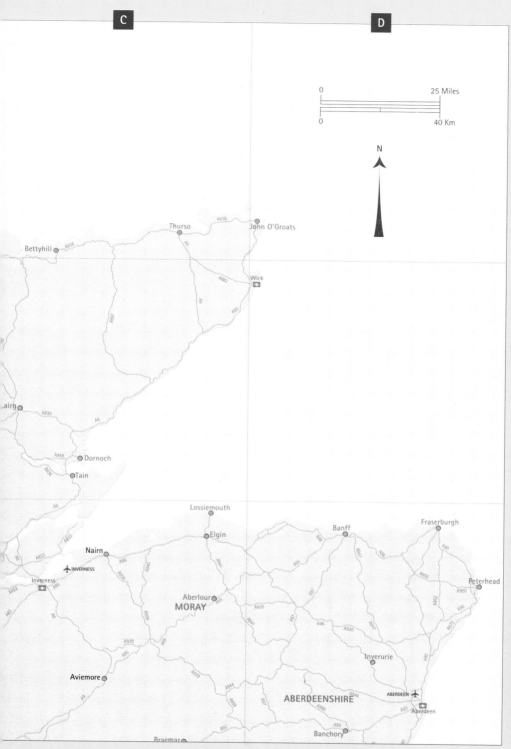

MAP 8

All place names in black offer parks in this guide.

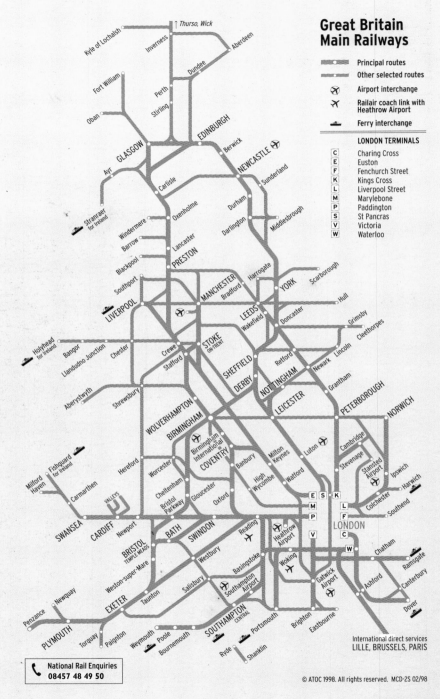

Great Britain Main Railways

Principal routes
Other selected routes
Airport interchange
Railair coach link with Heathrow Airport
Ferry interchange

LONDON TERMINALS

C	Charing Cross
E	Euston
F	Fenchurch Street
K	Kings Cross
L	Liverpool Street
M	Marylebone
P	Paddington
S	St Pancras
V	Victoria
W	Waterloo

National Rail Enquiries
08457 48 49 50

International direct services
LILLE, BRUSSELS, PARIS

01/MRE/1134